PETER NORTON'S®
COMPUTING FUNDAMENTALS

Second Edition

► PETER NORTON'S®
COMPUTING FUNDAMENTALS

Second Edition

Glencoe
McGraw-Hill

NEW YORK, NEW YORK ■ COLUMBUS, OHIO
MISSION HILLS, CALIFORNIA ■ PEORIA, ILLINOIS

A Division of The McGraw-Hill Companies

Library of Congress Cataloging-in-Publication Data

Norton, Peter, 1943–
   [Computing Fundamentals]
   Peter Norton's computing fundamentals.— 2nd ed.
    p.   cm.
   Includes index.
   ISBN 0–02–804337–5
   1. Computers. 2. Computer software.   I. Title.
QA76.5.N675   1996
004—dc20   96–32936
                                 CIP

Glencoe/McGraw-Hill

*A Division of The **McGraw·Hill** Companies*

Send all inquiries to:

Glencoe/McGraw-Hill
936 Eastwind Drive
Westerville, OH 43081

ISBN: 002–804337–5   with CD-ROM
ISBN: 002–804339–1   without CD-ROM

   3 4 5 6 7 8 9   066   01 00 99 98 97

Christina A. Martin	*Executive Editor, Glencoe/McGraw-Hill*
Pete Alcorn and Karen Lamoreux	*Development Management*
Kari Popović and Janet Andrews	*Production Management*
Janet Bollow and Janet Hansen	*Interior Design and Composition*
Stuart Kenter	*Photo Research*
Richard Sheppard	*Electronic Illustration*
James Bray	*Screen art*
Kayla Sussell	*Copyediting*
Anne Leach	*Index*
Black Dot Group	*Color Separation and Photo Scans*

BRIEF CONTENTS

This new edition of *Peter Norton's Computing Fundamentals* brings you a completely revised textbook and supplements package. The result is an innovative instructional system designed to help you teach and to help your students learn about computer technology.

World renowned computer expert, software developer, and author, Peter Norton has once again joined Glencoe in developing an integrated learning system that emphasizes life-long productivity with computers. Peter's straight forward, easy-to-follow writing style is a known winner! His successful books *Inside the IBM PC* and *Peter Norton's DOS Guide* have defined user-friendly computer instruction. Now students can benefit from his unique ability to teach computer concepts in a way that demystifies computing. Norton's "Glass Box Approach" truly comes to life in this edition! Our enhanced integrated package combines text, 3-dimensional graphics, animation, full-motion video, and sound to put students in touch with what actually happens inside the computer. This learning system will improve your ability to help students learn not only the basics of computing but also valuable tools for a lifetime of productivity.

▶ THE SECOND EDITION

Peter Norton's Computing Fundamentals, SECOND EDITION retains all the high-quality features that made the first edition a success! Since our primary goal is to present students with technology that they are likely to encounter at school and on the job, personal computers (PCs) are used in examples throughout. Other platforms (e.g., Mac, OS/2) and sizes of computers (e.g., mainframes) are discussed in the context of how they are used today.

Our emphasis is on productivity. Every computer concept is presented with guidelines on how to use the technology to be more productive at school, at work, and at home. To keep pace with computer technology, we've thoroughly revised every chapter to reflect the latest developments. We've also added coverage on emerging topics such as the Internet, networking, and multimedia. Changes and additions to this new edition are:

- **Reorganization of material.** Coverage of ergonomics and ethics have been moved to an appendix so that students can get to the core topics sooner.

- **Three entirely new chapters.** In response to new technologies, we've added new chapters on the Internet and the online world, computer graphics, and multimedia.

- **Completely revised text.** All other chapters have been completely revised to reflect the latest technology.

- **Special 3-D transvision in Chapter 1.** This detailed 3-D illustration, along with acetate transparencies, helps students identify and remember key components of a personal computer.

- **All new photographs, 3-D illustrations, and software screen shots.** Colorful, 3-D illustrations help students visualize computer components. New photographs depict the latest chip technology and models of computers.

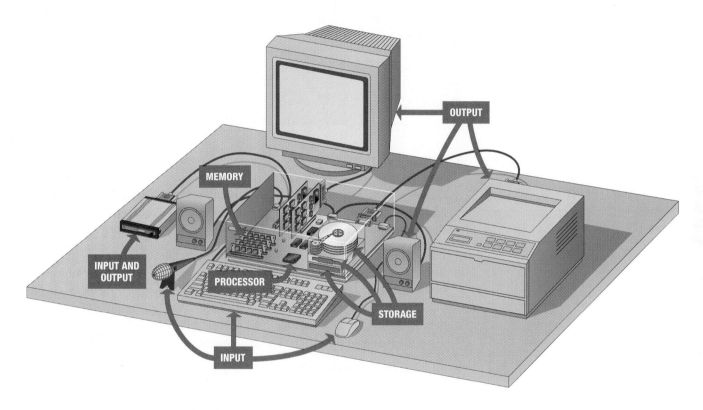

- **31 New feature boxes.** Throughout the text, you'll find three different types of feature articles each focusing on an aspect of technology. These 1-page articles are designed to help students relate the concepts they're learning to real world applications of technology. The **Norton Notebook** feature emphasizes practical uses of technology in the real world. **Techview** features insights into new technology areas. **Productivity Tip** articles offer practical guides to using technology to be more productive at school, at work, and at home.

NORTON NOTEBOOK   TECHVIEW   PRODUCTIVITY TIP

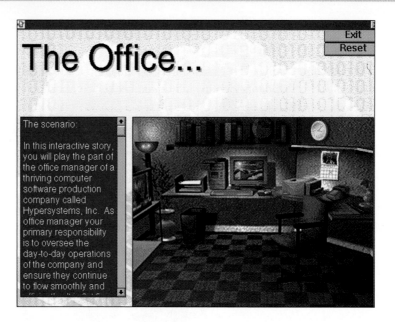

NORTON INTERACTIVE

■ **New end-of-chapter features.** Our new **Visual Summary** incorporates key graphics and illustrations into a bulleted summary of chapter concepts. This makes an excellent review and study tool for students. **Key Terms List with Page Number References** helps students quickly locate definitions for key terms. The **Key Term Quiz** challenges students to use the key terms they've learned. We included more comprehensive **Review Questions** and **Discussion Questions**.

■ **Norton Interactive.** A student CD-ROM available with *Peter Norton's Computing Fundamentals* contains full interactive multimedia modules for each chapter! These modules contain instruction, simulations, and interactive activities. For a demonstration of this exciting interactive learning tool, visit our Web site: **www.glencoe.com/ps/norton** or **www.hgcorp.com/nint.htm**

■ **Visual history timeline.** The history of the personal computer is captured in a visual presentation.

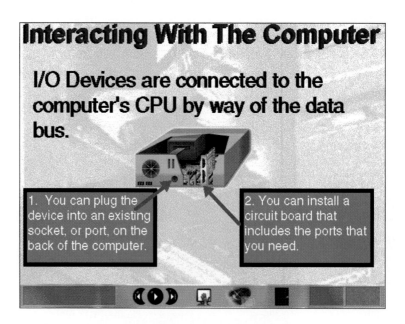

 COMPUTER CONCEPTS STUDY GUIDE ON CD-ROM

To enhance retention, Glencoe has developed a multimedia Study Guide on CD-ROM. This product includes a pre-test and post-test, and a review of all major concepts in the text.

▶ INSTRUCTOR SUPPORT

Glencoe appreciates the challenges involved in teaching computer technology. We've put together an innovative instructor's support system designed to help you meet the challenge! Updates to these materials, including content updates and projects, can be found on our Web site, **www.glencoe.com/ps/norton**

The Instructor's Productivity Center

The focal point of our instructor support, the *Instructor's Productivity Center*, is designed to help you prepare for class, present concepts, assess the performance of your students, and use technology in the classroom. The *Instructor's Productivity Center*, or *IPC*, consists of the Instructor CD-ROM, a printed catalog of test questions (Testbank), and an instructor's manual.

The IPC CD-ROM

The IPC CD-ROM contains all the technology tools you need to present computer concepts effectively:

- A complete **online guide to the IPC** and how to use technology in the classroom.

- An **electronic version of the instructor's manual** opens in the word processing program of your choice and allows you to modify teaching notes.

- **Classroom Presentations**. PowerPoint presentations, including diagrams and illustrations, are provided for each chapter in the book. Comes with a slide sorter.

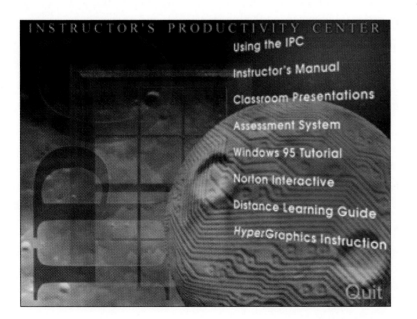

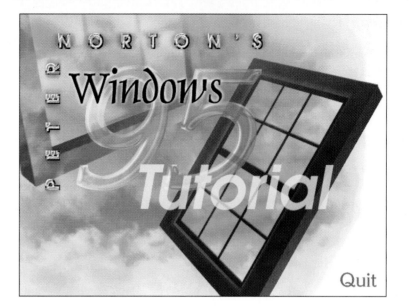

NORTON INTERACTIVE

■ The new Glencoe **Assessment System** is a windows-based test generator that allows you to produce and print out tests or deliver them online via your local area network. Contains over 2500 test questions and a built-in grading feature. Questions include True/False, Multiple Choice, Completion, Matching, and Short Answer for each chapter. All questions are rated by difficulty level, and are coded by learning objective and subject area.

■ A special multimedia **Windows 95 Tutorial** can be used as a classroom presentation or individualized instruction for your students.

■ A copy of the **Norton Interactive** multimedia modules with installation options allows you to install to a hard drive or your local area network.

■ **Distance Learning Guide**. An information bulletin for instructors that focuses on defining distance learning and Internet course delivery. Contains practical guidelines on how to set up distance learning facilities, what equipment is required, and how to enhance enrollments using the Internet.

■ *Hyper*Graphics Instruction. A demonstration of our interactive classroom instructional system. For more information, access **www.hgcorp.com** on the World Wide Web.

The Instructor's Manual and Key

A printed version of the Instructor's Manual, this comprehensive supplement contains detailed lesson plans and outlines, complete with teaching and assessment strategies. Everything is correlated to SCANS competencies. You'll also find answers to all the end-of-chapter questions and a guide to Internet sites. Page references to the textbook help you coordinate your lecture.

The Testbank

This is a printed catalog of the over 2500 test questions in the Glencoe Assessment System. The testbank includes True/False, Multiple Choice, Completion, Matching, and Short Answer questions for each chapter. All questions are rated by difficulty level.

The Annotated Instructor's Edition

The *Annotated Instructor's Edition* contains valuable teaching tips with additional information, discussion notes, and classroom projects to help you supplement the student textbook during your lecture.

▶ SOFTWARE TUTORIALS

Glencoe offers a full line of software tutorials to accompany this textbook. Each tutorial is designed to teach the basics of the software package with an emphasis on practical skills and productivity. Large screen shots and guided exercises help students learn basic skills. Enhanced application projects challenge students to create documents, spreadsheets, and databases using the skills they've learned.

Each tutorial is accompanied by an Instructor's Manual which includes teaching tips, additional projects, and sample quizzes and tests. Our new tutorials for Windows 95 software also include test generators with over 350 test questions.

Ask your Glencoe sales representative about our software tutorials and our Software Upgrade program!

▶ HYPERGRAPHICS INSTRUCTIONAL SYSTEM

Glencoe and its software development partner, *Hyper*Graphics Corporation, have developed a high-tech learning program for *Peter Norton's Computing Fundamentals,* SECOND EDITION. *Hyper*Graphics is an innovative educational system that utilizes interactive computer technology to teach and reinforce computer concepts, and then test and track students' understanding of important concepts.

With classroom presentation software and hand-held student response pads, students can answer questions in real time. Every response is recorded by the system to allow the instructor to monitor both individual and class progress. A variety of assessment tools are built-in, including objective questions after each concept is presented and group challenges for each chapter of material.

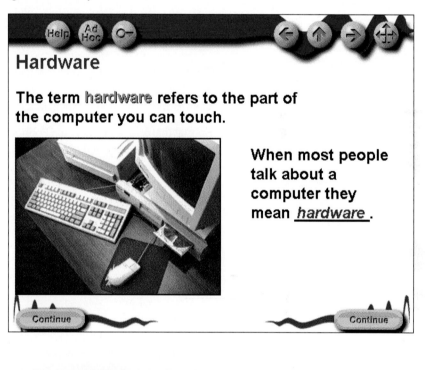

The student workbook, called *Textnotes*, allows students to create their own study guides based on the classroom instruction.

Contact your Glencoe sales representative for more information, or visit the *Hyper*Graphics Web site, **www.hgcorp.com**

◢ OUR SOFTWARE IS DISTANCE LEARNING READY!

The *Hyper*Graphics system is specially designed to help you implement a distance learning program in computers! Both hardware and software are fully compatible with SMART Technologies' SMART Boards and a variety of video conferencing systems.

In addition, Glencoe and *Hyper*Graphics Corporation support Internet delivery of our material. Ask your Glencoe sales representative about **Internet Course Packs.**

◢ ACKNOWLEDGMENTS

The following individuals contributed to the content and development of this project: Kim Bobzien, Elizabeth Collins, Mark Crosten, Ellen Finkelstein, Ron Gilster, Robert Goldhamer, Marianne Karinch, Mary Lambert, Terry O'Donnell, and John Ross.

Special thanks goes to Corinne Folino and Kim Harvey at Glencoe whose dedication and hard work help make the Peter Norton series a success. For their help and support throughout the project and especially at the eleventh hour, a personal thank you to the entire Glencoe Postsecondary Marketing Department, Dave Kunkler, Alan Hensley, and especially Colleen Morrissey.

Last, but by no means least, it was a privilege to work with Kari Popović, Janet Bollow, and Stuart Kenter. Their professionalism is reflected in the quality of their work.

September 1996

EDITORIAL CONSULTANTS

Dolores Pusins
Hillsborough Community College

Peter Irwin
Richland College

Wesley E. Nance
Cerritos College

REVIEWERS

Janet Ashall
University of Western Ontario

Patsy Blankenship
North Lake Community College

Ron Burgher
Metropolitan Community College

Kris Chandler
Pikes Peak Community College

Susan Demuro
New Hampshire Technical College

Ward Deutschman
Briarcliffe College

Kevin Duggan
Midlands Technical College

Clay Gehring
Montana State University, College of Technology

Michelle Hechman
Mt. Hood Community College

Doug MacNeil
Grand Rapids Community College

Dori McPherson
Schoolcraft College

William McTammany
Florida Community College at Jacksonville

Ann Robertson
Mitchell College

Judith Scheeren
Westmoreland County Community College

Wesley Scruggs
Brazosport College

Jack Stephens
Gadsden State Community College

Mary Valenti
Harford Community College

John Walker
Donna Ana Community College

Roger Yohe
Estrella Mountain Community College

CONTENTS

CHAPTER 2

Processing Data   38

CHAPTER 3

Interacting with the Computer   64

CHAPTER 4
Storing Information in a Computer   98

PRODUCTIVITY TIP
Backing Up Your Files   102

TECHVIEW
**PC Card: A Hard Disk the Size
of Your Driver's License**   118

NORTON NOTEBOOK
RAID — Not Just a Bug Spray   122

CHAPTER 5
Networks and Data Communications   128

NORTON NOTEBOOK
**What Do Brain Surgery, ET,
and the Stock Market Have
in Common?**   131

USING MICROCOMPUTER SOFTWARE   162   PART II

CHAPTER 6

The Operating System and the User Interface   164

CHAPTER 7

Word Processing and Desktop Publishing 202

CHAPTER 8

Spreadsheets 238

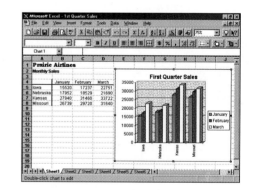

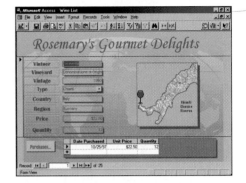

CHAPTER 9
Database Management   264

TECHVIEW

NORTON NOTEBOOK

CHAPTER 12
The New Media 348

APPENDIXES

PETER NORTON'S
COMPUTING FUNDAMENTALS

Second Edition

CHAPTER 1

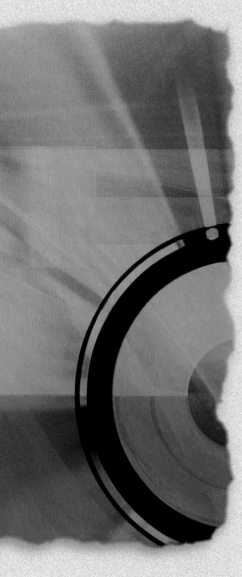

OBJECTIVES

When you complete this chapter, you will be able to do the following:

- Discuss some of the many ways computers have an impact on our lives.
- List the four parts of a computer system.
- Recognize four kinds of computer hardware.
- Explain the purpose of software.
- List the common types of computers available today and describe what kind of job each does best.

The computer is a truly amazing machine. Few tools help you perform so many different tasks in so many areas of your life. Whether you want to track an investment, publish a newsletter, design a building, or practice landing an F14 on the deck of the aircraft carrier *USS Enterprise*, you can use a computer to do it.

These powerful tools built of silicon, metal, and plastic have become so pervasive that virtually no business or organization can function effectively without them. Even in private homes, computers are becoming indispensable tools.

In this chapter, you will see some of the many ways computers help shape daily life. You will also take a peek under the hood of these magnificent machines to see what makes them tick. Finally, you will learn about the various types of computers and which tasks each does best.

▶ THE MULTIPURPOSE TOOL

The most prevalent type of computer is the personal computer.

In general terms, a **computer** is a group of electronic devices used to process data. In the 1950s, computers were massive, special-purpose machines that only huge institutions such as governments and universities could afford. Primarily, these early computers performed complex numerical tasks, such as calculating the precise orbit of Mars, or planning the trajectories of missiles, or processing statistics for the Bureau of the Census. Although computers were certainly useful for tasks like these, it soon became apparent that they could also be helpful in an ordinary business environment.

In the 1960s, modern computers began to revolutionize the business world. IBM introduced its System/360 mainframe computer in April 1964 and ultimately sold over 33,000 of these machines. As a result of the commercial success of its System/360, IBM became the standard against which other computer manufacturers and their systems would be measured for years to come.

In the 1970s, Digital Equipment Corporation (DEC) took two more giant steps toward bringing computers into mainstream use with the introduction of its PDP-11 and VAX computers. These models came in many sizes to meet different needs and budgets. Since then, computers continue to shrink in size while providing more power for less money. Today, the most common type of computer you will see is called a **personal computer**, or **PC**, because it is designed to be used by just one person at a time. Despite its small size, the modern personal computer is more powerful than any of the room-sized machines of the 1960s.

Computers in Business

Computers are so fundamental to modern society that without them, our economy would grind to a halt. They are such flexible tools that most people in the business community use them every day. Office workers use them to write letters, keep employee rosters, create budgets, communicate with coworkers, find information, manage projects, and so on. Step into any office building and you will probably see a computer on almost every desk.

In some cases, such as air traffic control, computers play a critical role in protecting peoples' lives.

Many businesspeople who work away from the office also use computers. For example, salespeople use computers to manage accounts and make presentations. Most salespeople who are on the road now carry portable computers, known as **laptops**, or **notebooks**, which can be every bit as powerful as models that sit on a desk. With a laptop, a salesperson can write letters, track travel expenses, update customer files, and create colorful multimedia presentations to help sell a product.

Computers are also vital in accounting departments. For organizing and manipulating large sets of numbers, which accounting departments do on a daily basis, computers are now considered essential. Accountants use computers to juggle budgets, create purchase orders, set up employee files, track expenses and income, and pay taxes. Today even tiny businesses—which can be as small as a single person—can afford to set up sophisticated accounting systems using a personal computer.

Salespeople often carry laptop computers to give presentations to potential customers.

As a customer, you have many opportunities to interact with computers. The device shown here, which lets you quickly pay for gas using a credit card, contains a computer.

Even if you do not work in a business, the way businesses use computers affects you every day. Any time you go to the bank, renew a subscription, call information for a phone number, or buy something out of a catalog, you are benefiting from the power and speed of computers. Even when you buy groceries and gasoline, you are interacting with computers.

Medicine and Health Care

In medicine today, computers are used for everything from diagnosing illnesses and monitoring patients at their bedside to controlling the movement of robotic surgical assistants.

Several innovative medical applications use small, special-purpose computers. For example, pacemakers are computers that operate within the human body to help it

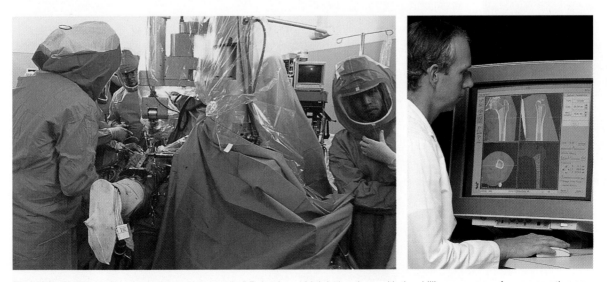

These doctors are using a computer system called Robodoc, which helps them with the drilling necessary for an operation on the patient's hip. Part of the process is illustrated on the screen in the photo on the right.

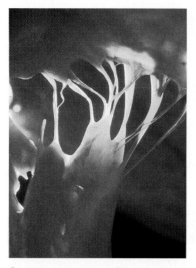

Computers can be used to control tiny remote cameras, which take pictures inside the body and help doctors make diagnoses.

function better. In addition, computers so tiny they can be swallowed are proving to be valuable diagnostic tools. Because these remotely controlled machines can navigate the twists and tight spaces in the body, they can take and transmit photographs of internal problems, such as blood clots and tumors, that previously could be seen only during exploratory surgery.

Education

In the last 15 years, computers have sparked a revolution in education. People from all walks of life from preschool children to senior citizens now put computers to work for their own intellectual benefit. You will find computers in classrooms, museums, and libraries, where they have become as essential to the learning process as books, paper, and pens.

In the classroom, students use computers to develop science projects, prepare reports, and gather information from electronic sources around the world. At the library, people read magazines and journals directly from a computer terminal, without having to search the shelves for paper originals. In museums, computers enable visitors to explore topics in depth and receive textual information accompanied by sound and video.

Many teachers are enthusiastic about the computer as an interactive learning tool. Unlike recorded television shows, computer-aided education programs can prompt students for feedback and then respond with new information. Computerized tutorials can teach, test for understanding, and reteach based on how much the student has learned. Simulation software lets students tackle real-world problems without leaving the classroom. For example, SimCity 2000, a program developed by Maxis, brings urban planning alive, letting would-be mayors and city planners use extensive city development and budget management tools to cope with such problems as natural and man-made disasters, crime, and rapid urban growth.

Computers are used at the Smithsonian in Washington, D.C. to guide museum goers and tell them about the exhibits.

This screen shows part of a city that a student designed using SimCity 2000.

Science

Scientists use computers to help develop hypotheses, collect and test data, and exchange information electronically with colleagues around the world. Researchers can access databases in distant locations without traveling any farther than the closest computer.

Scientists also use computers to simulate complex events, such as predicting how earthquakes will affect buildings or how pollution will change weather patterns. Sophisticated software even allows intricate molecules to be designed, diagrammed, and manipulated.

These photos were taken at 2.5-second intervals on July 22, 1994 from the *Galileo* spacecraft. The bright spot that appears on the dark side of Jupiter is the impact made by the largest fragment of the Shoemaker-Levy comet.

It would be impossible to explore outer space without computers. Satellites and space probes have beamed back to Earth a wealth of information about our solar system and the cosmos. For example, in 1994, NASA's *Galileo* spacecraft was on its way past Jupiter. Shortly before it arrived, astronomers calculated that fragments of a comet named Shoemaker-Levy were going to hit the planet. Unfortunately, all the fragments were going to hit the back side of Jupiter, so the impacts were not going to be visible from Earth. However, the impacts were going to be visible from *Galileo*. NASA's scientists communicated with the spacecraft's computers and redirected its cameras toward the impact areas. As a result, scientists were able to witness a spectacular astronomical event. Computer networks made it possible for the whole world to see the photographs almost instantaneously.

Engineering

Although drafting tables and T squares are still around, their days are numbered. An engineer designing a product can be far more productive with a computer than with pencil and paper.

When designing a product with a computer, engineers create an electronic model by describing all three dimensions of the object. If they want to see the object from a different perspective, they just tell the computer to display another view. On paper, they would have to produce a different drawing for each view. If they changed the design later, they would have to redraw every affected view.

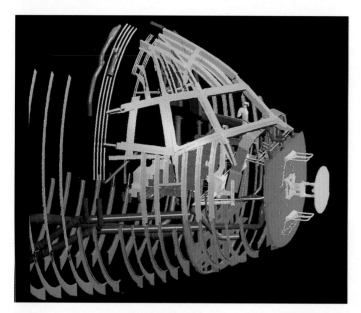

Designers of Boeing's 777 used an advanced type of CAD, known as CATIA (Computer-Aided, Three-dimensional, Interactive Application), to model every piece of the plane. For example, in this picture, the green ribs represent the airplane structure, and the red pipes are part of the flight control system. Designers can pre-assemble, or mock up, portions of the airplane on the computer screen to detect misalignments and other interference problems. This capability greatly improves accuracy, reduces the need for full-scale mock-ups, and enhances the overall quality of the airplane.

Designing objects with a computer is called **computer-aided drafting** or **computer-aided design (CAD)**. Specialized CAD systems are available for designing almost anything—from houses, cars, and buildings to molecules and spacecraft. Knowledge of CAD is now required for many engineering jobs.

One of the most extensive uses of CAD in recent years was the development of Boeing's new 777 airplane. Creation of a new commercial jet is a $3- to $4-billion process. Boeing decided that the best way to save time and money on this job was to use computers as much as possible.

The company began by building a massive computer—one of the largest ever. Then the 230 engineering design teams went to work, making a computerized model of the entire plane that included every single part. For previous planes, Boeing had built full-size models to test how everything fit together. With the 777, they were able to test everything using the computerized model.

One reason the CAD model of the 777 saved the company money was that it allowed the engineers to redesign parts as quickly as changes were required. For example, the doors of the 777 took three months to design the first time. When the shape of the plane's body changed and the doors had to be redesigned, the work took only one month. When the shape of the plane changed a second time, the redesign of the doors took only one week.

Using computers to help design the 777 also enabled the engineers to create the lightest and strongest plane possible. With sophisticated **computer-aided engineering (CAE)** software, which allows designers to specify the type of material to be used for each part, they were able to calculate whether the part could withstand the necessary stresses and temperatures. This type of testing was critical to guaranteeing the safety of the plane.

Manufacturing

In addition to product design, computers play an ever-increasing role in manufacturing. In some factories, computers control virtually everything. For example, consider a power plant that generates steam for electricity. In this kind of factory, a computer monitors pressures and temperatures at hundreds of critical points

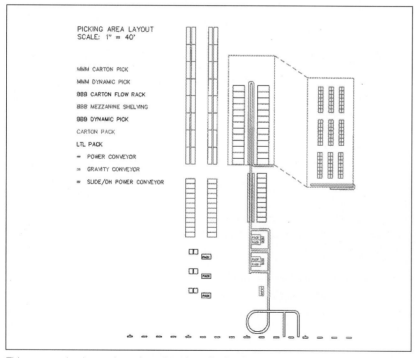

This screen simulates what takes place in a distribution warehouse.

Stephen Hawking Expresses Himself

In 1982, Stephen Hawking faced a serious financial challenge. He needed money to pay for his daughter's school tuition. His solution: write a popular book about the origins and evolution of the universe.

Known as the greatest theoretical physicist since Albert Einstein, Hawking was certainly up to the task. Yet he faced a serious obstacle. He couldn't write, at least not in the mechanical sense. From the time he was a 21-year-old graduate student, his towering intellect has inhabited a body withering from amyotrophic lateral sclerosis (ALS), also known as Lou Gehrig's disease. Over the years, he has gradually lost more and more motor control, leaving him confined to a wheelchair with severely limited use of his hands.

In 1984, emergency surgery caused the loss of his voice. Without the ability to talk, and barely able to move any part of his body, how could he complete this ambitious project? How could he continue lecturing at Cambridge University, where he was Lucasian professor of mathematics, as Sir Isaac Newton had been centuries before? The fate of his book—*A Brief History of Time: From the Big Bang to Black Holes*—and indeed of his entire career—looked bleak.

Walt Woltosz, a computer expert from Palmdale, California, heard of Hawking's plight from a colleague and sent him a program he'd written, called Equalizer. Originally developed by Woltosz for his mother-in-law, who also had ALS, it allows the user to select words from a computer screen with only the slightest movement. This method of entering data—called "keyboard emulation"—can be adapted to respond to any voluntary motion, such as a breath or the blink of an eye.

Using Equalizer, Hawking completed his book and it became a best seller, hailed for its clear and simple explanations of complex theories. In a movie based on his life, Hawking said that he—more than anyone—was surprised that his physical disabilities had actually

expanded his capabilities: "Much to my surprise, I found I was able to communicate much better than before."

This is how Hawking's system works: A cursor moves across the upper part of the screen, from one column of alphabetized words to the next. Hawking stops it by squeezing a switch that rests in his left hand. By doing so, he designates which words should move to the bottom of the screen. From these words he builds sentences, which he can send to a speech synthesizer or a disk. A formatting program called TEX enables him to prepare drafts of articles and papers. He writes equations in words, then the program translates them into symbols and prints them on paper in the appropriate type.

The vocabulary programmed into Hawking's computer contains about 2,500 words, including hundreds of technical ones. The vocabulary is periodically updated, but there is no real need to expand it. According to Woltosz, Hawking prefers Equalizer

to its successor, Scanning WSKE (pronounced "whiskey," an acronym for Words + Software Keyboard Emulator), because he "knows the screens by heart."

At first, Hawking ran Equalizer only on his desktop computer. Then, when a portable computer and speech synthesizer were configured for his wheelchair, the program enabled him to take his voice wherever he went. As of 1995, Hawking's setup included a Toshiba 1200XE run from a battery under his wheelchair. The screen was mounted on the arm of the wheelchair where he can see it. There is also a cellular phone, which allows him to receive and make calls through the computer.

Using his portable setup, he "starred" in the movie named after his famous book, and made a guest appearance on the television series *Star Trek: The Next Generation*. In the episode, he played poker with Sir Isaac Newton and Albert Einstein—and won.

Stephen Hawking arrives for the premiere of the movie based on his best-selling book. On the left is Errol Morris, director of the movie.

Most robots perform repetitive manufacturing jobs. Here, a robotic arm paints an automobile.

throughout the plant. If the pressure or temperature in a pipe or tank exceeds a specified level, the computer can regulate the process by instructing valves to turn and burners to adjust.

Factories also use computerized robotic arms to do physical work that is hazardous or highly repetitive. For example, automobile plants use robots to perform tasks such as painting, welding, and cutting and bending sheet metal for body parts. Manufacturing with computers and robotics is called **computer-aided manufacturing (CAM).** More recently, **computer-integrated manufacturing (CIM)** has given computers an additional role in designing the product: They can now order parts and plan production. This means that computers can coordinate the entire production process, from design to manufacturing.

Another use of computers in manufacturing is known as **automated fabrication,** or "autofab," a process that enables designers to make quick design changes to customize a product. Levi Strauss & Co. uses autofab to offer custom-made jeans to women. Using a system developed by Custom Clothing Technology Corp., Levi salespeople first enter a customer's measurements (waist, hips, rise, inseam) into a computer. Then, when the salesperson and customer find the prototype that fits the customer perfectly, the number of the prototype is sent, via computer,

to a factory in Mountain City, Tennessee. There, a team constructs the custom-tailored jeans. When the jeans are delivered three weeks later, they contain a Personal Pair customer number. That way, when customers want a new pair, they can simply call the local Levi store, give the customer number, and charge the jeans to a credit card.

On the left, a woman tries on a pair of prototype jeans at a Levi's retail store. On the right, a salesperson works with the customer to find exactly the right prototype.

Legal Practice

The legal profession also makes extensive use of computers today. Computer services such as LEXIS and Westlaw allow attorneys to search quickly through huge collections of information, called **databases,** for case information. Using a computer reduces the time required to complete such a search from days or hours to minutes or even seconds.

Computer technology does not stay in the attorney's office. Today, you can see it right in the courtroom. For example, a computer can instantly translate all the statements from the court reporter's stenography into readable text. Attorneys working on small, portable computers can make their own notes on the court reporter's record and see the results on their computer screens just seconds after the actual statement is made.

Some attorneys create their own databases for large cases involving thousands of documents and hundreds of depositions. By transferring this information to a portable computer, attorneys can walk into a courtroom with a comprehensive case file at their fingertips.

Law Enforcement

Many police departments use mobile computers, sometimes called **mobile data terminals (MDTs)**, in squad cars. When a police officer pulls a car over, the mobile computer, given just the vehicle license number for reference, can tell the officer who owns the car, whether it has been reported stolen, and other relevant information. Using the driver's license number of the person behind the wheel, the officer can find out if the license has expired or whether a warrant is outstanding for the driver's arrest. With a mobile computer, police can avoid calling in such information requests to a dispatcher, thereby keeping their radios free for emergencies.

Other areas of law enforcement use even more advanced techniques. The technique commonly known as DNA fingerprinting, for example, can positively identify someone from traces of blood, skin, or hair left at a crime scene, thereby helping to confirm the guilt or innocence of the accused.

Government

Approximately 270 million people live in the United States. Three ways the federal government uses computers to collect, process, and store vast amounts of information about its citizens are through the Social Security Administration, the Bureau of the Census, and the Internal Revenue Service.

Attorneys use the LEXIS database to search for information about federal and state case law. The service has 45 specialized libraries covering the major fields of practice, including tax, securities, banking, environmental, and international law. There are also libraries of English, French, and Canadian law.

The police officer is using a mobile data terminal, which provides quick access to information, such as license plate numbers of stolen cars.

Social Security numbers are issued to each U.S. citizen and to other people who work or bank in the United States. Computers can correlate and update information about these people's earnings throughout their lives. Then, based on these figures, the government calculates the retirement benefits that should be paid to each person.

Intuit Turbo Tax for Windows.

┌───┐
│ JAMES.TAX - TurboTax for Windows - [Form 1040: Individual Tax Return] │
│ File Edit Forms EasyStep Tools Window Help   │
│   │
│ Form **1040**   **U.S. Individual Income Tax Return**   **1995** │
│   │
│   For the year January 1 - December 31, 1995, or other tax year │
│   beginning _____, 1995, ending _____, 19 ____. │
│   │
│ Your first name   MI   Last name   Your SSN   │
│ James   B   Cortez   562-91-7159   │
│ Spouse's first name MI Last name   Spouse's SSN │
│ Home address (number and street). If a P.O. box, see instructions. Apt No. │
│ 21 Tamal Vista Blvd.   215   │
│ City, town or post office. If a foreign address, see instructions. State ZIP Code │
│ Corte Madera   CA   94925   │
│   │
│ **Presidential Election Campaign**   │
│   Yes No   Note: Checking │
│ Do you want $3 to go to this fund? .... □   X 'Yes' will not change │
│ If a joint return, does your spouse want $3 to go to this fund? ...... your tax or reduce │
│   your refund. │
│ Form 1040   Calculated Value │
└───┘

TurboTax, a program from Intuit, provides electronic tax forms. The program performs all the arithmetic, and you can send the completed forms to the IRS electronically using your telephone and modem.

The military is often at the forefront of technology. This man is using an Airborne Warning and Aircraft Control (AWAC) system to track the in-flight progress of missiles and jets.

The Bureau of the Census has counted people and surveyed their life conditions in the United States every ten years since 1790. In fact, it was the first civilian arm of government to use computers on a large scale. Early Bureau of the Census computers used stacks of punched cards to enter data into their databases. Today, much more powerful computers assemble this information. Government planners and social scientists use them for calculating the number of representatives each state sends to Congress, for keeping tabs on the rise and fall of personal income, for tracking the housing and migration patterns of different groups, and for many other purposes. Individuals and businesses can also tap into this information—for example, to find out the average income or family size in a certain neighborhood.

The Internal Revenue Service uses its computers to record income tax returns for millions of individuals and businesses every year. As you may suspect, the Internal Revenue Service does not just take your word for the amount you claim you owe when you file your taxes. Its computers check and cross-check tax returns with information received from many sources throughout the year.

Today, many people are also using computers to prepare their tax forms and send them electronically to the IRS. Not only does this capability free you from long lines at the post office, your return is less likely to contain mathematical errors, and it is processed more quickly. If the IRS owes you a refund, you will get it faster if you use a computer.

The Military

In 1946, ENIAC (Electronic Numerical Integrator and Calculator)—the first large-scale computer ever developed—was created for the United States Army. That machine contained 18,000 vacuum tubes and occupied 1,800 square feet, or as much space as a medium-sized house. Initially, it was used to compute artillery-shell trajectories for different distances and weather conditions—figures that used to be calculated painstakingly by hand. Today, the military uses much more compact computers in a variety of ways aboard ships, submarines, and airplanes, as well as on battlefields and in certain weapons and satellites. For example, computers in the "smart bombs" (which were actually missiles) used during the 1991 Persian Gulf War directed them at targets as small as a few square feet. Computers in the field communicate by radio with land-based networks that tie all the systems together.

Of course, the military also uses computers in many of the same ways businesses and other organizations do. In fact, military computers keep track of what may be the largest payrolls and human-resource management systems in the world.

Music

Computers have become a creative tool for musicians. The **Musical Instrument Digital Interface (MIDI)** is a well-established standard for synchronizing hardware and software that produce electronic notes. Simply stated, MIDI allows electronic instruments and computers to be connected. A musician can touch one synthesizer key to produce the sound of a violin and another to create a cymbal crash. Using MIDI, music software can turn notes from an instrument into sheet music, recording not only the notes themselves, but what instrument made them. This means that a composer can play various parts for the same piece of music on a MIDI keyboard and then put them together to create something as complex as a symphony. When the piece is complete, the composer simply tells the computer to print the sheet music.

This musician is writing an original piece of music with the help of a computer and a MIDI keyboard. The computer is recording the notes as he plays them. He can then go back and edit the music, making any changes or corrections he wants.

Computers also enable precise editing of all kinds of sounds, from music to sound effects to human speech. Combined with MIDI, this capability means a composer can control the exact sound of each instrument before combining it with other instruments.

Theater, Film, and Television

The next time you attend a play or watch a film or TV show, consider that often-unnoticed computer enhancements contribute to your enjoyment. At the theater, technicians use coordinated computer-controlled lighting cues to brighten or dim the stage. Some performing artists even use computers to control the images and sounds of the performance itself.

The motion picture industry has achieved astounding computerized special effects, and the same techniques quickly made their way into television programming, advertising, and even home video editing. Movies now contain many visual tricks that could never be accomplished without the aid of computers. Firms such as Industrial Light and Magic (ILM) and Pixar have been at the forefront in pioneering cinematic effects. At ILM, technicians use high-powered computers to create the illusion of a locomotive flying through the air or a robot transforming itself into a human being.

The computers in the foreground of this photo are being used to establish and control the lighting for the stage production of *Showboat*.

This scene from *Jurassic Park* combines computer animation and traditional film-making. The actors, the car, and the background were filmed using traditional techniques. The tyrannosaurus on the left was created at Industrial Light and Magic using advanced computer animation techniques.

The scenes (including the characters and the backgrounds) in the movie *Toy Story* were created entirely with computers. A technique called motion tracking is used to make the characters move realistically.

Every year, these companies invent new techniques for computerized special effects. Techniques that are now well established include computer animation, motion tracking, and digital composition.

Usually, computer animation involves creating images of people or other creatures on a computer and then making the images appear to move against a real or computer-generated background. For example, the dinosaurs in *Jurassic Park* and the toys in *Toy Story* were created using computer animation.

One of the biggest problems with computer animation is making computer-generated characters move realistically. One popular solution to the problem is called motion tracking. With this technique, sensors are attached to many of the joints and limbs of an actor or a marionette-style puppet. When the actor or puppet moves, the information collected from the sensors is sent to a computer. That same information is then applied to the corresponding joints and limbs of the computer-generated character to create a realistic illusion of movement. *Jurassic Park* took advantage of this technique, as did the 1995 film *Toy Story*.

Even in movies that do not involve computer-generated characters, computers often play a large role, especially in the area of digital editing, a field that involves a huge variety of techniques. One of the most popular for creating special effects is digital composition—the layering of one scene on top of another. For example, digital composition makes it possible to animate computer-generated characters against a real background and makes it easier to produce objects that look much bigger or smaller than they actually are. The movie *Apollo 13* used digital composition to show actors standing in front of what appeared to be a full-sized rocket. In fact, the rocket was just a 5-foot or 12-foot model (depending on the scene) that was filmed separately and then digitally composed with the scene containing the actors. *Forrest Gump* used digital composition to combine scenes of Tom Hanks with historic news clips.

About 160 years ago, a man named Maelzel traveled throughout the U.S. exhibiting a mechanized Chess Player, a human-like automaton dressed in a Turkish turban and robes.

The automaton, positioned behind a large cabinet upon which rested a chessboard, took on all challengers, winning most of its games. Maelzel's Chess Player created a sensation. Wherever it went, it evoked the same eerie question: Could the most esteemed aspect of the human mind (thought and logic) be replaced by a mere machine?

The poet Edgar Allan Poe exposed the machine as a hoax in 1836 (a small, chess-playing man was concealed in the fake apparatus inside the cabinet), but the emotions stirred by this illusion remained strong. Witnessing humans lose to what they thought was a machine worked up audiences into hot debates over the matters of meaning and the dignity of human life.

These same emotions surfaced during the first-ever chess match between world chess champion Garry Kasparov and an amazing IBM computer named Deep Blue from February 10–17, 1996, the 50th birthday of the first full-fledged computer, ENIAC.

Deep Blue had a brute force computing speed that could examine *200 million chess positions per second.* The human mind pales by comparison. It fires information signals at a maximum rate of *200 times per second.* And Deep Blue doesn't get tired. It can keep up its same amazing computing speed indefinitely. For example, it can easily examine *50 billion positions* in three minutes.

Deep Blue's initial victory (it won the opening game, but lost the match 4 to 2), deeply disturbed many people who wondered if a staple notion in science fiction was coming true: Artificial intelligence would prove to be more powerful than human intelligence.

Kasparov himself said: "I believe that for the first time in the history of mankind, we saw—definitely I saw—something similar to the artificial intellect."

Bill Gates, head of Microsoft, doesn't buy it. "Believe me," he writes, "there is no artificial intellect at work inside Deep Blue. It's just a computer running clever software."

Stuart Dreyfus, former chess champion and professor of engineering at the University of California, Berkeley, concurs: "Chess is played with a finite number of moves. It isn't like any other form of intelligence. Even a triumph by the computer should not reflect on [human] capabilities."

Deep Blue's strength came from its tremendous computing power—it can calculate more deeply into a chess match faster than any computer before it. It also has some powerful evaluation capabilities.

But Kasparov detected its weakness: Its inability to grasp the long-range, to conceive an original plan. "I was able to exploit the traditional shortcomings of computers," he said. "I changed slightly the order of a well-known opening sequence. Because the computer was unable to compare the new position meaningfully with similar ones in its database, it calculated endlessly but never originated a plan. I could figure out its priorities and adjust my play. It couldn't do the same to me. So, although I did see some signs of intelligence, it's an inflexible kind that makes me think I have a few years left."

The many who took Kasparov, who is generally considered the greatest chess player of all time, as the standard bearer for the collective mind of the human race in this contest, celebrated the day. The human mind prevailed!

And what happened to the loser? Deep Blue, a research computer with special purpose hardware and software and parallel computing systems, went back to serving humanity rather than challenging it. This computer, says IBM, may be useful for conducting research for financial markets, dealing with scheduling at the world's largest airports, or formulating molecular configurations for the pharmaceutical industry.

World chess champion Garry Kasparov ponders his chess move during a match with the IBM supercomputer, Deep Blue, in 1996.

The controls on a typical microwave oven are connected to a small computer. The brown board with the wires connected to it is the computer.

Computers at Home

It is a rare home these days that does not use computers in some form. Although personal computers have become common in people's homes, the majority of "home computers" are actually hidden, or embedded, inside household appliances. For example, televisions contain small computers that automatically fine-tune the image, select the brightness, and correct the color tones. Washing machines, microwave ovens, dishwashers, and sewing machines also use small computers to help them run more efficiently.

You are probably familiar with some of the advancements that computers have brought to home entertainment. VCR and stereo systems that incorporate Surround Sound use computers to simulate the acoustics in a large movie theater or concert hall. Game systems from companies such as Sega and 3DO, are really just specialized personal computers. Now, these new game systems let you play games with a friend who may live next door or across town.

Computer communication has also made the Internet popular among home computer users. The Internet is a world-wide network of computers that enables people to find and share information, discuss topics of common interest, and even advertise and sell products. Home users now use the Internet to shop, do their banking, get advice, send messages to friends, or check the weather in the next state. Essentially, the Internet allows people to stay connected with the people and events that matter to them.

AN OVERVIEW OF THE COMPUTER SYSTEM

The computers you read about in the last few pages come in all shapes and sizes, from the common personal computer, to embedded computers that work inside appliances, to the huge, room-sized machines used by the IRS. Despite the differences in size and use, all of these computers have several characteristics in common. First of all, any computer must be part of a system. As shown in Figure 1.1, a **computer system** consists of four parts:

- Hardware, also known simply as the computer
- Software, also known as programs
- Data, which the system converts into information
- People, also known as users

The term **hardware** refers to the part of the computer you can touch. It consists of interconnected electronic devices that control everything the computer does. When most people talk about a *computer*, they mean hardware.

The term **software** refers to sets of electronic instructions that tell the hardware what to do. These sets of instructions are also known as **programs**, and each of them has a specific purpose. For example, you will probably use a word processing program to enter, edit, and format text documents, such as letters, memos, and reports. WordPerfect and Microsoft Word are two popular word processing programs.

Data refers to the raw facts the computer can manipulate. Data can consist of letters, numbers, sounds, or images. However, no matter what kind of data is entered into a

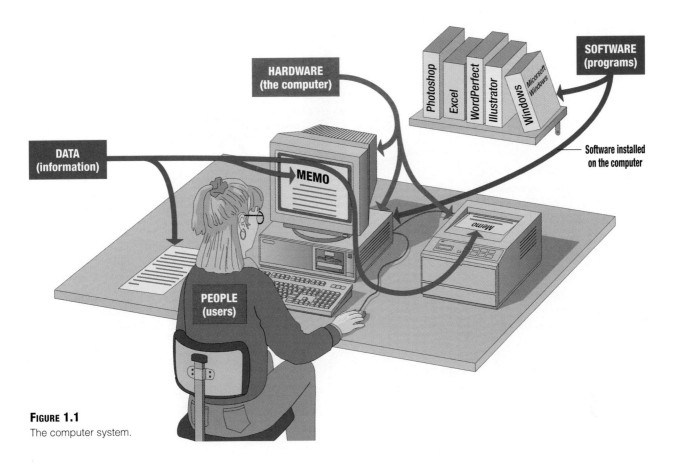

FIGURE 1.1
The computer system.

computer, the computer converts it into numbers. Consequently, computerized data is **digital,** meaning it has been reduced to digits, or numbers. Within the computer, data is organized into files.

A computer **file** is simply a set of data or program instructions that has been given a name. A file containing data is often called a **document**. Although many people think of documents simply as text, a *computer* document can include many kinds of data. For example, a computer document can be a text file (such as a letter), a group of numbers (such as a budget), or a video clip (which includes images and sounds). Programs are organized into files as well, but because programs are not considered data, these are not document files.

The last part of the computer system is the person who uses the computer. In discussions about computers, people are usually referred to as **users**.

▶ LOOKING INSIDE THE MACHINE

The computer itself—the hardware—has many parts, but each piece falls into one of four categories:

1. Processor
2. Memory
3. Input and output devices
4. Storage devices

Figure 1.2 shows the most common pieces of hardware, labeled according to these four categories.

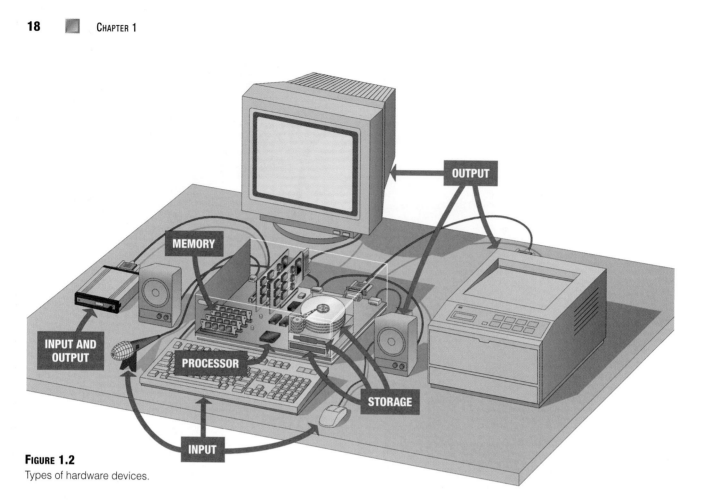

FIGURE 1.2
Types of hardware devices.

The Processor

The complex procedure that transforms raw data into useful information is called **processing.** To perform this transformation, the computer uses two components: the processor and memory.

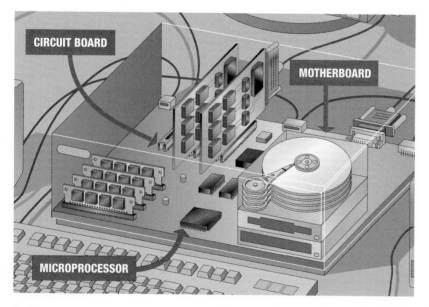

FIGURE 1.3
Processing devices.

The **processor** is like the brain of the computer, the part that organizes and carries out instructions that come from either the user or the software. In a personal computer, the processor usually consists of one or more **microprocessors**, which are slivers of silicon or other material etched with many tiny electronic circuits. As shown in Figure 1.3, the microprocessor is plugged into a **circuit board**—a rigid rectangular card containing the circuitry that connects the processor to the other hardware. The circuit board to which the microprocessor is connected is called the **motherboard**.

In some powerful computers, the processor consists of many chips and the circuit boards on which they are mounted. The term **central processing unit (CPU)** refers to a computer's processing hardware, whether it consists of a single chip or several circuit boards. This "vital organ" occupies an amazingly small space in a PC.

Memory

Memory is the computer's electronic scratchpad. Programs are loaded into and run from memory. Data used by the program is also loaded into memory for fast access. The most common type of memory is called **random access memory**, or **RAM** (see Figure 1.4). As a result, the term *memory* is commonly used to mean *RAM*.

Perhaps the most important thing to remember about RAM is that it is volatile, so it needs a constant supply of power. When you turn off a computer, everything in RAM disappears. As you will soon learn, this is why you frequently have to save everything you are working on to a storage device.

One of the most important factors affecting the speed and power of a computer is the amount of RAM it has. Generally, the more RAM a computer has, the more it can do. The most common measurement unit for describing a computer's memory is the **byte**—the amount of memory it takes to store a single character. When people talk about memory, the numbers are often so large that it is useful to use a shorthand term to describe the values:

- **kilobyte (KB)** approximately 1,000 bytes
- **megabyte (MB)** approximately 1,000,000 bytes
- **gigabyte (GB)** approximately 1,000,000,000 bytes

Today's personal computers commonly have from 8 to 32 million bytes of memory, or 8 to 32 MB.

FIGURE 1.4
Random Access Memory (RAM).

The CPU of a modern computer is a tiny device. The chip is about the size of a fingernail.

Input and Output Devices

Computers would be useless if they did not provide a means to interact with users. They could not receive instructions or deliver the results of their work. **Input devices** accept data and instructions from the user, and **output devices** return processed data back to the user. The generic term **device** refers to any piece of hardware.

Over the years, input devices have been built in many forms for many special purposes. The most common input device is the **keyboard**, which accepts letters, numbers, and commands from the user. In addition, people often use a **mouse**, which lets them draw on the screen and give commands by moving the mouse on a flat surface and pressing its buttons. Some other input devices are **trackballs**, **joysticks**, **scanners**,

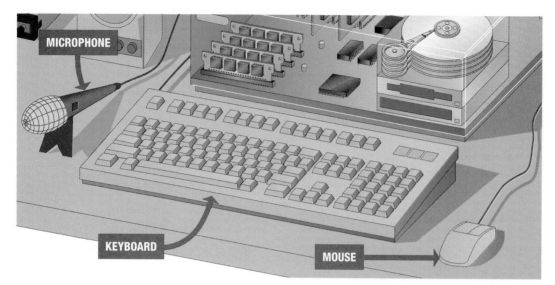

FIGURE 1.5
Input devices.

digital cameras, and **microphones**. The keyboard, mouse, and microphone are labeled in Figure 1.5.

The mouse and trackball allow you to draw or point on the screen. For playing quick-moving video games, the joystick is especially well suited. A scanner can copy a printed page into the computer's memory, eliminating the time-consuming step of keying input manually. Digital cameras record live images that can be viewed and edited on the computer. Similarly, attaching a microphone or CD player to the computer allows you to add the sound of a voice or a piece of music.

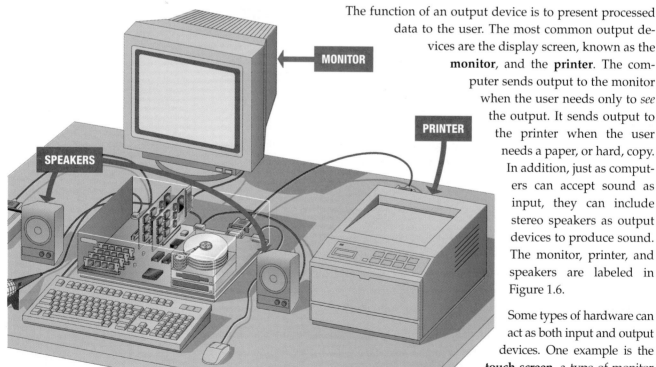

The function of an output device is to present processed data to the user. The most common output devices are the display screen, known as the **monitor**, and the **printer**. The computer sends output to the monitor when the user needs only to *see* the output. It sends output to the printer when the user needs a paper, or hard, copy. In addition, just as computers can accept sound as input, they can include stereo speakers as output devices to produce sound. The monitor, printer, and speakers are labeled in Figure 1.6.

Some types of hardware can act as both input and output devices. One example is the **touch screen**, a type of monitor that displays buttons you can touch.

FIGURE 1.6
Output devices.

The most common types of devices that can perform both input and output, however, are **communication devices**, which connect one computer to another—a process known as **networking**. Among the many kinds of communication devices, the most common are **modems**, which allow computers to communicate through telephone lines, and **network interface cards**, which let users connect a group of computers to share data and devices.

Storage

It is possible for a computer to function with just processing, memory, input, and output devices. To be really useful, however, it also needs a place to keep program files and related data when it is not using them. The purpose of **storage** is to hold data.

It is helpful to think of storage as an electronic file cabinet and to think of RAM as an electronic worktable. When you need to work with a program or a set of data, the computer locates them in the file cabinet and puts a copy on the table. After you have finished working with the program or data, you put the new version into the file cabinet. There are three major distinctions between storage and memory:

1. There is more room in storage than in memory, just as there is more room in a file cabinet than there is on a tabletop.
2. Storage retains its contents when the computer is turned off, whereas the programs or the data you put into memory disappear when you shut down the computer.
3. Storage is much cheaper than memory.

The most common storage medium is the **magnetic disk**. A disk is a round, flat object that spins around its center. **Read/write heads**, which are similar to the heads of a tape recorder or VCR, float above and below the disk near its surface.

Over the years, diskettes have shrunk while their capacity has greatly increased. The 3.5-inch diskette can hold more data than can either of the larger two diskettes.

The device that holds a disk is called a **disk drive**. Some disks are built into the drive and are not meant to be removed, and other kinds of drives allow you to remove and replace disks. Most personal computers have a nonremovable hard disk. In addition, there are usually one or two diskette drives, which allow you to use removable diskettes. Typically, a hard disk can store far more data than a diskette can, so the hard disk serves as the computer's primary filing cabinet. Diskettes are used to load new programs or data onto the hard disk, to trade data with other users, and to make backup copies of the data on the hard disk.

Because you can remove diskettes from a computer, they are encased in a plastic or vinyl cover to protect them from fingerprints and dust. The first diskettes, commonly used in the late 1970s, were 8-inch diskettes (they were 8 inches in diameter). Because the vinyl cover was very thin, the diskette was flimsy, or floppy. Hence, came the name of **floppy disk**. Next came the 5.25-inch diskettes that were common in the early PCs. Finally, the 3.5-inch diskette with its hard plastic shell appeared.

Other types of storage devices include CD-ROM drives, tape drives, optical drives, removable hard drives, and many others. The CD-ROM drive is the most common type after the hard and diskette drives. Compact disks, or CDs, are a type of optical storage device, identical to audio CDs, that can store about 650 MB, or about 450 times

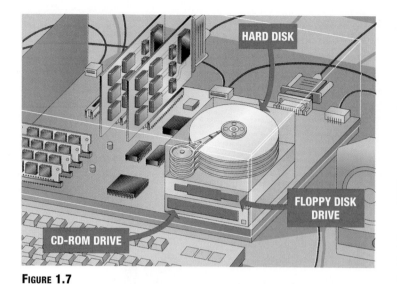

FIGURE 1.7
Storage devices.

as much information as a diskette. The type used in computers is called a CD-ROM, which stands for "compact disk read-only memory." The name implies that you cannot change the information on the disk, just as you cannot record over an audio CD. The hard disk, diskette drive, and CD-ROM drive are shown in Figure 1.7.

▶ SOFTWARE BRINGS THE MACHINE TO LIFE

For the most part, computers are general-purpose machines. You can use them just as effectively to calculate numbers as you can to create documents or drawings or to control other machines. The ingredient that allows a computer to perform a certain task is the software, which consists of electronic instructions. A specific set of the instructions that drive a computer to perform a specific task is called a program. When a computer is using a particular program, it is said to be **running** or **executing** that program. Because programs tell the machine's physical components what to do, without them a computer could not do anything. It would be just a box of metal and plastic.

Although the array of programs available is vast and varied, most software falls into two major categories: **system software** and **application software**. One major type of system software, called operating system software, tells the computer how to use its own components. Application software tells the computer how to accomplish specific tasks for the user, such as word processing or drawing. Figure 1.8 shows the relationship between the two types of software and the hardware, user, and data.

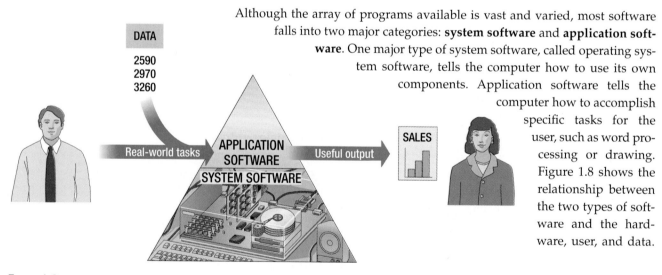

FIGURE 1.8
Application software and system software.

Operating Systems

When you turn on a computer, it goes through several steps to prepare itself for use. The first step is a self-test. The computer identifies the devices that are attached to it, counts the amount of memory available, and does a quick check to see whether the memory is functioning properly. This routine is initiated by a part of the system software located in **read-only memory (ROM)**, a chip that contains brief, permanent instructions for getting the computer started.

Next, the computer looks in the diskette drive and then on the hard drive for a special program called an **operating system**. The operating system tells the computer how to interact with the user and how to use devices such as the disk drives, keyboard, and monitor. When it finds the operating system, the computer loads that program into memory. Because the operating system is needed to control the computer's most basic functions, it continues to run until the computer is turned off.

After the computer finds and runs the operating system, it is ready to accept commands from an input device—usually the keyboard or a mouse. At this point, the user can issue commands to the computer. A command might, for example, list the programs stored on the computer's disk or make the computer run one of those programs. Table 1.1 shows the process the computer goes through at startup.

TABLE 1.1		
The Startup Process		
STEP	**SOURCE OF INSTRUCTION**	**TYPE OF INSTRUCTION**
❶	ROM	System self-check
❷	Hard disk	System software loaded into memory
❸	User	Control hardware by issuing operating system commands *OR* Load an application from the hard disk

Most personal computers run one of six popular systems written by various software companies: Microsoft Windows 95, Microsoft Windows NT, the Macintosh OS, MS-DOS, UNIX, or OS/2.

Application Software

A computer that is running only an operating system is not very useful because the operating system exists mostly for the benefit of the computer. Other programs are required to make the computer useful for people. The term *application software* describes programs that help people accomplish specific tasks. Application software has been written to do almost every task imaginable, from word processing to selecting a college to attend.

With thousands of applications available, categorizing them all is a task for an encyclopedist. There are, however, some major categories you are likely to encounter. These categories are:

- Word processing software
- Desktop publishing software
- Spreadsheets
- Database management software
- Graphics, multimedia, and presentation applications
- Entertainment and education software
- Utilities
- Communications software

Word Processing Programs

Although you can think of a **word processing program** as a computerized version of a typewriter, these programs are actually far more capable than their mechanical predecessors. Most word processors not only allow you to make changes and corrections to text easily, they let you check the spelling and grammar in your document, change the appearance of the type, add graphics, merge address lists with letters for

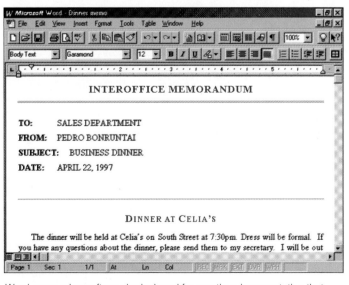

Word processing software is designed for creating documentation that consists primarily of text.

Spreadsheet programs are perfect for setting up budgets. Each cell can contain text, a number, or a formula for calculating a number.

group mailings, and generate indexes and tables of contents. You can use a word processor to create almost any kind of document. Term papers, business letters, legal documents, newsletters, and even books are produced on word processors.

Desktop Publishing Software

Software that handles page layout, or desktop publishing, is a very useful companion for a word processor. Combining the functions of a traditional typesetter and a layout artist, a desktop publishing program merges the output of word processors and graphics programs to produce professional-looking pages that are ready for the printer. Although many word processors can do this to some extent, **desktop publishing programs** have many more sophisticated features. Businesses use them to create advertisements and sales catalogs. Publishers use them to lay out magazines and books. This book, for example, was produced using QuarkXpress.

Spreadsheets

Spreadsheet programs are number crunchers. A **spreadsheet program** displays a large grid of columns and rows that you can view one portion at a time. The areas where columns and rows meet are called **cells**. You can put text, numbers, or formulas into cells to create a worksheet, which is a kind of computerized ledger. When your entries are complete, you can change any of them to produce instant "what-if" calculations—that is, you can plug different numbers into a spreadsheet to test different outcomes. Spreadsheets can also generate graphs and charts to show the relationships among numbers more vividly.

Like most elements in the world of computers, spreadsheets have come a long way since they were first developed. Today, many spreadsheets are three-dimensional, allowing you to create not just a single worksheet, but a stack of them that resembles an entire pad of ledger paper, with each sheet linked electronically to the others.

Spreadsheet programs provide excellent tools for graphing numerical data.

Database Management Software

Database management software extends your ability to organize collections of data stored in your computer and provides tools for listing subsets of the data that meet specified criteria. For example, when you organize information with index cards, you generally arrange it in some logical order, such as alphabetically by name. You can do this sorting with a database as well, but you are not limited to organizing just by name. You can file the same information by several categories, such as company, geographical region, or birth date. Then, when you need to retrieve information from the database, you can look it up using any of the categories you have established. For example, if you are unable to remember a name but you know where that person works, you can find that employee by entering the employer's name. You can also use the computer to select only those records that meet certain conditions. For example, a business could use a database program to list the names of all employees whose salaries fall within a certain range.

Graphics, Multimedia, and Presentation Applications

Programs that manipulate images are known as **graphics programs**, and they come in several forms. With some, you can create illustrations from scratch, using an electronic pointing device such as your pencil or brush. Such programs are referred to as either *paint* or *draw* programs, depending on how the software creates the image.

One important use of the images that are created or manipulated with graphics software is in multimedia, a type of application that incorporates images, text, sound, computer animation, and video (motion sequences, like what you see on TV or in movies). The programs that create multimedia are known as **multimedia authoring software**. This type of application lets you combine different types of media (print, images, sound) in interesting ways. Multimedia authoring software also includes special tools for synchronizing sound with moving images, and for projects such as computer animation and music videos.

Presentation graphics applications are another specialized type of graphics software. These programs help you create professional-looking visual aids for an audience. The visual aids can be computer images, paper printouts, or photographic transparencies. With presentation software, you can import numerical data from a spreadsheet and convert it to colorful graphs and charts. You can orchestrate images and even sounds to produce automated "slide shows."

CAD software, discussed earlier in this chapter, is still another type of graphics software. CAD programs are often used by architects and engineers to draw designs of buildings or products before the actual construction or manufacturing gets under way.

This screen shows a database of names and addresses organized by last name. Database management software makes it easy to reorganize data. For example, you could easily sort this list by city or ZIP code.

Multimedia authoring applications like Macromedia® Director® let you organize graphic elements into a sequenced presentation.

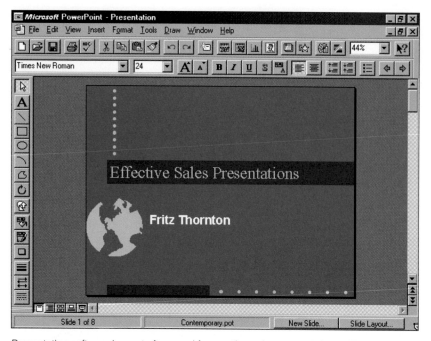

Presentation software is most often used for creating sales presentations, although it can be effective for any type of electronic slide show.

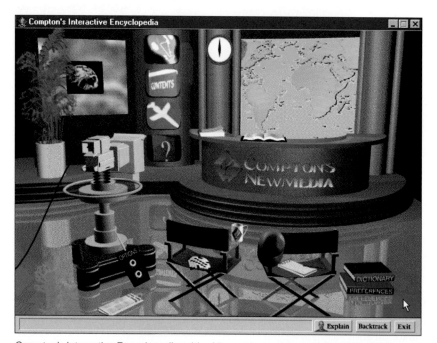

Compton's Interactive Encyclopedia adds video and sound to encyclopedia entries. Users can begin to explore the entries by clicking on objects in this virtual newsroom.

Entertainment and Education Software

Tutorials, games, and simulations are a few examples of the many types of entertainment programs that are available. Many educational programs can also be considered **entertainment software** and have been nicknamed "**edutainment**" programs. For example, programs that teach children how to do mathematics, how to recognize the alphabet, or how to read whole words and sentences are almost always presented as games with rewards for correct answers. These programs can be superb educational tools. While children enjoy playing, they learn fundamental skills. Educational programs are not limited to the three Rs, though. Older children and adults can use foreign-language tutors that test pronunciation and electronic encyclopedias that incorporate video and sound. Astronomy programs can re-create the night sky on your computer screen, with the stars and planets in their correct positions from the perspective of any point on Earth, and at any date or time. There are even games that teach you about the human body by allowing you to perform electronic "surgery."

Utilities

Utilities are useful programs that assist in the operation of your computer. Some help you back up data, remove outdated files, or recover data that has been accidentally erased. Others make it easier to find and arrange the information you need. Today, the most popular utilities are usually included as part of the operating system. For example, Windows 95 comes with half a dozen tools for taking care of your disks, including a backup utility and an anti-virus utility.

It is a sad truth that every new device, operating system, and application package that comes to market brings with it a new set of problems and dilemmas. Utilities bridge the gaps by helping to solve the problems and maximize your computer's potential.

Communications Software

Applications that put your computer in touch with others are called **communications programs**. The first type of communications software created for PCs allowed them to use modems, which are hardware devices for sending data across the telephone lines. With a modem and a piece of communications software, a user can exchange information with another user.

Another kind of communications software, called **network software**, lets users create a **network**, which is simply a group of connected computers. During the past ten years, networks using Novell NetWare and Microsoft's Windows NT have become extremely popular, and they are now considered almost a necessity for business computing.

The communication program shown here lets you send a document in the form of a fax to anyone who has a fax machine or a computer with a fax modem.

Other types of communications software include fax software, which lets a computer and a printer work like a fax machine, and the software distributed by the online service providers, such as CompuServe, America Online, and Microsoft Network, which lets you use a modem to connect your computer to the service.

THE SHAPES OF COMPUTERS TODAY

General-purpose computers come in many sizes and with varying capabilities. The terms that describe the different types of computers have been around for some time, although the capabilities of each type have changed quickly. These are the terms:

- Supercomputer
- Mainframe
- Minicomputer
- Microcomputer, or personal computer

All these types of computers can be connected to form networks of computers, but each individual computer, whether it is on a network or not, falls into one of these four categories.

Supercomputers

Supercomputers are the most powerful computers made. They are built to process huge amounts of data. For example, scientists build models of complex processes and simulate the processes on a supercomputer. One such process is nuclear fission. As a fissionable material approaches a critical mass, the researchers want to know exactly what will happen during every nanosecond of a nuclear chain reaction. A supercomputer can model the actions and reactions of literally millions of atoms as they interact.

Cray supercomputers are among the most powerful computers made. This model is the Cray T3E.

Another complex study for which scientists used a supercomputer involved air pollution in Los Angeles. A model that comprised more than 500,000 variables, including geographic elevations, temperatures, and airborne chemicals, was required to create an accurate simulation of the Los Angeles Basin and to predict the effects of various strategies for pollution control. This simulation would have taken many hours using a less powerful computer, but the supercomputer did it in half an hour.

Because computer technology changes so quickly, the advanced capabilities of a supercomputer today may become the standard features of a PC a few years from now, and next year's supercomputer will be vastly more powerful than today's. Contemporary super-computers generally cost upwards of $20 million, and they consume enough electricity to power 100 homes.

Mainframe Computers

The largest type of computer in common use is the mainframe. **Mainframe computers** are used where many people in a large organization need frequent access to the same information, which is usually organized into one or more huge databases. For example, consider the Texas Department of Public Safety, where people get their drivers' licenses. This state agency maintains offices in every major city in Texas, each of which has many employees who work at computer terminals. A **terminal** is a keyboard and screen wired to the mainframe. It does not have its own CPU or storage; it is just an **input/output (I/O)** device that functions as a window into a computer located somewhere else. The terminals at the Public Safety offices are all connected to a common database on a mainframe in the state capital. The database is controlled by a mainframe computer that handles the input and output needs of all the terminals connected to it. Each user has continuous access to the driving records and administrative information for every licensed driver and vehicle in the state—literally millions of records. On smaller systems, handling this volume of user access to a central database would be difficult and more time consuming.

Mainframe computers can cost anywhere from $35,000 to many millions of dollars. It used to be common for mainframe computers to occupy entire rooms or even an entire floor of a high-rise building. Typically, they were placed inside glass offices with special air conditioning to keep them cool and on raised floors to accommodate all the wiring needed to tie the system together. This setup is not used much anymore. Today, a typical mainframe computer looks like an unimposing file cabinet—or a row of file cabinets—although it may still require a somewhat controlled environment.

No one really knows where the term *mainframe* originated. Early IBM documents explicitly define the term *frame* as an integral part of a computer: "the housing, . . . hardware support structures, . . . and all the parts and components therein." It may be that when computers of all sizes and shapes began to appear in computer environments, the big computer was referred to as the *main frame*, as in the *main computer*, and that eventually the term was shortened to one word, *mainframe*.

Mainframe CPU

Mainframe terminals

The two employees in the foreground of this photo are working on mainframe terminals. Each terminal consists of a monitor and a keyboard. Processing for the terminals is carried out by the mainframe's CPU, which is visible in the background.

Minicomputers

When Digital Equipment Corporation (DEC) began shipping its PDP series computers in the early 1960s, the press dubbed these machines minicomputers because of their small size compared to other computers of the day. Much to DEC's chagrin, the name stuck. (Later, when even smaller computers built around microprocessors came out, they were first called **microcomputers** but, eventually, they were named *personal computers*.)

The best way to explain the capabilities of a **minicomputer** is to say that they lie somewhere between those of mainframes and those of personal computers. Like mainframes, minicomputers can handle a great deal more input and output than personal computers can. Although some minis are designed for a single user, many can handle dozens or even hundreds of terminals.

Minicomputers cost anywhere from $18,000 to $500,000 and are ideal for many organizations and companies because they are relatively inexpensive but have some of the desirable features of a mainframe. A company that needs the power of a mainframe but cannot afford such a large machine may find that a minicomputer suits its needs nicely. The major minicomputer manufacturers include DEC, Data General, IBM, and Hewlett-Packard.

This box, which is about the size of a large file cabinet, contains the CPU of an IBM AS400 minicomputer.

Personal Computers

When people use the terms *personal computer*, *PC*, and *microcomputer*, they mean the small computers that are commonly found in offices, classrooms, and homes. Personal computers come in many shapes, sizes, and brands. Although most models sit on desktops, others stand on the floor, and some are portable.

The terms *microcomputer* and *personal computer* are interchangeable; however, *PC*—which stands for *personal computer*—sometimes has a more specific meaning. In 1981, IBM called its first microcomputer the IBM PC. Within a few years, many companies were copying the IBM design, creating "clones" or "compatibles" that aimed at functioning just like the original. For this reason, the term *PC* has come to mean the family of computers that includes IBMs and IBM-compatibles. The vast majority of the microcomputers sold today are part of this family. The Apple Macintosh computer, however, is neither an IBM nor a compatible. It is another family of microcomputers, made by Apple Computer. So, it is accurate to say that a Macintosh is a personal computer, but some people consider it misleading to refer to the Macintosh as a PC. In this book, however, we will use the term *PC* as a simple abbreviation for *personal computer*, referring to both IBM-compatible models and Apple's Macintosh line.

This woman is using a minicomputer called the DEC Alpha Server 8400. Most of the computer is housed in the cabinet in the background.

One of the sources of the PC's popularity is the rate at which improvements are made in the technology. Microprocessors, memory chips, and storage devices keep getting faster and bigger. For example, compared to the typical PC of 10 years ago, a machine of the same price today will have at least 8 times as much RAM, about 50 times more storage capacity, and a microprocessor that is at least 75 times as fast. What's more, many analysts believe that this pace of change is going to continue for another 10 or 20 years!

One result of increasing PC power is that the differences between mainframes, minis, and microcomputers are not as great as they once were. In fact, the processing power of PCs often rivals that of current mainframes. (Mainframes are still popular because they can handle the input and output needs of many users at once, so they are still the right choice for the massive databases that many people need to use at the same time.)

Desktop Models

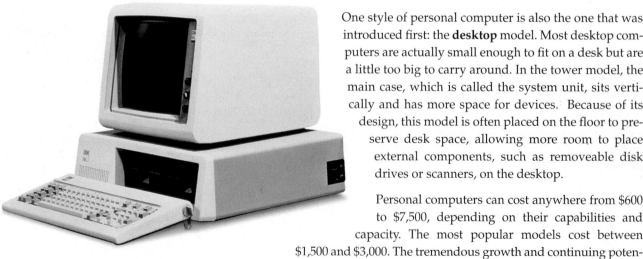

One style of personal computer is also the one that was introduced first: the **desktop** model. Most desktop computers are actually small enough to fit on a desk but are a little too big to carry around. In the tower model, the main case, which is called the system unit, sits vertically and has more space for devices. Because of its design, this model is often placed on the floor to preserve desk space, allowing more room to place external components, such as removeable disk drives or scanners, on the desktop.

Personal computers can cost anywhere from $600 to $7,500, depending on their capabilities and capacity. The most popular models cost between $1,500 and $3,000. The tremendous growth and continuing potential of the PC market has brought many manufacturers into this arena. A

The first IBM PC was released in 1981.

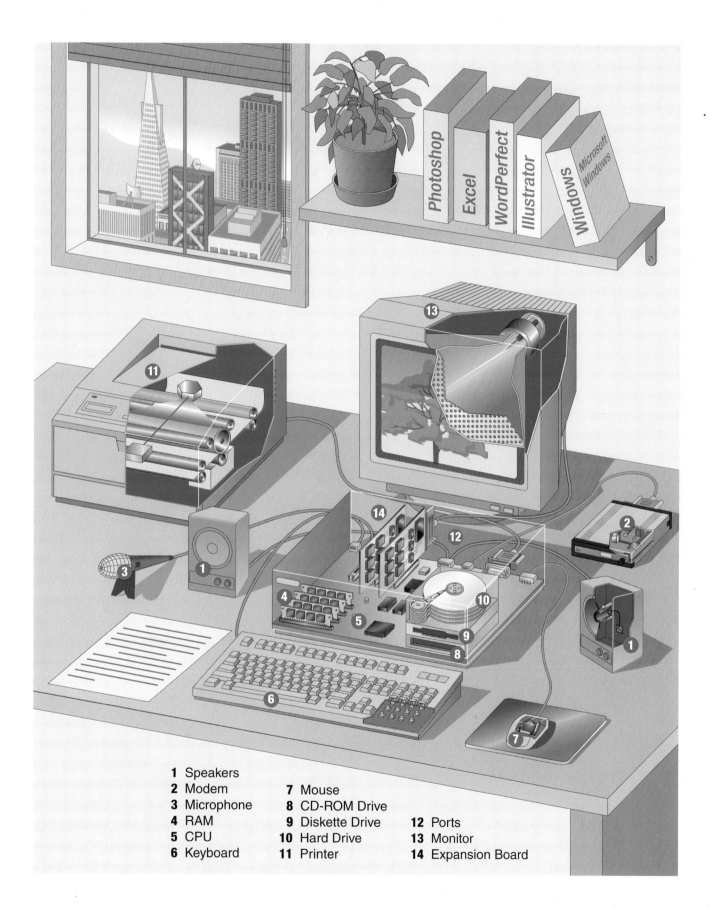

1 Speakers

2 Modem

3 Microphone   **7** Mouse

4 RAM   **8** CD-ROM Drive

5 CPU   **9** Diskette Drive   **12** Ports

6 Keyboard   **10** Hard Drive   **13** Monitor

                 11 Printer   **14** Expansion Board

Two common designs for PCs are shown here. On the left is the more traditional desktop model, with the monitor sitting on top of the system unit. On the right is a tower model, with the system unit sitting vertically. To save space, system units for tower models are often placed under a desk.

few of the major personal computer manufacturers are Apple, IBM, Compaq, Dell, and Hewlett-Packard.

Notebook Computers

Notebook computers, as their name implies, approximate the shape of an 8.5 by 11-inch notebook and can fit easily inside a briefcase. Also called laptops, they can operate on plug-in current or with special batteries. Notebooks are fully functional microcomputers; the people who use them need the power of a full computer wherever they go. Some models can plug into a "dock" that includes a large monitor, a full-sized keyboard, and sometimes an additional disk drive.

Personal Digital Assistants

Personal digital assistants (PDAs) are the smallest of portable computers. Often, they are no larger than a checkbook. PDAs, also sometimes called **palmtops**, are much less powerful than notebook or desktop models. They are normally used for special applications, such as creating small spreadsheets, displaying important telephone numbers and addresses, and keeping track of dates and agendas. Many can be connected to larger computers to exchange data.

This area of computing is evolving quickly. Some PDAs come with an **electronic pen** that lets users write on a touch-sensitive screen. The latest generation of PDAs can use infrared light to communicate with nearby computers. They may also have built-in cellular telephone, fax, and electronic mail capabilities.

The people who use PDAs generally want to avoid carrying a lot of weight and do not need a full array of applications while away from home or the office. Most use inexpensive standard batteries, the kind sold everywhere. Because of their limited power, however, PDAs usually have no disk drives. Instead, most use devices called PC cards, each about the size of a credit card, to store programs and data. These cards have proved so handy that the makers of notebook and desktop computers have adopted them as well.

The IBM ThinkPad is a notebook computer. When the computer is not being used, the top folds down and the keyboard collapses. The whole computer becomes about the size and weight of a thick pad of paper.

Many PDAs are pen-based computers. You interact with the computer by "writing" on the screen.

Buying a computer these days can seem a little like choosing from the dozens of flavors in an ice cream store; there are so many different models and options from which to choose! But the choice of a computer is not just a matter of taste. Some models actually will meet your needs better than others.

When deciding which computer to buy, one of the first questions to ask is: Do I want the power and wide-reaching capabilities of a desktop system, or the ease and convenience of a portable? Here are some simple guidelines to help you make up your mind.

First you must decide: What do I want a computer *for?* What do I want to *do* with it? Generally speaking, you will probably lean toward a **desktop model** if you plan to use it for:

■ *Graphic work or desktop publishing.* A desktop system will give you maximum monitor display size and color quality.

■ *Multimedia use.* A desktop will provide the best sound, video, CD-ROM speed, and flexibility for running multimedia products. You can get away with a high-end portable for *playing* multimedia products, but for the *creation* of multimedia, a desktop model is still the most practical.

■ *Scientific calculation or intensive 3-D graphics.* A desktop offers maximum processing speed.

■ *Complex configuration of peripherals or add-ons.* A desktop system can easily support adding on such specialized peripherals as circuit boards for sound, accelerators, networking access, mainframe connections, and various external devices.

You will be more satisfied with a **portable model** if you want to:

■ *Carry your data with you.* Do you need to keep schedules, addresses, work materials or study notes with you at all times? Will you be doing any "road warrior" work, such as sales or scientific field investigation? Portables make field work easy.

■ *Be able to work anywhere.* Do you want to do your banking at the beach, term papers in an airport terminal, or access databases in the restaurant? With portables, you can work anywhere in confined spaces, such as airplane seats.

■ *Present your work.* Do you want to be able to show your professor work-in-progress, display your artwork to prospective clients, or demonstrate your product line in your customers' offices? Portables can be the answer for on-the-spot presentations and demonstrations.

■ *Communicate instantly.* Is it important to you to have e-mail, faxes, and Internet tools always available? Portables coupled with cellular communications offer instant communication—to anywhere, from anywhere.

In case you still haven't made up your mind, there is a way to have the best of both worlds, though it requires a larger cash investment: Buy a high-quality monitor that resides on a desk and a cable to attach it to the "external video port" of your portable computer. (Not all portables have one. Ask when you buy.) This way, you can use your portable on the road, and have the convenience of a bigger display while at home or at work.

Or, buy a portable that has a "docking station" which allows you to plug your portable into a larger system effectively. A docking station also lets you build your own permanent system around your portable. For example, you can add disk drives, a bigger monitor, networking circuits and expansion slots for add-on peripherals.

Either way—with external monitor or docking station—you will have the best of both worlds: the advantages of portability when you are away from your desk, and a larger, more powerful system when you are at your desk.

Laptop computers allow you to work almost anywhere, whether your "office" is Ringling Brothers Circus...

...or a construction site.

Workstations

At the other end of the spectrum, in terms of PC power, are the machines sometimes called **workstations**. It is usually scientists, engineers, graphic artists, and programmers who use these powerful machines—that is, users who need a great deal of number-crunching power. In days past, workstations implied certain differences in terms of chip design and operating system. However, just as the distinctions between mainframes, minis, and microcomputers have become less clear, so have the differences between workstations and other PCs. This is all the result of the incessant increase in the power and popularity of the PC.

This personal computer is actually a powerful Ultra 1 workstation from Sun Microsystems.

▶ WHAT TO EXPECT IN THE FUTURE

These days, people just assume that in the future, computers will give them more power for less money and that computer manufacturers will pack more power into smaller packages. It is also a good bet that, given the multitude of software packages available for specialized tasks, your job will somehow involve using a computer.

Perhaps the most important change likely to take place in our society as a result of the computer industry is a continued explosion in connectivity. In other words, the computers you use, whether at home, at school, or at work, are going to be connected to the computers other people use. In one respect, this growth in connectivity will mean that you will be able to send e-mail—electronic messages transmitted on a network—to virtually anybody. You will be able to shop from home, bank from home, and conduct library research without going to the library.

These capabilities assume that everyone will be using the world-wide network known as the Internet. The fact that other types of electronic networks are going to be popping up all over the place is equally important, in terms of social impact. Remember, the telephone system, the cable system, and the electrical utility system are all networks. The companies that own these systems are watching the growth of the Internet and trying to figure out how to use their own infrastructures to offer more services to homes and businesses. As they do, you are going to experience a technical revolution that will affect

- How and where you work.
- How and where you and your children go to school.
- How you communicate with other people.
- How and where you shop and how you pay for goods.
- How you obtain and share information.

▶ VISUAL SUMMARY

The Multipurpose Tool

- The first modern computers were used for complex numerical tasks.
- Computers began to revolutionize the business world in the 1960s.
- Modern medicine uses computers in many ways. One of the most interesting is computerized diagnostic equipment that is so small it can be swallowed.
- Educators are interested in computers as tools for interactive learning.
- The scientific community uses computers to do research and to exchange information with colleagues around the world.
- Engineers and architects use computers to design objects and structures with the help of CAD techniques.
- Attorneys use computers to access and create databases that contain records of old cases and data related to current ones.
- Major governmental uses of computers include the Social Security system, the Bureau of the Census, the military, and the Internal Revenue Service.
- Musicians can use MIDI to combine or create sounds electronically, either in the recording studio or during live performances.
- Computers are used in theater and film to control stage lighting, create special effects, and streamline the film-editing process.

An Overview of the Computer System

- Computer systems include hardware, software, data, and people.
- Hardware consists of electronic devices, the parts you can see.
- Software, also known as programs, consists of organized sets of instructions for controlling the computer.
- Data consists of text, numbers, sounds, and images that the computer can manipulate.

Looking Inside the Machine

- The hardware, or physical components, of a computer consist of a processor, memory, input and output (I/O) devices, and storage.
- The processing function is divided between the processor and memory.
- The processor, or CPU, is the brain of the machine.
- Memory holds data as the CPU works with it.
- The most common units of measure for memory are the byte, kilobyte, megabyte, and gigabyte.
- The role of input is to provide data from the user or some other source.
- The function of output is present processed data to the user.

- Communication devices perform both input and output, allowing computers to share information.
- Storage holds data that is not currently being used by the CPU.

Software Brings the Machine to Life

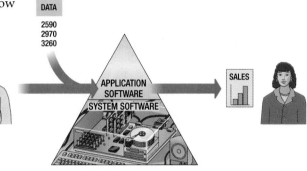

- Programs are electronic instructions that tell the computer how to accomplish certain tasks.
- When a computer is using a particular program, it is referred to as running or executing the program.
- The operating system tells the computer how to interact with the user and how to use the hardware devices attached to the computer.
- Application software tells the computer how to accomplish tasks the user requires.
- Eight important kinds of application software are word processing programs, desktop publishing, databases, spreadsheets, graphics, education and entertainment applications, utilities, and communications.

The Shapes of Computers Today

- There are four types of computers: supercomputers, mainframes, minicomputers, and personal computers.
- Supercomputers are the most powerful computers in terms of processing. They are useful for problems requiring complex calculations.
- Mainframe computers, which generally have many terminals connected to them, handle massive amounts of input, output, and storage.
- Minicomputers are smaller than mainframes but larger than microcomputers. They usually have multiple terminals.
- Personal computers are also called microcomputers. The term PC often denotes microcomputers that are either IBM PCs or compatibles. The term can also to refer to personal computers made by other manufacturers.
- Desktop computers, including the newer tower models, are the most common type of personal computer.
- Laptops (notebooks) and PDAs are used by people who need portable computing power outside the office.

- The most powerful PCs, which are used by engineers, scientists, and graphic artists, are known as workstations.

VISUAL SUMMARY AND EXERCISES

▶ KEY TERMS

After completing this chapter, you should be able to define the following terms:

application software, 22
automated fabrication, 10
byte, 19
cells, 24
central processing unit (CPU), 18
circuit board, 18
communication devices, 21
communications programs, 27
computer, 4
computer-aided drafting (computer-
    aided design or CAD), 8
computer-aided engineering (CAE), 8
computer-aided manufacturing (CAM), 10
computer-integrated manufacturing
    (CIM), 10
computer system, 16
data, 16
databases, 10
database management software, 24
desktop, 30
desktop publishing programs, 24
device, 19
digital, 17
digital cameras, 20
disk drive, 21
document, 17
edutainment, 26
electronic pen, 31
entertainment software, 26
executing, 22

file, 17
floppy disk, 21
gigabyte (GB), 19
graphics programs, 25
hardware, 16
input devices, 19
input/output (I/O), 28
joysticks, 19
keyboard, 19
kilobyte (KB, 19
laptops, 4
magnetic disk, 21
mainframe computers, 28
megabyte (MB), 19
memory, 19
microcomputer, 29
microphones, 20
microprocessor, 18
minicomputer, 29
mobile data terminals (MDTs), 11
modem, 21
monitor, 20
motherboard, 18
mouse, 19
multimedia authoring software, 25
Musical Instrument Digital
    Interface (MIDI), 13
network, 27
networking, 21
network interface cards, 21

network software, 27
notebooks, 4
operating system, 22
output devices, 19
palmtops, 31
personal computer (PC), 4
personal digital assistants (PDAs), 31
presentation graphics applications, 25
printer, 20
processing, 18
processor, 18
programs, 16
random access memory (RAM), 19
read-only memory (ROM), 22
read/write heads, 21
running, 22
scanners, 19
software, 16
spreadsheet program, 24
storage, 21
supercomputers, 27
system software, 22
terminal, 28
touch screen, 20
trackballs, 19
users, 17
utilities, 26
word processing program, 23
workstations, 33

▶ KEY TERM QUIZ

Fill in the missing word with one of the terms listed in Key Terms:

1. A(n) _____ enables a computer to communicate through a telephone line.

2. Electronic instructions that tell the hardware what to do are known as _____.

3. A(n) _____ is a powerful type of PC, usually used by scientists, engineers, graphic artists, or programmers.

4. Portable computers that can fit easily inside a briefcase are called _____.

5. A(n) _____ is a group of computers connected together.

6. A(n) _____ is a device that holds a disk.

7. The _____ refers to the combination of hardware, software, data, and people.

8. A keyboard and screen that are wired to a mainframe are known as a(n) _____.

9. A(n) _____ is a set of data or software that has been given a name.

10. A(n) _____ is a group of electronic devices used for processing data.

REVIEW QUESTIONS

1. Name three everyday places, outside of school or work, where you would be likely to encounter a computer, and describe how it is used in each setting.

2. Consider the types of work situations discussed in this chapter, and describe briefly how computers contribute to safer working environments for people.

3. List the four key components of a computer system. For each, provide an example and define its function.

4. Describe the relationship that exists between a computer's processor and its memory.

5. For each of the following devices, describe the type of component it is and briefly describe its function within a computer system.

   a. Laser printer
   b. Mouse
   c. Modem
   d. 1.2 GB hard drive
   e. CPU

6. Name at least three categories of application software that could be used to produce a publication such as a brochure or newsletter. Describe briefly how each can contribute to the final product's development.

7. Describe at least two ways in which storage complements memory.

8. Suppose you want to determine the materials needed to build a deck, including types, amounts, and costs. What category of application software do you think would be well suited for planning this project? Describe briefly how it can be used.

9. What are the four size categories for computers? Which one do you think would be best suited for an employee database in a company employing 250 employees at a single location?

10. Which type of computer provides a user with mobility as well as essentially the same processing capabilities as a desktop personal computer?

DISCUSSION QUESTIONS

1. Do you envision computers in the home being used more extensively over the next five to ten years for such everyday tasks as shopping, banking, and communicating with others? If so, list two or three reasons that support this direction; if not, explain why you think this is not likely to occur.

2. Will the "explosion" of connectivity that is now occurring have an impact on your own career goals? In what ways do you think using the Internet might contribute to your productivity in the career you imagine pursuing?

3. Consider some of the improvements that computers have brought to our lives, as addressed in this chapter. What key factors or characteristics do you believe make computers an essential part of our lives in today's world?

4. This chapter states that networks have become "almost a necessity for business computing." What do think about the growing impact that networks are having on industries? List at least two advantages for business that you think networked systems provide over systems that are not networked.

NORTON INTERACTIVE

Complete the Norton Interactive module for this chapter.

PROCESSING DATA

CONTENTS

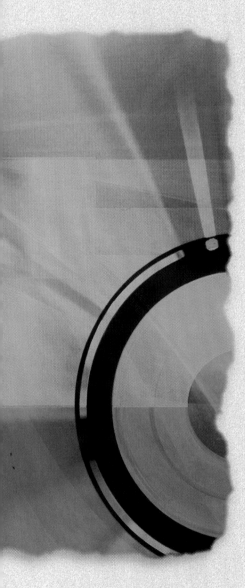

OBJECTIVES

When you complete this chapter, you will be able to do the following:

- Discuss the difference between data and information.
- Explain why computers use the binary number system.
- Describe the two main parts of the CPU and explain how they work together to process data.
- Differentiate between RAM and ROM.
- Describe the hardware features that affect processing speed.
- Compare members of the best-known families of CPUs.

Even people who have been using computers for years still marvel at what they can do: how at lightning speed and with amazing accuracy they can sort a mailing list, balance a ledger, typeset a book, or create lifelike models of objects that have never existed.

Just how a computer does all this may seem magical, but in fact it is a process based on simple concepts. All the words, numbers, and images you put into and get out of the computer are manipulated in relatively simple ways by the computer's processing components.

In this chapter, you'll find out what data is, how it differs from information, and what form it takes in the computer. Then, you'll explore the two processing components: the central processing unit (CPU) and memory. You'll also learn about the most important factors affecting a computer's speed. Finally, you'll look at the microprocessors made by the biggest chip manufacturers, with an emphasis on the families of chips from Intel and Motorola.

▶ TRANSFORMING DATA INTO INFORMATION

It often seems as though computers must understand us because we understand the information that they produce. However, computers cannot *understand* anything. All they can do is recognize two distinct physical states produced by electricity, magnetic polarity, or reflected light. Essentially, all they can understand is whether a switch is on or off. In fact, the "brain" of the computer, the CPU, consists primarily of several million tiny electronic switches, called **transistors**.

A computer only appears to understand information because it contains so many transistors and operates at such phenomenal speeds, assembling its individual on/off switches into patterns that are meaningful to us.

The term used to describe the information represented by groups of on/off switches is data. Although the words *data* and *information* are often used interchangeably, there is an important distinction between them. In the strictest sense, *data* consists of the raw numbers that computers organize to produce information.

You can think of data as facts out of context, like the individual letters on this page. Taken individually, they do not tell you a thing. Grouped together, however, they convey specific meanings. Just as a theater's marquee can combine thousands of lights to spell the name of the current show, a computer turns meaningless data into useful information, such as spreadsheets, graphs, and reports.

How Computers Represent Data

To a computer, everything is a number. Numbers are numbers, letters and punctuation marks are numbers, sounds and pictures are numbers; even the computer's own

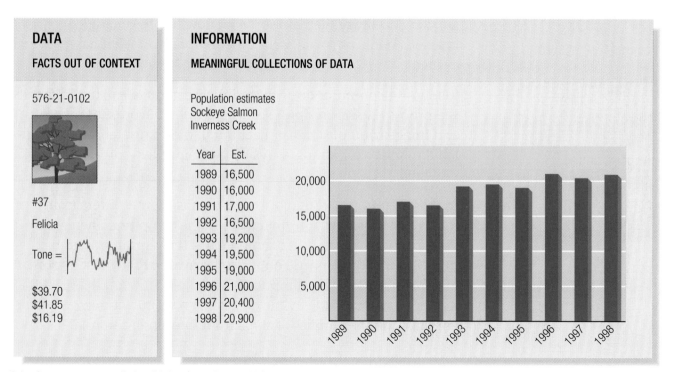

It is often necessary to distinguish between data and information.

instructions are numbers. This might seem strange since you have probably seen computer screens with words and sentences on them, but it is true. When you see letters of the alphabet on a computer screen, what you are seeing is just one of the computer's ways of representing numbers. For example, consider this sentence:

Here are some words.

It may look like a string of alphabetic characters to you, but to a computer it looks like the string of ones and zeros shown in Figure 2.1.

Computer data looks especially strange because people normally use base 10 to represent numbers. The system is called *base 10*, or the **decimal system** (*deci* means 10 in Latin) because ten symbols are available: 1, 2, 3, 4, 5, 6, 7, 8, 9, and 0. When you need to represent a number greater than 9, you use two symbols together, as in 9 + 1 = 10. Each symbol in a number is called a digit, so 10 is a two-digit number.

In a computer, however, all data must be reduced to electrical switches. A switch has only two possible states—"on" and "off"—so it has only two numeric symbols. 0 stands for "off," and 1 stands for "on." Because there are only two symbols, computers are said to function in base 2, which is also known as the **binary system** (*bi* means two in Latin).

When a computer needs to represent a quantity greater than 1, it does the same thing you do when you need to represent a quantity greater than 9: it uses two (or more) digits. To familiarize yourself with the binary system, take a look at Table 2.1, which shows how to count in base 10 and base 2.

Bits and Bytes

When referring to computerized data, each switch—whether it is on or off—is called a **bit**. The term *bit* is a contraction of *binary digit*. A bit is the smallest possible unit of data. To represent anything meaningful, that is, to convey information, the computer needs groups of bits.

H	0100 1000
e	0110 0101
r	0111 0010
e	0110 0101
	0010 0000
a	0110 0001
r	0111 0010
e	0110 0101
	0010 0000
s	0111 0011
o	0110 1111
m	0110 1101
e	0110 0101
	0010 0000
w	0111 0111
o	0110 1111
r	0111 0010
d	0110 0100
s	0111 0011
.	0010 0001

Figure 2.1
1s and 0s representing a sentence.

Table 2.1	
Counting in Base 10 and Base 2	
BASE 10	**BASE 2**
0	0
1	1
2	10
3	11
4	100
5	101
6	110
7	111
8	1000
9	1001
10	1010

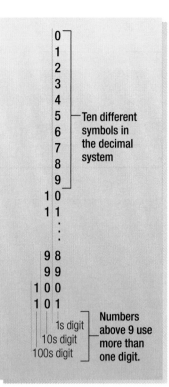

The decimal system uses ten symbols and multiple digits for numbers above 9.

Computers represent data with electrical switches. An "on" switch represents a 1. An "off" switch represents a 0.

After the bit, the next larger unit of data is the **byte**, which is a group of 8 bits. With one byte, the computer can represent up to 256 different values because it is possible to count from 0 to 255 with 8 binary digits.

The byte is an extremely important unit because there are enough different eight-bit combinations to represent all the characters on the keyboard, including all the letters

1 bit

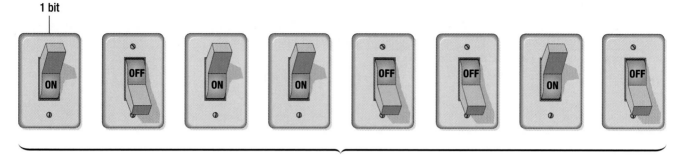

8 bits = 1 byte

One byte is composed of eight bits.

(uppercase and lowercase), numbers, punctuation marks, and other symbols. If you refer back to Figure 2.1, you'll notice that each of the characters (or letters) in the sentence "Here are some words." is represented by one byte of data.

Text Codes

Early in the history of computing, programmers realized they needed a standard code—a system they could all agree on—in which numbers stood for the letters of the alphabet, punctuation marks, and other symbols. EBCDIC, ASCII, and Unicode are three of the most popular systems that were invented.

EBCDIC

The BCD (Binary Coded Decimal) system, defined by IBM for one of its early computers, was one of the first complete systems to represent symbols with bits. BCD codes consisted of six-bit codes, which allowed a maximum of 64 possible symbols. BCD computers could work only with uppercase letters and with very few other symbols. For those reasons this system was short-lived.

The need to represent more characters led to IBM's development of the EBCDIC system. **EBCDIC**, pronounced "EB-si-dic," stands for Extended Binary Coded Decimal Interchange Code.

EBCDIC is an eight-bit code that defines 256 symbols. EBCDIC is still used in IBM mainframe and mid-range systems but is rarely encountered in personal computers. By the time small computers were being developed, the American National Standards Institute (ANSI) had swung into action to define standards for computers.

ASCII

The ANSI organization's solution to representing symbols with bits of data was the **ASCII** character set. ASCII stands for the American Standard Code for Information Interchange. Today, the ASCII character set is by far the most common. Table 2.2 shows the ASCII codes.

The characters from 0 to 31 are control characters; from 32 to 64, special characters and numbers; from 65 to 90, uppercase letters; from 97 to 127, lowercase letters, plus a handful of common symbols. Because ASCII, a seven-bit code, specifies characters up to only 127, there are many variations that specify different character sets for codes 128 through 255. The ISO (International Standards Organization) standard offers different sets of characters for different language groups. ISO 8859-1, for

TABLE 2.2

The ASCII Table

ASCII CODE	DECIMAL EQUIVALENT	CHARACTER	ASCII CODE	DECIMAL EQUIVALENT	CHARACTER	ASCII CODE	DECIMAL EQUIVALENT	CHARACTER
0000 0000	0	Null	0010 1011	43	+	0101 0110	86	V
0000 0001	1	Start of heading	0010 1100	44	,	0101 0111	87	W
0000 0010	2	Start of text	0010 1101	45	-	0101 1000	88	X
0000 0011	3	End of text	0010 1110	46	.	0101 1001	89	Y
0000 0100	4	End of transmit	0010 1111	47	/	0101 1010	90	Z
0000 0101	5	Enquiry	0011 0000	48	0	0101 1011	91	[
0000 0110	6	Acknowledge	0011 0001	49	1	0101 1100	92	\
0000 0111	7	Audible bell	0011 0010	50	2	0101 1101	93	]
0000 1000	8	Backspace	0011 0011	51	3	0101 1110	94	^
0000 1001	9	Horizontal tab	0011 0100	52	4	0101 1111	95	–
0000 1010	10	Line feed	0011 0101	53	5	0110 0000	96	`
0000 1011	11	Vertical tab	0011 0110	54	6	0110 0001	97	a
0000 1100	12	Form feed	0011 0111	55	7	0110 0010	98	b
0000 1101	13	Carriage return	0011 1000	56	8	0110 0011	99	c
0000 1110	14	Shift out	0011 1001	57	9	0110 0100	100	d
0000 1111	15	Shift in	0011 1010	58	:	0110 0101	101	e
0001 0000	16	Data line escape	0011 1011	59	;	0110 0110	102	f
0001 0001	17	Device control 1	0011 1100	60	<	0110 0111	103	g
0001 0010	18	Device control 2	0011 1101	61	=	0110 1000	104	h
0001 0011	19	Device control 3	0011 1110	62	>	0110 1001	105	i
0001 0100	20	Device control 4	0011 1111	63	?	0110 1010	106	j
0001 0101	21	Neg. acknowledge	0100 0000	64	@	0110 1011	107	k
0001 0110	22	Synchronous idle	0100 0001	65	A	0110 1100	108	l
0001 0111	23	End trans. block	0100 0010	66	B	0110 1101	109	m
0001 1000	24	Cancel	0100 0011	67	C	0110 1110	110	n
0001 1001	25	End of medium	0100 0100	68	D	0110 1111	111	o
0001 1010	26	Substitution	0100 0101	69	E	0111 0000	112	p
0001 1011	27	Escape	0100 0110	70	F	0111 0001	113	q
0001 1100	28	Figures shift	0100 0111	71	G	0111 0010	114	r
0001 1101	29	Group separator	0100 1000	72	H	0111 0011	115	s
0001 1110	30	Record separator	0100 1001	73	I	0111 0100	116	t
0001 1111	31	Unit separator	0100 1010	74	J	0111 0101	117	u
0010 0000	32	Blank space	0100 1011	75	K	0111 0110	118	v
0010 0001	33	!	0100 1100	76	L	0111 0111	119	w
0010 0010	34	"	0100 1101	77	M	0111 1000	120	x
0010 0011	35	#	0100 1110	78	N	0111 1001	121	y
0010 0100	36	$	0100 1111	79	O	0111 1010	122	z
0010 0101	37	%	0101 0000	80	P	0111 1011	123	{
0010 0110	38	&	0101 0001	81	Q	0111 1100	124		
0010 0111	39	'	0101 0010	82	R	0111 1101	125	}
0010 1000	40	(	0101 0011	83	S	0111 1110	126	~
0010 1001	41	)	0101 0100	84	T	0111 1111	127	
0010 1010	42	*	0101 0101	85	U			

example, covers Western European languages. There are many other character sets, however, for other languages, such as Russian, that use the Cyrillic alphabet.

Unicode

A new and evolving standard for data representation, called **Unicode Worldwide Character Standard**, provides two bytes—16 bits—to represent each symbol. With two bytes, a Unicode character could be any one of more than 65,536 different characters or symbols—enough for every character and symbol in the world, including the vast Chinese, Korean, and Japanese character sets and those found in known classical and historical texts. If a single character set were available to cover all the languages in the entire world, computer programs and data would be interchangeable. Because this is certainly a worthwhile goal, a widespread effort to replace ASCII with Unicode may someday take effect.

▶ HOW A COMPUTER PROCESSES DATA

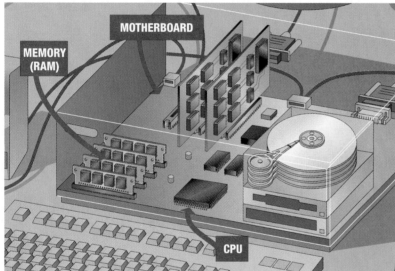
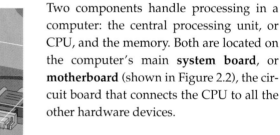

FIGURE 2.2
Processing devices.

Two components handle processing in a computer: the central processing unit, or CPU, and the memory. Both are located on the computer's main **system board**, or **motherboard** (shown in Figure 2.2), the circuit board that connects the CPU to all the other hardware devices.

The CPU

The CPU is the brain of the computer, the place where data is manipulated. In a microcomputer, the entire CPU is contained on a tiny chip called a microprocessor that is no larger than your smallest fingernail. The chip is mounted on a piece of plastic with metal wires attached to it. Every CPU has at least two basic parts, the control unit and the arithmetic logic unit.

CPU

This circuit board is the motherboard for a PC.

The Control Unit

All the computer's resources are managed from the **control unit**. You can think of the control unit as a traffic cop directing the flow of data. It is the logical hub of the computer.

The CPU's instructions for carrying out commands are built into the control unit. The instructions, or **instruction set**, list all the operations that the CPU can perform. Each instruction in the instruction set is expressed in **microcode**—a series of basic directions that tell the CPU how to execute more complex operations. Before a program can be executed, every command in it must be broken down into instructions that correspond to the ones in the CPU's instruction set. When the program is executed, the CPU carries out the instructions, in order, by converting them into microcode. Although the process is

Comic book detective Dick Tracy always used one piece of technology that seemed out of place—his watch. Decades before police officers could call headquarters from computers in their patrol cars, Dick Tracy maintained audio and video contact via his watch.

Now the day of the Dick Tracy watch is here, made possible by advances in miniaturization. Such a watch is definitely not commonplace, but all the technology is, and devices similar to it already exist.

Several companies have already built prototypes of this futuristic marvel, and some are about to market them. They vary widely in sophistication, from simple pagers that receive data over FM radio waves, to complex arrays of sensors and communicators.

The Timex Data Link, introduced in 1994, is an example. The watch works with special software that transforms information from a desktop computer into flashing bar codes on the computer's screen. The user types information, such as a business appointment, into Microsoft's Schedule+ program on a PC, then presses the command button to ready the watch for communication.

The user then selects the Timex command icon in Schedule+, and holds the watch up about a foot away from the PC screen. A sensor built into the watch reads the bar codes. Then a chip in the watch stores the information, which can include appointments, phone numbers, birthdays, or to-do lists. The watch owner can then go anywhere, taking the information with him.

On the high end of Dick Tracy watch technology is an experimental watch created by the United States Advanced Research Projects Agency (ARPA) in the mid-1990s. Strapped to a soldier's wrist, it monitors vital signs such as blood pressure and oxygen level, and uses the satellite-based Global Positioning System to pinpoint the soldier's location. Should the soldier be wounded in action, a hospital monitoring the battlefield could dispatch aid immediately.

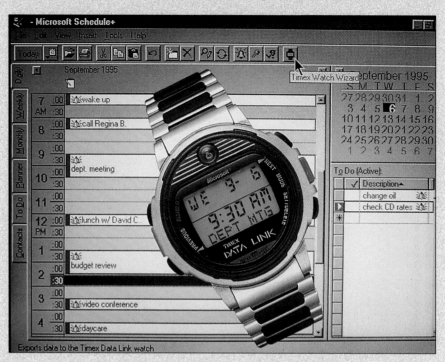

A tiny computer in the Timex Data Link watch connects to a PC via its own software or a commercial program like Microsoft's Schedule to keep track of appointments, to-do lists, or phone numbers.

A medic arriving on the scene would remove the electronic "dog tag" component of the watch and slip it into a handheld diagnostic computer. Because this "dog tag" would hold the soldier's medical history as well as the body's current vital signs, treatment could begin immediately.

At the Media Lab of the Massachusetts Institute of Technology, scientists are developing tiny computers for belt buckles, tie clasps, and shoes. In the near future you will be able to clip on such a computer that will inform your office or household computer system of your whereabouts.

These computers will also perform a variety of functions that may seem fantastic now: You will be able to alter your climate, send and receive messages from anywhere by voice and touch, or see and talk with your branch managers around the world simultaneously.

Manufacturers predict these wearable computers will become part of a person's wardrobe. Picture yourself in a few years: You will walk into a store and ask for a crystal pin with so many megabytes of memory. Or you will open a fashion magazine to read how XYZ-network-compatibility is all the rage in women's shoes this season. Computers, which once filled entire rooms, will reside quite comfortably in a ring on your finger.

Computers are small enough to fit in a ring on your finger, like this Decoder Ring made by Dallas Semiconductor.

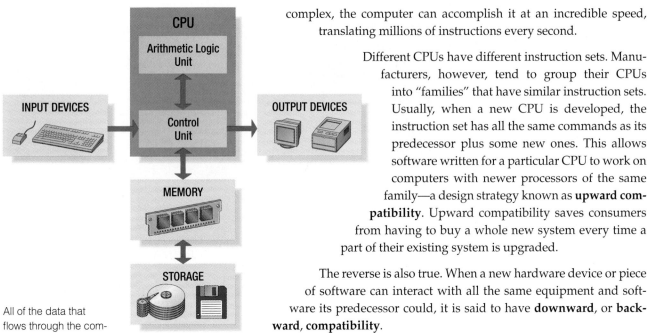

All of the data that flows through the computer is directed by the control unit in the CPU.

complex, the computer can accomplish it at an incredible speed, translating millions of instructions every second.

Different CPUs have different instruction sets. Manufacturers, however, tend to group their CPUs into "families" that have similar instruction sets. Usually, when a new CPU is developed, the instruction set has all the same commands as its predecessor plus some new ones. This allows software written for a particular CPU to work on computers with newer processors of the same family—a design strategy known as **upward compatibility**. Upward compatibility saves consumers from having to buy a whole new system every time a part of their existing system is upgraded.

The reverse is also true. When a new hardware device or piece of software can interact with all the same equipment and software its predecessor could, it is said to have **downward**, or **backward**, **compatibility**.

The Arithmetic Logic Unit

Because all computer data is stored as numbers, a lot of the processing that takes place involves comparing numbers or carrying out mathematical operations. In addition to establishing ordered sequences and changing those sequences, the computer can perform only two types of operations: arithmetic operations and logical operations. Arithmetic operations include addition, subtraction, multiplication, and division. Logical operations include comparisons, such as determining whether one number is equal to, greater than, or less than another number. Also, every logical operation has an opposite. For example, in addition to "equal to" there is "not equal to." Table 2.3 shows the symbols for all the arithmetic and logical operations.

It is important to remember that some of the logical operations can be carried out on text data. For example, when you want to search for a word in a document, the CPU carries out a rapid succession of "equals" operations to find a match for the sequence of ASCII codes that make up the word for which you are searching.

Many instructions carried out by the control unit involve simply moving data from one place to another—from memory to storage, from memory to the printer, and so forth. However, when the control unit encounters an instruction that involves arithmetic or logic, it passes that instruction to the second component of the CPU, the **arithmetic logic unit, or ALU**. The ALU includes a group of **registers**—high-speed memory locations built directly into the

TABLE 2.3			
Operations Performed by the Arithmetic Logic Unit			
ARITHMETIC OPERATIONS		**LOGICAL OPERATIONS**	
+	add	=, ≠	equal to, not equal to
−	subtract	>, ≯	greater than, not greater than
×	multiply	<, ≮	less than, not less than
÷	divide	≥, ≱	greater than or equal to, not greater than or equal to
∧	raise by a power	≤, ≰	less than or equal to, not less than or equal to

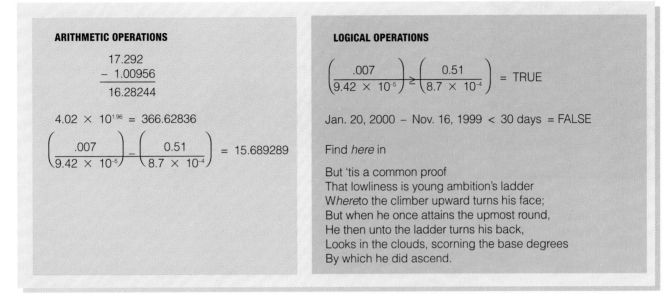

ARITHMETIC OPERATIONS

$$\begin{array}{r} 17.292 \\ -\ 1.00956 \\ \hline 16.28244 \end{array}$$

$$4.02 \times 10^{1.96} = 366.62836$$

$$\left(\frac{.007}{9.42 \times 10^{-5}}\right) - \left(\frac{0.51}{8.7 \times 10^{-4}}\right) = 15.689289$$

LOGICAL OPERATIONS

$$\left(\frac{.007}{9.42 \times 10^{-5}}\right) \geq \left(\frac{0.51}{8.7 \times 10^{-4}}\right) = \text{TRUE}$$

Jan. 20, 2000 – Nov. 16, 1999 < 30 days = FALSE

Find *here* in

But 'tis a common proof
That lowliness is young ambition's ladder
W*here*to the climber upward turns his face;
But when he once attains the upmost round,
He then unto the ladder turns his back,
Looks in the clouds, scorning the base degrees
By which he did ascend.

Examples of arithmetic and logical operations.

CPU that are used to hold the data currently being processed. For example, the control unit might load two numbers from memory into the registers in the ALU. Then, it might tell the ALU to divide the two numbers (an arithmetic operation), or to see whether the numbers are equal (a logical operation).

Memory

The CPU contains the basic instructions needed to operate the computer, but it does not have the capability to store entire programs or large sets of data permanently. The CPU does contain registers, but these are small areas that can hold only a few bytes at a time. In addition to the registers, the CPU needs to have millions of bytes of space where it can hold programs and the data being manipulated. This area is called **memory**.

Physically, memory consists of chips either on the motherboard or on a small circuit board attached to the motherboard. This electronic memory allows the CPU to store and retrieve data very quickly.

There are two types of built-in memory, permanent and nonpermanent. Some memory chips always retain the data they hold even when the computer is turned off. This type of memory is called **nonvolatile**. Other chips—in fact, most of the memory in a microcomputer—do lose their contents when the computer's power is shut off. These chips have **volatile** memory.

ROM (nonvolatile)

RAM (volatile)

CPU

Motherboard

ROM

Nonvolatile chips always hold the same data—the data in them cannot be changed. In fact, putting data

The CPU is attached to two kinds of memory: RAM, which is volatile, and ROM, which is nonvolatile.

ROM chip

ROM usually consists of a small chip, located near the CPU on the motherboard.

RAM chips

In personal computers, RAM chips are normally mounted on a small circuit board, which is plugged into the motherboard.

permanently into this kind of memory is called "burning in the data," and it is usually done at the factory. The data in these chips can only be read and used—it cannot be changed—so the memory is called **read-only memory (ROM)**.

One important reason a computer needs ROM is so it knows what to do when the power is first turned on. Among other things, ROM contains a set of start-up instructions that check to see that the rest of memory is functioning properly, check for hardware devices, and check for an operating system on the computer's disk drives.

RAM

Memory that *can* be changed is called **random-access memory (RAM)**. When people talk about computer *memory* in connection with microcomputers, they usually mean the volatile RAM memory. The purpose of RAM is to hold programs and data while they are in use. Physically, RAM consists of some chips on a small circuit board.

A computer does not have to search its entire memory each time it needs to find data because the CPU stores and retrieves each piece of data using a **memory address**. This is a number that indicates a location on the memory chips, much as a post office box number indicates a slot into which mail is placed. Memory addresses start at zero and go up to one less than the number of bytes of memory in the computer.

The ability to access each byte of data directly is the reason that this type of memory is referred to as "random access," hence the name random-access memory (RAM). Actually, though, read-only memory (ROM) is "random access" as well, so the names for the two types of memory can be misleading. It is best simply to remember that the contents of ROM do not change; the contents of RAM do.

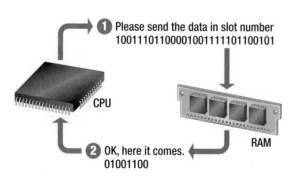

1 Please send the data in slot number
100111011000010011111101100101

CPU

2 OK, here it comes.
01001100

RAM

To request a byte of data, the CPU sends a memory address to RAM.

▶ FACTORS AFFECTING PROCESSING SPEED

Although all microcomputers have a CPU and memory, all microcomputers are by no means the same. Over the past 15 years, the power of microcomputers has increased dramatically. When people talk about computing power, they usually mean the speed with which the computer processes data. Therefore, more computing power really means faster processing.

The circuitry design of a CPU determines its basic speed, but several additional factors can make chips already designed for speed work even faster. You have already been introduced to some of these, such as the CPU's registers and the memory. In this section, you will see how these two components, as well as a few others such as the cache memory, clock speed, data bus, and math coprocessor affect a computer's speed. Figure 2.3 shows how these components might be arranged on the computer's motherboard.

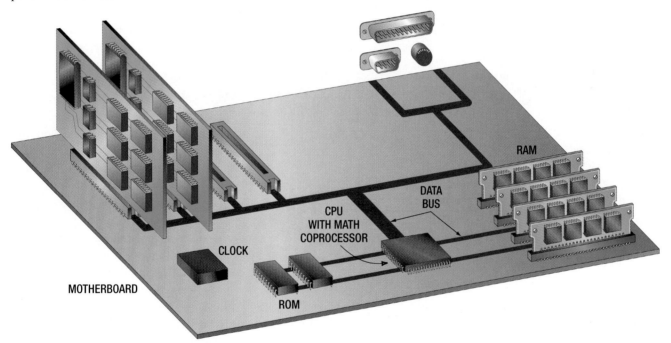

FIGURE 2.3
Devices affecting processing speed.

How Registers Affect Speed

The registers in the first PCs could hold two bytes—16 bits—each. Most CPUs sold today, for both PCs and Macintosh computers, have 32-bit registers. Some powerful computers, such as the newest minicomputers and some high-end workstations, have 64-bit registers, and this trend may soon work its way down to mainstream PCs.

The size of the registers, which is sometimes called the **word size**, indicates the amount of data with which the computer can work at any given time. The bigger the word size, the more quickly the computer can process a set of data. Occasionally, you will hear people refer to "32-bit processors," or "64-bit processors," or even

"64-bit computers." This terminology refers to the size of the register in the processor. If all other factors are kept equal, a CPU with 32-bit registers can process data twice as fast as one with 16-bit registers.

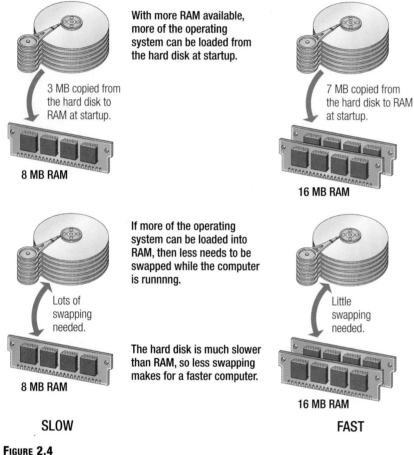

With more RAM available, more of the operating system can be loaded from the hard disk at startup.

3 MB copied from the hard disk to RAM at startup.

8 MB RAM

7 MB copied from the hard disk to RAM at startup.

16 MB RAM

If more of the operating system can be loaded into RAM, then less needs to be swapped while the computer is runnnng.

Lots of swapping needed.

The hard disk is much slower than RAM, so less swapping makes for a faster computer.

8 MB RAM

Little swapping needed.

16 MB RAM

SLOW

FAST

FIGURE 2.4
How RAM affects speed.

Memory and Computing Power

The amount of RAM in a computer can have a profound effect on the computer's power. For one thing, more RAM means the computer can use bigger, more powerful programs, and those programs can access bigger data files.

More RAM also can make the computer run faster. The computer does not necessarily have to load an entire program into memory to run it, but the more of the program it can fit into memory, the faster the program will run. For example, a PC with 8 MB of RAM is capable of running Microsoft Windows, even though the program actually occupies about 40 MB of disk storage space. When you run Windows, the program does not need to load all its files into memory to run properly. It loads only the most essential parts into memory. When the computer needs access to other parts of the program on the disk, it can unload, or **swap out**, nonessential parts from RAM back to the hard disk and load, or **swap in**, the program code or data it needs. However, as shown in Figure 2.4, if your PC has 16 MB of RAM or more, you will notice a dramatic difference in how fast Microsoft Windows 95 runs, because the CPU will need to swap program instructions between RAM and the hard disk much less often.

Fortunately, if you decide that you need more RAM than you have, you can buy more, open up your computer, and plug it in. In today's computers, chips are usually grouped together on small circuit boards called SIMMs (Single In-Line Memory Modules) or DIMMs (Dual In-Line Memory Modules). Each SIMM or DIMM can hold between 1 MB and 64 MB of RAM. Currently, the cost of upgrading the memory of a computer is between $25 and $40 per megabyte, so this is often the most cost-effective way to get more speed from your computer.

The Computer's Internal Clock

Every microcomputer has a **system clock**, but the clock's primary purpose is not to keep the time of day. Like modern wristwatches, the clock is driven by a piece of quartz crystal. When electricity is applied, the molecules in the quartz crystal vibrate

On the left is a SIMM; on the right is an example of a DIMM.

millions of times per second, a rate that never changes. The speed of the vibration is determined by the thickness of the crystal. The computer uses the vibrations of the quartz in the system clock to time its processing operations.

Over the years, clock speeds have increased steadily. For example, the first PC operated at 4.77 megahertz. **Hertz** is a measure of cycles per second. One clock cycle means the time it takes to turn a transistor off and back on again. **Megahertz (MHz)** means "millions of cycles per second." Today, the fastest PCs have clock speeds of more than 200 MHz. All other factors being equal (although they never are), a CPU operating at 133 MHz can process data twice as fast as the same one operating at 66 MHz.

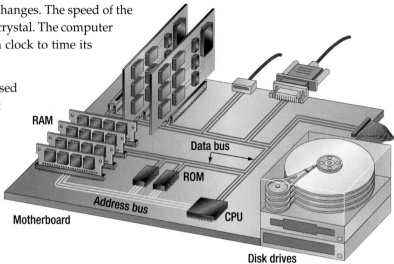

The motherboard includes an address bus and a data bus. The address bus leads from the CPU to memory (RAM and ROM). The data bus connects the CPU to memory, as well as all of the storage, input/output, and communication devices.

The Bus

In microcomputers, the term **bus** refers to the paths between the components of a computer. There are two main buses in a computer, the data bus and the address bus. The one that you hear the most about is the data bus, so when people just say "the bus," they usually mean the data bus.

The Data Bus

The **data bus** is an electrical path that connects the CPU, memory, and the other hardware devices on the motherboard. Actually, the bus is a group of parallel wires. The number of wires in the bus affects the speed at which data can travel between hardware components, just as the number of lanes on a highway affects how long it takes people to get to their destinations. Because each wire can transfer one bit at a time, an eight-wire bus can move eight bits at a time, which is a full byte. A 16-bit bus can transfer two bytes, and a 32-bit bus can transfer four bytes at a time.

PC buses are designed to match the capabilities of the devices attached to them. When CPUs could send and receive only one byte of data at a time, there was no point in connecting them to a bus that could move more data. As microprocessor technology improved, however, chips were built that could send and receive more data at once, and improved bus designs created wider paths through which the data could flow.

When IBM introduced the PC-AT in 1984, the most dramatic improvement was an enhanced data bus that was matched with the capabilities of a new

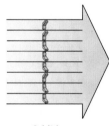

8-bit bus
1 byte at a time

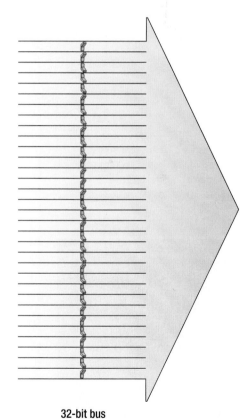

32-bit bus
4 bytes at a time

With a wider bus, the computer can move more data in the same amount of time (or the same amount of data in less time).

microprocessor, the Intel 80286. The data bus of the AT was 16 bits wide and became the *de facto* standard in the industry. It is still used for PC devices that do not require more than a 16-bit bus. The AT bus is commonly known as the **Industry Standard Architecture**, or **ISA**, **bus**.

Two years later, however, when the first 80386 chips (commonly abbreviated as the 386) began shipping, a new standard was needed for the 386's 32-bit bus. The first contender was **Micro Channel Architecture,** or the **MCA bus,** from IBM. Then came the **Extended Industry Standard Architecture (EISA) bus** from a consortium of hardware developers who opposed IBM's new standard because it was not backward compatible. The winner of the bus wars was neither MCA nor EISA. It was the **Peripheral Component Interconnect**, or **PCI, bus**. Intel designed the PCI bus specifically to make it easier to integrate new data types, such as audio, video, and graphics.

The Address Bus

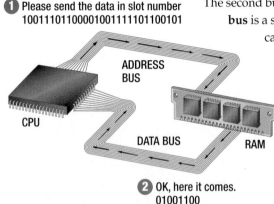

❶ Please send the data in slot number 100111011000010011111101100101

ADDRESS BUS

CPU

DATA BUS

RAM

❷ OK, here it comes. 01001100

Requests for data are sent from the CPU to RAM along the address bus. The request consists of a memory address. The data comes back to the CPU via the data bus.

The second bus that is found in every microcomputer is the address bus. The **address bus** is a set of wires similar to the data bus that connects the CPU and RAM and carries the memory addresses. (Remember, each byte in RAM is associated with a number, which is the memory address.)

The reason the address bus is important is that the number of wires in it determines the maximum number of memory addresses. For example, recall that one byte of data is enough to represent 256 different values. If the address bus could carry only eight bits at a time, the CPU could address only 256 bytes of RAM. Actually, most of the early PCs had 20-bit address buses, so the CPU could address 2^{20} bytes, or 1 MB, of data. Today, most CPUs have 32-bit address buses that can address 4 GB (over 4 billion bytes) of RAM. Some of the latest models can address even more.

One of the biggest hurdles in the evolution of PCs was that DOS, the operating system used in the vast majority of PCs for more than a decade, was designed for machines that could address only 1 MB of RAM. When PCs began to contain more RAM, special software had to be devised to address it. Programmers came up with two devices called expanded memory and extended memory. Windows 95 largely did away with these, although extended memory still exists in the operating system for purposes of backward compatibility.

Cache Memory

Cache memory chips

Most cache memory is visible on the motherboard as a group of chips next to the CPU.

Moving data back and forth between RAM and the CPU's registers is one of the most time-consuming operations a CPU must perform simply because RAM is much slower than the CPU.

A partial solution to this problem is to include a cache memory in the CPU. **Cache** (pronounced "cash") **memory** is similar to RAM, except that it is extremely fast compared to normal memory, and it is used in a different way.

Figure 2.5 shows how cache memory works with the CPU and RAM. When a program is running and the CPU needs to read data or instructions from RAM, the CPU first checks to see whether the data is in cache memory. If the data that it needs is not there, it reads the data from RAM into its registers, but it also loads a copy of the data into cache memory. The next time the CPU needs that same data, it finds it in the cache memory and saves the time needed to load the data from RAM. Knowing the size of most programs and many data files, you might think that the odds of the CPU finding the data it needs in the cache memory are small, but it actually does find the data it needs there often enough to improve the performance of a PC.

Program instructions are a good example of the kind of data the CPU often finds in cache memory. Frequently, programs ask computers to do the same operation repeatedly until a particular condition is met. In computer language, such a repetitive procedure is called a *loop*. For example, when a word processing program searches for a specific word, it must check each word in the document until it finds a match. If the instructions that tell the arithmetic logic unit how to find a match are in cache memory, the control unit does not have to load them from RAM each time. As a result, the search is completed more quickly.

Since the late 1980s, cache memory has been built into most PC CPUs. The first CPU caches came with 0.5 KB, then 8 KB, then 16 KB, then 32 KB. Today, some chips have as much as 64 KB built in. In addition to the cache memory built into the CPU, now cache is also added to the motherboard. Many of the PCs sold today have 256 KB or more of motherboard cache memory. Cache memory clearly provides performance benefits, so you can expect to see the new chips and new motherboards continue to leapfrog the old with more cache memory.

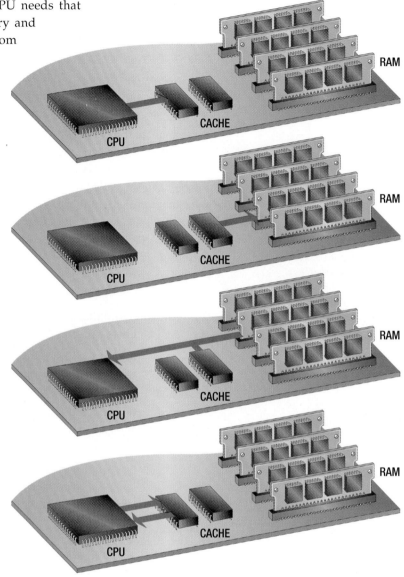

FIGURE 2.5

The cache speeds up processing by storing frequently used data or instructions in its high-speed memory. Whenever the CPU requests information from RAM, the cache controller intercepts the request and searches its own memory for the requested information. If the information is not there, the CPU retrieves the required data from the RAM memory and also sends a copy back to the cache. The next time the CPU needs the same information, the cache finds that information, and quickly sends it to the CPU, leaving RAM out of the loop.

Passing Math Operations to the Math Coprocessor

Some computers speed up certain kinds of processing by adding a math coprocessor to the CPU. A **math coprocessor** is a chip that is specially designed to handle complicated mathematical operations. Newer CPUs have math coprocessors built in. Earlier CPUs did not have them, so many users chose to upgrade their machines by adding them.

The ALU (arithmetic logic unit), which handles most processing operations, can manipulate binary code representing numbers, text, images, sound—any form of data that the computer can store. In terms of processing, the ALU is a generalist.

The problem with the general-purpose ALU is that is has difficulty performing certain mathematical operations. For example, say the processor needs to compute $(314.15927)^4$. The ALU is designed to manipulate whole numbers that are not too large or small. If it is forced to work with decimals, it can really get bogged down. The math coprocessor, on the other hand, is a processing specialist designed to work with exactly these kinds of numbers. It can execute arithmetic routines much more quickly than the ALU because it uses **floating-point arithmetic**, a computer technique that translates numbers into scientific notation. (In some computers, the math coprocessor is called the **Floating-Point Unit**, or **FPU**.) In floating-point arithmetic, the computer represents

$$0.0000586 \quad \text{as} \quad 5.86 \times 10^{-5}$$

$$\text{or} \quad 128,610,000,000 \quad \text{as} \quad 1.2861 \times 10^{11}$$

This technique simplifies complex arithmetic because the computer is not forced to store large numbers of decimal places.

When the computer must do a lot of floating-point arithmetic, the presence of a math coprocessor's floating-point unit can speed up processing considerably. Applications that benefit from math coprocessors include spreadsheets and drawing programs. Software for computer-aided design (CAD) and 3-D rendering generally will not even run without a math coprocessor because each point in a complex design must be plotted numerically.

CPUs Used in Personal Computers

The two biggest players in the PC CPU market are Intel and Motorola. Intel has enjoyed tremendous success with its processors since the early 1980s. Most PCs are controlled by Intel processors. The primary exception to this rule is the Macintosh. All Macs use chips made by Motorola. In addition, there are several firms, such as AMD and Cyrix, that make processors which mimic the functionality of Intel's chips. There are also several other chip manufacturers for workstation PCs.

The Intel Processors

The Intel Corporation is the largest manufacturer of microchips in the world, in addition to being the leading provider of chips for PCs. In fact, Intel invented the microprocessor, the so-called "computer on a chip," in 1971 with the 4004 model. It was this invention that led to the first microcomputers that began appearing in 1975. However, Intel's success in this market was not guaranteed until 1981, when IBM released the first IBM PC, which was based on the Intel 8088. Since then, all IBM machines and the compatibles based on IBM's design have been created around Intel's chips. A list of those chips, along with their basic specifications, is shown in Table 2.4. Although the 8088 was the first chip to be used in an IBM PC, IBM actually used an earlier chip, the 8086, in a subsequent model, called the IBM PC XT. The chips that came later—the 286, 386, 486, and even the Pentium—correspond

Ted Hoff, inventor of the microprocessor.

Intel's first microprocessor, the 4004.

to certain design standards that were established by the 8086. This line of chips is often referred to as the 80×86 line.

The steady rise in bus size, register size, and addressable memory illustrated in Table 2.4 has also been accompanied by increases in clock speed. For example, the clock attached to the first PCs ran at 4.77 MHz, whereas clock speeds for Pentium chips started at 60 MHz in 1993 and quickly rose to 100, 120, and 133, 150, and 166 MHz.

TABLE 2.4

Intel Chips and Their Specifications

MODEL	YEAR INTRODUCED	DATA BUS CAPACITY	REGISTER SIZE	ADDRESSABLE MEMORY
8086	1978	16 bit	16 bit	1 MB
8088	1979	8 bit	16 bit	1 MB
80286	1982	16 bit	16 bit	16 MB
80386	1985	32 bit	32 bit	4 GB
80486	1989	32 bit	32 bit	4 GB
Pentium	1993	64 bit	32 bit	4 GB
Pentium Pro	1995	64 bit	32 bit	64 GB

It is important to realize that these statistics do not convey all the improvements that have been made. The basic design of each chip, known as the architecture, has grown steadily in sophistication and complexity. For example, the architecture of the 386 contained 320,000 transistors, and the 486 contained 1.2 million. With the Pentium, that number grew to more than 3.1 million, and the Pentium Pro's architecture brought the total number of transistors on the chip to 5.5 million.

The growing complexity of the architecture allowed Intel to incorporate some sophisticated techniques for processing. One major improvement that came with the 386 is called virtual 8086 mode. In this mode, a single 386 chip could achieve the processing power of 16 separate 8086 chips each running a separate copy of the operating system. The capability for virtual 8086 mode enabled a single 386 chip to run different programs at the same time, a technique known as multitasking. All the chips that succeeded the 386 have had the capacity for multitasking.

The 486

Introduced in 1989, the 80486 did not feature any radically new processor technology. Instead, it combined a 386 processor, a math coprocessor, and a cache memory controller on a single chip. Because these chips were no longer separate, they no longer had to communicate through the bus—which increased the speed of the system dramatically.

The Pentium

The next member of the Intel family of microprocessors was the **Pentium**, introduced in 1993. With the Pentium, Intel broke its tradition of numeric model names—partly to prevent other chip manufacturers from using similar numeric names, which implied that their products were functionally identical to Intel's chips. The Pentium, however, is still considered part of the 80×86 series.

The Intel Pentium.

The Pentium chip itself represented another leap forward for microprocessors. The speed and power of the Pentium dwarfed all of its predecessors in the Intel line. What this means in practical terms is that the Pentium runs application programs approximately five times faster than a 486 at the same clock speed. Part of the Pentium's speed comes from a **superscalar** architecture, which allows the chip to process more than one instruction in a single clock cycle.

The Intel Pentium Pro.

The Pentium Pro

Introduced in 1995, the **Pentium Pro** reflected still more design breakthroughs. The Pentium Pro can process *three* instructions in a single clock cycle—one more than the Pentium. In addition, the Pentium Pro can achieve faster clock speeds—the earliest model available was packaged with a 133 MHz clock.

Intel coined the phrase "dynamic execution" to describe the specific innovation that distinguishes the Pentium Pro. Dynamic execution refers to the chip's ability to execute program instructions in the most efficient manner, not necessarily in the order in which they were written. This out-of-order execution means that instructions that cannot be executed immediately are put aside, while the Pentium Pro begins processing other instructions. This is in contrast to the original Pentium chip that can stall because it executes instructions in strict sequence.

The Motorola Processors

Motorola Corporation is the other major manufacturer of microprocessors for small computers. As mentioned earlier, Apple's Macintosh computers use Motorola processors. Other computer manufacturers, including workstation manufacturers, such as Sun Microsystems, have also relied heavily on Motorola chips. They were an early favorite among companies that built larger, UNIX-based computers, such as the NCR Tower series and the AT&T 3B series.

Table 2.5 shows the specifications for the most popular Motorola processors.

As you can see, Motorola offers two families of processor chips. The first is known as the "680×0 family," similar to the way that Intel's group of PC processors is known as the "80×86 family." The second, designated MPC, has a different architecture and is known as the PowerPC family.

The 680×0 Series

Although the 68000 chip is best known as the foundation of the original Macintosh, it actually predates the Mac by serveral years. In fact, IBM considered using the 68000 in the first IBM PC. (IBM's decision to use the Intel 8088 chip in its first PC was apparently driven by cost considerations.) Although Motorola's 68000 chip was more powerful than Intel's 8088, subsequent improvements to the Motorola chip were made in smaller increments than Intel's giant performance leaps. By the time Motorola introduced the 68060 chip, Intel was promoting the Pentium. In an attempt to regain market share, Motorola initiated the development of the new PowerPC chip.

TABLE 2.5

Motorola Processors for Personal Computers

ADDRESSABLE MODEL	YEAR INTRODUCED	REGISTER SIZE	DATA BUS CAPACITY	MEMORY
68000	1979	32 bit	16 bit	16 MB
68010	1983	32 bit	16 bit	16 MB
68020	1984	32 bit	32 bit	4 GB
68030	1987	32 bit	32 bit	4 GB
68040	1989	32 bit	32 bit	4 GB
68060	1993	32 bit	32 bit	4 GB
MPC 601	1992	64 bit	32 bit	4 GB
MPC 603	1993	64 bit	32 bit	4 GB
MPC 604	1994	64 bit	32 bit	4 GB
MPC 620	1995	128 bit	64 bit	1 TB*

*terabyte, equal to 1000 GB

Classified ad: 486/66, 8MB/540HD, 14"VGA, 3.5/5.25, Mouse, 1Yr. old, Good starter. Cost-$2500. Yours for $900. Call 555-8911.

The above advertisement, or one like it, is commonplace these days. You can expect that a computer system bought a year ago will decrease by half its value a year from now.

Last year's computer also can perform like a "tortoise" compared with the speedy "hare" of a newer model. For example, a state-of-the-art computer in 1994 with 8 MB of RAM, a 540 MB hard disk, a 14.4 Kbps modem, and a 486/33 processor—is considered slow compared to today's new systems.

Given this quick drop in both the value and the relative performance of a new computer, a good question to ask before buying is: Do I really need to buy a new computer, or can I get enough improved performance by upgrading what I already have?

Currently, if your computer has the equivalent of a 486 processor or better, an upgrade can be a viable option. Upgrading earlier models, by and large, will not bring you up to current standards and may be more trouble than it is worth, unless your needs are very specific and limited.

A PC can be upgraded in several different ways. The processor chip, system memory (RAM), cache memory, hard disk, and video display card can all be upgraded relatively easily and inexpensively. In fact, everything in a computer can be upgraded—floppy drives, motherboard, mouse or other pointing devices, and monitor—can all be replaced to change the performance of your computer.

Processor (CPU) upgrades are often the quickest way to a faster computer. Current upgrade packages can, for example, increase a 486/33 MHz

computer (486 indicates the CPU and 33 MHz indicates the processor speed) to a 486/66 MHz CPU for around $60, and to a 63 MHz Pentium CPU for less than $200. A processor upgrade can be as simple as removing the current processor chip and inserting the new one in the same socket. Generally, the necessary tools are included with a processor upgrade kit. However, for novices, it is usually best to let a computer shop install any upgrade components.

System memory (RAM) upgrade is another step you can take for faster processing. More memory means more room to keep information on hand for the processor. With today's personal computers and software, 8 MB of memory has become the practical minimum, with 16 MB yielding faster performance and at least 32 MB for high-end multimedia use. A RAM upgrade can be as easy as adding one or two additional SIMM (Single Inline Memory Module) modules to the memory banks on the motherboard.

Another possible upgrade is to add to or replace a hard disk, which can provide faster access to stored data

and/or more storage capacity. Managing large databases and graphics files are classic reasons for hard disk upgrades.

You can use "cache" upgrades to get better performance out of the software you already use. Cache memory is a small amount of very fast memory used to hold the most frequently accessed information, instead of having the computer access it from the relatively slow hard drive. For home use, a 256 KB cache is adequate. If you have less than that, improving your cache is a good place to start your upgrade.

Changing the video display card is another easy upgrade—just replace the current card with a newer one. Computer systems sold as recently as the mid-1990s may have video display cards with as little as 256 KB of video memory (VRAM). The minimum VRAM recommended by 1996 was 1 MB, and 2 MB is rapidly becoming the norm.

Upgrading doesn't give you the flashy excitement of a brand new computer. But, like the faithful tortoise, it may get you where you need to go.

486 100 MHz Intel overdrive upgrade processor.

Motorola's PowerPC 601 chip.

Motorola's PowerPC 604 chip.

A RISC chip from NEC, the V_R4000.

This Ultra 1 workstation from Sun Microsystems is based on a RISC microprocessor called the UltraSPARC. The Ultra 1 is designed for exceptionally high performance for networking and graphics programs.

The PowerPC Series

The PowerPC chip had an unusual beginning. Two industry rivals, IBM and Apple, joined forces with Motorola in 1991, ostensibly to dethrone Intel from its preeminence in the PC chip market. The hardware portion of their efforts is centered around the PowerPC chip, the first of which was the 601. Following closely on its heels was the 603, a low-power processor suitable for notebook computers. Its successor, the 604, is a high-power chip designed for high-end desktop systems. With the introduction of the 620 late in 1995, PowerPC chips established a new performance record for microprocessors. A handful of small 620-based machines working together offers about the same computing power as an IBM 370 mainframe. As you will see in the next section, PowerPC chips are different than the earlier 68000 series from the ground up.

RISC Processors

Both the Motorola 680×0 and Intel 80×86 families are **complex instruction set computing (CISC) processors**. The instruction sets for these CPUs are large, typically containing 200 to 300 instructions.

A newer theory in microprocessor design holds that if the instruction set for the CPU is kept small and simple, each instruction will execute much faster, allowing the processor to complete more instructions during a given period. CPUs designed according to this theory are called **reduced instruction set computing (RISC) processors**. The RISC design, which is used in the PowerPC but was first implemented in the mid-1980s, results in a faster and less expensive processor. Because of the way the Pentium Pro and its spin-offs process instructions, they are called RISC-like, but their architecture is still based on complex instruction set computing (CISC).

RISC technology has been the engine of mid-size computers such as the IBM RS/6000 and high-end UNIX workstations such as those built by Sun Microsystems, Hewlett-Packard, and NCR. RISC CPUs are also found in printers and other devices that have their own internal CPUs. The PowerPC processor reflected a major move on the part of industry giants toward using RISC technology in desktop and notebook computers.

Motorola is not alone in producing both RISC and CISC processors. In 1989, Intel introduced the i860, which was a 64-bit RISC chip that earned the distinction of being the first chip to contain more than one million transistors. Other RISC processors include the Intel i960, the Motorola 88100, NEC Electronics' V_R4000 series, and the DEC Alpha. Sun Microsystems also produces a RISC processor, known as SPARC, which it uses in its UNIX workstations. Members of the NEC V_R4000 family are meant to be used by the same range of computers as the PowerPC chips, namely, for machines from notebooks through high-end systems.

Whether CISC or RISC technology will be the basis of most future microprocessors has yet to be determined, but early bets are on models of RISC chips with reduced power consumption.

Parallel Processing

Another school of thought on producing faster computers is to build them with more than one processor. This is not a new idea in the mainframe and supercomputer arena. In fact, the IBM 3090 has two to four processors, and the Cray X MP 4 has four

Parallel Processing: On the Fast Track

In the race to make computers faster and more powerful, the CPU (central processing unit) is the star athlete, and it's already going just about at top speed. So what's next?

The answer: teams of CPUs. This is what technology calls "parallel processing," where multiple processors work together in a single system.

The processor is the crucial determinant of a computer's speed because it is involved in every computer task from scientific or engineering calculations to the placement of colors and character fonts on screen. There are several ways to make a faster processor. One is to increase the number of bits of information a chip can handle at once. Where computers once handled only 8 bits at a time, today, few handle less than 16 bits, many handle 32 bits, and advanced systems can handle as many as 64 bits.

Another is to increase the *pace* at which the chip handles these bits. This "clock rate" of the computer is measured in megahertz (MHz) which stands for millions of clock ticks per second. With each tick, a processor takes another step in calculating. Where computers once operated at 1 MHz or less, many now crank along at 66 MHz, some reach 200 MHz, and 1 GHz (GigaHertz or 1000 MHz) processors are currently on design boards.

However, the race to make the CPU go faster is slowing down; partly because each increase in processing speed is harder to accomplish. For example, moving from 64 bits to 128 bits was a much greater technological challenge than going from 8 to 16 bits. And processing at the GHz clock speeds causes electrical troubles, such as radio wave interference with the computer's electronics.

Another way to increase speed is to increase the number of CPUs in a system. This is parallel processing, also called a "multiprocessing" (MP) or "symmetric multiprocessing" (SMP).

In fact, most of today's computer processors actually have some measure of "parallel processing" built in. This is called "pipelining"—overlapping some of the steps of processing within a single processor.

MP (multiprocessor) systems are already common among high-end servers and workstations. Some of the fastest computers—including the nCube and the Connection Machine—use hundreds, even thousands of individual processors.

Why hasn't parallel processing moved into mainstream PC computing? Two reasons: cost and software complexity.

Microprocessors are one of the most expensive components in a PC. Putting in more than one raises prices substantially.

Also, operating systems and software traditionally have been designed to be used by one processor. Putting more processors into mainstream PCs would not improve their speed until operating systems and software programs capable of using more than one processor simultaneously (called multithreaded) are in current use.

It is widely believed, however, that multiprocessing will usher in the next generation of computers whose speed is expected to make today's computers look like snails. Some technology experts predict that computers will become so fast that speed will cease to be a determining factor for the mainstream user.

Just as the ordinary user of a car is not overly concerned with how much faster than 100 mph a car can go, the ordinary computer user of the future may discount speed in favor of such issues as budget, utility, and design.

Here is a cutaway look at a multiprocessor from Daystar.

processors. Some companies are developing computers with 256, 512, and even thousands of microprocessors, known as **massively parallel processors**. For example, Intel now has a contract with the U.S. Department of Energy to build what is being touted as "the world's fastest supercomputer." It will contain 9,000 Pentium Pro chips. It is remarkable that plans for the most powerful supercomputers revolve around the same chips that can be found in ordinary desktop computers.

At the other end of the spectrum, dual-processor and quad-processor versions of PCs are available today. Unfortunately, the DOS operating system is unable to make use of an additional processor. Some UNIX programmers, however, have developed software that takes advantage of an additional processor. One of Microsoft's operating systems, Windows NT, can also make use of parallel processor computers. These computers are often based on the Pentium Pro, and they look very much like ordinary desktop PCs.

▶ WHAT TO EXPECT IN THE FUTURE

For 20 years, advances in CPU technology have driven the rapid increases in computer power and speed. CPUs have doubled in performance roughly every 2 years, so today's fastest chips are about 1,000 times faster than those of 20 years ago. Although some industry analysts claim that this trend has to taper off soon, others predict that it will continue for another 15 years.

Naturally, such a prediction raises the question: What technological advancements will allow the chip manufacturers to keep up the pace? There are several possible answers.

First, there will probably be a continuation of existing trends; more cache built into the motherboard, faster clock speeds, and more instructions executed in each clock cycle. There may also be continued growth in register and bus size. Chip manufacturers may continue to reduce the size of the electrical pathways on the chip. If they can do that, they will be able to squeeze more and more transistors onto the microprocessor chip. There are already chips that hold more than five million transistors. The technology now exists to fit ten times that many onto the same space. As the technology marches along, the numbers will only grow.

Second, many analysts predict that RISC technology will be a major factor in CPU improvements. RISC architecture is only half the age of CISC architecture, and the makers of RISC chips say there is still a lot of room for improvements.

The greatest boost in CPU speed may come from multiprocessing, a design innovation that builds more than one chip into the CPU. In microcomputers, multiprocessing systems appeared first as network servers, the machines that form the hub of some computer networks. Currently, these machines are expensive and specialized. However, the cost of technology invariably falls, so you are soon likely to see multiprocessing systems on the desktop—if the performance gains justify the cost of multiple chips.

All of these technological improvements, as they occur, will be big news in the hardware industry. Ordinary computer users, of course, will hear less about the technology and more about the innovations that increased computing power makes possible. When you hear about great leaps forward in speech recognition, foreign-language translation programs, virtual reality, and full-screen, full-motion, full-color video, you should realize that the capabilities of the latest CPUs are as responsible for these advancements as the genius of software developers.

▶ VISUAL SUMMARY

Transforming Data into Information

- Computer data is reduced to binary numbers, because computer processing is performed by transistors that have only two possible states, on and off.
- The binary numbering system works the same way as the decimal system, except it has only two available symbols instead of 10.
- A single unit of data is called a bit; eight bits make up one byte.
- In the most common character-code set, ASCII, each character consists of one byte of data.

How a Computer Processes Data

- A microcomputer's processing takes place in the CPU, the two main parts of which are the control unit and the ALU.
- Within the CPU, program instructions are retrieved and translated with the help of an internal instruction set and the accompanying microcode.
- CPUs in the same family are made with backward compatibility in terms of instruction sets, so that a new CPU can work with all the same programs that the old CPUs used.
- The actual manipulation of data takes place in the ALU, which is connected to registers that hold data.
- Memory called ROM is nonvolatile (or permanent): it is used to hold instructions that run the computer when the power is first turned on.
- The biggest part of memory, called RAM, is volatile (or temporary): programs and data can be written to and erased from RAM as needed.
- The CPU accesses each location in memory with a unique number, called the memory address.

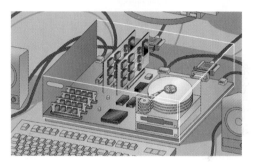

Factors Affecting Processing Speed

- The size of the registers, also called word size, determines the amount of data with which the computer can work at a given time.
- The amount of RAM can also affect speed, because the CPU can keep more of the active program and data in memory, rather than in storage.
- The computer's system clock sets the pace for the CPU using a vibrating quartz crystal.
- There are two kinds of buses, the data bus and the address bus, both of which are located on the motherboard.
- The width of the data bus determines how many bits at a time can be transmitted between the CPU and other devices.
- Bus architecture in the PC has evolved from the ISA bus to the PCI bus.
- The size (or width) of the address bus determines the number of bytes of RAM the CPU can access.
- The cache is a type of high-speed memory that contains the most recent data and instructions that have been loaded by the CPU.
- A CPU relies on either a math coprocessor or an integrated floating-point unit to perform floating-point arithmetic.

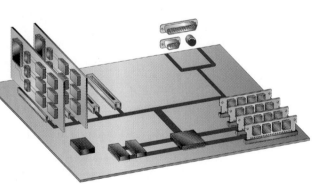

CPUs Used in Personal Computers

■ Since 1978, Intel's processors have evolved from the 8086 and the 8088 to the 286, the 386, the 486, the Pentium, and the Pentium Pro.

■ Motorola makes the CPUs used in Macintosh and PowerPC computers: the 68000, 68020, 68030, and 68040 were for Macintosh; the PowerPC series is now used in the Power Macintoshes.

■ Instruction sets for RISC chips are kept smaller than CISC chips, so that each instruction executes more quickly.

■ Some high-end micros and mid-size computers use RISC chips, as well as a growing number of PCs.

■ One trend in computer architecture is to incorporate parallel processors.

▶ KEY TERMS

After completing this chapter, you should be able to define the following terms:

address bus, 52
arithmetic logic unit (ALU), 46
ASCII, 42
binary system, 41
bit, 41
bus, 51
byte, 41
cache memory, 52
Complex Instruction Set
　Computing (CISC) processors, 58
control unit, 44
data bus, 51
decimal system, 41
downward (backward) compatibility, 46
EBCDIC (Extended Binary Coded
　Decimal Interchange Code), 42
EISA (Extended Industry Standard
　Architecture) bus, 52

Floating-Point Unit (FPU), 54
floating-point arithmetic, 54
Hertz, 51
Industry Standard Architecture
　(ISA) bus, 52
instruction set, 44
massively parallel processors, 60
math coprocessor, 53
Megahertz (MHz), 51
memory, 47
memory address, 48
microcode, 44
Micro Channel Architecture
　(MCA) bus, 52
motherboard, 44
nonvolatile, 47
Pentium, 55
Pentium Pro, 56

Peripheral Component Interconnect
　(PCI) bus, 52
random-access memory (RAM), 48
read-only memory (ROM), 48
registers, 46
Reduced Instruction Set
　Computing (RISC) processors, 58
superscalar, 55
swap in, 50
swap out, 50
system board, 44
system clock, 50
transistors, 40
Unicode Worldwide Character
　Standard, 44
upward compatibility, 46
volatile, 47
word size, 49

▶ KEY TERM QUIZ

Fill in the missing word with one of the terms listed in Key Terms:

1. The base 2 number system used by computers is known as the _____.

2. A(n) _____ is the common path between the components of a computer.

3. The smallest possible unit of data is called a(n) _____.

4. The _____ is the circuit board that connects the CPU to all the other hardware devices.

5. _____ is the most common character-code set.

6. A location in the memory chip is indicated by the _____.

7. A(n) _____ is a chip designed to handle complicated mathematical operations.

8. Tiny electronic switches in the CPU that register on or off are known as _____.

9. _____ is the ability of a new hardware device or piece of software to interact with the same equipment and software as its predecessor.

10. High-speed memory locations built directly into the CPU that hold data currently being processed are called

_____.

▶ REVIEW QUESTIONS

1. What is a CPU composed of primarily?
2. Describe how the letter *b* is considered meaningless data.
3. What characterizes a binary system? Explain briefly why it is used to represent data in a computer.
4. Which is the most common character set in use today?
5. Name the device that connects the CPU to a computer system's other hardware devices. What two processing components reside on it?
6. Explain briefly the roles of the CPU's control unit and arithmetic logic unit.
7. Explain briefly what the phrase "upward compatibility" means.
8. Under what conditions does the CPU's arithmetic logic unit (ALU) receive an instruction from the control unit?
9. How does cache memory speed up the computer?
10. What is a register, and what aspect of processing does it most affect?

▶ DISCUSSION QUESTIONS

1. Do you think the international interchange of data provided by the Unicode character set is a worthwhile goal for computing technology? Do you see any other benefits to Unicode's widespread implementation?

2. Why do you think the CPU is commonly referred to as a computer's brain? Can the CPU really "think" like a human's brain?

3. What significant factor led to advancements in bus technology, such as the EISA and PCI architectures?

4. Consider the evolving power of newer CPUs and the parallel increase in the number and arrangement of transistors they contain. Do you think there is a physical limit to the number of transistors in a CPU's design? What significant factor common to today's PCs occurred in the evolution of CPUs, beginning with the 80386 processor?

NORTON INTERACTIVE

Complete the Norton Interactive module for this chapter.

CHAPTER 3

INTERACTING WITH THE COMPUTER

CONTENTS

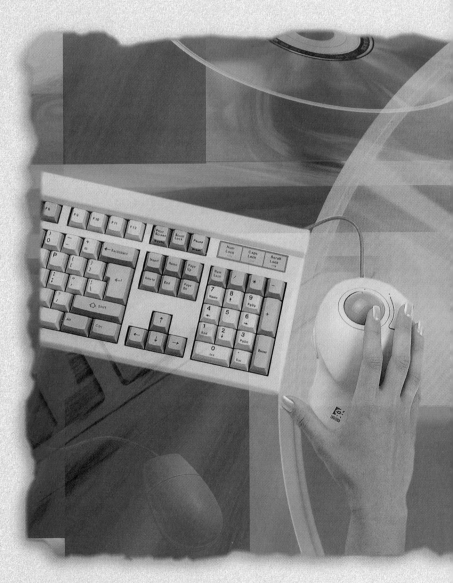

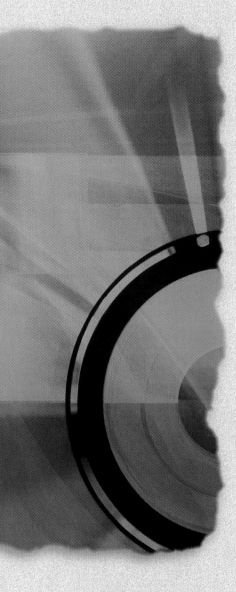

OBJECTIVES

When you complete this chapter, you will be able to do the following:

- Describe the most common input and output devices.
- Understand how a video monitor displays images.
- Discuss the advantages and disadvantages of different types of printers.
- Explain how input and output devices communicate with the other parts of the computer.

If the CPU is the brain of the computer, then the input and output devices are the eyes, ears, mouth, and hands. From the user's point of view, input and output (I/O) devices are just as important as the CPU—more so, in fact, because after you have purchased and set up the computer, you can take the CPU for granted. I/O devices, however, are the parts with which you interact, so your ability to use them effectively is critical to how well you can use the whole system.

The first part of this chapter is devoted to input devices, the second to output. The focus is on the hardware you will use the most: the keyboard, mouse, monitor, and printer. You will learn which types are available and the advantages of each. In addition, you will read about many other types of input and output devices, such as scanners, trackballs, speakers, and plotters. At the end of the chapter, you will learn how ports, expansion cards, and expansion slots are used to connect I/O devices to the rest of the computer.

▶ THE KEYBOARD

The **keyboard** is the primary input device for entering text and numbers. It is a relatively simple device, consisting of about 100 keys, each of which sends a different character code to the CPU. It was one of the first peripherals to be used with PCs, and it is still the most common—you will find a keyboard either built into or attached to every PC.

If you have not used a computer keyboard or a typewriter, you will find out one important fact very quickly: you can use a computer much more effectively if you know how to type. The skill of typing, or **keyboarding**, as it is often called today, implies the ability to enter text using all ten fingers without having to look at the keys. Certainly you can use a computer without being able to type, in fact, many people do. Some people claim that when computers can understand handwriting and speech, typing will become unnecessary. For now, typing is the fastest way to enter text and other data into a computer.

The Standard Keyboard Layout

Keyboards for personal computers come in a number of styles. The various models differ in size, shape, and feel, but except for a few special-purpose keys, most keyboards are laid out almost identically. The most common keyboard layout used today was established by the IBM Enhanced Keyboard. It has 101 keys arranged in four groups, as shown in Figure 3.1.

The **alphanumeric keys**—the parts of the keyboard that look like a typewriter—are arranged the same way on virtually every keyboard and typewriter. Sometimes this common arrangement is called the **QWERTY** layout because the first six keys on the top row of letters are *Q, W, E, R, T,* and *Y.* In addition to letters and punctuation

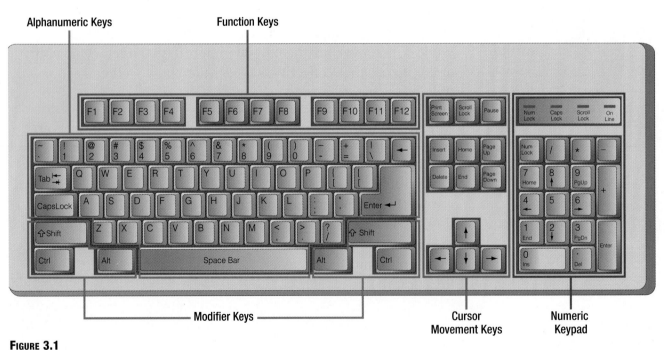

FIGURE 3.1

The standard keyboard layout.

marks, the alphanumeric keys include the **modifier keys**, so named because they are used in conjunction with the other keys. You press a letter or number while holding down one of the modifier keys. On a PC, the modifier keys are Shift, Ctrl (an abbreviation of "Control"), and Alt (an abbreviation of "Alternate"). The modifier keys on a Macintosh are Shift, Ctrl, Option, and ⌘ (Command).

① Alt
② Shift
③ Control

The **numeric keypad**, which is usually located on the right side of the keyboard, is the part that looks like an adding machine, with its ten digits and mathematical operators (+, −, *, and /).

The third part of the keyboard consists of the **function keys**. The function keys (F1, F2, and so on) are usually arranged in a row along the top of the keyboard. They allow you to give the computer commands without having to type long strings of characters. What each function key does depends on the program you are using. For example, in most programs, F1 is the help key. When you press it, a screen displays information about using the program.

The fourth part of the keyboard is the set of **cursor movement keys** which let you change the position of the cursor on the screen. When you use a word processing program, there is a mark on the screen where the characters you type will be entered. This mark, called the **cursor** or **insertion point**, can appear on the screen as a box, a line, or a symbol that looks like a capital I, known as the **I-beam cursor**. Figure 3.2 shows a typical cursor.

The cursor shows where the next letter typed on the keyboard will appear.

FIGURE 3.2
The cursor.

To edit text, you must first position the cursor in the displayed document. The cursor movement keys allow you to do so quickly.

With the introduction of Windows 95, manufacturers began adding keys to support specific functions of the new operating system. The two keys that were added allow fast typists to perform certain actions that otherwise would be possible only by using the mouse or a series of keyboard actions. One key activates the same shortcut menu that appears when you press the

Pressing this key opens the Windows 95 Start menu.

Pressing this key displays a shortcut menu.

Two new keys appear on some keyboards designed for use with Windows 95.

right mouse button; the other opens the Windows Start menu, which is used to launch programs.

How the Computer Accepts Input from the Keyboard

When you press a key on a keyboard, you might think the keyboard simply sends that letter to the computer—after all, that is what appears to happen. Actually, it is more complex than that, as shown in Figure 3.3.

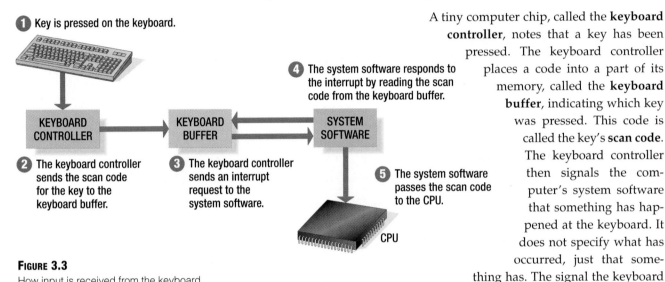

1 Key is pressed on the keyboard.

4 The system software responds to the interrupt by reading the scan code from the keyboard buffer.

KEYBOARD CONTROLLER → KEYBOARD BUFFER ⇄ SYSTEM SOFTWARE

2 The keyboard controller sends the scan code for the key to the keyboard buffer.

3 The keyboard controller sends an interrupt request to the system software.

5 The system software passes the scan code to the CPU.

CPU

FIGURE 3.3
How input is received from the keyboard.

A tiny computer chip, called the **keyboard controller**, notes that a key has been pressed. The keyboard controller places a code into a part of its memory, called the **keyboard buffer**, indicating which key was pressed. This code is called the key's **scan code**. The keyboard controller then signals the computer's system software that something has happened at the keyboard. It does not specify what has occurred, just that something has. The signal the keyboard sends to the computer is a special kind of message called an **interrupt request**. The keyboard controller sends an interrupt request to the system software when it receives a complete keystroke. For example, if you type the letter *r*, the controller immediately issues an interrupt request. (If you hold down the Shift key before typing *R*, the controller waits until the whole key combination has been entered.)

When the system software receives an interrupt request, it evaluates the request to determine the appropriate response. When a keypress has occurred, the system reads the memory location in the keyboard buffer that contains the scan code of the key that was pressed. It then passes the key scan code to the CPU.

Actually, the keyboard buffer can store a number of keystrokes at once. This is necessary because some time elapses between the pressing of a key and the computer's reading of that key from the keyboard buffer. Also, programmers must put instructions into their programs to read keystrokes (reading does not happen automatically) because the program might be doing something else at the moment a key is pressed. With the keystrokes stored in a buffer, the program can react to them when convenient.

▪ THE MOUSE

If you had bought a personal computer in the early 1980s, a keyboard would probably have been the only input device that came with it. Today, all new PCs come with some kind of pointing device as standard equipment. If the computer is a desktop or tower model, the pointing device is usually a mouse. A **mouse** is an input device that rolls around on a flat surface (usually on a desk) and controls the pointer. The **pointer**

Mouse

Most modern personal computers now come equipped with a mouse.

is an on screen object, usually an arrow, that is used to select text, access menus, move files, or interact with other programs, files, or data that appear on the screen.

The mouse first gained widespread recognition when it was packaged with the Apple Macintosh computer in 1984. Initially, some users scoffed at this simple tool, but it quickly became apparent that the mouse is very convenient for entering certain types of input. For example, a mouse lets you position the cursor anywhere on the screen quickly and easily without having to use the cursor movement keys. You simply move the pointer to the on screen position you want, press the mouse button, and the cursor appears there. A mouse also allows you to create graphic elements on the screen, such as lines, curves, and freehand shapes, and it makes using menus and interactive message boxes easier. With this new capability, the mouse helped establish the computer as a versatile tool for graphic designers, starting what has since become a revolution in that field.

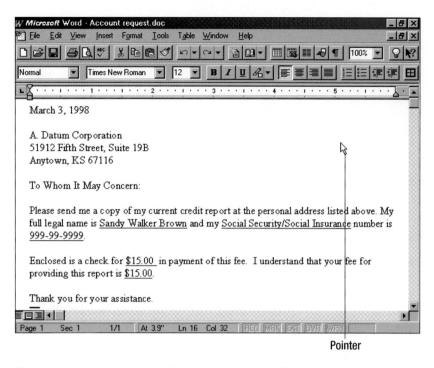

Pointer

The mouse controls the pointer, which is used to interact with items on the screen.

Using the Mouse

You use a mouse to point to a location on the screen. Push the mouse forward, and the pointer goes up; move the mouse to the left, and the pointer goes to the left. To point to an object or location on the screen, you simply use the mouse to place the pointer on top of the object or location.

Everything you do with a mouse you accomplish by combining pointing with four other techniques: clicking, double-clicking, dragging, and right-clicking. Clicking, double-clicking, and dragging are illustrated in Figure 3.4.

"click"   "click click"

Click   Double-click   Drag

FIGURE 3.4
Three mouse techniques.

To **click** on something with the mouse means to move the pointer to the item on the screen and to press and release the mouse button once. To **double-click** on an item means to point to it with the cursor and to press and release the mouse button twice in rapid succession. To **drag** an item, you position the mouse cursor over the item, then depress the mouse button and hold it down as you move the mouse.

Although most mice have two buttons, clicking, double-clicking, and dragging are usually carried out with the left mouse button. The mouse usually sits to the right of

FIGURE 3.5
Right-handed users generally keep the mouse to the right of the keyboard, so they can manipulate the mouse with their right hand.

the keyboard (for right-handed people) and the user maneuvers the mouse with the right hand, pressing the left button with the right forefinger, as shown in Figure 3.5. For this reason, the left mouse button is sometimes called the primary mouse button.

If you are left-handed, you may want to use the operating system to set the right mouse button as the primary button. This lets you place the mouse to the left of the keyboard, control the mouse with your left hand, and use your left forefinger for most mouse actions.

Although the primary mouse button is used for most mouse actions, an increasing number of programs also use the right mouse button. Windows 95, for example, uses the right mouse button extensively to open shortcut menus. Using the right mouse button is known as **right-clicking**.

The Inner Workings of a Mouse

A mouse is really a simple device. The most common type has a ball inside it that extends just below the housing. When you slide the mouse around on a flat surface, such as a desktop or a mouse pad, the ball rolls. Figure 3.6 shows the inside of a mouse.

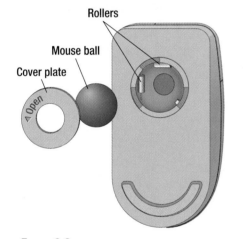

Rollers

Mouse ball

Cover plate

On two sides of the ball, at a 90-degree angle from each other, are two small rollers that touch the mouse and spin when the ball rolls. Figure 3.7 shows how moving a mouse diagonally causes the rollers to rotate.

A sensor detects how much each roller spins and sends this information to the computer. The computer translates the information and changes the position of the on screen pointer to correspond to the position indicated by the mouse.

FIGURE 3.6
Cover plate and mouse ball removed to show rollers.

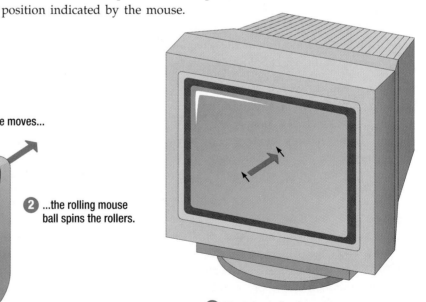

❶ When the mouse moves...

❷ ...the rolling mouse ball spins the rollers.

❸ The information from the spinning rollers is sent to the system software, which controls the pointer.

FIGURE 3.7
How the mouse controls the pointer.

Like the keyboard, a mouse does not actually send a message directly to the program that the computer is running. Rather, it sends an interrupt request to the CPU. The program that is running checks regularly to see whether the mouse has been used; if it has, the program reads a memory location to see what happened, then reacts appropriately.

Although most mouse units are connected directly to computers with a cord, some are not. A cordless mouse communicates with a special controller in or near the computer by transmitting a low-intensity radio or infrared signal. Cordless mice are more expensive than their tailed cousins, but many people like the freedom of movement they allow without the restriction of a cord.

Another difference between mice is the way in which they sense movement. Most track the rotation of rollers, but a few track movement optically by sensing the movement of dots or a grid on the mousepad. These optical models are generally more expensive. They are also less versatile, because they can be used only on their own special pads. Their chief advantage is that they are highly sensitive and therefore more accurate than standard mice.

Taking Care of a Mouse

A mouse rolls around on the surface of a mouse pad or a desk, so it tends to pick up tiny objects that are scattered there, such as dust and hair. After a while, the mouse will not work well because it is dirty. The pointer will seem to get stuck on the screen, and the mouse will bump along as though it had a flat tire. When this happens, it is time to clean your mouse.

To clean the mouse, turn it over and find the cover plate (see Figure 3.8). Rotate the cover plate in the direction of the arrows about a quarter turn, then turn the mouse over in your hand. The cover plate and the mouse ball should fall out. Wipe the mouse ball with a dry, clean cloth, then set it aside.

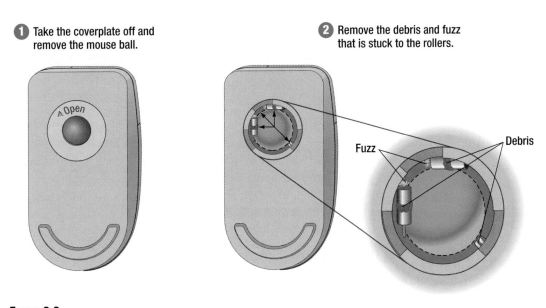

1 Take the coverplate off and remove the mouse ball.

2 Remove the debris and fuzz that is stuck to the rollers.

Fuzz

Debris

FIGURE 3.8
Cleaning the mouse ball.

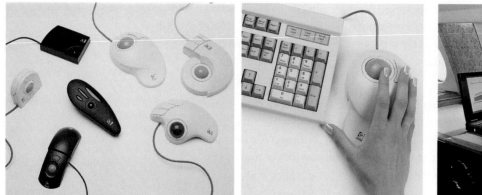

Trackballs come in many different shapes and sizes.

A notebook computer with a trackball can be very convenient in a small workspace, such as a seat on an airplane.

The Trackman Live, from Logitech, is a remote control trackball. It is especially handy for giving stand-up presentations.

The problem with the mouse is almost certain to be with the rollers. Use a pair of tweezers to remove any debris that is stuck to or wrapped around the rollers. When they are clean, replace the ball and coverplate. That should get you rolling smoothly again.

The Trackball

A **trackball** is a pointing device that works like an upside-down mouse. You rest your thumb on the exposed ball and your fingers on the buttons. To move the cursor around the screen, you roll the ball with your thumb. Because you do not move the whole device, a trackball requires less space than a mouse, so when space is limited, a trackball can be a boon. Trackballs gained popularity with the advent of laptop computers, which typically are used on laps or on small work surfaces without room for a mouse.

Some trackballs, such as the Trackman Live from Logitech, are not even attached to the computer and act like a remote control for the pointer. They are especially useful when giving presentations, because the presenter often walks around the room rather than sitting at a computer.

The Trackpad

The **trackpad** is a stationary pointing device that many people find less tiring to use than a mouse or trackball. The movement of a finger across a small touch surface is translated into cursor movement on the computer screen. The touch-sensitive surface may be just 1.5 – 2 inches square, so the finger never has to move far. The size also makes it well suited for a notebook computer.

Pointers in the Keyboard

This NEC VERSA 2205C comes with a trackpad rather than a trackball.

Several companies now offer another space-saving pointer device, consisting of a small joystick positioned near the middle of the keyboard, typically between the *g* and *h* keys. The joystick is controlled with either forefinger. Two buttons that perform the same function as mouse buttons are just beneath the spacebar and are

New computer users are often perplexed by the option to use keyboard commands to navigate through the maze of computer commands. How do you know what the commands do, and how do you possibly remember them all? Isn't a mouse a lot easier?

Now that GUIs (graphical user interfaces) are fairly standard in computing, a mouse is easy and intuitive to use. The only problem with a mouse is: It's slow.

When you use a mouse to open a menu, interact with a dialog box, or scroll through the document you are editing, you have to take your hand off of the keyboard to use the mouse, and then return your hand to the home row of the keyboard—every time. By the end of a day, these movements can add up to a lot of time.

Instead of using the mouse, you can get to the same place or execute the same commands by using combinations of keystrokes on your keyboard, known as *keyboard commands*, or hotkeys, or shortcut keys. The obvious advantage to keyboard commands is that your hands

do not leave the keyboard, and your actions are therefore faster.

Keyboard commands can accomplish almost any single action the computer can take. For example, in a standard word processing program, you can use hotkeys to open, close, save and print files, format, find, replace, delete, copy, insert, select, navigate, outline, add an annotation, access Help, and start your spelling or grammar checker. Once you become accustomed to using hotkeys, you spend less time moving your hands, and your whole computing process speeds up.

Hotkeys usually include a combination of the Alt, Ctrl, and Shift keys, coupled with a letter of the alphabet. Often there is an additional key included in the hotkey combination which is native to a particular platform. For example, PC keyboards contain a Windows-symbol key, and Macintosh keyboards have an Apple symbol key, referred to as the Command key. The Windows key and the Macintosh Command key are used in the same manner as the Alt, Ctrl, and Shift keys.

Keyboard commands are not as difficult to learn as they might seem at first. Often, the alphabetical letter in the command is directly correlated to the first letter of the command. For example, in a Macintosh system, to Print, you press the Command key plus the letter *P*. The Windows operating system has expanded this concept so that you can access any menu command by pressing Alt + the letter underlined in the menu name, and then pressing the underlined letter of the particular option you want.

A software standard known as Common User Access (CUA) has led to standardization of many of the commonly used hotkeys across different programs, and even across different environments, such as Windows and Macintosh. This means, for example, that the hotkey for opening a file in Word is basically the same as in Excel,

Ctrl + O, whether you are using a PC or Macintosh, the only possible difference being the "special key" of the particular platform you are using.

Here are some examples of common shortcut keys shared by the Windows and Macintosh environments:

Mac	Windows	Function
⌘+N	Ctrl+N	Open the New file dialog box.
⌘+O	Ctrl+O	Open the Open file dialog box.
⌘+S	Ctrl+S	Save a currently open and selected file.
⌘+P	Ctrl+P	Open the Print dialog box.
⌘+Z	Ctrl+Z	Undo an editing command.
⌘+C	Ctrl+C	Copy selected text or data to the Clipboard.
⌘+V	Ctrl+V	Paste text or data from the Clipboard into the current file.
⌘+F	Ctrl+F	Open the Find dialog box.

To learn hotkey formulas, also check pull-down menus which have many hotkey commands listed, or look up "shortcut keys" in the Help system of a particular application. Most programs have their entire series of keyboard commands listed.

Edit	
Can't Undo	⌘Z
Repeat Close	⌘Y
Cut	⌘X
Copy	⌘C
Paste	⌘V
Paste Special...	
Clear	Clear
Select All	⌘A
Find...	⌘F
Replace...	⌘H
Go To...	⌘G
AutoText...	
Bookmark...	⌘⇧F5
Links...	
Object	
Publishing	▶

Shortcut keys are shown beside commands in drop-down menus of many computer programs.

Microsoft Word	
Help Topics	Back	Options

Apply formatting using shortcut keys

Format characters using shortcut keys

To	Press
Change the font	CTRL+SHIFT+F
Change the font size	CTRL+SHIFT+P
Increase the font size	CTRL+SHIFT+>
Decrease the font size	CTRL+SHIFT+<
Increase the font size by 1 point	CTRL+]
Decrease the font size by 1 point	CTRL+[

To	Press
Change the case of letters	SHIFT+F3
Format letters as all capitals	CTRL+SHIFT+A
Apply or remove bold formatting	CTRL+B
Apply or remove an underline	CTRL+U
Underline single words	CTRL+SHIFT+W
Double-underline text	CTRL+SHIFT+D
Apply or remove hidden text	CTRL+SHIFT+H
Apply italic formatting	CTRL+I

These are some of the formatting shortcut keys available in Microsoft Word.

TrackPoint pointing device

TrackPoint buttons

IBM's ThinkPad comes with the TrackPoint pointing device. The pointer is controlled by pushing the red TrackPoint device forward, back, left, or right. Commands are executed by clicking on the TrackPoint buttons.

pressed with the thumb. Because it occupies so little space, the device is built into several laptop models. Another advantage is that users do not have to take their hands off the keyboard, so the device saves time and effort.

No generic term has emerged for this device yet, although several manufacturers are referring to it as an "integrated pointing device." On the IBM laptop called the ThinkPad, the pointing device is called the TrackPoint.

To interact with the Newton Message Pad, users point, tap, draw, and write with a pen.

OTHER INPUT DEVICES

Although the keyboard and mouse are the input devices with which people work most often on the desktop, there are a number of other ways to get data into a computer. Sometimes the tool is simply a matter of choice. In many cases, however, the usual tools may not be appropriate. For example, in a dusty factory or warehouse, a keyboard or mouse would become clogged with dirt pretty quickly. Also, alternative input devices are important parts of some special-purpose computers.

Pens

Pen-based systems use an **electronic pen** as their primary input device. You hold the pen in your hand and write or print on a special pad or directly on the screen. You can also use the pen as a pointing device, like a mouse, to select commands. It is important to realize here that the screen is the input device, not the pen. The screen detects pressure, light, or an electrostatic charge that comes from the pen and then stores the position of that signal.

Although pen-based systems would seem like a handy way to get text into the computer for word processing, perfecting the technology to decipher people's handwriting with 100 percent reliability is so complex that pens are not generally used to enter large amounts of text. They are more commonly used for data collection, where the touch of a pen might select a "yes" or "no" box, or to mark a box next to a part that must be ordered or a service that has been requested. Another common use is inputting signatures or messages that are stored and transmitted as a graphic image, such as a fax. The computer may not be able to decipher your scrawled note, but if it appears on your coworkers' screens and they can read it, that is all that is required. When delivery-service drivers make deliveries, they often have recipients sign their names on such a computer-based pad. As handwriting-recognition technology becomes more reliable, pen-based systems will undoubtedly become more common.

When you receive a package via UPS, you sign your name on a pen-based computer, which stores a digital image of your signature.

Touch Screens

Touch screens allow the user to point directly at the computer display, usually to select from a menu of choices on the screen. Most touch-screen computers use sensors in, or near, the computer's screen that can detect the touch of a finger.

Touch screens are appropriate in environments where dirt or weather would render keyboards and pointing devices useless, and where a simple, intuitive interface is important. They are well suited for simple applications such as automated teller machines or public information kiosks. Touch screens have become common in department stores, drugstores, and supermarkets, where they are used for all kinds of purposes, from creating personalized greeting cards to selling lottery tickets. There are even computerized touch screens on slot machines in gambling casinos.

A student obtains campus information at a public information kiosk.

Bar Code Readers

The most widely used input device after the keyboard and mouse is the flatbed or hand-held **bar code reader** commonly found in supermarkets and department stores. These devices convert the bar code, which is a pattern of printed bars on products, into a product number by emitting a beam of light—frequently a laser beam—that reflects off the bar code image. A light-sensitive detector identifies the bar code image by recognizing special bars at both ends of the image. Once the detector has identified the bar code, it converts the individual bar patterns into numeric digits. The special bars at each end of the image are different, so the reader can tell whether the bar code has been read right-side up or upside down.

After the bar code reader has converted a bar code image into a number, it feeds that number to the computer, just as though the number had been typed on a keyboard.

To enter prices and product information into a cash register, a cashier passes groceries over a bar code reader. The bar code reader projects a web of laser beams onto the bar code and measures the pattern of the reflected light.

Hand-held bar code readers are used to track Federal Express packages.

Image Scanners and Optical Character Recognition

The bar code reader is actually just a special type of image scanner. **Image scanners** convert any image into electronic form by shining light onto the image and sensing the intensity of the reflection at every point. Figure 3.9 illustrates the process.

Color scanners use filters to separate the components of color into the primary additive colors (red, green, and blue) at each point. Red, green, and blue are known as primary additive colors because they can be combined to create any other color.

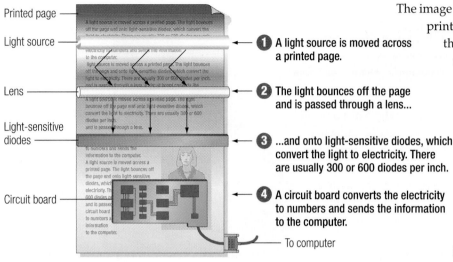

Printed page

Light source

Lens

Light-sensitive diodes

Circuit board

1. A light source is moved across a printed page.

2. The light bounces off the page and is passed through a lens...

3. ...and onto light-sensitive diodes, which convert the light to electricity. There are usually 300 or 600 diodes per inch.

4. A circuit board converts the electricity to numbers and sends the information to the computer.

To computer

Figure 3.9
How an image is scanned.

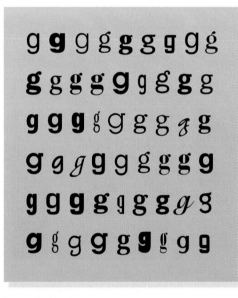

Figure 3.10
A few of the ways that a lowercase *g* can appear in print.

To use a hand-held scanner, you roll the end of the scanner across the image. If the image is wider than the scanner, you can make multiple passes.

The image scanner is useful because it translates printed images into an electronic format that can be stored in a computer's memory. You can then use software to organize or manipulate the electronic image. For example, if you have scanned a photo, you could use Adobe Photoshop—a graphics program—to increase the contrast or to adjust the colors. If you have scanned a text document, you might want to use **Optical Character Recognition (OCR)** software to translate the image into text that you can edit. When a scanner first creates an image from a page, the image is stored in the computer's memory as a bitmap. A **bitmap** is a grid of dots, each dot represented by one or more bits. The job of OCR software is to translate that array of dots into text (i.e., ASCII codes) that the computer can interpret as letters and numbers.

To translate bitmaps into text, the OCR software looks at each character and tries to match the character with its own assumptions about how the letters should look. Because it is difficult to make a computer recognize an unlimited number of typefaces and fonts, OCR software is extremely complex. For example, Figure 3.10 shows a few of the many ways the letter *g* can appear on a printed page.

Despite the complexity of the task, OCR software has become quite advanced. Today, for example, many programs can decipher a page of text received by a fax machine. In fact, computers with fax modems can use OCR software to convert faxes they receive directly into text that can be edited with a word processor.

Scanners come in a range of sizes, from hand-held models to flatbed scanners that sit on a desktop. **Hand-held scanners** are less expensive but typically require multiple passes over a single page because they are not as wide as letter-size paper. They do, however, have the advantage of portability.

Flatbed scanners are more expensive than hand-held scanners but offer higher quality reproduction, and they can scan a page in a single pass. (Multiple scans are sometimes required for color, however.) To use a flatbed scanner, you place the printed image on a piece of glass similar to the way a page is placed on a photocopier.

This student has just scanned an image using a flatbed scanner.

The Visioneer PaperPort Vx is useful for scanning text pages.

There are also medium-size scanners, such as the PaperPort Vx, from Visioneer, in which the sheet is fed through the scanner, in a manner similar to the way a page is fed through a fax machine.

Microphones and Voice Recognition

Now that sound capabilities are a standard part of computers, microphones are becoming increasingly important as input devices. Sound is used most often in multimedia, where the presentation can benefit from narration, music, or sound effects. In software, sounds are used to alert the user to a problem or to prompt the user for input.

For this type of sound input, a digitized recording is all that is required. All you need to make such a recording are a microphone (or some other audio input device, such as a CD player) and a **sound card** that translates the electrical signal from the microphone into a digitized form that the computer can store and process. Sound cards can also translate digitized sounds back into analog signals that can then be sent to the speakers.

There is also a demand for translating spoken words into text, much as there is a demand for translating handwriting into text. Translating voice to text is a capability known as **voice recognition** (or **speech recognition**). With it, you can speak to the computer rather than having to type, and you can control the computer with simple commands, such as "shut down" or "print status report."

Voice recognition software takes the smallest individual sounds in a language, called phonemes, and translates them into text or commands. Even though English uses only about 40 phonemes, a sound can have several different meanings ("two" versus "too," for example) making reliable translation difficult. The challenge for voice recognition software is to deduce a sound's meaning correctly from its context and to distinguish meaningful sounds from background noise.

▶ THE MONITOR

Although there are many kinds of input devices, there are currently just three common types of output devices: monitors, printers, and sound systems. Of the three, monitors are the most important because they are the output devices with which users interact most often.

Indeed, users often form opinions about a computer just from the look of the monitor alone. They want to know: Is the image crisp and clear? Does the monitor display colorful graphics? Two important elements determine the quality of the image a monitor displays: the monitor itself and the video controller. In this section, you will learn about both of these elements in detail and find out how they work together to display text and graphics.

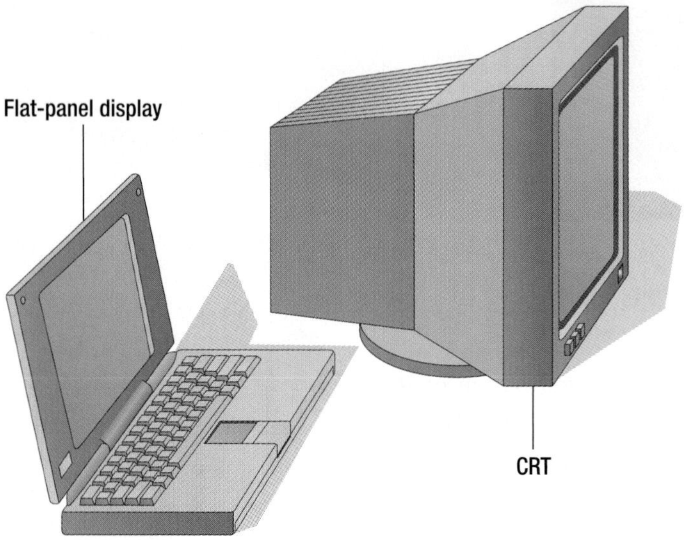

Two basic types of monitors are used with PCs. The first is the typical monitor that you see on a desktop computer—it looks a lot like a television screen and works the same way. This type uses a large vacuum tube, called a **cathode ray tube (CRT)**. The second type, known as a **flat-panel display**, is used with notebook computers. Either of these types can be **monochrome**, displaying only one color against a contrasting background (often black); **grayscale**, displaying varying intensities of gray against a white background; or **color**, displaying anywhere from four to millions of colors. Today, most new monitors display in color.

Flat-panel display

CRT

The two most common types of monitors.

How a CRT Monitor Displays an Image

Figure 3.11 shows how a typical CRT monitor works.

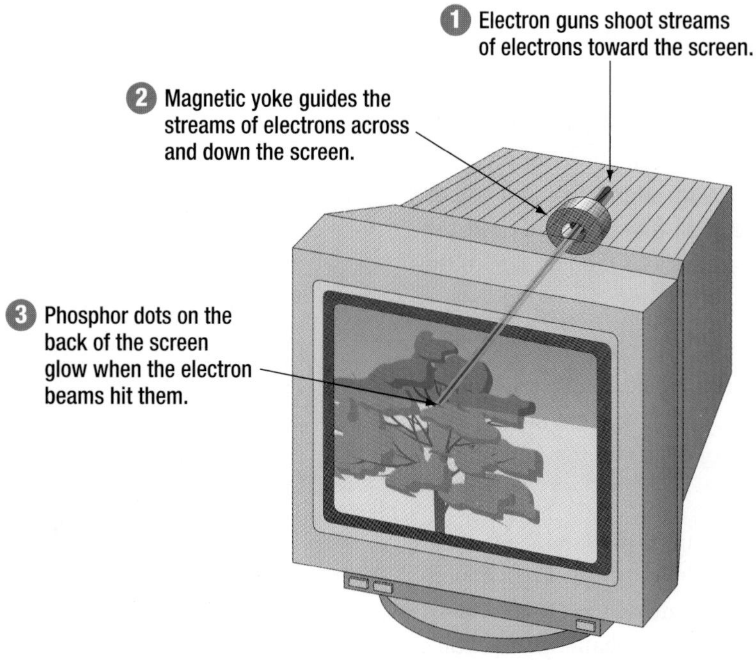

Near the back of a monochrome or grayscale monitor housing is an electron gun. The gun shoots a beam of electrons through a magnetic coil, which aims the beam at the front of the monitor. The back of the monitor's screen is coated with phosphors, chemicals that glow when they are struck by the electron beam. The screen's phosphor coating is organized into a grid of dots. The smallest number of phosphor dots that the gun can focus on is called a **pixel**, a contraction of *pic*ture *el*ement. Modern monochrome and grayscale monitors can focus on pixels as small as a single phosphor dot.

Actually, the electron gun does not just focus on a spot and shoot electrons there. It systematically aims at

1 Electron guns shoot streams of electrons toward the screen.

2 Magnetic yoke guides the streams of electrons across and down the screen.

3 Phosphor dots on the back of the screen glow when the electron beams hit them.

FIGURE 3.11
How a CRT monitor creates an image.

Life brings physical challenges to many people. Before the rise of personal computers, people with physical disabilities often had great difficulty performing everyday tasks, and had limited opportunities for employment. Today, an astonishing array of software and other devices are available to assist those with a broad range of disabilities. Although by no means a panacea, the personal computer is helping thousands of physically challenged people to enter mainstream occupations, and to express themselves in sports and in the arts.

For example, consider the case of a person with multiple sclerosis who has lost almost all muscle coordination. If even the use of a single muscle is retained, this person can do anything on a computer from writing simple letters to developing full-range multimedia productions. Electrical switches allow such a person to use almost any part of his or her body that is able to move (such as lips, chin, cheek, shoulder, arm, hand, foot—even eyebrows!) to use a joystick mounted on an adjustable extension arm of a wheelchair to control the on screen cursor and enter text via an on screen keyboard.

An office environment might seem insurmountable for a person paralyzed from the neck down. How could he or she use devices like telephones or computers? With current off-the-shelf computer technology, the solution is simple. A computer equipped with voice recognition software and an on screen keyboard, plus an ordinary modem, permit this individual to make telephone calls, read and write e-mail, letters, access spreadsheets and databases, and even to "surf the Net" for information.

Examples of other kinds of computer technology for the physically challenged include:

■ **Headwands or mouthsticks** allow a user to enter text on an on screen keyboard by head movements and puffing on a straw connected to a small headset.

■ **Optical pointing devices** allow a user to make on screen selections by simply staring at an image—a word, character, or picture—for as little as half a second.

■ **TongueMouse Keyboard**, made by New Abilities Systems, enables users to control the computer with their tongue. A custom-made dental retainer, fitted to the roof of the mouth, sends radio frequencies to a small receiver connected to the computer, and the mouse cursor moves accordingly.

■ **Voice recognition systems** allow computers to respond to spoken commands.

■ **Speech synthesizers** speak for those who can't. When the user points to or types a message on screen, the computer speaks it. Newer artificial voices are now clear enough so that some non-speaking individuals are able to place orders over the phone.

■ **Braille keyboards and translators** allow blind users to input data via Braille and send output to special printers that emboss Braille characters on paper.

■ **Tactile mouse** allows a blind person to "read" a computer screen through electronic impulses fed back to his or her fingertips.

■ **On screen telephones** allow people to use any pointing device, such as a mouse, headset, or joystick to operate a telephone on their computer screen. Other software allows a person to control most appliances, including telephones, lights, TVs, fans, thermostats, and alarm clocks, through the computer.

Although these products may seem remarkable, in reality they are no different from any other piece of computer hardware or software. For people who have disabilities, as for all people, computers provide tools that enhance the development of individual talents.

A blind person uses speech synthesis software to enter data on a computer.

1 The electron gun scans from left to right,

2 and from top to bottom,

3 refreshing every phosphor dot in a zig-zag pattern.

FIGURE 3.12
The scanning pattern of the CRT's electron gun.

every pixel on the screen, starting at the top-left corner and scanning to the right edge, then dropping down a tiny distance and scanning another line, as shown in Figure 3.12.

Like human eyes reading the letters on a page, the electron beam follows each line of pixels from left to right until it reaches the bottom of the screen. Then it starts over. As the electron gun scans, the circuitry driving the monitor adjusts the intensity of each beam to determine whether a pixel is on or off or, in the case of grayscale, how brightly each pixel glows.

A color monitor works just like a monochrome one, except that there are three electron beams instead of just one. The three guns represent the primary additive colors (red, green, and blue), although the beams they emit are colorless. Each pixel on the screen is made up of three tiny red, green, and blue phosphors arranged in a triangle. When the beams of each of these guns are combined and focused on a point on the screen, the phosphors at that point light up to form a tiny spot of white light. Different colors can be displayed by combining various intensities of the three beams. All monitors use masks with holes in them to align the beams. The holes in most monitors are arranged in triangles. Taking a slightly different approach, Sony Trinitron monitors, another popular model, use a single gun and a mask with parallel slots to align the beam on the colored phosphors.

Comparing CRT Monitors

When it is time to shop for a monitor, it is very important to do some comparison shopping. More than just being esthetically pleasing, a good monitor is easier on your eyes, allowing you to work longer and more comfortably. A poor monitor will cause eyestrain and headaches and can even cause long-term vision problems.

The first thing to do when shopping for a monitor is to take a close look at the display. Look at a screenful of text and examine how crisp the letters are, especially near the corners of the screen. Also, if you are going to work with graphics, display a picture with which you are familiar and see whether the colors look accurate.

Even if the monitor looks good (or if you are buying it through the mail), you need to check several specifications. These are the most important specifications:

- Size
- Resolution
- Refresh rate
- Dot pitch

Monitor Size

The physical size of the picture tube has an obvious bearing on how well you can see everything. With a large monitor, as shown in Figure 3.13, you can make the objects on the screen appear bigger, or you can fit more of them on the screen. In other words, bigger is better. Naturally, though, bigger costs more.

Monitors, like televisions, are measured in inches across the diagonal of the front of the tube. For example, a 15-inch monitor measures 15 inches from the lower-left to the upper-right corner. Actually, the picture that appears on a monitor is smaller than

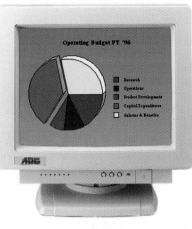

15-inch monitor

The image on the 17-inch monitor is 29 percent larger than on the 15-inch monitor.

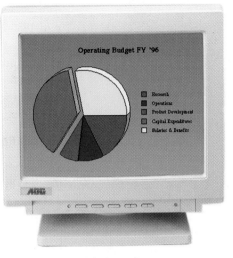

17-inch monitor

FIGURE 3.13
Comparison of a 17-inch monitor with a 15-inch monitor.

is indicated by the monitor size, because the image cannot extend too far into the corners of the CRT without becoming distorted. The picture on a 15-inch monitor, for example, usually measures about 13 inches diagonally.

Today, most new desktop systems are sold with monitors that measure about 15 inches. Over time, this measurement has gradually increased, so the norm may soon creep up to 17 inches.

Resolution

The **resolution** of a computer monitor is classified by the number of pixels on the screen, expressed as a matrix. For example, a resolution of 640 × 480 means there are 640 pixels horizontally across the screen and 480 pixels vertically down the screen. Because the actual resolution is determined by the video controller, not by the monitor itself, most monitor specifications list a range of resolutions. For example, most 15-inch monitors have pixel grids that allow for three settings: 640×480, 800×600, and 1024×768, as shown in Figure 3.14.

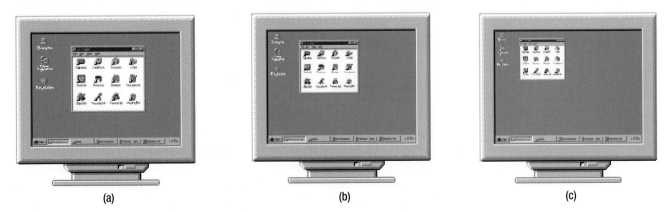

(a)   (b)   (c)

FIGURE 3.14
Windows 95 uses this picture of a monitor to show how screen items appear at different resolutions.
(a) shows the monitor at a resolution of 640x480. (b) shows it at 800x600. (c) shows it at 1024x768. Notice that more items can fit on the screen at higher resolutions, but the items appear smaller.

640×480 was the **VGA** (Video Graphics Array) standard established by IBM in the mid-1980s. The **SVGA** (Super VGA) standard expanded the resolutions to 800×600 and 1024×768. A few 15-inch monitors, and any good monitor bigger than 15 inches, will include even higher settings. However, higher settings are not always better, because they can cause objects on screen to appear too small. Most users with 15-inch monitors set them to display either 640x480 or 800x600. Users with 17-inch monitors will often use the higher settings.

Refresh Rate

When shopping for a monitor, the size and resolution are simple choices. The size is likely to be determined by your budget (although you may want to spend more on a big monitor if you are working with graphics). The resolutions tend to be standard. The refresh rate of the monitor, however, is neither obvious nor standard. **Refresh rate** is the number of times per second that the electron guns scan every pixel on the screen. Refresh rate is measured in Hertz (Hz), or in cycles per second.

The refresh rate is an important concern, because phosphor dots fade quickly after the electron gun passes over them. Therefore, if the screen is not refreshed often enough, it appears to flicker, and flicker is one of the main causes of eyestrain. The problem is compounded because you may not even detect the flicker: nevertheless, in the long run, it can still cause eyestrain.

Opinions vary as to what is an acceptable refresh rate. In general, a refresh rate of 72 Hz or higher should not cause eyestrain. However, note that some monitors have different refresh rates for different resolutions. Make sure the refresh rate is adequate for the resolution you will be using.

Dot Pitch

The last critical specification of a color monitor is the **dot pitch**, the distance between the phosphor dots that make up a single pixel (see Figure 3.15).

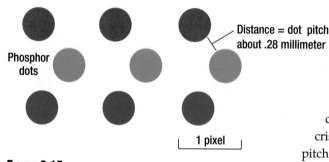

Phosphor dots

Distance = dot pitch about .28 millimeter

1 pixel

FIGURE 3.15
Dot pitch.

Recall that, in a color monitor, there are three dots in every pixel—one red, one green, and one blue. If these dots are not close enough together, the images on the screen will not be crisp. Once again, it is difficult to detect slight differences in dot pitch, but blurry pixels will cause eyestrain anyway. In general, when you are looking for a color monitor, look for a dot pitch no greater than 0.28 millimeter.

The Video Controller

The quality of the images that a monitor can display is defined as much by the video controller as by the monitor itself. The **video controller** is an intermediary device between the CPU and the monitor. It contains the video-dedicated memory and other circuitry necessary to send information to the monitor for display on the screen. It consists of a circuit board, usually referred to simply as a card ("video card" and "video controller" mean the same thing), which is attached to the computer's motherboard. The processing power of the video controller determines, within the constraints of the monitor, the refresh rate, the resolution, and the number of colors that can be displayed.

During the 1980s, when most PCs were running DOS and not Windows, the screen displayed ASCII characters. Doing so took very little processing power, because there were only 256 possible characters and 2,000 text positions on the screen. Rendering each screen required only 4,000 bytes of data.

Windows, however, is a graphical interface, so the CPU must send information to the video controller about every pixel on the screen. At the minimum resolution of 640×480, there are 307,200 pixels to control. Most users run their monitors at 256 colors, so each pixel requires one byte of information. Thus, the computer must send 307,200 bytes to the monitor for each screen.

If the user wants more colors or a higher resolution, the amount of data can be much higher. For example, for the maximum amount of color (24 bits per pixel will render millions of colors) at 1024×768, the computer must send 2,359,296 bytes to the monitor for each screen.

The result of these processing demands is that video controllers have increased dramatically in power and importance. There is a microprocessor on the video controller, and the speed

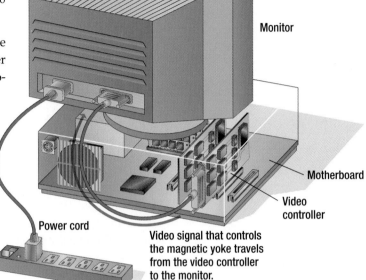

Monitor

Motherboard

Video controller

Power cord

Video signal that controls the magnetic yoke travels from the video controller to the monitor.

The video controller connects the CPU, via the data bus on the motherboard, to the monitor.

of the chip limits the speed at which the monitor can be refreshed. Most video controllers today also include at least 2 MB of **video RAM**, or **VRAM**. (This is in addition to the RAM that is connected to the CPU.) VRAM is "dual-ported," meaning that it can send a screenful of data to the monitor while at the same time receiving the next screenful of data from the CPU. It's faster and more expensive than **DRAM** (Dynamic RAM), the type of memory chip used as RAM for the CPU. Users with large monitors or with heavy graphics needs usually will want even more than 2 MB of VRAM.

Flat-Panel Monitors

CRT monitors are the standard for use with desktop computers because they provide the brightest and clearest picture for the money. There are, however, two major disadvantages associated with CRT monitors. They are big, and they require a lot of power. CRT monitors are not practical for notebook computers, which must be small and need to run off a battery built into the computer. Instead, notebooks use flat-panel monitors that are less than one-inch thick.

There are several types of flat-panel monitors, but the most common is the **liquid crystal display (LCD) monitor**. The LCD monitor creates images with a special kind of liquid crystal that is normally transparent but becomes opaque when charged with electricity. If you have a hand-held calculator, it probably uses liquid crystal. One disadvantage of LCD monitors is that, unlike phosphor, the liquid crystal does not emit light, so there

Most laptops have liquid crystal display (LCD) monitors because they are thinner, lighter, and require less power than a CRT.

is not enough contrast between the images and their background to make them legible under all conditions. The problem is solved by backlighting the screen. Although this makes the screen easier to read, it requires additional power.

There are two main categories of liquid crystal displays: active matrix and passive matrix. **Passive matrix LCD** relies on transistors for each row and each column of pixels, thus creating a grid that defines the location of each pixel. The color displayed by each pixel is determined by the electricity coming from the transistors at the end of the row and the top of the column. The advantage of passive matrix monitors is that they are less expensive than active matrix, a major consideration in laptops, where the monitor can account for one-third the cost of the entire computer. One disadvantage is that the pixels can be seen only if you are sitting directly in front of the monitor. In other words, the monitor has a narrow viewing angle. Another disadvantage is that passive matrix displays do not refresh the pixels very often. If you move the pointer too quickly, it seems to disappear, an effect known as submarining. Also, animated graphics can appear blurry.

Most notebooks that use passive matrix technology now refer to their screens as dual-scan LCD. In **dual-scan LCD**, the problem of the refresh rate is lessened by scanning through the pixels twice as often. Thus, submarining and blurry graphics are much less troublesome than they were before the dual-scan technique was developed.

Active matrix LCD technology assigns a transistor for each pixel, and each pixel is turned on and off individually. This allows the pixels to be refreshed much more rapidly, so submarining is not a problem with these monitors. In addition, active matrix screens have with a wider viewing angle than dual-scan screens.

▶ Printers

Besides the monitor, the other important output device is the printer. Two principal types of printers have become the standards with PCs: laser printers and ink jet printers. In years past, the dot-matrix printer was also a popular choice because it was once far less expensive than the other types. However, ink jet printers now offer much higher quality for about the same price, so dot-matrix printers are used only when physical impact with the paper is important, such as when the user is printing to carbon-copy forms.

In evaluating printers, three criteria are most important:

1. *Image quality.* Image quality, also known as print resolution, is usually measured in dots per inch (dpi).
2. *Speed.* Printer speed is measured in the number of pages of text the computer can print each minute. Pages per minute is abbreviated as ppm.
3. *Cost of operation.* The cost of ink or toner, and maintenance, varies with the type of printer.

Ink Jet Printers

Ink jet printers create an image directly on paper by spraying ink through tiny nozzles (see Figure 3.16). Ink jet technology has been around since before the PC boom, but the popularity of ink jet printers jumped around 1990 when the speed and quality improved and the price plummeted. Today, good ink jet printers are available for as little as $200. These models typically attain print resolutions of at least 360 dots per inch, comparable to that of most laser printers sold before 1992, and they can print from two to four pages per minute (only slightly slower than the slowest laser printers). The operating cost of an ink jet printer is quite low. Expensive mainte-nance is rare, and the only part that needs replacement is the ink cartridge, which typically costs less than $20 for black (color cartridges cost slightly more).

Another improvement in ink jet printers has been in the paper they require. For many years, they needed a special paper, and each sheet had to dry before you could touch it. Today, you can run normal photocopy paper through most ink jet printers (although glossy paper looks slightly better), and the ink is dry within a few seconds.

Finally, ink jet printers offer by far the most cost-effective way to print in color. Color ink jet printers have four ink nozzles: cyan (blue), magenta (red), yellow, and black. These four col-ors are used in almost all color printing, because it is possible to combine them to create any color in the visible spectrum. (Notice, however, that the colors are different than the primary additive colors (red, green, blue) used in monitors. This is because printed color is the result of light bouncing off the paper, not color transmitted directly from a light source. Consequently, cyan, magenta, yellow, and black are sometimes called subtractive colors.) For this reason, color printing is sometimes called four-color print-ing. Color ink jet printers continue to drop in price. "Last year's model" can be found for less than $250. Color ink jet printers have been a boon to home users and small offices, where cost is usually a more important consideration than speed.

Paper

Sprayed ink forms character

Color Ink Jet

Ink droplets

Horizontal plates

Nozzle

Vertical plates

Ink fountain

Electrically charged plates control direction of ink jet spray.

FIGURE 3.16
How an ink jet printer creates an image.

HP DeskJet 1600C

Color ink jet printers cost far less than color laser printers.

Laser Printers

Laser printers are more expensive than ink jet printers, their print quality is higher, and most are faster.

As the name implies, a laser is at the heart of these printers. A separate CPU is built into the printer to interpret the data that it receives from the computer and to control the laser. The

A laser printer produces its high-resolu-tion output quickly and quietly. However, they tend to cost more than ink jet print-ers. Color laser printers, such as this HP Color LaserJet LJ, can cost several thousand dollars.

result is a complicated piece of equipment, using technology similar to that in photocopiers.

Figure 3.17 shows how a laser printer works.

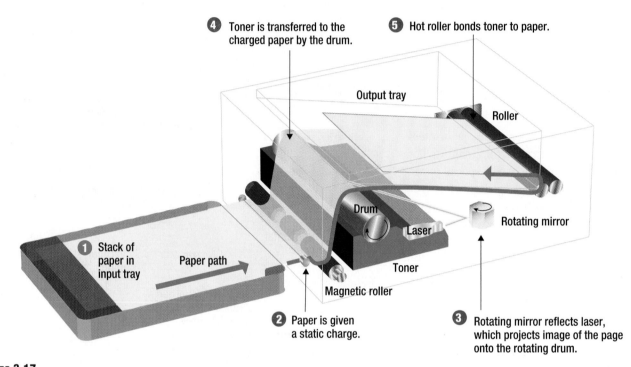

FIGURE 3.17
How a laser printer creates a printed page.

Just as the electron gun in a graphics monitor can target any pixel, the laser in a laser printer can aim at any point on a drum, creating an electrical charge. **Toner**, which is composed of tiny particles of oppositely charged ink, sticks to the drum in the places the laser has charged. Then, with pressure and heat, the toner is transferred off the drum to the paper. Also like a monitor and its video controller, laser printers contain special memory to store the images they print.

A color laser printer works like a single-color model, except that the process is repeated four times, and a different toner color is used for each pass. The four colors used are the same as in the color ink jet printers: cyan, magenta, yellow, and black.

Single-color (black) laser printers typically can produce between 4 and 16 pages of text a minute. However, if you are printing graphics, the output can be a great deal slower. The most common laser printers have resolutions of 600 dpi, both horizontally and vertically, but some high-end models have resolutions of 1200 or 1800 dpi. The printing industry stipulates a resolution of at least 1200 dpi for top-quality professional printing. It is difficult, however, to detect the difference between text printed at 600 dpi and 1200 dpi. The higher resolution is most noticeable in graphics reproduction, such as photographs and art work.

The quality and speed of laser printers make them ideal for office environments where several users can share the same printer easily via a local area network (LAN).

Convenience is another advantage of laser printers. Most can use standard, inexpensive copy paper, which is loaded into a paper tray. The disadvantages of laser printers are the price and the cost of operation. Laser printers start at about $500 and go up dramatically if you want speed, high resolution, or color. In addition, laser printers require new toner cartridges after a few thousand pages, and toner cartridges cost from $40 to $80 for black toner.

On the other hand, the cost of laser printers has come way down. In 1990, a 300 dpi laser printer that printed 4 pages per minute cost about $1,000. Today, you can get 600 dpi and about the same speed for $500. At the same time, color laser printers have also become more affordable, although most still cost several thousand dollars.

Other High-Quality Printers

Although most offices and homes use ink jet or laser printers, there are a variety of other types used for special purposes. These types are often used by publishers and small print shops to create high-quality output, especially color output. The last type discussed below, the plotter, is designed specifically for printing CAD documents.

Thermal-Wax Printers

Thermal-wax printers are used primarily for presentation graphics and handouts. They create bold colors and have a low per-page cost for pages with heavy color requirements. The process provides vivid colors because the inks it uses do not bleed into each other or soak specially coated paper. Thermal-wax printers operate with a ribbon coated with panels of colored wax that melts and adheres to plain paper as colored dots when passed over a focused heat source.

Thermal-wax printers, such as the Calcomp Colormaster Plus XF, are designed to produce bold, vivid colors.

Dye-Sub Printers

Desktop publishers and graphic artists get realistic quality and color for photo images using **dye-sub** (for *dye sub*limation) **printers**. In dye-sublimation technology, a ribbon containing panels of color is moved across a focused heat source that is capable of subtle temperature variations. The heated dyes evaporate from the ribbon and diffuse on specially coated paper where they form areas of different colors. The variations in color are related to the intensity of the heat applied.

Dye-sub printers create extremely sharp images, but they are slow and costly since the special paper required can make the per-page cost as high as $3 to $4.

Fiery Printers

One high-quality form of printing takes advantage of digital color copiers. The **fiery print server** is a special-purpose computer that transmits documents to a digital color copier, where they are printed. Fiery prints are used in print shops as an alternative to press printing.

IRIS Printers

IRIS printers are used by print shops to produce high-resolution presentation graphics and color proofs that resemble full-color offset printed images. The IRIS is a

IRIS printers use ink jet technology to achieve print resolutions as high as 1800 dpi.

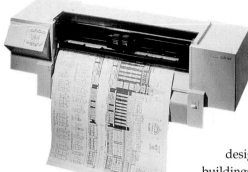

A plotter uses a robotic arm to draw with colored pens on oversized paper. Here, an architectural rendering is being printed.

high-tech form of ink jet printing in which individual sheets of paper are mounted onto a drum. The nozzles on the ink jet printing head pass from one end of the spinning drum to the other spraying minute drops of colored ink to form the image. This type of printer can produce an image with a resolution of 1800 dpi.

Plotters

A **plotter** is a special kind of output device. It is like a printer in that it produces images on paper, but it does so in a different way. Plotters are designed to produce large drawings or images, such as construction plans for buildings or blueprints for mechanical objects.

A plotter uses a robotic arm to draw with colored pens on a sheet of paper. The instructions that a plotter receives from a computer consist of a color and the beginning and ending coordinates for a line. With that information, the plotter picks up the appropriate pen, positions it at the beginning coordinates, drops the pen down to the surface of the paper, and draws to the ending coordinates. Plotters draw curves by creating a sequence of very short, straight lines.

▶ SOUND SYSTEMS

Just as microphones are now important input devices, speakers and their associated technology are key output systems. Today, when you buy a **multimedia PC**, you are getting a machine that includes a CD-ROM drive, a high-quality video controller (with plenty of VRAM), speakers, and a sound card.

The speakers attached to these systems are similar to ones you connect to a stereo. The only difference is that they are usually smaller and they contain their own small amplifiers. Otherwise, they do the same thing any speaker does: They transfer a constantly changing electric current to a magnet, which pushes the speaker cone back and forth. The moving speaker cone creates pressure vibrations—in other words, sound (see Figure 3.18).

The more complicated part of the sound output system is in the sound card. The sound card translates digital sounds into the electric current that is sent to the speakers. Sound is defined as air pressure varying over time. To digitize sound, the waves are converted to an electric current measured thousands of times per second and recorded as a number. When the sound is played back, the sound card reverses this process, translating

1 Electric current from the sound card...

2 ...is applied to an electromagnet.

Sound card

Electromagnet

Magnet

3 The changing magnetic field pushes a magnet back and forth...

4 ...which is attached to the speaker cone.

5 The moving speaker cone creates changes in the air pressure which your brain interprets as sound.

FIGURE 3.18
How a speaker creates sound.

How Does Your Spreadsheet Sound?

Business documents have become multimedia presentations. In the modern business world it is no longer possible to compose even the commonplace report or presentation only with text. Corporate communications are dressed in spiffier business attire than ever before. Spreadsheets have found their way into word processed reports, graphics pop up in spreadsheets, simple proposals have full-scale digital slide presentations attached—even the lowly memo can include at least one piece of clip art.

Now, sound is also becoming ordinary in business documents. You can include sound clips in all kinds of communications: letters, spreadsheets, databases, e-mail, and more. All you need is a computer equipped with a sound card and the accompanying software, which come bundled with newer computers, or as an upgrade to older models.

Computers were once mute, except for an occasional beep. But the increasing demand for multimedia—to make games more exciting, presentations more inviting, Web sites more interesting, and applications easier to learn—has made sound an important element in nearly every new computer and many software applications.

Computer sound comes out of a speaker. That speaker may be tiny enough to fit inside a pair of headphones or big enough to rattle an auditorium. The speaker's power is measured in watts, the same as other sound devices. It produces frequencies of sound from sub-woofer tones of 20 Hz to 100 Hz, through woofer and mid-range tones of 100 Hz to 6000 Hz, to high-range tweeter tones of 6000 Hz to 20,000 Hz, the outer limits of human hearing.

The commands to recognize and to produce the sound come from programs, routed through special software and the operating system. The software may receive input from musical instruments, special effects, or even human speech.

These programs are incredibly detailed, capable of specifying the frequencies and volumes of the sound through each fraction of a second.

Sound can be used in a computer as both input and output. Sound can be used as input in computers for disabled people who are unable to use the standard keyboard or mouse. For example, using voice recognition software combined with a soundboard, when a user speaks the words "File" and "Open," the application opens the Open file dialog box.

The possibilities for using sound as output are just as varied and interesting. For example, the instructions for filling out a sales forecast sheet in a spreadsheet program can be included in the worksheet as a sound clip. A cell in the worksheet might display an icon resembling a speaker that the user clicks to hear verbal instructions.

Or, as a data-entry specialist moves from one field to another completing a database form, verbal feedback might include instructions to the specialist for filling out the next field. Or the feedback could repeat the data he or she just typed into a field as a means of data verification.

The sound capabilities of computers also can be used interactively. For example, you might receive a memo over your company's e-mail system. When you click on a sound icon in the Subject box, your co-worker could ask you for instructions to accomplish a task. You could then create a reply message and record your instructions into the new memo.

Or, the playing of the sounds can be made automatic, no longer requiring that a button be clicked. When the memo is opened, a short clip of Bach's Toccata in D Minor might hint at the importance of the subject in the memo.

Due to the large size of sound clips and the complexity of hardware and software needed to create and to use them, memos such as this are rarely seen (and heard) in office environments. But the technology is available, and such documents will probably become commonplace in the not-too-distant future.

High-quality computer sound systems can be complex and sophisticated.

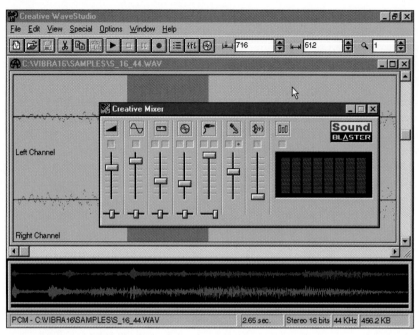

the series of numbers into electric current that is sent to the speakers. The magnet moves back and forth with the changing current, creating vibrations.

With the right software, you can do much more than simply record and play back digitized sound. Utilities that are built into Windows 95 provide a miniature sound studio, allowing you to view the sound wave and edit it. In the editing you can cut bits of sound, copy them, amplify the parts you want to hear louder, cut out static, and create many exotic audio effects.

This utility lets you edit sound files. For example, you can select sections of the frequency pattern (shown along the bottom of the screen), then amplify that section, repeat it, or cut it from the file.

▶ CONNECTING I/O DEVICES TO THE COMPUTER

In Chapter 2, you learned that all the components of a computer tie into the computer's CPU by way of the data bus. When you need to add a new piece of hardware to your computer, you need to know how to connect it to the bus. There are two basic ways. In some cases, you can plug the device into an existing socket, or **port**, on the back of the computer. Most computers have several types of ports, each with different capabilities and uses. The most common types are shown in Figure 3.19.

When a port is not available, you will need to install a circuit board that includes the port you need.

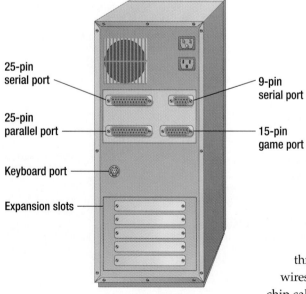

25-pin serial port

25-pin parallel port

Keyboard port

Expansion slots

9-pin serial port

15-pin game port

Serial and Parallel Ports

Internally, a PC's components communicate through the data bus which consists of parallel wires. Similarly, a **parallel interface** is a connection where there are eight or more wires through which data bits can flow simultaneously. Most computer buses transfer 32 bits simultaneously. However, the standard parallel interface for external devices like printers usually transfers eight bits (one byte) at a time over eight separate wires.

With a **serial interface**, data bits are transmitted one at a time through a single wire (however, the interface includes additional wires for the bits that control the flow of data). Inside the computer a chip called a **UART** converts parallel data from the bus into serial data that flows through a serial cable. Figure 3.20 shows how data flows through a 9-pin serial interface.

FIGURE 3.19

Standard ports on a PC.

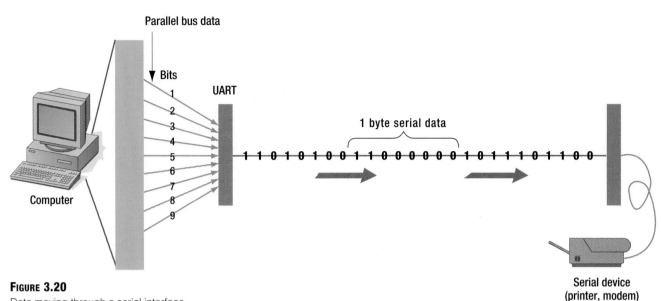

Parallel bus data

FIGURE 3.20
Data moving through a serial interface.

**Serial device
(printer, modem)**

Serial ports are most often used to connect a mouse or a modem. The current standard for serial communications is called **RS-232**, but there are many variations. For instance, a serial port can have either 9 or 25 pins. The PC shown earlier in Figure 3.19 has two RS-232 serial ports, one 9-pin and one 25-pin. This is a common configuration. Most serial devices come with a cable and an adapter so that you can use whichever type of port is available.

As you would expect, a parallel interface can handle a higher volume of data than a serial interface, because more than one bit can be transmitted through a parallel interface simultaneously. Figure 3.21 shows how data moves through a parallel interface.

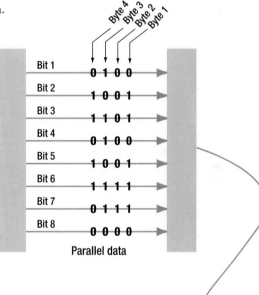

FIGURE 3.21
Data moving through a parallel interface.

**Parallel device
(printer)**

Parallel ports are most often used for printer interfaces, although some other products use them as well. Parallel ports have a 25-pin connector at the computer end. The printer end of a parallel printer cable has a 36-pin **Centronics interface**, developed by the first manufacturer of dot-matrix printers.

Two serial ports, one parallel port, and one port for a mouse or other pointing device, and a joystick for playing games, is a typical rear-panel configuration.

Expansion Slots and Boards

PCs are designed so that users can adapt, or **configure**, the machines to their own particular needs.

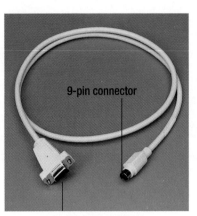

9-pin RS-232 connector

This cable has two different 9-pin serial connectors, allowing the user to link a Macintosh and PC through their serial ports.

9-pin connector

This modem cable has a 9-pin connector that plugs into the serial port on the back of the computer and a 25-pin RS-232 connector that plugs into the modem.

This small PC card is a modem that plugs into a notebook computer. The cord plugs into a standard telephone jack.

PC motherboards have two or more **expansion slots**, which are extensions of the computer's bus that provide a way to add new components to the computer. The slots accept circuit boards, also called **cards**, adapters, or sometimes just boards. Modern notebook computers are too small to accept the same type of cards that fit into desktop models. Instead, new components for notebooks come in the form of **PC cards**, small devices—about the size of credit cards—that fit into a slot on the back or side of the notebook. Figure 3.22 shows a PC expansion board being installed. The board is being attached to the motherboard—the main system board to which the CPU, memory, and other components are attached.

FIGURE 3.22

An expansion card being inserted into an expansion slot.

The expansion slots on the motherboard are used for three purposes:

1. To give built-in devices such as hard disks and diskette drives access to the computer's bus via controller cards.

2. To provide I/O (input/output) ports on the back of the computer for external devices such as monitors, external modems, printers, and the mouse (for computers that do not have a built-in mouse port).

3. To give special-purpose devices access to the computer. For example, a computer can be enhanced with an **accelerator card**, a self-contained device that enhances processing speed through access to the computer's CPU and memory by way of the bus.

The first and second of these are input/output (I/O) functions. Adapters that serve these purposes provide a port to which devices can be attached and serve as a translator between the bus and the device itself. Some adapters also do a significant amount of data processing. For example, a video controller is a card that provides a port on the back of the PC into which you can plug the monitor. It also contains and manages the video memory and does the processing required to display images on the monitor. Other I/O devices that commonly require the installation of a card into an expansion slot include sound cards, internal modems or fax/modems, network interface cards, and scanners. The third type, the accelerator cards, are often installed to speed up the CPU or the display of video.

SCSI

One device interface that takes a different approach from those discussed so far goes a long way toward overcoming the constraints of a limited number of expansion slots on the motherboard. This device is called **small computer system interface** (**SCSI**, pronounced "scuzzy"). Instead of plugging cards into the computer's bus via the expansion slots, SCSI extends the bus outside the computer by way of a

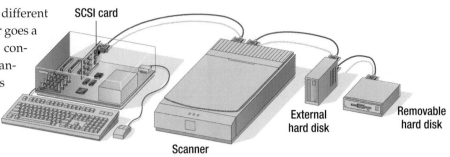

SCSI peripherals daisy-chained together.

cable. In other words, SCSI is like an extension cord for the data bus. Just as you can plug one extension cord into another to lengthen a circuit, you can plug one SCSI device into another to form a daisy chain.

IBM developed SCSI in the 1970s as a way to give mainframe computers access to small computer devices and vice versa. Since then, SCSI has undergone many changes. The emerging standard is SCSI-3 which far exceeds the SCSI-2 limit of six devices that could be daisy-chained on a single SCSI port. SCSI-3 can potentially link up as many as 127 devices.

To provide a PC with a SCSI port, you insert a SCSI adapter board into one of the PC's available expansion slots. Many devices use the SCSI interface. Fast, high-end hard disk drives often have SCSI interfaces, as do scanners, tape drives, and optical storage devices such as CD-ROM drives.

Whereas SCSI is an option for PCs, a SCSI port is built as a standard interface into Macintosh computers and into many UNIX workstations. In fact, with some Macintosh models, you do not have any other access to the computer's bus. Ports for a mouse, modem, and monitor are all built into the computer. Any other devices you want to add—such as an external hard drive, scanner, or CD-ROM drive—can be daisy-chained on the built-in SCSI port.

The PCI SCSI Master kit from Adaptec includes a SCSI adapter board and software for a computer with a PCI bus. Once it is installed, you can attach SCSI peripherals to your computer.

▶ WHAT TO EXPECT IN THE FUTURE

Among input devices, major advances of the future will probably be in the area of natural human-interface technologies, namely, voice recognition and handwriting recognition. The limitations here are in the realm of software rather than hardware, because it is quite difficult to program handwriting and voice recognition software.

Handwriting recognition software is already available, but it is not 100 percent reliable. Rapid progress is being made, however, because the makers of Personal Digital Assistants (hand-held portable computers) need this technology for the PDA to become a successful product. Even when handwriting recognition becomes reliable, you still will not see many handwriting tablets attached to desktop computers. Once you know how to type, typing is faster than writing, so the keyboard will remain the input device of choice wherever there is room for a keyboard.

Voice recognition, on the other hand, will eventually make its way to the desktop. In fact, there are already programs that can understand simple commands and clearly enunciated speech (although still not with a high degree of reliability). It is only a matter of time before the reliability of the software becomes acceptable and the microphone becomes an input device to rival the keyboard. However, as Paul Saffo, at the Institute for the Future in Menlo Park, California, likes to say, "You should never mistake a clear vision as a short distance." In other words, just because voice recognition is certainly in our future, it may be many more years before the technology becomes commonplace.

Among output devices, the new technologies will probably be limited to advancements in the old technologies: bigger monitors, faster printers, and more uses for sound. For years, some technologists have been touting the coming of the "paperless office," a work environment in which documents are circulated electronically, and no printing is necessary. To the extent that e-mail and workgroup computing are growing in popularity, the flow of electronic documents is on the rise. However, people generally still prefer to read from a printed page rather than from a screen. What's more, as far as the "paperless office" goes, the ability to edit documents quickly and easily often means that users print every draft of a document, using far more paper than they would if they did not have access to a computer. (Check the recycling bin of any office to vouch for the increased use of paper since the computer's advent.)

The biggest change in output over the next few years will probably be in more elaborate and less expensive printing options, especially the use of color.

▶ VISUAL SUMMARY

The Keyboard

- There are four parts to the standard keyboard: the alphanumeric keys, the numeric keypad, the function keys, and the cursor movement keys.

The Mouse

- The mouse is a pointing device that lets you control the position of the pointer on the screen without using the keyboard.
- Using the mouse involves a total of five techniques: pointing, clicking, double-clicking, dragging, and right-clicking.
- Most mice operate with a ball that spins a set of rollers. If the mouse does not operate properly, you can clean it by removing the coverplate and ball and removing any debris, such as dust, from the ball itself and the rollers.
- A trackball provides the functionality of a mouse but requires less space on the desktop.
- A trackpad provides the functionality of a mouse but requires less space and less movement.

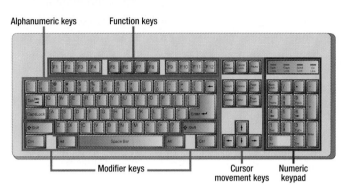

Alphanumeric keys   Function keys

Modifier keys   Cursor movement keys   Numeric keypad

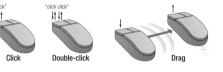

Click   Double-click   Drag

Other Input Devices

- With pen-based systems, you use an electronic pen to write on a special pad or directly on the screen.
- Touch-screen computers accept input directly through the monitor.
- Bar code readers, such as those used in grocery stores, can read bar codes, translate them into numbers, and input the numbers.
- Image scanners convert printed images into digitized formats that can be stored and manipulated in computers.
- An image scanner equipped with OCR software can translate a page of text into a string of character codes in the computer's memory.
- Microphones can accept auditory input and turn it into text and computer commands with voice recognition software.

The Monitor

- Computer monitors are roughly divided into two categories: CRT and flat-panel monitors.
- A CRT monitor works with an electron gun that systematically aims a beam of electrons at every pixel on the screen.
- When purchasing a monitor, you must consider the size, resolution, refresh rate, and dot pitch.
- The video controller is an interface between the monitor and the CPU.
- Most LCD displays are either active matrix or passive matrix (dual-scan).

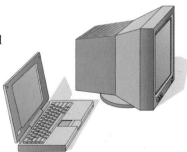

Printers

- Most printers are either ink jet printers or laser printers.
- Ink jet printers are inexpensive for both color and black printing, have low operating costs, and offer quality and speed comparable to low-end laser printers.
- Laser printers produce higher-quality print and are fast and convenient to use, but they are also the more expensive type of printer.

- Thermal-wax, dye-sub, fiery, and IRIS printers are used primarily by print shops and publishers to create high-quality color images.
- Plotters create images with a robotic arm that picks up pens and draws lines on a large sheet of paper.

Sound Systems

- Multimedia PCs generally come with sound systems, which include a sound card and speakers.
- The sound card translates digital signals into analog ones that drive the speakers.

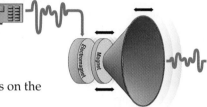

Connecting I/O Devices to the Computer

- External devices such as those used for input and output are connected via ports on the back of the computer.
- Expansion slots on a PC's motherboard give built-in devices access to the computer's bus via controller cards and provide I/O ports on the back of the computer for external devices.
- Most computers come with both serial and parallel ports.
- A SCSI port extends the bus outside the computer by way of a cable, which allows devices to be connected to one another in a daisy chain.

▶ KEY TERMS

After completing this chapter, you should be able to define the following terms:

accelerator card, 92
active matrix LCD, 84
alphanumeric keys, 66
bar code reader, 75
bitmap, 76
cards, 92
cathode ray tube (CRT), 78
Centronics interface, 91
click, 69
color (monitor), 78
configure, 91
cursor, 67
cursor movement keys, 67
dot pitch, 82
double-click, 69
drag, 69
DRAM, 83
dual-scan LCD, 84
dye-sub printer, 87
electronic pen, 74
expansion slots, 92
fiery print server, 87
flat-panel display, 78
flatbed scanners, 76
function keys, 67

grayscale (monitor), 78
hand-held scanners, 76
I-beam cursor, 67
image scanners, 75
ink jet printers, 84
insertion point, 67
interrupt request, 68
IRIS printer, 87
keyboard, 66
keyboard buffer, 68
keyboard controller, 68
keyboarding, 66
laser printers, 85
liquid crystal display (LCD)
    monitor, 83
modifier keys, 67
monochrome (monitor), 78
mouse, 68
multimedia PC, 88
numeric keypad, 67
Optical Character Recognition (OCR), 76
parallel interface, 90
passive matrix LCD, 84
PC card, 92
pixel, 78

plotter, 88
pointer, 68
port, 90
QWERTY, 66
refresh rate, 82
resolution, 81
right-clicking, 70
RS-232, 91
scan code, 68
serial interface, 90
small computer system interface
    (SCSI), 93
sound card, 77
SVGA (Super VGA), 82
thermal-wax printer, 87
toner, 86
touch screens, 75
trackball, 72
trackpad, 72
UART, 90
VGA (Video Graphics Array), 82
video controller, 82
video RAM (VRAM), 83
voice recognition (speech
    recognition), 77

▶ KEY TERM QUIZ

Fill in the missing word with one of the terms listed in Key Terms:

1. The _____ indicates where the characters you type will appear on screen.

2. A(n) _____ image is stored in the computer's memory as a grid of dots.

3. The vacuum tube used in PC monitors is known as a(n) _____.

4. The number of pixels on the screen, expressed as a matrix, is called the _____.

5. The _____ is the number of times per second that electron guns scan every pixel on the monitor's screen.

6. A(n) _____ printer is used primarily for producing boldly colored presentation graphics and handouts.

7. A(n) _____ chip converts parallel data from the bus into serial data.

8. _____ are devices used to translate printed images into electronic format that can be stored in a computer's memory.

9. _____ software translates a scanned image into text that you can edit.

10. An intermediary device between the CPU and the monitor that sends information to the monitor for display on screen is called a(n) _____.

▶ REVIEW QUESTIONS

1. Describe briefly how a parallel interface handles a higher volume of data than a serial interface.
2. Describe briefly how a sound card digitizes sounds.
3. List and describe at least three factors that have made ink jet printers so popular over the last ten years.
4. List and describe the most important specifications to consider when purchasing a monitor.
5. Name the primary display characteristics that influence the crispness or sharpness of on screen objects.
6. What are the three important criteria for evaluating printers?
7. What device interface acts, in one sense, like an extension cord for the computer's data bus?
8. What input device significantly revolutionized the graphic design field?
9. What is the biggest challenge facing developers of voice recognition software?
10. Why are pens currently not an optimal input device choice for word processing tasks?

▶ DISCUSSION QUESTIONS

1. Despite the rapid advancements being made with handwriting recognition software, do you think that the keyboard will continue to be the preferred input device for generating text? Which alternative—voice recognition through a microphone or handwriting recognition through a pen and tablet—do you think has a better chance of ultimately replacing the keyboard as the primary device for inputting text?

2. Suppose you are responsible for computerizing a gourmet restaurant's order-entering system. What type of input device do you think would be best-suited for the waitperson staff to input orders to the kitchen? What type of output device do you think would best serve the kitchen staff? What factors would you consider in your decision making?

3. When you think about the two most frequently used output devices for computers—monitors and printers—why do you think it stands to reason that color technology for printers will become more commonplace, more affordable, and more necessary to many users?

4. In your view, what primary factors led to the development of more sophisticated video controllers? Can you cite one or two current examples that indicate which video controller technology will continue to evolve?

NORTON INTERACTIVE

Complete the Norton Interactive module for this chapter.

CHAPTER 4

STORING INFORMATION IN A COMPUTER

CONTENTS

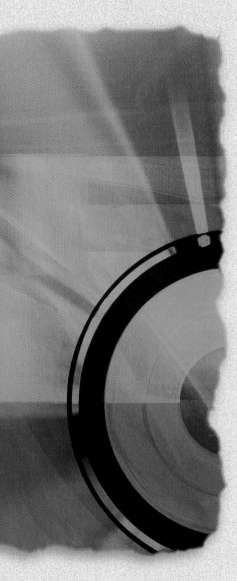

Objectives

When you complete this chapter, you will be able to do the following:

- List the most common types of storage devices.
- Explain how diskette and hard disk drives work.
- Understand how data is organized on a disk.
- Explain how tape drives work.
- Describe various optical storage devices.
- Discuss disk drive interface standards.

The physical components, or materials, on which data is stored are called **storage media**. The hardware components that write data to, and read it from, storage media are called storage devices. For example, a diskette is a storage medium ("medium" is the singular form of "media"), while a diskette drive is a storage device. Storage media and devices have evolved dramatically since computers were in their infancy, and this pace has accelerated since the introduction and growing popularity of PCs.

Two of the most widely used storage devices and accompanying media have been around for at least 15 years. The first to appear on PCs, the **diskette** (or floppy disk), is a flat piece of plastic, coated in iron oxide, and encased in a vinyl or plastic cover. The computer reads and writes data on a diskette with a **diskette drive**. A **hard disk** is like a diskette, but it consists of one or more rigid metal platters that are permanently encased in the **hard disk drive**.

The personal computers of the late 1970s and early 1980s generally included one or two diskette drives and no hard disk. This was true of the first IBM PC. Some early PCs also included attachments for tape drives, which could store data on ordinary audio cassette tapes.

It did not take long, however, before PC manufacturers found it necessary to include better storage technology that allowed users to keep most of their files and programs in one place. The solution was to build hard disks into the computers. In 1983, IBM recognized the need for bigger, faster, built-in storage, and added a 10 MB hard disk to their second-generation PC, the IBM PC XT.

Compared to the diskette drives of the day, those early hard disk drives were lightning quick, and could store amazing amounts of data. The XT hard disk held the equivalent of almost 30 360 KB diskettes. One of the basic truths of computing, however, is that there is never enough storage space. As soon as users began storing their files—and especially their programs—on their hard disks, they began to need hard disks with even more storage capacity. Soon 20 MB disks became the norm and then 40 MB. By 1990, new PCs often came with about 100 MB of storage. Most now come equipped with at least 1,000 MB, or 1 gigabyte (1 GB).

Today, the hard disk continues to be the data warehouse of the PC world, although the perpetual need for more storage has spawned the development of many new technologies. In this chapter, you will learn about the most important storage media and devices and find out what each is best suited for, how they work, and which offer the most speed and capacity.

◢ TYPES OF STORAGE DEVICES

Two main technologies are used to store data today: magnetic and optical storage. Although devices that store data typically employ one or the other, some combine both technologies. The primary types of magnetic storage are as follows:

- Diskettes
- Hard disks
- Removable hard disks
- Magnetic tape

The primary types of optical storage are:

- CD-ROM
- WORM
- Magneto-optical disks

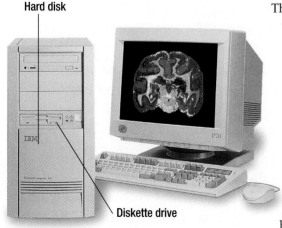

Hard disk

Diskette drive

The most common storage devices are diskette drives and hard disk drives. Both are referred to as **magnetic storage** because they record data as magnetic fields. The difference between diskette drives and hard disk drives is that diskettes are small and portable (they can be removed from diskette drives), but most store only 1.44 MB. Typically, hard disks are built into the computer, so they are not portable (unless the entire computer is). However, most hard disks can store at least 100 times as much data as a diskette. Hard disk drives are also much faster than diskette drives. Almost all PCs sold today come with a hard disk and at least one diskette drive.

The tape drive is another popular magnetic storage device. A **tape drive** is an add-on that is often used to create a backup copy of a hard disk, preserving the contents in case the hard disk is damaged.

Most new PCs come with a diskette drive and a hard disk drive.

Seagate Tape Drive

This tape drive from Seagate Peripherals is designed for backing up hard
disks.

Syquest Disk Drive

The removable hard disk combines the
portability of diskettes with speeds and
storage capacities comparable to hard
disks.

CD-ROM/Magneto-optical Drive

The Panasonic disk drives can be used
as CD-ROM drives and magneto-optical
drives.

Some storage manufacturers offer another type of device that combines some of the
benefits of diskette drives and hard disks—the removable hard disk drive.

Optical devices are also gaining popularity. The best-known optical device is the
CD-ROM (Compact Disk Read-Only Memory) drive, which uses the same technology as audio CD players. Other optical storage devices include write once, read
many (WORM) drives, magneto-optical drives, and recordable CD drives.

▶ MAGNETIC STORAGE DEVICES

Because all use the same medium (the material on
which the data is stored), diskette drives, hard disk
drives, and tape drives use similar techniques for
reading and writing data. The surfaces of diskettes,
hard disks, and magnetic tape are all coated with a
magnetically sensitive material (usually iron oxide)
which reacts to a magnetic field.

You may remember from high school science projects that one magnet can be used to make another.
For example, you can make a magnet by taking an
iron bar and stroking it in one direction with a
magnet. The iron bar eventually becomes a magnet
itself because its iron molecules align themselves in
one direction. The iron bar becomes **polarized**; that
is, its ends have opposite magnetic polarity (see
Figure 4.1).

Magnetic storage devices use a similar principle
to store data. Just as a transistor can represent binary data as "on" or "off," the orientation of a magnetic field can be used to represent data. A magnet

Another way to make a magnet is
to wrap a wire coil around an iron
bar and send an electric current
through the coil. This produces an
electromagnet.

If you reverse the direction of
the current, the polarity of the
magnet also reverses.

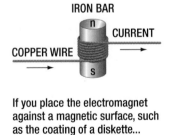

If you place the electromagnet
against a magnetic surface, such
as the coating of a diskette...

...the electromagnet's pole
induces an opposite field on
the magnetic surface.

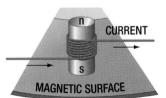
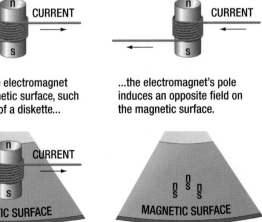

FIGURE 4.1
How an electromagnet creates a field on a magnetic surface.

You have been working all week on a presentation, and it is due at noon. You take a break—confident that your work is done. When you return, you see that a disk error has corrupted your hard drive. You can forget about making that deadline.

It won't happen? If not a disk error, then software bugs, power surges, data corruption, fire, viruses, and myriad other unpredictable assailants can destroy your files in the blink of an eye. That's why backing up files should be as much a part of your routine as brushing your teeth. Neither activity is very rewarding at the time, but eventually, they pay off.

Start your backup program by asking yourself these questions and then by making these decisions:

What kind of backup medium will I use?

Currently, the most popular options are floppy disks, tape drives, removable hard disks, magneto-optical (MO) disks, and recordable CDs. The medium you choose depends on how much storage you need and your budget. Floppy disks are a quick, convenient backup choice for small amounts of data. In most modern business settings, roomier media such as tape, removable hard disks, MO disks, or CDs are used.

Convenience is another factor. For example, tape drives are much less expensive than MO drives, but they are also slower and more cumbersome to use. Beware of substituting economy for convenience. If your backup system is too much trouble to use, you may be tempted to skip it—to your eventual regret.

What kind of software do you need?

For backups onto a floppy disk, removable hard drive or MO drive, the file-management program that comes with your operating system may be all

you need. For greater convenience, programs like *Microsoft Backup* allow you to schedule backups ahead of time and to back up either to disk or tape.

What will your backup procedures be?

Will you back up hourly, daily, weekly, or monthly? Will you back up your entire hard disk, or just the files that have changed since the last full or partial backup? Will you set up your system to perform backups automatically at a certain time, or will you remind yourself to do it manually?

One thing that's certain is that your backup procedure should start with a full backup, which should be repeated once a week. Beyond that, you can do a series of partial backups—either incremental (files that have changed since the last partial backup) or differential (files that have changed since the last full backup).

Just how much backup is enough? Here are some suggestions for deciding:

■ For a home computer used mainly for games and children's education, you might need backups only of your programs, made when first installed, plus occasional monthly backups of

any drawings and reports your children made for school.

■ If you have a home-office computer used for accounting, word processing, and some faxing, you could probably get by with weekly backups.

■ If you have a small office computer used every day for word processing, personal scheduling, and budgeting, you should back up incrementally every day, at the end of the day, with a second set of full backups weekly.

■ If you have a network server computer handling the documents of a half-dozen people in a work group, you'll need a full backup every day.

Where will you store your data?

Where will you keep your disks or tapes, so that when an unforeseen emergency like a fire, flood, or earthquake strikes, your data won't perish with your office? Some organizations routinely ship their media to a distant location, such as a home office or a commercial warehouse, or store them in weatherproof, fireproof, bombproof vaults. Home users may want to keep their backups in a safe-deposit box. Companies often keep three or more full sets of backup, all at different sites. Such prudence may seem extreme, but where crucial records are at stake, backups can mean the life or death of a business.

New Script

Manual Execution...
(use "run documents" as an execution shortcut)

[Cancel]   [Execute]

◉ Execute Now
○ Make a "run document"

Action: [Normal Backup ▼]

Using script *New Script* :
Do **Normal Backup**

The Retrospect program is software used to back up networks.

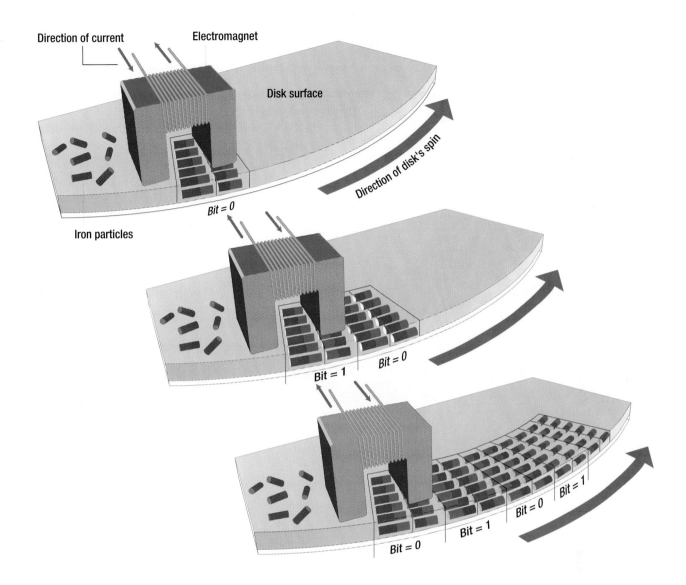

Direction of current   Electromagnet

Disk surface

Direction of disk's spin

Iron particles

Bit = 0

Bit = 1   Bit = 0

Bit = 0   Bit = 1   Bit = 0   Bit = 1

has one important advantage over a transistor: It can represent "on" and "off" without a continual source of electricity.

The surfaces of disks and magnetic tapes are coated with millions of tiny iron particles so that data can be stored on them. Each of these particles can act as a magnet, taking on a magnetic field when subjected to an **electromagnet**. The **read/write heads** of a hard disk drive, diskette drive, or tape drive contain electromagnets, which generate magnetic fields in the iron on the storage medium as the head passes over the disk (hard disk or diskette) or tape.

As shown in Figure 4.2, the read/write heads record strings of 1s and 0s by alternating the direction of the current in the electromagnets.

To read data from a magnetic surface, the process is reversed. The read/write head passes over the disk or tape while *no* current is flowing through the electromagnet. Since the storage medium has a magnetic field but the head does not, the storage medium charges the magnet in the head, which causes a small current to flow through the head in one direction or the other depending on the polarity of the field. The disk or tape drive senses the direction of the flow as the storage medium passes by the head, and the data is sent from the read/write head into memory.

FIGURE 4.2

Data being recorded by a read/write head.

Diskette Drives

Figure 4.3 shows a diskette and a diskette drive.

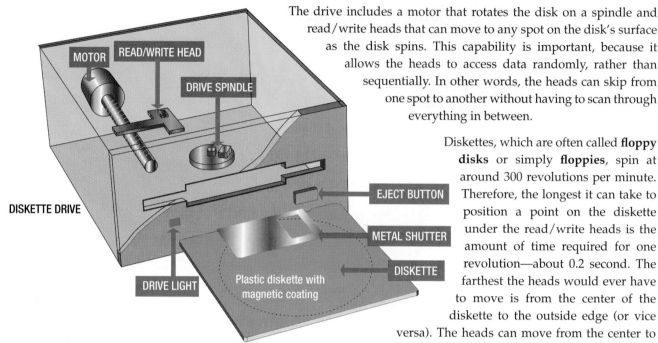

The drive includes a motor that rotates the disk on a spindle and read/write heads that can move to any spot on the disk's surface as the disk spins. This capability is important, because it allows the heads to access data randomly, rather than sequentially. In other words, the heads can skip from one spot to another without having to scan through everything in between.

Diskettes, which are often called **floppy disks** or simply **floppies**, spin at around 300 revolutions per minute. Therefore, the longest it can take to position a point on the diskette under the read/write heads is the amount of time required for one revolution—about 0.2 second. The farthest the heads would ever have to move is from the center of the diskette to the outside edge (or vice versa). The heads can move from the center to the outside edge in even less time—about 0.17 second. Since both operations (rotating the diskette and moving the heads from the center to the outside edge) take place simultaneously, the maximum time to position the heads over a given location on the diskette—known as the maximum access time—remains the greater of the two times, or 0.2 second (see Figure 4.4).

FIGURE 4.3
Parts of a diskette and diskette drive.

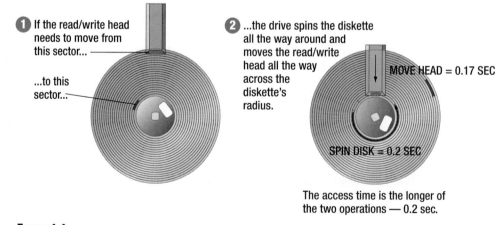

① If the read/write head needs to move from this sector...

...to this sector...

② ...the drive spins the diskette all the way around and moves the read/write head all the way across the diskette's radius.

MOVE HEAD = 0.17 SEC

SPIN DISK = 0.2 SEC

The access time is the longer of the two operations — 0.2 sec.

FIGURE 4.4
Maximum access time for a diskette drive.

Actually, though, the maximum access time for diskettes can be even longer, because diskettes do not spin when they are not being used. It can take as much as 0.5 second to rotate the disk from a dead stop.

The most common uses of diskettes are as follows:

◼ *Moving files between computers that are not connected through communications hardware:* One of the easiest ways to move data between computers is to copy the data to a diskette, remove the diskette from the first computer's drive, and insert it in another computer's drive.

◼ *Loading new programs onto a system:* Although large programs are often delivered on CD-ROM, many programs are still sold on diskettes. When you buy a program from a software retailer, you **install** it by copying the contents of the diskettes onto your hard disk drive, or by running a small program on the diskettes that installs the files on your hard drive automatically.

◼ *Backing up data or programs, the primary copy of which is stored on a hard disk drive:* **Backing up** is the process of creating a duplicate set of programs and/or data files for safekeeping. Most people rely on a hard disk drive for the bulk of their storage needs, but what if the hard drive malfunctions or is damaged? To protect against data loss, it is always wise to back up a hard disk. One common way to do so is to copy files onto diskettes.

Types of Diskettes

During the 1980s, most PCs used 5.25-inch diskettes. Today, though, the 3.5-inch diskette has largely replaced its 5.25-inch cousin. The size refers to the diameter of the disk, not to the capacity. The 5.25-inch type, shown in Figure 4.5, is encased in a flexible vinyl envelope with an oval cutout that allows the read/write head to access the disk.

The 3.5-inch type, shown in Figure 4.6, is encased in a hard plastic shell with a sliding metal cover. When the disk is inserted into the drive, the cover slides back to expose the diskette to the read/write head. It is important to realize that both these types are diskettes. The term *diskette* refers to the disk inside, not to the square plastic protector.

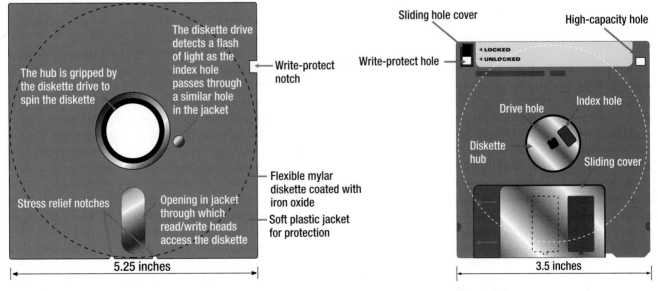

FIGURE 4.5
5.25-inch diskette.

FIGURE 4.6
3.5-inch diskette.

TABLE 4.1		
Diskette Capacities		
DIAMETER	**TYPE**	**CAPACITY**
5.25 inches	Double density	360 KB
5.25 inches	High density	1.2 MB
3.5 inches	Double density	720 KB
3.5 inches	High density	1.44 MB (most common)
3.5 inches	High density	2.88 MB

Both types of diskette have evolved from lower to higher densities. The **density** of the disk is a measure of the quality of the disk surface: The higher the density, the more closely the iron-oxide particles are packed, and the more data the disk can store. Thus, a diskette marked "high density" can store more data than one marked "double density." Table 4.1 shows the capacity, in bytes, of each kind of diskette.

The sizes given in the table are for DOS- and Windows-based machines. The Macintosh never used 5.25-inch disks. A double density diskette with a Macintosh format holds 800 KB, not 720 KB—a result of the different ways the two machines use the disks. A Macintosh high density disk holds 1.44 MB, the same capacity as a DOS- or Windows-based diskette.

As you can see from Table 4-1, the physically smaller disks can actually hold more data than the larger ones, thanks to newer technology. Because of their hard plastic shell and the sliding metal cover, the 3.5-inch diskettes are also more durable. As a result, the 5.25-inch diskette has virtually disappeared.

How Data Is Organized on a Disk

When you buy new diskettes (or a new hard drive), the disks inside are nothing more than simple, coated disks encased in plastic. Before the computer can use them to store data, they must be magnetically mapped so that the computer can go directly to a specific point on the diskette without searching through data. The process of mapping a diskette is called **formatting** or **initializing**. Today, many diskettes come preformatted for either PCs or Macs. If you buy unformatted diskettes, you must format them before you can use them. The computer will warn you if this is the case, and will format the diskette for you if you wish.

The first thing a disk drive does when formatting a disk is to create a set of magnetic concentric circles called *tracks*. The number of tracks on a disk varies with the type (most high density diskettes have 80). The tracks on a disk do not form a continuous spiral like those on a phonograph record—each one is a separate circle. Most tracks are numbered from the outermost circle to the innermost, starting from zero, as shown in Figure 4.7.

Each track on a disk is also split into smaller parts. Imagine slicing up a disk the way you cut a pie. As shown in Figure 4.8, each slice would cut across all the disk's tracks, resulting in short segments, or **sectors**. All the sectors on the disk are numbered in one long sequence, so the computer can access each small area on the disk with a unique number. This scheme effectively simplifies what would be a set of two-dimensional coordinates into a single numeric address.

When people refer to the number of sectors a disk has, the unit they use is *sectors per track*—not just sectors. If a diskette has 80 tracks and 18 sectors per track, it has 1440 sectors (80×18)—not 18 sectors.

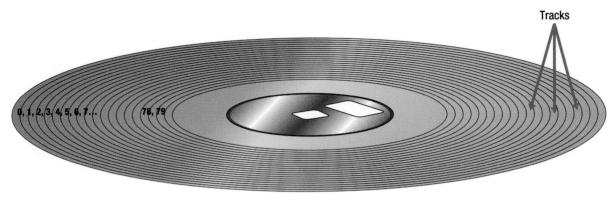

FIGURE 4.7
Tracks are concentric circles, numbered from the outside in.

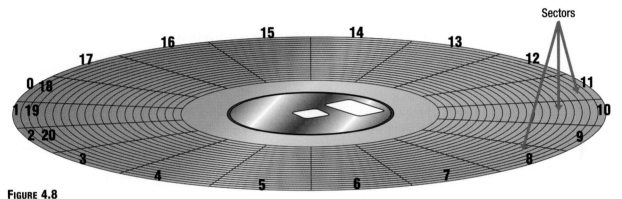

FIGURE 4.8
Sectors on a disk, each with a unique number.

Like any flat object, a disk has two sides. Some early drives could read data on only one side, but today, all disk drives can read and write data on both sides of a disk. To the computer, the second side is just a continuation of the sequence of sectors. For example, the 3.5-inch, 1.44-MB diskette has a total of 2880 sectors (80 tracks per side × 2 sides × 18 sectors per track).

On most diskettes, a sector contains 512 bytes, or 0.5 KB. The different capacities of diskettes are generally a function of the number of sides, tracks, and sectors per track. Table 4.2 shows how the capacities of diskettes relate to the dimensions.

A sector is the smallest unit with which any disk drive (diskette drive or hard drive) can work. Each bit and byte within a sector can have different values, but the drive

TABLE 4.2

Formatting Specifications for Various Disks								
DIAMETER (INCHES)	**SIDES**	**TRACKS**	**SECTORS/ TRACK**	**SECTORS**	**BYTES/ SECTOR**	**BYTES**	**KB**	**MB**
5.25	2	40	9	720	512	368,640	360	.36
5.25	2	40	18	1440	512	737,280	720	1.2
3.5	2	80	15	2400	512	1.228,800	1,200	.7
3.5	2	80	18	2880	512	1,474,560	1,440	1.44
3.5	2	80	36	5760	512	2,949,150	2,880	2.88

can read or write only whole sectors at a time. If the computer needs to change just one byte out of 512, it must rewrite the entire sector.

Because files are not usually a size that is an even multiple of 512 bytes, some sectors contain unused space after the end of the file. In addition, the DOS and Windows operating systems allocate groups of sectors, called **clusters**, to each of the files they store on a disk. Cluster sizes vary, depending on the size and type of the disk, but they can range from 4 sectors for diskettes, to 64 sectors for some hard disks. A small file that contains only 50 bytes will use only a portion of the first sector of a cluster assigned to it, leaving the remainder of the first sector, and the remainder of the cluster, allocated but unused.

How the Operating System Finds Data on a Disk

A computer's operating system is able to locate data on a disk (diskette or hard drive) because each track and sector is labeled, and the location of all data is kept in a special log on the disk. The labeling of tracks and sectors is called performing a **logical** or **soft format**. A commonly used logical format performed by DOS or Windows creates these four disk areas:

- The boot record
- The file-allocation table (FAT)
- The root folder or directory
- The data area

The **boot record** is a small program that runs when you first start the computer. This program determines whether the disk has the basic components of DOS or Windows that are necessary to run the operating system successfully. If it determines that the required files are present and the disk has a valid format, it transfers control to one of the operating system rograms that continues the process of starting up. This process is called **booting**—because the boot program makes the computer "pull itself up by its bootstraps."

The boot record also describes other disk characteristics, such as the number of bytes per sector and the number of sectors per track—information that the operating system needs to access the data area of the disk.

Boot record

FAT (copy 1)

FAT (copy 2)

Data area

Root directory

Unused area

When a disk is formatted, these four data areas are defined.

The **file-allocation table (FAT)** is a log that records the location of each file and the status of each sector. When you write a file to a disk, the operating system checks the FAT for an open area, stores the file, and then identifies the file and its location in the FAT.

The FAT solves a common filing problem: What happens when you load a file, increase its size by adding text to it, and then save it again? For example, say you need to add 5000 bytes to a 10,000-byte file that has no open space around it. The disk drive could move the surrounding files to make room for the 5000 bytes, but that would be time-consuming. Instead, the operating system checks the FAT for free areas, and then places pointers in it that link together the nonadjacent parts of the file. In other words, it splits the file up by allocating new space for the overflow.

When the operating system saves a file in this way, the file becomes **fragmented**. Its parts are located in nonadjacent sectors. Fragmented files do cause undesirable side effects, the most significant being that it takes longer to save and load them.

Users do not normally need to see the information in the FAT, but they often use the folder information. A **folder**, also called a **directory**, is a tool for organizing files on a disk. Folders can contain files or other folders, so it is possible to set up a hierarchical system of folders on your computer, just as you have folders within other folders in a file cabinet. The top folder on any disk is known as the root. When you use the operating system to view the contents of a folder, the operating system lists specific information about each file in the folder, such as the file's name, its size, the time and date that it was created or last modified, and so on. Figure 4.9 shows a typical Windows 95 folder listing.

The part of the disk that remains free after the boot sector, FAT, and root folder have been created is called the **data area** because that is where the data files (or program files) are actually stored.

Hard Disks

Although a shift toward optical technology is occurring, the hard disk is still the most common storage device for all computers. Much of what you have learned about diskettes and drives applies to hard disks as well. Like diskettes, hard disks store data in tracks that are divided into sectors. Physically, however, hard disks look quite different from diskettes.

A hard disk is a stack of one or more metal platters that spin on one spindle, like a stack of rigid diskettes. Each platter is coated with iron oxide, and the entire unit is encased in a sealed chamber. Unlike diskettes, where the disk and drive are separate, the hard disk and drive is a single unit. It includes the hard disk, the motor that spins the platters, and a set of read/write heads (see Figure 4.10).

Since you cannot remove the disk from its drive (unless it is a removable hard disk, which you will learn about later), the terms *hard disk* and *hard drive* are used interchangeably.

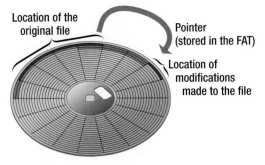

Location of the original file

Pointer (stored in the FAT)

Location of modifications made to the file

When new data needs to be added to a file, and there is no more room next to the cluster where the original data is stored, the operating system records the new information in an unused cluster on the disk. The FAT lists both clusters, and a pointer at the end of the first cluster connects it to the second.

Name	Size	Type	Modified
Address Book1.mdb	244KB	Microsoft Acces...	3/11/96 4:36 PM
Book1.xls	8KB	Microsoft Excel ...	1/16/96 4:20 PM
db1.mdb	80KB	Microsoft Acces...	10/25/95 11:58 AM
db2.mdb	84KB	Microsoft Acces...	11/27/95 4:46 PM
disk schedule.4xls.xls	5KB	Microsoft Excel ...	1/3/96 11:49 AM
disk schedule.xls	18KB	Microsoft Excel ...	11/21/95 9:42 AM
Event Mangement1.mdb	1,118KB	Microsoft Acces...	9/21/95 3:45 PM
James Screen.xls	17KB	Microsoft Excel ...	3/11/96 4:06 PM
Mscreate.dir	0KB	DIR File	7/17/95 1:05 PM

My Documents — File Edit View Help — 9 object(s) 1.53MB

FIGURE 4.9
Windows 95 directory listing.

These two photos show the inside of a hard disk drive. The hard disk itself is on the left. On the right is the circuitry that controls the drive. When they are installed in the computer, the circuitry is screwed to the top of the case that contains the hard disk.

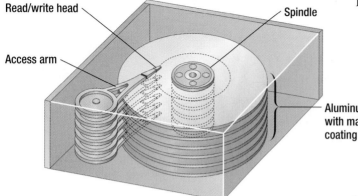

Read/write head
Access arm
Spindle
Aluminum platters with magnetic coating

FIGURE 4.10
Parts of a hard disk.

Hard disks have become the primary storage device for PCs because they are convenient and cost-efficient. In both speed and capacity, they far out-perform diskettes. A high-density 3.5-inch diskette can store 1.44 MB of data. Hard disks, in contrast, range in capacity from about 80 MB on up. Most PCs now come with hard disks of at least 1,000 MB, or 1 GB.

Two important physical differences between hard disks and diskettes account for the differences in performance. First, hard disks are sealed in a vacuum chamber, and second, the hard disk consists of a rigid metal platter (usually aluminum), rather than flexible mylar.

The rigidity of the hard disk allows it to spin much faster—typically more than ten times faster—than diskettes; a hard disk spins between 3,600 rpm and 7,200 rpm, instead of a diskette's 300 rpm. The speed at which the disk spins is a major factor in the overall performance of the drive.

The rigidity of the hard disk and the high speed at which it rotates allow a lot more data to be recorded on the disk's surface. As you may recall, waving a magnet past an electric coil like the one in a drive's read/write head causes a current to flow through the coil. The faster you wave the magnet, and the closer the magnet is to the coil, the larger the current it generates in the coil. Therefore, a disk that spins faster can use smaller magnetic charges to make current flow in the read/write head. The drive's heads can also use a lower-intensity current to record data on the disk.

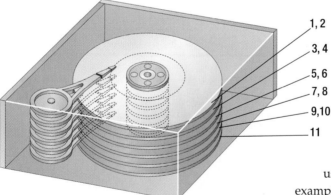

1, 2
3, 4
5, 6
7, 8
9,10
11

Not only do hard disks pack data more closely together, they also hold more data, because they often include several platters, stacked one on top of another. To the computer system, this configuration just means that the disk has more than two sides; in addition to a side 0 and side 1, there are sides 2, 3, 4, and so on. Some hard disk drives hold as many as 12 disks, but both sides of the disks are not always used.

With hard disks, the number of sides that the disk uses is specified by the number of read/write heads. For example, a particular hard disk drive might have six disk platters (that is, 12 sides), but only eleven heads, indicating that one side is not used to store data. Often, this is the bottom side of the bottom disk, as shown in Figure 4.11.

FIGURE 4.11
Read/write heads on each side of each platter, except the bottom of the bottom platter.

Because hard disks are actually a stack of platters, the term **cylinder** is used to refer to the same track across all the disk sides, as shown in Figure 4.12. For example, track 0 (the outermost track) on every disk is cylinder 0.

Like diskettes, hard disks generally store 512 bytes of data in a sector, but because of their higher tolerances, hard disks can have more sectors per track—54, 63, or even more sectors per track are not uncommon.

The computation of a hard disk's capacity is identical to that for diskettes—but the numbers are larger. Here's the breakdown for a disk that is sold as a 541 MB disk:

1,632 cylinders × 12 heads (sides)   = 19,584 tracks
19,584 tracks × 54 sectors/track   = 1,057,536 sectors
1,057,536 sectors × 512 bytes/sector = 541,458,432 bytes

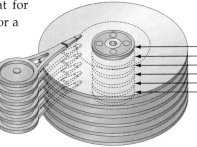

A cylinder consists of a vertical stack of tracks, one track on each side of each platter.

FIGURE 4.12
A cylinder on a hard disk.

In spite of all the capacity and speed advantages, hard disks have one major drawback. To achieve optimum performance, the read/write head must be extremely close to the surface of the disk. In fact, the heads of hard disks fly so close to the surface of the disk that if a dust particle, a human hair, or even a fingerprint were placed on the disk it would bridge the gap between the head and the disk, causing the heads to crash. A **head crash**, in which the head touches the disk, destroys the data stored in the area of the crash and can destroy a read/write head, as well. Figure 4.13 shows the height at which a hard disk head floats, compared to the sizes of dust particles, hair, and fingerprints.

Removable Hard Disks

Removable hard disks and drives attempt to combine the speed and capacity of a hard disk with the portability of a diskette. There are many different types of devices in this category. Choosing the best type is usually a matter of balancing your needs for speed, storage capacity, compatibility (will it work in different computers?), and price.

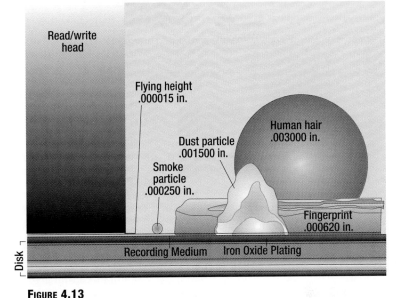

FIGURE 4.13
Distance between a hard disk's read/write head and the disk's surface, compared to the size of possible contaminants.

Hot-Swappable Hard Disks

At the high end, in terms of both price and performance, are **hot-swappable hard disks**. These are sometimes used on high-end workstations that require large amounts of storage. They allow the user to remove (swap out) a hard disk and insert (swap in) another while the computer is still on (hot).

Hot-swappable hard disks are like removable versions of normal hard disks: the removable box includes the disk, drive, and read/write heads in a sealed container.

Hard Disk Cartridges

Most removable hard disks that are used with PCs are very different than the hot-swappable design. Most work a bit like a diskette, with a disk in a plastic case that is inserted into or removed from the drive. The disk and case are often called a hard disk cartridge. Currently, the most common drives with removable hard disks are SyQuest drives.

The original SyQuest disk was the same diameter as an old floppy: 5.25 inches. During the early and mid-1990s, the standard sizes were 44 MB, 88 MB, and 200 MB. A newer design uses a smaller, 3.5-inch disk that can fit 105 MB or 270 MB. SyQuest chose to license their design to other hardware manufacturers, so many companies have made SyQuest-type disks and drives. During the early 1990s, this factor made SyQuest disks highly compatible and helped to make the SyQuest a popular standard.

Price was also a factor that helped popularize the SyQuest drive. The drive typically costs between $300 and $400, and the disk cartridges cost between $60 and $90. The major drawbacks of the SyQuest disks are that the older models are noticeably slower than a built-in hard disk, and data errors and degeneration of data over time are more of a problem.

This man is replacing a hot-swappable hard disk in a large storage device.

Although the storage medium is flexible, not hard, the Zip drive is a competitor to the SyQuest drive. It is manufactured by Iomega Corporation. The Zip drives are slower than SyQuests, but have gained popularity due to low prices. Typically, the drive costs about $200, and the disks cost as little as $15 for a 100 MB cartridge. Iomega is also pushing up the storage capacity and speed of removable hard disks. Their Jaz drive, for example, is as fast as some internal hard disks and can store 1 GB of data.

The Bernoulli Drive

This SyQuest drive records and reads data from small 3.5-inch cartridges that can store up to 270 MB.

Another technology that competes with the SyQuest drives is the Bernoulli drive, also made by Iomega. This drive, which dates back to 1983, is actually not a removable hard disk, because the disk itself is made of plastic, similar to a diskette. When the disk spins, air pressure bends the disk up toward the read/write head but maintains a thin layer of air between the heads and the disk. The very first Bernoulli disks held 5 MB, but more recent versions can store up to 230 MB and are almost as fast as an internal hard disk.

Tape Drives

The Iomega Jaz drive can store up to 1.0 GB of data on a removable cartridge.

Tape drives read and write data to the surface of a tape the same way an audio cassette recorder does. The difference is that a computer tape drive writes digital data instead of analog data—discrete "1s" and "0s" instead of the finely graduated signals created by sounds in an audio recorder.

The best use of tape storage is for data that you do not use very often, such as backup copies of your hard disk (which you will need only if your hard drive malfunctions or you accidentally delete a valuable file). Because a tape is a long strip of magnetic material, the tape drive has to write data to it sequentially—one byte after another. Sequential access is inherently slower than the direct access provided by media such as disks. When you want to access a specific set of data on a tape, the drive has to scan through all the data you do not need to get to the data you want. The result is a slow access time. In fact, the access time varies depending on the speed of the drive, the length of the tape, and the position on the tape to which the head wrote the data in the first place.

Despite the long access times, however, tape drives are well suited for certain purposes, especially for backing up your system's entire hard disk. Because hard disks usually have capacities much greater than diskettes, backing up or restoring a system with diskettes can be a long and tedious process requiring dozens or even hundreds of diskettes. Backing up using removable hard disks is usually very expensive. Tape, however, offers an inexpensive way to store a lot of data on a single cassette.

Shown here are three tape drives from Seagate Peripherals. The two on the left are internal drives, designed to be installed inside the system unit. On the right is an external drive that is connected to one of the ports on a PC.

Tape was one of the first widely used media for mass storage. Early mainframe computers used reel-to-reel tape systems, such as the one pictured in Figure 4.14.

Today, most tapes are housed in cassettes that contain both reels of the tape. The cassettes come in many sizes, but most are about the same size or smaller than an audio cassette. Oddly, you cannot tell much about the capacity of a tape from the cassette's size. Some of the largest cassettes have capacities of only 40 to 60 MB, whereas some of the smallest microcassettes can hold as much as 8 GB of data.

Generally, the highest capacities are achieved by **digital audiotape (DAT)** drives. DAT drives typically have two read heads and two write heads built into a small wheel (or cylinder) that spins near the tape at about 2,000 rpm—at the same time, the tape itself moves past the wheel at a relatively slow speed (about 0.34 inches per second). The write heads on the spinning wheel each write data with opposite magnetic polarities on overlapping areas of the tape. Each read head reads only one polarity or the other. The result is a very high data density per inch of tape. Although DAT cassettes are inex-

Figure 4.14
An old, reel-to-reel tape storage system.

pensive (they usually cost from $5 to $10), the DAT drives often cost more than $1,000. Individual users are more likely to buy less expensive systems. Today, tape systems for backing up a 1 GB hard disk can be purchased for about $200.

▶ Optical Storage Devices

Because of the continuing demand for greater storage capacity, hardware manufacturers are always on the lookout for alternative storage media. Today, the most popular alternatives to magnetic storage systems are optical systems.

Optical storage techniques make use of the pinpoint precision that is possible only with laser beams. A laser uses a concentrated, narrow beam of light, focused and directed with lenses, prisms, and mirrors. The tight focus of the laser beam is possible because the light is all the same wavelength.

There are two common types of optical technology. The most widely used type is compact disk (CD) technology, which is used in CD-ROM, WORM, PhotoCD, and CD-Recordable. The other type, which has been steadily gaining in popularity over the past few years, is a hybrid that combines magnetic and optical technology. These devices are known as magneto-optical drives.

CD-ROM

You put a CD-ROM in a computer the same way you put a CD in your stereo. You press a button, the tray slides out, you put the CD-ROM label-side-up in the tray and push the button again to slide the tray back in.

The familiar audio compact disk is a popular medium for storing music. In the computer world, however, the medium is called **compact disk, read-only memory (CD-ROM)**. CD-ROM uses the same technology that is used to produce music CDs. In fact, if you have a sound card and speakers connected to your computer, you can play CDs with your PC.

The CD-ROM drive for music or data reads 0s and 1s off a spinning disk by focusing a laser on the disk's surface. Some areas of the disk reflect the laser light into a sensor, whereas others scatter the light. A spot that reflects the laser beam into the sensor is interpreted as a 1, and the absence of a reflection is interpreted as a 0.

Data is laid out on a CD-ROM in a long, continuous spiral that starts at the outer edge and winds inward to the center. Data is stored in the form of **lands**, which are flat areas on the metal surface, and **pits**, which are depressions or hollows. A land reflects the laser light into the sensor, and a pit scatters the light (see Figure 4.15).

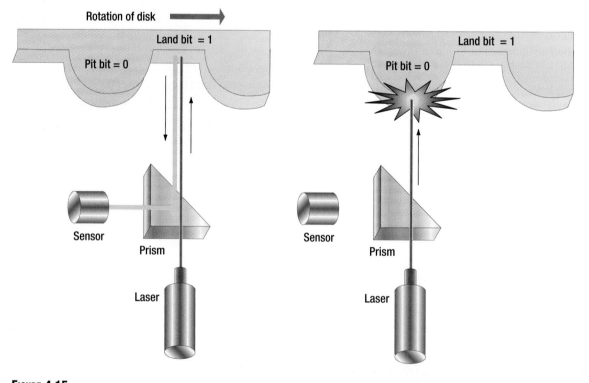

FIGURE 4.15
How data is read from a CD-ROM.

Compared to hard disk drives, CD-ROM drives are quite slow, in part because the laser reads pits and lands one bit at a time. Another reason has to do with the changing rotational speed of the disk. Like a track on a magnetic disk, the track of an optical disk is split into sectors. However, as shown in Figure 4.16, the sectors are laid out quite differently than they are on magnetic disks.

As you can see, the sectors near the middle of the CD wrap further around the disk than those near the edge. For the drive to read each sector in the same amount of time, it must spin the disk faster when reading sectors near the middle, and slower when reading sectors near the edge. Changing the speed of rotation takes time—enough to seriously impair the overall speed of the CD-ROM drive. The first CD-ROM drives read data at 150 KBps (kilobytes per second)—"single speed". This is much slower than a typical hard drive at 5–15 MBps (megabytes per second). Today's CD-ROM drives read data two (300 KBps), four (600 KBps), six (900 KBps), or eight (1200 KBps) times faster than the first models.

Even with the changing speed of the disk, though, reading data from an optical medium is a relatively simple undertaking. Writing data, however, is another matter. The medium is a foil disk that is physically pitted to reflect or scatter the laser beam. The disk is covered in a plastic coating, and it is very difficult to alter the surface of the disk once it has been stamped.

The fact that you cannot write data to a CD-ROM does not mean that this storage medium is not useful. In fact, many applications rely on huge volumes of data that rarely change. For example, dictionaries, encyclopedias, medical, legal, and other professional reference libraries, music, and video all require tremendous amounts of data that you would not normally want to alter even if you could.

In addition to these uses, software companies can distribute their products on CD-ROM. Because of the high precision and data density possible with CD-ROM, a single CD typically can hold about 650 MB of data. Because of their high capacity and the fact that one CD is much cheaper to produce than a set of diskettes, many software publishers regard CDs as the distribution medium of choice. For example, the Microsoft Office suite of applications is available on a single CD that also includes an online version of the printed manuals. Instead of having to install the programs from a series of 22 diskettes (or more), the user needs to insert only a single CD.

CDs may soon take a new direction with the advent of **DVD, digital video disk**, a high density medium that is capable of storing a full-length movie on a single disk the size of a CD. (Actually, it uses both sides of the disk.) In fact, DVDs look like CDs, and DVD-ROM drives are able to play current CD-ROMs. A slightly different player, the DVD Movie player, connects to your TV and plays movies like a VCR. The DVD Movie player will also play audio CDs.

Each side of a DVD can hold up to 4.7 GB. Therefore these two-sided disks can contain as much as 9.4 GB of data.

SECTORS ON A MAGNETIC DISK

SECTORS ON A CD-ROM

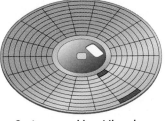

Sectors are wider at the edge than they are near the middle.

Sectors form a continuous spiral and each sector is the same width.

FIGURE 4.16
How sectors are laid out on a CD-ROM versus a magnetic disk.

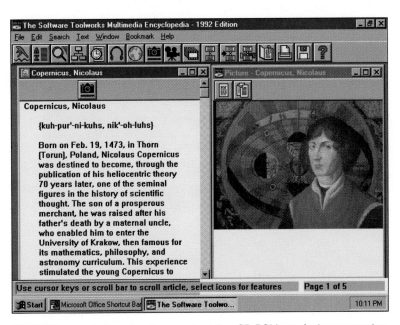

CD-ROM is a perfect medium for encyclopedias. CD-ROMs are far less expensive to print than a set of books, and the CD-ROM can contain video and sound, in addition to text and pictures.

When you buy software on CD-ROM, the CD is often the only thing in the box. Both the software and the documentation are on the disk.

CD-Recordable, WORM disks, and PhotoCD

CD-R drives can record data on special CDs. The disks can then be read by any CD-ROM drive.

For large quantities, CD-ROM disks can be produced by manufacturers with expensive duplication equipment. For fewer copies or even single copies, a **CD-recordable (CD-R) drive** can be attached to a computer as a regular peripheral device. CD-R drives allow you to create your own CD-ROM disks which can be read by any CD-ROM drive. Once information has been written to a part of the CD, that information cannot be changed. However, with most CD-R drives, you can continue to record information to other parts of the disk until it is full.

One popular form of recordable CD is PhotoCD, a standard developed by Kodak for storing digitized photographic images on a CD. Many film developing stores now have PhotoCD drives that can store your photos and put them on a CD. You can then put the PhotoCD in your computer's CD-ROM drive (assuming it supports PhotoCD, and most do) and view the images on your computer. Once there, you can also paste them into other documents. With a PhotoCD, you can continue to add images until the disk is full. Once an image has been written to the disk, however, it cannot be erased or changed.

Before CD-R and PhotoCD existed, the first ventures into developing a more flexible optical technology resulted in the **write once, read many (WORM) drive**. As with the CD, once data has been etched into the surface of a WORM disk, it cannot be changed. WORM is an ideal medium for making a permanent record of data. For example, many banks use WORM disks to store a record of each day's transactions. The transactions are written to an optical disk and become a permanent record that can be read but never altered.

Once your pictures have been processed and stored on a PhotoCD, you can see them on your computer screen and copy them into documents.

Magneto-Optical Drives

Magneto-optical (MO) disks combine some of the best features of both magnetic and optical recording technologies. An MO disk has the capacity of an optical disk but can be rewritten with the ease of a magnetic disk.

This magneto-optical drive from Maxoptix can store 1.3 GB on a removable disk.

The medium that MO disks use is unlike that of either an optical or a magnetic disk. The disk is covered with magnetically sensitive metallic crystals sandwiched inside a thin layer of plastic. In its normal state, the plastic surrounding the crystals is solid, preventing them from moving. To write data to the disk, an intense laser beam is focused on the surface of the medium, which very briefly melts the plastic coating enough to allow a magnet to change the orientation of the crystals (see Figure 4.17). The magnet has an effect at only the precise focal point of the laser, where the heated coating allows the crystals to be reoriented.

When the magnet changes the orientations of the metallic crystals on the surface of an MO disk, some crystals are aligned so that they will reflect the laser beam into a sensor; others are oriented so that they will not reflect into the sensor. To read data from the disk, the MO drive focuses a less intense laser beam on the track of crystals.

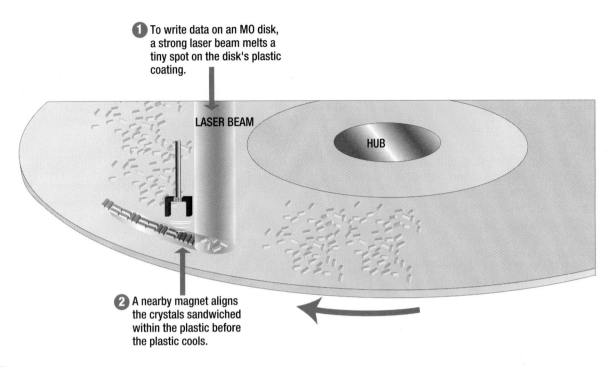

1 To write data on an MO disk, a strong laser beam melts a tiny spot on the disk's plastic coating.

LASER BEAM

HUB

2 A nearby magnet aligns the crystals sandwiched within the plastic before the plastic cools.

FIGURE 4.17
How a magneto-optical drive records data.

As the track spins under the beam, some spots reflect light into the sensor and others do not, creating the stream of 1s and 0s the computer recognizes as data (see Figure 4.18).

MO disks are available today in various sizes and capacities. Some of them look identical to 3.5-inch diskettes but have capacities of more than 1 GB and are comparable in speed to hard disks. Also, MO disks are portable and the data on them cannot be corrupted by magnets, heat, or humidity.

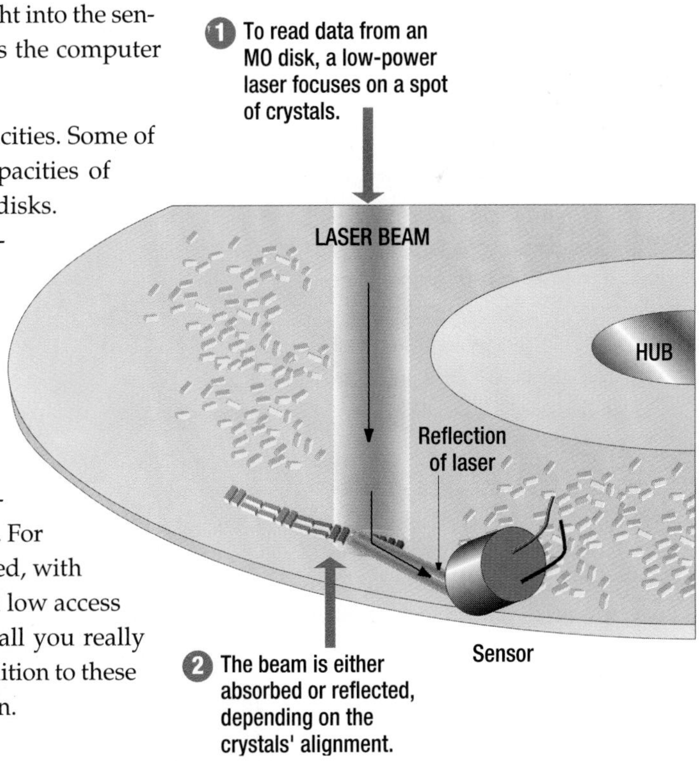

▶ MEASURING DRIVE PERFORMANCE

When evaluating the performance of common storage devices, you need to be aware of two common measures: the average access time and the data-transfer rate. For random-access devices (all the storage devices discussed, with the exception of magnetic tapes), you generally want a low access time and a high data-transfer rate. With tape drives, all you really need to worry about is convenience and capacity. In addition to these factors, the drive interface is an important consideration.

Average Access Time

The **average access time** of a device is the amount of time it takes the device to position its read or read/write heads over any spot on the medium. It is important that the measurement be an average because

1 To read data from an MO disk, a low-power laser focuses on a spot of crystals.

LASER BEAM

HUB

Reflection of laser

2 The beam is either absorbed or reflected, depending on the crystals' alignment.

Sensor

FIGURE 4.18
How a magneto-optical drive reads data.

PC Card: A Hard Disk the Size of Your Driver's License

Today's gigantic software applications can seem like the bull in the china shop. They take up a lot of room and tend to disrupt things in small spaces.

Put just a few of them on your PC, and you may soon find yourself with barely enough room to store your e-mail messages and multimedia presentations, let alone all your everyday work, not to mention the storerooms of data you're downloading every day from the Internet.

On top of this, how do you share the gargantuan files they produce? Network access probably lets you share your projects in the office, but what do you do when you want to take that presentation for tomorrow's meeting home with you tonight to fine-tune on your home computer? Often a standard floppy disk won't hold even one modern graphic file, let alone a whole presentation.

There are many types of *removable mass storage* devices available to meet these challenges, and one of the most interesting is the PC Card. PC Cards, also referred to as PCMCIA (Personal Computer Memory Card International Association) cards, are credit card sized expansion devices that are inserted into slots in your personal computer (primarily portable models). Although PC Card adapters are available for desktop computers, the size of the PC Cards makes them ideal for portable computers.

PC Card hard disk storage capacities currently range from 170 MB to 510 MB of data. Considering that the capacity of the entire hard disk of a desktop PC starts where these cards leave off, at around 500 MB, the capacity of these tiny devices is astonishing. This means that you can carry an additional hard disk with you like a credit card in your wallet!

PC Cards are credit card size in their length and width; however they tend to be thicker than a credit card. There are three types of PC Cards: Type I, II, and III, varying in thickness from about .16 inch to about .5 inch.

PC Card storage devices will serve adequately as either *removable storage* (this means you can take it with you) or *secure removable storage* (this means you keep a copy of your data separate from your computer as a backup or as an alternate storage site if your hard drive is full). PC Cards work well to share or transfer data, since they can be unplugged from one computer and then plugged into another.

In addition to storage, PC Cards are available for a variety of other functions described below:

- **Digital Video PC Cards** transform a laptop computer into a multimedia platform capable of recording, displaying, and transmitting real-time, full-motion video.
- **Audio PC Cards** let you add music or sound to presentations or enjoy an audio environment with recording and playback capabilities.
- **SCSI/Audio Multimedia Combo PC Cards** add 16-bit CD-quality sound and SCSI capabilities on a single card. This lets you listen to your favorite CD by connecting a CD-ROM drive to the SCSI interface. Or add music, sound, even voice annotation to your word processing documents and spreadsheet applications, all while you're on the road.
- **Cellular-Ready Fax/Modem PC Cards** allow mobile executives and field professionals to use their cellular telephones to send and receive data and faxes, anywhere, anytime.
- **Network PC Cards** in conjunction with remote access technology allow travelers instant access to their company network for sharing all kinds of files or communications.
- **Global Positioning System PC Cards** (with appropriate software) allow mobile businesspeople to map their route, find addresses, trace a route, or determine their position and speed—ideal for remote field work.

PC cards provide varied add-on functionality to laptop computers.

access times can vary a great deal depending on the distance between the heads' original location and their destination. To measure the access time of a drive effectively, you must test many reads of randomly chosen sectors—a method that approximates the actual read instructions a disk drive would receive under normal circumstances.

Access time is the combination of two factors: the speed at which a disk spins (revolutions per minute, or rpm), and the time it takes to move the heads from one track to another. In the section on diskettes, you saw that the longest it takes the head to access any point is about 0.2 second, which is the amount of time it takes the disk to complete one revolution at 300 rpm. Access times are measured in **milliseconds (ms)**, or 0.001 second. The maximum access time for diskettes—0.2 second—is 200 milliseconds. The average seek time is about one half of the maximum, or 100 milliseconds.

Average access times for hard drives can vary, but most good ones generate rates of 8 to 12 milliseconds. If you compare these figures to those for diskette drives, you will see that access times for hard disks are generally at least 8 to 10 times faster than diskette drives.

Access times for CD-ROM and WORM drives tend to be quite slow by hard disk drive standards, ranging from 100 to 300 milliseconds.

With removable hard disks and magneto-optical disks, access times can vary greatly. The best models compete with good hard disks, while the mediocre ones are about half as fast as a slow hard disk.

Data-Transfer Rate

The other important statistic for measuring drive performance is the speed at which it can transfer data—that is, how long it takes to read or write data. Speeds are expressed as a rate, or as some amount of data per unit of time. For **data-transfer rates**, time is measured in seconds, but units of data may be measured in bytes, KB, MB, or GB.

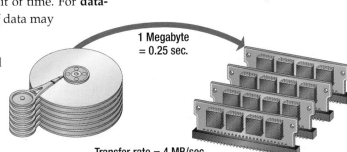

1 Megabyte = 0.25 sec.

Transfer rate = 4 MB/sec.

Once again, speeds can vary greatly. Speeds for hard disks are generally high, from about 5 MB per second (abbreviated MBps) up to 15 MBps for the high-end drives designed for networks. When buying a hard disk, the data-transfer rate is at least as important a factor as the access time.

Data-transfer rate is the time required to move a specific amount of data (for example, 1 MB) from one device to another, such as from the hard disk to memory.

CD-ROMs and diskettes are the slowest storage devices. CD-ROMs range from 300 KBps for a double-speed player, up to 900 KBps for a 6X drive (six times faster than a single speed drive). Diskette drives average about 45 KBps. Removable hard disks and magneto-optical disks range from about 1.25 MBps up into the hard disk range.

Note: Some drive manufacturers and dealers advertise their drive's data transfer rates in units of MBps, but others may express them in mega*bits* per second, or Mbps. When comparison shopping, make sure you notice whether the rate specified is "MBps" or "Mbps."

The speeds for various common storage devices are summarized in Table 4.3:

TABLE 4.3

Average Access Times and Data-Transfer Rates for Common Storage Devices

	HARD DISKS	REMOVABLE HARD DISKS	MAGNETO-OPTICAL	DISKETTES	CD-ROMS
Avg. Access Time (ms)	8–12	12–30	15–30	100	100–300
Data-Transfer Rate (MBps)	5–15	1.25–5.5	2–6	0.045	0.3–0.9

Drive-Interface Standards

Another important factor in determining how quickly a drive can read and write data is the type of controller that the drive uses. Just as a video monitor requires a controller to act as an interface between the CPU and the display screen, storage devices also need a controller to act as an intermediary between the drive and the CPU. A disk controller is connected directly to the computer's bus. On most computers, part of the disk controller is an integral part of the computer's main motherboard, and the rest is built into the drive itself. On some older computers, the controller is an expansion board that connects to the bus by plugging into one of the computer's expansion slots.

The ST-506 Standard

In 1979, Shugart Technology, which would later become Seagate Technology, developed the first standard for interfacing hard disks with PCs. That interface became known as ST-506, after the original hard disk drive that used it. The first ST-506 drives used a data-encoding scheme called modified frequency modulation (MFM). A **data-encoding scheme** is the method that a disk drive uses to translate bits of data into a sequence of flux reversals (changes in magnetic polarity) on the surface of a disk.

Because of MFM's inherent limitations, ST-506 drives that used this scheme had a maximum capacity of 127.5 MB and a maximum data-transfer rate of about 655 KB per second.

The second generation of ST-506 drives employed a new data-encoding scheme called run-length limited (RLL). The RLL encoding scheme made more efficient use of the surface space on a hard disk. With RLL encoding, the maximum drive capacity of the ST-506 increased to 200 MB, and the data-transfer rate improved to almost 800 KB per second.

Integrated Drive Electronics

The **integrated drive electronics (IDE) interface** places most of the disk controller's circuitry on the drive itself to provide a simpler interface with the computer and more reliable operation than was possible with the older ST-506 drives.

In 1983, Compaq Computer came up with the idea of integrating the disk controller circuitry onto the hard disk drive itself. The result was IDE, a simpler and more reliable standard than ST-506. Originally, IDE was capable of providing data-transfer rates of about 1 MB per second under ideal conditions, but this capacity grew to 8.3 MBps, which was faster than the data-transfer rates of most hard disks at that time. Enhanced IDE (EIDE) upgraded the standard and currently supports rates up to 16.6 MBps. When you shop for a system, you can generally assume that IDE really means EIDE. Enhanced IDE is currently the most popular drive interface for PCs.

Enhanced Small Device Interface

Also in 1983, the Maxtor Corporation developed its own improvement on the ST-506 interface. Like IDE, the **enhanced small device interface (ESDI)** (pronounced "es-dee") incorporates much of the circuitry of the controller directly into the drive.

This kit includes the hardware and software necessary to install a 2.0 GB hard disk in a PC.

Early ESDI controllers could transfer data at a rate of 1.25 MB per second, and the standard was improved to support transfers up to 3 MB per second—almost five times the rate of the earlier ST-506 drives. However, ESDI gradually lost market share to Enhanced IDE and it has largely disappeared.

Small Computer System Interface

The history of the **small computer system interface (SCSI)** goes back to the 1970s. SCSI (pronounced "scuzzy") was originally developed as a way to connect third-party peripheral devices to mainframe computers—specifically IBM mainframe computers. SCSI went through many transformations before the American National Standards Institute (ANSI) established a definition for the interface in 1986. Since then, the definition of SCSI continued to evolve, first with SCSI-2, and most recently with SCSI-3.

SCSI takes an approach that is different than IDE and ESDI. Because the original concept of SCSI was to provide peripherals (not just hard disk drives) access to the computer system's bus, one way to think of SCSI is as an *extension* of the computer's bus. As such, all interface circuitry needed by the device has to be on the device itself.

One benefit of SCSI is that bringing the computer's bus directly into the drive improves efficiency. It allows even higher data-transfer rates than are possible with EIDE. SCSI-2 began by supporting transfer rates up to 5 MBps, but variations allow up to 20 MBps. SCSI-3 raised the ante again to a range of 10–40 MBps.

Another benefit of SCSI is that it can accommodate multiple devices—as many as the bus can handle. SCSI-2 allows up to 7 devices, and SCSI-3 allows up to 127 devices. Also, because a SCSI interface is an extension of the bus, any type of device can be linked (or daisy-chained) on a single SCSI port. Remember, devices that use SCSI interfaces include not only hard disk drives, but also optical drives, tape drives, removable hard drives, printers, plotters, and scanners.

Despite the capabilities of SCSI, there are certain pitfalls. If you add a SCSI device to a PC, you should make sure that the device driver is supported by the SCSI card in your PC. In addition, some SCSI devices must be placed at the end of a SCSI chain, so you cannot have more than one such device on a single chain.

In the modern business environment, a "crash" of the company file server elicits panicked shouts or, at the very least, sorrowful groans. As more and more data and applications become centralized on file servers, a file server crash can paralyze many day-to-day business operations.

If the file server goes "down," the book-keeper cannot access data to produce the financial month-end report. The marketing department cannot examine district sales reports. The development team is unable to analyze each other's status reports. Secretaries cannot access standard forms for letters. Hardly anyone can do any work, since almost all of the company's shared data is on the file server.

RAID, a multiple-disk storage system, can be used as a solution to this problem. RAID stands for Redundant Array of Independent Disks, which, at first, sounds like a confusing mouthful. It translates as a storage system that links any number of disk drives to act as a single disk. In this system, information is written to two or more disks simultaneously to improve speed, reliability, and to ensure that data is available to users at all times.

RAID's capabilities are based on three techniques—(1) mirroring, (2) striping,

and (3) striping-with-parity. In a mirrored system, data is written to two or more disks simultaneously, providing a complete copy of all the information on a drive, should one drive fail. Striping provides the user with speedy response by spreading data across several disks. Striping alone, however, does not provide backup if one of the disks in an array fail. Striping-with-parity provides the speed of striping with the reliability of parity. Should a drive in such an array fail, the disk that stores the parity information can be used to reconstruct the data from the damaged drive. Some arrays using the striping-with-parity technique also offer a technique known as "hot swapping," which enables a system administrator to remove a damaged drive while the array remains in operation.

The use of these techniques varies with the end user's demands, because not all applications of RAID perform in the same way. For example, although mirroring is the simplest form of RAID, it also is the slowest—often slower than a single mechanism drive. Speed improves using the striping method but there is no *data redundancy*, or double-writing of data to ensure backup. Striping-with-parity solves both of these problems, but these systems are very expensive.

RAID systems are designed to meet the widely varying storage needs of many different kinds of enterprises. There are currently six levels in common use. The levels are numbered, 0–5, respectively. The two most popular levels of RAID are 0 and 1, primarily because they cost less than the systems that can support higher RAID levels.

Different RAID level systems can operate side-by-side to meet the needs of different business environments. For example, you might see a video digitizing system, which needs a lot of speed, using RAID-0. This works efficiently but it has no redundancy capability, so an additional tape backup is added for data security. On the other hand, the same company's accounting system, which has to be totally secure, uses RAID-1 which stores identical data on two different disks.

Currently, most RAID users are large corporations with large or mid-range system servers. However, as more and more people from all walks of life have begun to use computers, RAID has inched its way onto the PC desktop and one day soon may be a common desktop storage system.

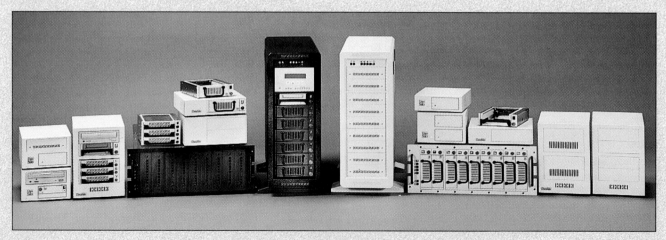

This is the line of hard drives developed for RAID applications by Kingston Technology.

▶ WHAT TO EXPECT IN THE FUTURE

Some of the most important changes in computer hardware over the next few years are likely to occur in the area of storage technology.

The first major change could result from removable hard disk and magneto-optical technologies that are finally competing with hard disk technology on the three crucial fronts: speed, capacity, and price. If there were a device that was equal to a good hard disk in all three of these categories, most customers probably would prefer to have a device with a removable disk. That way, they could easily expand the total storage capacity of their systems, trade large data files with others, and replace drives when they malfunction.

Other changes will arrive soon in the form of new standards and new technologies. Recent improvements in CD technology are increasing the capacity of the disk to about 4.5 GB. Another new approach is to record multiple layers of information on CDs using holographic images that are recorded in a crystal. Also, holographic techniques are being developed for storing terabytes (thousands of gigabytes) in crystals the size of sugar cubes. This technology is still in the lab and probably will not appear in common use until after the end of the century.

Although the trend in storage technology for many years has been to bring ever greater speeds and capacities to the desktop, there is also a groundswell of industry experts and companies that are advocating computers that do not include any storage devices at all. This idea has been driven by the popularity of the Internet. The theory is that people will buy inexpensive diskless machines, known as dumb Internet terminals. These computers will include high-speed communication links to the Internet and will obtain most of their software from it each time they are turned on. Many other industry experts scoff at the notion of computers without storage capacity. Only time will tell if this idea catches on.

▶ VISUAL SUMMARY

Types of Storage Devices

- Storage devices can be classified as magnetic or optical.
- The most common magnetic storage devices are diskettes, hard disks, magnetic tape, and removable hard disks.
- The most common optical devices are CD-ROM, WORM, and magneto-optical disks.

Magnetic Storage Devices

- Magnetic storage devices work by polarizing tiny pieces of iron on the magnetic medium.
- Read/write heads contain electromagnets that create magnetic charges on the medium.
- Diskette drives, also known as floppy disk drives, read and write to diskettes.
- Diskettes are most often used to transfer files between computers, as a means for distributing software, and as a backup medium.
- Diskettes come in two sizes: 3.5-inch, and 5.25-inch.
- Before a disk (diskette or hard disk) can be used, it must be formatted, or initialized—a process in which the read/write heads record tracks and sectors on the disk.
- At the same time as the physical formatting is taking place, the computer's operating system in a PC establishes the disk's logical formatting by creating the boot sector, the FAT, the root folder, and the data area.
- Hard disks can store more data than diskettes because the high-quality media, the high rotational speed, and the tiny distance between the read/write head and the disk surface permit densely packed data and rapid access.
- Removable hard disks combine high capacity with the convenience of diskettes.
- The best removable hard disks are now as large and fast as good internal hard disks.
- Because data stored on magnetic tape is accessed sequentially, it is most appropriate for backup, when the cost and capacity of the medium are of concern, but speed is not.

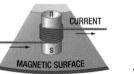

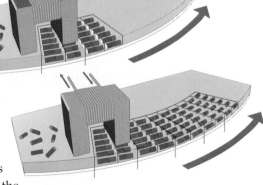

Optical Storage Devices

- CD-ROM uses the same technology as a music CD does; a laser reads lands and pits from the surface of the disk.
- CD-ROM disks can store 650 MB, but they cannot be written to.
- WORM disks and CD-Recordable disks can be written to once, but not rewritten or erased.
- Magneto-optical drives write data with a high-powered laser capable of melting the plastic on the disk coating and a magnet that aligns the crystals under the melted area. A less powerful laser reads the alignment of the crystals.

Measuring Drive Performance

- When considering the performance abilities of storage devices, you must know the average access time and the data-transfer rate.
- The average access time is the average time it takes a read/write head to move from one place on the recording medium to any other place on the medium.
- The data-transfer rate is a measure of how long it takes the device to read or write a given amount of data.
- The best access times and data-transfer rates are provided by hard disks and some of the latest removable hard disks and magneto-optical disks. CD-ROMs have the slowest access times. Diskettes have the slowest data-transfer rates by far.

Drive-Interface Standards

- A disk controller, the interface hardware between the CPU and the disk drive, usually conforms to one of the common interface standards: IDE, ESDI, or SCSI.
- IDE has been upgraded to Enhanced IDE. The upgraded interface standards support data-transfer rates as high as 16.6 MBps.
- SCSI, the second most common drive interface, essentially extends the capacities of the computer's bus.
- The most recent versions of SCSI support data-transfer rates from 10 to 40 MBps.

▶ KEY TERMS

When you have finished this chapter, you should be able to define the following terms:

average access time, 117
backing up, 105
boot record, 108
booting, 108
CD-recordable (CD-R) drive, 116
cluster, 108

compact disk, read-only memory (CD-ROM), 114
cylinder, 110
data area, 109
data-encoding scheme, 120
data-transfer rate, 119

density, 106
digital audiotape (DAT), 113
digital video disk (DVD), 115
directory, 109
diskette, 99
diskette drive, 99

electromagnet, 103
enhanced small device interface
    (ESDI), 121
file-allocation table (FAT), 108
floppies, 104
floppy disk, 104
folder, 109
formatting, 106
fragmented, 109
hard disk, 99
hard disk drive, 99

head crash, 111
hot-swappable hard disk, 111
initializing, 106
install, 105
integrated drive electronics (IDE)
    interface, 120
lands, 114
logical format (soft format), 108
magnetic storage, 100
magneto-optical (MO) disk, 116
millisecond, 119

pits, 114
polarized, 101
read/write head, 103
removable hard disk, 111
sector, 106
small computer system interface
    (SCSI), 121
storage media, 99
tape drive, 100
write once, read many (WORM)
    drive, 116

▶ KEY TERM QUIZ

Fill in the missing word with one of the terms listed in Key Terms:

1. The process of mapping a disk is called _____.

2. A(n) _____ disk has the capacity of a CD-ROM but it can be rewritten like a magnetic disk.

3. The amount of time it takes a device to position its read or read/write heads over any spot on the medium is known

    as _____.

4. _____ is the process of creating a duplicate set of programs and data for safekeeping.

5. You use a(n) _____ to organize files on a disk.

6. The internal process of starting up the computer is known as _____.

7. The _____ is the primary storage device for microcomputers.

8. A statistic for measuring how long a drive takes to read or write data is called the _____.

9. Another name for a diskette is a(n) _____.

10. A(n) _____ is the smallest segment of a track on a disk.

▶ REVIEW QUESTIONS

1. Name and describe briefly two widely used storage devices for PCs.
2. Describe how a removable hard disk offers the benefits of both diskettes and hard disks.
3. What is an important advantage that a magnet has over a transistor?
4. Describe briefly how a read/write head is able to pass data to and from the surface of a diskette.
5. What is a diskette's *density* a measure of?
6. Describe briefly how a computer's operating system is able to locate data on a disk's surface.
7. Describe briefly the process in which new data added to an existing file is stored on disk. What important component makes this process seamless to a user?
8. Describe the functions of lands and pits on the surface of a CD-ROM.

9. List and describe some of the benefits and disadvantages of using CD-ROMs over diskettes.
10. In what way is SCSI regarded as an extension of a computer's bus? What primary benefit does SCSI provide for storage drives?

▶ DISCUSSION QUESTIONS

1. Why do you think a "basic truth" in computing is that one never has enough data storage space? To what factors do you attribute to the need for storage devices that hold increasingly larger amounts of data?
2. Suppose you are considering the best storage medium for backing up data on a hard disk. What important considerations must you take into account? Would serial, or sequential, data access be preferable, or would random access be better for this purpose?
3. Why is it necessary that access times be averaged to measure the performance of a storage device accurately?
4. What do you think about the notion of using a computer that is simply a dumb Internet terminal?

NORTON INTERACTIVE

Complete the Norton Interactive module for this chapter.

NETWORKS AND DATA COMMUNICATIONS

CONTENTS

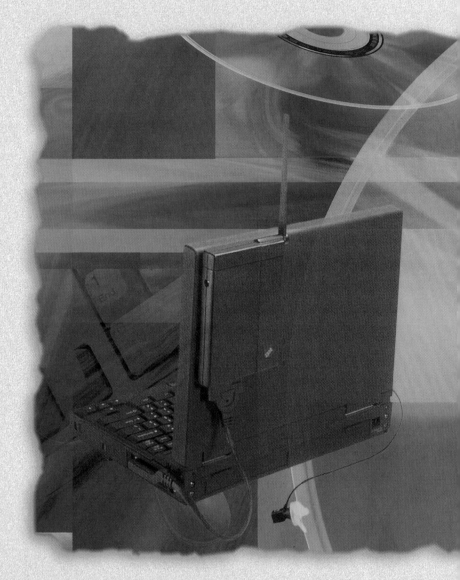

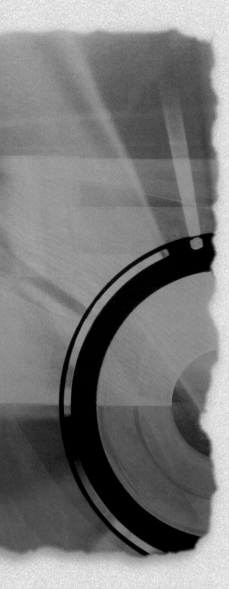

OBJECTIVES

When you complete this chapter, you will be able to do the following:

- List four major benefits of connecting computers to form a network.
- Differentiate between a LAN and a WAN.
- Differentiate among file server, client/server, and peer-to-peer computing.
- Describe the physical layout of networks based on bus, star, and ring topologies.
- Describe four common media for connecting the computers in a network.
- Compare the Ethernet, Token Ring, and ARCnet protocols.
- Describe the most popular reasons for connecting computers through the telephone lines.
- Explain how a modem works and what distinguishes one modem from another.
- List the most common types of digital lines and the basic characteristics of each.

When PCs first began appearing in the business environment, and software applications were simple and designed for a single user, the advantages of connecting PCs were not so compelling. As these machines spread throughout business, and as complex, multiuser software appeared, connecting PCs became a paramount goal. **Data communications**, the electronic transfer of information between computers, became a major focus of the computer industry. The rapid growth of the worldwide computer network called the Internet further spurred the spread of data communications.

Computers communicate in two main ways: through modems and through networks. Modems enable computers to use telephone lines, cellular connections (the kind that mobile telephones use), or even satellite links to exchange data. Networks connect computers directly, at higher speeds, either through special wiring or by some form of wireless transmission. The process of connecting a computer to a network is known as going **online**. Networking lets organizations maximize the value of computers, so it is not difficult to imagine a day when virtually every organization, large or small, will be part of a computer network.

◤ THE USES OF A NETWORK

The word *network* has several definitions. The most commonly used meaning describes the methods people use to maintain relationships with friends and business contacts. Applied to computers, it has a similar definition. A **network** is a way to connect computers together so that they can communicate, exchange information, and pool resources.

In business, networks have revolutionized the use of computer technology. Many businesses that used to rely on a centralized system with a mainframe and a collection of terminals now use computer networks in which every employee who needs a computer has one. Computer technology and expertise are no longer centralized in a company's mainframe and information systems departments. The technology and expertise are distributed throughout the organization among a network of computers and computer-literate users.

In education, schools have also shifted to strategies built around networks. These include local area networks, such as a network that connects the computers and printers in a computer lab, and wide area networks—especially the Internet.

Most offices have a personal computer on nearly every desk. The computers are connected to form a network.

Whatever the setting, networks provide tremendous benefits. Four of the most compelling benefits are:

- Allowing simultaneous access to critical programs and data
- Allowing people to share peripheral devices, such as printers and scanners
- Streamlining personal communication with e-mail
- Making the backup process easier

The next section will examine each one of these advantages in a little more detail.

Simultaneous Access

It is a fact of business computing that multiple employees, using a computer network, often need access to the same data at the same time. If employees keep separate copies of data on different hard disks, updating the data becomes very difficult. As soon as a change is made to the data on one machine, a discrepancy arises, and it quickly becomes very difficult to know which set of data is correct. Storing data that is used by more than one person on a shared storage device makes it possible to solve the problem.

It is also true that most office workers use the same programs. With a network, businesses can save thousands of dollars by purchasing special **network versions** of the

Answer: A network. In this computer age, activities that seem as different as night and day often share the common thread of being network-based. Networks of all kinds connect our world today, and they provide the means to accomplish widely divergent tasks never before possible. Here are some interesting examples.

Long-Distance Brain Surgery

A Pennsylvania hospital organization is using its network to transmit real-time video coverage of live surgery, distance education (online classes), and collaborative applications between multiple sites. A recent demonstration of the network capabilities involved the transmission of live video coverage of brain surgery.

The network, administered by the Allegheny Health, Education, and Research Foundation, connects 22 video conferencing sites between two hospitals in Philadelphia and Pittsburgh.

The network supports four three-way fully interactive video conferences at a time. AT&T provided its InterSpan ATM (asynchronous transfer mode) service as the core network-transmission medium, while the Warrendale, Pennsylvania company, Fore Systems, Inc., and the hospital system designed the network.

ET Online

Steven Spielberg has introduced a network-based electronic playground for seriously ill children where they can travel to virtual worlds guided by an on screen animated host. The network, demonstrated by Spielberg himself at a recent Digital World trade show, was developed by the Starbright Foundation, a charity for children that provides entertainment, technology, and medicine.

The pilot program was developed jointly by a variety of high tech companies. Worlds, Inc. produced the software that creates play spaces for the children to visit online. The high-speed telecommu-

nications equipment and workstations were provided jointly by Sprint Corp., Intel Corp., and UB Networks. Starbright intends the pilot program to evolve into a nationwide, multiuser interactive network.

To demonstrate the network, Spielberg, who is chairman of Starbright Foundation, sat at a computer and traveled to several "virtual worlds" resembling a tropical island, a cave, and the sky, using his alien creation ET as on screen host. Children in remote hospital settings animated different characters on screen. Over the network, ET and the children's characters played games with each other.

Stock Market Updates

The Bank of Boston uses a network and special software to transfer live TV news coverage to their traders' PCs on the stock market trading room floor. This way, the traders can keep abreast of up-to-date news on TV via their PCs without the chaos and noise that numerous TV monitors stationed in the trading room would cause.

Until recently, there were TV monitors mounted on the walls for traders to watch breaking news events that affect

fast-changing markets. These TVs, necessary as they were, often created problems, including physical obstructions, logistical cable nightmares, and increases to the already deafening noise level.

Television-capable PCs with direct hookups to cable TV were introduced in 1994 and are now widely available. However, the Bank of Boston, a multinational banking firm, wanted to upgrade its present equipment rather than buy new computers.

The solution came in the form of a unique software program called InSoft Network Television (INTV). This program transfers either live or recorded digital video from a server to client machines over a network, allowing traders to watch cable TV in a small window on their monitors while simultaneously running other programs.

Now, traders have their own private TVs at their fingertips, complete with remote control to select channels and adjust volume. Traders say they usually have the news running all the time and are able to respond to market changes immediately.

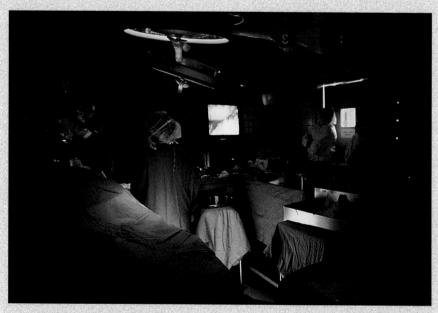

Live brain surgery is transmitted over a computer network at Allegheny General Hospital.

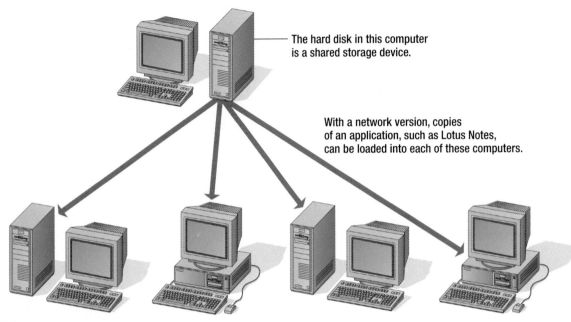

The hard disk in this computer is a shared storage device.

With a network version, copies of an application, such as Lotus Notes, can be loaded into each of these computers.

FIGURE 5.1
Using multiple copies of a network version of an application.

most commonly used programs rather than having to buy separate copies for each machine. When employees need to use a program, they simply load it from a shared storage device into the RAM of their own desktop computers, as shown in Figure 5.1.

A network version is also a more efficient use of hard disk space, since a large number of users can access a single shared copy, rather than storing separate copies on each user's hard disk.

Some software designed for networks is classified as **groupware**. This type of software includes scheduling and calendar software, e-mail, and document management software. Groupware allows multiple users on a network to cooperate on projects. Users can work on the same documents, share their insights, and keep each other abreast of their schedules so that meetings can be set up easily. Lotus Notes is perhaps the best-known example of groupware, although there are many competitors.

Screen Shot [©1994] Lotus Development Corporation. Used with permission of Lotus Development Corporation. Lotus 1-2-3, and Lotus Notes are registered trademarks of Lotus Development Corporation.

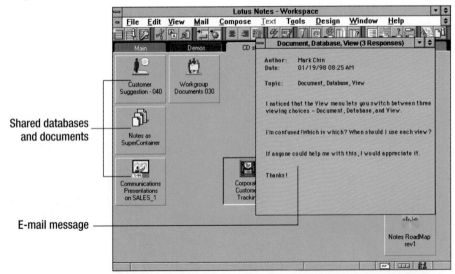

Shared databases and documents

E-mail message

This screen shows two features of Lotus Notes. On the left are several databases and sets of documents that employees are sharing. On the right is an e-mail message in which an employee is asking for help about how to use several features of the program.

Shared Peripheral Devices

Perhaps the best incentive for small businesses to link computers in a network is to share peripheral devices, especially expensive ones such as laser printers, large hard disks, and scanners, as shown in Figure 5.2.

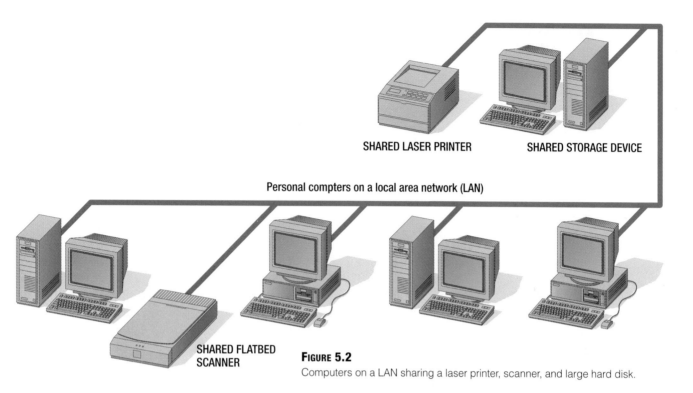

SHARED LASER PRINTER   **SHARED STORAGE DEVICE**

Personal compters on a local area network (LAN)

**SHARED FLATBED
SCANNER**

FIGURE 5.2
Computers on a LAN sharing a laser printer, scanner, and large hard disk.

Many laser printers cost well over $1,000, so it is not very cost-effective for each user to have one. Sharing a laser printer on a network makes the cost much less prohibitive.

An added benefit of sharing peripherals is that they can prolong the usable life of older computers. For example, older computers often do not have enough storage for modern software and data. If the computer is connected to a large central computer called a **network server** (also called a **file server**, or simply a **server**), excess data can be stored there. This solution is often less expensive than buying and installing new hard disks for older computers.

Personal Communication

One of the most far-reaching applications of data communications is **electronic mail (e-mail)**, a system for exchanging written messages (and increasingly, voice and video messages) through a network. E-mail is something of a cross between the postal system and a telephone answering system. In an e-mail system, each user has a unique address. To send someone an e-mail message, you enter the person's e-mail address and then type the message. When you are done, the message is sent to the e-mail address. The next time that user accesses the e-mail system, it reports that mail has arrived. Some systems notify the recipient as each message arrives by flashing a message on the computer screen or beeping. After reading the message, the recipient can save it, delete it, pass it on to someone else, or respond by sending back a reply message. Figure 5.3 shows the process for sending and receiving e-mail.

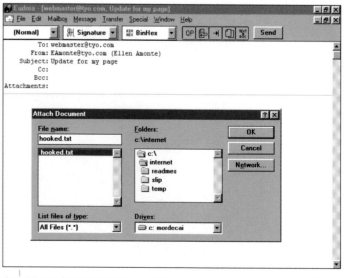

Attaching a document to an e-mail message is a simple way to trade files with coworkers.

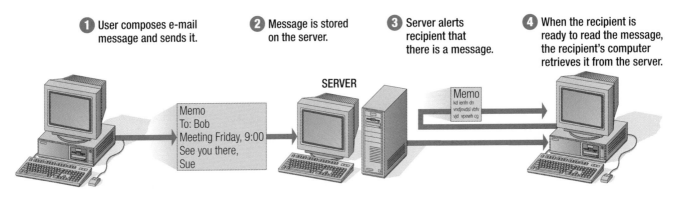

① User composes e-mail message and sends it.

② Message is stored on the server.

③ Server alerts recipient that there is a message.

④ When the recipient is ready to read the message, the recipient's computer retrieves it from the server.

SERVER

Memo
To: Bob
Meeting Friday, 9:00
See you there,
Sue

Memo
kd ienfm dn
vndjnvdsl vbfv
vjd vpewh cg

FIGURE 5.3
Sending and receiving e-mail.

In addition to sending a page or pages of mail text, many systems allow you to attach data such as spreadsheet files or word processed documents to your message. This means that an e-mail system allows people to share files even when they do not have access to the same storage devices. For example, a local area network also may have a connection to a large information network, such as CompuServe, Microsoft Network, America Online, or the Internet. In this case, the person on the local network can share files with anyone on the large information network.

E-mail is both efficient and inexpensive. Users can send written messages without worrying about whether the other user's computer is currently running. On centralized networks, the message is delivered almost instantaneously, and the cost of sending the message is negligible. E-mail has provided the modern world with an entirely new and immensely valuable form of communication.

In addition to e-mail, the spread of networking technology is adding to the popularity of teleconferencing and video conferencing. A **teleconference** is a virtual meeting in which a group of people in different locations conduct a group discussion by typing messages to each other. Each message can be seen by all the other people in the teleconference. Teleconference software has become more sophisticated, gradually adding such features as a shared scratch pad where diagrams or pictures can be drawn or electronically pasted.

The spread of networking is adding to the popularity of collaborative software, which allows users to connect with one another over LAN or modem links so they can see what's happening on other users' computers. It lets people send messages, exchange files, and sometimes even allows people to work on the same document at the same time. Figure 5.4 shows Timbuktu, a collaborative program, being used by a Windows 3.1 computer to a access a Macintosh through a LAN.

Windows 3.1 running Timbuktu

This window shows the screen of a Mac on the same LAN.

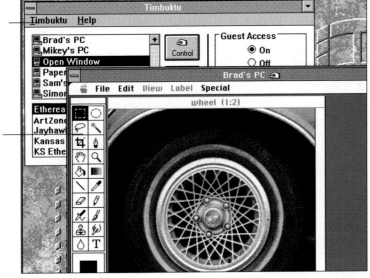

FIGURE 5.4
Collaborative software.

If users have the necessary hardware and software, they can actually see and speak to each other as they meet online (rather than merely typing messages). This is a process known as **video conferencing**. Video conferencing can also refer to a live video communication between just two people, as shown in Figure 5.5.

Easier Backup

In business, data is extremely valuable, so making sure that employees back up their data is critical. One way to address this problem is to keep all valuable data on a shared storage device that employees access through a network. Often the person managing the network has the responsibility of making regular backups of the data on the shared storage device.

▶ CATEGORIES OF NETWORKS

To understand the different types of networks and how they operate, it is important to know something about how networks can be structured. First, there are two main types of networks, distinguished by size. There are local area networks (LANs) and wide area networks (WANs). Second, either one of these types can be classified according to the logical relationships among the computers. There are file server networks, client/server networks, and peer-to-peer networks.

Courtesy of Cornell University

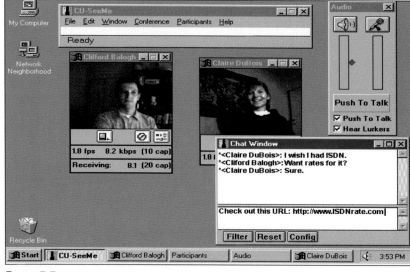

FIGURE 5.5

A video conference between two people using a program called CU-SeeMe.

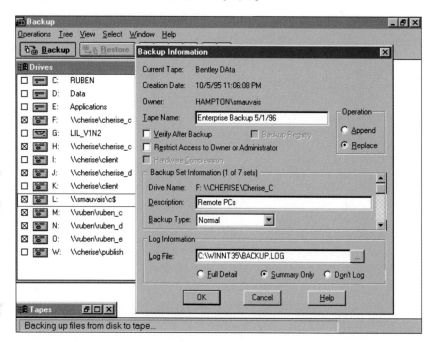

Backup systems like the one shown here can be used to back up a server and individual personal computers on the network.

Local Area Networks

A network of computers located relatively near each other and connected by a cable (or a small radio transmitter) is a **local area network (LAN)**. A LAN can consist of just two or three PCs connected together to share resources, or it can include several hundred computers of different kinds. Any network that exists within a single building, or even a group of adjacent buildings, is considered a LAN.

A LAN permits all the computers connected to it to share hardware, software, and data. The most commonly shared resources are disk storage devices and printers. To LAN users, the network is, or should be, completely transparent, which means that the shared devices on it seem to be directly connected to the user's computer as if

One of the biggest decisions a company makes about a new technical product is how to *deliver* it. The planning that goes into the development of a multimedia product, for example, must include how to get it to the users. One common delivery vehicle is a network—either an internal company network or the public Internet.

When modern multimedia products are transmitted over a network, they often meet the stumbling block of *limited bandwith*, or limitations in the amount of data that can be transfered by the various network media. Modern multimedia products are often beyond the capabilities of even the fastest modems.

It is the video component of multimedia that puts it beyond the capability of modem transfer. Full-screen, full-motion video requires more bandwidth than either a 28.8 Kbps modem or an ISDN connection can receive. As a result, it is difficult to deliver multimedia over the Internet to users who have dial-up connections via their telephone lines.

On the other hand, people have been receiving video images through their television sets for years, and a television doesn't even have a modem. This is because the television signal traditionally comes in an analog format. Today, however, cable companies are switching to digital networks so they can offer customers a wider range of services including:

■ **Video-enhanced phone conversations**, currently known as video conferencing. Put a camera beside your TV or computer and have a face-to-face conversation with anyone in the world.

■ **Interactive games** based on realistic video. Play with friends around the world, or join a game already in progress on the Internet.

■ **High-speed networks.** Run an extension of the cable around your home or office, then set up a LAN inside the building with a high-speed connection to a backbone outside the building that can support multimedia applications.

■ **Private radio or TV stations.** Set up your own sound or video broadcasts and distribute your multimedia brochures to potential clients.

■ **Home shopping.** Online shopping services have begun to support on-demand video presentations of products and online credit card purchases.

All these services have become possible because coaxial cable, the type of cable that connects to your television, can carry about 900 times as much data as a standard, twisted-pair telephone wire. This is enough bandwidth to bring digital, full-screen, full-motion video and CD-quality stereo audio to your television or your computer.

However, in addition to the coaxial cable and a cable provider that offers digital service, you will also need a *cable modem* to access these services. In one respect, the cable modem is like a modem for the phone lines. It can translate digital signals into analog ones that your television can display. A cable modem will also have to provide several other features:

■ digital input and output capability
■ a tuner that can differentiate between the different signals
■ built-in data encryption capability to ensure privacy

Naturally, then, cable modems are a lot more expensive than modems for telephone lines. They can be more expensive than many television sets. However, because the potential demand for a digital network capable of supporting multimedia is so huge, cable companies probably will find a way to make it affordable. When they do, television, the Internet, and your telephone service are going to be offered through a single system, and none of those services will ever be the same again.

This woman is using a cable modem to integrate digital communication and video on her computer.

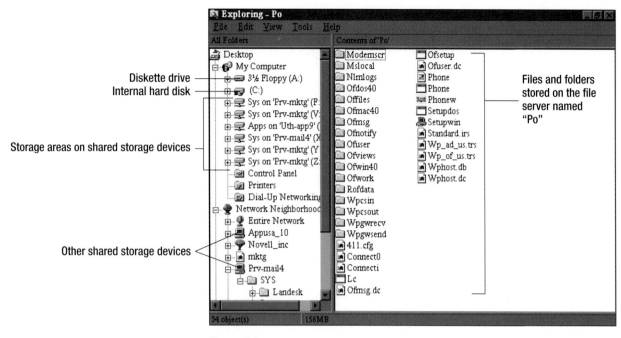

FIGURE 5.6
Accessing shared storage devices on a network.

they were merely peripherals. For example, a file server should appear to the LAN user simply as another disk drive, as shown in Figure 5.6.

In addition to shared hardware, LANs can provide all the other benefits of networks, including simultaneous access, enhanced personal communication, and easier backup.

Connecting Networks

It is often helpful to connect different LANs together. For example, two different departments in a large business may each have their own LAN, but if there is enough need for data communication between the departments, then it may be necessary to create a link between the two LANs.

To understand how this can be accomplished, you must first know that, on a network, data is sent in small groups called packets. A **packet**, also called a **frame**, is a group of bits that includes a header and a payload, as shown in Figure 5.7.

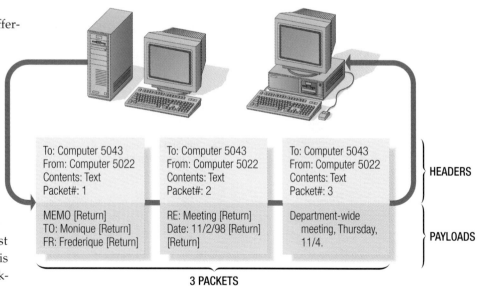

FIGURE 5.7
E-mail message, divided into packets.

The **payload** is the part that contains the actual data being sent. The header contains information about the type of data in the payload, the source and destination of the data, and a sequence number so that data from multiple packets can be reassembled at the receiving computer in the proper order.

Each LAN is governed by a protocol, a set of rules and formats, for sending and receiving data. If two LANs are built around the same communication rules, then they can be connected with a bridge or a router. A **bridge** is a relatively simple device that looks at the information in each packet header and rebroadcasts data that is traveling from one LAN to another. A **router** is a more complicated device that stores the addressing information of each computer on each LAN and uses this information to act like an electronic post office, sorting data and sending it along the most expedient route to its destination.

In some cases, a router can also be used to connect two different types of LANs. However, a router only "routes" data: it knows how to send it to the correct location, and that's all. If you need a more sophisticated connection between networks, you need a **gateway**, a computer system that connects two networks and translates information from one to the other. Packets from different networks have different kinds of information in their headers, and the information can be in different formats. The gateway can take a packet from one type of network, read the header, then encapsulate the entire packet into a new one, adding a header that is understood by the second network, as shown in Figure 5.8.

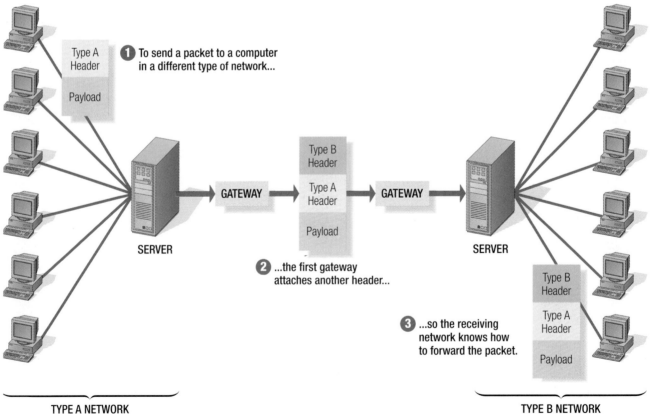

Figure 5.8
How a gateway forwards a packet to a different type of network.

Wide Area Networks

Typically, a **wide area network (WAN)** is two or more LANs that are connected together, generally across a wide geographical area. For example, a company may have its corporate headquarters and manufacturing facility in one city and its marketing office in another. Each site needs resources, data, and programs locally, but it also needs to share data with the other site. To accomplish this feat of data communication, the company could attach a router to each LAN to create a WAN. Figure 5.9 shows a typical WAN connecting two LANs.

The Internet is the ultimate WAN, since it connects many thousands of computers and LANs around the world. Most of the commercial online services and large bulletin boards were not WANs when they started out, because, typically, users dialed in to a single computer or a group of computers housed at a single site. However, today most of these systems provide connections to other specialized services and to the Internet, so they are now more like WANs.

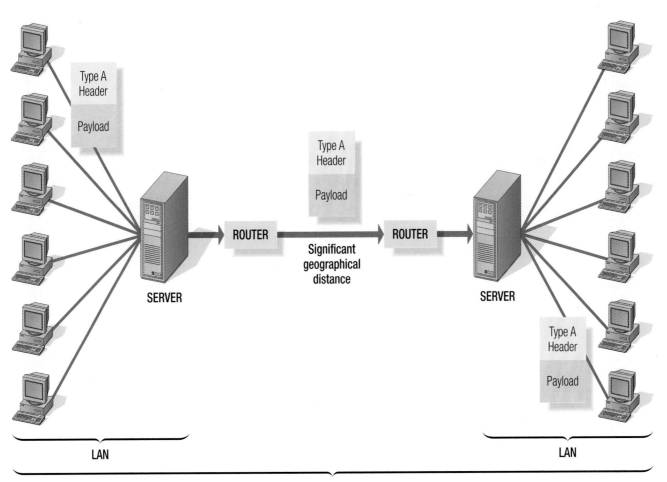

FIGURE 5.9
Combining two LANs to form a WAN.

File Server Networks

Describing a network as a LAN or a WAN gives a sense of the physical area the network covers. However, this classification does not tell you anything about how individual computers on a network, called **nodes**, interact with other computers on the network.

Many networks include not only nodes but also a central computer with a large hard disk that is used for shared storage. This computer is known as the file server, network server, or simply, server. Files used by more than one user (at different nodes) are generally kept on the server.

One relatively simple implementation of a network with nodes and a file server is a **file server network**. This is a hierarchical arrangement in which each node can have access to the files on the server but not necessarily to files on other nodes. When a node needs information on the server, it requests the entire file containing the information. In other words, the file server is used simply to store and forward (send) files (see Figure 5.10).

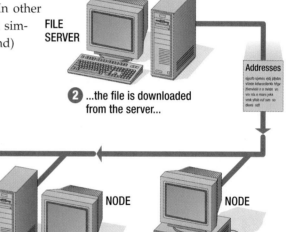

FILE SERVER

Addresses

2 ...the file is downloaded from the server...

1 If the user on this computer needs information from a shared address file...

NODE   NODE   NODE   NODE

3 ...and this computer searches the file for the desired information.

FIGURE 5.10
A simple LAN with a file server.

Client/Server Networks

Another approach for organizing nodes on a network is called **client/server** computing, a hierarchical strategy in which individual computers share the processing and storage workload with a central server. This type of arrangement requires specialized software for both the individual node and the network server. It does not, however, require any specific type of network. Client/server software can be used on LANs or WANs, and a single client/server program can be used on a LAN where all the other software is based on a simple file server relationship.

The most common example of client/server computing involves a database that can be accessed by many different computers on the network. The database is stored on the network server. Also stored on the server is the server portion of the database management system (DBMS), the program that allows users to add information to, or extract it from, the database. The user's computer (which can be called the node, workstation, or client) stores and runs the client portion of the DBMS.

Now, suppose the user wants information from the database. For example, suppose the database is a list of customer purchases, and the user needs to know the names of customers in the Wichita area who made purchases of more than $500. The user uses the client software to describe the information that is needed and sends the request to the server. The server software searches the database, collects the relevant customer names, and sends them back to the client. The client software then presents the information to the user in a way that makes sense. This process is shown in Figure 5.11.

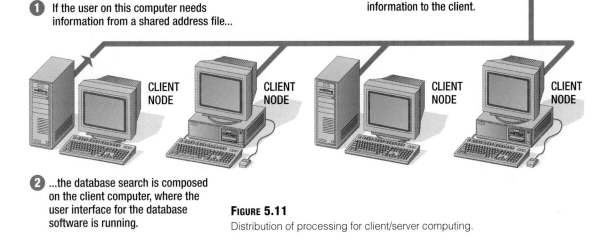

1 If the user on this computer needs information from a shared address file...

2 ...the database search is composed on the client computer, where the user interface for the database software is running.

3 The server processes the search and returns just the requested information to the client.

FIGURE 5.11
Distribution of processing for client/server computing.

Client/server software is valuable to large, modern organizations because it distributes processing and storage workloads among resources efficiently. This means that users get the information they need faster.

Client/server computing is also a commonly used model on the Internet. Users typically have client software that provides an easily used interface for interacting with this giant WAN. Other types of processing, such as receiving, storing, and sending e-mail messages, are carried out by remote computers running the server part of the relevant software.

Peer-to-Peer Computing

A third arrangement is a **peer-to-peer network**, in which all nodes on the network have equal relationships to all others, and all have similar types of software. Typically, each node has access to at least some of the resources on all other nodes, so the relationship is nonhierarchical. If they are set up correctly, Windows 95 and its predecessor, Windows for Workgroups, give users access to the hard disks and printers attached to other computers in the network. A peer-to-peer network is shown in Figure 5.12.

In addition, some very high-end peer-to-peer networks such as networks of UNIX computers allow **distributed computing**, which enables users to draw on the processing power of other computers in the network. That means people can transfer tasks that take a lot of CPU power—such as creating computer software—to available computers, leaving their own machines free for other work.

Peer-to-peer LANs are commonly set up in small organizations (less than 50 employees) or in schools, where the primary benefit of a network is shared storage, printers,

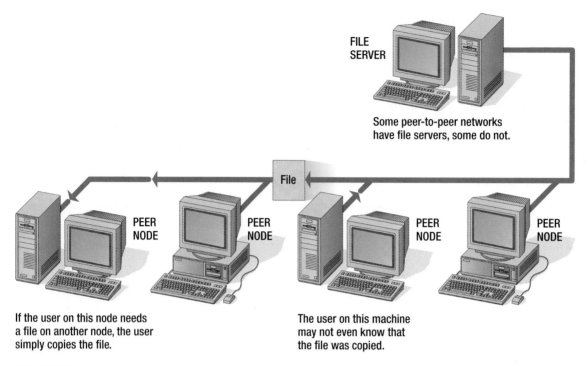

FILE
SERVER

Some peer-to-peer networks
have file servers, some do not.

File

PEER
NODE

PEER
NODE

PEER
NODE

PEER
NODE

If the user on this node needs
a file on another node, the user
simply copies the file.

The user on this machine
may not even know that
the file was copied.

FIGURE 5.12
Peer-to-peer network.

and enhanced communication. Where large databases are used, LANs are more likely to include client/server relationships.

It is important to realize that a peer-to-peer network can also include a network server. In this case, a peer-to-peer LAN is very similar to a file server network. The only difference between them is that the peer-to-peer network gives users greater access to the other nodes than a file server network does. (See Figure 5.12.)

▶ NETWORK TOPOLOGIES FOR LANS

In addition to the size of a network and the relationship between the nodes and the server, another distinguishing feature among LANs is the **topology**—the physical layout of the cables that connect the nodes of the network. There are three basic topologies: bus, star, and ring. Network designers consider a number of factors in determining which topology, or combination of topologies, to use. Among the factors considered are the type of computers currently installed, the type of cabling currently in place (if any), the cost of the components and services required to implement the network, and the speed with which data must travel around the network.

The Bus Topology

A **bus network**, like the bus of a computer itself, is a single conduit to which all the network nodes and peripheral devices are attached (see Figure 5.13). Nodes on a bus network transmit data at any time, regardless of any data being sent by other nodes. If one set of data happens to collide with another set of data transmitted by other nodes, that is, if two nodes try to send data at the same time, each node waits a small, random amount of time and then attempts to retransmit the data.

NETWORKS AND DATA COMMUNICATIONS

Although the bus topology is one of the most common, it has inherent disadvantages. Keeping data transmissions from colliding requires extra circuitry and software, and a broken connection can bring down (or "crash") all or part of the network, rendering it inoperable so that users cannot share data and peripherals until the connection is repaired.

The Star Topology

A **star network** places a hub in the center of the network nodes. Groups of data are routed through the central hub to their destinations. This scheme has an advantage in that the hub monitors traffic and prevents collisions, and a broken connection does not affect the rest of the network. If you lose the hub, however, the entire network goes down. Figure 5.14 shows the star topology.

The Ring Topology

The **ring topology** connects the nodes of the network in a circular chain in which each node is connected to the next. The final node in the chain connects to the first to complete the ring, as shown in Figure 5.15.

With this methodology, each node examines data that is sent through the ring. If the data is not addressed to the node examining it, that node passes it along to the next node in the ring.

The ring topology has a substantial advantage over the bus topology. There's no danger of collisions because data always flows in one direction. One drawback to the ring, however, is that if a connection is broken, the entire network goes down.

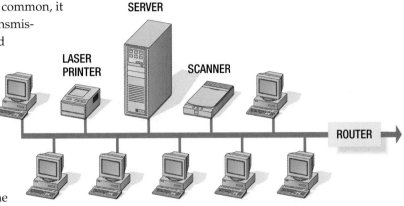

FIGURE 5.13
LAN with bus topology.

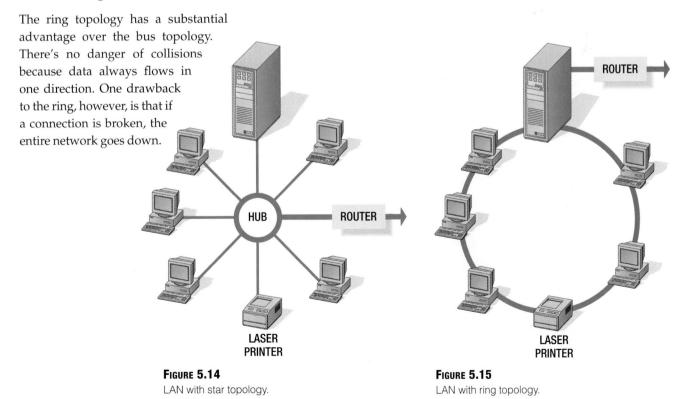

FIGURE 5.14
LAN with star topology.

FIGURE 5.15
LAN with ring topology.

▶ NETWORK MEDIA AND HARDWARE

No matter what their structure, all networks rely on *media* to link them together. You may recall that when referring to data storage, the term *media* refers to materials for storing data, such as magnetic disks and tape. In network communications, however, *media* refers to the wires, cables, and other means by which data travels from its source to its destination. The most common media for data communication are twisted-pair wire, coaxial cable, fiber-optic cable, and wireless links.

Twisted-Pair Wire

Twisted-pair wire normally consists of four or eight copper strands of wire, individually insulated in plastic, then twisted around each other in braided pairs and bound together in another layer of plastic insulation. (There were originally just two wires, rather than four or eight, hence the name *twisted-pair*.) Except for the plastic coating, nothing shields this type of wire from outside interference, so it is also called *unshielded twisted-pair (UTP)* wire. Some twisted-pair wire is further encased in a metal sheath and therefore is called *shielded twisted-pair (STP)* wire. Figure 5.16 shows what UTP and STP look like.

Indoor wiring for telephones uses twisted-pair wire, so twisted-pair is often called telephone wire. Because it was readily available and inexpensive, telephone wire gained early favor as a conduit for data communications. Today, however, some twisted-pair wire used for communication is made to more demanding specifications than voice-grade telephone wire.

Sometimes network media are compared by the amount of data they can transmit each second, a measurement known as **bandwidth**. Twisted-pair wire was once considered a low-bandwidth media, but networks based on twisted-pair wires now support transmission speeds up to 150 megabits per second (Mbps), and even faster speeds are on the horizon.

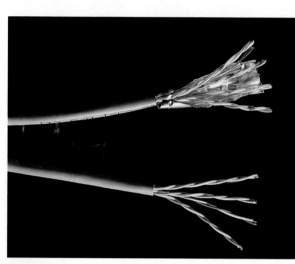

FIGURE 5.16
Shielded (top) and unshielded (bottom) twisted-pair wire is the most common medium for computer networks.

Coaxial Cable

Coaxial cable, sometimes called **coax** (pronounced "co-axe"), is widely used for cable TV and is used in some networks (however, the connectors are different for TV and networks). There are two conductors in coaxial cable. One is a single wire in the center of the cable and the other is a wire mesh shield that surrounds the first wire with an insulator in between (see Figure 5.17).

Coaxial cable can carry more data than older types of twisted-pair wiring, and it is less susceptible to interference from other wiring. However, it is also more expensive and has become less popular as twisted-pair technology has improved. Two types of coaxial cable are used with networks: thick and thin. Thick coax is the older standard and is seldom installed in new networks.

Central wire
Insulator
Wire mesh

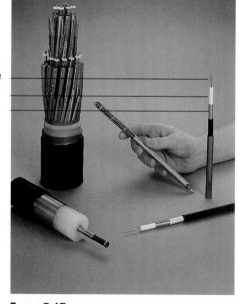

FIGURE 5.17
Coaxial cable.

Fiber-Optic Cable

A **fiber-optic cable** is a thin strand of glass that transmits pulsating beams of light instead of electric frequencies (see Figure 5.18). When one end of the strand is exposed to light, the strand carries the light all the way to the other end—bending around corners with only a minute loss of energy along the way.

Because light travels at a much higher frequency than electrical signals, fiber-optic cable can easily carry data at more than a billion bits per second—usually 1300 Mbps. Fiber-optic cable is also immune to the electromagnetic interference that is a problem for copper wire.

The disadvantage of fiber-optic cable is that it is more expensive than twisted-pair and coax, and it is more difficult to install because it does not bend around corners as easily. As costs have come down, however, fiber-optic cable has become increasingly popular, and it is now revolutionizing a number of communications industries. Telephone and cable television companies, especially, have been moving from twisted-pair wire and coaxial cables to fiber-optic cables.

Strands of glass

FIGURE 5.18
Fiber-optic cable.

Wireless Links

Today, wireless communication is competing with twisted-pair, coaxial, and fiber-optic cable. The advantage of wireless communication is the flexibility that it offers in terms of the network layout. **Wireless communication** relies on radio signals for transmitting data. It is important to remember that radio frequencies form part of the electromagnetic spectrum, including X-rays, ultraviolet light, the visible spectrum, infrared, microwaves, and the longer waves that are used by commercial radio stations.

There are four common uses of wireless communication in networks:

1. Office LANs can use radio signals to transmit data between nodes.
2. Laptops can be equipped with cellular telephone equipment and a modem so that business people can stay in touch with the office network, no matter where they travel.

This device uses infrared light to connect a laptop to a LAN.

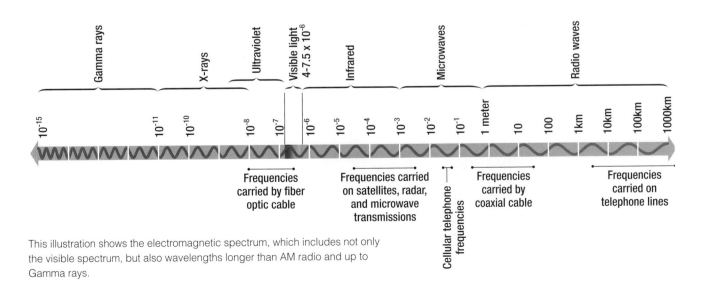

This illustration shows the electromagnetic spectrum, which includes not only the visible spectrum, but also wavelengths longer than AM radio and up to Gamma rays.

This man is logging on to his office network by attaching the modem in his notebook computer to a cellular phone.

3. Corporate WANs often use microwave transmission to connect two LANs within the same metropolitan area. If a company has buildings on opposite sides of town, it can set up a microwave antenna on top of each one to move data back and forth quickly. This type of communication, however, requires an unobstructed line of sight between the two antennas.

4. WANs that cover long distances often use satellites and microwave communication. Television and telephone companies have used satellites for many years, but big businesses use them for their computer networks as well.

The Network Interface Card and Network Protocols

Cables or radio waves may link a network together, but each computer on the network still needs hardware to control the flow of data. The device that performs this function is the **network interface card (NIC)**. The NIC is a type of expansion board—a printed circuit board that fits into one of the computer's expansion slots and provides a port on the back of the PC to which the network cable attaches. The computer also requires network software to tell the computer how to use the NIC.

Both the network software and the NIC have to adhere to a network protocol, which is a set of standards for communication. A **network protocol** is like a language computers use for communicating data. For computers to share data, they must speak the same language.

As is often the case with computer technologies, protocols are in a continual state of flux. Whenever someone comes up with a new standard, someone else invents another that does the same job faster and more reliably. Today, the most common protocols used in networks are Ethernet, Token Ring, and ARCnet. Each of these is designed for a certain kind of network topology and has certain standard features.

Ethernet

Currently, **Ethernet** is the most common network protocol. Ethernet was originally designed for a bus topology and thick coaxial cable. More recent implementations have moved to the star topology and twisted-pair wires.

Ethernet requires each computer or workstation on the network to take its turn to send data. When a computer needs to send data to another computer or to a peripheral device, it must first check to see whether the network is available. If the network is in use by another node, it waits a tiny fraction of a second and tries again. If two nodes inadvertently transmit simultaneously, the conflict is detected and they retransmit one at a time. This approach to network communication is called

Connecting LANs using microwave requires a direct line of sight between the two antennas.

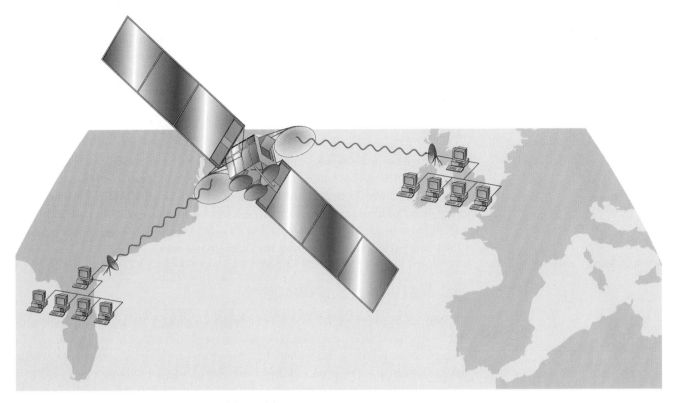

Satellites can be used to connect LANs around the world.

CSMA/CD (Carrier Sense Multiple Access/Collision Detection). As you might guess, when there are many computers on an Ethernet network, access time can become noticeably delayed.

The original implementations of Ethernet, which used coaxial cable, were called 10Base-5 and 10Base-2. The most popular implementation of Ethernet currently is called **10Base-T**. It uses a star topology and twisted-pair wires and can achieve transmission speeds up to 10 Mbps. 100Base-T, also known as Fast Ethernet, is available using the same media and topology, but different network interface cards are used to achieve speeds of up to 100 Mbps. Hewlett-Packard's 100Base-VG competes with 100Base-T. Still other implementations of Ethernet are pushing transmission speeds even higher.

Token Ring

IBM's network protocol is the **Token Ring**. The controlling hardware in a Token Ring network transmits an electronic token—a small set of data that includes an address—to each node on the network many times each second. If the token is not currently in use, a computer can copy data into the token and set the address to which the data should be sent. The token then continues around the ring. Each computer along the way looks at the address until the token reaches the computer with the address that was recorded in the token. The receiving computer then copies the contents of the token and resets the token status to empty.

Token Ring networks have the advantage of data traveling through the ring in one direction in a controlled manner. With this approach, data cannot

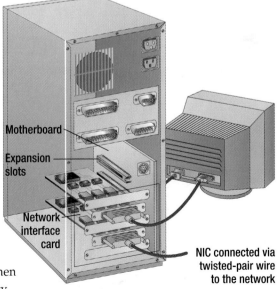

Motherboard

Expansion slots

Network interface card

NIC connected via twisted-pair wire to the network

The network interface card is an expansion board that plugs into an expansion slot. It contains a jack for connecting the network cable.

collide, so a complex scheme like CSMA/CD is not necessary. However, the network hardware is not cheap: Token-ring adapter cards can cost as much as five times more than other types of network adapters. Token Ring networks once operated at either 4 or 16 Mbits per second, but, as with Ethernet, new technology has pushed the transmission rate up to 100 Mbits per second.

ARCnet

ARCnet (Attached Resource Computer network) has both a topology and protocol all its own. ARCnet uses either twisted-pair wire or coaxial cable, and the star topology is formed with hubs attached to the network. The original ARCnet protocol was very slow, but it became popular because it was inexpensive, reliable, and easy to set up and to expand. Fast ARCnet, like Fast Ethernet, increased the transmission rate to 100 Mbits per second and includes the ability to use fiber-optic cable.

▶ NETWORK SOFTWARE

Most of the networking terms you have seen so far—with the exception of the protocols discussed in the previous section—have referred to hardware. As with every other part of the computer system, however, there must be software to control the hardware. The group of programs that manages the resources on the network is often called the **network operating system**, or **NOS**.

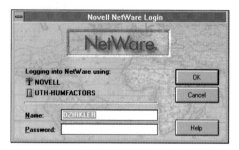

FIGURE 5.19

The Novell NetWare Login dialog box.

The most popular NOS, NetWare, from Novell, can be used to run networks with different protocols, including Ethernet, Token Ring, and ARCnet. NetWare also includes support for various hardware platforms, such as Mac, PC, and UNIX nodes and servers. The Novell NetWare Login dialog box is shown in Figure 5.19.

One of NetWare's competitors, Banyan's VINES, offers similar flexibility. Some other NOSs, such as Windows NT Server, DECNet, LANtastic, and AppleShare are designed to implement specific network protocols on specific types of machines.

▶ DATA COMMUNICATION OVER TELEPHONE LINES

Network hardware and software offer a way to establish ongoing data communication, generally over media (twisted-pair wire, coaxial cable, fiber-optic cable, and so forth) specifically set up for the network and known as *dedicated* media. The alternative to using dedicated media is to use the telephone system for data communication. This is possible because the telephone system is really just a giant electronic network owned by the telephone companies.

Although it is designed to carry two-way electronic information, the network of telephone lines is significantly different than a typical computer network. Remember, the phone system was originally designed to carry voice messages, which are analog signals. Increasingly, however, phone lines are being used to send digital data.

The reason for this trend is simple. By connecting your computer to the telephone, potentially you can send data to anyone else in the world who has a computer and telephone service, and you do not need to set up a network to do it. You simply pay the phone company for the time you spend connected to the other computer. This trend has important implications for users as well as for phone companies. Typically, the analog lines that carry voice signals are not very well suited for carrying data because the limit for transmission speeds over analog lines is only about .005 as fast as a 10Base-T Ethernet network. As a result, the phone companies now offer digital lines that are specifically designed for data communication.

Soon after the introduction of the PC, users recognized the value of trading data and software over telephone lines. In response to this user demand, Hayes Microcomputer Products, Inc. developed the first modem for personal computers, the Smartmodem. Introduced in 1978, the modem connected a computer to a standard telephone line and allowed the transmission of data. This technological innovation started an explosion of digital connectivity for both businesses and individual users.

Hayes created the first modem for personal computers in 1978. It transmitted data at about .01 the speed of today's modems.

◤ MODEMS

Although digital telephone lines are gaining popularity, most people still have analog phone lines attached to their homes and businesses. Attaching a computer to an analog phone line requires a modem, so it is important to know a few things about how modems work and what to look for when you buy one.

How a Modem Works

In standard phone service, a telephone converts the sound of your voice into an electric signal that flows through the phone wires. The telephone at the other end converts this electric signal back into sound, so that the person you are talking to can hear your voice. Both the sound wave and the telephone signal are analog signals—they vary continuously with the volume and pitch of the speakers' voices. Since a computer's "voice" is digital—consisting of on/off pulses representing 1s and 0s—the device called a **modem** (short for *mo*dulator-*dem*odulator) is needed to translate these digital signals into analog signals that can travel over standard phone lines. In its modulation phase, the modem turns the computer's digital signals into analog signals. In its demodulation phase, the reverse takes place. Figure 5.20 shows how computers communicate through modems and a phone connection.

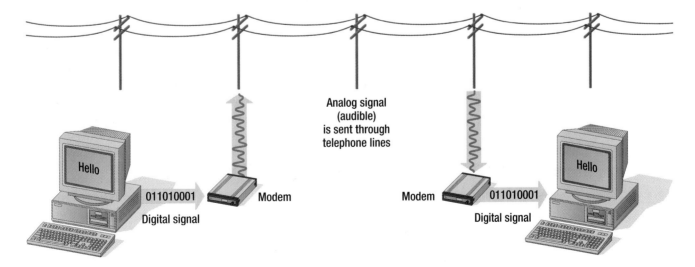

FIGURE 5.20
How modems connect computers through telephone lines.

Choosing a Modem

A modem can be a simple circuit board—an expansion card—that plugs into one of the PC's expansion slots, or it can be an external device that plugs into a serial port.

Choosing a modem is far from simple. The modem industry, like the computer telecommunications industry in general, is plagued by a very bad case of alphabet soup addiction—a dizzying array of specifications, acronyms, and numbers that can confuse even the most experienced computer users. Terms such as V.22, V.32, V.32bis, V.34bis, V.34, V.42bis, CCITT, MNP4, and MNP5 are just a few that you will encounter. This confusion is due to the proliferation of new standards—telecommunications technology improves so swiftly that companies continually develop products that exceed the capabilities of existing ones.

When you buy a modem, there are four areas to consider:

- Transmission speed
- Data compression
- Error correction
- Internal versus external

By far the most important consideration is the transmission speed. With early modems, transmission speed was measured in baud rate, a measure of how fast the signal could modulate. However, the correct way to measure how fast data is transmitted is **bits per second**, or **bps**. Today, if you see a modem that lists a baud rate, it is really just a misnomer for bps.

The first modems transmitted data at 300 bps, then evolved to 1200 bps and 2400 bps. Then, the makers of modems found ways to build data compression capabilities into their modems. **Data compression** uses mathematical algorithms to analyze groups of bits and represent them with shorter groups of bits. It soon became obvious that standards were necessary so that modems could understand the data compression schemes used by other modems. The first standard was called V.32, and it achieved transmission speeds of 9600 bps—four times the speed of a 2400 bps modem. A subsequent standard called V.32bis enabled modems to transmit at 14,400 bps. Following that came the V.34 standard, which allowed for a 28,800 bps transmission rate.

With modem communications, when bits per second are large numbers, they are abbreviated Kbps, which stands for 1000 bits per second. Thus, 14,400 bps is abbreviated 14.4 Kbps. Today, 28.8 Kbps is the preferred standard for modems, especially among people who communicate over the Internet. Generally, you want your modem transmission speed to be as high as possible. Of course, with a fast modem, you can still connect to any slower modem—a fast modem just gives you the option to go faster when you can.

When computers communicate through telephone lines, data moves through the line so quickly that even the smallest amount of static can introduce significant errors. Noise you could not hear if you were using the telephone line for a conversation can wreak havoc with computer data. As a result, modems and communications software use **error-correction protocols** to recover from transmission errors.

When you purchase a modem, you will generally find the error-correction protocols listed. The common ones are MNP2, MNP3, MNP4, MNP5, and V.42bis, which incor-

This is an external modem from U. S. Robotics. On the back are connections for attaching it to the computer, a telephone jack, and a telephone. There is also a plug for a power cord, because external modems require their own power supply.

porates the MNP protocols. Nearly all commercially available modems incorporate these standards, so consumers rarely need to concern themselves with the error-correction protocols supported by a particular modem.

One other issue to consider when buying a modem is whether to buy an internal or external modem. An **external modem** is a box that houses the modem's circuitry outside the computer. It connects to the computer through a serial port and to the telephone system with a standard telephone jack. An **internal modem** is a circuit board that plugs into one of the computer's expansion slots. An internal modem saves desktop space but occupies an expansion slot.

Modems also come in the form of a PC card for use with laptop computers. Some use standard phone lines, but others include a cellular phone, which enables completely wireless transmissions.

Most modems used with personal computers can also emulate a fax machine. Called **fax modems**, these devices can exchange faxes with any other fax modem or fax machine. With the proper software, users can convert incoming fax files into files that can be edited with a word processor—something that stand-alone fax machines cannot do.

Telephone jacks

An internal modem plugs into one of the computer's expansion slots. When it is installed, all you can see is the metal edge with the two telephone jacks. One jack is used to attach the modem to the telephone jack on the wall. The other can be used to connect a telephone, so you can still use the telephone line for calls, even though the line goes through the modem.

Connecting with a Modem

A computer that is equipped with a modem and connected to a standard telephone line can dial up and communicate with any other computer that has a modem and a telephone connection. These are some common uses for data communication over the phone lines:

■ Direct connections with other users
■ Connections with office LANs
■ Connections with BBSs, online services, and the Internet

This notebook computer is equipped with a modem in the form of a PC card. The modem comes equipped with a cellular unit, so the user can log into a network without using a phone line.

Direct Connections with Other Users

Suppose you are writing an article on commercial fishing in Puget Sound. Before you submit the article to *Field and Stream*, you want a friend to read what you have written. At first, you consider printing out the article, finding an envelope and stamps, and going to the post office to mail it. Fortunately, you remember that your friend has a computer and a modem, so it would be much easier to send the article electronically. You call your friend and explain that you want to modem the file. This is the process for sending it:

1. You launch the software that controls your modem.
2. You enter your friend's phone number, and your computer dials the number.
3. Your friend's computer picks up the line, and the two computers establish a connection through the two modems.
4. You use your modem software to send the file to your friend's computer.
5. You tell your computer to hang up the phone.

Modems can be used to connect your computer to a friend's computer.

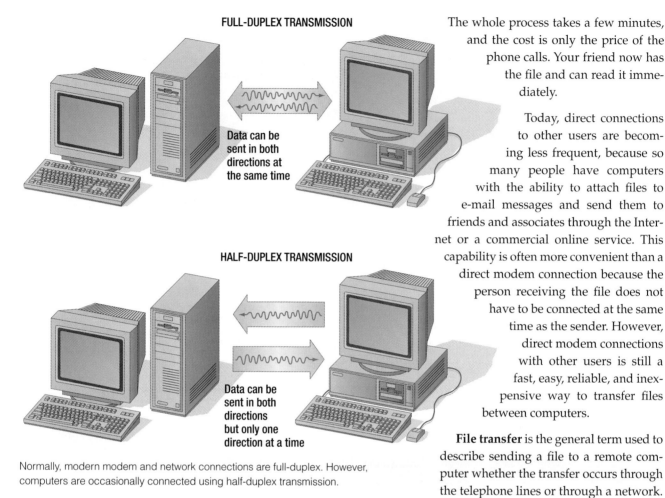

FULL-DUPLEX TRANSMISSION

Data can be sent in both directions at the same time

HALF-DUPLEX TRANSMISSION

Data can be sent in both directions but only one direction at a time

Normally, modern modem and network connections are full-duplex. However, computers are occasionally connected using half-duplex transmission.

The whole process takes a few minutes, and the cost is only the price of the phone calls. Your friend now has the file and can read it immediately.

Today, direct connections to other users are becoming less frequent, because so many people have computers with the ability to attach files to e-mail messages and send them to friends and associates through the Internet or a commercial online service. This capability is often more convenient than a direct modem connection because the person receiving the file does not have to be connected at the same time as the sender. However, direct modem connections with other users is still a fast, easy, reliable, and inexpensive way to transfer files between computers.

File transfer is the general term used to describe sending a file to a remote computer whether the transfer occurs through the telephone lines or through a network. The act of sending a file to another user or to a network is known as **uploading** the file. Copying a file from a remote computer is known as **downloading** the file. For a file to be transferred from one computer to another through a pair of modems, both computers must use the same **File Transfer Protocol (FTP)**—the set of rules or guidelines that dictates the format in which data will be sent. The most common File Transfer Protocols for modems are called Kermit, Xmodem, Ymodem, and Zmodem.

One of the important functions of the File Transfer Protocol is to check for errors as a file is being sent. Normally, modem communication is **full-duplex**, which means data can travel in both directions at the same time. Sometimes, however, modem communication can be **half-duplex**, which means that data can be sent in both directions but only one direction at a time. In either type of communication, the receiving computer can respond to the sender and verify that the data it received contained no errors. If there are errors, the computer sending the data retransmits whatever portion is incorrect. Each File Transfer Protocol uses its own method to check for errors. Some are more efficient than others and therefore can transmit data faster.

Connections with Office Networks

These days, more and more people are **telecommuting**, working at home or on the road and using telecommunications equipment—telephones, modems, fax machines, and so forth—to stay in touch with the office.

The advantages of telecommuting over working in an office can be compelling. The telecommuter is spared the time and expense of traveling to work. This savings can include gas, automobile maintenance (or the cost of riding the bus or train), and sometimes the cost of insurance. As more workers telecommute, traffic congestion and air pollution are somewhat alleviated. Many companies and employees also find that telecommuters are more productive, presumably because there are fewer distractions at home during the day. As a result, many companies have instituted programs that encourage employees to work from home during part of the week.

For the telecommuter, setting up a home office almost always requires a computer and a modem. With the right software, the home user can then dial into the office network and upload or download files at any time. Dialing into the network has the same effect as logging onto it at the office, except that transmitting files takes place more slowly. The home office computer should also be able to act as a fax machine unless the user has a stand-alone fax machine and a separate phone line for it. Finally, many people with home offices find it necessary to buy a copier.

Home offices now have access to multifunctional machines, such as this model from Panasonic, which can act as a printer, copier, fax machine, and scanner.

▶ USING DIGITAL TELEPHONE LINES

As you learned in the modem section, standard telephone lines transmit analog signals, in which sound is translated into an electrical current. As a result, you need a modem to translate data into a form that can be sent over the phone lines. In addition, telephone lines operate at about 3100 Hz, which means that data has to be compressed to travel at more than about 2400 bps. Data compression has become quite sophisticated, so modems can often transmit data at rates as high as 56 Kbps (56,000 bps). Nevertheless, this can create a severe bandwidth bottleneck, considering that typical network transmission speeds are at least 10 Mbps (10,000,000 bps)—about 200 times as fast.

The phone companies recognized this problem a number of years ago and began the long process of converting an analog system into a digital system. The massive data channels that connect major geographical regions are already digital, but the phone lines running under or above most city streets are still analog. This combination of digital and analog lines makes for an extremely confusing system, especially when you are transmitting data through a modem.

However, when the phone companies complete the transition and digital lines are installed to every building, the data transmission system will be a lot simpler.

The transformation from analog to digital lines will affect most users in three simple ways:

1. You will need a different phone—a digital one that translates your voice into bits rather than an analog signal.
2. You will not need a modem to send data. Instead, you will use an adapter that simply reformats the data so that it can travel through the phone lines.
3. You will be able to send data much more quickly.

ISDN, T1, and T3

There are many different kinds of digital service that are offered by the phone companies. The best known are called ISDN, T1, and T3.

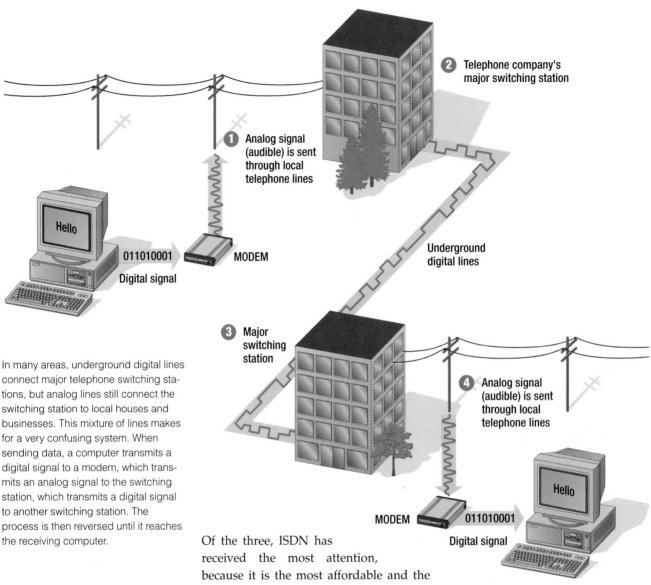

① Analog signal (audible) is sent through local telephone lines

② Telephone company's major switching station

Digital signal

011010001

MODEM

Underground digital lines

③ Major switching station

④ Analog signal (audible) is sent through local telephone lines

MODEM

011010001

Digital signal

Hello

Hello

In many areas, underground digital lines connect major telephone switching stations, but analog lines still connect the switching station to local houses and businesses. This mixture of lines makes for a very confusing system. When sending data, a computer transmits a digital signal to a modem, which transmits an analog signal to the switching station, which transmits a digital signal to another switching station. The process is then reversed until it reaches the receiving computer.

Of the three, ISDN has received the most attention, because it is the most affordable and the one most likely to make its way into homes and small businesses. **ISDN**, which stands for **Integrated Services Digital Network**, is a system that replaces all analog services with digital services.

When most people talk about ISDN, they are referring to a particular level of service called BRI (Basic Rate ISDN). BRI provides three communication channels on one line—two 64 or 56 Kbps data channels and one 19 Kbps channel that is used to set up and control calls. The two data channels can carry voice or data, and they can be used simultaneously, so you can transmit data and carry on a conversation at the same time on the same line. Also, the channels can be combined so that BRI service can be used to transmit data at rates as high as 128 Kbps without compression.

Some phone companies now offer BRI service in some locations especially in large metropolitan areas. Installation can be expensive, but the cost of service is slowly coming down to compete with the basic rates offered for analog lines.

A higher level of service for ISDN is called Primary Rate ISDN, or PRI. In this country, PRI provides 24 channels at 64 Kbps each, a total bandwidth of 1.544 Mbps. This

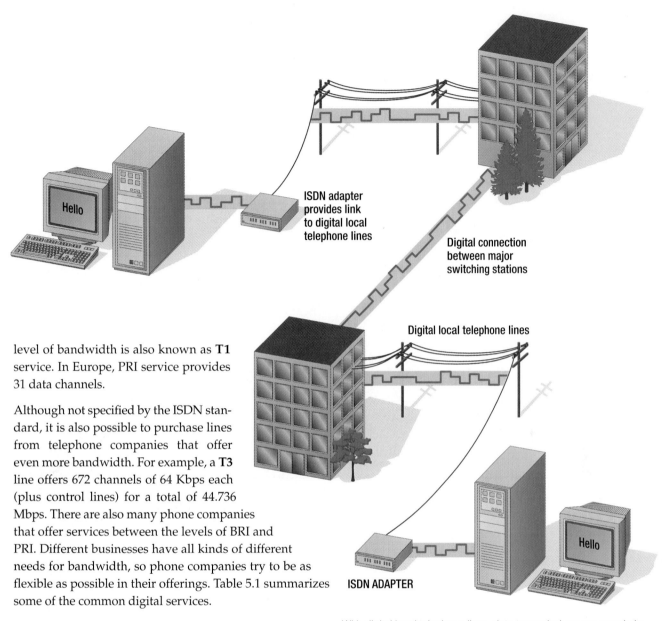

ISDN adapter provides link to digital local telephone lines

Digital connection between major switching stations

Digital local telephone lines

ISDN ADAPTER

level of bandwidth is also known as **T1** service. In Europe, PRI service provides 31 data channels.

Although not specified by the ISDN standard, it is also possible to purchase lines from telephone companies that offer even more bandwidth. For example, a **T3** line offers 672 channels of 64 Kbps each (plus control lines) for a total of 44.736 Mbps. There are also many phone companies that offer services between the levels of BRI and PRI. Different businesses have all kinds of different needs for bandwidth, so phone companies try to be as flexible as possible in their offerings. Table 5.1 summarizes some of the common digital services.

With digital local telephone lines, data transmissions can remain in a digital format all the way from the sending computer to the receiving computer.

ATM

ISDN, T1, and T3 can all be used effectively to set up WANs, as long as the networks are used primarily for transferring the most common types of data—files, e-mail messages, and so on. However, these types of services are not well suited for transmitting live video and sound. As a result, phone companies are beginning to offer a service called ATM, which stands for **Asynchronous Transfer Mode**.

ATM is a protocol designed by the telecommunications industry as a more efficient way to send voice, video, and computer data over a single network. It was originally conceived as a way to reconcile the needs for these different kinds of data on the telephone system, but the proponents of ATM argue that it can be implemented on computer LANs and WANs, as well. In fact, ATM is a network protocol—and therefore is similar to Ethernet and Token Ring.

TABLE 5.1

Digital Telephone Services

TYPE OF SERVICE	SPEEDS AVAILABLE	DESCRIPTION
ISDN	BRI = 128 Kbps PRI = 1.544 Mbps	BRI is a dial-up digital service, called *dial-up* because the line is open only when you make a call. Service is relatively inexpensive, but user pays for usage and long distance. PRI is a continuous, or dedicated, connection.
T1	1.544 Mbps	Can refer to several types of service, including ISDN PRI and private, leased lines between two points (usually to form a WAN).
T3	44.736 Mbps	Service equivalent to 28 T1 lines. Requires that fiber-optic cable be installed.
Frame Relay	Many speeds avail., from 56 Kbps up to 1.536 Mbps.	A fast, packet-switching technology. Signal is carried to a frame relay circuit at the phone company's branch office. Groups of data are encapsulated in packets and forwarded to their destination. Frame relay service typically implies a permanent virtual circuit between two points (usually to form a WAN). However, frame relay switches can also be used with dial-up, ISDN lines.
SMDS	Many speeds, from 1.17 Mbps up to 34 Mbps	Switched Multimegabit Digital Service. Another fast, packet-switching technology, similar to frame relay service but catering to higher-end users.
ATM Cell Relay	51.84 Mbps up to about 10,000 Mbps now, with higher speeds in the future.	Yet another switching technology. Because it is fast, flexible, and very well suited for all types of data (including sound and video), ATM may become the technology used in the backbones connecting telephone company branch offices.

ATM is one of the technologies that the telecommunications industry is examining for contributing to what is popularly known as the **information superhighway**, a worldwide network that will be capable of supporting high-bandwidth data communication to virtually every home, school, and business.

To understand the significance of ATM, you need to think about how most telephone lines work. With a **circuit-switched** line, you call a number, the phone system connects you, and you have complete access to that connection until you hang up. This arrangement is vastly different than most computer networks, which transmit packets of data and are therefore referred to as **packet-switched** systems. In circuit-switched lines, you and the person at the other end of the line have a fixed amount of bandwidth available. Even if you do not say anything to each other—or in the case of modem transmission, if you do not send any data, the bandwidth is still available.

This type of communication can be inefficient, because data communication tends to be erratic. For example, consider two office LANs, connected using the telephone system. Every few minutes, a person in one office might send a file to a person in another office. During this time—maybe just a few seconds—the necessary bandwidth is very high. During the remaining time, however, no bandwidth is required at all. Yet the phone line remains active, reserving the same amount of bandwidth.

Clearly, voice and data have different bandwidth requirements. Other types of communication, such as transmission of a digital video signal, have still different types of requirements. ATM addresses the needs of different kinds of communication by

E-mail has become the combination letter/phone call/appointment/ meeting/ social get-together of the computer age. E-mail is popular largely because of its reputation for informality and wit, but there still exists a standard etiquette expected in e-mail communication. Here are a few beginning guidelines.

Keep It Simple

Remember that e-mail may arrive on a very wide variety of computers. Any extended ASCII characters in your e-mail message may come through garbled, or not at all.

Watch Your Language

Your message will be better received if it is written in grammatically clear, concise, articulate language, even though this aspect of e-mail is sometimes ignored in favor of speed and informality. Complete sentences are not necessary, but try to think through your message ahead of time to some degree, and then write. No one likes to wade through lines of rambling, incoherent thought.

Need to Know Basis

Send your message only to the specific person(s) who need to know the information, not to everybody in your office. Similarly, send ccs (carbon copies) only to those who really need copies. Unneeded messages are the equivalent of "junk mail" and can be annoying.

Don't Yell

In e-mail manners, writing a message in all capital letters is the equivalent of shouting. Consequently, capitals should be used sparingly—never just for emphasis.

Be Careful with Emotional Outbursts

In general, e-mail is not the best medium for heated, emotional communication. The conversational style of e-mail can lead you to believe that you are talking to someone online, but an e-mail conversation is different from a person-to-person conversation. Stripped of the context, body language, tone and facial expressions of usual conversation, e-mail can be interpreted more intensely.

Short and Sweet

Think "postcard" rather than "letter" and keep your messages short. Unlike postal "snail mail," for which the writer pays the cost of delivery, recipients often must pay online charges to receive e-mail. A long message can be both boring and expensive. Because e-mail messages are characteristically short, abbreviations, or acronyms, are commonplace. Here are a few you can use to shorten your e-mail communications.

Here is an example of e-mail done in Lotus cc:Mail for the World Wide Web.

Common E-mail Acronyms

ACRONYM	TRANSLATION
BTW	By the way
FWIW	For what it's worth
FYI	For your information
g	Grin—usually in brackets or angles \<g\> or [g]
gd&h	Grinning, ducking, and hiding
gd&r	Grinning, ducking, and running
gd&r,vvf	Grinning, ducking, and running, very very fast
IMO	In my opinion
IMHO	In my humble opinion
LOL	Laughing out loud
NOYB	None of your business
OTL	Out to lunch
OTOH	On the other hand
PMFJI	Pardon me for jumping in
PTB	Powers that be
ROTFL	Rolling on the floor laughing
TANJ	There ain't no justice
TANSTAAFL	There ain't no such thing as a free lunch
TIA	Thanks in advance
TIC	Tongue in cheek
WOA	Work of art
WYSIWYG	What you see is what you get

Keep It Light

E-mail is known for its lightness and wit. When reading mail on the big online services, you may see some strange sets of characters in messages, such as :-).

These are called "emoticons," or emotional icons. They are often used to convey light-heartedness and humor. Emoticons were originally used on the early mainframe computer systems when everything was text-based, and it was not possible to display graphics. They are still widely used in e-mail communications, even though modern e-mail programs often have graphical emoticons.

Emoticons are used to express feelings or to describe yourself in e-mail communications. Self-descriptive emoticons are used especially over the Internet where you often never meet the recipients of your correspondence in person and want to tell them a little about yourself.

Common E-mail Emoticons

EMOTICON	TRANSLATION
;-)	I don't believe it!
(:-)	Smiley big-face
:-'I	User has a cold
:-)8	User is well-dressed
:-o	User is shocked
:-Y	A quiet aside
:-W	Speak with a forked tongue
:I	Not funny!
{}	No comment
:-(	Sad
:~-(	Crying
#-)	Partied all night
%+{	Lost a fight
%-(l)	Laughing out loud
%-6	Braindead
:-#	User's lips are sealed.
l-)	User is asleep/bored

providing different kinds of connections and bandwidth on demand. Rather than reserving a fixed amount of bandwidth whether data is being transmitted or not, an ATM network transmits packets, known as cells, that include information about where they should go, what type of data is included, and what order the packets should follow. Cells can be sent in clumps, by different routes if necessary, even out of order (since the packet includes enough information to put the data back into proper order). Unlike standard phone transmission, which is based on circuit switching, ATM is based on cell switching.

Because the volume of cells being transmitted can vary with the bandwidth of the incoming signal, ATM is considered an ideal way to combine voice, data, and video transmission on the same high-bandwidth network. As a result, it is one of the most widely used industry buzzwords of the decade. Whether it will capture the telecommunications and data communications industries, however, is yet to be determined.

▶ WHAT TO EXPECT IN THE FUTURE

It is probably safe to say that networking and data communications is the future of computing. Currently we are witnessing a race toward global connectivity, with progress being made on almost every front:

- Networking technology is growing more sophisticated, and transmission speeds are increasing rapidly.
- All of the telecommunications industries—telephone companies, cable companies, Internet service providers, online services, and so on—are working to offer high bandwidth to homes and businesses.

The last point is especially notable. Both the consumers of information and the telecommunications industry are rushing toward the common goal of massive connectivity. Each group sees a future where bandwidth will be cheap so that people can stay in touch no matter where they are, and the variety of available information will be virtually unlimited.

In the middle of all this enthusiasm, however, there is a missing link that some people find frightening and others find truly enchanting. People want connectivity, and the telecommunications industry wants to sell it to them, but people do not want to pay much just for bandwidth. They are only going to pay for information.

Well, what kind of information will people pay for? The more pessimistic pundits predict "500 channels and nothing on." Perhaps even worse, they see "infoglut," a world so saturated with information that it will be almost impossible to find the information you want.

On the other hand, the situation offers almost boundless opportunities for creative entrepreneurs with the vision to predict accurately and then supply the kinds of information for which people will pay.

▶ VISUAL SUMMARY

The Uses of a Network

- Networks allow users simultaneous access to shared programs and data.
- Networks also allow users to share peripheral devices, such as printers and hard disks, and thereby prolong the usable life of many machines.
- Networks usually include the ability to send e-mail, and many e-mail systems let users attach files to their messages.
- Some networks also aid communication by providing tools for teleconferencing and video conferencing.
- Connecting computers to form a network makes it easier to perform backups of the data on all the networked hard disks.

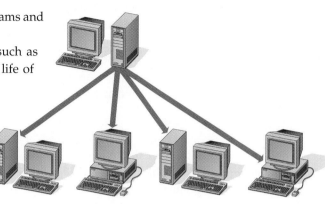

Categories of Networks

- LANs connect computers that are relatively close together, while WANs join multiple LANs that are spread over a large geographical area.
- LANs are connected using bridges, routers, and gateways.
- Nodes and a file server can be connected to create file server, client/server, and peer-to-peer networks.

Network Topologies for LANs

- The physical layout of a LAN is known as the topology.
- LAN topologies can be a bus, star, or ring.

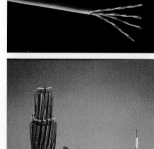

Network Media and Hardware

- The three most common wires used to connect computers are twisted-pair wires, coaxial cable, and fiber-optic cable.
- Increasingly, computers also communicate through wireless links; the most common types are cellular and microwave links.
- In addition to the media that connect the computers in a network, each computer also needs a network interface card.
- To communicate directly, the computers in a network must also use the same network protocol, the language used to communicate data.
- The most common network protocols are Ethernet, Token Ring, and ARCnet.

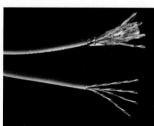

Network Software

- The software that manages the resources on a network is called the network operating system, or NOS.
- The most popular NOS is NetWare, from Novell.

Data Communications Over Telephone Lines

■ Increasingly, phone lines are being used to send digital data, because the phone system is, in effect, a pre-existing network connecting a vast number of people around the world.

■ In 1978, Hayes Microcomputer Products, Inc., introduced the first modem that allowed PC users to transmit data through a standard phone line.

Modems

■ A modem is used to translate the computer's digital signals into analog signals that can travel over standard phone lines; a modem attached to the receiving computer translates the analog signal back into a digital one.

■ The most important consideration in choosing a modem is the speed at which it can send data, but other important considerations are the data compression and error-correction techniques it uses, and whether the modem is internal or external.

Digital Telephone Lines

■ Analog phone lines are slow and not well suited for sending data, so telephone companies have gradually been switching to digital service.

■ The best known type of digital service is called ISDN.

■ ISDN service is available in many urban areas, with the lowest-level service, BRI, providing a bandwidth of 128 Kbps.

■ T1 and T3 offer higher bandwidth: 1.544 Mbps and 44.736 Mbps, respectively.

■ The hottest buzzword in the telecommunications industry today is ATM, which promises a system designed to meet the needs of transmitting voice, data, and video data.

▶ KEY TERMS

After completing this chapter, you should be able to define the following terms:

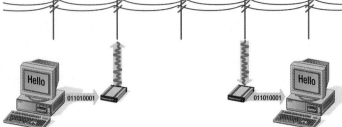

10Base-T, 147	Ethernet, 146	internal modem, 151
ARCnet, 148	external modem, 151	local area network (LAN), 135
Asynchronous Transfer Mode (ATM), 155	fax modem, 151	modem, 149
bandwidth, 144	fiber-optic cable, 145	network, 130
bits per second (bps), 150	file server, 133	network interface card (NIC), 146
bridge, 138	file server network, 140	network operating system (NOS), 148
bus network, 142	file transfer, 152	network protocol, 146
circuit-switched, 156	File Transfer Protocol (FTP), 152	network server, 133
client/server, 140	frame, 137	network versions, 130
coaxial cable (coax), 144	full-duplex, 152	nodes, 140
data communications, 129	gateway, 138	online, 130
data compression, 150	groupware, 132	packet, 137
distributed computing, 141	half-duplex, 152	packet-switched, 156
downloading, 152	information superhighway, 156	payload, 138
electronic mail (e-mail), 133	Integrated Services Digital Network (ISDN), 154	peer-to-peer network, 141
error-correction protocols, 150		ring topology, 143

▶ KEY TERM QUIZ

Fill in the missing word with one of the terms listed in Key Terms:

1. A system for transmitting written messages through a network is known as _____.

2. A(n) _____ is a network of computers that serves users located relatively near each other.

3. You can connect computers together to communicate and exchange information using a(n) _____.

4. The physical layout of the wires that connect the nodes of the network is the _____.

5. Copying a file from a remote computer is called _____.

6. A(n) _____ is a central computer that includes a large disk-storage device on a LAN.

7. The group of programs that manages the resources on the network is known as the _____.

8. A unit of measurement indicating how fast data is transmitted is called _____.

9. _____ are the individual computers on a network.

10. The act of sending a file to another user or to a network is called _____.

▶ REVIEW QUESTIONS

1. List and describe briefly the benefits that networks provide.
2. How do networks help businesses save money?
3. How does groupware benefit users? Name and describe briefly at least three of its components.
4. Describe how an e-mail system emulates the postal system and a telephone-answering system.
5. List and describe briefly the four types of data communications media that link networks.
6. How is access time affected in an Ethernet network that links many computers?
7. List and describe the three most common network protocols.
8. Describe what takes place during a modem's demodulation phase.
9. What aspects should you consider when purchasing a modem?
10. Describe the ways in which replacing analog phone lines with digital phone lines will simplify data communications.

▶ DISCUSSION QUESTIONS

1. Describe at least two ways in which video conferencing can save money for businesses.
2. Does a business save money by encouraging employees to telecommute? Despite the convenience aspects discussed in the chapter, are there any negative aspects to conducting business in this manner?
3. Suppose a significant part of your job requires sending and receiving large-sized graphic files to different locations. What kind of features, hardware, and specifications should you consider in setting up a home office to handle this aspect of your job?
4. In what significant ways does asynchronous transfer mode affect data communications? Describe some possible changes people are likely to see over the next ten years, if ATM is implemented widely on the information superhighway.

NORTON INTERACTIVE

Complete the Norton Interactive module for this chapter.

PART II

USING MICROCOMPUTER SOFTWARE

THE OPERATING SYSTEM AND THE USER INTERFACE

CONTENTS

OBJECTIVES

When you complete this chapter, you will be able to do the following:

- Define operating system.
- Explain the importance of the user interface.
- Discuss other major functions of the operating system, such as managing hardware and managing files.
- Understand how utility software supports the operating system.
- Define multitasking and explain how it saves time for a user.
- Review the important Microsoft operating systems, starting with MS-DOS.
- List other significant operating systems, such as the Macintosh operating system, UNIX, and OS/2.

On August 24, 1995, Microsoft Corporation founder and CEO Bill Gates stepped up to the podium at Microsoft headquarters in Redmond, Washington, and announced that Microsoft Windows 95 was beginning to ship to customers. Within four days the first million copies had already gone out. It was the biggest product announcement in the history of computers—notifying the public of a new operating system.

What is an operating system? Why should a user be familiar with the operating system? What is the Windows 95 operating system? How could the announcement of an operating system be what many considered to be "a shot heard 'round the world" for computers?

In this chapter, you will explore the operating system—what it does for you as you work and what it does in the background with other programs and hardware. You will look at the evolution of operating systems from Microsoft, the operating system leader. Then you will briefly review some of the other players in the operating system game: IBM's OS/2, Apple Computer's Macintosh operating system, and UNIX (originally developed by AT&T). In the Norton Workshop section at the end of the chapter, you will see how operating systems are used to manage files, load programs, and perform multitasking operations.

▶ WHAT IS AN OPERATING SYSTEM?

An **operating system (OS)** is a software program, but it is different from word processing programs, spreadsheets, and all the other software programs on your computer. It is the master control program.

The release of Windows 95 turned out to be a huge media event. Here, Bill Gates addresses the crowd.

When you turn on a computer, the machine looks for an operating system to "boot" (jargon for "pull itself up by its bootstraps") before it runs any other programs. Once the OS starts up, it takes charge until you shut down the computer. The operating system performs the following functions:

■ Provides the instructions to display the on screen elements with which you interact. Collectively, these elements are known as the **user interface**.
■ Loads programs (such as word processing and spreadsheet programs) into the computer's memory so you can use them.
■ Coordinates how programs work with the CPU (central processing unit), keyboard, mouse, printer, and other hardware as well as with other software.
■ Manages the way information is stored on and retrieved from disks.

Also, the functionality of the OS can be extended with the addition of utility software.

▶ THE USER INTERFACE

When you start an operating system, the on screen items you see and interact with are defined as the user interface. In the case of most current operating systems, including Windows 95 and the Macintosh OS, the user interface looks like a collection of objects on a colored background. Figure 6.1 shows what you see when you start a computer running Windows 95.

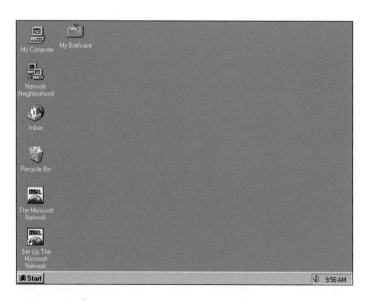

FIGURE 6.1
The screen you see when you start Windows 95.

Note: Most of the screens in this chapter show Windows 95 because it is currently the best-selling operating system for IBM-type computers. However, the concepts discussed and the terms defined in the first half of this chapter apply equally well to earlier versions of Windows, the Mac OS, OS/2, and to most versions of UNIX (except where specifically noted).

Parts of the Interface

Figure 6.2 shows the Windows 95 interface with the Start menu open, a program running and a dialog box. These features are discussed in the sections that follow.

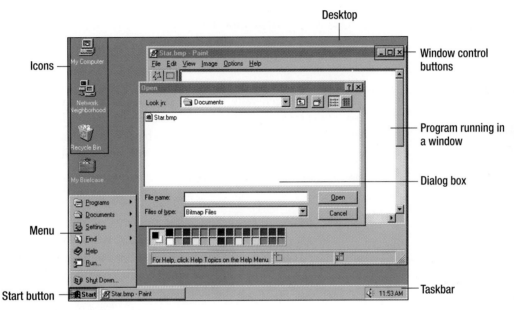

FIGURE 6.2
Common features of the operating system.

The Desktop

Software makers call the colored area you see on screen the **desktop**, because they want you to think of it just as the surface of a desk. The pictures, too, stand for things you might have in your office—in the case of Windows, a Recycle Bin, an Inbox, and a Briefcase. These pictures are called **icons**, a word that means *image*.

Because you point at graphics on the screen, programmers sometimes refer to the interface as a **graphical user interface**, or **GUI** (pronounced "gooey"). People also refer to it as a point-and-click interface, because you use a mouse to point at on screen objects and then click on them. Apple Computer introduced the first successful GUI with its Macintosh computer in 1984.

To do things on the desktop, you control the icons using the mouse and its on screen pointer. Sometimes you simply point at the icons; sometimes you click on them once; sometimes you double-click (click twice in rapid succession). Sometimes you slide an icon across the desktop by moving the mouse while holding down a mouse button—an operation known as dragging.

Icons

Icons represent the parts of the computer you work with—printers, fonts, document files, folders (a way to organize files into logical groups), disk drives, etc. Software

Each of these icons represents programs that you can launch from the Start menu in Windows 95.

FIGURE 6.3
The Start button.

designers try to make the icons look like what they represent, so it is easy to identify the icon you need.

There are fairly consistent rules for using the mouse to interact with icons.

- You click once on an icon to **select** it. That indicates you plan to work with it.
- You double-click on an icon to **choose**, or **activate**, it. For instance, you double-click on the icon of a word processing program to load that program into memory and start using it.
- If you click on an icon and hold down the mouse button, you can drag the mouse to move the icon to another location on the desktop. Sometimes you drag an icon to another icon to perform an action. For instance, you drag an icon for a file to the Recycle Bin to delete the file.
- If you right-click on many parts of the desktop, you will see a shortcut menu containing the most common commands associated with that part.

Although icons generally look like what they represent, another class of symbols, called buttons, generally look the same from program to program. **Buttons** are areas of the screen you can click to cause something to happen. Most buttons have a name or icon (or both) surrounded by a black border. The Start button in Figure 6.3 is one such button. When you click on it, you cause the Start menu to appear.

The Taskbar and the Start Button

Whenever you start a program in Windows 95, a button for it appears on the **Taskbar**—an area at the bottom of the screen whose purpose is to hold and display the buttons for the programs you are running. When you have multiple programs running, you can shift from one to the other by clicking on a program's button on the Taskbar, as shown in Figures 6.4 and 6.5. The program in the foreground with the highlighted button in the Taskbar is called the **active program**.

Excel is on top, ready to be used, and its button is highlighted in the Taskbar.

Word is in the background, and its button in the Taskbar is not highlighted.

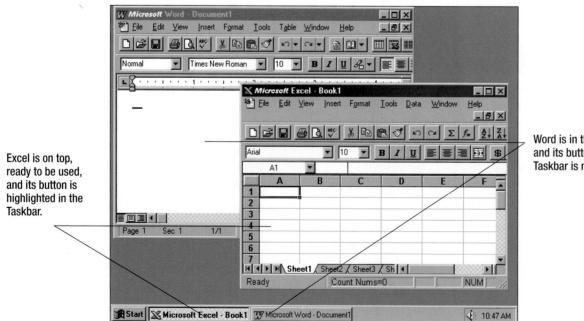

FIGURE 6.4
Two programs running, Excel is active.

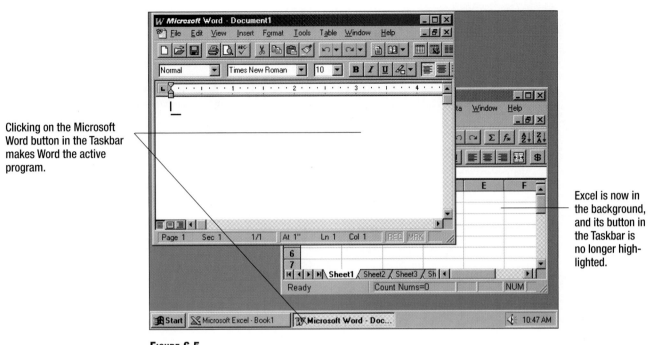

Clicking on the Microsoft Word button in the Taskbar makes Word the active program.

Excel is now in the background, and its button in the Taskbar is no longer highlighted.

FIGURE 6.5
Two programs running, Word is active.

The **Start button** is a permanent feature of the Taskbar. After you click on it (Figure 6.6), you can click on a program icon to start a program, on Help to find information to assist you as you work, or on Shut Down when you are ready to turn off your computer.

Note: The Taskbar and the Start button are unique to Windows 95. They do not appear in any other operating systems except upgrades to Windows 95 and some recent versions of Windows NT.

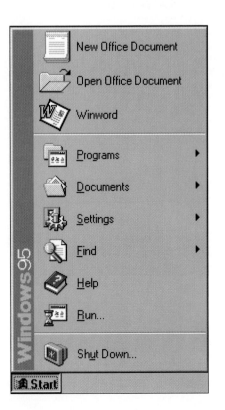

FIGURE 6.6
Typical contents of the Start menu.

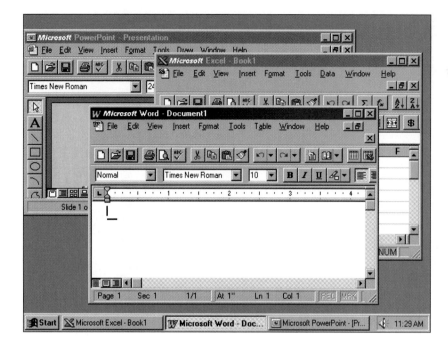

Programs Running in Windows

After you have double-clicked a program icon to load a program into memory, when the program appears, it may take up the whole screen or it may appear in a rectangular frame on the screen known as a **window**. By manipulating these windows on the desktop, you can see multiple programs that have been loaded into memory at the same time. For example, in Figure 6.7, you can see three open windows displaying three different programs.

FIGURE 6.7
Three open windows.

Although each of the programs displayed in the different windows is running concurrently, you still need a way to tell Windows which one you want. To do this, you simply click in the desired window, or click on its button on the Taskbar.

The title bar of the active window is highlighted.

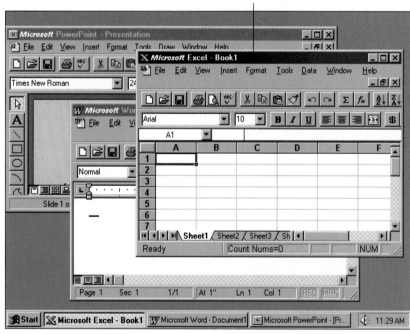

As shown in Figure 6.8, the window's title bar becomes highlighted to show that it is the **active window**—the window where your next actions will take effect. Most windows share many of the same characteristics. For example, all windows include a **title bar** across the top that identifies what the window contains. In addition to providing useful information, the title bar has another useful purpose. You can move the entire window by clicking on the title bar and dragging the window to a new location on the desktop.

Bars below the title bar often contain menus or buttons that help you to tell the program what you want it to do.

FIGURE 6.8
Changing the active window.

In all versions of Microsoft Windows, windows also have adjustable borders and corners. If you drag the corners or sides of the windows, you can make them larger or smaller so you see more or less of their contents. As shown in Figure 6.9, many windows also have **scroll bars** to view the different parts of the program or file that are longer or wider than what can be displayed in its window.

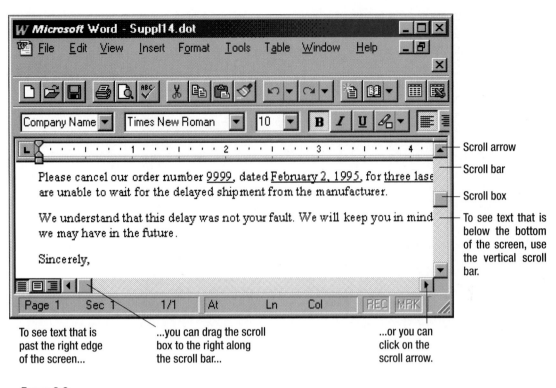

Scroll arrow

Scroll bar

Scroll box

To see text that is below the bottom of the screen, use the vertical scroll bar.

To see text that is past the right edge of the screen...

...you can drag the scroll box to the right along the scroll bar...

...or you can click on the scroll arrow.

FIGURE 6.9
Scroll bars.

Window Control Buttons

In the top-right corner of a window in Windows 95 are three buttons for manipulating the windows (see Figure 6.10).

Close button

Minimize button   Maximize button

FIGURE 6.10
The window control buttons for Windows 95.

- You click the single line—the Minimize button—to reduce the program to a button on the Taskbar;
- You click the picture of a box—the Maximize button—to restore the window to its previous size;
- You click the X—the Close button—to close the window altogether.

In Windows 3.1, Windows for Workgroups, and many versions of Windows NT, these buttons look different. The window control buttons for these programs are shown in Figure 6.11.

FIGURE 6.11
Window control buttons for Windows 3.1.

Double-click here to close the window (clicking once opens a Control menu).

Minimize button

Maximize button

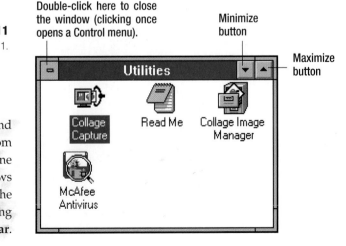

Menus

Although you initiate many tasks by clicking on icons and buttons, you can also start tasks by choosing commands from lists called **menus**. You have already seen one menu, the one that appears when you click on the Start button in Windows 95. The more standard type of menu, however, appears at the top of many windows (in all of the popular GUI operating systems) in a horizontal list of menus called the **menu bar**.

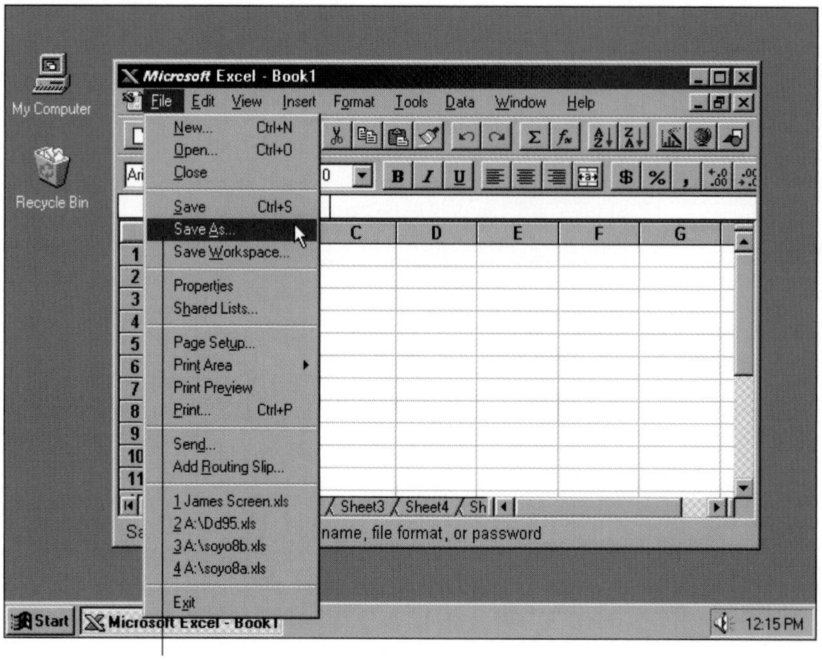

The user is selecting the Save As command from the File menu.

When you click on an item in the menu bar, a menu "drops down" and displays a list of commands (for this reason, these menus are sometimes called *pull-down menus* or *drop-down menus*). For example, the File menu in Windows programs typically contains commands for opening, closing, saving, and printing files. Figure 6.12 shows such a pull-down menu in Excel. To execute or run one of the commands listed in the menu, you click on it.

FIGURE 6.12
The File menu in Excel.

As a shortcut, you also can execute many commands from the keyboard, bypassing both the mouse and the pull-down menus. For example, in Windows programs, one letter in the name of each menu command is underlined. If you hold down the Alt key and type that underlined letter, you can activate the command just from the keyboard (see Figure 6.13). Once in an open menu, you just press the underlined letter in the command you wish to execute. For example, in Figure 6.13, you could just press Alt+O or O to display the Open dialog box, where you specify the file you want to open.

The underlined *F* indicates that you can press Alt+F to open the File menu.

With the File menu open, you can press Alt+O, or simply the letter *O*, to execute the Open command.

As a one-step shortcut, you can press Ctrl+O to execute the Open command without opening the File menu.

Dialog Boxes

Dialog boxes are special-purpose windows that appear when you need to tell the program (or operating system) what to do next. For example, if you choose Find, and then choose Files or Folders from the Windows Start menu, a dialog box will appear that asks you to describe the file or folder you want to find. A dialog box is called that because it conducts a "dialog" with you as it seeks the information it needs to perform a task. Figure 6.14 shows a typical dialog box and explains how to use the most common dialog box features.

FIGURE 6.13
Shortcuts for initiating menu commands.

Radio buttons let you select one option from a set of choices.

Clicking on a tab displays different sections of the dialog box. The Index section is currently visible.

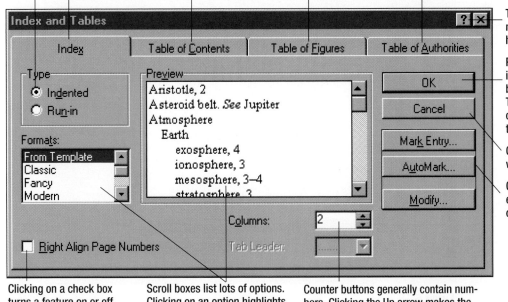

The Help button provides information about this dialog box and how to use it.

Pressing Enter on the keyboard is a shortcut for clicking on the button with the thick border. The OK button applies the options you have selected in the dialog box.

Cancel closes the dialog box without making any changes.

Clicking on a button with ellipses (...) after the name opens another dialog box.

Clicking on a check box turns a feature on or off. This box is empty, so the Right Align Page Numbers feature is currently off.

Scroll boxes list lots of options. Clicking on an option highlights it, making it the active choice.

Counter buttons generally contain numbers. Clicking the Up arrow makes the value increase. The Down arrow makes it decrease. Also, you can click on the value to highlight it, then type a different value.

FIGURE 6.14
Dialog box features.

Becoming Familiar with the Interface

A well-designed GUI offers more than a set of easy-to-use, point-and-click tools. It also offers consistency and familiarity for the user, because it forces the applications that run under the operating system to use the same tools.

For example, take a look at the two screens shown in Figures 6.15 and 6.16.

FIGURE 6.15
Microsoft Excel, a spreadsheet.

They show very different kinds of software. Figure 6.15 shows a spreadsheet program, and Figure 6.16 shows a programming environment. Notice how many elements of the interface are the same. Both screens have the same window dressing—they both

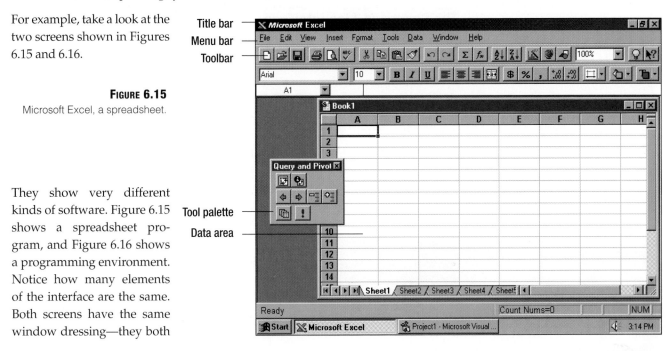

Title bar
Menu bar
Toolbar
Tool palette
Data area

Title bar

Menu bar

Toolbar

Tool palette

Data area

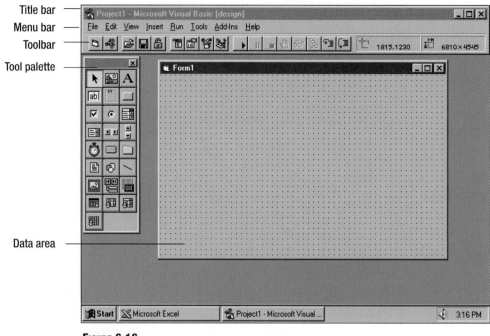

FIGURE 6.16
Microsoft Visual Basic, a programming environment.

have window control buttons, menu bars, and toolbars. The names of some of the menus differ, and the buttons look different, but all the menus and buttons are accessed in the same way.

This level of consistency in the interface is an important part of making the computer system intuitive and easy to use. It is known as **common user access (CUA)**. Once users learn how to use the basic tools, they can move from one program to the next with much more ease then they could if all the aspects of the interface for each application were different.

The Command-Line Interface

The graphical user interface has become the standard because the Macintosh and Windows operating systems use it. However, for more than a decade, computer operating systems used command-line interfaces. The most popular of these during the 1980s were Microsoft's MS-DOS and its near twin PC-DOS from IBM. "DOS" is pronounced "doss" and stands for "Disk Operating System." Users interact with a **command-line interface** by typing strings of characters at the appearance of a prompt on screen. In DOS, the prompt usually includes the identification for the active disk drive (a letter followed by a colon), followed by a greater-than symbol as in C:>. Figure 6.17 shows the DOS prompt, which is still available in Windows 95 for those who want to run DOS programs or to work with DOS keyboard commands.

```
C:\>ver

Windows 95. [Version 4.00.950]

C:\>
```

FIGURE 6.17
The DOS prompt.

Some experienced users of command-line interfaces argue that they are simpler, faster, and provide better information than GUI operating systems. However, GUIs became the standard because most users preferred them, in part because they are easier to learn. Finding and starting programs from a command-line prompt can be compared to traveling at night with a road map in your head. Instead of pointing and clicking at icons, you type a series of *memorized* commands. For instance, in DOS, you type DIR at the prompt to see a list of the files in a particular "directory" (the equivalent of a folder), as shown in Figure 6.18. The section "Microsoft Operating Systems," later in this chapter, describes working with DOS and the limitations that led to the popularity of GUI operating systems such as Windows 95.

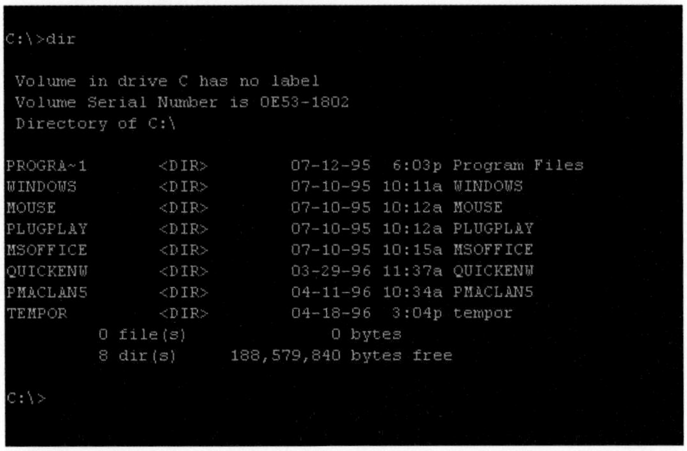

FIGURE 6.18
The results of the DIR command in DOS.

▶ RUNNING PROGRAMS

Just as the operating system can provide a consistent interface for running programs on the computer, it is also the interface between those programs and other computer resources (such as computer memory, a printer, or another program such as a spreadsheet application).

When programmers write computer programs, they build instructions into them—called **system calls**—that request services from the operating system. (They are "calls" because the program has to call on the operating system to provide some information or service.)

For example, when you want your word processing program to retrieve a file, you use the Open dialog box to list the files in the folder that you specify (see Figure 6.19).

FIGURE 6.19
The Open dialog box in Word.

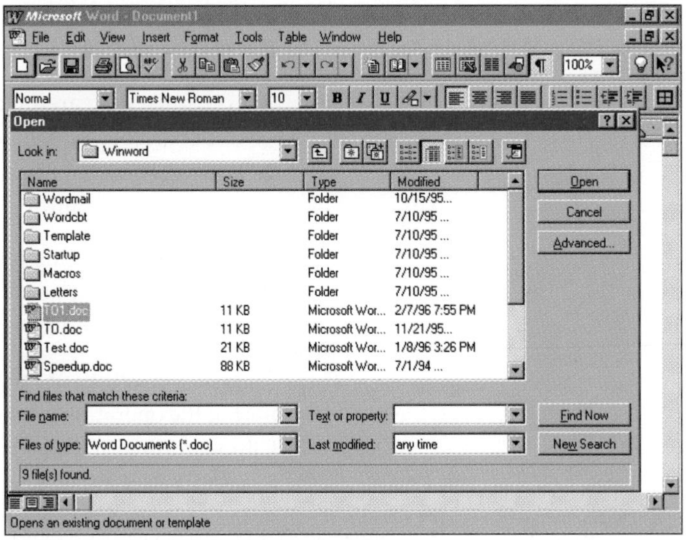

To provide the list, the program calls on the operating system. The OS goes through the same process to build a list of files whether it receives its instructions from the desktop or from another application. The difference is that when the request comes from an application, the operating system sends the results of its work to the application instead of to the desktop.

Some of the other services that an operating system provides to programs, in addition to listing files, are as follows:

- Saving the contents of files to a disk for permanent storage.
- Reading the contents of a file from disk into memory.
- Sending a document to the printer and activating the printer.
- Providing resources that let you copy or move data from one document to another, or from one program to another.
- Allocating RAM among various programs that you may have open.
- Performing the seemingly simple activity of recognizing keystrokes or mouse clicks and displaying characters or graphics on the screen.

Sharing Information

As soon as you begin using a word processing program—or almost any other type of application—you'll discover the need to move chunks of data from one place in a document to another. For example, you might look at a letter and realize that it would make more sense if the second paragraph were moved to page 2. One of the beauties of using a computer is that this type of editing is not only possible but simple.

Most operating systems, including Windows 95, Windows NT, and the Macintosh OS, accomplish this feat with an operating system feature known as the Clipboard. The **Clipboard** is a temporary storage space for data that is being copied or moved. For example, to move a paragraph in a word processed document, you perform the actions as shown in Figure 6.20.

Often, instead of using the **Cut** command, which removes data and places it on the Clipboard, you will want to use **Copy**, which makes a copy of the data and stores it on the Clipboard but does not remove the original. In either case, you use the **Paste** command to copy the contents of the Clipboard back into your document.

Note: The Clipboard stores only one set of data at a time, although the set of data can be almost any size or length. The contents of the Clipboard are cleared each time you select a new set of data and choose either the Cut or Copy commands again. This fact has two important consequences:

1. You must be careful not to erase valuable data that has been placed in the Clipboard or you will lose it.
2. You can Paste data from the Clipboard as many times as you like (until you choose Cut or Copy again).

As you might imagine (or already know), the Clipboard also can be used to move data from one document to another. For example, you can copy an address from one letter to another and thereby avoid retyping it.

The real versatility of the Clipboard, however, stems from the fact that it is actually part of the operating system, not a particular application. As a result, you can use the Clipboard to move data from one program to another. For example, say you created a chart in a spreadsheet program and want to paste it into a report that you created with your word processing program. As shown in Figure 6.21, you can do it easily with the Clipboard.

The versatility of the Clipboard has been further extended with a feature known in Windows as **OLE**, which stands for **Object Linking and Embedding**. A simple cut

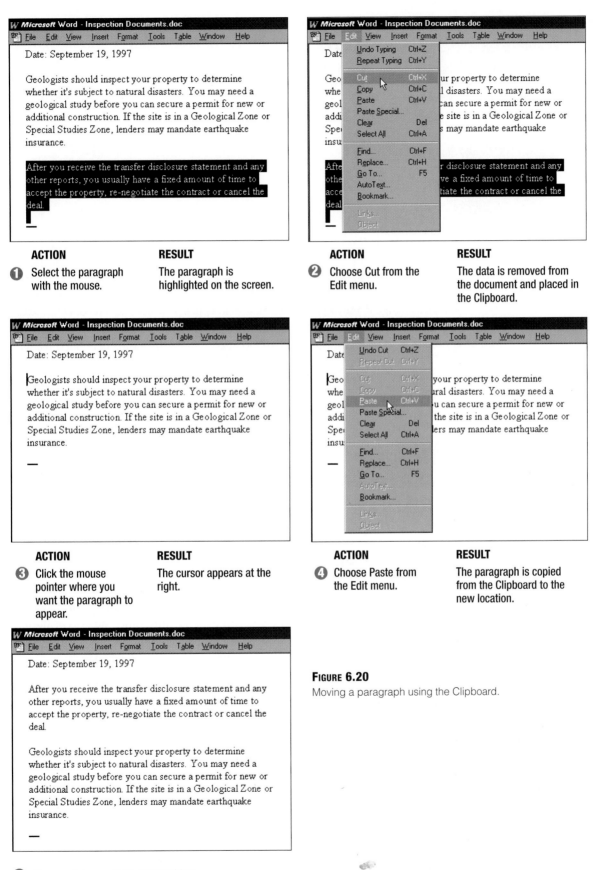

ACTION

① Select the paragraph with the mouse.

RESULT

The paragraph is highlighted on the screen.

ACTION

② Choose Cut from the Edit menu.

RESULT

The data is removed from the document and placed in the Clipboard.

ACTION

③ Click the mouse pointer where you want the paragraph to appear.

RESULT

The cursor appears at the right.

ACTION

④ Choose Paste from the Edit menu.

RESULT

The paragraph is copied from the Clipboard to the new location.

FIGURE 6.20

Moving a paragraph using the Clipboard.

⑤ Paragraph is now in its new position.

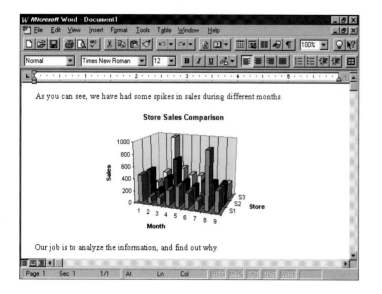

and paste between applications results in **object embedding**. The data, which is known as an object in programming terms, is embedded in a new type of document. It retains the formatting that was applied to it in the original application, but its relationship with the original file is destroyed—it is simply part of the new file.

FIGURE 6.21

A spreadsheet chart pasted into a word processing document.

Object linking, however, adds another layer to the relationship: The data that is copied to and from the Clipboard retains a link to the original document, so that a change in the original document also appears in the linked data. Object linking can be a boon to business users, who must create daily, weekly, or monthly reports. For example, suppose the report shown in Figure 6.21 is generated weekly, and it always contains the same chart, updated with the correct numbers for the current week. With object linking, the numbers in the spreadsheet from which the chart is generated can be updated, and the chart in the report will automatically reflect the new numbers.

Multitasking

Besides being able to run programs and share data across applications, Windows and Macintosh operating systems have joined OS/2 and UNIX in achieving a long-sought goal of personal computers: multitasking, which is a computer's version of being able to "walk and chew gum at the same time." **Multitasking** means much more than the ability to load multiple programs into memory (although even that was quite difficult for earlier operating systems). Multitasking means being able to perform two or more procedures at the same time—such as printing a multipage document, sending e-mail over the Internet, and typing a letter—all simultaneously.

Software engineers use two methods to develop multitasking operating systems. The first requires cooperation between the operating system and application programs. Programs that are currently running will periodically check the operating system to see whether any other programs need the CPU. If any do, the running program will relinquish control of the CPU to the next program. This method is called **cooperative multitasking** and is used by the Macintosh operating system to allow such activities as printing while the user continues to type or use the mouse to input more data.

Multitasking lets you do more than one thing at once. Here, the computer is starting the modem and printing a picture while the user composes an e-mail message.

The second method is called **preemptive multitasking**. With this method, the operating system maintains a list of programs that are running and assigns a priority to each program in the list. The operating system can intervene and modify a program's priority status, rearranging the priority list. With preemptive multitasking, the operating system can preempt the program that is running and reassign the time to a higher priority task. Preemptive multitasking thereby has the advantage of being able to carry out higher priority programs faster than lower priority programs. Windows 95, Windows NT, OS/2, and UNIX employ preemptive multitasking.

▶ MANAGING FILES

The files that the operating system works with may be programs or data files. Most programs you purchase come with numerous files—some may even include hundreds. When you use the programs, you often create your own data files, such as word processing documents, and store them on a disk under names that you assign to them. A large hard disk often holds thousands of program and data files. It is the responsibility of the operating system to keep track of all these files so it can copy any one of them into RAM at a moment's notice.

To accomplish this feat, the operating system maintains a list of the contents of a disk on the disk itself. As you may recall there is an area called the File Allocation Table, or FAT, that the operating system creates when you format a disk. The operating system updates the information in the FAT any time a file is created, moved, renamed, or deleted. In addition, the operating system keeps track of different disks or disk drives by assigning names to them. On IBM and compatible computers, diskette drives are assigned the letters *A* and *B* and hard disk drives are designated as the *C* drive and up. CD-ROM drives have the first available letter following the hard drives—often the letter *D*. Operating systems not created by Microsoft use slightly different schemes for keeping track of disks and their contents, but each of the different schemes accomplishes the same task.

In Windows 95, there are actually two different programs for viewing and managing the contents of a disk, the My Computer window and the Windows Explorer. In either one, you select the icon that represents a disk drive, and a window appears with the list of files on that disk (see Figure 6.22).

When there are hundreds of files on a disk, finding the one you want can

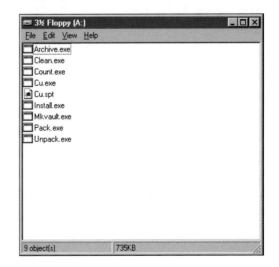

FIGURE 6.22
My Computer window, showing the contents of a diskette.

The meteoric rise of the World Wide Web in this decade is changing the way that people think about computer operating systems, and what they expect their operating systems to do.

An operating system (OS) manages a computer's processes, memory, files, and any external devices, such as a mouse, printer, or network interface.

With the rise of the biggest network of all, the Internet, people have come to expect more than just basic interfacing capabilities. They want the ability to access, retrieve, and display all the varieties of information available on the World Wide Web. These functions require a browser, a special software navigational tool designed to access the Web through the network connections provided by the OS.

Currently, there is also a wide variety of "helper apps," software tools that enable the browser to display the many kinds of files encountered on the Web, such as graphics, sound, video, and program content like the Java applets. Finding these tools—either by downloading them from the Web or by purchasing software—can be time consuming. Once found, even helper apps must be configured to function with a user's browser, network connection, operating system, and hardware platform.

But this may not be the case for long. In early 1996, Microsoft announced its intention to release an "Internet add-on kit" that will work specifically with Windows 95 to provide users with a greater integration of the operating system and Internet functions. A few months later, at the Tech Ed 96 conference in Los Angeles, Microsoft demonstrated pre-release versions of two more products designed to integrate Internet functionality with Windows 95.

The first one was a program called Peer Web Services that allows users to convert existing documents to documents containing the HTML coding needed for Web viewing. It also allows users to set up their own small Web server using their desktop PCs.

The other new product was a Web page authoring tool called WebPost, enabling users to create Web pages featuring rich content and then to post these pages to another Web server by taking advantage of features that are already built into Windows 95.

Whether these products make it to the market in their current forms remains to be seen. Microsoft's direction is clear, however; it wants the OS to absorb the browser.

On the other hand, browser manufacturers want to keep their distance from the OS. They have found that operating a level up from the OS is an advantage, and they do not want to be bound to a particular OS's limitations.

Browser manufacturers are best exemplified by the Mountain View, California company, Netscape, manufacturers of the Navigator browser. Netscape has announced plans to expand its browser capabilities via its open, plug-in architecture. This allows third parties to write software that plugs into Navigator's existing feature set, making new Web features such as sound, animation, and video easy to implement as they become available.

One of the Web's founding fathers, Tim Berners-Lee, suggested a broader perspective on the whole issue in a 1996 interview published in the *San Francisco Examiner*. Berners-Lee (who now directs a consortium establishing technical standards for the Web), believes that it no longer makes sense to differentiate between operating systems and browsers.

"It is more logical to think of the local information [on a computer] as just one part of the world of information," he said. "That way, the browser and the desktop become one. Whether you think of that as the browser making the desktop obsolete or the desktop making the browser obsolete, that might depend on where you currently have a large market share." ("Battle of the Browsers," Evan Ramstad, *San Francisco Examiner*, March 17, 1996)

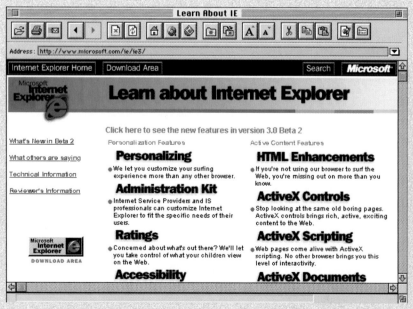

Microsoft's Explorer is one of the many available Internet browsers.

be time consuming. To find files quickly, you can organize them using folders. Figure 6.23 shows a listing of the main folder of a hard disk. Notice how file names are accompanied by the file sizes in bytes, and the date and time when the files were last modified.

Also notice that there are several folders in the list. Folders can contain other fold-

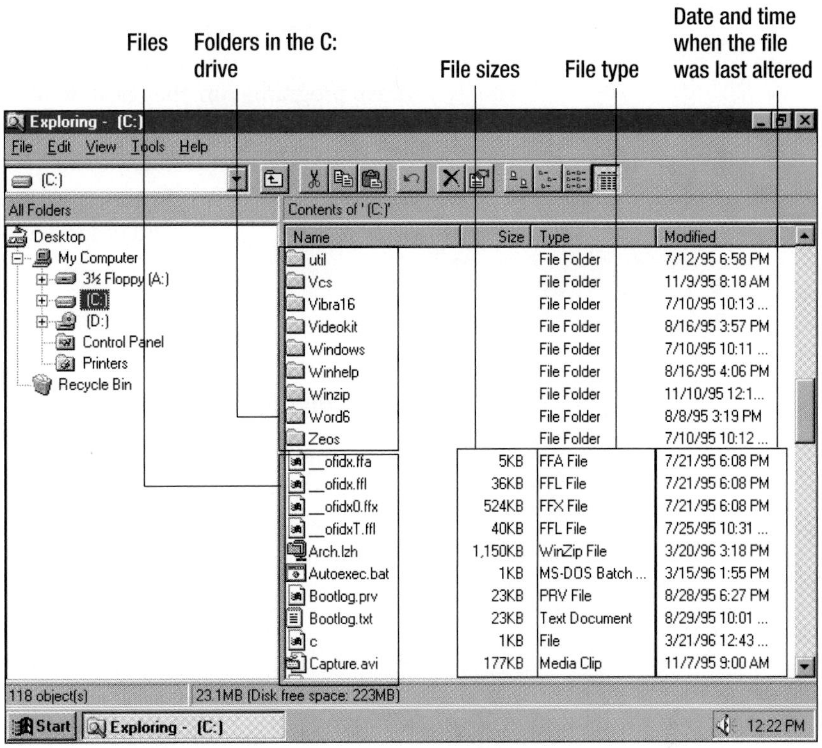

FIGURE 6.23

The Exploring window, showing the contents of the hard disk.

ers, so you can create a structured system known as a **hierarchical file system**. A diagram for a hierarchical file system is shown in Figure 6.24.

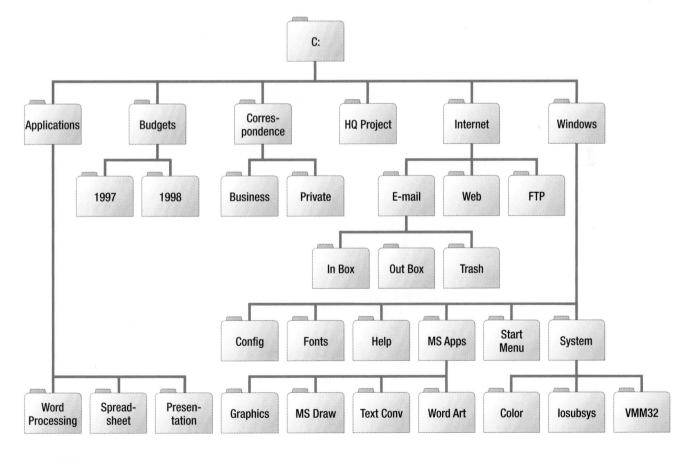

FIGURE 6.24

A hierarchical file system.

▶ MANAGING HARDWARE

When programs run, they need to use the computer's memory, monitor, disk drives, and other devices, such as a printer, a modem, or a CD-ROM drive. The operating system is the intermediary between programs and hardware. In a computer network, the operating system also mediates between your computer and other devices on the network.

In the next sections, you will see three ways in which the operating system serves as the go-between to keep hardware running smoothly.

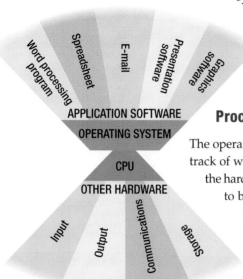

The operating system acts as an intermediary between the application software and all of the hardware.

Processing Interrupts

The operating system responds to requests to use memory and other devices, keeps track of which programs have access to which devices, and coordinates everything the hardware does so that various activities do not overlap and cause the computer to become confused and stop working. The operating system uses **interrupt requests** to help the CPU coordinate processes. For example, if you tell the operating system to list the files in a folder, it sends an interrupt request to the computer's CPU. The basic steps in this process are shown in Figure 6.25.

The interrupt request procedure is a little like using parliamentary procedures in a large meeting. At first, it may seem like an extra layer of unnecessary formality. In fact, this formality is needed to keep everyone from talking at once—or in the case of interrupt requests, to keep the CPU from becoming overwhelmed with a barrage of possibly conflicting processing procedures.

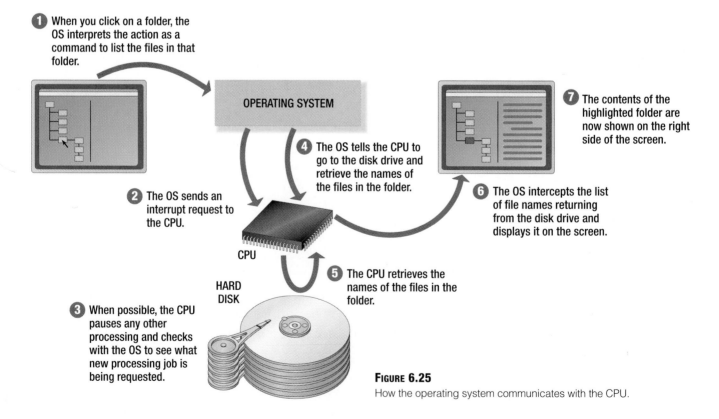

① When you click on a folder, the OS interprets the action as a command to list the files in that folder.

② The OS sends an interrupt request to the CPU.

③ When possible, the CPU pauses any other processing and checks with the OS to see what new processing job is being requested.

④ The OS tells the CPU to go to the disk drive and retrieve the names of the files in the folder.

⑤ The CPU retrieves the names of the files in the folder.

⑥ The OS intercepts the list of file names returning from the disk drive and displays it on the screen.

⑦ The contents of the highlighted folder are now shown on the right side of the screen.

FIGURE 6.25
How the operating system communicates with the CPU.

Providing Drivers

In addition to using interrupts, the operating system often provides complete programs for working with special devices, such as printers. These programs are called **drivers** because they allow the operating system and other programs to activate and use, that is, "drive" the hardware device. In the days when DOS reigned, drivers had to be installed separately for each program used. With modern operating systems such as Windows 95 and the Macintosh's OS, drivers are an integral part of the operating system. This means that most of the software you buy will work with your printer, monitor, and other equipment without requiring any special installation.

Networking

Besides providing interrupt requests and drivers for working with individual devices, the OS also can allow you to work with multiple computers on a network.

On a network, usually each person has a separate PC with its own operating system. The network server also has its own operating system, which manages the flow of data on the file server and around the network. The leading network operating system for PCs today is a system dedicated just to networking—Novell NetWare. However, most of the PC operating systems have some limited networking capabilities.

In Windows 95, other computers on a LAN appear as part of the Network Neighborhood.

▶ ENHANCING THE OPERATING SYSTEM WITH UTILITY SOFTWARE

Operating systems are designed to let you do most of the things you normally would want to do with a computer—manage files, load programs, print files, multitask, and so on. These programs (actually, sets of programs) are sold by the behemoths of the software industry: Microsoft, Apple, IBM, Santa Cruz Operation (SCO), and Novell. However, there are many other talented software firms that are constantly finding ways to improve operating systems. The programs they create to do this are called utilities. In the 1980s, when utilities for PCs first appeared, some of the most popular were those that helped the user to back up files, detect computer viruses (rogue programs that can destroy data files), and retrieve files that have been deleted. A few utility programs actually replace parts of the operating system, but the vast majority simply add helpful functionality.

Because they aid the inner workings of the computer system, utilities are grouped with the operating system under the category of **system software**. Utilities are not considered application software because they do not let you create any tangible result. Their purpose is relevant only to the computer system itself.

Software makers began to provide utility programs to remedy perceived limitations in operating systems. However, over the years, makers of operating systems have integrated many utilities into the system itself. Generally, this year's utility programs become next year's operating system features.

Today, popular utilities range from programs that can organize or compress the files on a disk to programs that help you remove programs you no longer use from your

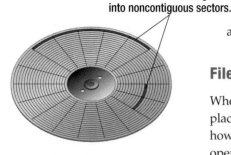

This file has been fragmented into noncontiguous sectors.

FIGURE 6.26

File fragmentation.

hard disk. The categories of utilities covered in the sections that follow include file defragmentation, data compression, backup, data recovery, antivirus, and screen savers.

File Defragmentation

When you first copy a file to a disk, the operating system tries to put it all in one place, in one or more contiguous sectors. If you later go back and add data to the file, however, the sectors next to the original may no longer be available. In this case, the operating system puts the new data somewhere else on the disk (see Figure 6.26).

A file that is split up this way is said to be fragmented because its parts are physically separated. The problem with fragmented files is that it takes the hard drive longer to read and write them because the disk must reposition its read-write heads several times while working with the same file.

A utility program that defragments files on a disk can speed up the disk drive quite noticeably. Windows 95 comes with a **defragmentation utility** called Disk Defragmenter. Before you use this or any other defragmentation utility, however, you should be sure to back up your data.

This dialog box shows the progress being made by the Disk Defragmenter utility as it defragments the files on the hard disk.

Data Compression

Data compression, the ability to reduce the storage requirements of a file using mathematical algorithms, has several applications, including data communications and multimedia. As you may recall, data compression techniques are built into modems so they can send files faster.

Another use for data compression is to fit more data on a disk. Doing so usually requires a **data compression utility**, a program specifically designed to abbreviate sequences of bits in order to make files as small as possible. Data compression utilities come in different types, depending on how they will be used. Some utilities compress files on demand, usually to fit data onto a small disk, such as a diskette, or to reduce the amount of hard disk space taken up by files that are rarely accessed. PKZip and WinZip for the PC and Stuff It for the Macintosh are some of the most popular data compression utilities.

Another type of utility compresses all the data as it is stored on your hard disk, effectively doubling the capacity of the disk. The user need not even know that data compression and decompression are going on, except that in some cases opening files may be slower. DriveSpace, which is built into Windows 95, is an example of this type of utility.

The files listed on this screen have been compressed and stored in a file named old_figs.zip. The ratio column shows that the files have been compressed by as much as 98 percent. A file with a 98-percent compression ratio means that the data in the file now occupies only 2 percent as much space as it did when it was not compressed.

Backup Software

Data compression is also built into backup software, another type of utility. **Backup software** is designed to help you copy large groups of files from your hard disk to some other storage media, such as diskettes, magnetic tape, removable hard disks, magneto-optical disks, or recordable CDs.

Once again, backup software was originally sold by independent software firms but is now often found as part of the operating system. For example, Microsoft Backup was originally developed by Symantec as a separate utility, but it is now packaged with all the different Microsoft operating systems, including MS-DOS, Windows 95, and Windows NT.

Users can and should back up their data. The real purpose of this utility is to make the backup process as painless as possible. For example, most backup software lets you set a timer and automatically copy the contents of your hard disk to magnetic tape or the network server when you are not using your computer, usually late at night.

Data Recovery Software

Once in a while, you may erase a file from a disk and then realize that you still need it. This is when you need a **data recovery utility**, also called an **unerase program**, which can recover data files that have been mistakenly deleted or somehow rendered unusable.

Both the Macintosh operating system and Windows 95 try to help with the problem of mistakenly erased files by providing the Trash (Mac) and the Recycle Bin (Windows 95); these are areas to which you can move files that you no longer need. The operating system does not actually erase the files until you give the command to Empty Trash or Empty Recycle Bin.

Even then, however, the computer does not actually destroy the data in the files. All it does is mark each file in such a way that the operating system can write over it. Until the operating system actually does copy a new file to that area on the disk, the old file cannot be seen by the user, but it can be resurrected. Data recovery software is designed to make files that have been erased but not written over visible to the user. The user can select them and change their status back to a usable form.

The same type of software can also be used to examine a disk and look for damaged files. Files can become unreadable if they are damaged by an error in software or the disk drive, or if the storage media itself is damaged. Data recovery software can sometimes piece together the readable parts of such files and make those parts available again.

Here, Microsoft Backup is being used to create a backup copy of the hard disk.

This utility is used to bring back files that have been erased. Notice that the first character of each file is a ? or ~ (which are not acceptable characters for file names in DOS or Windows). When you recover the file, all you are really doing is changing the first character back to one that the computer understands as part of a file name.

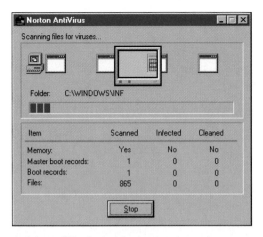

Antivirus utilities look at the boot sector and every executable file on a disk and report how many are infected with viruses.

Antivirus Utilities

A **virus** is a parasitic program buried within another legitimate program or stored in a special area of a disk called the *boot sector*. Executing the legitimate program or accessing the disk activates the virus without the user's knowledge. Viruses can be programmed to do many things, including copy themselves to other programs, display information on the screen, destroy data files, or erase an entire hard disk. If you occasionally transfer files or trade diskettes with other computer users, you can spread the virus unknowingly.

Tracking viruses down, eradicating them, and preventing their spread is the major objective of **antivirus utilities**. Antivirus programs examine the boot sector and every file on a disk, identify any viruses, and attempt to remove them. You can also configure antivirus programs so that they are active at all times, searching for infected files or suspicious programs. Some common antivirus utilities are McAfee, ViruScan, Symantic Antivirus, Norton Antivirus, Virex, and Disinfectant.

Screen Savers

Another popular type of utility is the **screen saver**, a program that displays moving images on the screen if no input is received for several minutes. Screen savers originally gained popularity as a way to fight "ghosting," a hardware problem of computer monitors in the early 1980s in which an image that was displayed for many hours on the screen became "burned" into the phosphor dots and therefore was permanently visible on the screen's surface. However, even after the hardware was corrected and ghosting no longer took place, programmers had become so creative with the types of images displayed by screen savers that users began to buy them just for the sake of novelty, and to protect their data from being seen when they are away from their desks. Today, you can find screen savers that display Flying Toasters, *Far Side* comic strips, bizarre mathematical color patterns, and scenes from TV shows like *Star Trek* and *The Simpsons*.

Star Trek: The Screen Saver has been a long-time favorite. In addition to spaceships and exploding robots floating across your screen, other modules include scenes of Captain Kirk barking orders and security guards running away from creatures who drill through rocks.

▶ MICROSOFT OPERATING SYSTEMS

Although a number of companies have offered operating systems over the years, one company, Microsoft Corporation, has dominated the market for microcomputer operating systems. Microsoft itself has supplied what may seem an alphabet soup of operating systems. In practice, however, their products have evolved from one to another in a reasonably sequential fashion. The following is a brief summary.

MS-DOS

Microsoft's **MS-DOS**, along with the similar PC-DOS from IBM and competitors like DR DOS (originally from Digital Research and later purchased by Novell), was once the most common of all the PC operating systems. There was an overwhelming volume of software available that ran under DOS, and a large installed base of Intel-based PCs that ran DOS.

Although it ruled throughout the 1980s, initially DOS did not gain the upper hand without a fight. Its toughest early competitor was an operating system called CP/M, which stood for Control Program for Microprocessors. Its developer was Gary Kildall, the owner and founder of Digital Research. However, DOS won the early operating system marketing wars because it was finally accepted by IBM as the standard operating system for their IBM PC. It therefore became the operating system for the huge market of IBM-compatibles.

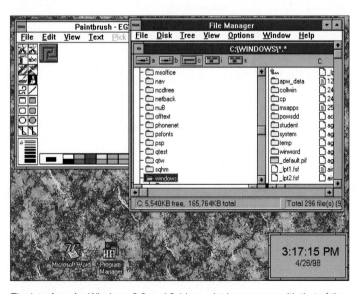

Most PCs during the 1980s and early 1990s ran DOS. This screen shows a set of help files being copied into a subdirectory named "work."

DOS was adequate for the IBM-compatible PCs of the early 1980s, but it has certain limitations that became more noticeable as PCs became more powerful. For example:

- Under DOS, you can load only a single program into memory at a time. To work with a second program, you have to close the first—a process that often hinders productivity.

- DOS was not designed to handle the large amounts of RAM that today's PCs typically use. As a result, you have to use utilities to access memory beyond the 640 KB limit imposed by DOS.

- DOS was designed for 16-bit CPUs and cannot take advantage of the 32-bit architecture of the 486, Pentium, and later chips. This forces computers to work at speeds below their capacity.

- DOS file names are limited to eight characters, plus a three-character "extension" following a period, as in the name "wordproc.doc". Windows 95 and the upgrades to Windows 95 have remedied this situation by allowing file names up to 256 characters long.

- Finally, as has been mentioned, the DOS command-line interface is more difficult to learn than a well-designed GUI. When Windows came along, most users were all too happy to stop typing commands and start clicking on icons.

Microsoft Windows 3.0, 3.1, and 3.11

In the mid-1980s, Microsoft accepted the popularity of the Macintosh computer and users' desire for a GUI.

The interface for Windows 3.0 and 3.1 has a lot in common with that of the Mac and Windows 95. Users work with files and programs by clicking on desktop icons to open windows.

Their solution was Microsoft Windows, a GUI that ran on top of DOS, replacing the command-line interface with a point-and-click system. Windows, therefore, was not originally an operating system but an **operating environment**, another term for an interface that disguises the underlying operating system.

The first version of Windows did not work very well and did not sell very well either, and the second version also was not a success. It was not until Microsoft released Windows 3.0 in 1990 that the program really took off.

Windows 3.0 was reasonably stable and succeeded in providing a GUI and the ability to load more than one program into memory at a time. During the early 1990s, **Windows 3.0**, **Windows 3.1**, and **Windows 3.11** (called Windows for Workgroups) became the market leaders. (DOS actually remained the most popular operating system, because it was required to run these operating environments.)

DOS, running in a window

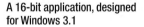

A 16-bit application, designed for Windows 3.1

Windows 95 is primarily designed to run 32-bit applications. However, it can also run the older, 16-bit applications that were designed for Windows 3.0, 3.1, and DOS.

Microsoft Windows 95 (and Upgrades)

In 1995, Microsoft released **Windows 95**, a complete operating system and a successor to DOS for desktop computers. Windows 95 is a 32-bit, preemptive multitasking operating system with a revised GUI. All the strengths of Windows 95, which followed the Windows 3.x series (all the versions of Windows 3—3.0, 3.1, and 3.11), had already existed in other operating systems—most notably the Macintosh and Windows NT. In fact, purists considered it a compromise because, unlike those 32-bit operating systems, Windows 95 contains a good deal of 16-bit code—needed to run older DOS and Windows programs. Though the 16-bit code may have represented a backward glance, it was probably Windows 95's greatest marketing strength.

As a result of the 16-bit code, Windows 95 can run almost any DOS or Windows program. Thus, if a company has already invested in many such programs, it can continue to use its familiar programs while migrating to the new operating system.

For users of Windows 3.1, Windows 95 has several attractions. First, it offers 32-bit processing. This means that for programs designed with 32-bit processing in mind, the operating system can exchange information with printers, networks, and files in 32-bit pieces instead of 16-bit pieces as in Windows 3.1 and DOS. For information moving around in the computer, the effect is like doubling the number of lanes on an expressway.

Second, Windows 95, like Windows NT, offers preemptive multitasking and not the less efficient cooperative multitasking of Windows 3.1 and the Macintosh. The self-contained 32-bit preemptive multitasking means that, if one program fails, you still have access to all the other programs loaded into memory. In most cases, you do not have to restart the computer to work with those programs, as you did with earlier versions of Windows.

Third (and probably first in the eyes of users), Windows 95 has a graphical interface that is a welcome improvement over Windows 3.1. The Windows Explorer, for example, improves on earlier Microsoft operating systems for working with files. Windows 95 also allows users to type file names of up to 256 characters and to have spaces in those names—freedoms that had not been available on DOS-based PCs.

In addition, Windows 95 offers a plug-and-play standard for connecting new hardware. With Windows 3.0 and 3.1, users often faced nightmare-like complexities when installing disk drives, sound cards, modems, printers, CD-ROM drives, and other hardware. Under **plug-and-play**, the manufacturers do all the compliance work in advance. You simply connect a Windows 95-certified device to your computer, and the operating system does everything else to make sure that it works properly with the computer.

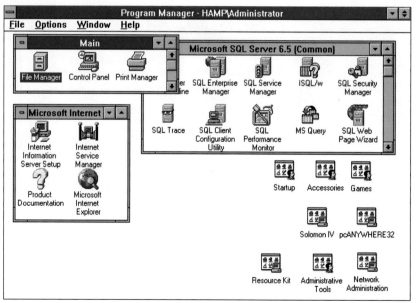

File names can be up to 256 characters long.

The Windows Explorer lists folders on the left side of the screen and the contents of folders on the right side.

Another Windows 95 asset is compatibility with networking software such as Novell NetWare and Microsoft Windows NT Server. With networks, too, you can simply identify the network operating system when you install Windows 95, and Windows 95 will be compatible with it.

As with any program, upgrades to Windows 95 will continue to improve on these advances, eliminating bugs from earlier versions and improving such features as network links, the Internet browser, and support for 3-D games.

Microsoft Windows NT

Although Windows 95 is considered the successor to DOS, Microsoft released **Windows NT**, a 32-bit operating system for PCs, in 1993. Windows NT was originally designed to be the successor to DOS, but by the time it was ready for release, it had become too large to run on most of the PCs in use at the time. As a result, Microsoft repositioned Windows NT to be a high-end operating system designed

The interface for Windows NT started out looking a lot like Windows 3.1. More recent versions resemble Windows 95.

designed primarily for powerful workstations and network servers. With Windows NT released, Microsoft went back to the drawing board to create Windows 95.

Windows 95 retained backward compatibility for users working with older machines and older programs. However, Windows NT addressed the market for the powerful 32-bit, networked workstations that use some of the most powerful CPUs on the market today.

▶ OTHER OPERATING SYSTEMS FOR PERSONAL COMPUTERS

Although Microsoft has become the unquestioned market leader in operating systems, that has not always been the case. Other operating systems have been popular, and some continue to keep their staunch supporters' loyalty.

The Macintosh Operating System

The Macintosh is a purely graphical machine. In its early days in the mid-1980s, its tight integration of hardware, operating system, and its GUI made it the favorite with users who did not want to deal with DOS's command-line interface. Another big advantage of the Macintosh was that all of its applications functioned similarly, applying the concepts of common user access and making them easier to learn than DOS applications. Now that GUIs have become the standard, it is hard to appreciate just how big a breakthrough this really was.

The **Macintosh operating system** was also ahead of Windows with many other features, including plug-and-play hardware compatibility and built-in networking. Nevertheless, the Mac operating system works only on Macintosh and compatible hardware, while DOS and all the varieties of Windows work only on IBM-compatible computers (which account for about 85 percent of the PC market). Still, the Mac remains the first choice of many publishers, multimedia developers, graphic artists, and schools. As of the mid-1990s, Apple controlled about a 10 percent share of the personal computer market—surpassing former rival IBM.

System Software 7.5.1. Apple Computer, Inc. Used with permission. Apple and the Apple logo are registered trademarks of Apple Computer, Inc. All rights reserved.

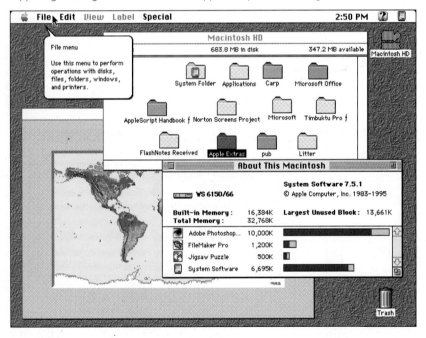

The Macintosh was the first commercially successful computer to come with a GUI operating system.

OS/2

Although they are now fierce rivals, IBM and Microsoft were once allies. After the introduction of the Intel 80286 processor in 1982, both companies recognized the need to take advantage of the new capabilities of this CPU. They teamed up to develop **OS/2**, a modern multitasking operating system for Intel microprocessors. The partnership did not last long. Technical differences of opinion and IBM's perception of Microsoft Windows as a threat to OS/2 (which proved to be accurate) caused a rift between the companies that ultimately led to the dissolution of the partnership.

IBM continued to develop and promote OS/2 as a strategic cornerstone of its System Application Architecture (SAA), a comprehensive plan for overall business computing.

Like Windows NT, OS/2 is a single-user multitasking operating system with a point-and-click interface. It is also a true multitasking system. Its designers claim that it is better than Windows 95 at running older DOS-based programs and that it performs more efficient multitasking.

Courtesy of International Business Machines Corporation. Unauthorized use not permitted.

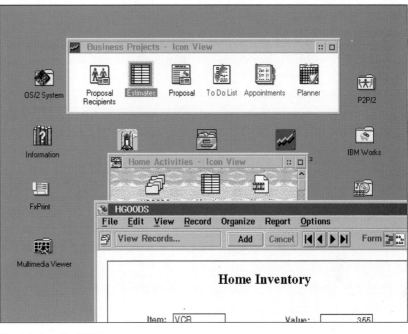

The interface for OS/2.

UNIX

UNIX is older than all the other PC operating systems, and in many ways it served as a model for them. Initially developed by Bell Labs and geared toward telecommunications, UNIX was sold to Novell in the early 1990s. Because of its early use in university settings, several versions were developed. The best known is Berkeley UNIX. Other versions include A/UX for the Mac and AIX for IBM high-end workstations.

UNIX was not just a multitasking system like the other operating systems in this chapter. It was also a multiuser and multiprocessing operating system. That is, it could allow multiple users to work from more than one keyboard and monitor attached to a single CPU, just as a mainframe with dumb terminals does. UNIX allowed for a PC with more than one CPU working at a time—an admirable feat by early PC standards.

UNIX runs on many different types of computers—on Cray supercomputers, PCs, and everything in between, including mainframes and minicomputers.

UNIX is a registered trademark in the United States and other countires, licensed exclusively through x/open Company, Ltd.

```
linex2> ls
Mail/          News/          brian/        mail/
Mailboxes/     ShopCart.dat   james.pl      public_html/
linex2> cd mail
linex2> ls
saved-messages     sent-mail          sent-mail-feb-1996
linex2> cd ..
linex2> ls
Mail/          News/          brian/        mail/
Mailboxes/     ShopCart.dat   james.pl      public_html/
linex2> ps
  PID TT STAT  TIME COMMAND
 3023 p8 S     0:00 -csh (csh)
linex2> ftp
ftp> open ftp.netscape.com
Connected to ftp20.netscape.com.
220 ftp20 FTP server (Version wu-2.4(17) Tue Feb 20 09:08:35 PST 1996) ready.
Name (ftp.netscape.com:swankman): anonymous
331 Guest login ok, send your complete e-mail address as password.
Password:
230-Welcome to the Netscape Communications Corporation FTP server.
230-
230-If you have any odd problems, try logging in with a minus sign (-)
230-as the first character of your password.  This will turn off a feature
230-that may be confusing your ftp client program.
230-
230-Please send any questions, comments, or problem reports about
230-this server to ftp@netscape.com.
230-
230-*********** October 13, 1995 **********
230-Private ftp is now only on ftp1.netscape.com.  Anonymous is supported on
230-ftp 2 through 8.  If you are accessing a named account please use ftp1.
230-
230 Guest login ok, access restrictions apply.
ftp> bye
221 Goodbye.
linex2> █
```

A screen from command line UNIX operating system looks a lot like DOS, with typed commands and command prompts. In fact, DOS borrowed several commands and features from UNIX.

The operating system (OS) basically determines what programs you can run on your computer. Applications must be compatible with the OS of the computer you use. Most applications are OS-specific, meaning that they run on one operating system only.

Most modern applications offer identical versions designed for different operating systems, but many do not.

Also, it can be frustrating trying to use files that were created in a different operating system from your own. Many major applications, such as Excel and Word, have built-in conversion abilities but these conversions are imperfect and sometimes alter formatting or introduce foreign characters.

In addition, many computers are platform-specific, which means, for example, that a PC computer may not be able to read a Mac disk.

For these reasons and more, it is necessary for the modern businessperson to learn to work in what is called *cross-platform environments*. This means that you must find ways to work with a variety of operating systems or with systems that are built to cross the boundaries of operating systems.

A simple example of a cross-platform environment that most computer users see every day is a network. A network can link certain functions of multiple operating systems over a local area or wide area network. For example, you can print files over a network from both Macintosh and Windows-based computers.

Users on different operating systems can also share files over a network. The computers must be equipped with utility programs that allow disks from other computers to be recognized in disk drives and with file formats that can be translated back and forth among operating systems and application programs.

Another option is to use applications that come in identical versions for each operating system. Then those applications can easily exchange files and the computer operators need learn only one application.

One recent development in cross-platform environments is called a *hardware plug-in*. Here, a computer is miniaturized to fit on a circuit board and then plugged into another computer. The plug-in computer doesn't need its own disk drives, monitor, or other such devices. It can share memory and

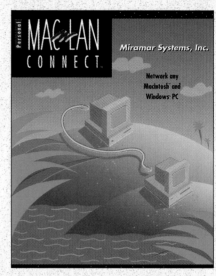

MacLan is a software program for linking Macintosh and Windows PC computers via a network.

hard drive space with the main computer.

Another common form of cross-platform environments is called *software emulation*. This involves a special kind of software program called an *emulator*, which makes one computer act like another, capable of running that other computer's operating system and applications. This is a relatively inexpensive way to get the benefits of more than one operating system and software library.

The latest wrinkle in cross-platform systems is a new *hardware specification* called Common Hardware Reference Platform, or CHRP. A hardware specification is a group of standards established for building a piece of hardware, most commonly the computer itself. Currently, the two most common standards are Mac OS and IBM-compatible or DOS-based.

CHRP is designed to support a variety of operating systems at once—for example, Windows, Macintosh, UNIX, and Windows NT. Computers based on CHRP certainly will earn points for flexibility; how easy they are to use, and how completely and consistently they will accommodate the various operating systems remains to be seen.

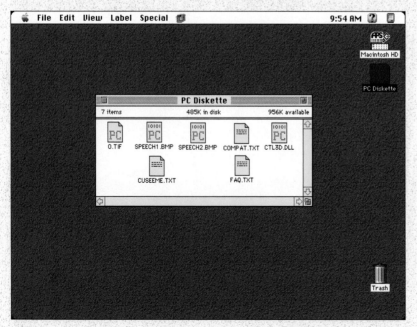

The Power Macintosh offers a cross-platform environment capable of reading this PC disk.

Because of its ability to work with so many kinds of hardware, UNIX became the backbone of the Internet. Thanks to its power and its appeal to engineers and other users of CAD and CAM software, UNIX has been popular for RISC workstations such as those from Sun Microsystems, Hewlett-Packard, IBM, and Silicon Graphics.

Although it is an extremely robust and capable operating system, command-line UNIX is not for the faint of heart, because it requires many commands to do even simple things. A UNIX windowing system called X-Windows has brought a GUI to UNIX computers, but it has remained an operating system for engineers and technical users. Although some of its capabilities have become mainstream, it has gradually lost ground to operating systems such as DOS, Windows, and the Mac, which generally have been perceived as easier to learn and use.

▶ NORTON WORKSHOP: MULTITASKING AND OLE

In this section you will watch as a scientific researcher named Steve Wu uses the operating system to accomplish tasks on his PC. Steve is a biology graduate student working on his dissertation. Today he needs to create a summary page for one of the data sets he has collected. To complete the summary he needs to do the following tasks:

- Locate the text file called Summary 1, Wk.1 and move it to a new folder.
- Open the file.
- Open a spreadsheet file called Results 1, Wk.1.
- Copy part of the spreadsheet to the Clipboard.
- Paste a linked version of the data into the text file.
- Save the text file containing the linked data.

In other words, Steve is going to use the operating system and Object Linking and Embedding (OLE) to create a linked summary containing text and spreadsheet data. In addition, he is going to be multitasking the entire time, because he wants to listen to an audio CD while he is working.

The first step is to start the CD. He begins from the Windows 95 desktop and locates the CD Player in the Start menu, as shown in Figure 6.27.

FIGURE 6.27

The CD Player program, one of the multimedia accessories in Windows 95.

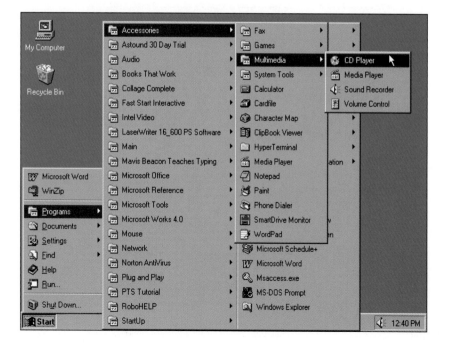

He launches the CD Player, puts the CD in his CD-ROM drive, and clicks on the play button. The CD Player is shown in Figure 6.28.

FIGURE 6.28
The CD Player.

Now Steve is ready to get to work. First he needs to locate the file that contains the text for his summary page. He begins by opening the Windows Explorer, the tool he uses to manage his files. The Explorer is shown in Figure 6.29.

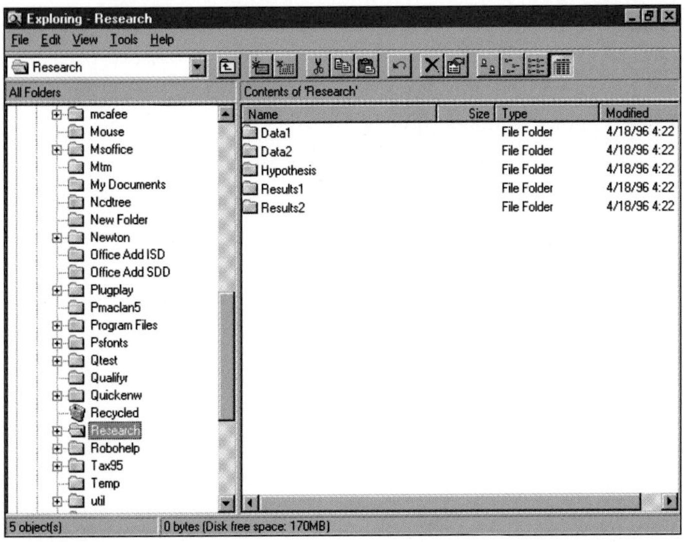

FIGURE 6.29
The Exploring window.

Unfortunately, he can't remember where he stored the file. To locate it, he uses the Find utility that is built into the operating system. He selects Find Files or Folders from the Tools menu to display the Find dialog box. He enters the name of the file, **Summary 1, Wk.1**, into the text field in the dialog box, and tells the utility to look in the C: drive. He clicks the Find Now button and the operating system locates the file. The dialog box showing the results is displayed in Figure 6.30.

FIGURE 6.30
The Find dialog box.

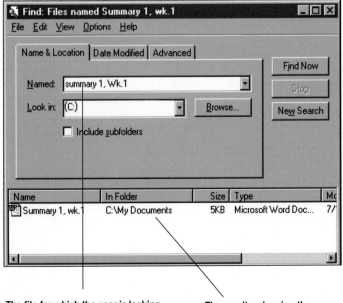

The file for which the user is looking

The results, showing the location of the file

To open the file, he simply double-clicks on the file. The open file is shown in Figure 6.31. Notice that you can still see the Taskbar below the word processing program.

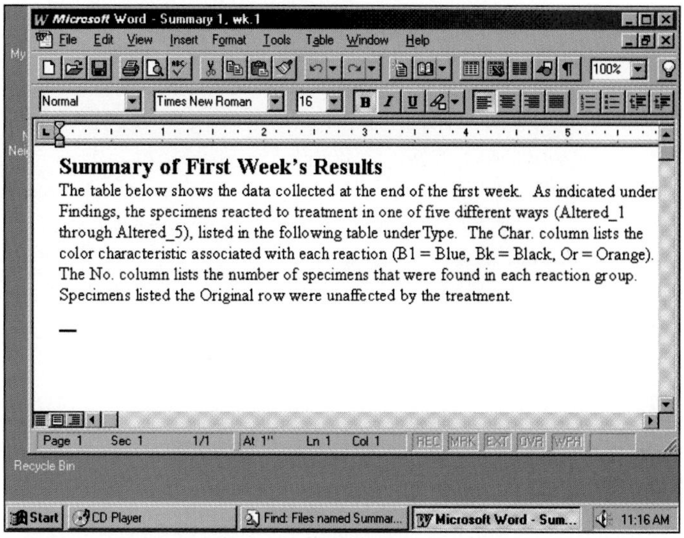

FIGURE 6.31
The Summary file.

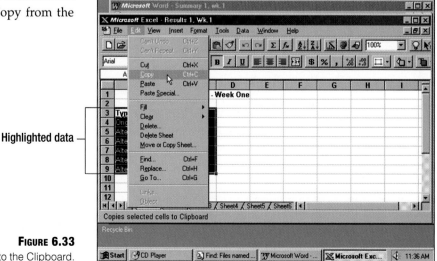

Now Steve needs to open the spreadsheet file containing the data he will link to his text file. This time, however, he knows where the file is. He navigates to the file using the Explorer and double-clicks to open it. The spreadsheet file is shown in Figure 6.32.

Spreadsheet file

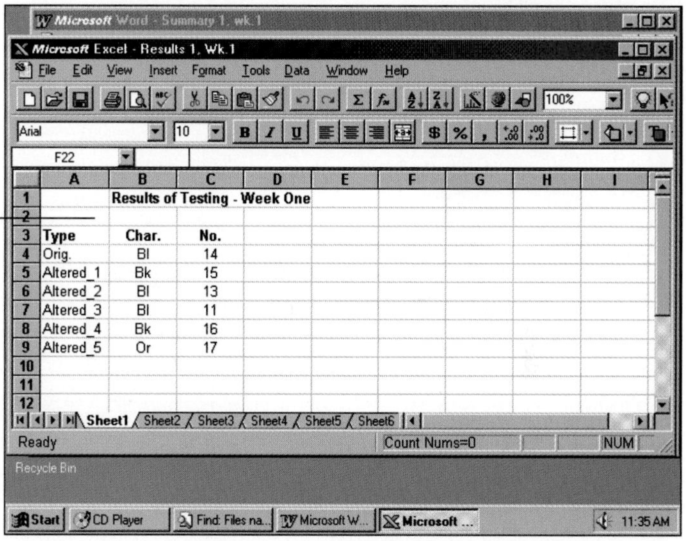

FIGURE 6.32
The spreadsheet file, showing the data for the first week.

The next step is to highlight the data he wants to link from the spreadsheet and to choose Copy from the Edit menu, as shown in Figure 6.33.

Highlighted data

FIGURE 6.33
Copying the Results data to the Clipboard.

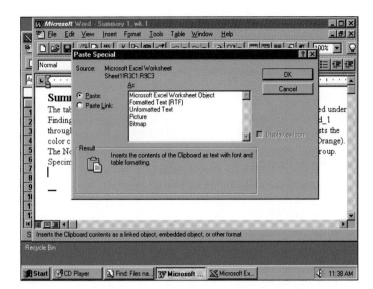

Now he goes back to the text document and moves the cursor to the place where he wants the linked data to appear. With the cursor in the correct position, he selects Paste Special from the Edit menu. The dialog box shown in Figure 6.34 appears.

FIGURE 6.34
The Paste Special dialog box.

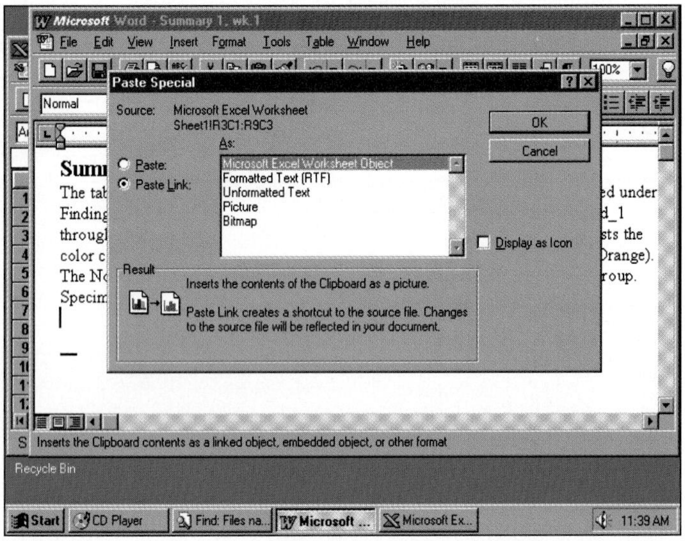

Here, it is important that he selects the Paste Link option and selects Microsoft Excel Worksheet Object, as shown in Figure 6.35.

FIGURE 6.35
The link is now set up.

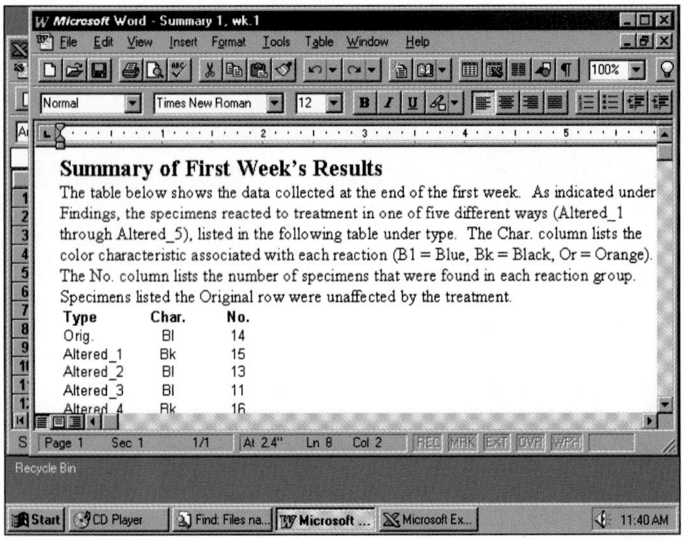

When he clicks on OK, the data is pasted into the text document, as shown in Figure 6.36.

FIGURE 6.36
The results are now in the word processing document but are still linked to the spreadsheet.

Now, whenever data is changed in the spreadsheet file, Results 1, Wk. 1, the corresponding table in the Word document will be automatically updated.

Steve is ready to save the document with a new name, in a new folder. He chooses Save As from the word processing program's File menu to display the Save As dialog box (see Figure 6.37).

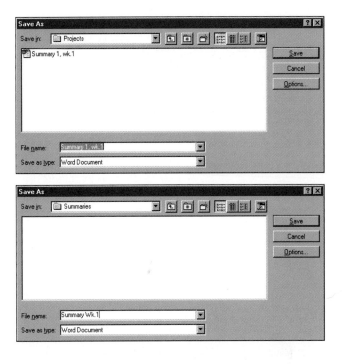

FIGURE 6.37
The Save As dialog box.

He wants to keep the linked reports in a folder within his Research folder. He navigates to the Research folder, clicks on the Create New Folder button, names the new folder "Summaries," moves to the new folder, and enters the name Summary Wk.1 as the new file name. The completed Save As dialog box is shown in Figure 6.38.

FIGURE 6.38
The completed Save As dialog box.

Steve has completed his work. He exits the spreadsheet software and the word processing program. Before he turns off the computer, he goes to the CD Player, clicks the Stop button, and removes the CD from the drive. To turn off the computer, he selects Shut Down from the Start menu. The operating system displays the dialog box shown in Figure 6.39.

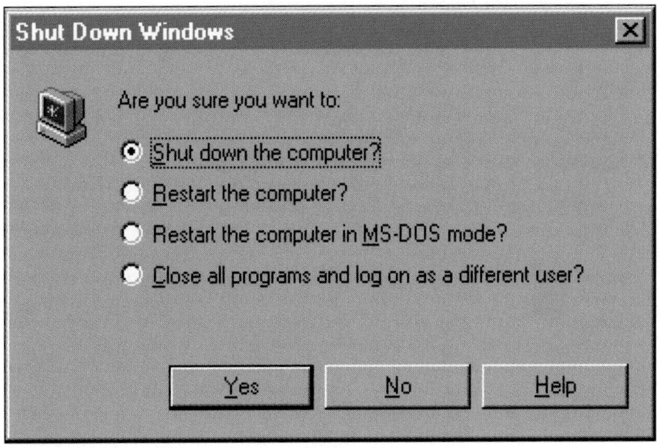

FIGURE 6.39
The Shut Down Windows dialog box.

He clicks on OK, waits until the computer gives the go-ahead, and turns off the power.

▶ WHAT TO EXPECT IN THE FUTURE

Operating system technology is one of the fastest-moving areas in the microcomputer world. Almost every year, the manufacturers of PC operating systems—primarily Microsoft, IBM, and Apple—come up with new, more capable versions of their operating systems.

For all of the contenders, certain technologies just beginning to emerge are likely to become standard parts of future operating systems. Current systems already offer the ability to connect with a network and share files and programs with others while protecting against loss of data. New versions will be increasingly good at networking, so that working in a workgroup on a network will become as easy as working on a stand-alone PC. Operating systems already allow people to connect with the Internet, but such connection will become increasingly common, easy, and feature-rich. Multimedia computing, still in its early stages compared to what it may one day become, will be a primary concern of operating systems. Operating systems will allow you to work with video, sound, and voice input as if you were in charge of your own movie studio.

As operating systems evolve, however, most believe that the operating system will still be the most important program in the computer. It affects all the other programs, it affects the user at all times, and it influences technical and marketing trends across the years.

If you consider the extent of the operating system's importance and the fact that Microsoft provides the operating system for about 85 percent of all PCs in this country, you will see that any move away from the Microsoft standard would constitute a fundamental change in this market. Such a change could occur as the result of two possible scenarios.

First, consider that the rest of the software industry resents Microsoft's power and has shown a tendency (though so far not successful) to "gang up" against Microsoft. If a major anti-Microsoft software alliance gained a foothold in an important core technology (such as Internet access), it could reverse one major trend in the industry—that more and more features are constantly being added to the operating system. A major software alliance could redefine the operating system as smaller, rather than as a set of programs that grow ever larger. The movement to build a low-cost "network computer" led by Larry Ellison of Oracle, a leading maker of database software, and others, is one such scenario.

A second scenario involves the "breakup" of Microsoft into at least two parts: an operating systems company and an applications company. Much like the breakup of AT&T into several regrouped "Baby Bells" decades ago, such a move would have to be justified as a breaking up of a monopoly.

Though neither of these scenarios seems likely in the immediate future, both seem increasingly possible if current trends continue. Ironically, even if one scenario were to occur, Microsoft's competitors would remain unhappy. Even a corporate breakup would leave the maker of the dominant operating system as the most powerful software company in the world.

Meanwhile, Microsoft continues to add features to its OS. In June of 1996, it announced plans that accelerate the incorporation of Internet tools, including a browser, into the Windows OS. How it succeeds against hordes of less powerful but energetic competitors will have profound impact on the end user in the years just ahead.

▶ VISUAL SUMMARY

What Is an Operating System?

- The operating system provides interfaces for the user, software, hardware, and for file management.
- The functionality of the operating system can be extended with the addition of utilities.

The User Interface

- Most modern operating systems employ a graphical user interface (GUI), in which users control the system by pointing and clicking on screen graphics.
- A GUI is based on the desktop metaphor, icons, sizable windows, menus, and dialog boxes.
- The applications designed to run under a particular operating system use the same interface elements, so users see a familiar interface or common user access (CUA) no matter what they are doing on the computer.
- Some older operating systems, such as DOS, use command-line interfaces, which the user controls by typing commands at a prompt.

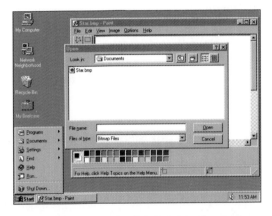

Running Programs

- The operating system manages all of the other programs that are running.
- It also provides system-level services to those programs, including file management, memory management, and printing.
- The operating system allows programs to share information. In Windows 3.1, 3.11, NT and 95, sharing is accomplished through the Clipboard and OLE.
- A modern operating system also makes multitasking possible.

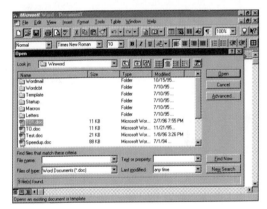

Managing Files

- The operating system keeps track of all the files on each disk. On a PC, Windows does this by constantly updating the FAT.
- Users can make their own file management easier by creating hierarchical file systems that include folders and subfolders.

Managing Hardware

- The operating system uses interrupt requests to maintain organized communication with the CPU and the other pieces of hardware.
- Each of the hardware devices is controlled by another piece of software, called the driver, which allows the operating system to activate and use the device.
- The operating system also provides the software necessary to link computers to form a network.

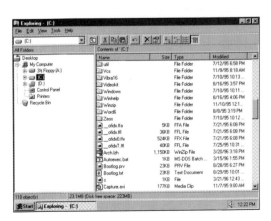

199

VISUAL SUMMARY AND EXERCISES

Enhancing the Operating System with Utility Software

- Operating systems have gradually included more and more utilities.
- The most common utilities are for file defragmentation, data compression, backup, data recovery, protection against viruses, and screen saving.

Microsoft Operating Systems

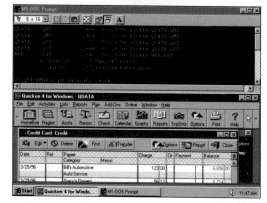

- DOS dominated the operating system market during the 1980s, but gradually became obsolete.
- Windows 3.0, 3.1, and 3.11 are operating environments that provided a GUI for computers running DOS.
- The strengths of Windows 95 are its simplified interface, 32-bit multitasking, and its ability to run older Windows and DOS programs.
- Microsoft Windows NT offered true 32-bit architecture and excellent networking capabilities.

Other Operating Systems for Personal Computers

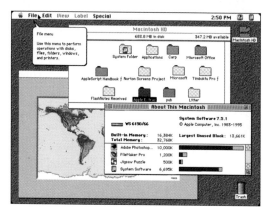

- The Macintosh has long been a favorite among GUI fans, as well as publishers, multimedia developers, graphic artists, and schools, primarily because of its consistent interface, built-in networking, and plug-and-play hardware capability.
- IBM's operating system is OS/2, a single-user, multitasking system for Intel-based machines.
- UNIX was the first multiuser, multiprocessing operating system on personal computers, but it has been losing market share.

▶ KEY TERMS

After completing this chapter, you should be able to define the following terms:

activate, 168
active program, 168
active window, 170
antivirus utilities, 186
backup software, 184
buttons, 168
choose, 168
Clipboard, 176
command-line interface, 174
common user access (CUA), 174
cooperative multitasking, 178
Copy, 176
Cut, 176
data compression utility, 184
data recovery utility, 185
defragmentation utility, 184
desktop, 167
drivers, 183

graphical user interface (GUI), 167
hierarchical file system, 181
icons, 167
interrupt request, 182
Macintosh operating system, 190
menu bar, 171
menu, 171
MS-DOS, 187
multitasking, 178
object embedding, 178
object linking, 178
Object Linking and Embedding (OLE), 176
operating environment, 188
operating system (OS), 166
OS/2, 191
Paste, 176
plug-and-play, 189
preemptive multitasking, 179

screen saver, 186
scroll bars, 170
select, 168
Start button, 169
system calls, 175
system software, 183
Taskbar, 168
title bar, 170
unerase program, 185
UNIX, 191
user interface, 166
virus, 186
window, 170
Windows 3.0, 188
Windows 3.1, 188
Windows 3.11, 188
Windows 95, 188
Windows NT, 189

▶ KEY TERM QUIZ

Fill in the blank with one of the terms listed in Key Terms:

1. When you double-click on an icon you _____ it.
2. The _____ is the master control program on your computer.
3. The _____ across the top of the window identifies the contents of the window.
4. The ability to perform two or more processes at the same time is known as _____.
5. When you copy or move data it is stored temporarily on the _____.
6. _____ is the process of cutting and pasting between applications.
7. You can drag the _____ to view different parts of a document.
8. A(n) _____ is designed to locate and eradicate a parasitic program or disk sector.
9. You use _____ to copy large groups of files from your hard drive to other storage media.
10. The on screen elements with which you interact are known as the _____.

▶ REVIEW QUESTIONS

1. Why is an operating system known as a master control program?
2. List and describe briefly the four functions performed by an operating system.
3. Why does the term *desktop* serve as a metaphor for the on screen interface of an operating system?
4. Describe briefly the four mouse techniques commonly used to work with on screen objects.
5. What does a window in a graphical user interface represent?
6. What device conducts a "dialog" with a user to gather the information necessary to perform a task?
7. What are two important characteristics of a well-designed GUI?
8. List and describe briefly at least three services that an operating system provides to active applications.
9. Describe briefly what occurs when an object in one document is linked to another document. How does this process contrast with a simple cut-and-paste operation?
10. List and describe briefly the various types of system utility programs that are provided with today's operating systems.

▶ DISCUSSION QUESTIONS

1. What does multitasking mean to a user? In what ways does the user benefit from the multitasking capabilities of an operating system?
2. In what ways have newer operating systems such as Windows 95, Windows NT, and the Macintosh OS simplified procedures such as managing files, hardware devices, and memory?
3. How can data that has been deleted from a disk still be recovered? Can erased data be recovered at any time, or is there variability to this process? What factors might render erased data unrecoverable?
4. Do you think that using an antivirus program is mandatory for anyone using a PC for business purposes? Are there any drawbacks to using antivirus software? Do you think such programs are 100 percent effective against all viruses? What do you think daily users of computers should do to ensure the best chances that their systems will remain clean?

NORTON INTERACTIVE

**Complete the Norton
Interactive module
for this chapter.**

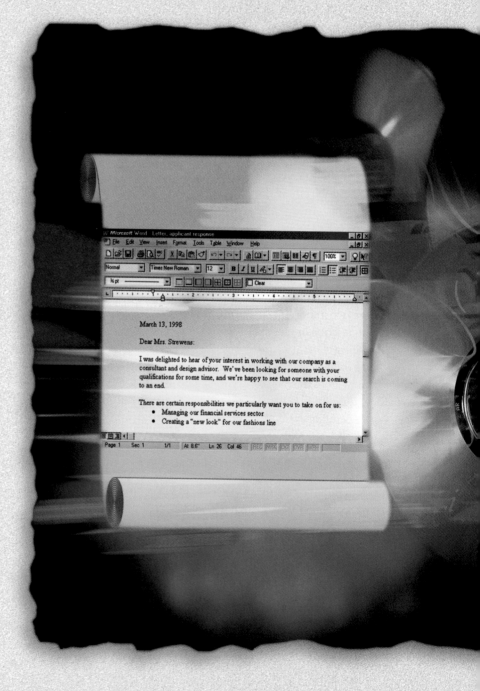

CHAPTER 7

WORD PROCESSING AND DESKTOP PUBLISHING

CONTENTS

OBJECTIVES

When you complete this chapter, you will be able to do the following:

- Describe the types of documents you can create with word processing software.
- Discuss the editing and formatting features of word processing software.
- Explain the purpose of HTML editing, the mail merge feature, style sheets, and the Print Preview window.
- Explain the difference between word processing and desktop publishing programs.
- Describe some of the important features of desktop publishing software.

For most people, writing is an everyday occurrence. It should come as no surprise that among the many types of application programs, two of the most popular are those that help you put text on a page: word processing and desktop publishing software. Word processing software, which provides a general set of tools for entering, editing, and formatting text, is the most common type of application found on PCs. Desktop publishing software is more specialized, offering powerful formatting tools, especially designed for documents, such as magazines, flyers, advertisements, and books.

In this chapter, you will be introduced to the kinds of documents that you can create with word processing software and the features that you will find within the programs. This chapter focuses on word processing software, because that is the type of program that most new users learn first. Toward the end of this chapter, you will be introduced to the advanced formatting capability of desktop publishing software. In the last section, the Norton Workshop, you will witness the creation of a professional memo using a word processing program.

► THE MANY USES OF WORD PROCESSING SOFTWARE

Word processing software gives users an extensive set of tools for working with text. It is used to create all kinds of documents, from simple notes and memos, to brochures, resumes, and 100-page reports. The four examples that follow illustrate some different types of documents you can create with word processing software.

Word processing software is one of the miracles of the modern age. Most people use it so often that it has become difficult to remember how they ever got along without it.

Robert Wagner
1254 Westlake Drive
San Francisco, CA 94959
(915)587-1473
May 8, 1997

Four Corners Real Estate Developers
Attn: Human Resources Dept.
53 Geneva Avenue
San Jose, CA 94009

Dear Human Resources Professional:

Enclosed please find a copy of my resume in response to the employment opportunities ad placed in the San Francisco Examiner on May 6. As you can see, I have experience and skills that I believe would be a benefit to your company. Please feel free to phone my references, or call me at any time for a personal interview. thank you in advance for your time.

Sincerely,

Robert Wagner

This is a simple text document—a letter sent in response to a job listing. The user has employed the power of word processing software to compose and edit the document, but has chosen to keep the format very simple. This is the preferred format for business letters. It includes a date, address, salutation, body, and closing.

This birthday card was also made using word processing software. It has colored text, rotated text, and even a picture.

1254 Westlake Drive
San Francisco, CA 94995
Work (916)587-1442
Home (415)555-1212

Robert Wagner

Objective

Seeking a full-time, permanent position with opportunity for personal growth and advancement

Education

1993 - 1996   San Francisco University   San Francisco, CA

BA, Economics

- Graduated 6th in class

Work experience

1996 - 1997   Redwood Real Estate   San Francisco, CA

Administrative Assistant

- Served as clerical and administrative assistant to a staff of 6 realtors. Duties included word processing, reception, filing, and maintenance of the computer system. Processed requests for credit history through TRW. Composed advertisements to be placed in local papers for new real estate listings. Expert PC user, with complete knowledge of WordPerfect, Lotus 1-2-3 and dBase.

Volunteer experience

American Red Cross; taught life-saving to thousands attending the CPR Saturday courses. Fully certified in CPR and Rescue Breathing.

California Coastal Commission. Organized local group for yearly Saturday Beach Cleanup, including task assignments and celebratory bar-b-que.

Interests and activities

Computers, Tropical Fish, and Community Activities

References

Mr. Nicolai Cosic, Supervisor, Redwood Real Estate (415) 955-4345

Ms. Elizabeth Waters, Student, (415) 945-9395

Ms. Juanita Escobar, Instructor, San Francisco University (415) 955-3549

This is a résumé—a listing of a person's qualifications for a job. More creative formatting is used here than in the business letter. There are bulleted lists, formatted headings, and different types of text alignment.

IN BRIEF

REPORTS ON TRIAL RESEARCH

VOLUME ONE   NUMBER ONE

In this issue . . .

Can the gender of the defense attorney have a bearing on the verdict in a rape case?

When the judge admonishes the jury to disregard inadmissible testimony, does it work?

Are contemporary juries acting tougher than judges?

How much faith do jurors have in testimony elicited hypnotically?

Does televising witnesses for public viewing affect their testimony?

The interval between pretrial publicity and the trial — is there an influence on jury behavior?

What is juror reaction to testimony that has to be translated into English?

Do jurors view aggressive female defense attorneys differently than they do aggressive male defense attorneys?

NOTE ON JURY AND LITIGATION RESEARCH   The intention of IN BRIEF is to bring the best of research in the area of social science and the law to the attention of trial attorneys. However, we caution that even well designed research with relevant variables nicely controlled may not generalize to real life situations that involve a multitude of uncontrolled factors. Jury research is almost never allowed to take place during actual courtroom proceedings because of the numerous difficulties and ethical problems involved. Consequently, investigators rely on "mock" or "simulated" jurors or juries. When we use the words "juror" or "jury" in this newsletter, we refer to the subjects utilized in social science experiments, unless otherwise indicated.

Can the gender of the defense attorney have a bearing on the verdict in a rape case?

Absolutely. This study revealed that a defendant on trial for rape was acquitted at a strikingly higher rate when his lawyer was a woman.

Findings

■ Appreciably more not guilty verdicts were given in this controlled simulation when the defense attorney was a woman (71%) than a man (41%).

■ Fault attribution analysis revealed that, when the defense attorney was a woman, *male jurors attributed more fault to the victim.* Female jurors, however, attributed fault evenly, *regardless of the gender of the defense attorney.*

■ When the victim was presented as elderly (over 60), however, female jurors tended to fault the defendant much more.

■ Nothing of consequence was determined regarding the physical attractiveness of the victim.

Conclusion

The finding that male jurors in a rape case seem much more susceptible to the influence of a woman defense attorney than female jurors seem to be obviously has important consequences regarding jury composition in these cases. Why a woman defense attorney should elicit so many more acquittals than her male counterpart is open to conjecture. Further attitude research may provide an answer.

[**Study design:** An equal number of men and women subjects were randomly assigned to eight mixed-sex groups, each of which heard one of two condensed audiotapes of an actual rape case, complete with testimony and attorney's summaries. One one tape, the voice of the defense attorney was male; on the other, female. All groups were shown the same photograph of the defendant, but each was shown a different picture of the victim (as either attractive, unattractive, young or old, to test the effects of these attributes). Subjects then responded to questionnaires. **Limiting factors:** For practical methodological reasons, subjects here decided verdicts on an individual basis, rather than in groups, as would occur in real jury decisions. Hence, there was no discussion with peers. Also, an audiotape cannot convey all of the complex visual cues present in an actual trial.]

Villemur, N. K. and Hyde, J. S., "Effects of Sex of Defense Attorney, Sex of Juror, and Age and Attractiveness of the Victim on Mock Juror Decision Making in a Rape Case," *Sex Roles* (1983)9,8:879-888.

When the judge admonishes the jury to disregard inadmissible testimony, does it work?

No — just the opposite seems to occur. Findings here suggest that when the judge specifically admonishes the jurors to disregard inadmissible testimony (critical testimony in this case), jurors tend to lean towards that testimony. In fact, the stronger the admonishment, the likelier it is that jurors *will* contemplate what they were told to disregard.

Findings

■ When the critical testimony was ruled to be admissible, jurors were strongly influenced to hold the defendant guilty.

■ If the judge did no more than define the testimony in question as inadmissible, there was negligible biasing effect; that is, a simple ruling of inadmissibility had little imapct on guilty verdicts.

■ If the judge ruled the testimony inadmissible, but *went on* to warn jurors to disregard it, such behavior biased the jurors in favor of such testimony.

Conclusion

Several psychological theories have been advanced to account for this phenomenon. One suggests that, when the judge simply rules testimony

---

This page from a newsletter demonstrates many of the formatting features in word processing software, but the effect is much more sophisticated than the birthday card.

▶ YOUR WINDOW INTO THE DOCUMENT

When you first start using word processing software, you find yourself in the main editing screen, which consists of a window through which you view your documents. On a computer with a sufficiently large monitor, you can open several windows, each with a different document or with different views of the same document. Most of the time, though, you will want to use a window that occupies the entire screen.

Figure 7.1 shows Microsoft Word for Windows, Version 7, currently the best selling word processing program. In addition to a document area, Word provides a menu bar across the top of the window and two rows of icons and tools that represent frequently used commands, such as those for printing and for selecting text styles. Word also offers a status bar across the bottom of the window with information related to your position in the current document, the page count, and the status of keyboard keys.

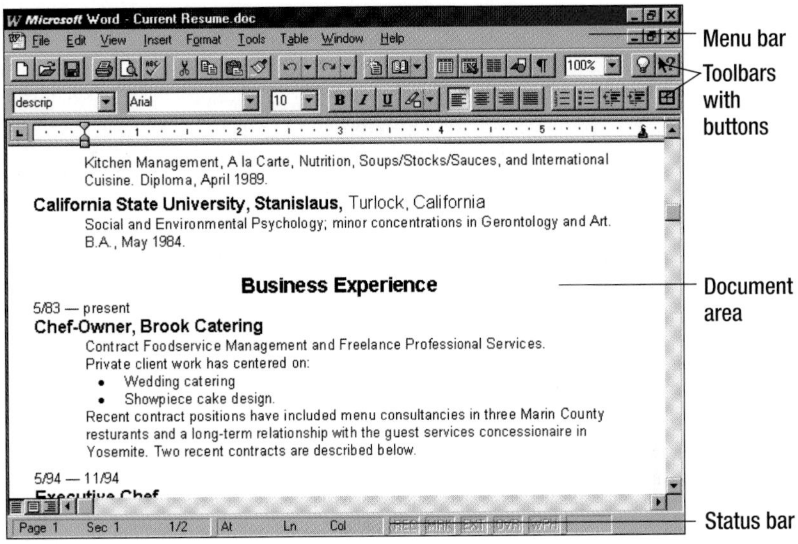

FIGURE 7.1
Parts of the Microsoft Word screen.

Word processors designed for graphical environments display text on screen in a manner that closely resembles what the printed document will look like. This feature is called **WYSIWYG** (pronounced "wiz-ee-wig"). It is an acronym for What You See Is What You Get. When the Macintosh was introduced in 1984, it was the first successful computer with the graphical power to be WYSIWYG, and the term was coined. Today, most word processors provide the WYSIWYG feature.

▶ ENTERING TEXT

You create a document by typing text on the keyboard. In a new document, the word processor will place a cursor in the upper-left corner of the document window. As you type text, the cursor advances across the screen, showing you where the next character will be placed.

Word Wrap

One of the great time-saving features of word processing software comes from the computer's ability to compute the length of each line of text as the text is entered. In other words, you do not have to press Enter (or Return) to move the cursor down to the next line as your text nears the right edge of the screen—the cursor will automatically drop down to the next line, as shown in Figure 7.2. This feature is called

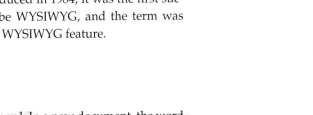

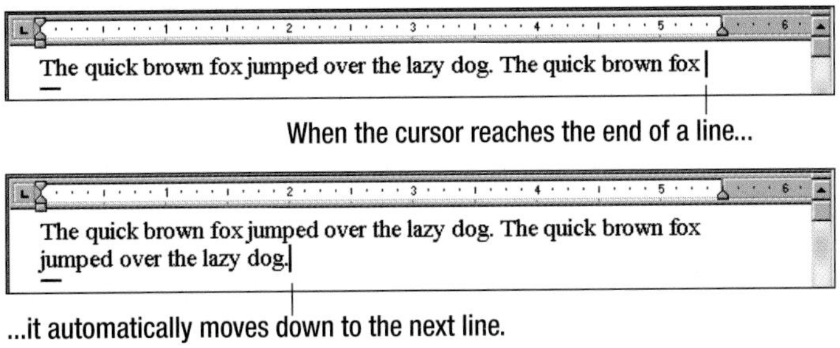

When the cursor reaches the end of a line...

...it automatically moves down to the next line.

FIGURE 7.2
Word wrap.

The word processing screen is a window into your document.

To scroll up or down through the document, you can use the scroll bars.

word wrap. Because the program automatically wraps text from one line to the next, the only time you need to press the Enter key is at the end of a paragraph.

Navigating Around a Document

When you get near the bottom of your word processor's screen or window, the top line on screen will move out of view, and the rest of the lines will move up to make room for a new line at the bottom. This is called **scrolling**, a term that comes from the concept of a continuous scroll of paper, as shown in Figure 7.3.

FIGURE 7.3
Scrolling through a document.

When your document is longer than can be shown in a document window, the screen functions like a window that you move up and down to see different parts of the document. Pressing the down-arrow key when the cursor is at the bottom of the screen causes the window to scroll down through the remainder of the document. Pressing the up-arrow key while the cursor is at the top of the screen causes the window to scroll up through the document.

Another way to move up and down is to use the mouse for scrolling. On the right edge of the screen there is a vertical bar, called the **scroll bar**, with arrow buttons at the top and bottom. The buttons are called **scroll arrows**. By clicking the mouse pointer on these buttons, you can scroll the window up and down, one line at a time, regardless of where the cursor is on screen.

Also located on the vertical scroll bar is a **scroll box**. When you are working in a large document, you can move quickly through it by dragging the scroll box up or down along the scroll bar to the relative position you want to go to. For example, to move quickly to the middle of a document, you can drag the scroll box to the middle of the scroll bar. To move up or down one screen at a time, you can also click in the scroll bar above or below the scroll box. Once you can see the part of the document you want to edit, you use the mouse to click on the spot where you want to place the cursor.

Finally, there are some widely accepted norms for the way the cursor movement keys work. For example, with most word processors, the Home key positions the cursor at the beginning of the current line and the End key positions it at the end of the line. Table 7.1 shows some of the most common actions of the other cursor movement and positioning keys. Note that these are general definitions. Keystroke actions for specific word processing programs may vary.

▶ EDITING TEXT

Perhaps the greatest advantage of word processing software over its predecessor, the typewriter, is its ability to change text without the user having to retype the entire page. Changing an existing document is called **editing** the document.

TABLE 7.1

Common Key Definitions in a Word Processor

KEY OR KEY COMBINATION	ACTION
Up arrow	Moves the cursor up one line
Down arrow	Moves the cursor down one line
Left arrow	Moves the cursor to the left
Right arrow	Moves the cursor to the right
Page up	Repositions the window up one screen
Page down	Repositions the window down one screen
Home	Moves the cursor to the beginning of the current line
End	Moves the cursor to the end of the current line
Insert	Toggles between inserting text or typing over existing text
Delete	Deletes the character under (or to the right of) the cursor
Ctrl + Home	Moves the cursor and the window to the top of the document
Ctrl + End	Moves the cursor and the window to the bottom of the document
Ctrl + Page Up	Moves the cursor to the beginning of the first line displayed in the window
Ctrl + Page Down	Moves the cursor to the end of the bottom line displayed in the window
Ctrl + Right Arrow	Moves the cursor to the beginning of the next word
Ctrl + Left Arrow	Moves the cursor to the beginning of the previous word
Shift + arrow key	Selects text (for formatting or moving, for example)
Shift + Delete	Cuts selected text and places it in the Clipboard
Shift + Insert	Inserts the text in the Clipboard at the current cursor position

Correcting a Typing Mistake

If you make a mistake as you type, there are several ways you can fix the error. If the mistake was in the last word you typed (just to the left of the cursor), you can use the Backspace key to move back up to the point where the mistake began. The Backspace key moves the cursor to the left and at the same time, removes each previous character it moves over. After deleting the characters you want to remove, you can then resume typing.

When typing, you may also need to correct an error in the middle of a sentence. For instance, say that you typed this phrase:

The quick brwon fox jumped

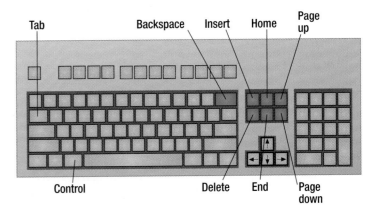

You can use the Backspace, Insert, or Delete keys such as those shown on this IBM-compatible keyboard to correct mistakes.

Using the Backspace key to correct the misspelling "brwon" would also erase the words "fox jumped," requiring you to type them again. In this situation, you might use the left-arrow key to return the cursor to the word with the mistake. The left-arrow key will move the cursor back without erasing characters. Then you could use Backspace to erase the *wo* and retype *ow*.

You also can use a mouse to make corrections by simply moving the mouse pointer over the first character you want to change and then clicking the mouse button. This moves the cursor directly to the error. As you gain experience with a word processor, you will gradually develop a sense of the easiest way for you to correct errors.

Selecting Blocks

Setting the position of the cursor and typing new text or pressing Backspace or Delete are techniques for making minor edits to documents. When larger changes are needed—for example, when you need to move a paragraph—you need more powerful tools. A **block** is a contiguous group of words, sentences, or paragraphs in your document that you earmark for one of several purposes. The marking process is called **selecting** the text. Most word processing software allows you to select a block of text by dragging the mouse pointer from the beginning to the end of the block. As you hold down the mouse button and move the mouse cursor over the text, the text will change color to indicate that the text is selected. The block is then said to be **highlighted**.

You can also double-click with the mouse button to select a single word or triple-click to select an entire paragraph.

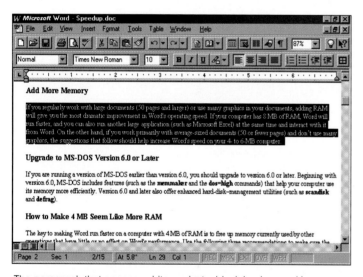

The paragraph that appears white against a black background is a highlighted block.

You can select text with the keyboard as well by holding down the Shift key and moving the cursor with the arrow keys. To use a mouse to deselect a block, click the mouse anywhere on the screen. The block will be displayed in normal colors. To deselect using the keyboard, press one of the cursor movement keys, such as an arrow key.

Working with Blocks of Text

Once a block is selected, there are many things you can do to it. You can erase the entire block by pressing the Delete key or by typing any other text over the selected block. Selecting and deleting a block is the fastest way to delete long passages of text.

You also can copy or move the block from one part of the document to another, or even from one document to another. With some word processors, moving text is as easy as dragging the block to a new location, a technique called **drag-and-drop editing**. The same effect can be accomplished by using the Clipboard to cut or copy the block, then pasting it to a new location.

Find and Replace

One exceptionally handy feature found in every word processor is **find and replace** (or **find and change**). With find and replace, you can make the program look for every occurrence of a sequence of characters—a word, name, or phrase—and replace each one with new text.

For example, say that you create a ten-page document, and then realize that you misspelled someone's name in dozens of places throughout the document. By choosing Find and Replace from the Edit menu, you can easily replace the name with the proper spelling everywhere it occurs. When you select the Replace menu option, a dialog box similar to the one shown in Figure 7.4 appears. In this dialog box, you enter the text for which to search, and the text with which to replace it. By clicking the Replace button, you can step through the document, replacing each occurrence one at a time, or click Replace All to replace all the misspelled names automatically.

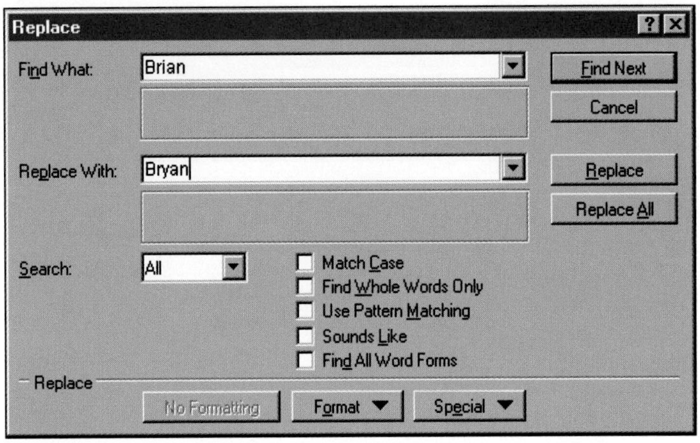

FIGURE 7.4
The Replace dialog box.

The Undo Command

When you are editing a document, you will occasionally make a mistake. There are two powerful tools for recovering from mistakes.

The first tool is the Save command. By saving your work every couple of minutes, you always have a recently saved copy of the document. If you make a big mistake, you can close the document without saving and then open the most recently saved version.

The second tool is the Undo command. In most cases, Undo offers a faster way to backtrack after making a mistake. You simply choose the Undo option from the Edit menu, and the last action you performed is undone. Most software now has a feature for undoing more than one mistake, as shown in Figure 7.5. In the menu, you select the command that you believe was a mistake, and the software returns your document to the condition it was in just before that command was issued.

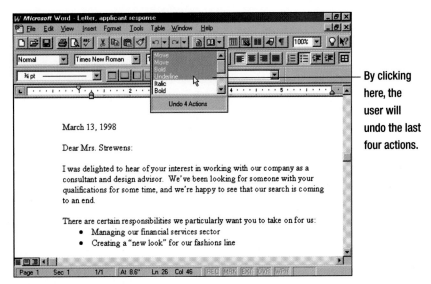

By clicking here, the user will undo the last four actions.

FIGURE 7.5
The multiple-undo feature.

Checking Spelling

Most word processing packages have a **spelling checker**, a software feature that compares each word in a document with the software's internal dictionary. The

The spelling checker has found this word in the document...

...and suggests that it be replaced with this word.

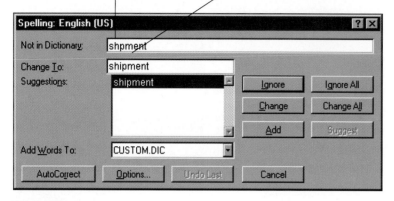

FIGURE 7.6
The spelling checker.

ability to check for misspellings in a document can add to your confidence that a document will be professional in every sense.

The dictionaries used by spelling checkers typically contain thousands of words. There are, however, many acceptable words that spelling checkers will question because they do not find them in their dictionaries—for example, the names of people and companies, and many abbreviations and acronyms. For this reason, a good spelling checker allows you to create your own custom dictionary that it can then use for further reference.

When a spelling checker identifies a word that it cannot locate in its standard and custom dictionaries, the program prompts you by displaying a dialog box or message, such as the one shown in Figure 7.6.

The dialog box suggests an alternative word if the spelling checker can find one fairly close to the word it suspects is misspelled. It may also display a list of other words that are similar to the suspect word. You can accept the suggested spelling of the word or you can choose one of the other similar words.

Unfortunately, spelling checkers are not yet smart enough to check for the context of a word. Some words will be considered correct even if the usage is wrong. For example, consider this sentence:

It was a pleasant seen.

Clearly, "seen" should be "scene." Unfortunately, the spelling checker will go right by it because "seen" is a correctly spelled word. Because spelling checkers can check only for spelling, not for usage, new products called **grammar checkers** have emerged on the market. These packages check for word usage, correct grammar, and sometimes even writing style. They are often sold separately, although the trend is to integrate them into word processing software.

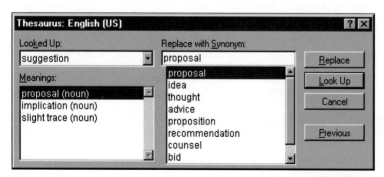

A thesaurus finds synonyms for words that you enter or highlight. Here, the thesaurus has listed synonyms for "suggestion."

Using a Thesaurus

An online thesaurus is a feature that has been a standard in word processors almost as long as spelling checkers. A computerized **thesaurus** lets you type in words and responds with a list of synonyms, or words with similar meanings. When you compose a document and think that a word is just not quite right, you can highlight the word and bring up the thesaurus to see a list of alternatives.

The paperless office, with all its information residing as electronic and magnetic bits on computer disks, has been a popular prediction for many years. It foretold an end to the frustration of filing cabinets, the intimidation of paper-archive warehouses, and the ecological damage caused by the production of paper.

There is, however, one big obstacle to creating a true paperless business. Many programs and computers are still unable to read what other programs and computers write. With printed documents, any person literate in the language that the document was written in can dig a page out of a briefcase, cabinet or warehouse, now or 50 years from now, and understand what it says.

Two computers or programs must agree upon the language, the storage medium, the file format for text, the file format for images, even the representation of fonts and colors for a document to be mutually readable.

The first step toward a universal electronic language was the ASCII code for exchanging pure text documents. But the standard ASCII character set cannot accommodate the complexity of today's computer documents. It cannot use styles, formatting, and other aspects of modern communication.

Individual programs began to incorporate "import and export" filters. These were functions that attempted to translate documents from their original state to the format of the application currently in use. As file formats proliferated and evolved, these filters became insufficient.

Designers then tackled operating systems as the next step in standardizing digital exchange. They established some rules on standard file formats and supported the translators of some of the major applications, such as Word or Excel.

Today, one of the promising developments toward the paperless office is the "portable document program," which first appeared commercially in 1993. Adobe's Acrobat, Corel's WordPerfect Envoy, No Hands' Common Ground, and Farallon's Replica are examples of such applications.

Portable document programs create electronic documents that carry all the necessary components with them: fonts, graphics, and a viewer. A viewer is a small program that can display and print a document with all of its details and styles. Using the viewer, people can read and print the document even if they aren't running the application on their computer. This feature makes portable documents ideal for workgroup collaboration where team members all have different computer systems.

However, portable document programs also have drawbacks. There are inconsistencies in their delivery—changing fonts, item positions, and other elements. Issues about cost (in some cases there is a charge for the viewer program) and ownership have still to be settled. Also, the documents can be read and printed only, not edited.

Other steps toward the paperless office involve a variety of technological advances including personal digital assistant computers (PDAs), paperless faxes, remote-access databases, and more. Here are a few recent examples of the trend:

■ Taco Bell streamlined its food quality inspection process by abandoning paper reports in favor of electronic inspections. Its inspectors now carry PDAs to access a preprogrammed electronic inspection form.

■ UPS (United Parcel Service) publishes all its internal software manuals and updates on CD-ROM with searchable keywords, requiring less employee time to find answers electronically than to page through the former paper manuals.

■ Sprint Corporation telephone service updated its order-entry system to eliminate paper. The salespeople now carry laptop computers from which they send orders directly to the company's internal database. Sprint reports that the new system is faster, cuts down on errors, and is user-friendly to both salespeople and customers.

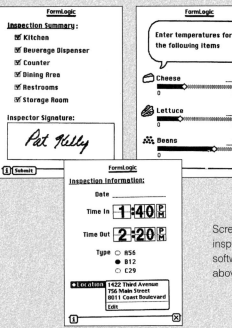

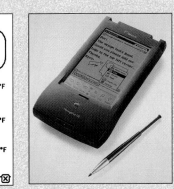

Screens from the Taco Bell food quality inspection software, by Wright-Strategies. This software runs on the Apple Newton shown above at right.

▶ FORMATTING TEXT

In word processing software, less than half of the features are devoted to editing. Most are for formatting the document, which includes controlling the appearance of text, the layout of text on the page, and the inclusion of pictures and other graphic elements, such as lines, boxes, and shading. Most formatting features fall into one of three categories:

- Character formats
- Paragraph formats
- Document formats

There are a few advanced tools, however, such as HTML scripting (formatting for the World Wide Web), which do not fall into these categories.

Character Formats

Character formats include settings that control the appearance of individual text characters, such as font, type size, type style, and color.

Fonts

The term **font** or **typeface** refers to the style of the letters, symbols, and punctuation marks in your document. Fonts have names like Times, Helvetica, and Palatino. In addition to those that come with the operating system, most word processors come with at least a handful of built-in additional fonts. You can also purchase additional fonts.

There are two general categories of fonts: monospace and proportional. Every character of a **monospace font** takes up exactly the same amount of horizontal space. Monospace fonts resemble a typewriter's output. This is a very useful characteristic if you need to line up columns of type. The most common monospace font is Courier.

```
This is the Courier font, which is monospaced.
```

This is the Arial font, which is proportional.

In a monospaced font, each character occupies the same amount of horizontal space. In a proportional font, characters take up only as much space as they need in order to be legible.

Serifs ◁ Times New Roman is a serif font.

Arial is a sans serif font.

Serif fonts have decorative lines and curls at the ends of strokes. Sans serif fonts do not.

Most fonts, however, are **proportional fonts**. With a proportional font, each character may have a slightly different width. Examples are seen in the letters M and I. The letter M is much wider than the letter I. In a proportional font, the I will take up less horizontal space than the M.

Typefaces also fall into two additional broad categories—**serif** and **sans serif**. Serif type fonts have fancy curls or extra decorative strokes at the ends of the strokes that make up each character; sans serif fonts do not (*sans* means "without" in French). According to general typesetting conventions, serif type is easier to read, and therefore more suitable for body text, while sans serif type is better for display text or headings. The headings in this book are set in a sans serif face; the text in this sentence is set in a serif face.

Type Size

The size of a font is measured in points. One point equals .02 inch in height. Therefore, 12-point type, the most common size used in business documents, is .17 inch tall, from the top of the tallest letters to the bottom of the letters that descend below the baseline (g, j, p, q, and y). Figure 7.7 shows a few common type sizes and how the type is measured.

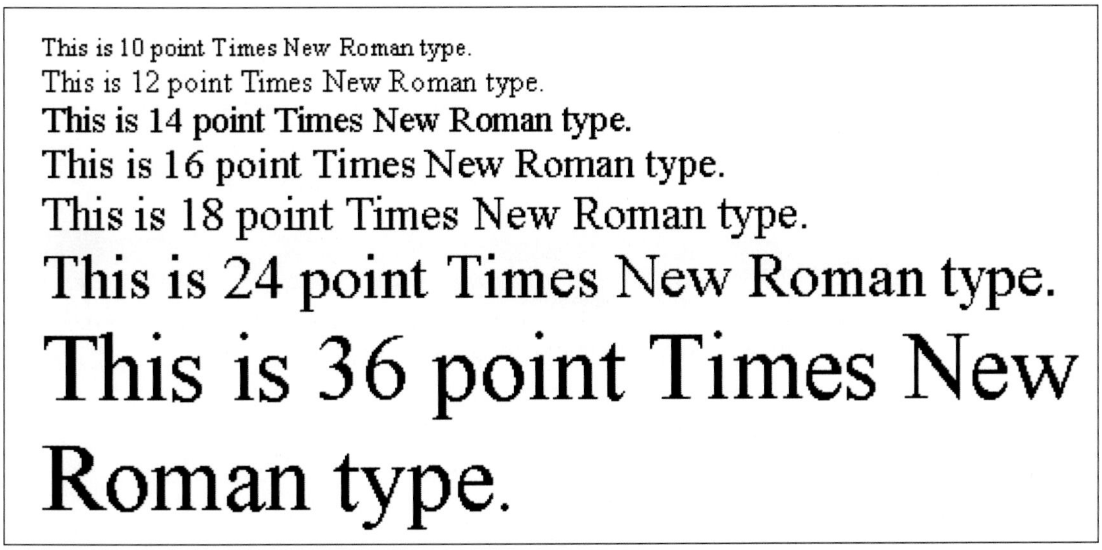

This is 10 point Times New Roman type.
This is 12 point Times New Roman type.
This is 14 point Times New Roman type.
This is 16 point Times New Roman type.
This is 18 point Times New Roman type.
This is 24 point Times New Roman type.
This is 36 point Times New Roman type.

FIGURE 7.7
Type sizes.

Type Styles

In addition to the font and type size, the appearance of characters can be controlled with type styles. The most common style attributes used in documents are bold, italics, and underlining. Examples of these styles, as well as several less common ones, are shown in Figure 7.8.

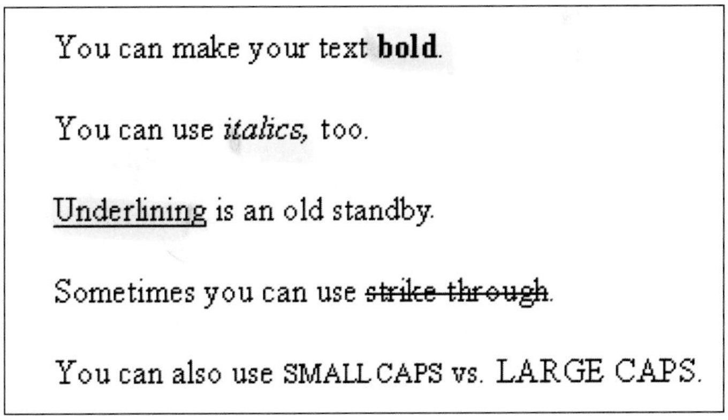

You can make your text **bold**.

You can use *italics*, too.

<u>Underlining</u> is an old standby.

Sometimes you can use ~~strike-through~~.

You can also use SMALL CAPS vs. LARGE CAPS.

FIGURE 7.8
Type styles.

Applying Character Formats to Your Document

When working with word processing software, there are two ways you can apply character formats (or any format, for that matter) to your text. You can select the formats as you enter text, or you can enter all the text first and then reformat it. In practice, you will probably use both methods.

When applying character formats, the best rule of thumb is to keep it simple. If you have too many different character formats, your document will look jumbled and unorganized. Even in complex documents with many different features, you should limit yourself to just a few different fonts and a few combinations of type sizes and styles.

Paragraph Formats

In word processing, the word *paragraph* has a slightly different meaning than it does traditionally. When using word processing software, you create a **paragraph** each time you press the Enter key. A group of sentences is a paragraph, but a two-word heading is defined as a paragraph as well.

Paragraph formatting includes settings that are applied only to whole paragraphs. These include line spacing, paragraph spacing, indents, alignment, tab stops, and borders and shading.

Line and Paragraph Spacing

With word processing software, you can have precise control over the amount of space between each line of text in a paragraph, a setting known as **line spacing**. Lines can be single-spaced or double-spaced, or set to any spacing you desire. Figure 7.9 shows examples of different line spacing.

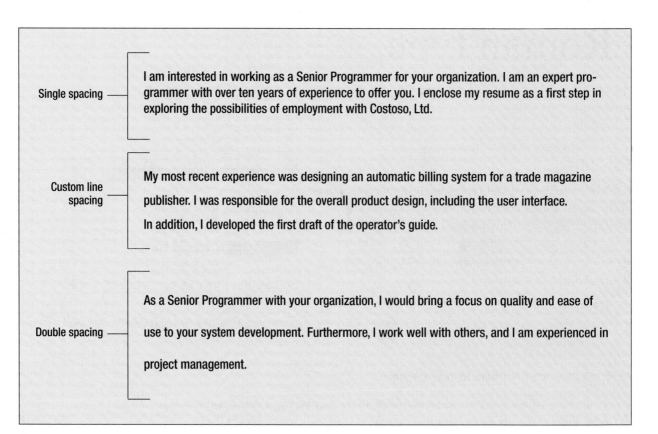

FIGURE 7.9
Samples of different line spacing.

Paragraph spacing refers to the amount of space between each paragraph. By default the paragraph spacing is usually the same as the line spacing. However, you can set the software so that extra space is automatically included at the end of each paragraph. For example, Figure 7.10 shows an extra 6 points of space added between the paragraphs.

> Your February 2, 1997, letter regarding the delivery of damaged merchandise was forwarded to me. I am looking into the situation, and I hope to have it resolved quickly. When I have finished my investigation, I will write or call you with a response.
>
> I assure you that we are taking your complaint very seriously. You are a valuable customer, and any dissatisfaction on your part indicates an opportunity for improvement on our part.
>
> If I need more information from you to help me in this matter, I will contact you. Thank you for your patience.

FIGURE 7.10
Single-spaced lines, with extra space between paragraphs.

Indents and Alignment

In a word processed document, the **margins** are the white borders around the edge of the page where the text is not allowed to go. **Indents** determine how close each line of a paragraph comes to the margins. **Alignment** refers to the orientation of the lines of a paragraph with respect to the margins. There are four alignment options: left, right, center, and justified or full justification. Alignment and indents are paragraph formats; the margins are part of the document formats. Together, the indents and alignment control the shapes of paragraphs. Figure 7.11 shows four examples of different indents and alignments.

Your February 2, 1997, letter regarding the delivery of damaged merchandise was forwarded to me. I am looking into the situation, and I hope to resolve it quickly. When I have finished my investigation, I will write or call you with a response. — No indent, justified

Your February 2, 1997, letter regarding the delivery of damaged merchandise was forwarded to me. I am looking into the situation, and I hope to resolve it quickly. When I have finished my investigation, I will write or call you with a response. — First-line indent, left-aligned

Your February 2, 1997, letter regarding the delivery of damaged merchandise was forwarded to me. I am looking into the situation, and I hope to resolve it quickly. When I have finished my investigation, I will write or call you with a response. — First-line indent, right-aligned

Your February 2, 1997, letter regarding the delivery of damaged merchandise was forwarded to me. I am looking into the situation, and I hope to resolve it quickly. When I have finished my investigation, I will write or call you with a response. — Hanging indent, left-aligned

FIGURE 7.11
Four paragraph shapes.

Tabs and Tab Stops

The keyboard's Tab key moves the text cursor forward (to the right) until it encounters a tab stop, inserting a fixed amount of space in the line. A **tab stop** is a position, both on screen and in the document, usually measured from the left margin of the document. When you create a new document, tab stops typically are defined at every fourth or fifth character, or at every .5-inch position. Most word processors allow you to change or remove the tab stops by displaying a ruler across the top or bottom of the screen that shows where tab stop positions are set. In some word processors, the ruler and tab stops are visible at all times.

Tabs are most often used to align columns of text accurately. For example, in Figure 7.12, the columns of text are separated by tab spacing (rather than by spaces inserted with the space bar). The first column is aligned with a left-aligned tab stop, the second column is aligned using a right-aligned tab stop, the third by a center tab stop, and the fourth using a decimal tab stop.

Left-aligned tab stop   Centered tab stop   Right-aligned tab stop   Decimal tab stop

		TODAY'S PURCHASES		
Department	Part Code	Description	Quantity	Cost.
Purchasing	4453HF	Disks	50	$12.50
Marketing	KD4323	Pens	2000	$50.24
Research	D387567	Test Tubes	1200	$2500.00
Admin.	DFG465	Binder Clips	100	$50.00
Research	DGK473	Rubber Gloves	500	$32.00
Day Care	H483GH	Diapers	100	$50.00

FIGURE 7.12
Four kinds of tab stops.

Borders and Shading

Finally, paragraphs can be formatted with borders or shading. A **border** is a line, often called a rule, that is drawn on one or more sides of a paragraph. **Shading** consists of a pattern or color that is displayed as a background to the text in a paragraph. Figure 7.13 shows a paragraph with a drop shadow, border and shading.

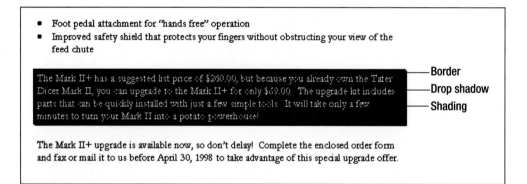

- Foot pedal attachment for "hands free" operation
- Improved safety shield that protects your fingers without obstructing your view of the feed chute

The Mark II+ has a suggested list price of $260.00, but because you already own the Tater Dicer Mark II, you can upgrade to the Mark II+ for only $69.00. The upgrade kit includes parts that can be quickly installed with just a few simple tools. It will take only a few minutes to turn your Mark II into a potato powerhouse!

— Border
— Drop shadow
— Shading

The Mark II+ upgrade is available now, so don't delay! Complete the enclosed order form and fax or mail it to us before April 30, 1998 to take advantage of this special upgrade offer.

FIGURE 7.13
Paragraph with a border, shading, and a drop shadow.

Document Formats

You already have been briefly introduced to margins, one of the most important of the document formats. Often, the first step of setting up a new document is to enter the width for each margin. In addition, the document formats include the size of the page, its orientation, and the headers, footers, and footnotes.

Page Size and Orientation

Normally, documents are set up to fit on 8.5 by 11-inch pieces of paper, a standard known as letter-size paper. However, you also can set up your document for other standard sizes, such as legal size (8.5 by 14 inches), assuming your printer is capable of handling that size paper. You can also set up your document for custom paper sizes.

The dimensions of the document are also determined by the orientation of the paper. By default, documents are set up with **portrait orientation**, in which the document is taller than it is wide. However, you can always switch to **landscape orientation**, in which the paper is turned on its side.

Vocational Software Company
655 Friedal Street
Gayle, South Dakota 55344
(934)554-3535
June 7, 1997

Lou Picard, Instructor
Best Training Facilities
1412 San Jose Avenue
Cloverdale, WA 89899

Dear Mr. Picard:

Thank you for the suggestions that you offered in your letter dated May 6, 1997. Your suggestions for enhancing the PC Basics Course were well thought out and clearly stated. I have forwarded them to our development department for consideration.

Although we can't promise that we will implement your suggestions, we appreciate them and will give them the serious consideration that they deserve. Thank you again for taking the time to share your ideas with us.

Sincerely,

Chris Fields

Landscape printing.

Vocational Software Company
655 Friedal Street
Gayle, South Dakota 55344
(934)554-3535
June 7, 1997

Lou Picard, Instructor
Best Training Facilities
1412 San Jose Avenue
Cloverdale, WA 89899

Dear Mr. Picard:

Thank you for the suggestions that you offered in your letter dated May 6, 1997. Your suggestions for enhancing the PC Basics Course were well thought out and clearly stated. I have forwarded them to our development department for consideration.

Although we can't promise that we will implement your suggestions, we appreciate them and will give them the serious consideration that they deserve. Thank you again for taking the time to share your ideas with us.

Sincerely,

Chris Fields
Account Representative

Portrait printing.

Headers, Footers, and Footnotes

Long documents generally include headers, footers, or both. Headers and footers are lines of text that run along the top and bottom of every page. They often include the name of the document and the page number. The date on which the document was printed and the name of the person who wrote it might also be included. For example, the header for the pages in this book includes the chapter number or the chapter name (depending on whether it is a left-facing page or a right-facing page) and the page number. There are no footers.

Footers should not be confused with footnotes, which are placed at the bottom of the page and annotate a specific place in a document. If you have ever had to write a term paper, you are probably familiar with footnotes. Word processing software includes tools for entering footnotes. As you edit or reformat the document, the software keeps the footnote on the correct page.

▶ ADVANCED WORD PROCESSING FEATURES

Naturally, there are a few formatting features and tools that do not fit into the categories described so far in this chapter. Some of these features, such as Print Preview and Mail Merge, are like utilities, giving you access to system-level features. Others, like HTML scripting and the ability to add graphics or sounds to your document, add functions that are almost like adding new software programs.

Print Preview

A feature many word processing programs provide, called **print preview**, gives you the ability to see exactly what your pages will look like before you print them. Print preview shrinks the view of your document down so you can see an entire page or facing pages on screen at the same time. (Sometimes your word processor can also magnify the page.)

In some programs, you cannot edit your text in print preview, but it is especially helpful for seeing how overall formatting characteristics, such as margin settings and headers and footers, will affect the appearance of your document before you waste paper to find out.

Figure 7.14 shows a document in print preview. Notice that the last sentence is printing on the next page, rather than at the end of the paragraph. Print preview allows you to see and correct situations like this before you print the document.

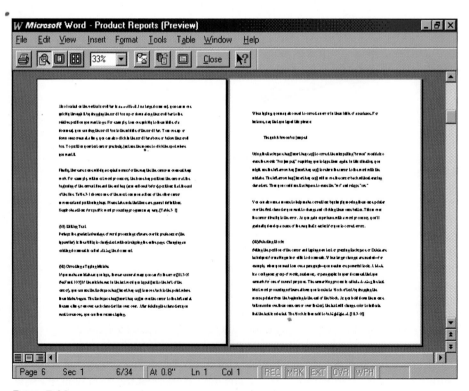

FIGURE 7.14
Print Preview screen.

Mail Merge

A **mail merge** is the process of combining a form letter with the contents of a database, usually a name and address list, so that each copy of the letter has one entry from the database printed on it. The mail merge feature makes it easy to send the same letter to a list of different people with the correct name and address printed on each letter.

To perform a mail merge, you first create a database of names and addresses, also known as a *secondary file*. The database can be created using a special tool in the word processing software, or it can be imported from a spreadsheet or database program.

When the database is set up correctly, the next step is to create the form letter. In addition to normal text, the form letter, sometimes referred to as the *primary file*, contains references to entries in the database. When the letter is set up, you are ready to merge the two files. The merge creates one copy of the letter for each entry in the database, as shown in Figure 7.15.

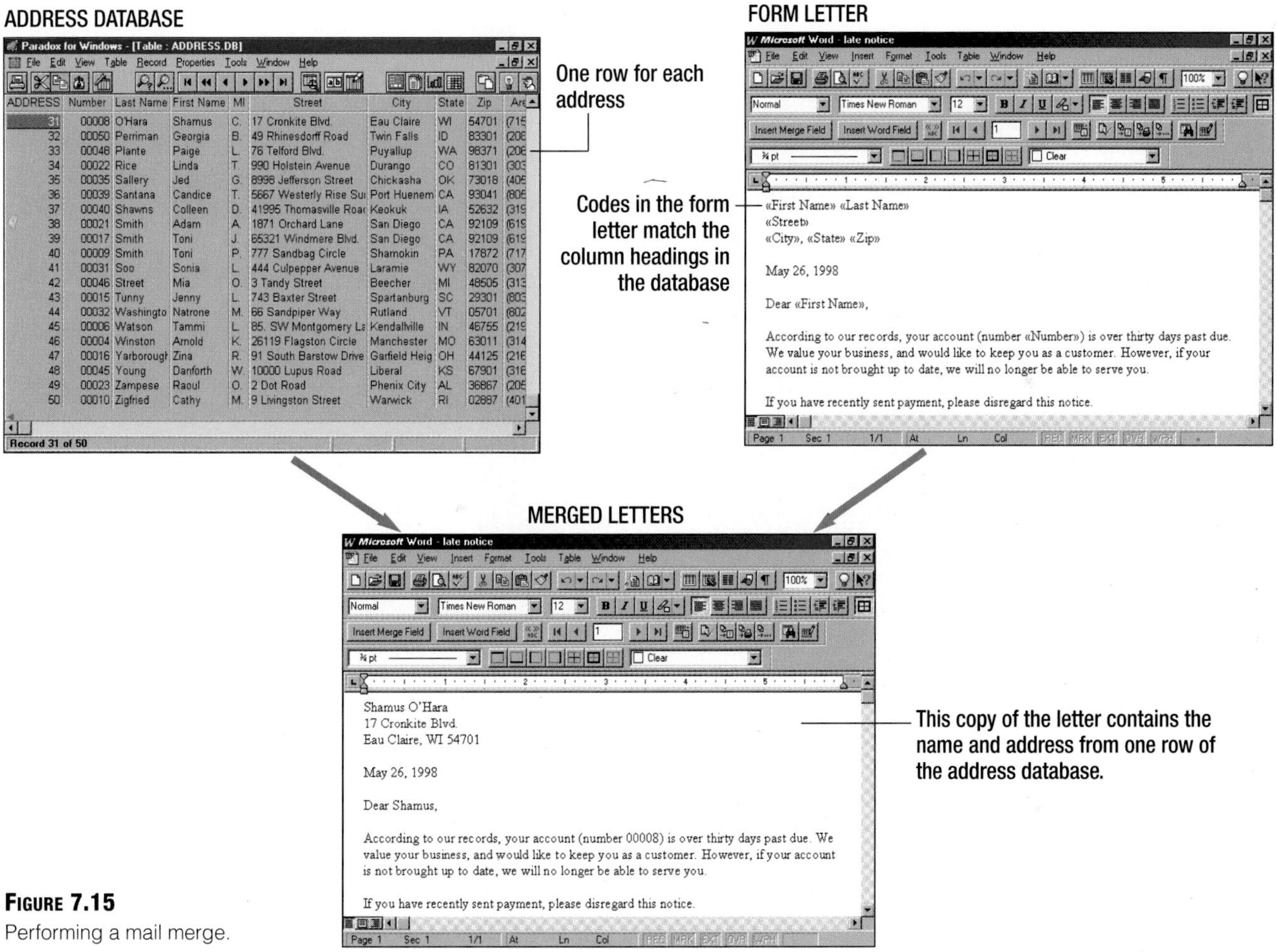

ADDRESS DATABASE

FORM LETTER

One row for each address

Codes in the form letter match the column headings in the database

MERGED LETTERS

This copy of the letter contains the name and address from one row of the address database.

FIGURE 7.15

Performing a mail merge.

The real benefit of the mail merge feature is realized if you use the address database more than once to send different letters. In this case, you are spared the work of re-entering all the names and addresses. Businesses send form letters frequently, so the mail merge feature has proved very popular.

Adding HTML Codes to Make World Wide Web Pages

In 1994 and 1995, many companies and individuals began creating electronic documents that can be accessed on the part of the Internet known as the World Wide Web. These documents are known as Web pages. Creating a page for the Web requires formatting the page using Hypertext Markup Language, or HTML.

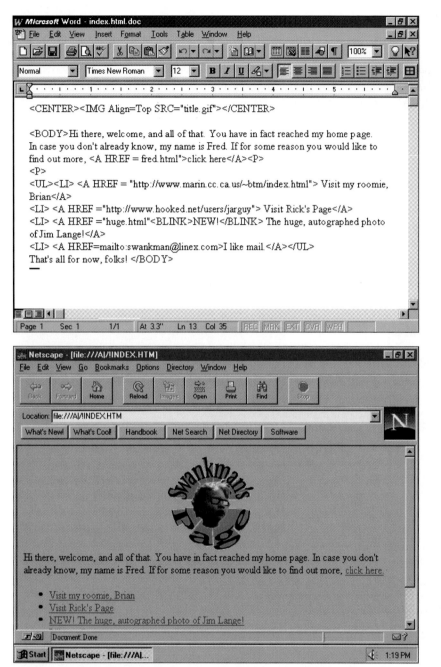

FIGURE 7.16
Document coded with HTML.

Today, some word processing software includes the ability to format documents using HTML so they can be turned into Web pages. An example of a document coded with HTML is shown in Figure 7.16. The resulting page, as it appears on the Web, is shown in Figure 7.17.

FIGURE 7.17
The HTML document, viewed using a browser for the World Wide Web on the Internet.

Adding Graphics and Sounds

As was mentioned earlier, it is possible to add graphic images—photos, drawings, or clip art—to your documents. In fact, the process is quite simple. You set the cursor where you want the graphic to appear, tell the word processing program that you want to insert a graphic, then locate the graphic file. The only catch is that the graphic must be in a format that the word processing software can understand. However, most word processing software can readily import the standard types. Once the graphic has been imported, you can move, size, crop, and add borders to it. You can even adjust the alignment so that your text flows around the picture.

In addition to graphics, some software now lets you attach sound files to word processed documents. In general, you attach the sound file in much the same way that you attach a graphic file. The only difference is that a button, displaying a speaker, appears in the document. Clicking on the button plays the sound file.

Click here to play the attached sound file. ——

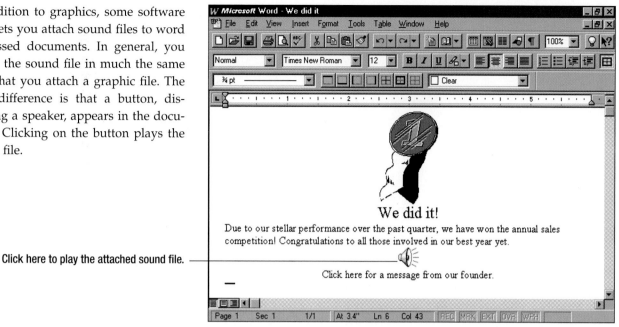

Documents in some word processing programs can contain both images and sounds.

Styles and Style Sheets

A **style** is a named collection of character and paragraph formats. For example, a style named Plain Text might include the following formatting settings:

Times, 12-point
Left alignment
Double-spacing

Another style named Headings might include these styles:

Helvetica Bold, 24-point
Center alignment
36-point spacing, plus 18 points after the
   paragraph
Bottom border

A **style sheet** is a collection of styles that can be applied to a group of similar documents. Styles and style sheets can save you a great deal of time with long documents that include lots of repetitive elements, such as headings. Once the styles are set up, you can apply them simply by selecting the style from a menu. Styles allow you to apply the same sets of formatting choices over and over with a single keystroke.

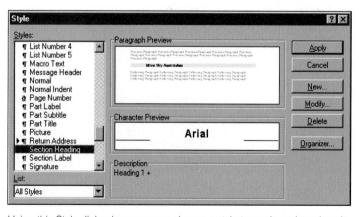

Using this Style dialog box, you can choose a style to apply and see how it will look in the Paragraph Preview box. When you have found the right style, you click on the Apply button.

Using style sheets can also be a tremendous time-saver when you want to make universal changes. Let's say you are using a style sheet and decide that the font for the headings should really be Palatino instead of Times New Roman. All you have to do is change the definition of that style, and every heading in the document will change automatically.

Modern word processing programs offer a variety of ways to style your document, or determine how it will look. Style choices can include any visual elements such as type font and size, line spacing, kerning, color, borders, tab settings, margins, and much more.

It can take a significant amount of time to apply each style, one by one, to your document. That's why there's a better way: styles and templates.

A style in desktop publishing language is a collection of formats stored under a name, generally referred to as a style name, or sometimes as a style sheet. For example, you may associate the 12-point Palatino font, the regular character format, and a half-inch paragraph indent for a style you name "Report." Every time you work on a term paper you use that style, and your text is automatically styled according to the format you previously defined.

Why use styles? Speed is the primary reason. Applying a single style to your document is much quicker than individually applying fonts, line spacing, character formatting, bullets, and all the rest of your formats, one at a time.

Styles also make it easy for you to change your mind. If you find yourself frequently changing the look of your document, styles are for you. With a single command you can change everything.

Styles also allow consistency in your documents. For example, if your company defines and uses a particular set of styles, all their documents will have a similar look, which people will come to associate with the company.

There are styles built into most word processing programs. Word, for example, currently has 75 built-in styles. One of these is referred to as the default style, which is the style in which your new documents automatically open. This style, called normal, can be modified or given a different name (called an alias), but never deleted. You may also create user-defined styles, such as the "Report" style discussed above, which can be both modified and deleted.

If you forget which style you have applied to your document, Word has a new way of showing you the style through the Help command. If you click the Help button on the Standard toolbar, the Help button icon appears with an arrow and a ? character. When you click this toolbar button and then click within your document text, a balloon appears describing the formatting for that particular location.

The next step up from styles is templates. A template is a group of elements stored in a special type of document which is then used to create other documents based on it. Templates can be used for any documents you plan to use over and over again, for example, letterhead, business cards, a company logo, or a newsletter.

In 1995, a computer virus called the Word Macro Virus appeared. It used Word's macro language to attack templates in the Microsoft Word program, thereby corrupting files. It was the first cross-platform virus, meaning that it infected both PC and Macintosh documents created with applications that used the Word Macro language. It served as another reminder to always use antivirus software on your computer.

Because the use of styles and templates can be daunting to the beginner, the current version of Microsoft Word includes a feature called a wizard which guides you through the process of creating common documents such as memos, letters, and reports, as well as sophisticated documents such as résumés or newsletters. You can also learn more about how to use styles and templates by looking them up in the Help index.

It may take you time and practice to become proficient in the use of styles and templates, but they will save you time in the long run and add a professional look to all of your work.

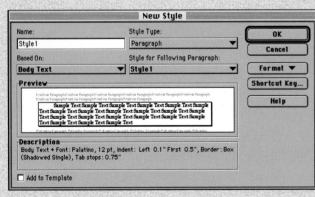

This dialog box from Microsoft Word allows you to define styles for your documents.

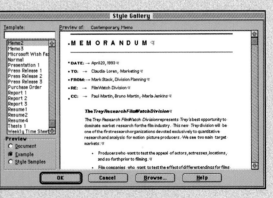

This shows some of the templates available in Microsoft Word. On the right is a preview of the Memo 2 template.

▶ DESKTOP PUBLISHING SOFTWARE

The introduction of **desktop publishing (DTP) software** revolutionized the publishing and graphic arts industries, bringing to ordinary users the power to produce professional-quality documents and publications. The impact of desktop publishing on the microcomputer market has influenced the ongoing development of word processing, spreadsheet, and database software, inspiring developers of the major business applications to include DTP features in their software.

Before DTP software arrived, producing publications of any kind, from simple newsletters to magazines or books, was a complex and time-consuming process involving the special skills of many different professionals. DTP software simplifies the process by including features to specify the publication's design, to set the type to be used, and to arrange type and graphics on pages so they are ready for the printer.

The impact of DTP software on PCs and the publishing industry was immediate and dramatic. Because it placed the means of production in the hands of one person, DTP software spawned a cottage industry of desktop publishers. Individuals (often with backgrounds in traditional design, typesetting, or paste-up businesses) bought computers and DTP software and went into the publishing business for themselves. In addition, since the integration of the publication process saved a great deal of time and money, newspaper, magazine, and book publishers turned to DTP software to increase their efficiency, production capacity, and profits.

Desktop Publishing Versus Word Processing

DTP software has influenced other software packages to improve features for graphics, layout, and publication, and none more so than word processing. Capabilities that were once the exclusive domain of DTP, such as importing graphics, are now incorporated into the major word processing programs. In fact, for many simple publishing jobs, you no longer need DTP software. DTP software, meanwhile, has added important word processing features, such as find and replace and spell checking, further blurring the line between the two types of applications.

However, DTP is still the best choice for professional-quality typesetting and page layout, for making sophisticated use of graphics or color, and for commercial-quality printing. Once you are comfortable with the features of DTP programs, you will find that they give you much better control over the look of your document than word processing programs do.

Type Controls

In addition to the many details for type that word processing programs let you specify, DTP software gives you two more essential controls for professional typesetting: kerning and tracking.

Kerning is making fine adjustments in the space between individual letters (called *letter*

SUSPECT VANISHES
West-Side Police Lose James in Corn Field

SUSPECT VANISHES
West-Side Police Lose James in Corn Field

With kerning, these
letters were moved
closer together.

Kerning can be especially important in headlines.

Eric Cantona wins footballer of the year!

Eric Cantona wins footballer of the year!

Eric Cantona wins footballer of the year!

Wide tracking spaces all the letters in a line further apart. Tight tracking moves them closer together.

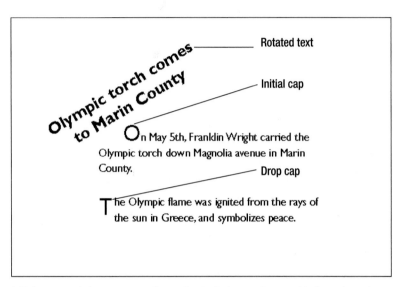

Olympic torch comes to Marin County ——— Rotated text

——— Initial cap

On May 5th, Franklin Wright carried the Olympic torch down Magnolia avenue in Marin County. ——— Drop cap

The Olympic flame was ignited from the rays of the sun in Greece, and symbolizes peace.

Initial caps and drop caps are decorative techniques often used in fancy layouts. Rotated text has many uses, but you should make sure it is clearly legible when it is printed.

MAJOR LEAGUE SOCCER FINALLY HERE!

Soccer returned with a bang today in typical American fashion. Parachuters jumped from the sky and landed in San Jose's Spartan Stadium to kick off the debut of Major League Soccer. The narrow field was bulging with American and foreign stars like Alexi Lallas, Carlos Valderrama, and Marco Etcheverry, who plays for the visiting team, D.C. United.

DTP programs provide many options for fancy borders and drop shadows. They also provide a high degree of control when wrapping text around pictures.

spacing). For example, you might move a capital *V* and a capital *A* closer together because they look too far apart. Or you might add space between an *r* and an *n* because they can look like an *m* when they are too close together. Adjusting the space between these and other pairs of letters can have great impact on the look of a headline, for instance, or in type that is set for a graphic effect.

Tracking also adjusts letter spacing, but rather than making adjustments between individual characters, tracking is a general setting for an entire block of text. Tighter tracking squeezes all the letters closer together, fitting more type into a given space. This can be very important when fitting text into a particular layout. Loose tracking expands the space between letters, making the page look less dense, which can be easier to read.

Other special text controls are often included in DTP software (as well as some word processing software). **Drop caps** and **initial caps** are enlarged capital letters at the beginning of a paragraph that either occupy two or more lines of type (drop cap) or stand higher than the rest of the line (initial cap). They are usually placed in the first word of a beginning paragraph. **Rotating text** lets you set type at any angle.

Graphics Controls

DTP software tends to be highly sophisticated and flexible with graphics. DTP and word processing programs both allow you to import a variety of graphics formats. In addition, DTP programs provide more direct control over the exact placement of the graphic on the page, and let you specify exactly what kind of border or shade you want around the graphic image. DTP programs also tend to be more versatile in wrapping text around an irregularly shaped graphic.

Other graphic controls exclusive to DTP software include applying color to a black-and-white or gray image; linking graphics to text elements so they will go with the text if it is moved; adjusting brightness, contrast, and halftone screens for scanned photos and other bitmap images; making negative images of imported graphics; and selecting color models on which to base color adjustments.

Page Layout and Document Controls

Designed for the publisher, DTP programs have sophisticated controls for setting up the format of documents, as well as coordinating multiple documents in a publication.

One of the most common elements for page layout in DTP software is called **master pages**. These are special pages within the document that are set aside for defining elements common to all pages in the document, such as page numbers, headers and footers, ruling lines, margin features, special graphics, and layout guides. Once the items are set on the master pages, they will be placed automatically on the document pages. Having all such elements on a master page lets you see the overall design of the document and adjust it intelligently, which greatly facilitates design and layout. DTP master pages also provide an easy way to create **templates**, documents that are preformatted, ready for text to be inserted quickly and easily.

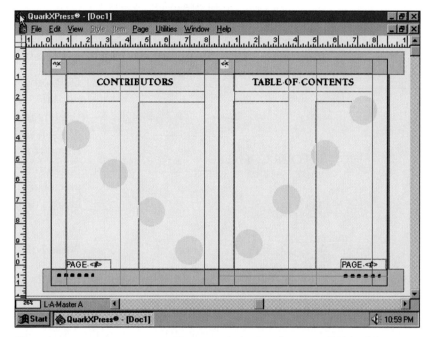

Shown here are two master pages. Each page in the Contributors and Table of Contents sections of the book being produced will have the elements on these pages.

Prepress Controls

Perhaps the most unique characteristic of DTP software is the ability to prepare your document for the printing press.

If you plan to use color in a document that is going to press, DTP is a must. DTP software lets you specify colors according to printing industry standards, such as Pantone and TruMatch, so both you and the printer understand precisely what colors are to be used. When documents are printed in color, separate pages must be created for each color on each page of the document. These are called **color separations**. There are two main types of color separations. If you want a specific color printed as a design element, DTP software can print **spot color separations**,

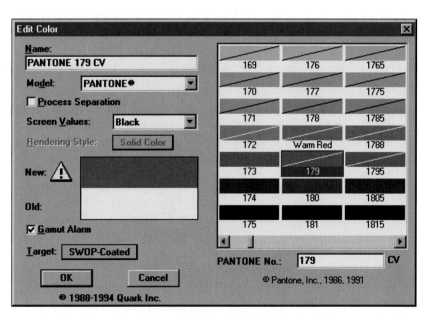

This dialog box gives the user precise control over the colors on the page. Pantone is an industry standard for specifying colors using numbers.

where each separation represents items in a particular color. Spot color separations are a good way to save money if, for example, you are printing a document that is mostly black and white but contains one additional color.

On the other hand, if you want full-color photos or artwork, DTP software can print **process color separations**, where, for each page, a separation is printed for each of the three primary printing colors (cyan (blue), magenta (red), and yellow), as well as black. This is also called **CMYK separation**. CMYK separations let the printer combine colored inks on the press to reproduce full-color art.

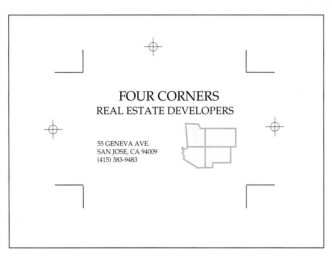

DTP software also handles other prepress issues. To align the different pages and separations properly on the press, printers use **crop marks** and **registration marks** (or **targets**) on each page. Crop marks show precisely where the corners of the page are (especially important for custom-page sizes), and registration marks (see Figure 7.18) allow precise alignment of color separations and multiple-page layouts used on the press.

FIGURE 7.18

A business card, ready for printing, with crop marks and registration marks.

Some DTP programs also have controls for **trapping**, the process of adding a tiny overlap to adjacent color elements on a page to account for possible misalignment in the press. Finally, most DTP packages come with custom setups for printing to digital image setters, which are used by the printer (or film manufacturer) to create film for the press without requiring the intermediate step of a process camera. Image setters work on the same principles as laser printers, but instead of fusing toner to paper, they use the laser to expose photographic film directly. They also operate at a much higher resolution than do laser printers, and thus result in a higher-quality product.

▶ NORTON WORKSHOP: CREATING A PROFESSIONAL MEMO

The memo is a ubiquitous business document. A memo is an informal, yet efficient, means of communicating with your colleagues. Most of the time, they are very plain (especially when they arrive as e-mail). However, for some memos, professional formatting can provide just the right touch for the message.

To give you a sense of how someone creates a memo using word processing software, read along as Marilyn puts together a note to her salespeople about an upcoming dinner for several important clients.

Her computer is already on, because she has been using it all morning. She starts her word processing software.

Marilyn uses many templates. She has one she normally uses for memos, but she needs something festive. She decides to look at the ones that come with the software.

In the Open dialog box, she clicks on a button to see previews of the different templates. She finally finds one she wants (see Figure 7.19).

FIGURE 7.19

The "Elegant Memo" selected.

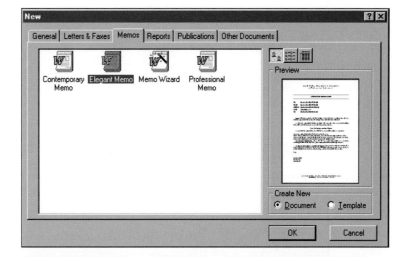

She double-clicks on the template, and a new, untitled file appears as shown in Figure 7.20.

FIGURE 7.20

The untitled memo template.

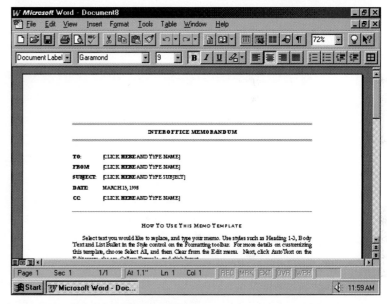

Marilyn wants to change the format a bit, but it is usually better to enter the content before worrying about formatting. She types the message into the template as shown in Figure 7.21.

FIGURE 7.21

The memo, entered into the template.

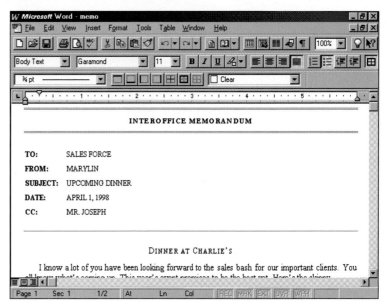

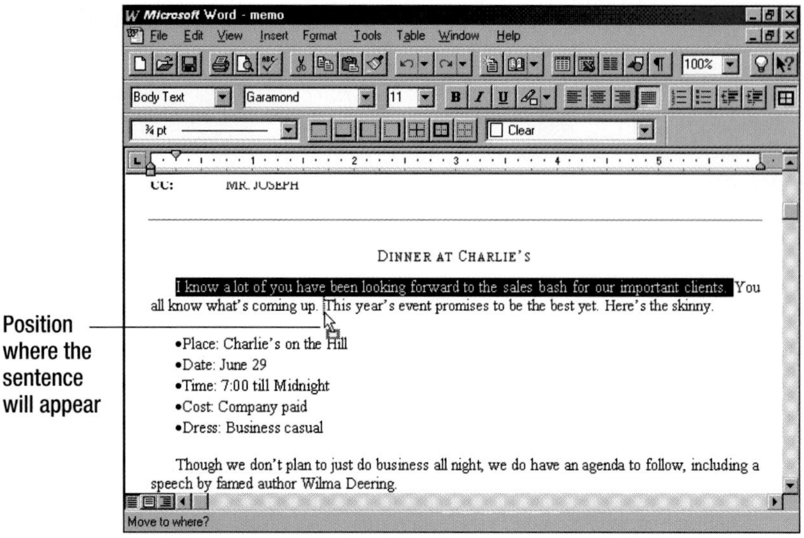

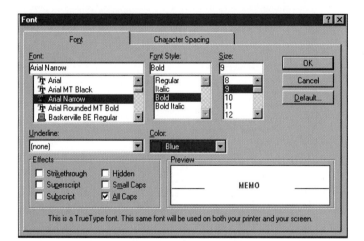

Position where the sentence will appear

She looks back at her work and sees a typo (a typing error) that needs fixing. She right-clicks on the misspelled word and corrects it. Next, she decides that the first sentence would make more sense if it came after the second. She highlights the first sentence and uses the drag-and-drop editing technique to move it. While she is dragging the block, the new cursor position appears as a faint gray line that moves around with the mouse pointer, as shown in Figure 7.22.

FIGURE 7.22
Using drag-and-drop to move the first sentence.

Normally, at this point she would use the spelling checker, but this memo is short, and she is sure there are no more typos. Instead, she moves on to reformat the word "Memo." She double-clicks to select the word, then chooses Font from the Format menu. The dialog box shown in Figure 7.23 appears.

FIGURE 7.23
The Font dialog box.

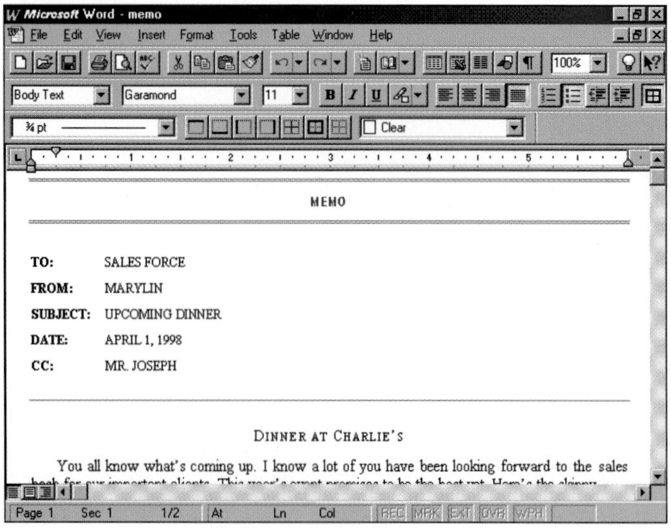

She knows she wants to use the font called Arial Narrow, but the text also needs color, and perhaps a shadow. The dialog box lets her combine different effects and view them in the Preview window. She finally settles on Arial Narrow, bold, blue. With all the character settings completed, she clicks on the OK button. So far, the document looks like Figure 7.24.

FIGURE 7.24
The memo heading reformatted.

Marilyn wants to inspire her salespeople by showing them a picture of the guest speaker at the upcoming dinner. She has used a scanner to create a .TIF (Tagged Image File Format) file of a photograph of the speaker (see Figure 7.25). Then, she chooses Picture from the Insert menu and selects the picture to insert into the memo.

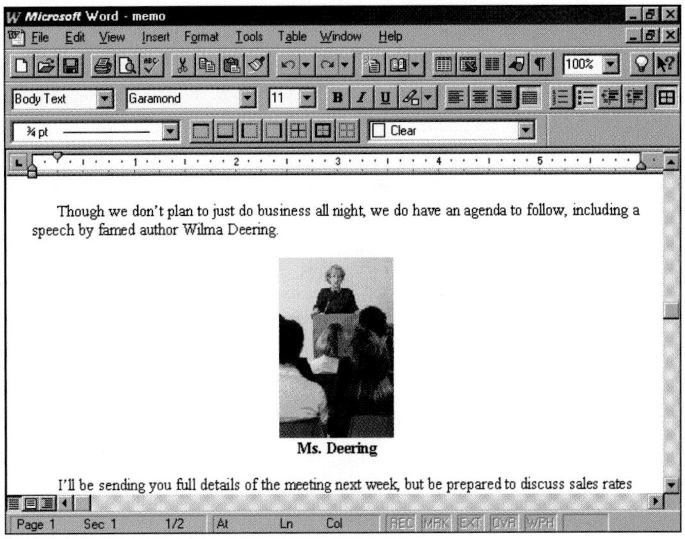

FIGURE 7.25

A .TIF file placed in the memo.

She knows that the salespeople have been curious about success rates for several of the products, so she creates a table showing the products and their rate of sales and inserts the table into the memo (see Figure 7.26).

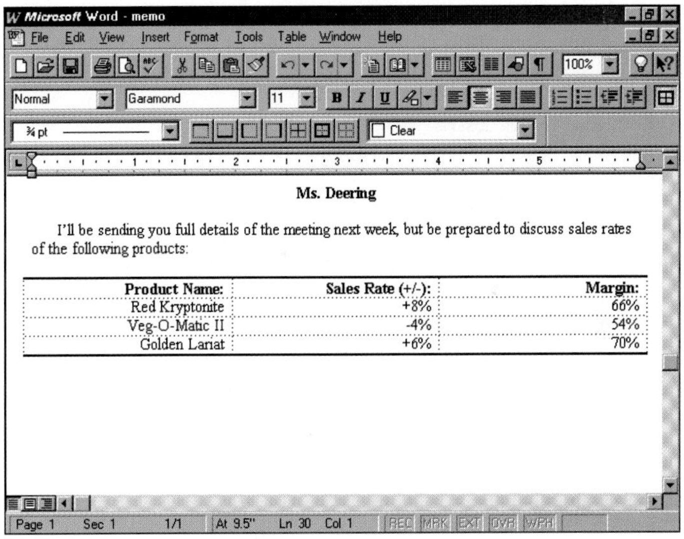

FIGURE 7.26

A table inserted into the memo.

Finally, Marilyn is ready for a final splash, a piece of her favorite clip art. Clip art consists of small images and icons, often sold commercially in large collections or provided free with software. First, she clicks the mouse to set the position of the cursor, and she opens the Insert Picture dialog box. She navigates to the picture, a graphic file called *Lightblb.wmf*. She selects it and checks the preview window to make sure it is the one she wants (see Figure 7.27).

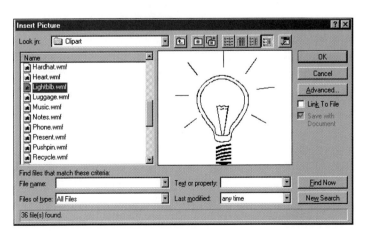

FIGURE 7.27

The Insert Picture dialog box.

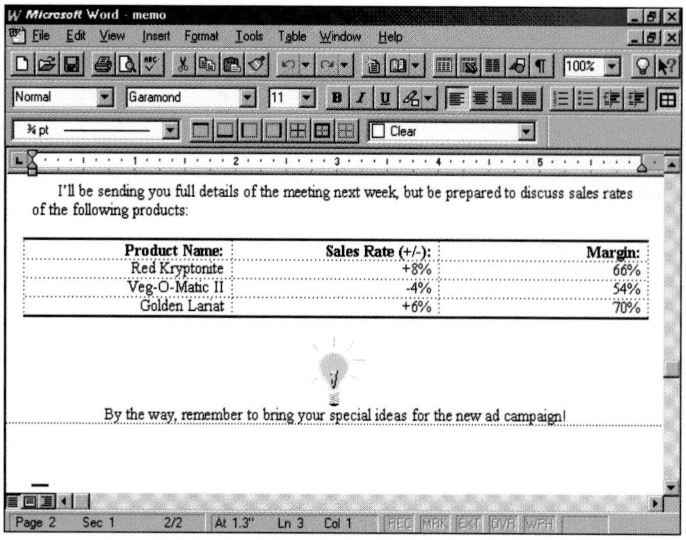

She clicks OK and the graphic appears in her memo. She drags it to a better place on the memo, as shown in Figure 7.28.

FIGURE 7.28
The light bulb placed in the memo.

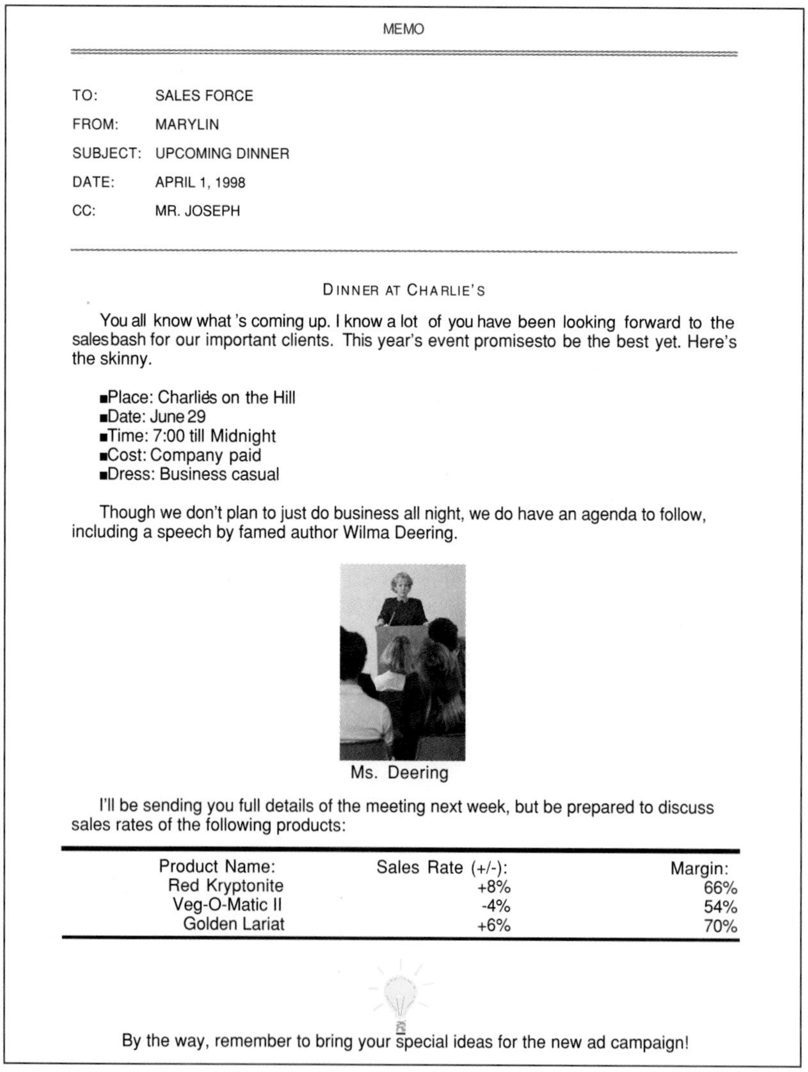

The lightbulb just needs to be a little bigger, and then she will be done. She puts the cursor over one of the corner boxes and drags it to extend the boundaries of the image. She's finally finished and prints the result as shown in Figure 7.29.

FIGURE 7.29
The finished memo.

MEMO

TO: SALES FORCE
FROM: MARYLIN
SUBJECT: UPCOMING DINNER
DATE: APRIL 1, 1998
CC: MR. JOSEPH

DINNER AT CHARLIE'S

You all know what's coming up. I know a lot of you have been looking forward to the sales bash for our important clients. This year's event promises to be the best yet. Here's the skinny.

- Place: Charlie's on the Hill
- Date: June 29
- Time: 7:00 till Midnight
- Cost: Company paid
- Dress: Business casual

Though we don't plan to just do business all night, we do have an agenda to follow, including a speech by famed author Wilma Deering.

Ms. Deering

I'll be sending you full details of the meeting next week, but be prepared to discuss sales rates of the following products:

Product Name:	Sales Rate (+/-):	Margin:
Red Kryptonite	+8%	66%
Veg-O-Matic II	-4%	54%
Golden Lariat	+6%	70%

By the way, remember to bring your special ideas for the new ad campaign!

▶ WHAT TO EXPECT IN THE FUTURE

As in the computer hardware marketplace, the trend in the software industry is to add features and to consolidate functionality. What does this mean for word processing and DTP? We are already seeing some of the effects of this trend. High-end word processors such as Microsoft Word provide page layout features in addition to graphics capabilities and integrated drawing programs. DTP systems are steadily becoming better suited for composition as well, integrating spelling checkers and other traditional features and tools of word processors.

If these trends continue, we are likely to see the lines that separate these distinct types of software blur further. When the dust settles, perhaps we will have a new class of software that seamlessly integrates word processing, drawing, color graphics, and typesetting.

On the other hand, there are many critics of this trend toward consolidation. One result has been what people call "bloatware." That is, software that gets bigger and more power-hungry with each new version, even though most users employ only a fraction of the features. Bloatware is a common criticism, and there are several responses to it.

One response comes from Microsoft, whom many blame as one of the bloatware culprits. Microsoft's approach has been to make more efficient use of the software tools installed on the computer. In past versions, for example, multiple programs had separate spelling checkers, each requiring several hundred thousand bytes of hard disk space. Today, if you use both Word and Excel, they share a common dictionary. The graphics tools in each of these programs are also shared.

A more aggressive response to bloatware is OpenDoc, a long-range software strategy initiated by other industry giants, including Apple and IBM. These companies see bloatware as a natural result of the current software market. Their response is a whole new framework for building applications in which small, specialized tools are purchased as needed. If OpenDoc is successful, then you could decide that you do not need, and do not want to pay for, tools like a grammar checker or automated guides that step you through the process of creating a résumé. If all you want is a text editor and basic formatting capabilities, you could buy just those components.

There is, however, one catch to this more aggressive response. Industry alliances among software companies rarely have succeeded. Making software is a complicated endeavor, so cooperation is especially difficult.

VISUAL SUMMARY AND EXERCISES

▶ VISUAL SUMMARY

The Many Uses of Word Processing Software

■ Word processing software is used to create documents that consist primarily of text.

■ With word processing software, users can create anything from simple letters and memos to brochures, résumés, and 100-page reports.

Your Window into the Document

■ When you are using word processing software, the screen is dominated by an editing window through which you view your documents.

■ The Word screen also includes a menu bar, toolbars, scroll bars, and a status bar.

Entering Text

■ Word wrap makes entering text easier, because you need only to press the Enter (or Return) key at the end of a paragraph.

■ The fastest way to navigate around a document is to use the scroll bar, scroll arrows, and scroll box. You can also use the cursor movement keys if you prefer them.

Editing Text

■ Editing is the process of changing an existing document. The term applies to many kinds of applications, not just to word processing.

■ If you make a mistake as you type, you can press the Backspace key to back up, erase your error, and retype the text.

■ You can also use the mouse or the arrow keys to position the cursor, then make corrections.

■ To correct larger errors, you can select blocks of text, then delete or move them.

■ Text blocks can be moved with drag-and-drop editing or by using the Clipboard.

■ Find and Replace helps you to find occurrences of a word (often a misspelled word) and change it to a different spelling.

■ The Undo command undoes your most recent actions; a multiple undo feature can undo a whole series of actions.

■ A spelling checker compares each word in a document to a dictionary.

■ A thesaurus provides a list of synonyms for a highlighted word.

Formatting Text

- Character formats include fonts, type size, type styles, and color.
- Fonts are described as either monospace or proportional, and as either serif or sans serif.
- In word processing, a paragraph is created every time you press the Enter key.
- Paragraph formatting includes line and paragraph spacing, indents and alignment, and borders and shading.
- Document formats include the margins, the page size, the page orientation, and the headers, footers, and footnotes.

You can make your text **bold**.

You can use *italics*, too.

Underlining is an old standby.

Sometimes you can use ~~strike-through~~.

You can also use SMALL CAPS vs. LARGE CAPS.

Advanced Word Processing Features

- The print preview feature lets you see what your document will look like when it is printed.
- Mail merge combines a form letter with the contents of a database (usually a name and address file), creating a separate copy of the letter for each entry in the database.
- Some word processing software lets you create World Wide Web pages that are formatted with HTML codes.
- Most word processing software allows you to add graphics and sounds to your documents.
- Styles are named sets of formatting options. You can use them to save time when you want to apply the same formatting options to recurring text elements.

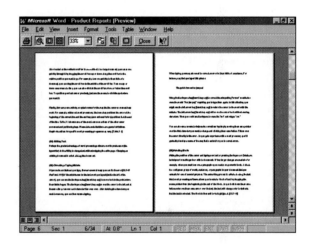

Desktop Publishing Software

- Desktop publishing software is used for sophisticated layouts incorporating text, graphics, and design features.
- Although word processing and DTP are becoming more like each other in their features, DTP is still best for professional-quality typesetting and page layout.
- DTP has type controls such as kerning, tracking, drop caps, initial caps, and rotating text.
- Graphics controls are used for publishing—quality placement, borders, and wrapped text.
- Master pages let you specify elements common to all pages in the document.
- Prepress controls include color separations, crop marks, registration marks, and output designed to go directly to digital image setters used by print shops.

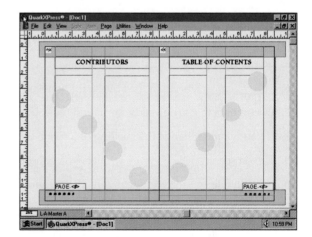

VISUAL SUMMARY AND EXERCISES

KEY TERMS

After completing this chapter, you should be able to define the following terms:

alignment, 217
block, 210
border, 218
CMYK separation, 228
color separation, 227
crop marks, 228
desktop publishing (DTP)
  software, 225
drag-and-drop editing, 210
drop cap, 226
editing, 208
find and change, 211
find and replace, 211
font, 214
grammar checker, 212
highlighted, 210
indent, 217
initial cap, 226

kerning, 225
landscape orientation, 219
line spacing, 216
mail merge, 221
margin, 217
master pages, 227
monospace font, 214
paragraph, 216
portrait orientation, 219
print preview, 220
process color separation, 228
proportional font, 214
registration marks, 228
rotating text, 226
sans serif, 214
scroll arrows, 208
scroll bar, 208
scroll box, 208

scrolling, 208
selecting, 210
serif, 214
shading, 218
spelling checker, 211
spot color separation, 227
style, 223
style sheet, 223
tab stop, 218
target, 228
template, 227
thesaurus, 212
tracking, 226
trapping, 228
typeface, 214
word wrap, 208
WYSIWYG, 207

KEY TERM QUIZ

Fill in the blank with one of the terms listed in Key Terms:

1. The _____ feature lets you enter text without having to press Enter to start the next line.

2. When you select text it is _____.

3. The style of the letters in your document is referred to as a(n) _____.

4. A(n) _____ font does not have decorative strokes on the characters.

5. If your document is wider than it is long, it is in _____ orientation.

6. _____ lets you adjust the space between individual letters.

7. Documents that are already formatted for your use are called _____.

8. If you want to change the spelling of a name throughout a document you can do so easily with _____.

9. The on screen _____ lets you choose an alternative word or synonym.

10. You can use _____ to accurately align columns.

REVIEW QUESTIONS

1. What makes up a block of text? Describe briefly three ways to select a block of text in today's word processing programs.
2. Which situation is a better candidate for using drag-and-drop editing, moving a paragraph from page 1 to page 36, or moving a sentence from the beginning of a paragraph to the end? Describe your answer briefly.

3. Describe two strategies for reversing word processing mistakes in documents.

4. What is a good general rule to follow when applying character formatting to your documents?

5. Which kind of page orientation would you want to select for a document containing a wide eight-column table? Explain your answer.

6. List the basic steps for setting up a mail merge operation.

7. Name and describe briefly at least three features that set DTP software apart from today's feature-packed word processing programs.

8. What is the purpose of master pages or templates?

9. Which type of application would likely be the better choice for manipulating graphic images in the design of a document?

10. List and describe briefly the types of controls at your disposal for controlling the appearance of text, including style, size, and density.

▶ DISCUSSION QUESTIONS

1. Why do you think features such as word wrap, scrolling, and WYSIWYG have become standard equipment with today's word processing programs?

2. Describe in general terms how you might use a find and replace operation to edit a phrase so that it appears capitalized in some situations and in lowercase letters in others.

3. Do you think that using a spelling checker, and perhaps a grammar checker, for all of your final documents is a sufficient substitute for proofreading? Explain why or why not.

4. Suppose you need to design and lay out a four-color brochure. Your job is to develop, write, and edit the text, lay out the pages, and incorporate the graphics and photographs—essentially, to take the project from blank page to finished product. Describe the processes you would use to complete the task, including the word processing features you would use to prepare the text, such as font selections, and the type of color separation you would employ to minimize your production costs.

NORTON INTERACTIVE

Complete the Norton Interactive module for this chapter.

SPREADSHEETS

CONTENTS

OBJECTIVES

When you complete this chapter, you will be able to do the following:

- List the major features of a spreadsheet program.
- Describe some common uses for spreadsheets.
- Explain the structure of a worksheet.
- List several number formats.
- Describe the syntax of a formula.
- Explain the rules of precedence for operators.
- Name the most common types of charts.
- Name several methods for analyzing data.
- Name some future trends for spreadsheets.

The first microcomputers appeared in 1975—strange contraptions lacking either keyboards or monitors, and appealing primarily to electronics hobbyists. Over the next few years, more usable microcomputers began to appear, including the Apple II in 1977. These computers began to interest a wider audience than the very first PCs, but they still did not gain much popularity among businesspeople. Then, in 1979, Dan Bricklin and Bob Frankston invented VisiCalc for the Apple II.

VisiCalc, "the visible calculator," was the first electronic spreadsheet, and it spelled success, not only for Bricklin and Frankston, but also for the Apple II. Suddenly, accountants, bookkeepers, managers, and anyone who had ever created a budget, analyzed statistics, or collected numerical research data had access to a powerful computational tool. It could save time, help avoid endless, brain-numbing arithmetic, and eliminate mathematical errors. Many people have said that the invention of the spreadsheet, more than any other event, launched the personal computer revolution.

▶ A TOOL FOR WORKING WITH NUMBERS

A **spreadsheet** is a software tool for entering, calculating, manipulating, and analyzing sets of numbers. A typical spreadsheet is shown in Figure 8.1.

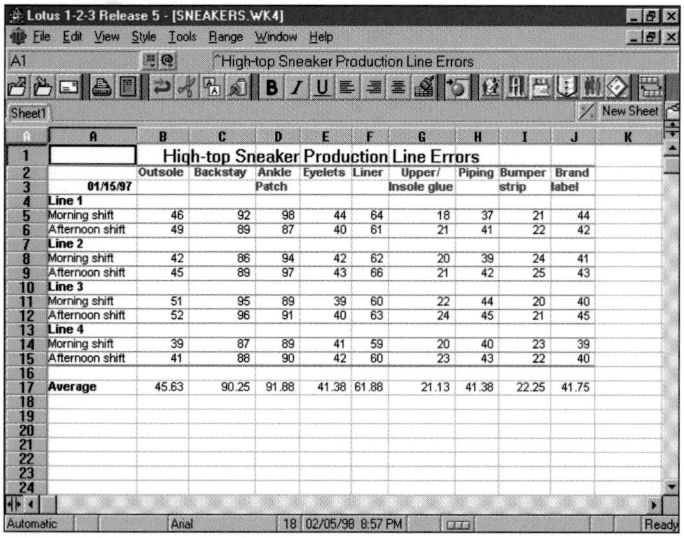

A spreadsheet without any data looks like a grid of

FIGURE 8.1
A spreadsheet.

rows and columns. The intersection of any **column** and **row** is called a **cell**, where you can place numbers, descriptive text, formulas, and more. The power of the spreadsheet lies in the fact that cells can contain **formulas**, which calculate numbers based on numbers or formulas in other cells. For example, if you enter a list of numbers into a column of cells, you can have the computer add the numbers by entering a formula containing the SUM function in a cell below your list of numbers. The formula will give you the total of those numbers (see Figure 8.2).

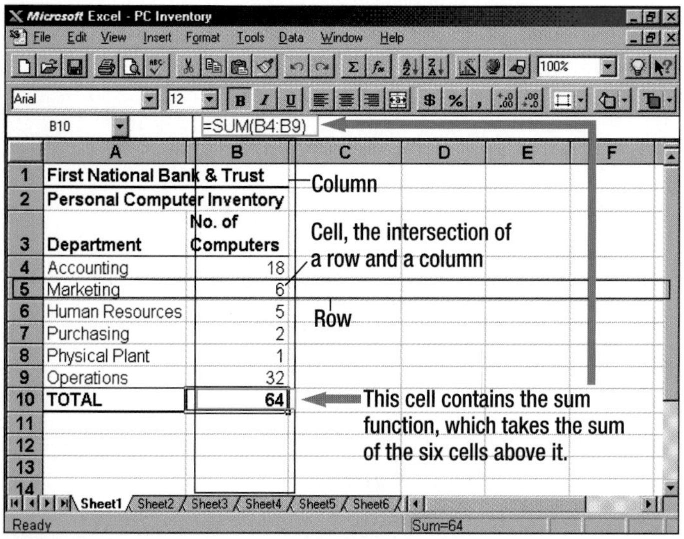

FIGURE 8.2
The SUM function.

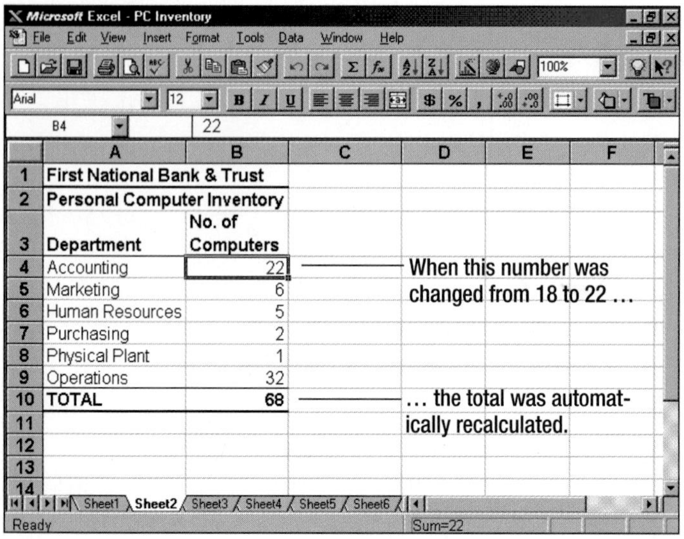

If you then change one of the numbers in your list, the spreadsheet recalculates the total automatically (see Figure 8.3).

FIGURE 8.3
Automatic recalculation.

A spreadsheet is like a grid of cells with a programmable calculator attached to each cell. The computer can perform calculations at a blinding speed. It does not matter how many numbers and formulas you put in a spreadsheet, the computer can recalculate every formula every time you change any number.

Note: Over time, the term *spreadsheet* has come to refer specifically to the software, while **worksheet** refers to the files that you create with spreadsheet software. This distinction is used throughout the remainder of this chapter.

Today, in addition to the basic tools for calculating numbers, spreadsheet programs offer you several additional features:

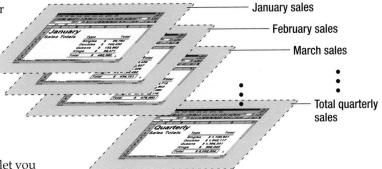
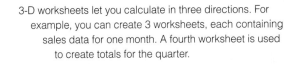

- 3-D worksheets, that are like a pad of worksheets, let you calculate not only on any one worksheet, but also from worksheet to worksheet. In Excel, all worksheets are 3-D, so they are called workbooks. The individual pages of the workbook are called sheets.
- Beautifully designed **charts**, which are graphic representations of numbers. Charts, also called **graphs**, are created from your data and can use dramatic graphic and 3-D effects.
- Analysis tools that allow you to draw meaningful conclusions from the numbers on the worksheet.
- Database management tools to organize information and create reports.
- A programming language for automating commands.
- User interfaces to create worksheets for employees or customers.
- Integration with other programs, so that you can insert a worksheet into a report created on your word processor, or a graphic into your worksheet.

3-D worksheets let you calculate in three directions. For example, you can create 3 worksheets, each containing sales data for one month. A fourth worksheet is used to create totals for the quarter.

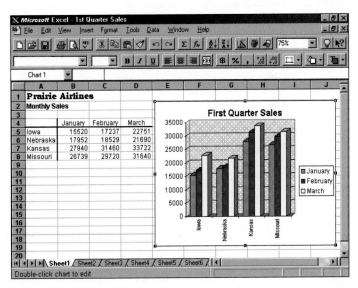

The chart on the right graphically represents the data on the left.

Spreadsheets in Business

Probably the most common use of spreadsheets is in business. Businesses large and small need to track income and expenses, forecast profits or losses, and analyze sales trends. The following list describes a few ways in which typical business departments use spreadsheets:

- Sales departments use spreadsheets to calculate sales commissions for their salespeople.
- Purchasing departments can create invoices that are built around spreadsheets, then use the information to create running totals of their costs.
- Manufacturing departments use spreadsheets to keep records of maintenance performed on equipment, and to record transfers of finished goods to warehouses.
- Personnel departments use spreadsheets to track wages and salaries paid to employees, as well as the costs of employee benefits.

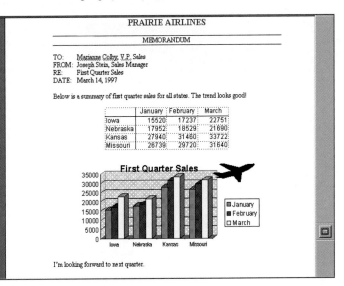

Here, the data and chart have been copied into a memo that was created with a word processing program.

This worksheet calculates commissions and bonuses for a sales department.

- Marketing departments often use spreadsheets to explore the costs of new projects. They also make presentations, which usually contain charts created with spreadsheets.
- Finally, although accounting systems today are, for the most part, database management systems, accounting personnel frequently take advantage of spreadsheets for preparing budgets and for financial planning.

Other Professional Uses

In engineering, spreadsheets are used for advanced calculations on data. For example, an automotive company testing electric motor prototypes compiles hundreds of pieces of data relating to the engines. The engineers determine the mean (average) high and low numbers using the mathematical, trigonometric, and statistical functions available in the spreadsheet program.

In the sciences, research is a major part of nearly everyone's job, and the result of research is data. Whenever the data consists of numbers, the spreadsheet is an important tool. Spreadsheets are especially valuable for applying statistical functions to large sets of numbers. For example, a biologist studying the salinity of water in a river might collect hundreds or even thousands of samples. Proving that certain observed fluctuations are more than accidents or meaningless aberrations requires computing a standard deviation based on all the numbers—a grueling task made much easier with a spreadsheet.

Spreadsheets for Home Users

Many people use spreadsheets at home, too. A spreadsheet is an ideal way to create a personal budget. Then you can track your actual expenses and compare them to your budget.

This budget has been set up by a family to track their income and expenses, month by month.

This amortization schedule shows how much of each month's mortgage payment goes to pay off the principal and interest on a $73,500 home loan. The data on this screen is for one year (12 months).

Formula bar

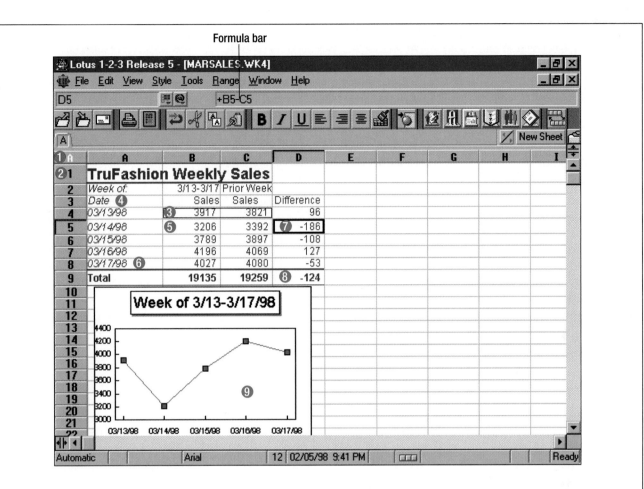

❶ Column headings use letters.

❷ Row headings are numbered.

❸ Cell. The cell is the basic unit of a worksheet. It can contain text, numbers, and formulas. Cells are referred to by combining their column and row headings. This cell is called B4, which is the cell's **address.**

❹ Text is called a **label,** because it often labels numerical data. Spreadsheet programs can distinguish between numbers and text. Only numbers can be calculated. Both numerical and text input can be aligned left, right, or centered in a cell, and can be formatted with different fonts and type sizes, or with bold, italicized, or underlined characters.

❺ Numerical entries are called **values.** Values can be formatted to display as dollars and cents, percentages, dates, times, and fractions. They can be shown with or without commas, decimal points, and so forth. You can even create your own custom formats. Formatting a number does not change its value. The spreadsheet program calculates numbers based on their values, not on their display.

❻ Date entry. Dates and times are also values, but they have their own formats. For example, a date can be shown as 7/1/97; July 1, 1997; or 07-01-97.

❼ Formula. A formula performs a calculation and must begin with a special symbol so that the program recognizes it as a formula. The formula used to calculate the number in this cell is +B5-C5. Quattro Pro and Lotus 1-2-3 formulas begin with a plus sign (+). Excel formulas begin with an equal sign (=). Once you have completed typing the formula in the **formula bar,** the cell shows only the result of the calculation. The formula bar continues to show the formula you entered.

❽ Function. Spreadsheet programs come with many built-in functions that are complex equations that you include in your own formulas. The function in this cell, called SUM, calculates the sum of the values in the cells D4, D5, D6, D7, and D8.

❾ Chart. Spreadsheet programs can create charts based on your data. They provide a choice of many types of charts, such as pie, line, and bar charts, in both 2-D and 3-D versions.

This worksheet calculates total sales for a brand of shoes. The numbers are illustrated in the graph.
See the callouts for an explanation of how the worksheet works.

Because an electronic spreadsheet provides an environment designed for the organization and manipulation of numerical data, it can help make even your most difficult number-crunching tasks easier and more accurate.

Its underlying concepts are found in the accountant's paper spreadsheets and columnar pads used to organize data into tables and matrices for calculations and cross-references. The first electronic spreadsheet program, VisiCalc, was developed by Dan Bricklin, a college professor, and his programmer friend, Bob Frankston. It was developed as an easy way to track students and their assignments in tabular form.

At first glance, the display of an electronic spreadsheet can be intimidating with all of its buttons, bars, menus, icons, list boxes, and so on. Of course, the challenge is learning to use this application tool effectively. The first step to using an electronic spreadsheet productively is essentially just a matter of orientation. Once you understand its functions and how each relates to a process you already know, you can become an effective user in a very short time.

As an example, look at how a spreadsheet could help manage a personal budget. Budgets have a number of entries used to compute the amount of money left over at the end of the month. If you were to do this budget on paper, you would list the names of each entry on the left followed by its amount. Each name and amount entry is a row in your budget. The descriptions are in one column and the amounts in another and, as often is the case, arithmetic mistakes are made. If you were to continue on to the next month, any mistakes you made are likely to be compounded. Also, if you change any amount, it is likely that your entire budget must be recalculated.

Item	Amount
Rent	$ 700
Food	$ 600
Car	$ 250
School	$ 150
Misc.	$ 100
Subtotal	$1,800
Income	$1,900
Net	$ 100

Sample Budget

To put the power of the electronic spreadsheet to work on your budget, you would enter each of your descriptions and numbers into a separate cell of the worksheet. Cells are the boxes formed by the intersecting columns and rows. A cell is referred to by the letter of the column and the number of the row that meet to form the cell. For example, the cell that is formed where column B meets row 4 is called cell B4.

After you have entered the budget item descriptions and amounts one below another in adjacent columns, you can use one of the spreadsheet's functions to calculate a subtotal of your expenses. It is then a simple matter to enter a formula to calculate the net of your income and expenses. This formula would be entered as "=B9-B8" to indicate that you wish the amount in cell B8 to be subtracted from the amount in cell B9.

Now that your budget is contained on a worksheet (a spreadsheet page), you can test possible changes to your budget. Changing any one, or all, of the entry amounts causes the totals to be automatically recalculated. A change to the Rent amount is instantly reflected in both the Expenses subtotal and the Net amounts.

One of the spreadsheet's best features is its ability to calculate "what-if" scenarios.

Another of its strong features allows you to create a graph of your budget. You can create pie, line, bar, column and area charts, even in 3-D if you wish.

The power of an electronic spreadsheet vastly exceeds the few features that have been discussed. Using a spreadsheet for such a simple task as this budget is a bit like using a Howitzer to attack a gnat, but it does provide a quick demonstration of the electronic spreadsheet's basic functions—arranging data in rows and columns to make calculations that reflect the latest changes in the data. Whether you are working on your personal budget or the national debt, the electronic spreadsheet is the most effective application to employ.

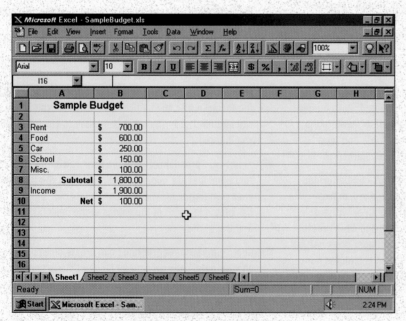

Here is the sample budget entered into a spreadsheet.

If you want to buy a car or a house, you can use a spreadsheet to calculate loan payments, the total interest, and the total principal paid. You can even create an amortization schedule, which details each payment and the principal remaining to be paid.

Many people also use spreadsheets as simple database managers. For example, you might want to keep track of your videotapes, CDs, or books. A person with a garden might create a database for a perennial flower garden. The gardener could create a list of perennials that includes their height, color, and flowering time. Then the list could be sorted by flowering time to make sure there will be some perennials flowering throughout the summer.

► CREATING A WORKSHEET

Creating a worksheet is a process that involves several steps, as shown in Figure 8.4.

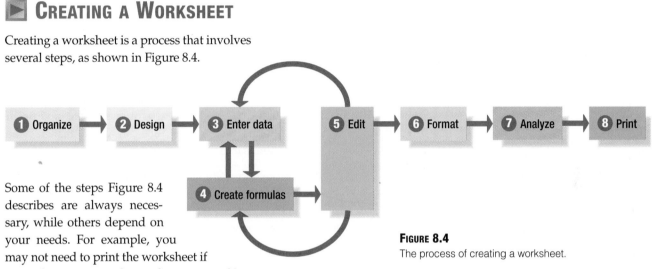

Some of the steps Figure 8.4 describes are always necessary, while others depend on your needs. For example, you may not need to print the worksheet if you only want to see the results on screen. You

FIGURE 8.4
The process of creating a worksheet.

may not want to format the worksheet if its purpose is only to provide you with a quick analysis of your data. However, if you want to present that analysis to a bank with a loan application, you will certainly want to format it to make the best possible impression. Also, you may not want to follow the steps described in the following sections in the same order listed. For example, editing a worksheet is a process that can be done at any time. In every case, you should lay out the data so it is clearly organized. Data should be labeled so you know what the numbers mean. The results of formulas should be labeled to indicate what type of process was performed on the numbers.

Organizing the Data

Your first task is to collect your data so you can decide how you are going to structure it. Suppose you are creating a worksheet containing monthly sales data. If you have access to the records for every sale, you could amass it all into one giant spreadsheet. In most cases, however, that kind of detail is not necessary. The sales total for each product your company produces might be all that you need.

Deciding which data is relevant is closely related to organizing it, and both decisions stem from the central purpose of the spreadsheet. If the purpose is to see which products are selling best, then you need to categorize the data by product. If the purpose is to determine which salespeople are most effective, and who is selling the most of which product, then you should organize the data by both product and salesperson.

This worksheet has been designed, but the data has not yet been entered.

The first value has now been entered.

Designing the Worksheet

Once you know what data you have and what results you want to generate, you can design how the data will appear on the worksheet. For example, for the monthly sales data, are you going to list the months across the top as column heads, or down the left side as row heads? You must decide if you would like quarterly subtotals or only annual totals. If the amount of data is extensive, you might use several worksheets and summarize the data on a grand total worksheet. Finally, you have to decide whether you want to create a graph and what kinds of analyses you want to do.

Sometimes it helps to plan a structure on paper first, although advanced users will be comfortable working out the design directly on the screen. Once you create a first draft, you can easily move, create, and delete columns and rows. You can even change your columns into rows and vice versa.

Note: Many financial worksheets involve time categories, such as months or years. Normally, time periods appear as column headings, arranged horizontally across the top of the worksheet.

The first step is to enter a main heading at the top of the worksheet and the text that labels your rows and columns. For example, your main heading might be *Fairfield Software 1997 Sales*. You might list the names of the months across the top, say in columns B through M. Down the first column, you might list the categories of software that you sell. Once these labels are in place, it becomes easy to see where to enter your data.

Entering Labels and Values

When you have established the worksheet structure, you are ready to enter the text and numbers that make up the worksheet. The **cell pointer**, a square covering one cell, identifies the *active* cell, the one in which the characters you type will appear. You set the position of the cell pointer by clicking the mouse on the cell or by using the arrow keys on the keyboard. The Tab, Home, End, Page Up, and Page Down keys also allow you to move around the worksheet using the keyboard.

Spreadsheet programs are number specialists, just as word processing programs are word specialists. Therefore, as soon as you type in a value, the program recognizes that value and allows you to perform calculations on it. Likewise, if you type in a word, the program recognizes it as a label and not meant for a calculation procedure. When typing numbers, you do not insert commas or dollar signs—these are created by using number formats, discussed later.

Creating Formulas

When you have entered the data into the worksheet, you are ready to perform calculations with that data. This is done using formulas, the true power of a spreadsheet program. In order to create formulas, you first need to know the required **syntax**, which is the term used to describe the sequence of characters used in a formula. The syntax of a formula begins with an equal sign (=) in Excel or a plus sign (+) in Lotus 1-2-3 and Quattro Pro. The + or = is followed by a combination of values, operators, and cell references.

Operators

Operators specify the type of operation that you want to perform on the parts of a formula. Arithmetic operators are the most common type of operator. They perform basic mathematical operations on numeric values, such as addition and multiplication, and thereby produce numeric results. The arithmetic operators are shown in Table 8.1.

TABLE 8.1

Arithmetic Operators in Spreadsheet Programs

ARITHMETIC OPERATORS	MEANING
+ (plus sign)	Addition
– (minus sign)	Subtraction (or negation, when placed before a value, for example, –1)
/ (forward slash)	Division
* (asterisk)	Multiplication
% (percent sign)	Percent, when placed after a value, for example, 20%
^ (caret)	Exponentiation (e.g., $2^3=8$)

TABLE 8.2

Comparison Operators

COMPARISON OPERATORS	MEANING
=	Equals
<>	Does not equal
>	Greater than
>=	Greater than or equal to
<	Less than
<=	Less than or equal to

A **comparison operator** compares the values or labels in two cells. The result of this formula is either TRUE or FALSE. For example, the formula = 4 > 2 will generate the result TRUE. Table 8.2 lists the comparison operators.

A **text operator** joins one or more text values into a single combined text value. The ampersand (&)—the only text operator—joins one or more labels into a single combined label. For example, the formula +A1&" "&B1 combines the labels in cells A1 and B1. (The quotation marks separated by a space are necessary to insert a space between the two text labels.) Translated into English, the formula means "in this cell, enter the label in A1 *and* a space *and* the label in B1."

The Order of Mathematical Operations

When arithmetic operators are used in formulas, spreadsheets calculate the results using the rules of precedence followed in mathematics. The order is as follows:

1. Exponentiation (^)
2. Negation (–)
3. Multiplication and division (*, /)
4. Addition and subtraction (+,–)

Otherwise, operators are evaluated from left to right. In order to change the order of precedence to suit your needs, you add parentheses around any part of the formula that you want to be calculated first. For example, in the expression 5+6*3, multiplication precedes addition, producing 23. However, if you want the addition to be calculated first, you must input (5+6)*3 to get a result of 33.

Cell References

When creating formulas, you will often want to refer to other values in the worksheet. To reduce time and errors, it is best to use a **cell reference** rather than to input the cell's data again. The most common method is to refer to the cell by its address, such as A1, B10, or Y254.

You can refer to individual cells as in the examples above, but sometimes you want to refer to a **range** or **block**, a rectangular group of contiguous cells. In Excel, this is indicated by the use of the colon (:) and in Lotus 1-2-3, it is done using two periods (..). For example, in Excel, the formula =SUM(B4,C4,D4) can be written =SUM(B4:D4).

Ranges can consist of a group of cells in a column, a row, or even a group that includes several rows and columns. For example, a range of B3..F18 (in Lotus 1-2-3) includes the whole block that has B3 as the upper-left corner and F18 as the lower-right corner, as shown in Figure 8.5.

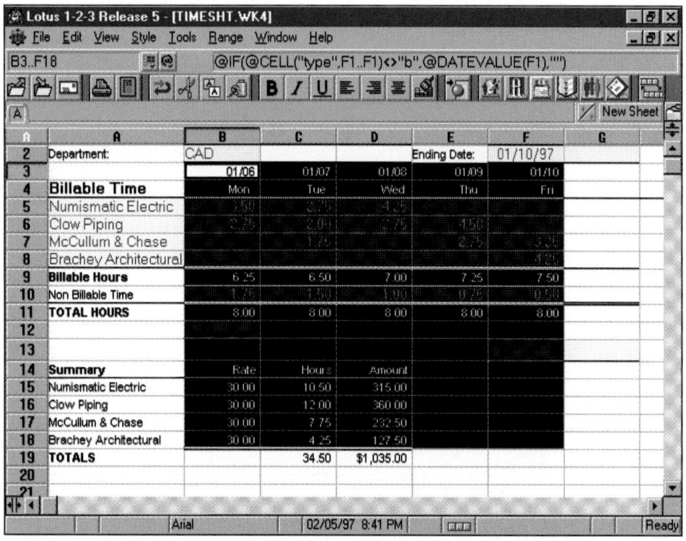

FIGURE 8.5
A highlighted range.

An important tool for referring to cells is naming cells or cell ranges. Once you assign a name to a cell, you can include the name in a formula instead of the cell address. The formula cited above, =SUM(B4, C4, D4), might then appear as =SUM(April_Income, May_Income, June_Income). This makes the formula much more comprehensible, since the words convey more meaning than the cell addresses.

Figure 8.6 shows several examples of formulas using arithmetic operators with named cell references.

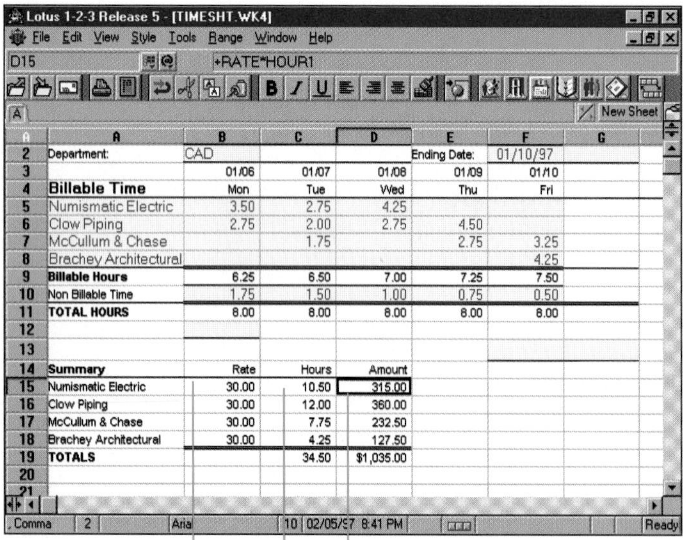

FIGURE 8.6
Named cells.

When you work with 3-dimensional spreadsheet programs, you need a way to refer to cells on other sheets. Normally, to do this, you simply use the sheet name as the first part of the cell reference, followed by a special character (the exclamation point (!) in Excel), then the rest of the reference. For example, to refer to cell G4 in an Excel sheet named Totals, you would use the reference Totals!G4.

This cell has been given the name RATE. This one is HOURS1.

The cell D15 contains the formula +RATE x HOURS1.

Functions

Spreadsheets come with many built-in formulas, called **functions**, that perform specialized calculations automatically. You can include these functions in your own formulas. Some functions are quite simple, such as the COUNT function, which counts how many values are in a range of cells. Many functions, however, are very complex. You may not know the mathematical equations for a loan payment or the depreciation of an asset using the double declining balance method, but by using spreadsheet functions you can arrive at the answer. You add **arguments** within the parentheses of the function. Arguments are the values (often cell references) which the function uses in its operation.

The most commonly used function is the SUM function which adds a list of numbers to get a total sum. In the following formula (using Lotus 1-2-3 syntax), the SUM function's argument is a range:

@SUM(B4..G4)

This formula adds the values in the six cells that comprise the range B4..G4.

Although the SUM function above can take any number of arguments, most functions have very specific types of arguments. For example, in Excel, a loan payment calculation requires the following syntax, with the arguments separated by commas.

=PMT(rate, nper, pv)

where "rate" is the interest rate per period (if the interest is 18% per year, but if you pay monthly, then the "rate" = 0.18/12 = 0.015)

"nper" is the number of periods (if the loan is for 10 years and you pay monthly, then "nper" = $10 \times 12 = 120$)

"pv" is the present value, i.e., the amount of the loan.

An actual formula using the PMT function might look like this:

=PMT(0.1, 12, 100000)

The result is $8,884.88. This function tells you that if you borrow $100,000 for one year at 12% interest, you will have to make monthly payments of $8,884.88 for 12 months.

The leading spreadsheets come with hundreds of these functions. Table 8.3 lists some of the most commonly used ones.

Editing the Worksheet

Once you have input the basic data and created a few formulas, you will often copy the formulas down a column or across a row. In addition, you may decide to change the structure of your worksheet. Spreadsheet programs make it easy to move, copy, or delete the contents of cells. You can also insert or delete rows and columns. You can even add new sheets to a 3-D file, or delete worksheets you no longer need.

TABLE 8.3

Common Functions

FUNCTION NAME	DESCRIPTION
ABS	Absolute (positive) value of an argument
AVERAGE/AVG	Average of arguments
COUNT	Count of numbers in a range of cells
IF	Specifies a logical test to perform, then performs one action if test result is true, another if it is false
LEN/LENGTH	Number of characters in a string of characters
MAX	Maximum value of arguments
MIN	Minimum value of arguments
PMT	Periodic payment for a loan or annuity
PV	Present value of an investment
ROUND	Number rounded to a specified number of digits
SUM	Total value of arguments

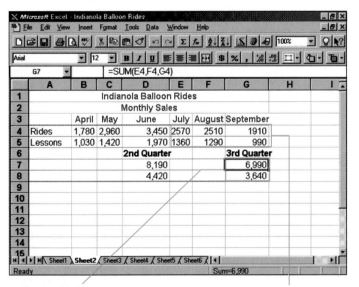

The formulas in these two cells,   **which compute totals for these two ranges...**

...were copied to these two cells.   **The resulting formulas automatically adjust to compute the totals for these two ranges.**

One helpful feature of spreadsheets is that when you move formulas and data to a new location, the spreadsheet automatically adjusts the cell references for formulas based on that data. For example, the second-quarter totals in Figure 8.7a in cells D7 and D8 can be copied to create third-quarter totals without having to re-enter the cell references. In Figure 8.7b, the second-quarter formulas were copied to create the third-quarter formulas. The spreadsheet program created the proper formulas, summing up the third-quarter months.

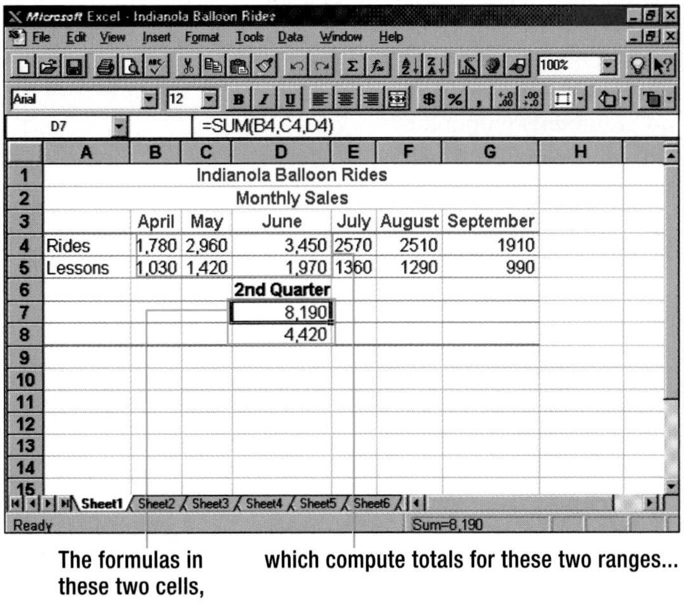

FIGURE 8.7A
Copying formulas.

Of course, you can move and copy text as well. Anything you input, you can change.

The reason the spreadsheet program changes the formulas when you copy them is it remembers that the formulas being copied will reference the same rows as the origin, but will automatically change the column reference when the formulas are moved to a new column. For this reason, when they are used in formulas, cell references such as B4 or D7 are called **relative cell references**. In Figure 8.7b, cell D7 contains the formula =SUM(B4,C4,D4). When it was copied to cell G7, the program automatically changed the formula to =SUM(E4,F4,G4) so that it would add up the July, August, and September Ride sales in row 4. This saved the time of having to type the formula. When you work with long lists of formulas, the time saved can be tremendous, and you will make fewer keyboard mistakes.

FIGURE 8.7B
The copied formula.

However, sometimes you don't want the formulas to change as you copy them. You want all the formulas, no matter where they are, to refer to a specific cell. For example, if the current interest rate is in cell A1, and a number of formulas are based on that rate, you want to be able to copy the formulas without the reference to A1 changing. In this case, you use an **absolute cell reference**, which is usually written using the dollar sign ($). For example, A1 is a relative cell reference and A1 is an absolute cell reference. Figure 8.8 shows a projection for third and fourth quarters. In this case, the user wanted to copy the formula from cell E8 to E9 to avoid retyping it, and then edit it based on the previous years' experience. But both the projections for the third and fourth quarters needed to refer to cell E6. This was accomplished using absolute cell references.

The formulas in these two cells are based on an absolute cell reference.

FIGURE 8.8
Absolute cell references.

Formatting Values, Labels, and Cells

Spreadsheet programs offer numerous formats specifically for numbers. Numbers can appear as dollars and cents, percentage, dates, times, and fractions. They can be shown with or without commas, decimal points, and so forth.

23791363.25679	no comma, any number of decimal places
23,791,363.25679	commas for thousands and millions, any number of decimal places
$23,791,363.26	dollar value, with commas
23,791,363	bound to an integer, with commas
25.68%	percentage
23791363	rounded to an integer, no commas
-23791363.26	no comma, rounded to two decimal places, minus sign for negative
(23,791,363.25679)	commas, negatives shown in red in parentheses

Eight different value formats.

Dates and times are a special category of numbers. In order to calculate dates (for example, to find out how many days there are between November 15, 1996, and March 2, 2002) spreadsheets turn dates into serial numbers, usually starting from January 1, 1900. Likewise, a typical way to calculate time is to treat time as a fraction of a day. You can still enter and display a time or date using a standard format such as 3/9/96.

In addition to number formats, spreadsheets also offer a choice of fonts and type styles, shadowed borders, and more. You can create special effects by adding graphics, such as clip art, to your worksheets. The latest versions of Lotus 1-2-3 and Excel come with maps that you can use to create unique charts based on your data. In addition, you can now automatically dress up your charts using professionally designed, prepackaged formats. Several of the figures in this chapter were formatted in this way. Figure 8.9 shows some of these effects.

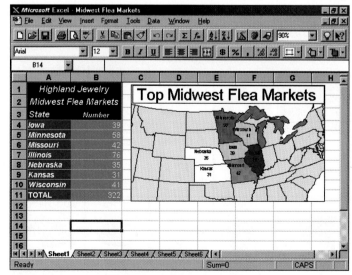

FIGURE 8.9
Type styles and a map.

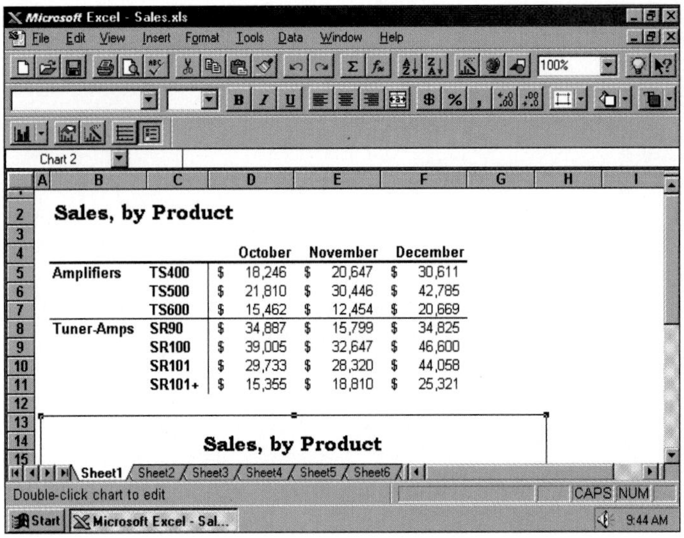

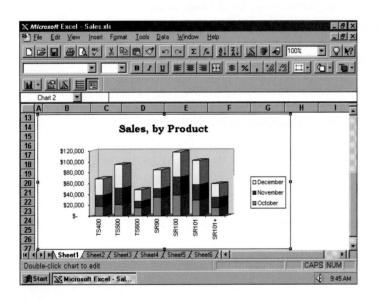

FIGURE 8.10
Stereo sales.

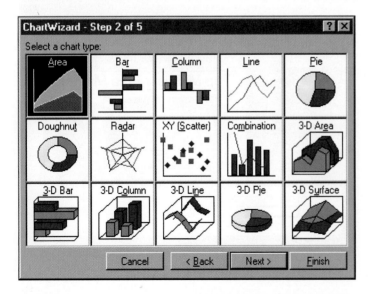

Adding Charts

One of the most popular features of spreadsheet software is the ability to generate charts based on numeric data. The purpose of a chart is to make the data easier to understand. This can be especially important when presenting data to an audience. As a result, you will often see charts in business presentations, yet you will rarely see the worksheets that were used to create the charts.

As an example of how charts make data easier to interpret, take a look at the worksheet in Figure 8.10, which lists total sales of various stereo components over a three-month period.

Making quick conclusions based on this data is difficult. You must look carefully and do some mental arithmetic to discover which products sold best and which month had the best sales. But watch what happens when the information is displayed in a chart, as in Figure 8.11.

FIGURE 8.11
Data summarized in a chart.

It is obvious that the SR100 model is the best-selling product. Without too much analysis, you can also see that December was the best month for sales.

With modern spreadsheets, the process of creating a chart is quite simple. The one in Figure 8.11 was created with eight mouse clicks. You select the data you want to chart, click on a chart button, then interact with a series of dialog boxes. Once the chart is created, you can continue to adjust its appearance, using a set of special chart tools.

The most important decision you make when creating a chart is the *type* of chart that you create. The most popular types are bar charts, line charts, pie charts, and scatter charts. As you can see in Figure 8.12, these basic types can take many forms. In fact, once you choose one of the 15 types shown in the figure, you are faced with another dialog box where you choose between 4 to 10 subtypes. The decisions you make are critical to how well the chart will illustrate your data.

FIGURE 8.12
Chart types in Excel.

Spreadsheets manipulate numbers for accounting, engineering, scientific research, and all sorts of everyday business and home-related tasks. Sometimes a table of numeric results is exactly what customers, employees, bosses, or colleagues need to see.

However, most presentations are more informative and persuasive when the numbers have been translated into graphs and charts. Information conveyed in images is often understood more easily. You can also use illustrations to better convey a focus or point you want to make within a large array of information.

Charts and graphs can be presented alone as a summary of the important trends or conclusions you are making, or as illustrations within your worksheet to guide readers to a particular focus of the material.

Because graphs and charts are so important, current versions of most major spreadsheet programs such as Lotus 1-2-3, Excel, and QuattroPro offer the capability to automatically convert numbers in your worksheets to visual graphs or charts that you can include as part of your presentation. You can enhance these visual graphics with colors, borders, text formats, special symbols, clip art, and even freehand drawing.

Separate business graphics programs such as Visio, Harvard ChartXL, ABC FlowCharter, and CorelFlow provide more sophisticated chart and graph-making capabilities for business users. These programs offer more complex diagramming elements such as freehand curves, drawing layers, preselected color palettes, and other features.

Although at first it may seem difficult to build charts and graphs, major spreadsheet and business graphics programs offer wizards (a guidance process within the application) to carry you through the task of graph and chart creation almost painlessly, even the first time.

The first decision you will face in chart and graph creation is when to use one and what kind to use. Here are some simple guidelines to help you decide:

1. Charts and graphs can be used effectively in any worksheet. Human beings notice visual patterns much more readily than patterns in a set of numbers.

2. Choose a graph or chart type appropriate for the information you are presenting. For example:

■ Pie charts are best for showing the relative fractions of a whole, such as the relative portions of a company's total income produced by each of the major departments.

■ Bar charts are best for comparing sizes of related items, such as the comparative amounts of the different inventory items stocked in a warehouse.

■ Line charts are best for showing changing totals over time, such as how profits for the company have varied over the past ten years.

3. Don't try to put too much information into one graph or chart. Too many items, such as too many bars or too many slices in the pie, obscure your point.

4. Use a scale in your graph or chart that reflects the point you want to make.

5. Be sure to completely label all elements of the graph or chart, including axes, data elements, scale, title, source, and dates.

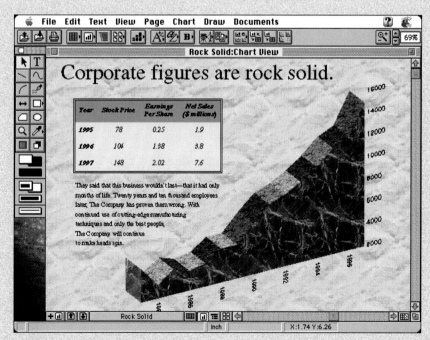

Charts can be used to produce a visual representation of a company's growth over time.

Analyzing the Data

When your worksheet's basic format is complete, and you have created any necessary charts, you can use the worksheet to *analyze* the data. Even adding up totals is a simple form of analysis, but sometimes you want more. In this section you will learn about three useful techniques: what-if analysis, goal seeking, and sorting.

What-If Analysis

When preparing a projection for next year's sales, you may want to test more than one set of assumptions. What happens if inflation goes up? What if interest rates go down? What if the local factory shuts down, putting many of your customers out of work? Using a spreadsheet to test how alternative scenarios affect numeric results is called **what-if analysis**.

All spreadsheets allow you to do simple what-if analysis. You can change one part of a formula, or a cell that it refers to, easily, and then see how that affects the rest of the worksheet. A more sophisticated type of what-if analysis, however, is to create a table that automatically calculates the results based on any number of assumptions. Figure 8.13 shows such a table which calculates the monthly mortgage payment for several possible interest rates.

B7		=PMT(B4/12,B5*12,-B3)					
	A	**B**	**C**	**D**	**E**	**F**	**G**
1	**Mortgage Payment Examples**						
2				Other Interest Rate Possibilities			
3	Total Mortgage	$ 125,000			$1,212.68		
4	Interest Rate	8.25%		7.50%	$1,158.77		
5	Years Paid	15		7.75%	$1,176.59		
6				8.00%	$1,194.57		
7	Monthly Payment	$1,212.68		8.25%	$1,212.68		
8				8.50%	$1,230.92		
9							

FIGURE 8.13
Monthly mortgage payments, based on different interest rates.

What-if analysis is such an important tool for business that spreadsheets offer yet another way to do it. You can create several scenarios or versions of the same spreadsheet, each one containing different assumptions reflected in its formulas. In the mortgage loan example, you can create a best-case scenario which assumes you will find a house for $100,000 and an interest rate of 7.5%. Your worst-case scenario might be a house for $150,000 and an interest rate of 9%. Then you can create a report that summarizes the versions.

Goal Seeking

Suppose you want to look at the problem and know what result you want to get. **Goal seeking** finds values for one or more cells that make the result of a formula equal to a value you specify. In Figure 8.14, cell B7 is the result of the Payment (PMT) formula. In this case, you know the maximum monthly payment you can afford is $1,200, so you want cell B7 to be your starting point. The bank is offering an interest rate of 8.25% over 15 years. The total mortgage, cell B3, can be calculated from the monthly payment, years paid, and interest rate. Figure 8.14 shows the result of this process—you can afford a mortgage of $123,693.

B3		123693.44191904					
	A	**B**	**C**	**D**	**E**	**F**	**G**
1	**Mortgage Payment Examples**						
2							
3	Total Mortgage	$ 123,693					
4	Interest Rate	8.25%					
5	Years Paid	15					
6							
7	Monthly Payment	$1,200.00					
8							

FIGURE 8.14
The result of a goal seek operation.

Sorting

Spreadsheet programs offer the ability to create, sort, and select from lists of data. They do not offer the same database capabilities as relational database management programs, but they can handle many simple database tasks. You can sort the data, or select only the records that meet certain criteria, and then perform calculations on the results.

Figure 8.15 shows the first few records of a simple database. It lists monthly sales of a copier store. Managers can select sales data for any one of their sales staff, or sort sales by name or amount. Then they can use the results to determine who sold the most.

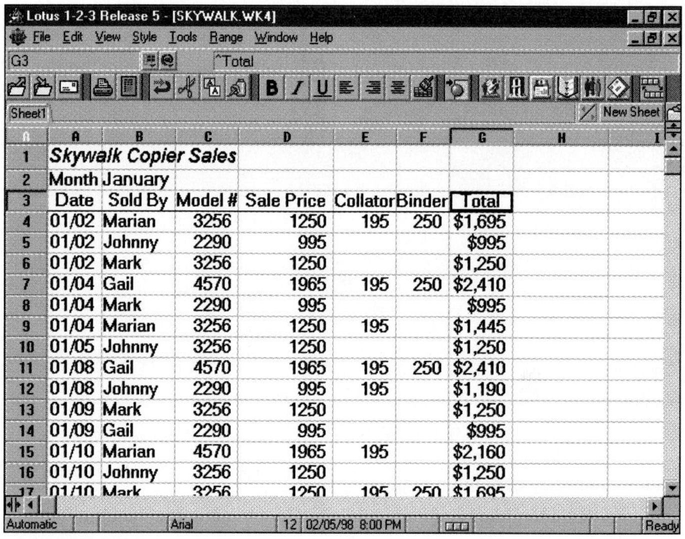

Printing the Worksheet

Of course, no spreadsheet program would be complete without allowing you to create a paper version of your worksheet. Because worksheets are not naturally the shape and size of your printer's ordinary paper, you need to prepare for printing carefully. The program will divide your worksheet into paper-sized segments, and then you can print it. Some helpful print options are printing to fit a page and scaling to a percentage of normal size. For spreadsheets that are wider than they are long, you may want to print sideways, in the setting known as landscape orientation. Most spreadsheet programs allow you to preview what your printed version will look like before you print, which is a wise precaution.

FIGURE 8.15
A database of sales transactions.

▶ ADVANCED TOOLS

If you use spreadsheets often, you will appreciate some of the special tools they offer for streamlining operations. Among the most valuable are macros, outlining, and auditing.

Spreadsheets were one of the first programs to offer **macros**—a series of recorded commands that automate a task. For example, suppose you are working on a spreadsheet where you must continually copy one full column to another. Doing this task manually could take you about 8 to 13 keystrokes. With a macro, you record the same sequence of keystrokes and give it a name, like Alt+A. Then every time you need to copy a column, you just press Alt+A and the macro will play back those keystrokes, copying the column.

You can use a macro to enter data, format worksheets or files, guide users through specific operations, calculate complex formulas with variable data, and so on. There are two ways to create a macro. The first is to record your keystrokes and mouse movements, the second is to use the macro programming language that comes with the spreadsheet program. These languages allow you to create complex programs within the spreadsheet program itself. Figure 8.16 shows a short program that makes the selected cell red and italic.

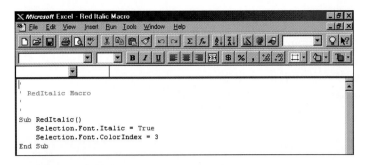

FIGURE 8.16
An Excel macro.

These symbols indicate that totals have been included for both rows and

The box containing the plus sign (+) indicates that the column data has been collapsed.

The box containing the minus sign (-) indicates that the outlining feature is currently expanded, showing the contents of each row.

The worksheet on the left is so wide that it will not fit on the screen. On the right, the Outlining tool has been used to collapse the data so that only the annual totals are shown.

When you create a macro, you must give it a name. You can also assign it to a keyboard shortcut (such as Alt+A), a menu item, or a toolbar icon. You can execute, that is play back, the macro by choosing the name of the macro from a list of macros, by using its keyboard shortcut, or selecting its menu item or toolbar icon.

Outlining is useful if you have a complex worksheet with several levels of data, such as monthly sales, quarterly subtotals, and annual totals. The outlining feature collapses the worksheet to show only subtotals and totals, or only totals. This helps you to analyze major trends and to see the structure of the worksheet clearly.

Spreadsheets can become complicated. Sometimes it is hard to recognize the tangled web of relationships. One formula may depend on a dozen cells. One cell can affect a dozen formulas. Therefore, it is necessary to have tools to sort out these relationships, especially when a problem surfaces and you need to find the cause. This is called **auditing**. Some of the available auditing tools are as follows:

- Zooming out to see the entire worksheet at one glance.
- Viewing the formulas in the cells instead of their results.
- Viewing explanatory notes that have been attached to cells.
- Automatically going to a cell that is referred to by a cell or that depends on another cell.
- Creating tracers, which show the relationships between cells graphically.

Tracers in this screen show that the Monthly Payment value has been computed using the values in B3, B4, and B5, and that the result has been copied to E3.

▶ NORTON WORKSHOP:
A WORKSHEET TO ANALYZE SALES

In this Norton Workshop, you will see how Eric Sawitsky, owner of Skywalk Copier Sales, creates a worksheet to analyze sales over the last three years and to project next year's sales. He wants to see the trends over the past three years (1995, 1996, and 1997) and analyze what factors relate most closely to his net profit. He has two theories that he wants to test:

- The more salespeople he has, the higher his net profit value.
- The more he spends on advertising, the higher his net profit value.

His data for the worksheet comes from three profit and loss statements, each of which he will place on separate sheets. He names the sheets *1995*, *1996*, and *1997*, and then imports the profit and loss statements to the three sheets. The 1995 statement is shown in Figure 8.17.

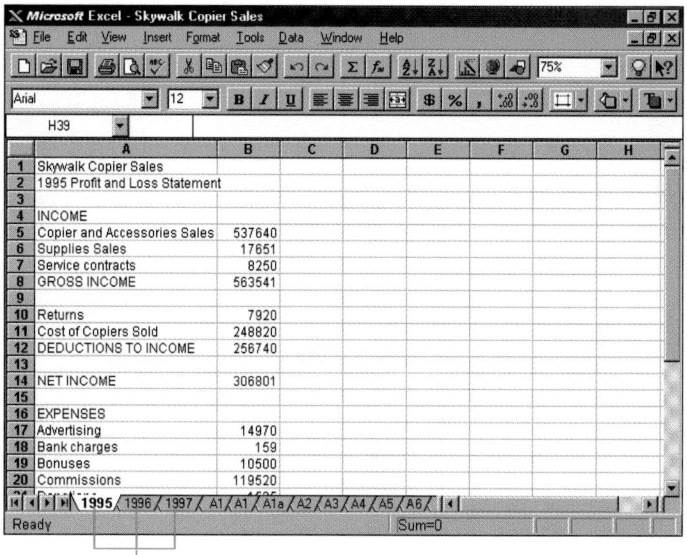

FIGURE 8.17
Profit and loss statement for 1995.

These 3 tabs label the 3 sheets
containing profit and loss statements.

Eric names a new sheet *Analysis* to consolidate information from the three sheets *1995*, *1996*, and *1997*. He then creates the basic structure shown in Figure 8.18.

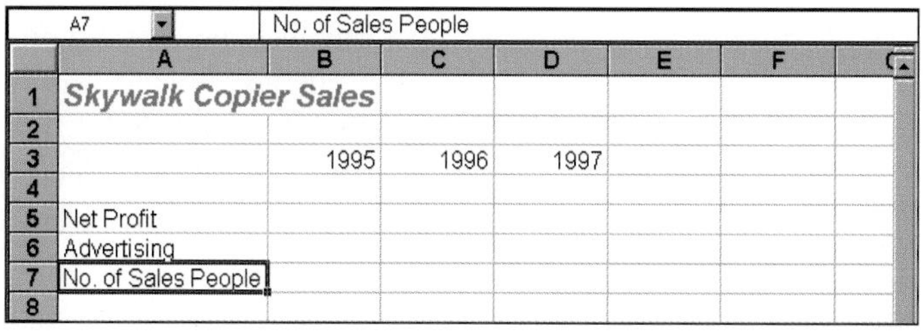

FIGURE 8.18
The new Analysis sheet.

Now he is ready to enter data. He clicks on cell B5 of the *Analysis* sheet, types an equal sign (=), and then clicks on cell B32 in sheet 1995. He presses Enter and the cell reference appears in the *Analysis* sheet, as shown in Figure 8.19.

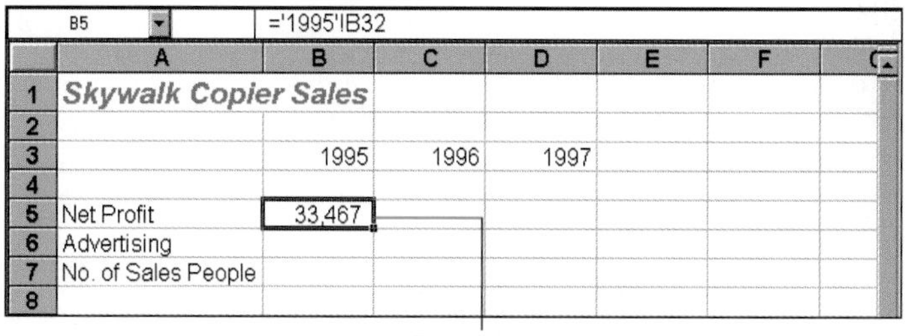

FIGURE 8.19
The first value, copied from the 1995 sheet.

The formula for the cell contains the name of the 1995 sheet and the cell reference B32.

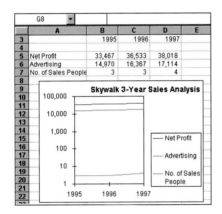

D7		4				
	A	**B**	**C**	**D**	**E**	**F**
1	*Skywalk Copier Sales*					
2						
3		1995	1996	1997		
4						
5	Net Profit	33,467	36,533	38,018		
6	Advertising	14,970	16,367	17,114		
7	No. of Sales People	3	3	4		
8						

Eric enters the six formulas in cells B5 through D6. Now he types in the number of salespeople for each year to complete the sheet, as shown in Figure 8.20.

FIGURE 8.20
The completed Analysis sheet.

Now, Eric is ready to do some analysis. He starts by making a graph. He selects the data and clicks on the Chart button. He decides to use a line graph, because it is useful for showing trends over a period of time. His first try is shown in Figure 8.21.

FIGURE 8.21
The first attempt at graphing the data.

The problem is that the scale of the number of salespeople is so different from the scale of the advertising and net profit. He double-clicks on the y-axis and chooses the Logarithmic Scale option in the Format Axis dialog box. A logarithmic scale is useful when the scales are as far apart as they are here. The result is shown in Figure 8.22.

FIGURE 8.22
The graph changed to a logarithmic scale.

Eric feels he needs more specific information about the relationship between net profit, advertising, and the number of salespeople. The first step is to calculate the percent change in his three variables from year to year. He decides to transpose the rows and columns and copy his data to a new sheet called *Percent Increase*. Then he inserts the *% Increase* label after 1996 and 1997. Now, he is ready to develop the formulas he needs, which are shown in Figure 8.23. The formula bar shows the formula for cell B6. Notice the parentheses, which are necessary to make the spreadsheet calculate the subtraction before the division.

B6		=(B5-B4)/B4				
	A	**B**	**C**	**D**	**E**	**F**
1	*Skywalk Copier Sales*					
2						
3		Net Profit	Advertising	No. of Sales People		
4	1995	33,467	14,970	3		
5	1996	36,533	16,367	3		
6	% Increase	9.2%	9.3%	0.0%		
7	1997	38,018	17,114	4		
8	% Increase	4.1%	4.6%	33.3%		
9						

FIGURE 8.23
The Percent Increase sheet.

It is now clear that net profit and advertising always increase in similar amounts, whereas the number of salespeople increases in a way that is not connected to net profit. Of course, he knows that he would have to examine the data for more years to be certain that the relationship is causal, but he is satisfied that he has found a clue to his profits.

Back in the *Analysis* sheet, Eric uses a statistical function, TREND, to see what 1998 might bring. He selects the cells that contain net profits for three years and asks for a fourth number. These are the arguments for the function. The result, seen in Figure 8.24, shows that if the current trend continues, his net profit will be $40,556 in 1998.

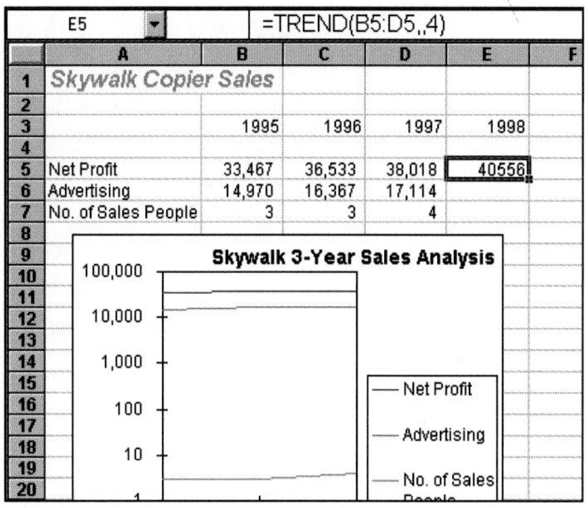

FIGURE 8.24

The result of the TREND function.

This is interesting and helpful information, but Eric is not willing to accept a continuation of the same trend. His goal is a 10 percent increase in net profits. He decides to use Goal Seek to find out the dollar amount of net profit if it increased by 10 percent.

Returning to his *Percent Increase* sheet, Eric adds labels for 1998 and % Increase. He copies the % Increase formula from cell B8 to cell B10 under Net Profit. Then he uses the Goal Seek command. In the Goal Seek dialog box he completes his request as shown in Figure 8.25.

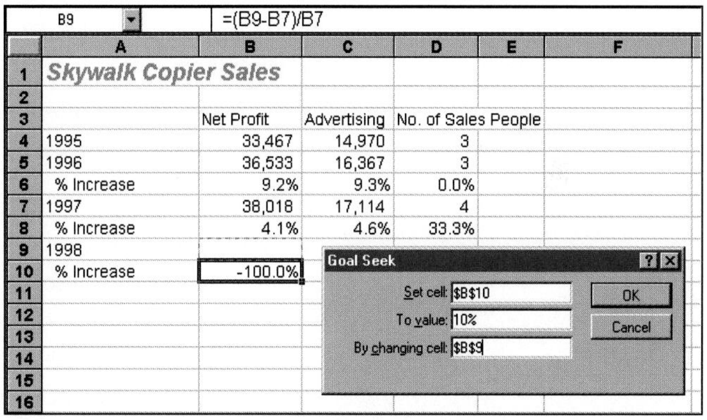

FIGURE 8.25

Using the Goal Seek dialog box.

Eric duplicates the process for advertising. He figures that if advertising and net profit are so closely related, this will provide him with useful information about how much to spend on advertising next year. The results are shown in Figure 8.26.

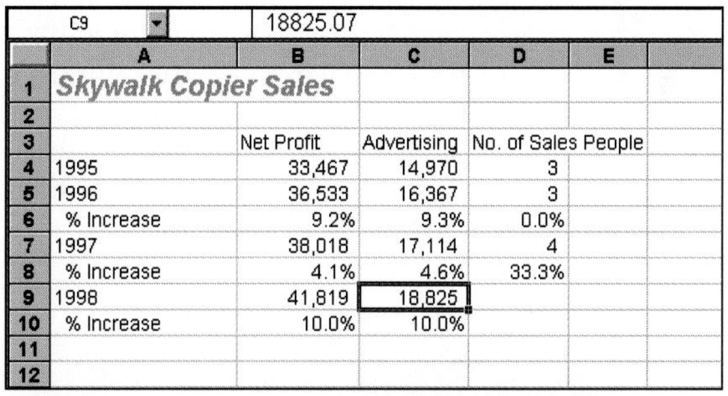

FIGURE 8.26

The results of using Goal Seek to compute advertising in 1998.

Finally, he is ready to format the tables. He chooses a suitable format from the list of built-in formats, using the preview box to decide which format he wants. The results for the first table are shown in Figure 8.27.

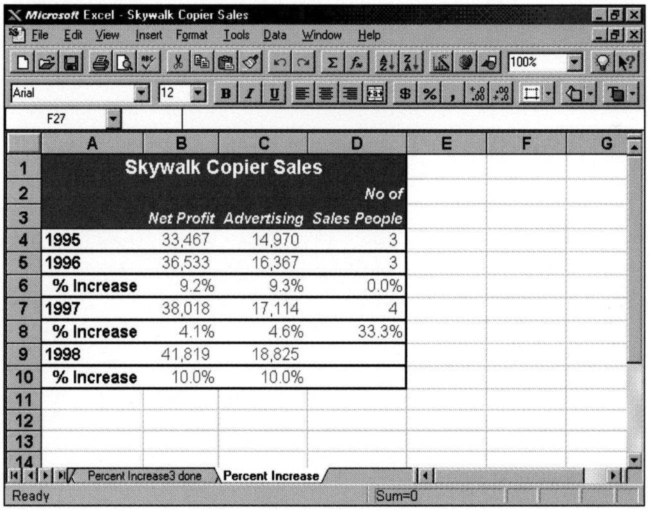

FIGURE 8.27

The formatted Percent Increase sheet.

▶ WHAT TO EXPECT IN THE FUTURE

As we move into the future, what are the trends for spreadsheet programs? To a large extent, these mirror the trends for the software industry in general. All three of the top spreadsheet programs are now available as part of "office suites" that package several programs together: the spreadsheet program, a word processor, a drawing or presentation graphics program, an organizer, and sometimes a database management program. Office suites provide integration between the spreadsheet program and the other applications in the suite. They also offer a common interface, including menus and toolbars, making it easy to learn and use all the programs together. More and more, you will use your spreadsheet program as part of cross-application projects, for example, collecting sales data in your database management program, importing it into your spreadsheet for analysis, and putting the resulting table and chart into a report you write with your word processor.

Group computing is another trend. As more companies create networks for their computers to share information, there is a need to allow more than one person at a time to work on a file. Lotus, a leader in this area, calls this Team Computing. Lotus' SmartSuite 96 offers several features designed to make it easy for groups to work together on a project.

Finally, the software companies are always searching for ways to make it easier for you to use their products. They research which tasks are performed most frequently and then they create icons or guides to help you complete those tasks. Excel's Wizards and Lotus' Assistants fall into this category. In addition, all the spreadsheet programs provide templates for many commonly used documents. Spreadsheets are even using word processing tools with spell checking, auto-correcting, and formatting features. Excel's AutoComplete assists you with repetitive data entry by automatically completing an entry when you start typing text that has already been typed in the same column.

For the future, you can expect spreadsheets to offer more special features for the advanced user while simplifying frequently used tasks for beginning and advanced users alike.

▶ VISUAL SUMMARY

A Tool for Working with Numbers

- A spreadsheet program is used to calculate and analyze sets of numbers.
- A spreadsheet is formatted in columns and rows of cells.
- Cells can contain values, labels, or formulas.
- A data file created with a spreadsheet is called a worksheet.
- Business uses for spreadsheets are financial analysis, tracking numerical data, simple databases, and worksheets designed for customer or employee use.
- Scientists and engineers use spreadsheets to do complex statistical, mathematical, and trigonometric calculations.
- Personal uses for spreadsheets include budgeting, loan calculations, and simple database management.

Creating a Worksheet

- The process of creating a worksheet can involve organizing the data, designing the worksheet, entering data, creating formulas, editing, formatting, adding charts, analyzing data, and printing the worksheet.
- A formula lets you create a value in one cell that is calculated based on the values in other cells.
- Formulas follow the order of mathematical operations: exponentiation, negation, multiplication and division, addition and subtraction.
- A cell is referred to by its address—created by combining its column and row headings, as in B4. Groups of cells can be referenced with a range, such as B4:G4. Single cells or ranges can also be given names. In 3-D spreadsheets, you can refer to cells on other worksheets. Finally, you can refer to cells in other files.
- Built-in functions include arguments, which are the values on which the function performs its operation.
- References to cells can be relative or absolute.
- Numbers can be formatted as dollars, percents, dates, times, fractions, and normal decimal numbers, with or without commas.
- You can format a worksheet using fonts, borders, maps, and graphics.
- Charts are used to make data easier to understand.
- The most common types of charts are bar charts, line charts, pie charts, and scatter charts.
- What-if analysis can be as simple as replacing a value in a cell that affects other cells, or it can involve the use of data tables, and scenarios or versions.
- Goal Seek allows you to specify a goal and arrive at the starting figure.
- Spreadsheets have database management capabilities including sorting, selecting, and printing out reports.

① Organize → ② Design → ③ Enter data → ⑤ Edit → ⑥ Format → ⑦ Analyze → ⑧ Print
④ Create formulas

23791363.25679
23,791,363.25679
$23,791,363.26
23,791,363
25.68%
23791363
-23791363.26
(23,791,363.25679)

Advanced Tools

■ A macro is a series of recorded commands that automate a task.

■ Macros can be created by recording keyboard and mouse actions or by using a macro programming language that comes with the application.

■ Outlining is used to summarize the data in a worksheet.

■ Auditing is used to demonstrate the logic behind the data and formulas in a complex worksheet.

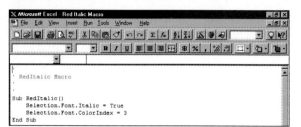

▶ KEY TERMS

After completing this chapter, you should be able to define the following terms:

absolute cell reference, 250	comparison operator, 247	range, 248
address, 243	formula, 240	relative cell reference, 250
argument, 249	formula bar, 243	row, 240
auditing, 256	function, 248	spreadsheet, 240
block, 248	goal seeking, 254	syntax, 247
cell, 240	graph, 241	text operator, 247
cell pointer, 246	label, 243	value, 243
cell reference, 248	macro, 255	what-if analysis, 254
chart, 241	operator, 247	worksheet, 241
column, 240	outlining, 256	

▶ KEY TERM QUIZ

Fill in the blank with one of the terms listed in Key Terms:

1. You can use a _____ to calculate and analyze sets of numbers.

2. Graphic representations of numbers are known as _____.

3. A(n) _____ refers to the file you create with spreadsheet software.

4. Numerical entries are also called _____.

5. The _____ identifies the active cell.

6. The _____ is the sequence of characters used in a formula.

7. You can automatically perform specialized calculations using _____.

8. To test more than one set of assumptions, you can use _____.

9. A(n) _____ is a series of commands that automates a task.

10. The combined cell column and row headings are known as the cell's _____.

▶ REVIEW QUESTIONS

1. Define briefly a spreadsheet and describe its basic structure.
2. List and describe the other features available with spreadsheet software in addition to its ability to calculate numbers.
3. What two preliminary steps are necessary before you design a worksheet? Describe the method recommended in this chapter for carrying out the design process.
4. When entering a formula in a cell, does it matter in which order you enter the values and operators? Explain your answer.
5. List and describe each component that makes up a built-in function.
6. What must you include in a formula to ensure that the formula will operate on a specific value no matter where the formula might be moved or copied? How do you do this with most spreadsheets?
7. Describe briefly why it is not necessary to include numeric symbols like dollar signs, commas, or percent signs when you enter a value in a cell.
8. What spreadsheet feature allows you to represent data visually as a data-analysis tool?
9. Name and describe the two spreadsheet features that allow you to analyze different sets of calculated results based on different assumptions.
10. Describe how *auditing* can be a useful worksheet troubleshooting tool.

▶ DISCUSSION QUESTIONS

1. The chapter's introduction voiced the claim by many "that the invention of the spreadsheet, more than any other event, launched the personal computer revolution." Do you agree with this statement? Based on what you read in the rest of this chapter, cite two or three reasons that support this claim.
2. Suppose you are working with a three-dimensional worksheet, and you want to create a consolidation sheet that calculates totals and averages for values in the other sheets. Describe how you would set up the consolidation sheet and build the formulas to accomplish the task.
3. What fundamental feature of spreadsheet software provides the real power behind its calculation abilities? Describe briefly at least one kind of common operation that demonstrates this ability.
4. List and describe as many reasons as you can for using a worksheet to store and manipulate certain kinds of data, such as names and addresses, rather than using a relational database manager program. Name any significant advantages or disadvantages.

NORTON INTERACTIVE

Complete the Norton Interactive module for this chapter.

DATABASE MANAGEMENT

CONTENTS

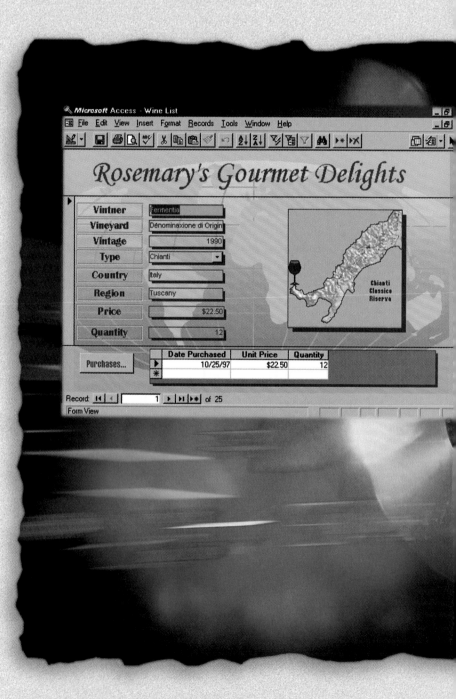

OBJECTIVES

When you complete this chapter, you will be able to do the following:

- Distinguish between data and information.
- Define database and database management system (DBMS) software.
- Describe the features of a DBMS.
- Describe the most common database structures: flat-file, relational, hierarchical, network, and object-oriented.
- Explain the purpose of the most common field types: text, numeric, date and time, logical, counter, memo, and binary.
- Discuss the methods for designing and implementing a DBMS.

Without question, our world contains vast amounts of data. Think of any kind of business, personal, or social pursuit, and you can be sure there is an associated data collection at its disposal and vital to its existence. To make large collections of data useful, companies use computers and an efficient data management system. The goal of database management software is to gather large volumes of data and process them into useful information.

In this chapter, you'll learn about the world of databases and database management systems. Like a warehouse, a **database** is a repository for collections of related data or facts. A **database management system (DBMS)** is a software tool that allows multiple users to access, store, and process the data or facts into useful information.

▶ DATA AND INFORMATION

As you look into the relationship between DBMSs and databases, you need to be aware of an important distinction that exists between data and information. Data consists of the raw facts or items that are gathered and stored. Information is the product or result of using a DBMS to assemble the data into a meaningful form.

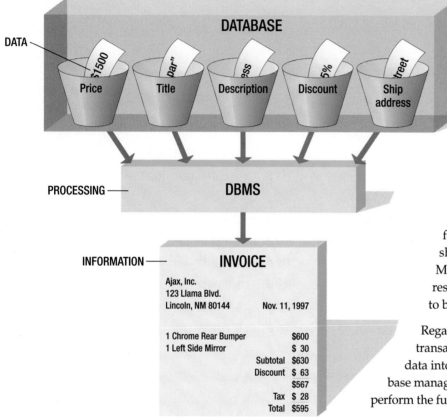

Data is gathered and assembled into useful information.

To illustrate, the surname "Lewis" and the amount "$1,500" are examples of raw data, single items that exist within a data collection. Through a DBMS, an art gallery, for example, can merge these two examples of raw data with additional data to generate an invoice. The invoice will detail Alice Lewis's purchase of a painting entitled *Approaching Storm*, for $1,500, plus $108.75 tax, that will ship to 1100 33rd Avenue in Santa Monica, California. The invoice is the result—the information—that is useful to both the purchaser and the seller.

Regardless of the type of business, business transactions involve lots of data. To turn the data into information, the businesses use database management systems, which are designed to perform the functions described in Table 9.1.

TABLE 9.1	
Functions of a DBMS	
DBMS FUNCTION	**COMPUTER SYSTEM FUNCTION**
Collect the relevant data	Input
Preserve the data for later use	Storage
Organize the data into logical and meaningful sets (information)	Processing
Create meaningful subsets of the data (information) for specific purposes	Processing
Obtain meaningful subsets of the data (information) in printed form	Output

▶ THE DATABASE-DBMS RELATIONSHIP

DBMSs are one of the primary reasons that people use computers. Many large companies and organizations rely heavily on commercial or custom DBMSs to

handle immense data resources. Banks, manufacturing companies, retail chains, government agencies, and health care institutions—to name just a few—store huge volumes of data every day. Organizations like these require sophisticated DBMSs to accommodate their data management needs. Often, these DBMSs are custom-made, proprietary, and programmed using standard programming languages such as COBOL and C. These programs are often designed to run on large, mainframe computers.

To process massive collections of data, employees in large organizations use networked PCs.

DBMSs are no less necessary for people and organizations who use networks and standalone personal computers. In these cases, the DBMS is often a commercial product, sold by the same companies that offer popular spreadsheets and word processing software. Some popular DBMSs for personal computers include:

- dBase for DOS, dBase for Windows, and Paradox from Borland International
- Access and Visual FoxPro from Microsoft
- FileMaker Pro from Claris
- Q & A from Symantec
- Lotus Approach
- R:BASE for Windows from Microrim.

This list is hardly a complete one. There are many other commercial DBMS products available for IBM-compatible PCs running DOS, Windows, UNIX, OS/2, Macintosh, and other systems.

Personal computers have brought database management to the desktops of individuals in businesses and private homes. Although the average individual at home may not need an inventory tracking system, home users use commercial DBMS products to maintain address lists of friends and business contacts, manage household purchases and budgets, and store data for home businesses.

More people are using computers at home to manage personal data with the help of a commercial DBMS.

A DBMS makes it possible to do many routine tasks that would be otherwise tedious, cumbersome, and time consuming without the services of a computer. For example, a DBMS can do the following tasks:

- Sort thousands of records by zip code prior to a bulk mailing.
- Comb the same database for all records of those New Yorkers who live in boroughs outside Manhattan.
- Print a list of selected records, such as all real estate listings that closed escrow last month.
- Invoice a customer's new car lease, adjust the dealership's inventory, and update the service department's mailing list—merely by entering the data for a single sales transaction.

The Database

A database contains a collection of related items or facts and arranges them in a specific structure. For example, data such as '96, *Yamaha*, *Virago 750*, *Black, 4*, and *$4,100* are all relevant to a motorcycle dealership's database. Any item of data imaginable can exist in a database: from a last name in a customer database, to a part number in an inventory database, to a conviction date in a criminal database.

Data in a database is most commonly viewed in a 2-dimensional table consisting of columns and rows, similar to the structure of a spreadsheet (see Figure 9.1).

Customer ID	Company	Title	Last Name	First Name	MI	Stre
ARCWY	Archway Centers	CIS Director	Winston	Arnold	K.	26119 Flagston
AZTDC	Aztec Day Care	Asst. Director	Smith	Adam	A.	1871 Orchard L
BGNGM	Beginning Methods	Director	Jarmen	Alexandria	U.	121 Kranston A
BLLAC	Bell Academy	Librarian	Smith	Toni	P.	777 Sandbag C
BGRSD	Big Rock School District	Administrator	Ford	Randolf	N.	2100 Seabright
BGSDV	Big Sky Development	Consultant	Landetta	Earl	K.	10 Funston Stre
BRNCH	Branching Out	Director	Jones	Janice	J.	465 Sunset Vie
BRKDC	Breakers Discovery Center	Attendant	Santana	Candice	T.	5667 Westerly
BDGDI	Bridgeway Data, Inc.	President	Tunny	Jenny	L.	743 Baxter Stre
CFVEX	Cabin Fever Express	Asst. Manager	Gamberoni	Michelle	U.	6903 Lakefront
CODIS	Coast Discovery	Educator	Zampese	Raoul	O.	2 Dot Road
DRPVM	Deer Park Village Museum	Curator	Jenkins	Radcliffe	F.	200 Zanzibar Cc
DMDBC	Diamond Back School	Principal	Clearwater	Maya	Z.	53 Diamondbac
DMPDC	Dimples Day Care	Care Provider	Zigfried	Cathy	M.	9 Livingston Str
DSCGL	Discs Galore	Manager	Melvin	Danforth	W.	10000 Lupus Rc
EDUIN	Edument Industries	Buyer	Mansville	Jane	B.	119 Burley Drive
FRYCC	Ferry Community Center	President	Lawrence	Jeremiah	W.	82109 Circle Rc
FLWPS	Flowerpot Schools	Teacher	Boyce	Joseph	D.	65 Larkspur Driv
FOYDC	Fountain of Youth	Director	Livingston	Mabel		82111 Young S
GDVLA	Gage Development Assoc.	Manager	Plante	Paige	I.	76 Telford Blvd

Record: 50 of 50

Unique code for each customer.

FIGURE 9.1
Database viewed as a 2-dimensional table.

The entire collection of related data in the table is referred to as a file. Each row represents a **record**, which is a set of data for each database entry. Each table column represents a **field**, which groups each piece or item of data among the records into specific categories or types of data. A set of recipe cards provides another way in which you can visualize the relationship between a database file, its records, and its fields, as shown in Figure 9.2.

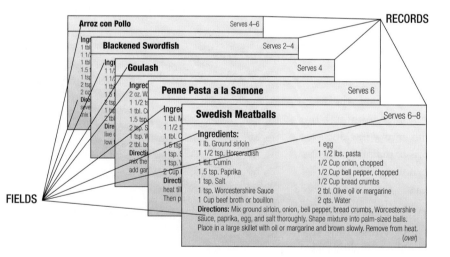

FIGURE 9.2
A database of recipes on index cards.

Notice that the table arrangement shown in Figure 9.1 consists of a set number of named columns and an arbitrary number of unnamed rows. The table organizes each record's data by the same set of fields, but the table can store any number of records. The only limit is the storage capability of the disk. Any one record in the table does not necessarily have data in every field. However, for a record to exist, it must have data in at least one field.

The order of fields in a table strictly defines the location of data in every record. A phone number field, for example, must contain a record's phone number—it cannot contain a phone number in some rows (in some records) and a person's name or zip code in others. Similarly, the set of fields in any one table provides a sensible definition of the database for those who must access its data. For instance, you would expect to find the part number for a radiator in an inventory of auto parts, but you should not expect to view an employee's payroll record in the same table.

Flat-File Databases

A database file that consists of a single data table is a **flat-file database**. Flat-file databases can be quite useful for certain single-user or small-group situations, especially for maintaining lists such as address lists or inventories. Data that is stored, managed, and manipulated in a spreadsheet is another example of a flat-file database.

Despite their simplicity, flat-file databases do have a significant limitation over databases consisting of multiple tables. They do not allow for more complex requests for data because there are no links to, or relationships with, other tables. This is fine if you merely need to locate a part or verify an address. However, very often you need to process more extensive information from multiple data tables. For instance, you might need to locate those customers in a specific sales region who ordered a specific quantity of a particular item. The customer data, the order data, and the inventory data would very likely exist in different tables—one for customers, one for orders, and one for products or inventory. Databases consisting of multiple tables can link or relate records according to one of four conceptual structures:

1. The Relational database
2. The Hierarchical database
3. The Network database
4. The Object-Oriented database

The Relational Database Structure

A database structure is a model or design that provides the conceptual foundation for a database. Like anything else with a specific structure, databases require precise planning before they are designed or built.

This chapter focuses primarily on the relational structure, which represents a database made up of a set of tables. In a **relational database**, a common field existing in any two tables creates a relationship between the tables. For instance, a Customer ID Number field in both a *customers* table and an *orders* table links the two tables (see Figure 9.3). The relational database structure is easily the most prevalent in today's business organizations.

There are endless examples of relational databases. A flooring company's database would be likely to contain data tables such as the following:

■ Customer names, addresses, and phone numbers
■ Orders
■ Vendors of carpeting, hardwood, and vinyl flooring products
■ Sales employees and installation contractors
■ On-hand inventory

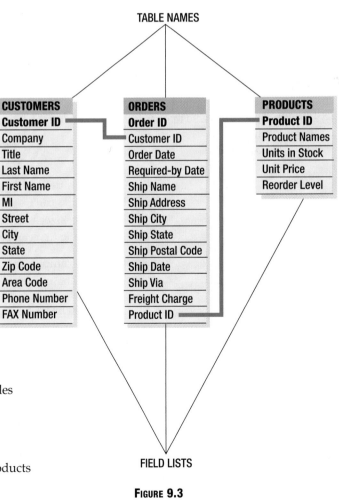

FIGURE 9.3
Linked fields in relational database tables.

Multiple tables in this kind of database make it possible to handle many data management tasks. For example:

■ The customer, order, and inventory tables can be linked to process orders and billing.
■ The vendor and inventory tables can be linked to maintain and track inventory levels.
■ The order and employee tables can be linked to control scheduling.

Other Database Structures

Although this chapter focuses on the relational structure, the other three types do bear mention. The hierarchical and network structures (or models) generally apply to older systems that are still in use today, primarily on mainframe computers. In a **hierarchical database**, records are organized in a tree-like structure by type. The relationship between record types is said to be a parent-child relationship, in which any *child* type relates only to a single *parent* type.

The **network database** is very similar to the hierarchical structure except that any one record type can relate to any number of other record types.

An **object-oriented database** is a newer structure that has been generating a great deal of interest in recent years. It represents a very different approach to the way data is treated by database developers and users. The object-oriented structure groups data items and their associated characteristics, attributes, and procedures into complex items called objects. Physically an object can be anything: a product, or event, such as a house, an appliance, a textile, an art piece, a toy, a customer complaint, or even a purchase.

An object is defined by its characteristics, attributes, and procedures. An object's characteristics can be text, sound, graphics, and video. Examples of attributes might be color, size, style, quantity, and price. A procedure refers to the processing or handling that can be associated with an object.

For example, imagine a database used at an electronics store. In the company's database, a television could be an object with the following properties:

Characteristics: text, graphics (information about the TV is text; pictures of the TV are graphics)

Attributes: brand name, screen size, model number, retail price, and images of the TV and a cutaway of the TV's interior

Procedure: adding the TV's product number, price, and sales tax to a sales invoice.

When a customer chooses to buy the television, the salesperson clicks on a button, which issues a message to the television object. The message initiates the procedure that adds the television to a sales invoice while updating the inventory database.

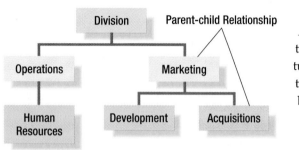

In a hierarchical database, record types are organized in parent-child relationships.

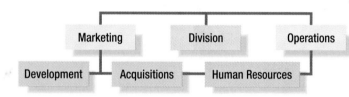

In a network database, a record type can relate to any number of other record types.

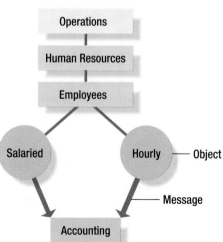

In an object-oriented database, messages are passed from one object to another.

The DBMS

Although databases come in a variety of sizes, almost any collection of data can become quite unwieldy as it receives and stores more and more data over time. Computers make it possible to harness large data collections efficiently using a DBMS. A DBMS is a program, or collection of programs, that allows any number of users to access data, modify it (if necessary), and construct simple and complex requests to obtain and work with selected records.

Perhaps a DBMS's biggest asset is its ability to provide extremely quick access and retrieval from large databases. Because database files can grow extremely large (many gigabytes on large systems), recalling data quickly is not a trivial matter. A DBMS, especially when it is running on powerful hardware, can find any speck of data in an enormous database in minutes—sometimes even seconds or fractions of a second.

Although there are many tasks you can perform with a DBMS, including creating and designing the database itself, data management tasks fall into one of three general categories:

- Entering data into the database.
- Reordering the records in the database (for example, obtaining an alphabetical list of customers).
- Obtaining subsets of the data.

Equally important, DBMSs provide the means for multiple users to access and share data in the same database by way of networked computer systems. For instance, a flooring company's bookkeeper or accounting clerk could use the DBMS to see the prior month's purchases. At the same time, a salesperson could be completing a sale and adding new purchase data to the database.

Data retrieved by a DBMS is sometimes brought into nondatabase software to be incorporated into other kinds of documents. For instance, a college administrator can import data from the school's course database into a word processing program to create a catalog for the upcoming term. Output from the word processor can be transferred to a desktop publishing program to lay out and print the new course catalog.

▶ WORKING WITH A DATABASE

The DBMS provides the vehicle that presents the data to the user and the tools required to work with the data. This is what is meant by the DBMS's interface. The **interface** is the visual tool you use to perform the important DBMS functions that manage data productively, namely:

- Creating tables.
- Entering and editing data.
- Viewing data using filters and forms.
- Sorting the records.
- Querying the database to obtain specific information.
- Generating reports to print processed information.

Drive the Internet Superhighway
In this hands-on, practical workshop you will learn all you need to know to navigate the Internet, including Internet vocabulary, jargon, nettiquette, obtaining access, E-mail, the World Wide Web, and more.
Instructor: Steve Foreman
Dates: May 9 & 16
Days: Thursdays
Time: 7-10pm
Where: Indian Valley Campus
Fee: $90
Course #6616

Build Your Own Website Using Adobe PageMill
Adobe's PageMill was specifically designed to address the needs of non-technical people; however, it is expected that students taking this class will have previous experience using a mouse driven interface (Windows or Macintosh) and experience on the World Wide Web
Instructor: Chris Salzman
Dates: April 18
Days: Thursdays
Where: Marin Community College
Fee: $45
Course: #6689

Creating Interactive Multimedia in Director
We will explore Director's capabilities and how different elements are integrated. We will cover control of animation, QuickTime and audio, and how the Lingo programming language is used to create an interactive application. Previous computer experience essential.
Instructor: Geoff Chang
Dates: May 6-20
Days: Mondays
Where: Berkeley Campus
Fee: $135
Course: #6968

This course catalog was created with database records exported to a word processing program.

An explosion in the number of databases has paralleled the fantastic growth in the use of computers. Today's businesses—especially large businesses—store massive amounts of data. They keep internal data about their company, their employees, and all of the business transactions they make. They also store external data about their competitors and their industry. Consequently, in today's business climate, a common problem is having too much information, a situation known as infoglut.

The usual approach to battling infoglut is to maintain well designed databases. At some point, however, the law of diminishing returns comes into play and there is simply too much information. It simply is not practical to create a new database and a new database management system (DBMS) for each new problem that comes along. So the newest approach to the problem of infoglut is to build a data warehouse and then to mine the data warehouse for critical information.

A data warehouse is a massive collection of corporate information, often stored in gigabytes or terabytes of data. It can include any and all data that is relevant to the running of a company.

However, setting up a data warehouse is much more complicated than simply dumping all kinds of data into one storage place.

A key step in setting up a data warehouse is scrubbing the data. This means sifting through it and performing such tedious tasks as eliminating duplications and incomplete records and making sure that similar fields in different tables are defined in exactly the same ways.

Once the data warehouse has been set up, it can be an invaluable resource for serving the needs of customers, outsmarting the competition, discovering trends in the market, and developing new products.

To accomplish these goals, a company needs more than just a data warehouse. It also needs software tools to sort through and perform advanced types of statistical analyses on the huge data collections stored in the warehouse. Typically, the goals of data mining fall into one of these two categories:

■ Discovering hidden relationships and trends. Statistical analysis on large sets of data often can reveal information that nobody would have thought to

look for. For example, what if statistical analysis on voting behavior showed that a high percentage of people who own motorcycles and vegetable juice extractors tend to vote with an independent party? This information would be invaluable to an independent candidate who wanted to target potential supporters.

■ Making predictions. If enough data is collected on customers, statistical analysis can point out those people who are likely to be repeat customers, and those who are likely to buy only once. Marketing efforts directed only at people who fit the repeat customer profile can save a company quite a lot of money.

Ultimately, the goal of data mining is to answer complex business questions. Whether a company uses the predictive method of analysis (knowing what the question is ahead of time) or exploratory analysis (framing the question only after mining the data has unearthed a trend or a piece of information)—the end result of data mining is that a company can put its vast storehouse of information to better business uses by finding out exactly what it knows, how to get to it, and what to do with it.

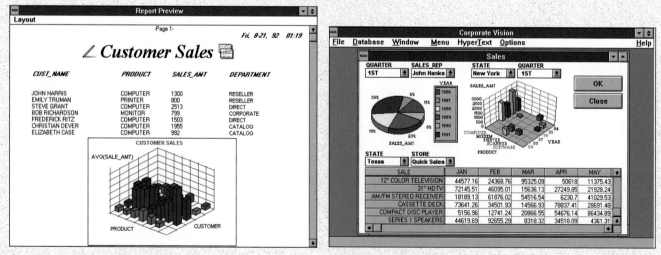

Once information has been organized, it can be used to produce reports like the ones shown above. The report on the left shows the types of sales, the amounts, and the department. The report on the right is an even more complex accounting of sales data.

Creating Tables

Once you determine the names and types of fields you need in a table, you enter the necessary specifications for each field. The specifications for a field include its name and the type of data it identifies and stores in the table. Other specifications for a field might include an optional description of the field's purpose, the number of characters it stores, instructions for entering the data, or other aspects that control the display format of the data.

Setting Field Data Types

To create a new database, you must first determine what kind of data will be stored in each table. In other words, you must define the fields. This is a three-step process:

1. Name the field
2. Specify the field type
3. Specify the field size

In Step 1, when you name the field, you should indicate, as briefly as possible, what the field contains. Figure 9.4 shows a database table with clearly named fields.

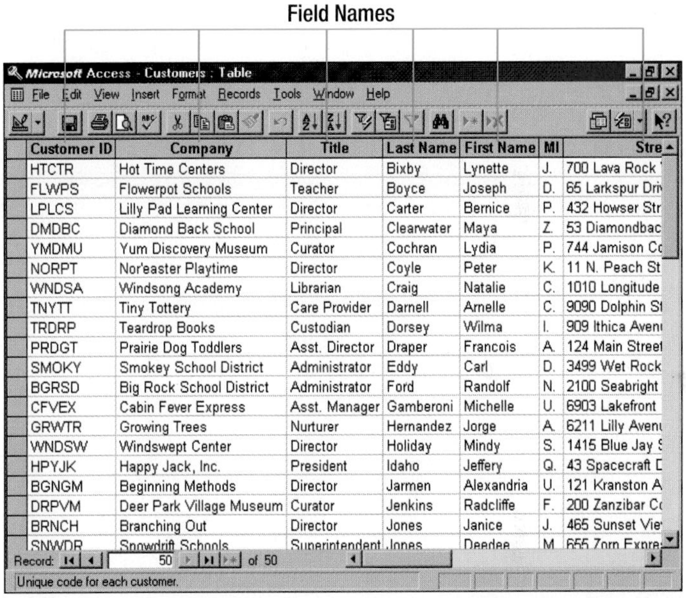

FIGURE 9.4
Clearly named fields.

Step 2, specifying the field type, requires knowledge of what kind of data the DBMS can understand. Most modern DBMSs can work with the following predefined field types:

- text
- numeric
- date and time
- logical
- binary
- counter
- memo

Figure 9.5 shows examples of each of these field types.

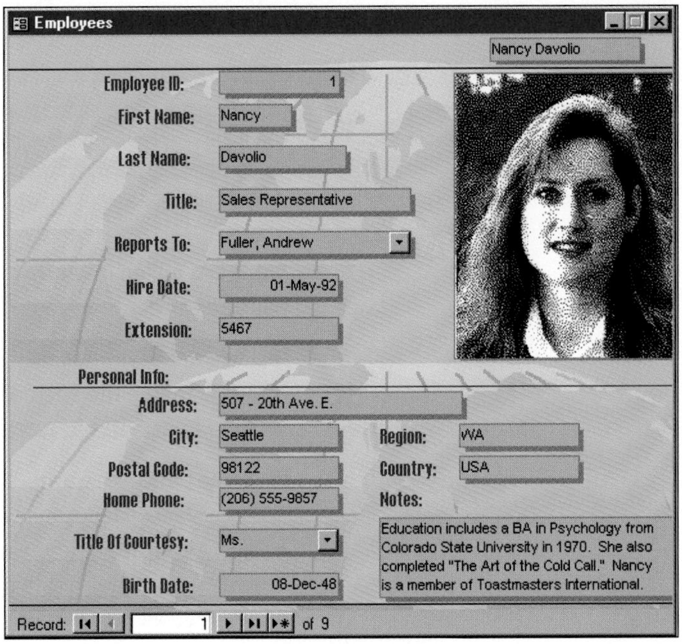

FIGURE 9.5
Field types.

Text or **character fields** (also called **alphanumeric fields**) accept any string of alphanumeric characters such as a person's name, a company's name, an address, a phone number, or any other textual data. Text fields also typically store entries consisting of numbers, like phone numbers or zip codes, that are not used in numeric calculations.

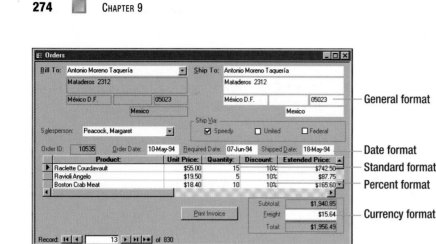

As in a spreadsheet, a database management system can format numbers in many different ways.

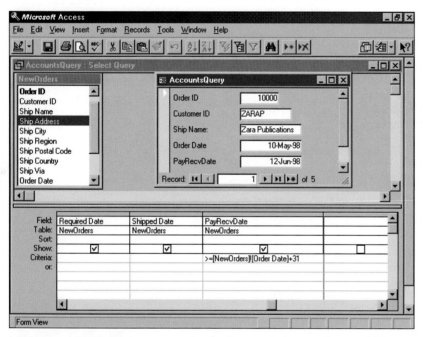

In this screen, the records in an accounting database are being tested to see which payments were received more than 31 days after the order. To accomplish this, the DBMS tests the Pay RecvDate (a date field listing when the payment was received) to see if it is greater than or equal to the Order Date (another date field) plus 31.

Numeric fields store purely numeric data. The numbers in a numeric field might represent currency, percentages, statistics, quantities, or any other value. The data itself is stored in the table strictly as a numeric value, even though the DBMS can display the value with formatting characters, like dollar or percent signs, decimal points, or comma separators.

A **date** or **time field** stores date or time entries. This field type converts a date or time entry into a numeric value, just as dates and times are stored internally as serial numbers in spreadsheet cells. In most DBMSs a date value represents the number of days that have elapsed since a specific start date. When you enter a date in a date field, the DBMS accepts your input, displays it in the format of a date, and converts it to a number that it stores in the database. Date and time fields typically include automatic error-checking features. For instance, date fields can verify a date entry's accuracy and account for the extra day in leap years. Date and time fields are quite handy for calculating elapsed time periods, such as finding records for invoices 31 days overdue.

In addition to these field types there are other specialized field types: logical, binary, counter, and memo fields.

Logical fields store one of only two possible values. You can apply almost any description for the data (yes or no, true or false, on or off, and so forth). For example, a Reorder field in a Products table can tell an inventory clerk whether or not a quantity has dipped below a certain value as a reminder to restock.

Binary fields store binary objects, or BLOBs. A **BLOB (Binary Large OBject)** can be a graphic image file such as clip art, a photograph, a screen image, a graphic, or formatted text. A BLOB can also be a sound track, a video clip, or other object.

In some DBMSs, **counter fields** store a unique numeric value that the DBMS assigns for every record. Because it is possible for two records to have identical data in some tables, a counter field ensures that every record will have a completely unique identification. Counter fields may also be used for creating records that number sequentially, such as invoices.

Because most field types have fixed lengths that restrict the number of characters in an entry, **memo fields** provide fields for entering notes or comments of any length.

Setting Data-Entry Validation

After determining the name and type for each field, the final step of setting up the table is to define the size of the fields. Doing so is generally a matter of examining the data that will be in the field and estimating its maximum size.

Exercise ID   7
Exercise Name   Biking
Exercise Description Burke-Gilman Trail.

Default Sets
Units   Meters
Def. Reps/Duration   10000
Def. Weight/Setting
Exercise Type   Cardiovascular

Drafting - Video Clip in Exer...

Example Footage

Binary field containing a video clip

Binary fields allow graphic images and other nontext items to be stored in a database.

Once the table has been set up, data can be entered. In most cases, entering data is a matter of typing characters at the keyboard. However, the process can have more pitfalls than you might expect, especially if it is being carried out by someone other than the user who set up the tables. For example, the DBMS might not handle a number correctly if the user enters it with a dollar sign—even though the number will be displayed as a dollar amount.

Most DBMSs allow you to set up a device that validates or converts what is typed at the keyboard so that the data is properly entered in the field. Such devices have different names and different capabilities, depending on the specific DBMS product. Some products call them **masks**, others call them **pictures** or **field formats**. Regardless of the name, the device accepts only valid characters and controls the entry's display format.

For example, you can set up a State field so that a state's two-letter code appears uppercase (TN), no matter how the data is typed (tn, Tn, tN, or TN). A phone number field's entry can be controlled similarly. Even though the user types only the phone number's ten digits, it will appear with the area code enclosed in parentheses, a space, and a hyphen following the prefix—for example, (818) 555-1234.

Viewing Records

The way data appears on screen contributes to how well users can work with it. You have already seen examples of data presented in 2-dimensional tables. With many DBMS products, the table, or Datasheet view, is what you use to create a database table and to modify field specifications. This view is also suitable for viewing lists of records that you group together in some meaningful way, such as all customers who live in Omaha.

Filtering Records

There are times, when viewing the entire table is unwieldy—there may simply be too many entries. Using a filter is one way to limit the information that appears on screen.

Filters are a DBMS feature for displaying and browsing a selected list or subset of records from a table. The visible records satisfy a condition that the user sets. It is

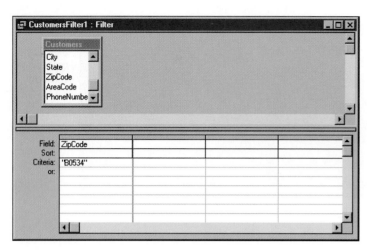

This simple filter, when applied to a database, will display only records that contain 80534 in the ZipCode field.

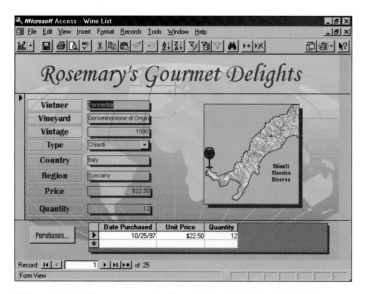

This customized form was created by placing objects, selecting colors, and inserting a graphic.

called a filter because it tells the DBMS to display those records that satisfy the condition, while hiding—or filtering out—those that do not.

For example, you can create a filter that displays only those records that have the data "80534" in the ZipCode field. This feature makes it easier to work with a related set of records, because you can focus on subsets that are relevant to your current needs. In most DBMSs you can redisplay the entire associated table by selecting a command that turns off the filter.

Using Forms

Although the display of data in columns and rows can be suitable for viewing records and performing small data-editing tasks, it is not as convenient for other data management tasks. For many users extensive data entry can be handled more conveniently with a customized form. A **form** is simply a screen that displays data for a single record, as shown in Figure 9.6. You can customize its appearance to your liking. A form can be associated with a single table or with multiple tables.

FIGURE 9.6
A data-entry form.

DBMSs also allow you to create forms to search out records that meet conditions that you specify. For instance, you can create a query to select records for products necessary to fill an order. Queries can perform other data management operations, such as performing a calculation to deduct the order quantity from the Stock on Hand field in an inventory table. A customized order form based on this query provides a convenient visual tool for users to complete this type of transaction simply by entering the relevant data.

Basically, forms in most DBMSs are customized by taking objects that represent fields and placing them in exact locations on a special layout area of the screen. In Windows-based DBMSs you do this in a window that provides the design tools for creating field control tools, like radio buttons, lists boxes, and scroll bars. These devices, or objects, make it possible for users to select data or define query conditions by making selections. You can further enhance a form with font selections, colors, graphics, and pictures or clip art.

Sorting Records

One of the most powerful features of DBMSs is their ability to sort a table of data rapidly, either for a printed report or for display on screen. **Sorting** arranges records according to the contents of one or more fields. For example, in a table of car parts, you can sort records into numerical order by part number or into alphabetical order by part name. To obtain the list that is sorted by part number, you define the condition for the Part Number field that tells the DBMS to rearrange the records in numerical order for this data (see Figure 9.7).

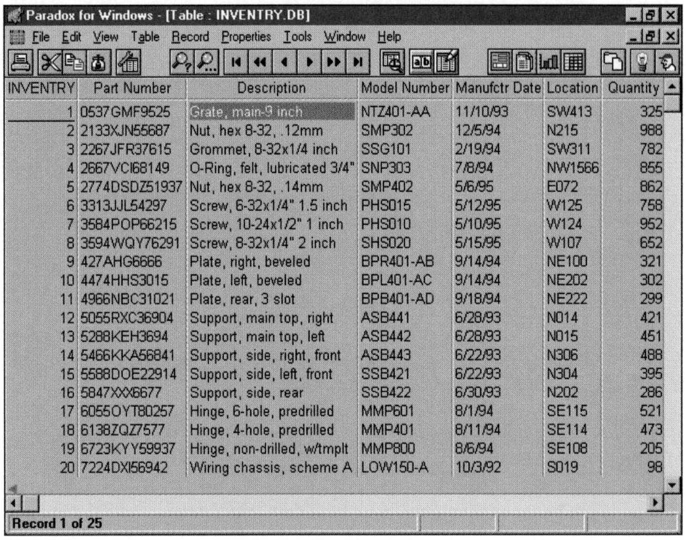

FIGURE 9.7
Records arranged numerically by part number.

When sorting records, one important consideration is determining the **sort order**. There are two sort orders for organizing records. An **ascending sort order** arranges records in alphabetical or numerical order according to the data on which the sort is based. For example, if you base an ascending sort on a Last Name field, the records will be arranged in alphabetical order by last name. Conversely, a **descending sort order** arranges records in the opposite order, that is, from Z to A or 9 to 0.

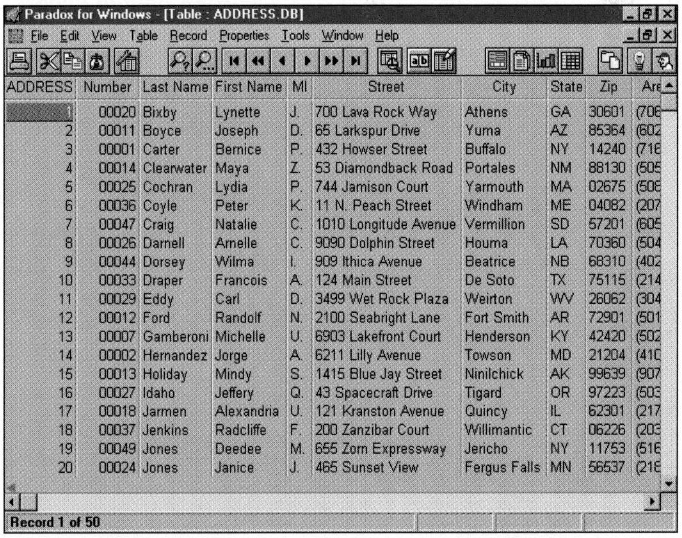

How a DBMS Locates Records

Sorting is convenient for users because, like using a phone directory, specific records are easier to find when the data is organized in some meaningful arrangement rather than listed randomly. However, the DBMS uses its own method to locate and access records quickly, no matter how the records have been sorted in a table.

In this database, the records have been arranged alphabetically according to the contents of the Last Name field.

For example, when you set conditions to find certain records, the DBMS must search the database to find the records that meet your conditions. Very often the order of the records has changed since the database was created. To determine the positions of specific records in a sorted table, DBMSs use a special table called an index. The **index** stores an association between one field and the physical record number in the original table. In most cases, the **record number** refers to the original position (row number) of the record.

Suppose you create an employee table containing hundreds of records, and the tenth record you create is for an employee named Alice Zucker. The index stores the

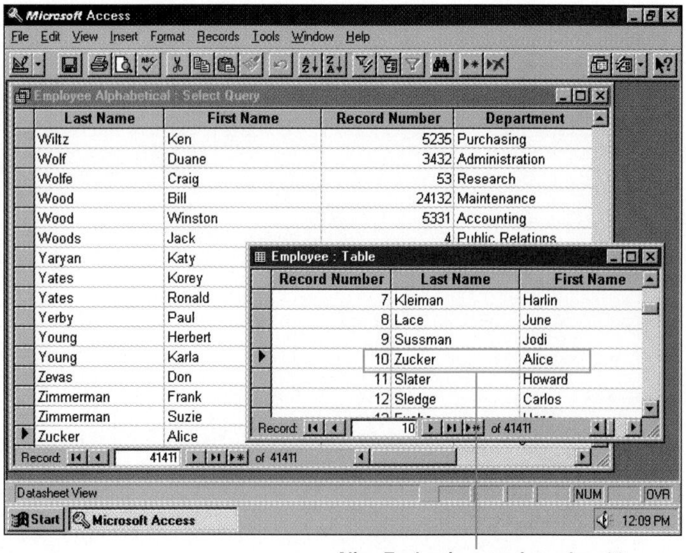

Alice Zucker is record number 10.

association between the last name field and the physical record number (record number 10, last name Zucker) in a separate table (see Figure 9.8).

FIGURE 9.8
An index and database table relationship.

Later, after you've created the entire table, suppose you sort the employee records alphabetically by last name. Even though Alice Zucker's record might end up in row 692, and another employee's record now occupies row 10, Alice Zucker's record is still considered record number 10 by the DBMS. During a search for Alice Zucker's record, the DBMS uses the index table to go directly to the row in the employee table that contains record number 10, no matter how the database records have been rearranged, and no matter how many employees named Zucker might be in the database.

Ensuring Unique Records with a Primary Key

Many DBMSs allow you to set a primary key for a table. The **primary key** is a field or set of fields that defines a default record order for the table. Records appear on screen or printed in a report in this order if no alternate order is specified. By definition, the primary key field stores values unique to each record, such as customer ID numbers. So, like an index, the primary key not only allows for quick access to particular records, it also confines the field to unique entries, ensuring that the table contains no records that are exact duplicates.

Because users frequently organize records according to the contents of fields other than the primary key field, it is often necessary to set sorting conditions for more than one field. For example, customer and employee tables, which store names of people, will likely have multiple records that contain the same last names—perhaps even some that have the same last and first names. To truly sort such tables alphabetically, the sort requires multiple conditions. One condition sets an ascending sort on the last name field, another sets an ascending sort on the first name field, and perhaps even another condition for the middle initial field. As you can see in Figure 9.9, under these sort conditions, records containing identical last names will arrange alphabetically by first name and, if necessary, by middle initial. Notice the records for Adam Smith, Toni J. Smith, and Toni P. Smith.

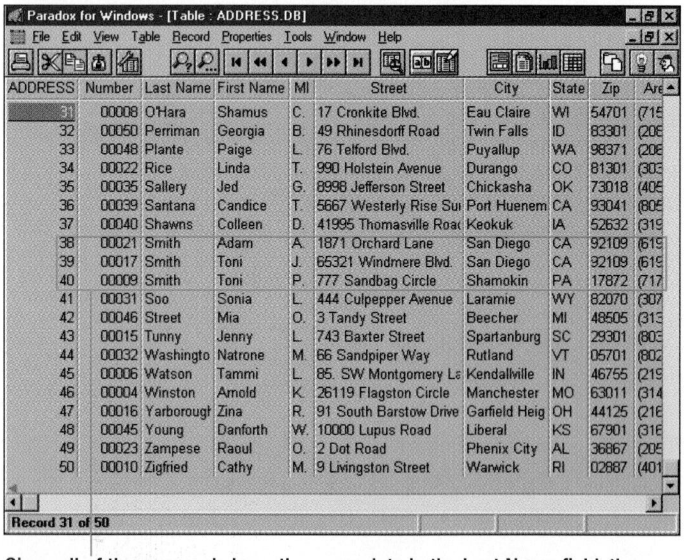

Since all of these records have the same data in the Last Name field, they were sorted according to First Name, then according to MI (middle initial).

FIGURE 9.9
Records sorted on multiple key fields.

A Gold Medal in Information Technology

The 1996 Centennial Olympic Games were expected to be the greatest media event in modern history. The anticipated numbers involved were staggering: 10,000 athletes from 197 countries, 15,000 journalists, 40,000 volunteers, 75,000 other participants, 11 million tickets, 271 events, and a television audience comprising two-thirds of the world's 5.6 billion inhabitants.

IBM, the official Olympic Information Technology Sponsor, developed its complex Olympic Technology Solution to direct more than three terabytes (1 million MB = 1 terabyte) of information during the three-week event through a complex maze of mainframes, minicomputers, PCs, 300 LANs (wired and wireless), Internet access points, 13,000 telephones, 10,000 televisions, 7,000 workstations, 1,000 desktop printers, 100 high-speed printers, 9,000 radios, 6,000 pagers, 8,000 cable installations, all supported by a $300-million technology budget.

Dennie M. Welsh, IBM's General Manager for Global Services, described the Olympic challenge with this colorful analogy.

"Imagine the largest hotel chain in the world all integrated together with reservations systems happening spontaneously on one information system, coupled with the largest restaurant chain, the largest medical information facility, and the biggest library activities, all of this operating simultaneously in a background environment, and then, put on top of that, two Super Bowls a day for 17 days."

The underlying framework for this technological wonder was its database. As John E. Jamieson, Manager of Application Solutions for the Games, pointed out at the pre-Olympic briefing: "The foundation for this whole architecture is the data foundation. Data integrity is the most important element. We've had to

assure that federations, the press, athletes, and the audience around the world all are able to get accurate, consistent information, across any venue in a very, very rapid period of time."

Complex and custom-developed, the Distributed Relational Database Architecture (DRDA) of the Olympic Games allowed event results to be posted within two minutes of validation by Olympic officials across 31 different Olympic venues. This was achieved with data replication software, so that when an event occurred in one venue, the information was transferred in nearly real-time to all other venues.

The results reporting system involved 37 applications specific to various sports linked by 250 Local Area Networks and two Wide Area Networks.

The database also allowed the approximately 150,000 accredited members of the Olympic "family" to access information in the 60-gigabyte database. By entering a user name and password, Olympic participants were able to share strategies for upcoming events, access historical background and reference materials, send e-mail, check changes in the afternoon schedule—or even

pick a restaurant for dinner—on touch screens at information kiosks.

The database was updated continually and simultaneously by 40,000 officials and volunteers entering data into pen-based ThinkPad notebook computers during events. For example, officials on the volleyball playing field recorded every play, score, foul, and miss as they occurred. This information was then transferred to the 31 venues, including scoreboards, workstations, and the Internet.

The database provided the foundation for the four key components of Olympic technology:

■ Games Management System—handled operational activities such as ticketing, accreditation, and network access privileges.
■ Results Management System—posted results to the 31 Olympic venues, plus the Internet.
■ Commentator Information System—posted games results, supplemented with athlete profiles and other statistical information.
■ Info '96—provided information access and retrieval for all Olympic participants (athletes, judges, and volunteers).

An Olympic official checks results history on the Olympic database program.

Querying a Database

In a manner similar to entering sort conditions, you can enter expressions or criteria that:

- Allow the DBMS to locate records.
- Establish relationships or links between tables to update records.
- List a subset of records.
- Perform calculations.
- Delete obsolete records.
- Perform other data management tasks.

Any of these types of requests is called a **query**, a user-constructed statement that describes data and sets criteria so the DBMS can gather the relevant data and construct specific information. In other words, a query is a more powerful type of filter that can gather information from multiple tables in a relational database.

This query is being set up to display the VIN, make, and model of cars that have been reported stolen in Tucson. The query is based on data in two tables, Active Policies and Pending Claims.

An insurance claims representative, for instance, might create a query to list vehicle information on automobiles reported stolen by insured clients in Tucson, Arizona. The query would include field names such as MAKE and MODEL from an "Active Policies" table, LOSS_TYPE and LOCATION from a "Pending Claims" table, and VIN (for Vehicle Identification Number), which is common to both tables. To get the desired information, the query requires the specific data or criteria that will isolate those records (autos stolen in Tucson) from all the records in both tables. In this case the claims representative would include matching VIN numbers, and "Theft," and "Tucson" as criteria.

Some DBMSs provide special windows or forms for creating queries. Generally, this window or form provides an area for selecting the tables the query is to work with and columns for entering the field names where the query will get or manipulate data.

This table shows the results of the Cars stolen in Tucson query.

SQL: The Language of a Query

Within every DBMS is a language that is similar to a programming language. This language is designed specifically for communicating with a database using statements that are closer to English than to programming languages. In many DBMSs this standardized language is known as **SQL**. SQL was based on an earlier query language called SEQUEL, which was an acronym for "Structured English QUEry Language." It is used to structure query statements.

An SQL statement provides a description of data contained in a database so the DBMS can locate and use the desired data as defined by the user. To understand how SQL works, you might examine a common query in which you request records matching certain criteria. For example, suppose you were to formulate the aforementioned query in the form of a question in English. It might look like this:

For all vehicle identification numbers in the Active Policies table that match those in the Pending Claims table, are there any records where the LOSS_TYPE field contains "Theft," and the LOCATION field contains "Tucson?"

From this question you could derive the necessary components to create an SQL SELECT statement, one of the most common query statements used with DBMSs. The SELECT statement is generally structured to tell the DBMS the following:

- The database table (or tables) with which it will be working.
- Which fields to work with.
- The criteria for selecting records.

When you build a query that must select data from multiple tables, the tables must be linked by a common field. In this example, the VIN (Vehicle Identification Number) field links the two tables referenced in the query. From the preceding question, then, the following SQL SELECT statement is created so that the claims representative receives the desired information:

```
SELECT      VIN, MAKE, MODEL
FROM        Active Policies JOIN Pending Claims
ON          [Active Policies]VIN = [Pending Claims]VIN
WHERE       LOSS_TYPE="Theft" AND LOCATION="Tucson"
```

Although the actual syntax varies between DBMS programs, the basic structure shown here is universal. This SQL statement forms the query that tells the DBMS to do the following:

1. Look in the Active Policies and Pending Claims tables (linked by the VIN field).
2. Locate VIN matches between the tables.
3. Return the VINs, makes, and models for all theft claims in Tucson.

Query by Example

Although SQL and query languages are an important part of a DBMS, very few PC and Macintosh users who work with a DBMS ever actually write an SQL (or any other query language) statement. DBMSs commonly provide an interface, like a form or a grid, that collects the facts about a query from the user and composes the SQL or query statements behind the scenes. This feature allows a user to **query by example (QBE)**, or to perform "intuitive" queries.

With QBE, you specify the search criteria by typing values or expressions into the fields of a QBE form or grid. On some systems, the QBE form looks just like a blank form that you might design for data entry. On others, it may be a window with a grid or a dialog box with a list of the fields in your tables.

Some QBE forms (such as those in Access) display check marks that indicate the fields you want

The Microsoft Access QBE grid lets users create queries by typing information into a form containing fields from existing tables.

This polished-looking invoice is a relatively simple database report.

This list of customers and their addresses is also a database report.

displayed. There is also an area where you can enter the criteria for your query. The criteria can include values and mathematical or logical operators (=, <, AND, and so forth) or text like "Theft."

Generating Reports

Not all DBMS operations have to occur on screen. Just as forms can be based on queries, so, too, can reports. A **report** is printed information that, like a query result, is assembled by gathering data based on user-supplied criteria. In fact, report generators in most DBMSs create reports from queries.

Reports can range from simple lists of records to customized formats for specific purposes, such as invoices. Report generators can use selected data and criteria to carry out automated mathematical calculations as the output is being printed. For example, relevant data can be used to calculate subtotals and totals for invoices or sales summaries. Reports are also similar to forms in that their layouts can be customized with objects representing fields and other controls.

▶ NORTON WORKSHOP: APPLYING A DBMS IN A BUSINESS ENVIRONMENT

In this Norton Workshop, you will explore a practical situation in which a user creates, modifies, and uses a database within a commercial DBMS product. Kelly owns and operates a home mail-order business to distribute three children's multimedia educational software products that she has developed. She needs to create an efficient system for keeping records of her customers and for processing and managing orders.

Designing the Database and Creating the Tables

Because most successful projects begin with a blueprint or plan, Kelly begins the design process by jotting down a rough diagram of the tables she will set up as separate database files. She uses the plan to think about the table names; the number, names, and types of fields that will organize the data each will store; and the relationships among the tables. The layout is shown in Figure 9.10.

FIGURE 9.10
Database table plans.

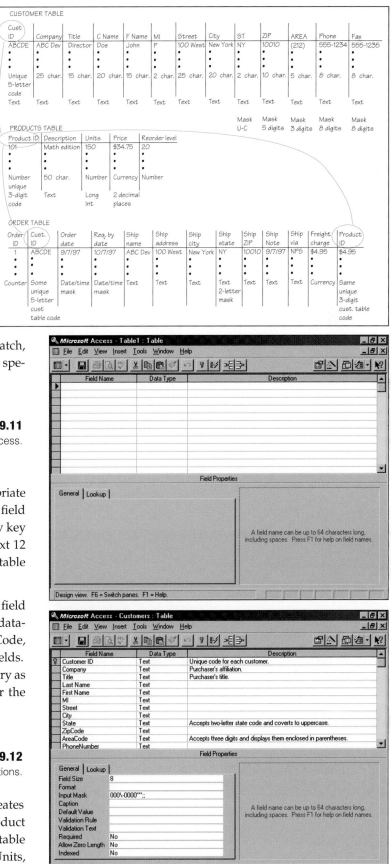

Because she is developing her database from scratch, Kelly begins by creating the table's structure in a special table design window (see Figure 9.11).

FIGURE 9.11
The Table design window in Access.

She enters the name of the first field in the appropriate location provided by the DBMS. She names this field Customer ID and sets it up as the table's primary key field. Then she enters the field names for the next 12 fields, which are all text fields. She names the table "Customers" and saves the table to disk.

Next, Kelly customizes the table by changing the field size limits for most of the fields and by creating data-entry masks for the Customer ID, State, ZipCode, AreaCode, PhoneNumber, and FAXNumber fields. The data-entry masks will help speed up data entry as she, or perhaps an assistant, enters the data for the records in the table (see Figure 9.12).

FIGURE 9.12
Completed Customers table specifications.

Before designing a form for data entry, Kelly creates two more database tables that will store her product inventory and purchase orders. The Products table contains five fields: Product ID, Description, Units, Price, and ReorderLevel. After creating this table,

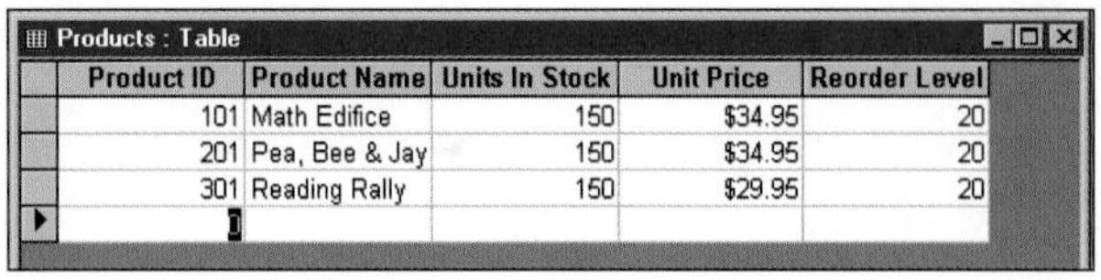

Products : Table

Product ID	Product Name	Units In Stock	Unit Price	Reorder Level
101	Math Edifice	150	$34.95	20
201	Pea, Bee & Jay	150	$34.95	20
301	Reading Rally	150	$29.95	20

Kelly uses Datasheet view to enter the records for her three multimedia titles directly in the Products table. The result is shown in Figure 9.13.

FIGURE 9.13
The completed Products table.

Her Orders table contains 13 fields for storing order data, such as the products purchased, shipping address, and order and shipping dates. Later she will create a form for entering records in this table.

Before designing and implementing forms, Kelly uses another special window to establish relationships among her tables. First she selects all three tables, represented by field list boxes, and then she drags the fields that are common to her tables from one field list box to the next to establish the links between them efficiently.

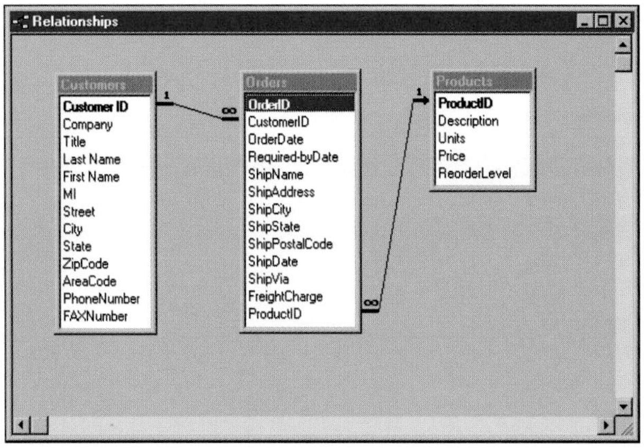

The DBMS product Kelly is using displays a "join" line between the field list boxes that represent the linked tables, as shown in Figure 9.14. She can always go back and edit the properties of each link later if she needs to.

FIGURE 9.14
Linked database tables.

Creating a Data-Entry Form

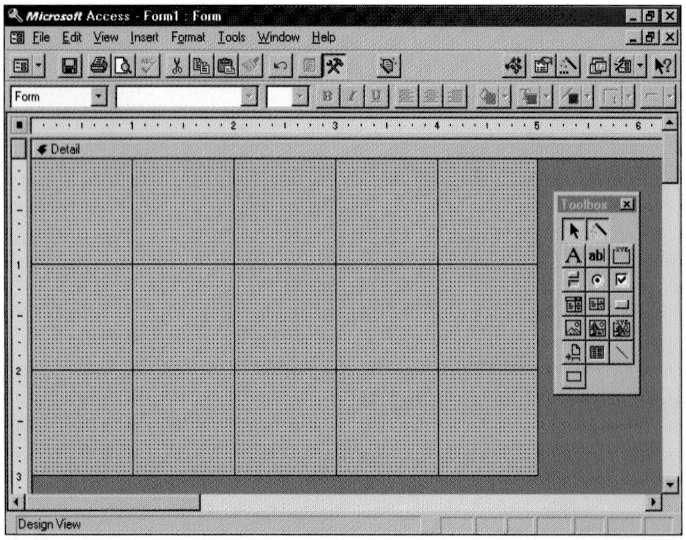

Now, Kelly creates a form for entering her customer records. Essentially, the window for designing the form that Kelly uses is a blank slate on which she can add objects representing fields and other design elements. The grid display (shown in Figure 9.15) helps Kelly align objects as she places them. To modify the appearance of each object, as well as control the display of data, Kelly selects one or more objects and then modifies their property settings.

FIGURE 9.15
A window for designing forms.

Kelly completes the form by

- Creating a header.
- Adding drop shadows behind the field boxes.
- Changing fonts, font attributes, and colors.
- Modifying and deleting labels.
- Adding a graphic object (see Figure 9.16).

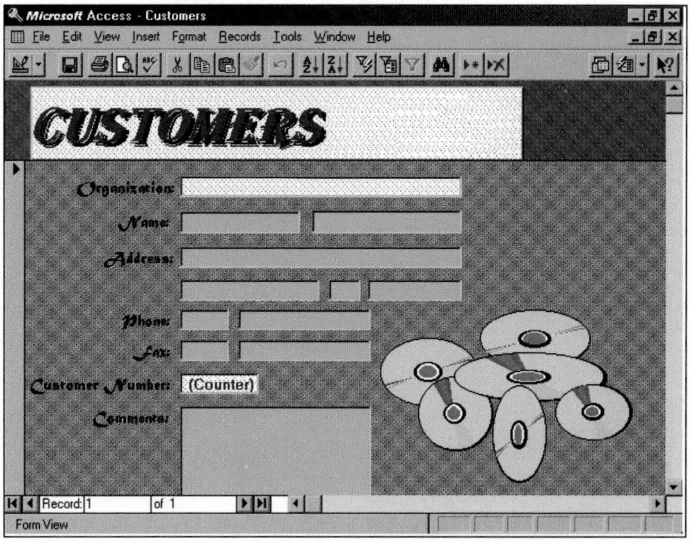

FIGURE 9.16
A completed data-entry form.

Entering and Modifying Data

Kelly uses her customized form to enter records for her customers. Now, whenever Kelly gets a new order by phone or mail, she simply starts the DBMS program, opens the Customers form, and goes straight to a blank form at the next sequential record position. There, she enters the data for a new record.

One day, an existing customer in Florida informs Kelly that they are shutting down the business at the end of the month, so Kelly needs to locate the obsolete record and delete it. She uses the DBMS's Find command to search for the characters "FL" in the State field. When the record she is searching for appears on the form, Kelly selects it and deletes it.

Kelly would like to filter her Orders table for the new orders she entered for the current day. She can do this by applying a filter that lists those records based on the criteria she enters, including two fields from the Orders table, the type of sort for arranging the records in the filtered list, and the current date for the Order Date, as shown in Figure 9.17.

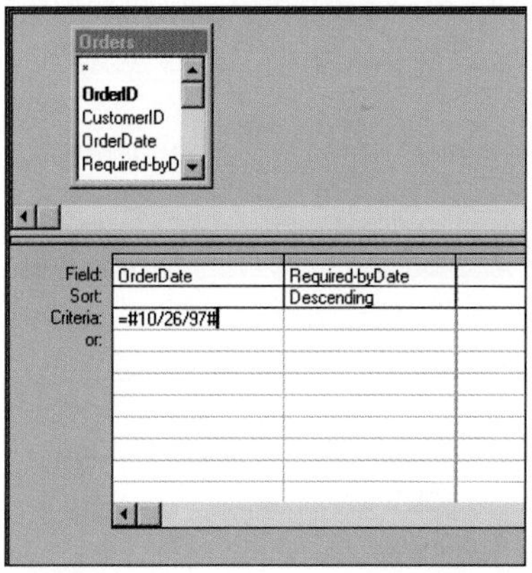

FIGURE 9.17
The criteria for creating a filter.

When she applies the filter, the DBMS presents her with a Datasheet view of only those records meeting her criteria in the Orders Table Window (see Figure 9.18).

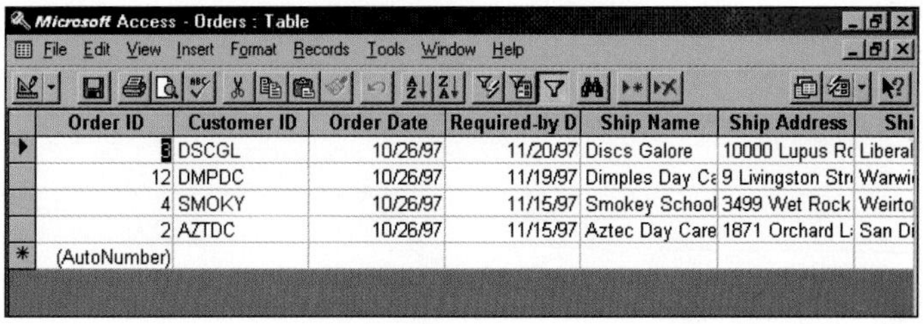

FIGURE 9.18
The filtered Orders list.

Querying the Database

In the course of running her mail-order enterprise, Kelly must do a variety of tasks using the DBMS to maintain the integrity of the database, process new orders, and follow up with existing customers. Many of these tasks require her to query the database for selected information.

For instance, Kelly wants to call all customers who have recently purchased her newest title, "Reading Rally." By using the query function to generate a list of these specific customers, Kelly can ensure that she calls all the right customers.

This task requires a Select query. Kelly begins by selecting the Customers table and the Orders table as well as the field names she wants to display and use for criteria in the DBMS's QBE grid. On the sort row, Kelly specifies an Ascending sort order for the AreaCode and State fields. The query's result will give her a list of records arranged to help her plan calls according to time zones. On the criteria row, Kelly enters =301, the ID number for the relevant product. She also turns off the display for this field so it will not appear in the resulting list (see Figure 9.19).

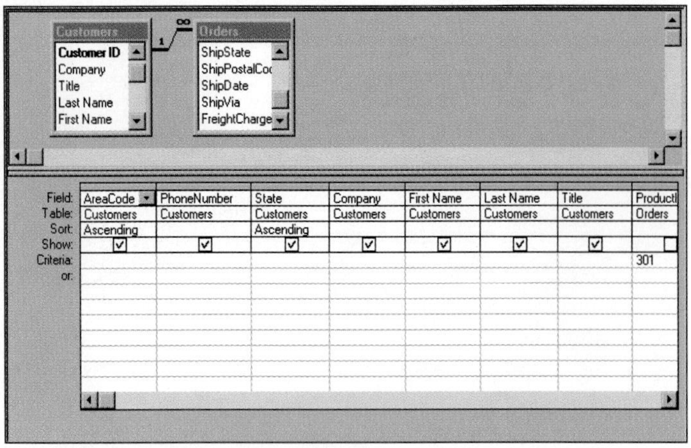

FIGURE 9.19
The QBE grid showing criteria.

With the query set up, Kelly runs it to display the list in Datasheet view (see Figure 9.20). Now all Kelly needs to do is print a hard copy of the list and then save the query.

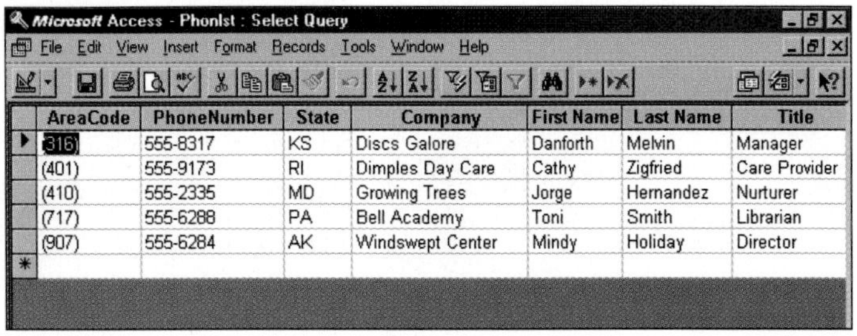

AreaCode	PhoneNumber	State	Company	First Name	Last Name	Title
(316)	555-8317	KS	Discs Galore	Danforth	Melvin	Manager
(401)	555-9173	RI	Dimples Day Care	Cathy	Zigfried	Care Provider
(410)	555-2335	MD	Growing Trees	Jorge	Hernandez	Nurturer
(717)	555-6288	PA	Bell Academy	Toni	Smith	Librarian
(907)	555-6284	AK	Windswept Center	Mindy	Holiday	Director

FIGURE 9.20
The Select Query's result.

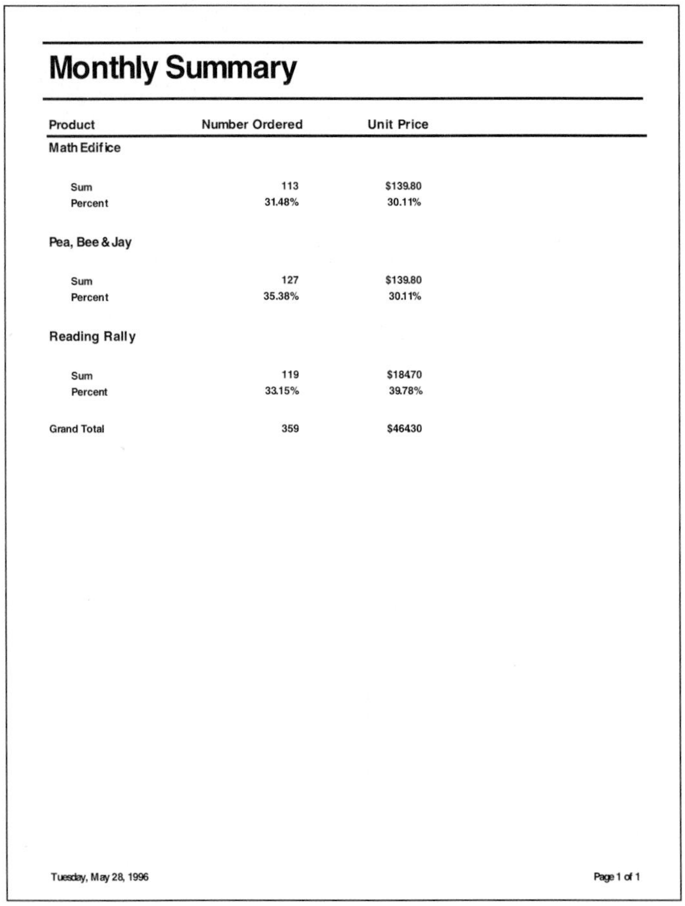

Monthly Summary

Product	Number Ordered	Unit Price
Math Edifice		
Sum	113	$139.80
Percent	31.48%	30.11%
Pea, Bee & Jay		
Sum	127	$139.80
Percent	35.38%	30.11%
Reading Rally		
Sum	119	$18470
Percent	33.15%	39.78%
Grand Total	359	$46430

Tuesday, May 28, 1996 Page 1 of 1

Generating a Summary Report

Kelly uses the DBMS's report generator to display and print a monthly summary that breaks down the current month's sales activity by product. Because the report will extract data from more than one table, Kelly bases the report on an existing query named Monthly Summary.

In a window for designing the report layout, Kelly drags selected fields from the query's field list box to the layout grid in very much the same way that she created her data-entry forms. As she builds her report page, Kelly periodically switches to a special preview window, provided by the DBMS, to see a visual representation of the page and to monitor her progress. When the report is to her liking, she can select the appropriate command to print it (see Figure 9.21).

FIGURE 9.21
The printed report.

▶ WHAT TO EXPECT IN THE FUTURE

This chapter introduced briefly object-oriented database structures as the newest conceptual model for building databases. In the next few years, expect relational databases to be refined with standards that will allow companies to marry objects with their existing relational databases. For users this will mean greater flexibility in managing data, customizing data management procedures, and using existing data resources in a variety of applications.

One of the biggest advantages of this migration to object-oriented applications is the aspect of reusability, in which many existing objects become standardized and available for building other objects. DBMS users will create universal elements that can be managed and manipulated in a variety of applications. Not only is the object-oriented model beneficial for more traditional data elements, it also allows users to manage more complex forms of data, such as sound and video. DBMS interfaces are likely to become much more "alive" with graphics, animation, and sound.

Now that graphical interfaces have become omnipresent and commercial applications are increasingly adopting object-oriented standards, look for automated procedures in many existing products to become more sophisticated. Data management tasks that are common to many organizations, but still complex for most users, will be set up and structured almost instantly. The "learning curve" for users will be reduced significantly as the design and data manipulation process becomes more of a customization task, tailoring procedures to the specific needs of organizations.

▶ VISUAL SUMMARY

Data and Information

- Data are raw facts collected, such as those collected by an organization to record transactions.
- Information consists of usable sets of data.
- A DBMS is used to assemble information from data.

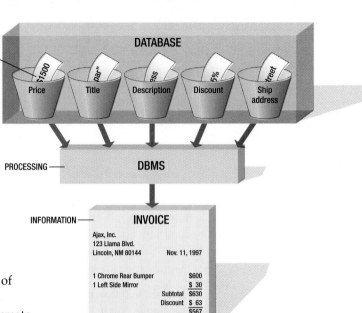

The Database-DBMS Relationship

- A database is a repository for collections of related items or facts.
- A DBMS is a software tool that allows users to create database tables and that provides access to multiple users.
- A database table arranges data in columns representing fields and rows representing records.
- Field types include text, numeric, and logical.
- Flat-file databases cannot form relationships with other tables and are best suited for home or small business uses.
- Relational databases are very powerful because they have the ability to form relationships between tables.
- Hierarchical and network structures are conceptual models for older systems that define databases used on mainframe systems.
- Object-oriented databases define data, data characteristics, attributes, and procedures as complex objects that can combine with other objects through messages.

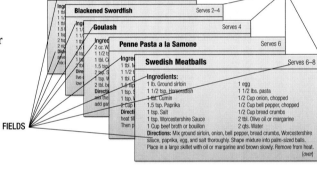

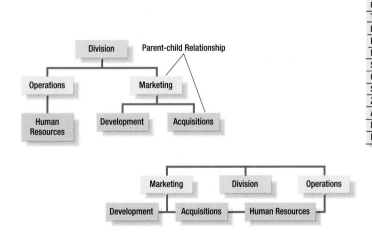

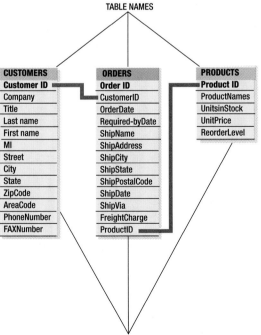

Working with a Database

- Table or Datasheet view is used to create a table's structure, view lists of records, and enter and edit data.
- Forms are custom screens for displaying and entering data that can be associated with database tables and queries.
- Masks, pictures, and other validation devices ensure that data is entered uniformly or converted to a proper field format.
- Filters let you browse through selected records that meet a set of criteria.
- Sorting arranges records in a table according to specific criteria.
- Indexes are special tables that DBMSs use to locate records quickly in a table that contains records arranged according to some condition.
- Queries are user-constructed statements that set conditions for selecting and manipulating data in one or more tables and assembling the criteria-matching data into information.
- SQL is a special query language for communicating with a database by describing data and sometimes instructing the DBMS to do something with the data.
- QBE is an interface for queries that allows the DBMS to collect the facts about a query from the user and to compose the query's SQL statement by itself.
- A report is printed information based on a query that gathers criteria-matching data and, in some cases, performs mathematical calculations.

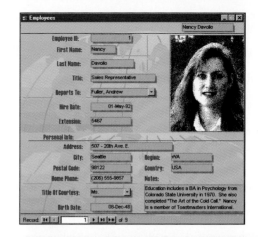

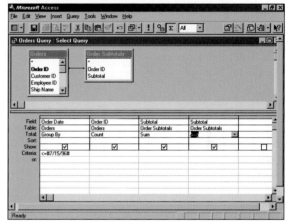

▶ KEY TERMS

After completing this chapter, you should be able to define the following terms:

ascending sort order, 277	filter, 275	primary key, 278
alphanumeric field, 273	flat-file database, 269	query, 280
binary field, 274	form, 276	query by example (QBE), 281
BLOB (Binary Large Object), 274	hierarchical database, 270	record, 268
character field, 273	index, 277	record number, 277
counter field, 274	interface, 271	relational database, 269
date field, 274	logical field, 274	report, 282
database, 265	mask, 275	sorting, 277
database management system (DBMS), 265	memo field, 275	sort order, 277
	network database, 270	SQL, 280
descending sort order, 277	numeric field, 274	text field, 273
field, 268	object-oriented database, 270	time field, 274
field format, 275	picture, 275	

▶ KEY TERM QUIZ

Fill in the blank with one of the terms listed in Key Terms:

1. A table column represents a(n) _____.

2. Data such as names, addresses, and phone numbers are stored in a(n) _____.

3. A row in a table represents a(n) _____.

4. A(n) _____ stores graphic images such as clip art, a photograph, or formatted text.

5. A program that allows any number of users to access and modify records is known as a(n) _____.

6. A screen that displays data for a single record is called a(n) _____.

7. You can arrange records in alphabetical or numerical order by _____.

8. A field that defines a default record arrangement for a table is known as a(n) _____.

9. A(n) _____ allows you to perform many data management tasks.

10. To perform "intuitive" queries, you use _____.

▶ REVIEW QUESTIONS

1. What is a database? What is a database management system?
2. What distinguishes information from data?
3. Describe briefly how data is structured within a database file.
4. List and define the three components that make up a database.
5. What primary characteristic distinguishes a flat-file database from a relational database?
6. Which database structure is characterized by parent-child relationships among record types?
7. List and describe the elements that make up an object in the object-oriented database model.
8. List the various field types that can exist in a database.
9. What does it mean to "filter" database records?
10. Describe what a query is and what it is used for.

▶ DISCUSSION QUESTIONS

1. In the chapter's discussion of DBMSs there are several examples mentioned where data input by one user is used in other transactions by other users. What do you think are some of the benefits to an organization when data can be shared by multiple individuals? What hardware requirements are necessary?
2. What do you think is the biggest asset to using DBMSs? Why do you think they are so important to businesses and other organizations?

3. Describe briefly how an SQL statement works. What important characteristic distinguishes SQL statements from programming languages?

4. Suppose you want to produce a list of customers whose accounts are 60 days overdue as of today. Describe in general terms how you would form queries by example to: (1) extract the criteria-matching records and (2) print a list of the relevant information.

NORTON INTERACTIVE

Complete the Norton Interactive module for this chapter.

THE INTERNET

CONTENTS

OBJECTIVES

When you complete this chapter, you will be able to do the following:

- Explain how the Internet got started.
- Understand the structure of Internet addresses.
- Describe the major features of the Internet: e-mail, News, Telnet, FTP, Archie, Gopher, Veronica, and the World Wide Web.
- Describe the ways in which a PC can access the Internet.

Some observers believe that the Internet is having the same kind of fundamental impact on modern society as the invention of the printing press had in the fifteenth century. The printing press expanded communication and the spread of information, making it possible to create many copies of a document quickly and cheaply. The Internet is encouraging a giant leap forward in the same process—it is increasing the availability of information and the ease and speed of communication. By connecting millions of computers, the Internet makes it possible for a computer user anywhere in the world to exchange text, pictures, movies, sound, computer programs, and anything else that can be stored in digital form with anyone else in the connected world. This chapter will focus on the history and development of the Internet, describe its most important functions and services, and explain how you can connect your own computer to the Internet.

▶ BACKGROUND AND HISTORY: AN EXPLOSION OF CONNECTIVITY

The seeds of the Internet were planted in 1969, when the Advanced Research Projects Agency (ARPA) of the U.S. Department of Defense began connecting computers at different universities and defense contractors. The goal of this early network was to create a large computer network with multiple paths between users that could survive a nuclear attack or other disaster. ARPA also wanted users in remote locations to be able to share scarce computing resources.

Soon after the first links in **ARPANET** (as this early system was called) were in place, the engineers and scientists who had access to this system began exchanging messages and data that were beyond the scope of the Defense Department's original objectives for the project. In addition to exchanging ideas and information related to science and engineering, people also discovered that they could play long-distance games and socialize with other people who shared their interests. The users convinced ARPA that these unofficial uses were helping to test the network's capacity.

ARPANET started with just a handful of computers, but it expanded rapidly. The network jumped across the Atlantic to Norway and England in 1973, and it never stopped growing. In the mid-1980s, another federal agency, the National Science Foundation (NSF), got into the act after the Defense Department dropped its funding of the Internet. NSF established five "supercomputing centers" that were available to anyone who wanted to use them for academic research purposes. NSF had expected that the people who used its supercomputers would use ARPANET to obtain access, but it quickly discovered that the existing network could not handle the load. In response, it created a new, higher-capacity network, called **NSFnet**, to complement the older and by then overloaded ARPANET. The link between ARPANET, NSFnet, and other networks was called the Internet.

NSFnet made Internet connections widely available for academic research, but the NSF did not permit users to conduct private business over the system. Therefore, several private telecommunications companies built their own network backbones that used the same set of networking protocols as NSFnet. Like the trunk of a tree or the spine of a human being, a network **backbone** is the central structure that connects other elements of the network. These private portions of the Internet were not limited by NSFnet's "appropriate use" restrictions, so it became possible to use the Internet to distribute business and commercial information.

Interconnections (known as **gateways**) between NSFnet and the private backbones allowed a user on any one of them to exchange data with all of the others. Other gateways were created between the Internet and other networks, large and small, including some that used completely different networking protocols.

The original ARPANET was shut down in 1990, and government funding for NSFnet was discontinued in 1995, but the commercial Internet backbone services have easily replaced them.

By the early 1990s, interest in the Internet began to expand dramatically. The system that had been created as a tool for surviving a nuclear war found its way into businesses and homes. Now, advertisements for new movies are just as common online as collaborations on particle physics research.

Today, the Internet connects thousands of networks and millions of users around the world. It is a huge, cooperative community with no central ownership.

▶ HOW THE INTERNET WORKS

The single most important thing to understand about the Internet is that it potentially can link your computer to any other computer. Anyone with access to the Internet can exchange text, data files, and programs with any other user. For all practical purposes, just about everything that happens across the Internet is a variation of one of these activities. The Internet itself is the pipeline that carries data between computers.

TCP/IP: The Universal Language of the Internet

The reason the Internet works at all is that every computer connected to it uses the same set of rules and procedures (known as **protocols**) to control timing and data format. The set of commands and timing specifications used by the Internet is called Transmission Control Protocol/Internet Protocol, universally abbreviated as **TCP/IP**.

The TCP/IP protocols include the specifications that identify individual computers and exchange data between computers. They also include rules for several categories of application programs, so programs that run on different kinds of computers can talk to one another.

TCP/IP software looks different on different kinds of computers, but it always presents the same appearance to the network. Therefore, it does not matter if the system at the other end of a connection is a supercomputer that fills a room, a pocket-size personal communications device, or anything in between; as long as it recognizes TCP/IP protocols, it can send and receive data through the Internet.

A Network of Networks—Backbones and Gateways

Most computers are not connected directly to the Internet—they are connected to smaller networks that connect through gateways to the Internet backbone. That is why the Internet is sometimes described as "a network of networks." Figure 10.1 shows a typical Internet connection.

The core of the Internet is the set of backbone connections that ties the local networks together and the routing scheme that controls the way each piece of data finds its destination. In most networking diagrams the Internet backbone is portrayed as a big cloud, because the routing details are less important than the fact that the data passes through the Internet between the origin and destination.

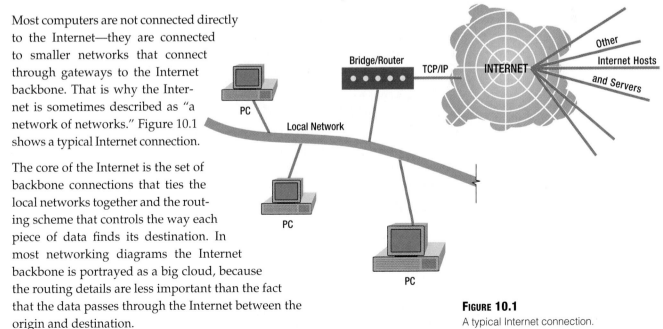

FIGURE 10.1

A typical Internet connection.

Addressing Schemes—IP and DNS Addresses

Internet activity can be defined as computers communicating with other computers using TCP/IP. The computer that originates a transaction must identify its intended destination with a unique address. Every computer on the Internet has a four-part numeric address, called the Internet Protocol address or **IP address**, which contains routing information that identifies its location. Each of the four parts is a number between 0 and 255, so an IP address looks like this:

205.46.117.104

Computers have no trouble working with big strings of numbers like this, but humans are not so skilled. Therefore, most computers on the Internet (except the ones used exclusively for internal routing and switching) also have an address called a **Domain Name System (DNS)**, an address that uses words instead of numbers.

DNS addresses have two parts: an individual name, followed by a **domain** (a name for a computer connected to the Internet) that generally identifies the type of institution that uses the address, such as *.com* for commercial businesses or *.edu* for schools, colleges, and universities. The University of Washington's DNS address is *washington.edu*, Microsoft's is *microsoft.com*.

Within the United States, the last three letters of the domain usually tell what type of institution owns the computer. Table 10.1 lists the most common types.

Some large institutions and big corporations divide their domain addresses into smaller **subdomains**. For example, a business with many branches might have a subdomain for each office—such as *boston.widgets.com* and *newyork.widgets.com*. You might also see some subdomains broken into even smaller sub-subdomains, like *evolution.genetics.washington.edu* (a contender for the Internet's longest DNS address).

Outside of the United States, domains usually identify the country in which the system is located, such as *.ca* for Canada or *.fr* for France. Sometimes, a geographic domain address will also include a subdomain that identifies the district within the larger domain. For example, there is a commercial Internet service provider in the Canadian province of British Columbia called Mindlink. Its DNS address is *mindlink.bc.ca*.

DNS addresses and numeric IP addresses identify individual computers, but a single computer might have many separate users, each of whom must have an account. Some of the largest domains, such as America Online (*aol.com*) may have more than a million different user names. When you send a message to a person rather than a computer, you must include that person's user name in the address. The standard format is the user name first, separated from the DNS address by an "at" symbol (@). Therefore, John Smith's e-mail address might be:

jsmith@widgets.com

You would read this as "J Smith at widgets dot com."

TABLE 10.1

Internet Domains

DOMAIN	TYPE OF ORGANIZATION
.com	business (commercial)
.edu	educational
.gov	government
.mil	military
.net	gateway or host
.org	other organization

Clients and Servers

The basic model for Internet tools is used for many functions: a **client** application on a user's computer requests information through the network from a **server**, a powerful computer, generally containing a large hard disk, which acts as a shared storage resource. In addition to containing stored files, a server may also act as a gatekeeper for access to programs or data from other computers.

▶ MAJOR FEATURES OF THE INTERNET

The technical details that make the Internet work are only part of the story—the reason so many people use the Internet has more to do with content than connectivity. As it exists today, there is a huge amount of information available through the Internet. For many users, it is a valuable source of news, business communication, entertainment, and technical information.

The Internet also has created hundreds of "virtual communities," made up of people who share an interest in a technical discipline, a hobby, or a political or social movement. There are online conferences of astronomers, toy train collectors, and house-bound mothers of two-year-olds. College students in Australia and Alabama come together on live Internet Relay Chat channels. Online conference services like the Well, based in northern California, resemble a kind of "cocktail party" where there are lots of interesting conversations happening at the same time.

As a business tool, the Internet has many uses. Electronic mail is an efficient and inexpensive way to send and receive messages and documents around the world within minutes. The World Wide Web is becoming both an important advertising medium and a channel for distributing software, documents, and information services. As a channel for business research, the databases and other information archives that exist online are frequently better and more up-to-date than any library.

E-Mail

The single most common use of the Internet is for the exchange of electronic mail, or **e-mail**. Anyone with an e-mail account can send messages to other users of the Internet and to many networks connected to the Internet through gateways. Most e-mail programs also permit users to attach data files and program files to messages.

E-mail is not a live connection between the originator of a message and its recipient. There is always a delay between the time a message is sent and the time it arrives. Sometimes that delay is just a few seconds, but it is always there, because e-mail works as a store-and-forward system. When you send a message, your computer passes it to a **post office server**, which identifies the destination address and passes it through the Internet to a **mail server**, where the message is stored in a mailbox until the recipient comes looking for it. Figure 10.2 shows the path of an e-mail message from origin to destination.

E-mail programs generally combine all of these features:

■ A text editor for writing and editing messages.
■ An address book for storing names and e-mail addresses.

The Microsoft Exchange client, the e-mail manager in Windows 95.

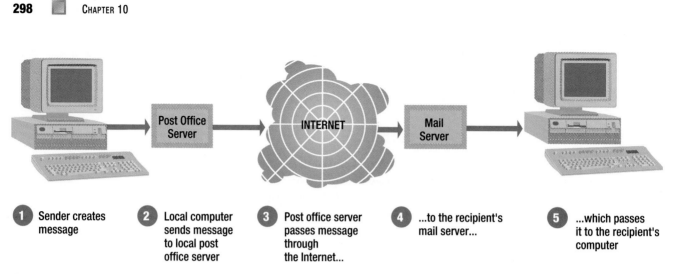

① Sender creates message

② Local computer sends message to local post office server

③ Post office server passes message through the Internet...

④ ...to the recipient's mail server...

⑤ ...which passes it to the recipient's computer

FIGURE 10.2
The progress of an e-mail message.

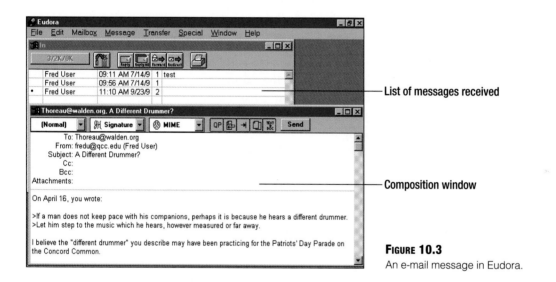

—— List of messages received

—— Composition window

FIGURE 10.3
An e-mail message in Eudora.

- Ability to transfer outbound messages to a post office server.
- Ability to transfer inbound messages from a mail server.
- A message manager that organizes and stores sent and received messages.

There is an e-mail program included in Windows 95, and many others are available separately.

One of the most popular e-mail programs is Eudora, which exists in versions for both Windows and Macintosh computers. Figure 10.3 shows a screen from the Windows version of Eudora, including a composition window for new messages and a list of messages received.

Besides one-to-one messages, Internet e-mail is also used for one-to-many messages, in which the same set of messages goes to a list of many names. One type of mailing list that uses e-mail is an automated list server, or **listserv**. Listserv systems allow users on the list to post their own messages, so the result is an ongoing discussion. Hundreds of mailing list discussions are in progress all the time on a huge variety of topics. For example, there are mailing lists for producers of radio drama, for makers of apple cider, and for members of individual college classes who want to keep up with news from their old friends.

News

In addition to the messages distributed to mailing lists by e-mail, the Internet also supports a form of public bulletin board called **News**. There are more than 10,000 news groups, each devoted to discussion of a particular topic.

Many of the most widely distributed news groups are part of a system called **Usenet**, but others are targeted to a particular region or to users connected to a specific network or institution, such as a university or a large corporation.

A news reader program—the client software—obtains articles from a news server, which exchanges them with other servers through the Internet. To participate in News, you must run a news reader program to log onto a server.

To see messages that have been posted about a specific topic, you must subscribe to the news group that addresses that topic. News groups are organized into major categories, called domains, and individual topics within each domain. The name of a news group begins with the domain and includes a description of the group's topic, such as *alt.food*. Some topics include separate news groups for related subtopics, such as *alt.food.chocolate*.

There are six major domains within the Usenet structure, and many more "alternative" domains. The major Usenet domains are listed in Table 10.2.

Anyone can contribute articles to a news group, and that is both the greatest strength and greatest weakness of the system. A good news group can have a strong spirit of community, where many people pitch in to work together. If you are looking for an obscure piece of information, there is a good chance that you can find it by asking in the right group. There is no "fact checking" in most news groups, so you cannot automatically assume that everything you read online is true. News groups are a relatively fast way to distribute information to potentially interested readers, and they allow people to discuss topics of common interest. They also can be a convenient channel for finding answers to questions. Many questions tend to be asked over and over again, so it is always a good idea to read the articles that other people have posted before you jump in with your own questions. Members of many news groups post lists of **Frequently Asked Questions**, or **FAQs**, every month or two.

TABLE 10.2	
Common Usenet Domains	
DOMAIN	**DESCRIPTION**
comp	Computer-related topics
sci	Science and technology (except computers)
soc	Social issues and politics
news	Topics related to Usenet
rec	Hobbies, arts, and recreational activities
misc	Topics that do not fit one of the other domains
The Most Important Alternative Topics Include	
alt	Alternative news groups
bionet	Biological sciences
biz	Business topics, including advertisements
clari	News from the Associated Press and Reuters, supplied through a service called Clarinet
k12	News groups for primary and secondary schools

As Figure 10.4 shows, subscribing to a news group is a three-step process.

STEP 1
Download of list of
available news groups.

STEP 2
Choose the group
that interests you.

STEP 3
Select the article
you want to read.

This is the article.

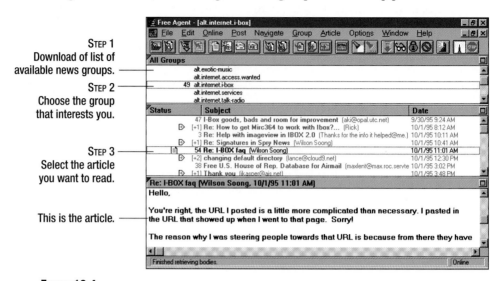

FIGURE 10.4
Subscribing to a news group.

You must download a list of available news groups from the server, choose the groups that interest you, and finally, select the articles that you want to read. In most news readers, you can choose to reply to an article by posting another article to the news group, or by sending a private e-mail message to the person who wrote the original article.

Telnet—Remote Access to Distant Computers

Telnet is the Internet tool for using one computer to control a second computer. Using Telnet, you can send commands that run programs and open text or data files. The Telnet program is a transparent window between your own computer and a distant host system—a computer that you are logging onto.

It sends input from your keyboard to the host, and displays text from the host on your screen.

Connecting to a Telnet host is easy; enter the address, and the Telnet program sets up a connection. When you see a log on message from the host, you can send an account name and password to start an operating session. Access to some Telnet hosts is limited to users with permission from the owner of the host, but many other hosts offer access to members of the general Internet public.

Telnet connections are useful for many purposes. For example, Figure 10.5 shows a Telnet connection to a library's online catalog. You can obtain

FIGURE 10.5
A Telnet connection to a library catalog.

information about books in the library's collection over the Internet as easily as you could from the library's own reference room.

Another common use for Telnet is to provide access to news groups that are not part of Usenet, such as the one in Figure 10.6.

FIGURE 10.6

A Telnet connection to an online conference service.

FTP

You can use Telnet to operate a distant computer by remote control through the Internet, but sometimes there is no substitute for having your own copy of a program or data file. **File Transfer Protocol**, or **FTP**, is the Internet tool used to copy files from one computer to another. When a user has accounts on more than one computer, FTP can be used to transfer data or programs between them.

There are also public FTP archives that will permit anyone to make copies of their files. These archives contain thousands of individual programs and files on almost every imaginable subject. Anyone with an FTP client program can download and use these files. Because these public archives require visitors to use the word "anonymous" as an account name, they are known as **anonymous FTP archives**.

Here are a few of the things that exist in FTP archives:

- Weather maps
- Programs for Windows, Macintosh, UNIX, and other operating systems
- Articles and reviews from scholarly journals
- Recipes
- Historic documents such as the United Nations Charter
- Digital images of paintings by Salvador Dali
- The Collected Poems of William Butler Yeats
- John von Neumann's 1945 report on the EDVAC, one of the earliest digital computing systems
- Maps from the United States Geological Survey

The list could fill this chapter four or five times over.

Using FTP is simple. Often, the hard part is locating a file that you want to download. One way to find files is to use **Archie**, the searchable index of FTP archives maintained by McGill University in Montreal. The main Archie server at McGill gathers copies of the directories from more than a thousand other public

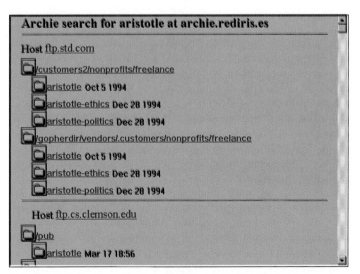

This is the index for an anonymous FTP archive at the University of North Carolina using an FTP program that displays subdirectories and files in a single list. The user clicks on the name of a file to download it. Other FTP programs use drag-and-drop graphic interfaces or separate text commands.

This screen shows the partial result of a search for files related to "Aristotle." The search identified several public archives that contain copies of Aristotle's writings.

FTP archives every month and distributes copies of those directories to dozens of other servers around the world. When a server receives a request for a "keyword search," it returns a list of files that match the search criteria along with the location of each file.

Once you have an address and file name, it is a simple matter to download a copy with an FTP client program.

Gopher

All kinds of information are available through the Internet, but much of it can be difficult to find without a guide. **Gopher** organizes directories of documents, images, programs, public Telnet hosts, and other resources into logical menus.

The first Gopher was created at the University of Minnesota (home of the Golden Gophers) to provide easy access to information on computers all over the university's campus. When a user selected an item from a Gopher menu, the Gopher server would automatically download that item to the user's computer. The system worked so well that other information providers created their own Gopher servers and linked them to the Minnesota menus.

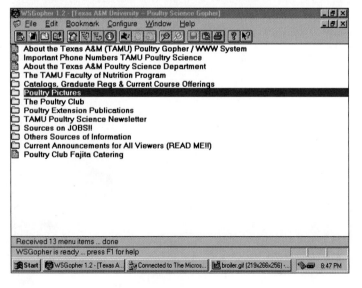

A Gopher menu can include links to anything on the Internet, including files of all kinds, host computers, and other Gopher menus. Some menus and submenus are organized by subject, and others list resources in a particular geographical region. Most menus also include pointers to the local server's top-level menu or to the "Mother Gopher" in Minnesota that lists all the Gopher servers in the world. Therefore, it is possible to start on almost any Gopher menu and jump to any other Gopher with just a few intermediate steps.

As an example, let's follow a series of Gopher menus. Figure 10.7 shows a Gopher menu that lists Gopher servers in Texas.

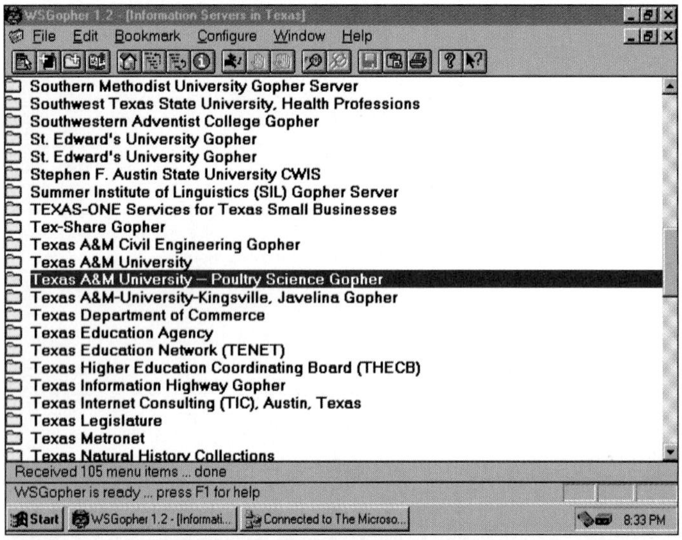

FIGURE 10.7
The top-level Texas Gopher menu.

When you select the Texas A&M Poultry Science Gopher from that menu, you get the menu in Figure 10.8, which lists specific services and additional menus.

FIGURE 10.8
The Texas A&M Poultry Science Gopher.

The "Poultry Pictures" directory leads to more than a dozen .GIF picture files including the picture of a broiler in Figure 10.9.

FIGURE 10.9
A picture from Texas A&M.

Gopher goes a long way toward making the Internet more accessible, but with more than 15 million items in Gopher menus, there is still a lot of territory to search. Like the Archie search tool for FTP archives, **Veronica** (Very Easy Rodent-Oriented Net-wide Index to Computer Archives) is a keyword search tool that finds and displays items from Gopher menus.

The World Wide Web

The **World Wide Web** (**the web** or **WWW**) was created in 1989 at the European Particle Physics Laboratory in Geneva, Switzerland, as a method for incorporating footnotes, figures, and cross-references into online **hypertext** documents in which a reader can click on a word or phrase in a document, and immediately jump to another location within the same document, or to another file. The second file may be located on the same computer as the original document or anywhere else on the Internet. Because the user does not have to learn separate commands and addresses to jump to a new location, the World Wide Web organized widely scattered resources into a seamless whole.

The Web was an interesting but not particularly exciting tool used by scientific researchers—until 1993, when Mosaic, a point-and-click graphic Web browser, was developed at the National Center for Supercomputing Applications (NCSA) at the University of Illinois. Mosaic, and the Web browsers that have evolved from Mosaic, have changed the way people use the Internet. Web pages are now used to distribute news, interactive educational services, product information and catalogs, highway traffic reports, and live audio and video, among many other things. Interactive Web pages permit readers to consult databases, order products and information, and submit payment with a credit card or other account number.

The latest generation of Web browsers, including Mosaic, Netscape Navigator, and Microsoft's Internet Explorer, can open file viewers and other application programs automatically when they receive graphic images, audio, video, and other files. Combined with distributed application languages, like Sun Microsystems' Java, users also can import live, interactive data (such as financial information that changes

This screen shows the results of a Veronica search for items related to Alan Turing, the pioneer computer scientist.

A typical Web page. Here the user clicks on the underlined word "pictures" to see photographs of the planets.

The Internet gives access to the biggest repository of information that has ever existed in the world. You can find almost anything you could ever want to know on the Internet.

Or can you? It's the age-old task of finding a needle in a haystack, only this haystack has, at the latest count, more than 7 million places to look, and more are being added every day.

Searching for information on the Net is enormously challenging because there is an astounding amount of information to sift through and it's always changing. Also, it is organized in a chaotic and complicated interconnected system of Web sites, Gopher and FTP sites, newsgroups and mailing lists.

The good news is that yes, it is possible to find specific information on the Net, and surprisingly quickly. There are a variety of different search engines designed to access information specified by the user. However, finding what you want requires solid research techniques and a good command of how to use search engines.

Each search engine has its own Web page containing forms into which you type the string of text relating to what you want to search for on the Web. Click a button, wait a little (hopefully) while, and the engine reveals its list of "hits," or information repositories that contain your string.

Your task as a researcher is to select words for your string that match the entries in your engine's index as closely as possible. Otherwise, you could wind up wading through literally thousands of unrelated "hits."

Becoming a Web researcher is a complex task. Here are some basic tips that can simplify your Web research right from the start:

Read instructions. Most engines provide a description of how they work and how to conduct a search.

Watch your language. Phrase your query string to maximize each particular search engine's capabilities. For example:

■ Some engines will search for whole phrases, or occurrences of a number of words together, instead of individual words.

■ Some engines let you use wild cards (* and ?) to find variations on a phrase.

■ Some engines let you use Boolean operators, or special terms, like AND, OR, or NOT to narrow and refine your search in terms of time and content.

■ Some engines "stem" your query words; for example, a query for parking will also find park.

Use more than one engine. Different engines yield different results. If one engine doesn't find what you want, another might.

Rewrite your query. If you don't get the results you want the first time, try rephrasing your query string to define more clearly what it is you want.

Spell Correctly. Search engines don't correct typos.

Try, try again. After the first pass, go to the most promising sites and look for words you can use in your query to narrow or enlarge your search. Rephrase your text string, and try your search again.

Try synonyms. There are many different ways to say something. If "running" doesn't get what you want, try "races" or "jogging."

Try metasearch engines. These are sites where you can use several search engines to launch queries. This saves the time of jumping from one engine to another.

Try specialized engines. Some engines search only a specific group of sites, such as commercial sites, government-sponsored sites, or Usenet newsgroups. If you know where you want to look, these specialized engines can save you lots of time.

Read the hit summaries. Most engines provide a summary of each "hit" they've found. These summaries can help you eliminate large numbers of entries without having to take the time to visit the pages.

Keep a trail of breadcrumbs. Use bookmarks to keep track of sites you want to visit again.

Keep up to date. Sites, engines, and the latest Web research tools change at least once every day. Stay informed.

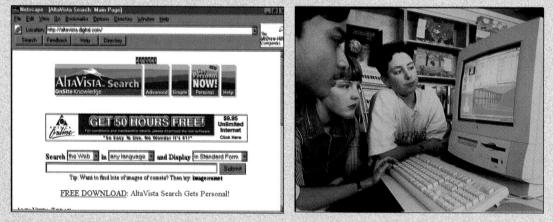

Research on the Internet is made possible by search engines like Alta Vista, which locate specific topics in the vast storehouse of information available on the World Wide Web.

frequently) and executable programs from the World Wide Web.

Some observers currently think that Java, or something like it, will move many computing applications out of individual desktop computers and onto Internet servers.

The internal structure of the World Wide Web is built on a set of rules called **Hypertext Transfer Protocol (HTTP)** and a page description language called **Hypertext Markup Language (HTML)**. HTTP uses Internet addresses in a special format called a **Uniform Resource Locator**, or **URL**. URLs look like this:

type://address/path

type specifies the type of server in which the file is located. *address* is the address of the server, and *path* is the location within the file structure of the server. So the URL for the University of Illinois is:

http://www.uiuc.edu

Files in other formats may also have URLs. For example, the URL for the SunSite FTP archive of PC software at the University of North Carolina is:

ftp://sunsite.unc.edu-/pub/micro/pc-stuff

Documents that use HTTP are known as **Web pages**. A typical Web page contains information about a particular subject with links to related Web pages and other resources. Many Web sites contain a top-level **home page** that has pointers to additional pages with more detailed information. For example, a university might have a home page with links to a campus guide, Telnet access to the library, and separate pages for individual departments and programs.

Hundreds of new Web pages appear every week, but they are not always easy to find. Unlike Gopher, which organizes information on the Internet into logical menus, the World Wide Web does not provide a basic structure for locating resources. As an attempt to fill this gap, an assortment of directories and search tools is available online. One of the best is Yahoo!, whose URL is *http://www.yahoo.com.* Yahoo! is an extensive directory with a menu that lists thousands of Web sites, organized by topic, and a search engine that looks for specified words in titles and addresses of the Web sites in the directories.

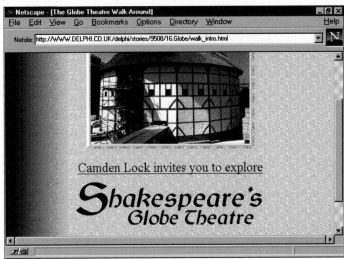

This Web site lets users explore the Globe Theatre in London, where Shakespeare's plays were originally performed.

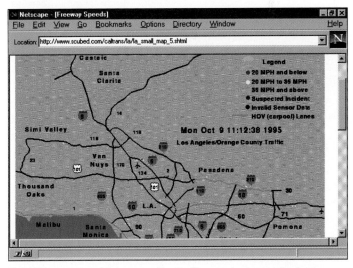

This Web page provides users with a traffic report covering the freeways in the Los Angeles area. This information is updated periodically throughout the day.

Online Services and BBSs

Today, many of the most exciting things you can do with a personal computer involve online services, bulletin board services (BBSs), and the Internet. In a world of information, these services are your passport.

TV shows have entertained us for years. Now the Internet is trying its hand at showtime. On the Net you can tune in anytime, custom-tailor the show the way you want it, and even talk to the characters!

Cybercasts, as Internet shows are called, are in their infancy. But already there are many talk shows, newscasts, and, of course, soap operas.

Cybercasts are different from TV and radio shows in that they are aired continuously (updating occurs in the background while you watch) and they are interactive—which means you finally get to talk back. You give your feedback in the form of e-mail or in live online chat rooms. If your computer system supports current video technology, you can even talk live to the "stars" of some cybercasts via video conferencing.

Linda Ellerbee, late-night NBC news anchor, is credited with hosting the very first cybercast show on the Internet, a monthly talk show called *On the Record*, in early 1996. The first installment originated from the @Cafe in New York City, where Ellerbee talked to two audiences—one live in person at the cafe, and one live Web-connected audience.

Other pioneer cybercasts on the Net include the Sci-Fi Channel cable network which simulcasts its TV programs on its Dominion Web site **(http://www.scifi.com)**; Discovery Channel Online's live! talk show **(http://www.discovery.com)**; and National Public Radio, which publishes portions of its daily radio programming online **(http://www.npr.org)**.

There is a large variety of news shows on the Net. One of the most interesting is PointCast News Network, which tailors the news just for you **(http:// www.pointcast.com).**

PointCast is somewhat different from other cybercasts in that it requires you to download client software, which allows you to pick the news, weather, sports, and business information you want to receive. Also, you can configure PointCast software to act like a screensaver and turn the news on for you whenever your PC is idle.

Another interesting new development in Internet cybercasts is multiple media, in which a company transmits a particular show in a variety of media, such as TV, radio, and the Internet. ClNet, a San Francisco company specializing in the coverage of computer-related news over the Internet, also hosts a cable TV show, a radio show, and a cybercast offshoot of the radio show called News Stream. **(http://www.cnet.com)**.

Another development in cybercasts is the streaming of live audio and video coverage, a method of file transfer that allows playback to begin before a download has been completed, giving the illusion of live broadcast. You can hear and see events as they happen in a live and interactive environment.

Streaming has permitted some landmark events in cyberhistory to take place. One was the real-time cybercast of President Bill Clinton and Vice-President Al Gore's remarks at a high school in California to celebrate Net Day 96 in March 1996. Live video and audio coverage was streamed over the Internet in real-time using a video conferencing tool called CU-SeeMe.

Another historical event was the cybercast of the Pope celebrating Papal Mass from Baltimore in October 1995, via Maryland Public TV's (MPT) Web site. The Mass was transmitted in real-time video and audio.

Closely related to cybercasts are e-zines, or online magazines. For example, at the Job Hunter e-zine **(http://www.collegegrad.com)** you will find information on landing your first job, plus you can post your résumé and browse through thousands of job listings.

For entertainment value, try StrangeMag e-zine **(http://www.cais.com/strangemag/ home.html)**, which includes articles on offbeat topics such as time travel, the Loch Ness Monster, and UFOs.

For TV "couch potatoes" on the verge of becoming Web "computatoes," be forewarned: All TV shows come to an end, but cybercasts are available 24 hours a day!

Linda Ellerbee hosts the first online cybercast, "On the Record", in 1996.

A screen of one of the online soap operas.

An **online service** is a company that offers access, generally on a subscription basis, to e-mail, discussion groups, databases on various subjects (such as weather information, stock quotes, newspaper articles, and so on), and other services ranging from electronic banking to online games. Most online services also offer access to the Internet. Currently, the most popular online services are America Online, CompuServe, Microsoft Network, and Prodigy. Users typically pay by the month, and the subscription gives them a limit on the number of hours they can use the service. If they use the service for more time, they pay by the hour. A BBS is similar to an online service, except that the services are normally limited to discussion groups. Also, many BBSs are run by individuals and can be accessed free (although you still have to pay for the phone call).

People subscribe to online services for all kinds of reasons. Many subscribe simply to have access to e-mail and the other kinds of communication that online services include, such as discussion groups and chat lines. A **discussion group** (also known as a **bulletin board** or a **news group**) is an electronic storage space where users can post messages to the other users. The discussion group lets users carry on extended conversations and trade information. Figure 10.10 shows messages posted to a discussion group.

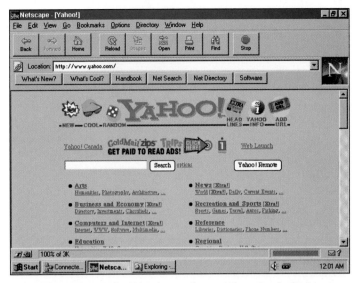

This is the home page for Yahoo!, an online search engine for finding information on the Web.

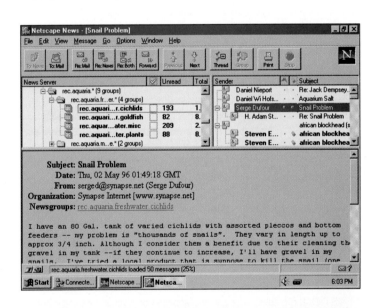

FIGURE 10.10

Message posted to a discussion group.

People tend to join discussion groups aimed at their professional or personal interests. Because different services have different kinds of discussion groups, the services tend to attract different kinds of users. For example, CompuServe attracts many computer professionals, because there are discussions that relate to specific pieces of software or hardware. Prodigy, on the other hand, tends to attract home users. Like e-mail, discussion groups are an inexpensive, efficient means for communication.

Many small services, usually known as bulletin board services or **BBSs**, exist only to provide specific discussion groups or groups of discussion groups. BBSs gained popularity almost as soon as modems became popular. At first, most were run privately, out of peo-

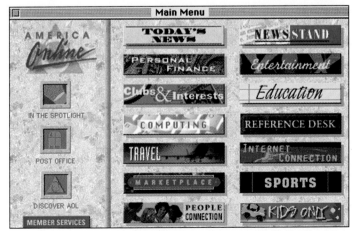

America Online offers a variety of information and services. Used by permission. America Online, Inc., 1996.

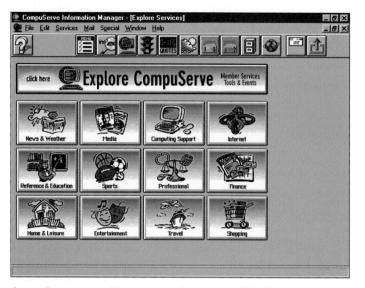

CompuServe is one of the popular online services. This is the screen you see when you log on. Each icon represents a category of information and services that the user can access online.

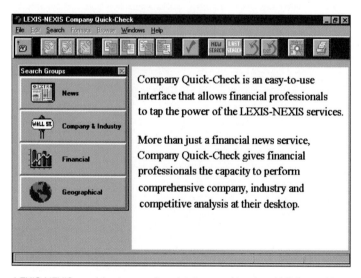

LEXIS-NEXIS provides huge online databases of legal and bibliographic information. The screen shown here, LEXIS-NEXIS Company Quick-Check, is a special software interface for looking up information about companies and industries.

ple's homes. During the 1980s and early 1990s, they spread to the commercial online services and the Internet. Today, the term system operator, or sysop, is used to describe the person who monitors group discussions.

Most of the online services also offer **chat lines**, which are similar to bulletin boards, except that they are live group discussions, more akin to a conference call than to a bulletin board. Although relatively new to computer networks (compared to bulletin boards), chat lines have a long history in the telephone system. In the early days of telephones, operators opened party lines where groups of people (usually women, and often in rural areas) could have a "virtual" party without leaving their homes.

Although the biggest online services are general in content and offer lots of features, others are much more specialized, offering access to specific databases. Perhaps the best known is LEXIS-NEXIS, a company that sells access to its two databases. LEXIS® is a legal database that researchers can use to find specific laws and court opinions. NEXIS® is a bibliographic database that contains information about articles on a wide range of topics.

Internet Features in Application Programs

The Internet tools described up to this point usually appear as either separate, stand-alone applications or integrated programs that combine several Internet client functions into a single graphic interface. As the Internet continues to become part of daily life for more and more computer users, many other application programs have begun to integrate Internet functions. For example, add-on programs for Word-Perfect, Microsoft Word, and other word processors and desktop publishing programs can import World Wide Web pages and other Internet files into documents. Many programs can also be used to create Web pages and browse the Web. Communications programs can send and receive messages through the Internet as easily as they use a telephone line. Spreadsheets and database managers can obtain information from Internet servers that they can analyze and display on a local computer. This trend is likely to continue and grow.

▶ ACCESSING THE INTERNET

Because the Internet connects so many computers and networks, there are many ways to obtain access to it. Some methods are appropriate for computers attached to a local area network in a college or corporation, while others are better for an isolated computer in a home office or small business.

One of the hottest new skills in the computer industry is the ability to create Web pages that hop, skip, sing, and ask what toppings you want on your pizza.

This capacity for motion and interactivity on a Web page is made possible by a growing number of tools. Java, the tool with the widest scope, has caused almost as much talk and excitement as the Internet itself. **(http://www.java.sun.com)**

Java is a programming language, a set of codes used for creating cross-platform programs. It was developed by Sun Microsystems in the mid '90s. Webmasters (as Web site developers are called) were looking for ways to extend the capabilities of HTML. Basically, all HTML can do by itself is format text and display .gif and .jpeg graphics. People want their Web pages to do more, such as move and interact.

This movement and interactivity is accomplished through applets, Java programs which are designed to run within something called a virtual machine. A virtual machine is the environment in which a computer of one type emulates another, and runs the applet inside of that. In theory, if a user has a virtual machine available, all Java applets will run inside of it, whatever the platform. To create these applets, programmers write programs in Java code, using an integrated development environment (IDE). An IDE is a specialized software package that provides developers the tools they need to write in a particular programming language. Examples of Java IDEs include Cafe by Symantec and the Java Developer's Kit by Sun Microsystems.

Accessing Java-enhanced Web sites requires a Java-compatible browser. Netscape has been Java-compatible since version 2.0. Sun also makes its own browser called HotJava.

To understand how Java-enhanced Web sites differ from traditional Web sites using only HTML, think of the Internet as an example of a client/server computing system. The Web site computer is the server, and your computer is the client, which accesses pages on the Web site using a Web browser. The browser translates the HTML code (with which the Web page is constructed) into a graphical format, so you can click on a link on the page. Your browser translates a link into an URL (or Internet address) and then goes to that address and brings back to you the item associated with the link.

This process becomes more complicated when you encounter a Web page that includes some advanced interactivity, such as a form that you fill out to complete a customer order. Before Java was developed, this kind of interactivity was accomplished by routing the information you fill in on the form to a DBMS (database management system) on the server, which then processed the order and passed the results back to you (the client) via the common gateway interface (CGI).

This process is time consuming, especially if the database on the server has to handle many requests simultaneously.

With Java, the process is completely different. When you click on the same Web page link, the server sends your computer not only the corresponding HTML document, but also a Java applet. The form you then fill out is part of the applet, and the processing is performed by the applet on the client machine. Once the applet has figured tax, totals, and so forth, only the necessary information is passed back to the server. Because the applet is doing the work on the client computer, not a database on the server, the process is much more efficient.

Java is like a morning cup of coffee for your Web page: It wakes things up, gets them out of bed, and puts them on the move.

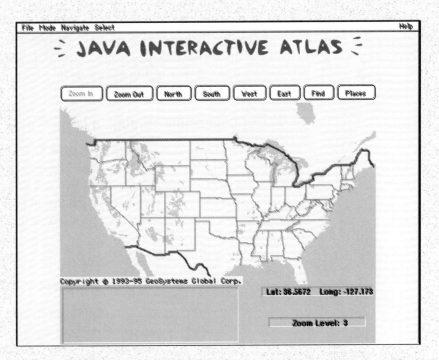

This Java applet allows users to connect to Telnet servers through a Web browser. Prior to Java, browsers required a "helper application" in another window to do this.

Direct Connection

In a direct connection, Internet programs run on the local computer, which uses the TCP/IP protocols to exchange data with another computer through the Internet. An isolated computer can connect to the Internet through a serial data communications port using either **Serial Line Interface Protocol (SLIP)** or **Point to Point Protocol (PPP)**, two methods for creating a direct connection through a phone line.

```
ls-lRt
ls-lRt.Z
00WELCOME.info
Copyright.info
226 Transfer complete.
243 bytes received in 0.02 seconds (9.96 Kbytes/s)
ftp> get README.online
200 PORT command successful.
150 Opening ASCII mode data connection for README.online (1880 bytes).
226 Transfer complete.
local: README.online remote: README.online
1929 bytes received in 0.36 seconds (5.22 Kbytes/s)
ftp> bye
221 Goodbye.
linex2> ls
Mail/          News/          brian/          public_html/
Mailboxes/     README.online  mail/           sandstone/
linex2> sz README.online
sz: 1 file requested:
README.online

Sending in Batch Mode
**B0000000000000
linex2>
```

With a remote terminal connection to a shell account, all information appears as text on the screen.

Remote Terminal Connection

A remote terminal connection to the Internet exchanges commands and data in ASCII text format with a host computer that uses UNIX or a similar operating system. The TCP/IP application programs and protocols all run on the host. Because the command set in UNIX is called a shell, this kind of Internet access is known as a **shell account**.

Gateway Connection

Many networks that do not use TCP/IP commands and protocols may still provide some Internet services, such as e-mail or file transfer. These networks use gateways that convert commands and data to and from TCP/IP format.

Although it is possible to connect a local network directly to the Internet backbone, it is usually not practical (except for the largest corporations and institutions) because of the high cost of a backbone connection. As a general rule, most businesses and individuals obtain access through an **Internet Service Provider (ISP)**, which supplies the backbone connection. ISPs offer several kinds of Internet service, including inexpensive shell accounts, direct TCP/IP connections using SLIP or PPP accounts, and full-time high-speed access through dedicated data circuits.

Connecting Through a LAN

If a Local Area Network (LAN) uses TCP/IP protocols for communication within the network, it is a simple matter to connect to the Internet through a **router**, another computer that stores and forwards sets of data (called packets) to other computers on the Internet. If the LAN uses a different kind of local protocol, a **bridge** converts it to and from TCP/IP. When a LAN has an Internet connection, that connection extends to every computer on the LAN.

Connecting Through a Modem

If there is no LAN on site, an isolated computer can connect to the Internet through a serial data communications port and a modem, using either a shell account and a terminal emulation program, or a direct TCP/IP connection with a SLIP or PPP account. TCP/IP connections permit users to run application programs with graphical user interfaces, rather than limiting them to ASCII text.

High-Speed Data Links

Modem connections are convenient, but their capacity is limited to the relatively low data-transfer speed of a telephone line. A 28.8 Kbps modem is fine for text, but it is really not practical for huge digital audio and video files. Furthermore, when many users are sharing an Internet connection through a LAN, the connection between the bridge or router and an ISP must be adequate to meet the demands of many users at the same time.

Fortunately, dedicated high-speed data circuits are available from telephone companies, cable TV services, and other suppliers. Using fiber optics, microwave, and other technologies, it is entirely practical to establish an Internet connection that is at least ten times as fast as a modem link. All it takes is money.

For small businesses and individual users, **ISDN (Integrated Services Digital Network)** is an attractive alternative. ISDN is a relatively new digital telephone service that combines voice, data, and control signaling through a single circuit. An ISDN data connection can transfer data at up to 128,000 bits per second. Most telephone companies offer ISDN at a slightly higher cost than the conventional telephone lines that it replaces.

Other Online Services

The Internet has overshadowed and absorbed some of the other online services, but it is not the only place to obtain information through a modem. Online information services such as America Online, Microsoft Network, and CompuServe provide their own conferences, live chat groups, news reports, online versions of magazines and newspapers, and huge libraries of downloadable files, along with Internet services such as e-mail, Usenet news, FTP file transfer, and access to the World Wide Web.

Access to the Internet through an online service usually costs a little more than an account with an ISP, but, so far, the added value of the online services, their conferences, news, and file libraries make them the preferred method for millions of users. All of the online services offer free trial memberships, so it is easy to sign up and look around without any risk.

▶ CONNECTING A PC TO THE INTERNET

Connecting a desktop computer to the Internet actually involves two separate issues: software and the network connection. The industry has developed a standard interface called Windows Sockets, or **Winsock**, that makes it possible to mix and match application programs from more than one developer. Figure 10.11 shows how applications, the Winsock interface, and network drivers fit together.

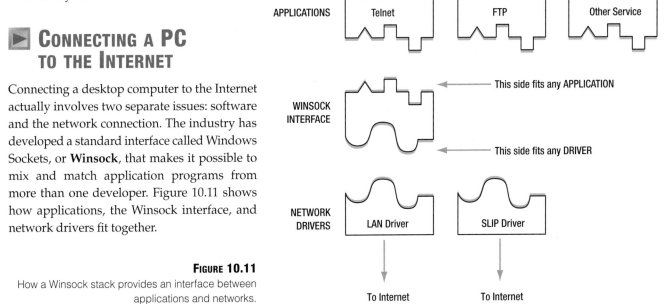

FIGURE 10.11
How a Winsock stack provides an interface between applications and networks.

Netcom is one of the companies offering an integrated package for accessing the Internet. The buttons along the top of the screen launch tools for using e-mail, the Web, FTP, chat, and so on.

Integrated Internet Software Packages

Many companies offer suites of Internet access tools. These packages usually contain client programs for e-mail, Telnet, FTP, and other applications, along with a World Wide Web browser and software for connecting to a network using dial-up modem connections, connection through a LAN, or both. In addition, some packages include sign-up utilities that will work with one or more Internet service providers who offer modem access through local telephone numbers in most major metropolitan areas.

The all-in-one-box approach has several advantages. In most cases, the applications in a suite share a common interface design, so they are easy to learn and use. Additionally, since all the applications come from the same source, there is a single point of contact for technical support and product upgrades. If a suite includes an account with a particular ISP, it is a safe bet that the service provider has worked with the software developer to make sure there are no incompatibilities between the software and the network.

▶ Norton Workshop: Research Using the Web

In this section, you will see how Emma, a student in New York City, did some free-form research by using the World Wide Web to find information about England and France for a vacation that she is planning.

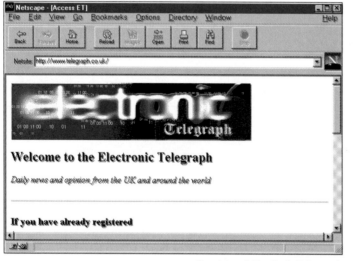

Courtesy of *The Daily Telegraph*

Through the Yahoo! search engine, Emma has found the URL for the *Electronic Telegraph*, an online version of a London newspaper. She logs on to her account with a local ISP, opens her Web browser, and enters the URL for the *Electronic Telegraph*. Her browser downloads the home page of the online publication, direct from London (see Figure 10.12).

FIGURE 10.12
The home page for the electronic version of *The Telegraph*.

The *Electronic Telegraph* requires visitors to register, but it will accept "guest" as both an account name and a password. After Emma logs in, the site offers a choice of sections, as shown in Figure 10.13.

FIGURE 10.13

Topic areas on the *Electronic Telegraph*.

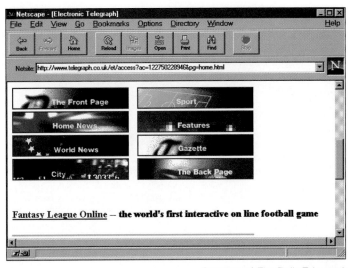

Courtesy of *The Daily Telegraph*

Each section includes headlines for individual stories in today's newspaper. Emma clicks on the Features icon to see the lists of feature stories. There she finds an article about touring Paris online. Since she will be going to Paris as well as London, she decides to jump directly to some of the links that are listed in the article. The first link takes her to a Paris home page, which contains many more links relevant to visiting Paris (see Figure 10.14).

FIGURE 10.14

The Paris Links page.

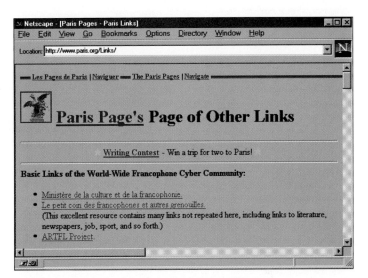

She scrolls down the page to see links to specific information about Paris, as shown in Figure 10.15.

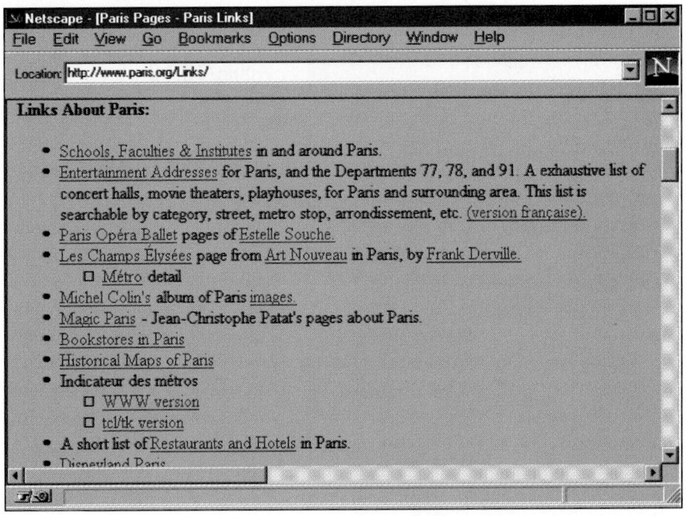

FIGURE 10.15

More links to pages about Paris.

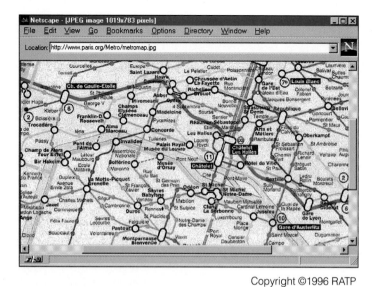

Copyright ©1996 RATP

Among other things, the Paris home page offers guides to concert halls, movie theaters, restaurants, and bookstores in Paris, and a map of the Paris Metro. As she does not yet have maps for her trip, she jumps to the Metro map (see Figure 10.16) and prints it.

FIGURE 10.16
A map of the Paris Metro.

The Metro map does not contain any other links, so Emma clicks on the Back button in her Web browser program to go back to the Paris home page. There she finds a link to "Museums," which has another link to "Musee du Louvre." This page contains buttons for many of the most famous objects in the Louvre. Emma clicks to see images of the Mona Lisa (Figure 10.17), the Venus de Milo (Figure 10.18), and the Winged Victory (Figure 10.19).

FIGURE 10.17
The Mona Lisa, an image file in the Louvre section of the Paris Pages.

FIGURE 10.18
Another object at the Louvre, the Venus de Milo.

FIGURE 10.19
The Winged Victory.

There is more to Paris than museums, so Emma returns to the Paris home page. There she finds links to many of the sights around town, including a list of monuments (see Figure 10.20).

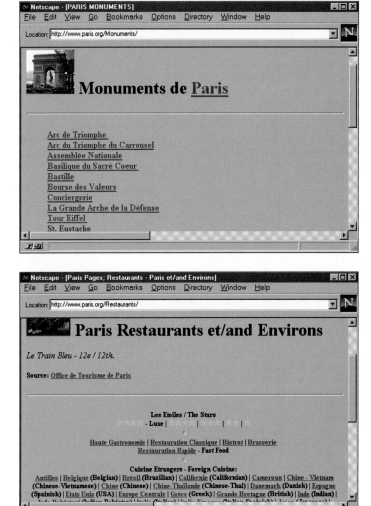

FIGURE 10.20

A page listing Paris monuments.

Finally, Emma uses the Paris home page to look for places to eat. The Paris Restaurants page lets visitors find bistros and haute cuisine, based on location, price, type of food, and other features (see Figure 10.21).

FIGURE 10.21

Restaurants in and around Paris.

Emma prints the details about a few of the most interesting restaurants and logs off.

You have just witnessed a fairly typical session of "Web surfing," exploring the vast stores of information on the World Wide Web simply by clicking from one URL to the next.

To be sure, there are more structured ways to find specific information. You can use a search engine, such as Yahoo!, to find sites that meet increasingly specific search words, until you find exactly what you are looking for.

But the Web, with its hypertext structure, is ideally suited for exploration. It can be a lot of fun simply to look around until you discover something that interests you. Perhaps more than any other aspect of the Internet, it is this capacity for exploration that continues to broaden the popularity of the online world.

WHAT TO EXPECT IN THE FUTURE

The state of the Internet today is like broadcast radio in the early 1920s. It is still searching for the best way to evolve from technical curiosity to mass medium. The basic technology is in place, but the content and business models are still developing. Over the next few years, the Internet will continue to expand and change in several important ways: faster connections, more users, new multimedia and "virtual reality" services, and distributed network-based applications. As cable TV and telephone companies provide affordable high-speed access, and as more homes and offices are connected, information providers will use the Internet to distribute digital audio and video services for education, entertainment, and business communication. Distributed application languages like Java will enable information providers to supply interactive services such as multimedia newspapers, live stock market tickers, and games to millions of subscribers. Other programs will notify users automatically when predesignated events take place anywhere on the Internet.

Many businesses will find ways to make money online, while others will go bankrupt trying. Some Internet services will be surrounded by advertisements, while others will require payment for access to their Web sites and FTP archives, or for individual downloads. Ten years from now, it is quite possible that the Internet will be as universal as radio and television are today.

▶ VISUAL SUMMARY

Background and History: An Explosion of Connectivity

■ The Internet was created for the U.S. Department of Defense as a tool for military communications, command, and control, and exchange of data with defense contractors.

■ It has continued to expand and grow by establishing interconnections with other networks around the world.

■ Today, the Internet is a network of networks that is interconnected through regional and national backbone connections.

■ The Internet carries messages, documents, programs, and data files that contain every imaginable kind of information for businesses, educational institutions, government agencies, and individual users.

How the Internet Works

■ All computers on the Internet use TCP/IP protocols to exchange commands and data.

■ Any computer on the Internet can connect to any other computer.

■ Individual computers connect to local and regional networks, which are connected together through the Internet backbone.

■ A computer can connect directly to the Internet, or as a remote terminal on another computer, or through a gateway from a network that does not use TCP/IP.

■ Every computer on the Internet has a unique numeric IP address, and most also have an address that uses the Domain Name System.

■ Most Internet application programs use the client-server model; users run client programs that obtain data and services from a server.

TABLE 10.1	
Internet Domains	
DOMAIN	TYPE OF ORGANIZATION
.com	business (commercial)
.edu	educational
.gov	government
.mil	military
.net	gateway or host
.org	other organization

Major Features of the Internet

■ The Internet is a source of news, business communication, entertainment, and technical information. It also supports "virtual communities."

■ Electronic mail is the most popular use of the Internet.

■ Telnet allows a user to operate a second computer from the keyboard of his or her machine.

■ FTP is the Internet tool for copying data and program files from one computer to another.

■ News and mailing lists are public conferences distributed through the Internet and other electronic networks.

■ Gopher is a hierarchical menu system that helps users find resources that may be anywhere on the Internet.

■ The World Wide Web combines text, illustrations, and links to other files in hypertext documents. The Web is the fastest growing part of the Internet.

- Online service companies and bulletin board services (BBSs) offer, in addition to Internet access, a wide variety of other features, such as e-mail, discussion groups, stock quotes, news, and online games.
- Other Internet tools and services can be integrated into word processors, database managers, and other application programs.

Accessing the Internet

- Users can connect to the Internet through local area networks (LANs) through direct TCP/IP connections, and through gateways from online information services.

Connecting a PC to the Internet

- The Winsock standard specifies the Windows interface between TCP/IP applications and network connections.
- Users can mix and match Winsock compatible applications.
- Internet application suites are available from many suppliers; they combine a full set of applications and drivers in a single package.

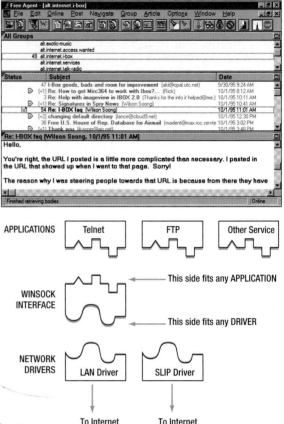

▶ KEY TERMS

After completing this chapter, you should be able to define the following terms:

anonymous FTP archives, 301	Gopher, 302	post office server, 297
Archie, 301	home page, 305	protocol, 295
ARPANET, 294	hypertext, 303	router, 310
backbone, 294	Hypertext Markup Language (HTML), 305	server, 296
BBSs, 307		shell account, 310
bridge, 310	Hypertext Transfer Protocol (HTTP), 305	Serial Line Interface Protocol (SLIP), 310
bulletin board, 307	Internet Service Provider (ISP), 310	
chat lines, 308	IP address, 296	subdomain, 296
client, 296	ISDN (Integrated Services Digital Network), 311	TCP/IP, 295
discussion group, 307		Telnet, 300
domain, 296	listserv, 298	Uniform Resource Locator (URL), 305
Domain Name System (DNS), 296	mail server, 297	Usenet, 299
e-mail, 297	News, 299	Veronica, 303
File Transfer Protocol (FTP), 301	news group, 307	Web page, 305
Frequently Asked Questions (FAQs), 299	NSFnet, 294	Winsock, 311
	online service, 307	World Wide Web (the Web or WWW), 303
gateway, 294	Point to Point Protocol (PPP), 310	

▶ KEY TERM QUIZ

Fill in the blank with one of the terms listed in Key Terms.

1. The central structure that connects elements of a network is known as the _____.

2. A(n) _____ is the set of rules and procedures used by all computers connected to the Internet.

3. The Internet is most often used for the exchange of _____.

4. There are thousands of _____ on the Internet devoted to different topics of discussion.

5. _____ lets you connect your computer to a distant host system.

6. You can use _____ to link to anything on the Internet.

7. _____ are documents that use HTTP.

8. A(n) _____ is a powerful computer that acts as a shared storage resource on a network.

9. A standard interface that makes it possible to mix and match applications from more than one developer is called _____.

10. Live group discussions online are carried out on _____.

► REVIEW QUESTIONS

1. According to this chapter, what is the single most important aspect to understand about the Internet?
2. What are protocols? What do they do?
3. What allows any size computer to be able to send and receive data through the Internet?
4. Explain briefly why the Internet is sometimes described as "a network of networks."
5. What is Archie used for primarily?
6. Describe the differences between an IP address and a Domain Name System address.
7. List and describe the five functions combined in an e-mail program.
8. What protocol is necessary for sharing data files between computers?
9. Describe how keyword search tools help users find information via the Internet.
10. What trend in application software is likely to continue to grow as the Internet grows in popularity?

► DISCUSSION QUESTIONS

1. What do you think about the claim that new languages like Java will move applications out of individual desktop computers to Internet servers? In what ways do you think such an occurrence might benefit businesses and other organizations? What do you think are some benefits to connecting a company's LAN to the Internet? Are there any detriments?
2. Based on what you read in this chapter about the Internet's history, what significant factor made it possible to conduct business and exchange commercial information over the Internet?
3. Despite the promise that the Internet will perhaps one day be as universal as radio and television, how do you feel about the growing "commercialization" of the Internet? Do you think the motive to use the Internet as a vehicle for profit will negatively impact it as a wealthy source of information?
4. Do you think that graphic web browsers have changed significantly the way people use the Internet? Do you think the graphic user interface programs for browsing the World Wide Web have contributed to the growing numbers of people who use the Internet?

NORTON INTERACTIVE

Complete the Norton Interactive module for this chapter.

GRAPHICS

CONTENTS

OBJECTIVES

When you complete this chapter, you will be able to do the following:

- Explain the purpose and use of graphics software.
- Differentiate between paint and draw programs.
- Discuss the differences between the major categories of graphics software.
- List the most common file formats for bitmap and vector graphics.
- Explain the appropriate uses of different graphics software packages.

Graphics software is used for many different purposes and by many different kinds of users. In fact, most people do not realize how much of the imagery they see during a typical day was created on a computer with graphics software. For example, a number of stamps were created for the United States Postal Service with a draw program on a Macintosh computer. The designs of the titles of many popular television shows were produced by graphic artists using common 3-D modeling programs. Furthermore, much of what you see in a daily newspaper was either assembled or retouched by photo-manipulation and draw programs.

With its ability to mimic traditional artists' media, graphics software also allows artists to do with a computer what they once did with brushes, pencils, and darkroom equipment. With a few keystrokes, the click of a mouse button, and some practice, a talented artist can create colorful and sophisticated images. Because the software is easy to use, even amateurs can produce striking visuals.

Although graphics software was a relative latecomer to the computer world, it has advanced a long way in a short time. In the early 1980s, most graphics programs were limited to drawing simple geometric shapes, usually in black and white. Today, graphics software offers advanced drawing and painting tools, plus color control that is virtually unlimited. In newspapers and magazines, on posters and billboards, in TV and the movies, you see the products of these powerful tools.

▶ WORKING WITH IMAGES

In today's publishing and design industries, it is not uncommon for an artist to take files created on a PC, convert them to Macintosh format, manipulate them with a whole series of graphics programs, then convert them back to a PC format. It is also common to do just the opposite, converting images to a PC format and then back to a Macintosh format. Just as traditional artists must know the capabilities of their paints and brushes, today's computer-based artist must have a wide knowledge of graphics software, the hardware platforms on which it runs, and the formats in which the data can be stored.

Many traditional artists have added a computer to their collection of tools.

Platforms

The 1984 introduction of the Apple Macintosh computer and a modest piece of software known as MacPaint ushered in the era of "art" on the personal computer. With a black-and-white display that showed images just as they would print, and a pointing device, the Macintosh computer allowed users to manipulate shapes, lines, and patterns with great flexibility.

Graphic artists also appreciated the Macintosh's easy-to-use graphical interface, with such enhancements as sophisticated typefaces and the ability to magnify images and undo mistakes. Within a few years, the graphics world had embraced the Macintosh as a serious production tool. With the release of more powerful graphics software and the advent of the **Postscript** printing language—which enabled accurate printing of complex images—the Macintosh became the tool of choice for a new breed of computer artists.

In the late 1980s, Microsoft's Windows brought many of the same capabilities to IBM PCs and compatibles, greatly expanding that market for graphics software. Today, PCs have achieved relative parity with Macintosh systems in the area of graphics software. Good programs are available for both platforms. Often, the same program comes in both Mac and PC versions. This has created a nice situation for users because now creative decisions can involve more thought and discussion about "creative" issues and less worry about "computer" capability.

Another important platform for computer graphics is the class of machines known as workstations. These specialized single-user computers possess extremely powerful and fast CPUs, large-capacity hard disks, high-resolution displays, and lots of RAM.

A high percentage of printed advertisements are created using graphics software.

Many use the UNIX operating system and some use graphics software written especially for the workstation. Two popular models of workstations are the Sun SparcStation and the Silicon Graphics Indigo2.

A workstation can be compared to a high-performance race car. Although it is fast and agile, its expense and complexity can make it seem impractical outside of specialized arenas. Accordingly, workstations typically are reserved for the most demanding graphics projects, such as complicated animation, high-resolution mapping, technical drafting, and cinematic special effects.

In recent years, the price of workstations has dropped dramatically, making their power more accessible to the average graphics user. At the same time, Macintosh and Windows-based computers have become much more powerful, greatly shrinking the gap between workstations and personal computers. These two factors can make choosing a hardware platform for graphics work difficult.

Sun Microsystems makes one of the most popular workstations for graphic applications, the SparcStation.

Often, the decision to purchase a particular type of computer rests as much on social or convenience factors as on what software you are going to use. If you are working as part of a team, and the rest of the team is using PCs, generally you will have an easier time trading files if you use a PC as well. On the other hand, if the work you plan to do can be done better and in one-third the time on a Sun workstation, then it is probably better to choose that platform and suffer the inconveniences of transferring files to other platforms when the need arises.

Types of Graphics Files

The issue of moving files between computers also brings up the topic of graphic file formats. As soon as you create or import an image and begin to work with it, you must determine the format in which you will save your file.

Many graphics programs save files in proprietary formats. For example, by default, Adobe Illustrator, Corel Draw, and Adobe Photoshop each saves files in a different format. Some programs can understand the proprietary formats of other programs, but some cannot. Fortunately, however, there are standard (nonproprietary) file formats used with graphic files on all types of computer systems. There are two basic groups into which these formats are divided: bitmap and vector formats.

Bitmaps Versus Vectors

Graphics files are composed of either

1. A grid of dots, called a **bitmap**, or
2. A set of **vectors**, which are mathematical equations describing the positions of lines.

In general, graphics programs fall into two primary categories along this division. Those that work with bitmaps are called **paint programs**. Those that work with vectors are called **draw programs**. Each category has advantages and drawbacks, depending on the kind of output needed.

When you use bitmap-based graphics software, you are using the computer to move pixels around. If you look very closely at a computer screen, you can see the tiny dots that make up images—these are **pixels**. Manipulating pixels can become very complex. For example, an 8 x 10-inch black-and-white image–if displayed at a typical screen resolution of 72 pixels per inch—is a mosaic of 414,720 pixels (see Figure 11.1). That means that the computer must remember the precise location of each and every one of those pixels as they are viewed, moved, or altered. If it is decided that the same 8 × 10-inch piece of artwork must have up to 256 colors in its makeup (which is considered minimal with today's technology), then the computer must keep track of the 414,720 pixels multiplied by the 8 bits per pixel that are necessary to identify 256 different colors. That equals 3,317,760 bits that the computer must keep track of for one image! (See Figure 11.2)

The animation in the film *Toy Story* was created using Silicon Graphics and Sun workstations. Silicon Graphics Indigo2 computers were used to build the characters. Sun Sparc 20 computers were used to add color and shading to the shapes.

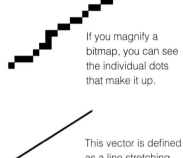

If you magnify a bitmap, you can see the individual dots that make it up.

This vector is defined as a line stretching between two endpoints, not as a set of dots.

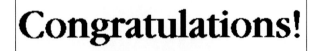

Congratulations!

This text has been generated with a paint program, so the text is actually composed of tiny dots, called pixels.

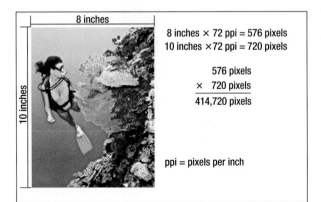

8 inches

10 inches

8 inches × 72 ppi = 576 pixels
10 inches × 72 ppi = 720 pixels

576 pixels
× 720 pixels
414,720 pixels

ppi = pixels per inch

FIGURE 11.1

8 × 10 image, displayed at standard screen resolution.

Unlike paint programs, which manipulate bitmaps, draw programs work their magic through mathematics. By using equations instead of dots to represent lines, shapes, and patterns, vector-based graphics software can represent highly detailed images with only a fraction of the computing power needed for bitmaps.

8 inches × 72 ppi = 576 pixels
10 inches ×72 ppi = 720 pixels

```
        576 pixels
    ×   720 pixels
    414,720 pixels
    ×      8 bits per pixel
    3,317,760 bits
```

ppi = pixels per inch

FIGURE 11.2

8 × 10 image, displayed in color.

Strictly speaking, the vectors used by draw programs are lines drawn from point to point. Vector-based software can use additional equations to define the thickness and color of a line, its pattern, and other attributes. Although a line on the screen is still drawn with pixels (because that is how all computer screens work), to the computer it is an equation. Thus, to move the line from Point A to Point B, all the computer does is substitute the coordinates for Point A with those for Point B. This saves the effort of calculating how to move thousands of individual pixels.

Whether you use a bitmap- or vector-based program depends on what you are trying to do. For example, if you want to be able to retouch each pixel in a photo, you will choose bitmap-based software. If you are making a line drawing of a car and want the capability of repositioning its wheels without having to redraw them, you will probably choose vector-based software. Or, if you need both capabilities, some graphics software allows you to create art that takes advantage of each kind of program.

Standard File Formats

If you need to share files with other users or move files between programs (you almost always do), you should be familiar with the standard file formats for graphics files, as shown in Table 11.1. Most standards are for bitmap graphics.

For vector graphics, the most common format by far is **Encapsulated Postscript,** or **EPS**. This format is based on the Postscript printing language, the most common standard for Macs and PCs communicating with laser printers and high-end reproduction equipment.

Getting Existing Images into Your Computer

The vast majority of graphics programs allow the user to create images from scratch, building

TABLE 11.1	
Standard Formats for Bitmap Graphics	
FORMAT	**DESCRIPTION**
BMP	(BitMaP) A graphics format native to Windows and the Windows applications created by Microsoft. Widely used on PCs but not Macs.
PICT	(PICTure) The native format defined by Apple for the Mac. Widely used on Macs but not PCs.
TIFF	(Tagged Image File Format) Bitmap format defined in 1986 by Microsoft and Aldus. Widely used on both Macs and PCs.
JPEG	(Joint Photographic Experts Group) A bitmap format common on the World Wide Web and often used for photos that will be viewed on screen.
GIF	(Graphic Interchange Format) A format developed by CompuServe. Like JPEG images, GIF images are often found on World Wide Web pages.

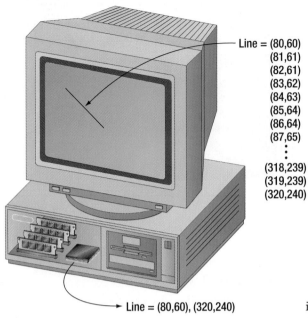

Line = (80,60)
(81,61)
(82,61)
(83,62)
(84,63)
(85,64)
(86,64)
(87,65)
⋮
(318,239)
(319,239)
(320,240)

Line = (80,60), (320,240)

To the monitor, a line is just a long list of individual pixels. With vector-based software, however, the CPU can represent the same line using just the end points.

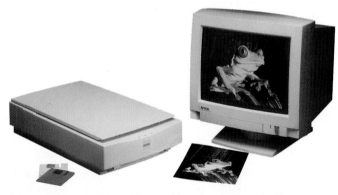

A scanner is a valuable tool for graphic artists, because it allows them to convert printed images into bitmapped files that can be stored on a computer and manipulated with graphics software.

A digital camera takes pictures just like a traditional camera. The difference is that the digital camera stores the image as a bitmapped file rather than an exposed piece of film.

simple lines and shapes into complex graphics. However, when using high-end graphics software, it is probably more common to begin with an existing image. If the image you start with is already a graphic file, then getting it into your computer is a matter of importing the file into the program that you want to use. Doing so simply requires that your program understands the file format in which the graphic is stored. There are, however, other building blocks with which you can start. The most common are clip art and printed images that you digitize (convert from an analog format to a digital one) using a scanner. If you do not have an image, you can use a digital camera to capture something in the real world quickly and import it into your computer.

Scanners and Cameras

A scanner is a little bit like a photocopy machine, except that instead of copying the image to paper, it transfers the image directly into the computer. If the image is on paper or a slide, a scanner can convert it into a digital file that a computer can manipulate. The scanner is attached to the computer by a cable and controlled by software that is often included with the graphics program. The result of scanning an image is a bitmap file (although software tools are available for translating these images into vector formats).

Digital cameras are another way to import images into a computer. These devices store digitized images in memory for transfer into a computer. Many are quite small and easy to use and include software and cables for the transfer process. Once again, the resulting file is generally a bitmap.

Advanced digital cameras have become very useful to a number of creative professionals mostly because they save the time, expense, and inconvenience of developing film and creating prints in a darkroom. Newspaper photographers use expensive versions to take pictures of late-breaking events, thereby saving the time it would take to develop film. Catalog photographers use digital cameras to record and store images of products directly into the same computers that are used to create their catalogs. Less expensive digital cameras are great for artists who need a quick picture for an illustration.

Electronic Photographs

Today, graphic artists use traditional photos translated into digital formats more often than they use photos from digital cameras. Digitizing a photo always involves some type of scanner, but the process has become very sophisticated in recent years.

Most often, professional-quality photos that need to be digitized are sent to special processing labs that scan the image and save the resulting file in a format called PhotoCD. Kodak created the **PhotoCD**, or **PCD**, format as a standard means for recording photographic images and storing them on a compact disk.

In fact, when you shoot a roll of film, you can now take the roll to almost any film developer, and they can send it out to be stored on a PhotoCD. In a few days, you can pick up the CD, take it home, and see the images on your computer (assuming you have a CD-ROM drive that is PhotoCD-compatible, which most are). Then, you can paste the photos into your electronic documents or manipulate the images with graphics software.

Today, there are many professional photographers who use PhotoCD, as well as many businesses that sell or distribute photos or samples of photos.

Clip Art

For the nonartist, or for the artist looking for an easy way to start or enhance digital artwork, clip art is available from many vendors. The term "clip art" originated with the existence of large books filled with page after page of professionally created drawings and graphics that could be cut out, or "clipped," from the pages and glued to a paper layout. Today, clip art is commonly available on CD-ROM, diskettes, or via commercial online services, and clip art can be found in both bitmap and vector formats. The variety of clip art is huge, ranging from simple line drawings and cartoons to lush paintings and photographs. People, animals, plants, architecture, maps, borders, patterns, textures, and business symbols are but a few of the many categories.

Clip art is valuable because it is relatively inexpensive, readily available, easy to use with graphics software, and generally of high quality. For example, if you are looking for a picture of a truck and you lack the skills or time to draw one yourself, you can simply copy a clip art drawing into your file. Clip art also can be used as a basis for larger pieces of artwork. When you need a map of Florida, which would you rather do—draw it by hand, or import a professionally rendered image with your graphics software? Answer this question, and you will understand why computerized clip art is so popular.

Copyright Issues

The ease with which computer users can acquire and manipulate images has brought another issue to the fore—copyright. Although clip art is often licensed for unlimited use, most images that you see in print or on screen are not. Instead, they are owned by the creator

The computer shown here is used to convert pictures and store them on PhotoCDs. The large tower unit to the woman's left scans photo film and stores the image as a bitmap. The box on the right side of the picture is the PhotoCD recorder.

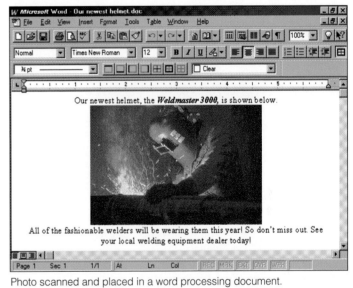

Photo scanned and placed in a word processing document.

All of these images come from a company that sells professionally made photographs. Buyers can purchase a bitmap image and copy it from a PhotoCD, or they can order a slide or print from the company.

Digital photography is taking the modern graphics industry by storm. Digital photos can be seen in just the minutes it takes to upload the image from your camera to your computer. Plus, you can alter the picture you just took—instantly!

A digital camera, also called a filmless camera, records images on a stamp-sized photosensitive semiconductor chip called a charge-coupled device (CCD) instead of the light-sensitive silver halide crystals of traditional photography. Physically, the structure of the camera is similar to a film-based camera, with lens, shutter, and diaphragm.

Currently, digital cameras are more expensive than film-based cameras, and the image quality they produce is generally far less satisfactory, especially with entry-level models. High-end digital cameras can produce excellent image quality with higher resolution and greater color depth.

Although prices of digital cameras are falling as digital technology advances, basic consumer models still have a way to go before they match film cameras in quality. Enlarged digital images often exhibit artifacts (stray marks) and pixelization (blotchy patches and sawtooth edges).

So why would the general consumer want to use a digital camera? One big reason is to make Web pages. Web publishing does not require high-quality imaging, and it's a lot of fun to post your own pictures on your Web page. There are motion video digital cameras on the market that allow you to post your home videos (saved in a format like QuickTime) on your Web site, too.

Another big use of digital photography is for business applications where immediacy is important. For example, law-enforcement personnel, insurance field agents, building inspectors, real

Lower-end digital camera by Connectix and serial cable for connecting to the computer.

Portable high-end digital camera.

estate agents, and security personnel all use digital cameras to obtain visual records of particular scenes.

Images for all sorts of documents such as newsletters, brochures, presentations, and school projects can also be done quite well with a digital camera.

Taking a digital picture is easy, as most digital cameras are simple point-and-shoot devices. You start by snapping the shutter of your digital camera just as you would a regular camera.

However, the image-saving process is quite different. In a digital camera, light strikes the CCD cells inside the camera, and activates them electronically. Digital data is then created by the circuitry in the camera. This data is compressed and saved to the camera's memory in the form of pixels, or picture elements.

Unlike film cameras, most digital cameras let you erase the most recent picture so you don't waste your camera's memory on unwanted shots.

The digital images must then be uploaded electronically to your PC. This is a fairly straightforward process of connecting camera and computer via a serial cable. Then you use the software program that comes bundled with the camera to send your images to your hard disk, where you can open the files

and see your pictures immediately. The process currently takes from five to twenty minutes.

With a modem and a cellular phone, it's possible for you to be anywhere in the world, say on a cruise ship in the South Pacific, and instantly transmit images to anywhere in the world, say to downtown Manhattan.

One of the most startling aspects of digital photography is that you can alter your images. You can cut and paste, crop or resize, change perspective, and colors and create all kinds of special effects.

To do all this, you need an image editor software program. These programs vary in sophistication from simple editors that come bundled with the digital camera or your computer operating system, to extremely sophisticated professional graphics programs such as Adobe Photoshop.

Look for inexpensive, disposable digital cameras and camcorders soon. The baby books and family albums of the future may very well be viewed on computer screens.

or publisher of the image, and are licensed for publication in a specific place for a set number of times. This means, for example, that if you scan a photograph from a magazine, place it in your work, and sell it to someone else, you are infringing on a copyright and could be fined or prosecuted. If you want to use an image you did not create solely on your own, and it is not part of a clip art package, you must contact the copyright holder for permission. Copyright law is complicated and there are many gray areas. If you are ever unsure, it is best to contact a lawyer or the person who created the image.

These six images are clip art.

▶ GRAPHICS SOFTWARE

Creating a digital image, or manipulating an existing one, can involve a huge variety of processes. No single piece of graphics software is capable of performing all the possible functions. In fact, there are five major categories of graphics software:

- Paint software
- Photo-manipulation software
- Draw software
- Computer-aided drafting (CAD) software
- 3-D modeling software

Of the five, the first two are bitmap-based paint programs, and the rest are vector-based draw programs. Grasping this difference will help you understand how artists use each type of program and why.

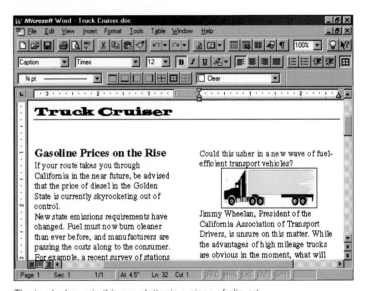

The truck shown in this newsletter is a piece of clip art.

Paint Programs

With software tools that have names like paintbrush, pen, chalk, watercolors, airbrush, crayon, and eraser, paint programs have a very familiar feel. However, since paint programs keep track of each and every pixel placed on a screen, they also can do things that are impossible with traditional artists' tools—for example, erasing a single pixel or creating instant copies of an image.

Paint programs lay down pixels in a process comparable to covering a floor with tiny mosaic tiles. Changing an image created with a paint program is like scraping tiles off the floor and replacing them with different tiles. This dot-by-dot approach allows a high degree of flexibility, but it has a few drawbacks. For example, once you create a circle or make an electronic brush stroke, you can erase or tinker with the individual pixels, making minor adjustments until the image is exactly what you want. On the other hand, you cannot change the entire circle or stroke as a whole, especially if you have painted over it. That is because the software does not think of bitmaps as a circle or brush stroke after they are created. They are simply a collection of pixels.

Paint programs are also not well suited to handling text. Even though many provide an easy way to add text to an image, once that text is placed it becomes just another

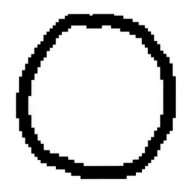

This circle was created using a paint program. As a result, the program has stored each tiny dot as separate information. The dots are not associated with each other, so the circle cannot be selected and moved.

Pencil pointer ——

To Do List:

This text has been converted to a bitmap. Consequently, you cannot erase it letter by letter. You have to erase the group of pixels that form each letter. The pencil pointer shown here is erasing each dot that makes up the *T*.

collection of pixels. This means that if you misspell a word, you cannot simply backspace over the faulty text and retype it. You must erase the word completely and start over.

These limitations aside, paint programs provide the tools to create some spectacular effects. As shown in Figure 11.3, some programs can make brush strokes that appear thick or thin, soft or hard, drippy or neat, opaque or transparent.

FIGURE 11.3
Painting tools in Fractal Design Painter.

Each of the buttons on this palette gives the artist a different tool, and therefore a different effect. There are pencils, pens, chalk, crayons, and an airbrush.

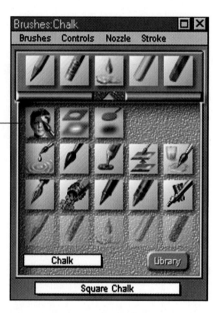

Some programs allow you to change media with a mouse click, turning your paintbrush into a chalk or a crayon, or giving your smooth "canvas" a texture like rice paper or an eggshell.

Unusual special effects abound in paint programs. For example, you can convert a scanned photograph into a pencil sketch or make it look like a Van Gogh oil painting, as shown in Figure 11.4.

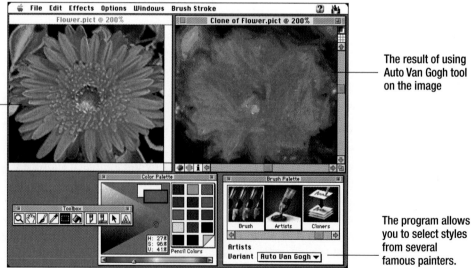

Original bitmap image

The result of using Auto Van Gogh tool on the image

The program allows you to select styles from several famous painters.

FIGURE 11.4
Photographic image, converted into a bitmap that resembles a Van Gogh painting.

Imagine how boring magazines and newspapers would be without pictures. How about your own publications? Do you often wish your documents had more personality?

You may not think of yourself as a publisher, but almost everyone these days "publishes" some kinds of documents—newsletters, brochures, business presentations, school papers, résumés, or letters ranging from job applications to family updates. Soon, you might expand your horizons to include multimedia projects or Web pages.

No matter how simple or complicated your projects are, art will enhance and enliven them. But what if you're no artist? The solution: clip art.

Clip art is a collection of electronic sketches, logos, and pictures which you can purchase, usually on CD. Or you can download shareware versions of clip art from the Internet. Also, some word processing programs, such as the latest versions of Word, come bundled with clip art. To use clip art in your documents, you just search through these digital collections using an "image browser" or cataloging software which may be part of the clip art collection. You just select the images you want to use and then copy, paste, or import them into your document just as you would text.

Image editing software is available if you wish to alter the art in various ways, such as smoothing lines, changing color, or deleting unwanted parts.

Most clip art is "royalty free," which means that you do not have to pay any rights fees to use it. You can print a piece of clip art to hang on your wall, publish it in your best-selling book, or post it on your Web site, all without paying anything more than the original price of the clip art program.

In this newly emerging age of multimedia, you may want more than just pictures in your projects. For example,

Images like these are available in clip art collections.

wouldn't it be fun to include a sound clip of a trumpet in your letters to your family to call attention to your infrequent letters? Or how about including a video clip of a busy office in your business proposal? Or, wouldn't it be a great attention getter to have an animated monster pop up in the children's story you're writing?

All of the these examples are possible through the use of clip media, which is becoming increasingly popular as the development of multimedia and Web pages increases. Clip media requires more sophisticated software and hardware than clip art, but it can add a dramatic, unforgettable flourish to your projects.

What should you look for when you buy clip art or clip media? The first criterion, of course, is what type of images you want. Some compilations have a specific focus, such as the environment, holidays, or sports. There are also soup-to-nuts collections containing all kinds of unrelated images. You can find clip art collections in catalogs, computer magazines, online, or at computer stores.

Here is a list of other criteria to consider:

System Compatibility. Know whether the collection is PC- or Mac-based, although some CDs these days work on both platforms. Make sure your system and your software will support the collection.

CD or floppy. If you're going to use much art, you'll want a CD-ROM drive. You can buy thousands of clips on a CD for as little as $10.

Get a good image browser. Try to get a collection with a good browser bundled in the package (most do).

Documentation. Look for a collection that comes with a hard copy visual index so you can see all the images before you print them.

Numbers aren't everything. Don't be swayed just by sheer numbers of images. Some clip art CDs are crammed with low-resolution, poor clips that you will probably never use.

Try experimenting with all kinds of clip media in your documents. Soon, your projects will sparkle with new life, and you'll be able to express yourself in new ways.

This image was created using software tools that mimic the use of watercolors.

This image was created using software tools that mimic the use of chalk.

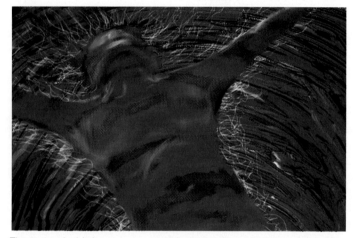

The texture in this image was created with a software tool that seems to repaint images with a blurring brush.

It is also possible to change the apparent lighting source, distort the image through a lens, and warp, curl, or marbleize it. Adobe SuperPaint and Fractal Design Painter are examples of paint programs.

Photo-Manipulation Programs

When scanners made it easy to transfer photographs to the computer at high resolution, a new class of software was needed to manipulate these images on the screen. A cousin of paint programs, **photo-manipulation programs** now take the place of a photographer's darkroom for many tasks. Although they are most often used for simple jobs such as sharpening focus or adjusting contrast, they are also used to modify photographs in ways far beyond the scope of a traditional darkroom. The picture shown in Figure 11.5, for example, has obviously been subjected to electronic manipulation.

Because photo-manipulation programs edit images at the pixel level, just as paint programs do, they can control precisely how a picture will look. They are also used to edit nonphotographic images and to create images from scratch. The advent of photo-manipulation programs has caused an explosion in the use of computers to modify images. Adobe Photoshop, Corel Photo Paint, and Micrografx Picture Publisher are some popular photo-manipulation programs.

FIGURE 11.5

This image demonstrates how a photo-manipulation program can be used to combine a traditional black-and-white photograph (the woman's face) with computer-generated graphic effects.

Photo-manipulation programs can accomplish some amazing things. After a photograph has been brought into the computer, usually by scanning or from a PhotoCD, the user can change or enhance the photo at will, down to individual pixels. For example, if a photo has dust spots, or someone's eyes look red from a flash, the airbrush tool can draw just the right number of appropriately colored pixels delicately into the affected areas to correct the problem (see Figure 11.6).

Small or large color corrections can be made in just seconds or minutes—for an entire photo or just a part of it. If someone's face appears too dark or too washed out, software tools can reveal hidden details—a job that formerly required minutes or hours in a darkroom.

FIGURE 11.6

Repairing a scratched image with an airbrush tool.

White lines come from scratches on the original film.

The airbrush tool can be used to smooth over sharp lines.

Photo-manipulation programs also contain tools that can alter the original image drastically, in effect causing photos to lie. For example, if a photograph of a group of people has been scanned into the computer, special tools can erase the pixels that form the image of one of these people, and replace them with pixels from the background area—effectively removing the person from the photo. There are even tools that can move objects in a scene or create a collage of several different images.

Today, almost every photograph you see in print has been scanned into a computer and enhanced by photo-manipulation programs. Most of the time, these changes are restricted to slight color corrections or to the removal of dust, but the potential for larger alterations is still there. The adage "photos don't lie" has become a relic of the past. In a society where image is everything, photo-manipulation programs represent genuine

Notice that the keyhole in this photo has been partially erased and replaced with parts of a new background—the cow.

The original photograph used to create this image was under-exposed. As a result, the balloon appears very dark. However, the top part of the balloon has been manipulated with a dodge tool that brightens some of the colors.

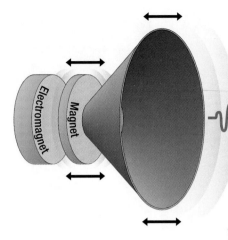

The hardware illustrations in this book were created using a draw program called Adobe Illustrator.

power. How far photo illustration artists will go, and in what direction, is limited only by their imagination and tempered only by their desire for credibility. Many newspapers and magazines have established written guidelines that limit the kinds of changes a photograph can undergo to include only the removal of dust spots or the correction of an unnatural cast of color.

Photo-manipulation programs are capable of outputting images at very high resolutions, producing output that is indistinguishable from a darkroom-produced photograph. What this means is that to make best use of most photo-manipulation programs, you need a powerful computer—one with a fast microprocessor, lots of RAM and storage space, and a high-quality display. All of this hardware does not come cheap, with the result that many people who have photo-manipulation programs are not capable of using the programs to their fullest extent.

Draw Programs

Draw programs are well suited for work where accuracy and flexibility are as important as gorgeous coloring and special effects. Although they do not possess the pixel-pushing capability of paint programs, they can be used to create images with an "arty" look and have been adopted by many designers as their primary tool. You see their output in everything from cereal box designs to television show credits, from business cards to newspapers. Macromedia FreeHand, Adobe Illustrator, and Corel-Draw are some popular draw programs.

Draw programs work by defining every line as a mathematical equation, or vector. Sometimes, draw programs are referred to as object-oriented programs because each item drawn, whether it be a line, square, rectangle, or circle, is treated as a separate and distinct object from all the others. For example, when you draw a square with a draw program, the computer remembers it as a square of a fixed size and not as a bunch of pixels that are in the shape of a square.

Draw programs offer two very big advantages over paint programs. The first is that when objects are created, they remain objects to the computer. After you draw a circle, you can return to it later and move it intact by dragging it with the mouse, even if it has been covered over with other shapes or lines. You can change the circle's shape into an oval or you can fill its interior with a color, a blend of colors, or a pattern.

Because this circle was created with a draw program, it can be filled with a color (black, in this case), moved, and copied.

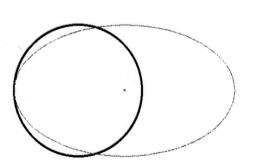

Simply by clicking and dragging, you can change a circle into an oval.

The other big advantage draw programs have is the ability to resize images easily, so that they match the dimensions of the paper on which they will be printed. Because bitmap images consist of a grid of dots, the only way to control the size of the image is to adjust the resolution, the number of dots per inch. However, lowering the resolution to make an image larger can make the image visibly rougher.

Vector graphics, on the other hand, are much easier to resize. The software mathematically changes all of the objects so they appear larger or smaller. When this is done, there is no change in the resolution, so there is no loss in the image's quality.

For similar reasons, draw programs are also superior to paint programs in their handling of text. Because the computer treats text characters as objects rather than as collections of dots, the text can be colored, shaded, scaled, tilted, or even joined to a curvy line with very little effort.

Today, however, the distinction between draw programs and paint programs is blurring very quickly. Attributes of paint programs have been incorporated into draw programs and vice versa, producing some software packages that can be used to handle almost any task involving graphic images. For example, most draw programs now include the ability to import photos or art created with paint programs, although for the most part they lack the ability to edit them at the pixel level.

Draw programs make it easy to color text.

Lines of text can be bent or distorted with draw programs.

Text can also be forced to follow a curvy line.

Computer-Aided Drafting Programs

Computer-Aided Drafting (CAD), also known as Computer-Aided Drawing or Computer-Aided Design, is the computerized version of the hand drafting process that used to be done with a pencil and ruler on a drafting table. Over the last 15 years, the drafting process has been almost completely computerized, as CAD programs have become easier to use and have offered more features. CAD is used extensively in technical fields, such as architecture, and in mechanical, electrical, and industrial engineering.

Unlike drawings made using paint or drawing programs, CAD drawings are usually the basis for the actual building or manufacturing process—a house, an engine gear, or an electrical system. To satisfy the rigorous requirements of manufacturing, CAD programs provide a high degree of precision. If you want to draw a line that is 12.396754 inches or a circle with a radius of .90746 centimeters, a CAD program can fulfill your needs.

This sextant was created using AutoCAD, a popular CAD program from Autodesk.

Another important feature of CAD programs is their ability to define layers, which are like transparent layers of film that you can place on top of each other. Layers permit CAD users to organize very complex drawings. For example, a structural engineer designing an office building might create layers such as Electrical, Plumbing,

Courtesy of Autodesk

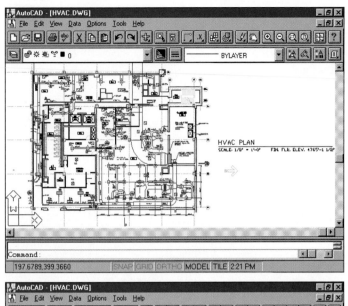

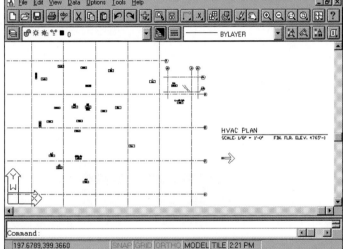

At the top is a complete HVAC (Heating, Ventilation and Air Conditioning) plan for a building. This figure shows a single layer of the plan.

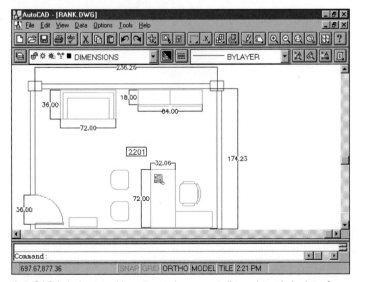

AutoCAD is being used here to produce exact dimensions, in inches, for an office floor plan.

Structural, and so on. The engineer can then show and hide these individual layers while different parts of the building are designed.

All CAD programs have the capability to add dimensions to a drawing. Dimensions are notations showing the measurements of an object and are usually placed on their own layer. Dimensioning is essential to the process of actually building or manufacturing the object being drawn. Most CAD programs can also perform calculations on your drawings. For example, they can calculate the area of a living room or the volume of a storage tank.

Most CAD programs also include (or offer as an extra) different ways to display or print 3-D objects. For example, **wireframe models** represent 3-D shapes by displaying their outlines and edges. Figure 11.7 shows an example.

FIGURE 11.7
Wireframe model.

For a solid-looking representation of the object, CAD programs can **render** the image, shading in the solid parts and creating output that looks almost real. Figure 11.8 shows a rendered image.

FIGURE 11.8
A rendered image.

Finally, advanced CAD software offers the ability to create a database from a drawing. This can be used to create the list of materials needed in the manufacturing process.

Hard copies of CAD drawings are usually created on plotters rather than on printers. Plotters can handle the large sheets of paper used for technical drawings and may use a different pen for each layer of the drawing.

Because CAD is such an essential part of the manufacturing process, it is often the first step in Computer-Aided Manufacturing (CAM). A CAD drawing can be turned into numerical code, which is then read by a cutting machine that cuts metal, stone, and other materials into the shape that was drawn.

CAD programs often come in different versions, depending on how many features are included. Full-featured programs can cost $2,000 or more, but the less expensive versions may fulfill your needs, and they start at about $100. The most popular program for professional engineers is Autodesk's AutoCAD. It is a full-featured program with 3-D rendering, programming language, and database capabilities. Other CAD programs include Drafix, AutoCAD LT, AutoSKETCH, CADKEY, Visio CAD, and Intergraph Microstation.

3-D Modeling Programs

Whether you are aware of it or not, you are constantly exposed to elaborate 3-D imaging in movies, television, and print. Many of these images are now created with a special

This architect is printing detailed building plans using a plotter.

type of graphics software, called **3-D modeling software**, which enables users to create electronic models of 3-dimensional objects without using CAD software. Fast workstations or PCs coupled with 3-D modeling programs have the ability to lend realism to even the most fantastic subjects. Widely used 3-D modeling programs include 3-D Studio, MacroModel, Ray Dream Designer, and Strata StudioPro.

There are four different types of 3-D modeling programs: surface, solid, polygonal, and spline-based. Each of the different types uses a different technique to create 3-dimensional objects. **Surface modelers** build objects by stretching a surface—like a skin—over an underlying wire-frame structure. **Solids modelers** do the same thing as surface modelers, but also understand thickness and density. This can be important if you need to punch a hole through an electronic object. **Polygonal modelers** combine many tiny polygons to build objects—similar to the way one would build a geodesic dome out of many perfectly fitted triangles.

Myst® is a registered trademark of Cyan, Inc. Copyright ©1993 Cyan, Inc.

3-D modeling can be used to create surrealistic landscapes, such as this scene from the game Myst.

This gear is an example of a CAD model rendered with surface modeling techniques.

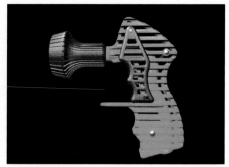

This CAD model of a spray nozzle for a hose was created using solids modeling techniques.

The structure supporting this bridge demonstrates how polygonal modeling techniques can be used.

Spline-based modelers build objects, either surface or solid, using mathematically defined curves, which are rotated on an axis to form a 3-D shape.

Regardless of their method of creation, 3-D objects can be modified to any shape using electronic tools akin to those used in woodworking. Just as wood can be cut, drilled, shaped, and sanded, objects created with a 3-D modeling program can be changed or molded with the click of a mouse. For example, holes can be drilled into computer-based 3-D objects, and corners can be made round or square by selecting the appropriate menu item. 3-D objects also can be given realistic textures and patterns, animated, or made to fly through space.

Because 3-D modeling places very high demands on hardware, it has long been the province of those who can afford workstations or ultra-high-end personal computers. Creative professionals believe that 3-D modeling programs are the wave of the future. As capable computers become less expensive, making the leap from realistic 2-D drawing to more realistic 3-D modeling will become even easier.

Using high-end workstations, architects, engineers, and artists create ever-more-complex objects with 3-D modeling software.

NORTON WORKSHOP: CREATING AN INFOGRAPHIC

Daily newspapers use graphics software for many purposes. At most newspapers, all of the photographs are cropped and color-corrected with photo-manipulation programs. Many advertisements are created with draw and paint programs. The design of individual section openers, such as the sports page, includes elements created with draw programs. Artists in editorial art departments use draw, paint, and photo-manipulation programs to create explanatory graphics that help readers understand the day's news.

Graphics journalists work under daily deadline pressure to create drawings called informational graphics, or **infographics**. To give you a better idea of how that is done, this Norton Workshop will take you step-by-step through the creation of a newspaper informational graphic that explains how a train derailment occurred.

Because the graphics journalist, Deanne, is unfamiliar with exactly how train tracks are put together, she takes a short walk to some train tracks near the newspaper building to take some pictures with a Polaroid camera. The photographs she takes are of the pieces of the tracks that are described in the incoming stories about the accident.

After taking the pictures, she searches through some reference books for information and drawings of the construction of train tracks. In one book she finds a perfect explanation, with a small drawing of a section of railroad track. The drawing in the book is photocopied and a flatbed scanner is used to scan the photocopied page into

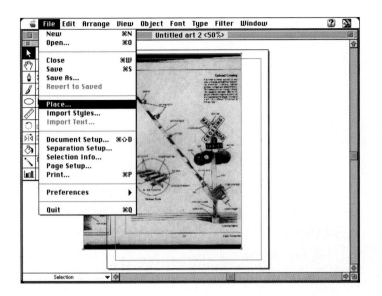

her computer. She saves the scanned image in a format her draw program can understand and brings it into the program. The imported drawing is shown in Figure 11.9.

FIGURE 11.9
The scanned image, imported into a draw program.

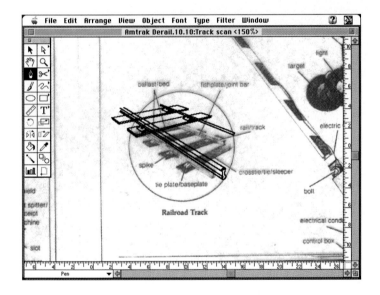

Using the **Bezier tool**, which allows the user to draw connected lines that can be manipulated into any shape, she traces over the scanned-in drawing of the railroad track (see Figure 11.10).

FIGURE 11.10
Tracing over scanned lines with the Bezier tool.

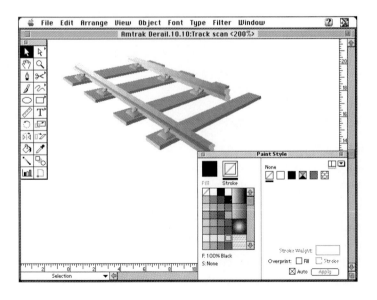

She fills in the shapes she traced with appropriate colors and also uses the blend tool to create realistic shadows (see Figure 11.11).

FIGURE 11.11
The finished tracks.

At this point, she decides that an actual photograph of the derailment scene might be helpful. She finds an aerial picture showing the train and the cars that have fallen off the tracks.

Importing photographs into draw and paint programs is easy, and she takes advantage of this capability to give readers a better idea of the overall scene along with the details of how the train became derailed. She opens the photograph with a photo-manipulation program, then crops and color-corrects it, changing the contrast and brightness to suit the output she envisions. Her results are shown in Figure 11.12.

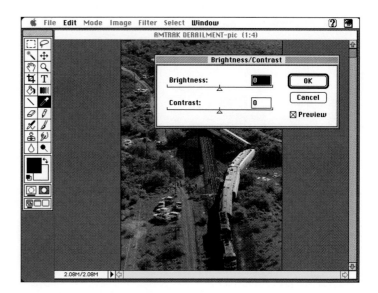

FIGURE 11.12

The derailment photo, scanned and corrected for brightness and contrast.

Deanne knows the informational graphic she is creating is going to be tall and narrow and that she needs to show the details of the railroad drawing. She uses the levels command in the photo-manipulation program to create a fog-like effect on either side of the picture of the derailment scene as shown in Figure 11.13. This lightens the background so that the text and train track drawing will be clearly readable.

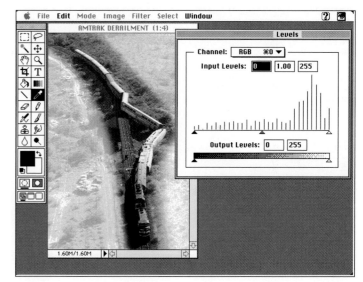

FIGURE 11.13

Lightening the background to make room for the drawing of the tracks.

By selecting the area that she does not want to change, and then inverting it, Deanne is able to affect just the areas she has selected. She then saves the file and imports it into the draw program document (see Figure 11.14).

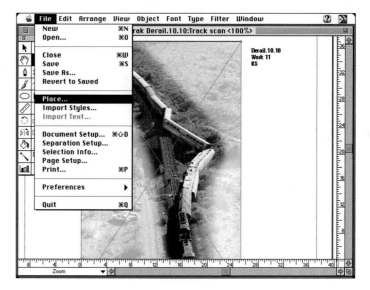

FIGURE 11.14

The drawings of the train tracks are behind the photo. After the photo is placed, the drawings are brought to the foreground.

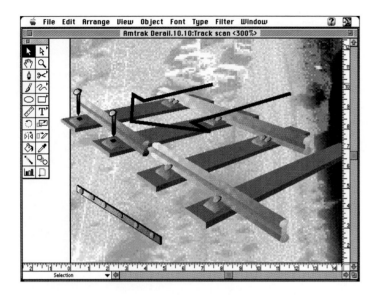

In the draw program, she duplicates the drawing of the railroad track she had made earlier, moves it below the original, and uses the knife tool to "cut" a piece of the railroad track to show the break created by the saboteurs who caused the crash. Then she uses the Bezier tool again to draw some spikes and a bar that held the track together. She then draws a directional arrow to show how the railroad track was moved (see Figure 11.15).

FIGURE 11.15
Details added to the tracks to show sabotage.

By this time, some descriptive text has been prepared to fit over other areas of the drawing, providing a short narrative for the reader to follow. Figure 11.16 shows where she places the text.

FIGURE 11.16
Text placed around drawings and photo.

Next, she adds a headline for the graphic and credit lines at the bottom of the completed drawing, and then prints it on a high-resolution laser printer for proofreading (see Figure 11.17).

FIGURE 11.17
A part of the finished illustration.

Finally, she transfers the graphic as a computer data file over the newspaper's network to be added to the completed page.

The description above is a good example of what an accomplished artist can do by combining the capabilities of different types of graphics software. Freedom is one of the most important advantages that current graphics software has provided for artists. As you have seen, a photograph worked on by a photo-manipulation program can be seamlessly and quickly transported into a draw program. Conversely, work created by a draw or paint program can be imported into a photo-manipulation or even a 3-D program. Artists have become experts in adding computers and software to their repertoire of tools. As they push the boundaries of what can be done, we will all benefit from the increased sophistication and beauty of the many images that surround us in the modern world.

▶ WHAT TO EXPECT IN THE FUTURE

Graphics software has already become an extremely sophisticated field. In fact, this chapter has barely scratched the surface of the many technical issues involved in creating and manipulating digital images. As a result, many of the upcoming developments in graphics software are also extremely technical and may appear in highly specialized programs. There are, however, two trends that are likely to accelerate in the most common graphics software packages.

The first is the integration of paint features into draw programs and vice versa. Each type, in its pure form, has important limitations. Users who need flexibility generally need both types. Naturally, programs that can combine the best of both types successfully are attractive for reasons of convenience and price.

The other emerging trend is in the area of graphics software providing animation features. In an animated series of frames, objects appear to move smoothly if they move a short distance in each successive frame. Graphics software can help you to create this effect of motion by supplying tools that allow you to see a series of frames at the same time. In addition, the software must let the user set the speed at which the frames will be displayed. Furthermore, animated images and video images have their own file formats, the most common being AVI, the Windows video standard, and MOV, also known as QuickTime. Graphics packages that provide tools for creating animation and video also will provide the ability to save files in these formats.

▶ VISUAL SUMMARY

Working with Images

- Most graphics software is available for different computer platforms, including both Macs and PCs. Some software is available only for workstations.
- Paint programs work with bitmaps. Draw programs work with vectors.
- The most common bitmap formats are BMP, PICT, TIFF, JPEG, and GIF. The most widely used vector format is Encapsulated Postscript, or EPS.
- Scanners, digital cameras, and clip art are three ways to input art into the computer.
- Professional-quality photographs are often stored on PhotoCD.
- Copyright issues are an important concern if artwork produced by someone else is to be used.

Graphics Software

- The five main categories of graphics software are paint programs, photo-manipulation programs, draw programs, CAD software, and 3-D modeling programs.
- Paint programs include tools like paintbrushes, ink and felt pens, chalk, and watercolors.
- Paint programs are not well suited to applications that require a lot of text.
- The specialty of paint programs is very natural and realistic effects that mimic art produced via traditional methods.
- Photo-manipulation programs have replaced many tools a photographer uses.
- Photo-manipulation programs can exert pixel-level control over photographs and images.

- With photo-manipulation programs, photographs can be altered with no evidence of alteration.
- Draw programs are well suited to applications where flexibility is important.
- Objects created with draw programs can be altered and changed easily.

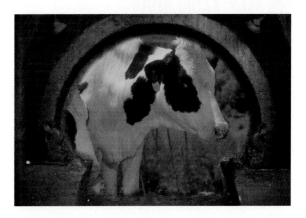

- Draw programs work with text very well.
- Computer-Aided Drafting (CAD) software is used in technical fields, such as architecture and engineering, to create models of objects that are going to be built.
- CAD software allows users to design objects in three dimensions.
- Output from CAD software can appear as a wireframe model or as a rendered object, which appears solid.

- 3-D modeling programs are used to create spectacular visual effects.
- 3-D modeling programs work by creating objects via surface, solids, polygonal, or spline-based methods.

▶ KEY TERMS

After completing this chapter, you should be able to define the following terms:

3-D modeling software, 337
Bezier tool, 340
bitmap, 324
BMP, 325
Computer-Aided Drafting (CAD), 335
draw program, 324
Encapsulated Postscript (EPS), 325
GIF, 325

infographic, 339
JPEG, 325
paint program, 324
PhotoCD (PCD), 326
photo-manipulation program, 332
PICT, 325
pixel, 324
polygonal modeler, 337

Postscript, 322
render, 336
solids modeler, 337
spline-based modeler, 338
surface modeler, 337
TIFF, 325
vector, 324
wireframe model, 336

► KEY TERM QUIZ

Fill in the blank with one of the terms listed in Key Terms.

1. Graphics programs that work with bitmaps are called _____.

2. A 3-D modeling program that also understands thickness and density is known as a(n)_____

3. With CAD programs you can produce _____ to represent 3-D shapes.

4. You can also _____ a solid-looking representation of an object using a CAD program.

5. A special type of graphics software used to create electronic models of three-dimensional objects is called _____.

6. To build an object by stretching a surface over a wire-frame structure, you would choose a(n) _____.

7. Graphics files are composed of either bitmaps or a set of _____.

8. _____ combine many tiny polygons to build objects.

9. A(n) _____ builds objects using curves which are rotated on an axis to form a 3-D shape.

10. Graphics journalists create drawings called _____.

► REVIEW QUESTIONS

1. According to the chapter, what two products "ushered" in the era of art on personal computers?
2. What kind of computers are the Sun SparcStation and the Silicon Graphics Indigo2, and in what ways do they benefit commercial graphic artists and designers?
3. Which kind of graphics program allows a user to work with vector images?
4. What devices can be used to convert images on paper or film into a digital file format?
5. What factors have contributed to the popularity of clip art?
6. What limitations are there with bitmap-based paint programs?
7. What distinguishing characteristic of vector images makes resizing them much easier and more precise than resizing bitmap images?
8. Describe briefly the manner in which an image rendered with a CAD program can be used as a first step in the manufacturing process? What is this process called?
9. What features are available in a CAD program that you do not find in other programs for manipulating graphic images, such as paint and draw programs?
10. List and describe the four types of 3-D modeling programs.

► DISCUSSION QUESTIONS

1. What tools and techniques, which were not required by graphic artists and illustrators in the past, do you think today's graphic artists must know and understand to be productive?

2. Discuss some of the implications that electronic retouching of photographs through the use of photo illustration software might create in today's society.

3. As cheaper and more powerful computers are developed, in what areas of our lives do you think we will see more sophisticated graphics imaging?

4. Suppose you want to be able to build a collection or library of images as you work that you can use again and again to save time when creating new images. What kind of graphics software do you think would best accomplish this? What kind of hardware requirements do you think you would need?

NORTON INTERACTIVE

Complete the Norton Interactive module for this chapter.

THE NEW MEDIA

CONTENTS

OBJECTIVES

When you complete this chapter, you will be able to do the following:

- Explain the concept of interactive multimedia and its role in new communications technologies.
- Describe the ways consumers receive multimedia content.
- Provide examples of multimedia applications for schools, businesses, and the home.
- Describe hypermedia and its role in multimedia presentations.
- Envision how you might use virtual reality.
- Explain the process of creating a multimedia presentation.
- Discuss the impact of digital convergence on the media being produced for mass consumption.

Today's high-powered yet affordable personal computers have encouraged businesses to reexamine the way they deliver information and entertainment to their customers. They invite people to explore new ways to communicate, get information, or be entertained. With text, graphics, animation, video, and sound being converted to digital signals for storage and editing on computers, these **media**—these channels for communication—can be combined to produce engaging, **multimedia** content for any audience.

For example, an encyclopedia does not have to be only pages of text and pictures. In a multimedia edition, the pictures can move and speak to the reader. By adding more media to the message, there is a greater likelihood that everyone in the audience will understand the message. If a multimedia encyclopedia can also entice the reader to participate—with a click of a mouse button or the typing of a few words on the keyboard—this new media involves its audience unlike any book, movie, or TV program.

▶ THE POWER OF INTERACTIVITY

The last time a new electronic medium captured the public's attention was in the late 1940s and early 1950s with the rapid and widespread popularity of television. Television was a new way to convey information and entertainment to a mass audience—adding moving pictures to the sounds of radio that had been coming into peoples' homes for decades.

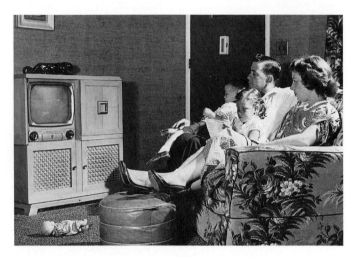

The "couch potato" appeared soon after the first televisions.

When television was introduced (and even today), critics said that presenting pictures along with sounds deprives the viewers of their powers of imagination. Instead of the audience having to visualize and imagine what the characters and scenes looked like, as in a radio drama or a book, TV programs left little to the imagination. By passively watching hour after hour of ready-to-digest material, people can become "couch potatoes," sitting silent and motionless on the sofa as programs pour out of the picture tube.

Interacting with Television

Today, the prevalence of inexpensive computers offers a way to change our passive response to electronic media. Computers make it possible to create **interactive media**, in which people can respond to—and even control—what they see and hear. Instead of passively accepting every sound bite, story line, or advertisement that appears on the video screen, viewers can become interactive users, searching for items of particular interest, digging deeper into a news story, or even choosing to view an alternative plot line for a situation comedy.

Part of the public's interest in interactivity can be directly related to the success of home video games. As millions of children and adults around the world have demonstrated, it is possible to turn off spoon-fed television programming, and instead guide a character sneaking through a 3-dimensional maze, manage a sports team on the field, or solve a computerized puzzle.

These home video games are called interactive because they include a feedback loop that does not exist in most commercial media such as television, print, and radio. Most media offer only one-way communication, as shown in Figure 12.1.

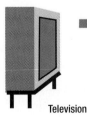

Information

Television

In a television broadcast, information flows in one direction, from the TV to the viewer.

FIGURE 12.1

Traditional media with one-way communication.

Interactive media, however, puts a computer in the hands of the viewer and thereby establish two-way communication—also known as a feedback loop. For an example, see Figure 12.2.

With a TV-based video game, the user has a computer (for example, a Sega, Nintendo, or 3DO system) and some type of controller, such as a joystick. As a result, the information that comes out of the television is constantly changing in response to the information coming from the user.

FIGURE 12.2
Interactive media with feedback loop.

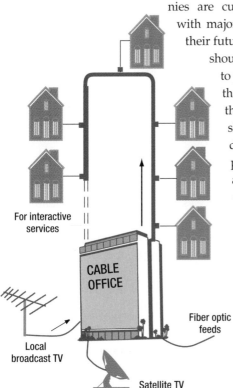

In the world of television broadcasting, however, the transition from one-way communication to two-way, interactive communication is slow. Traditional broadcast companies such as the popular television networks and cable television companies are currently wrestling with major decisions about their futures. For example, should they continue to produce programs that appeal only to the couch potato? Or should they instead develop new kinds of programming and media aimed at a generation of viewers whose appetite for interactivity has been whetted by playing with video games or personal computers? The problem of how to accommodate the interactive communication with the cable company is still a technical hurdle to be solved. Few cable systems today are equipped to handle such two-way communication.

For cable companies to provide interactive programming, they will have to extend the wiring that connects all the homes back to the cable office. This loop will establish a structure similar to the feedback loop in Figure 12.2.

Interacting with Computers

While consumers wait for the deployment of interactive television networks, many other content-delivery vehicles are already in place. Due to the large amount of information that typically is presented in an interactive production, the large electronic storage capacity of the CD-ROM has become popular for use with desktop personal computers.

Usually, each CD-ROM disk is a self-contained interactive program—a game, a self-paced learning program, or a course of instruction, such as one that shows you

Interactive video games are made for both computers and television. This game, Doom, is based on a well known formula: run through a maze of rooms and shoot at monsters.

how to add a redwood deck to your house. More interactive than just play-only videocassettes, these programs usually ask the viewers to use a mouse or keyboard to enter customized information about themselves or the problem they are trying to solve (like how to design the redwood deck to wrap around a corner of your house). The computer then uses programs and other materials on the CD-ROM disk to produce custom information just for the viewer (such as how much redwood deck planking to order).

Another increasingly popular delivery method for interactive material is a connection to an online service or the Internet. Unlike the broadcast world, commercial online services and the Internet were designed for high-volume, two-way information transfer. When a computer user connects to such a service, the service rarely does anything without some interaction—such as the user telling the service "where" to go by clicking an on screen button or typing a command. The user is entirely in control of navigating through the information.

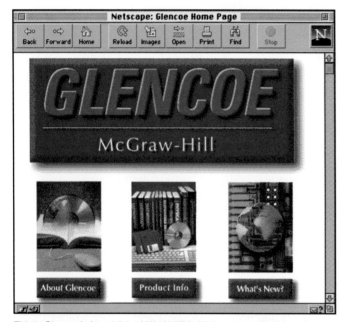

This is Glencoe's (a publisher) World Wide Web page on the Internet. Users can click on the buttons to look for related information.

Also, remember that interactivity includes interaction among real people—it is not just one individual interacting with a world of faceless computers. The most familiar form of electronic interactivity is a phone conversation. It is easy to forget, though, that a personal computer is also a communications device, letting people share ideas in a variety of forms. Connected to online services or the Internet, millions of people interact with others each day either in "live" conversations typed on the keyboard or via electronic mail.

For decades different media have been used together in various combinations in film, theater, and television. But the interactive component—where the viewer participates in the direction of action—distinguishes today's multimedia offerings from the past. Although interactive multimedia is a relatively new field, people have already identified a huge variety of potential uses.

Interactivity and Education

Education has embraced this new technology and is one of the first and best consumers of multimedia. In today's schools, multimedia computers are an integral part of many classrooms and bring a new level of interactivity to learning.

One major reform movement in education promotes active and cooperative learning. Computers and multimedia help students and teachers to make the transition to this new mode of learning. In the classroom, visual presentations that include animation, video, and sound motivate students to become active participants in the learning process. Interactive multimedia programs bring concepts to life and help students to integrate critical thinking and problem-solving skills. Some students are even learning how to create interactive term papers and projects using multimedia.

This approach to education also builds strong social skills and allows students with a wide range of learning skills to be successful. After all, some students learn best by reading, some by hearing, some by seeing, and some by doing. Teachers using

So you've finally put together your first multimedia project. What do you do with it now? There are basically two distribution vehicles for multimedia: CD-ROMs or the World Wide Web.

If you want a permanent, physical, and portable medium for your work, you will probably choose CD-ROM. Creating your own CD-ROM can seem intimidating, but taken one step at a time, it can be done even by beginners.

CDs provide an affordable storage medium—about a penny a megabyte—and, consequently, are showing up in all kinds of everyday business uses in addition to multimedia creation. This includes archiving, storage of financial data, and digital publishing.

A CD holds 650 MB of data (about 74 minutes of audio), enough to back up most hard drives with just one or two CD-ROMs, or store a database containing literally millions of records quite affordably. Also, CDs are readable worldwide on any computer with a CD drive, making them excellent transfer media.

If you plan to make your own CD, you can expect to go through the following three steps:

■ Authoring refers to the process of creating your CD content. Using authoring software, you can insert audio and video segments into your project to create interactive programs. If you are merely storing files on your CD or if your content consists of text only, you may not need authoring software.

■ Pre-mastering refers to the formatting and arranging of data to be burned onto your CD. This process is not yet as easy as the drag-and-drop process of copying files to a floppy. You will need to put files in proper recording sequence, manage data and digital audio tracks, calculate storage space required, and determine the best recording speed.

To do this, you must use a pre-mastering software program, probably the one that comes bundled with your CD-R (CD-recordable) drive, which is different from a regular CD-ROM drive.

The software manuals will probably be sufficient to guide you through the pre-mastering process.

■ Burning is the final step in which you make an actual CD that can be played in any standard CD-ROM drive. To do this you will need a CD-R drive and a blank CD.

There is a wide array of CD types to choose from, depending on what types of data you want to record: text, audio, graphics, interactive media, and various combinations. In addition to audio CDs and data CD-ROMs, other formats you will see include CD-ROM XA, Photo CD, CD-I (CD-Interactive), and Enhanced CD.

Somewhere along the line, you will probably encounter the dreaded buffer underrun. Everyone who makes a CD eventually does.

In current technology, if the flow of data between the PC and CD-R drive is interrupted for even a fraction of a second during the burning process, the disk is ruined, and you must begin again. This interruption, which can occur for all kinds of reasons, is called a buffer underrun.

The good news is that the process of making a CD is most likely going to become cheaper and easier in the near future. On the horizon are erasable disks that will be reusable just as floppy disks are today. Also, fresh off the drawing board is the DVD (digital video disk), a large-capacity CD-ROM type disk designed to hold a full-length feature movie, with enough room left for the soundtrack and an ad for T-shirts or coffee mugs.

A killer light show, multiple graphics and a hip-hop beat: Accounting cuts its first CD.

Introducing the HP SureStore CD Writer.

Excuse Accounting for acting a little cool, but they've just put together the hottest presentation in the company with the new HP SureStore CD-Writer.

And if they can do it, you can too.

The possibilities are endless. You could store an entire multimedia show, with moving images, music and graphics. Or distribute huge files, price lists, catalogs — even years of tax records. together

The HP SureStore CD-Writer has everything you need to easily create and launch your own CDs. You get 2x recording speed and a 4x reader in one. Universally accepted CDs offer 650 MB of space that can be read by millions of CD players worldwide.

So whether you're a major multimedia supplier, an in-house service, or one of those groovy cats in accounting, the HP SureStore CD-Writer is the best way to set you apart. For more information on how to cut your first CD, call 1-800-826-4111, ext. 1261.

Modern businesses use CDs for easy storage, transfer, and presentation of data.

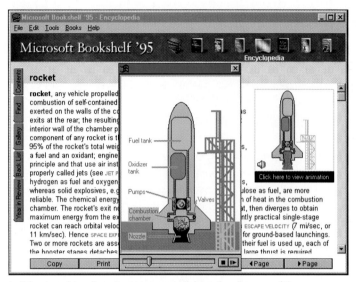

In this encyclopedia entry, users can click on the diagram of the space shuttle to see an animation of the propulsion system.

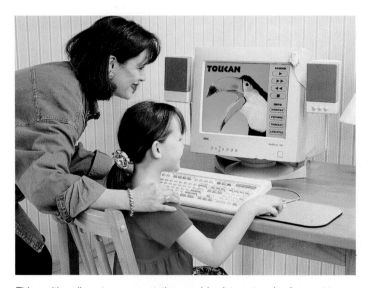

This multimedia nature presentation provides interest and enjoyment to everyone in the family.

interactive educational techniques and interactive multimedia are at the cutting edge of their profession.

One common interactive multimedia application for education is an electronic encyclopedia contained on a CD-ROM. If students have an assignment to write a report on a region of Africa, they can read about the history and geography, and at the click of the mouse button, they can see video clips of the hustle and bustle of a city, and hear audio clips of African languages or the sounds of tribal music. As a result, the information comes to life. A good encyclopedia may entice students to explore related topics with an ease and speed that would be unthinkable in a printed encyclopedia. Students may even have the software tools to produce their reports in the form of a multimedia presentation, borrowing some of the audio and video clips to illustrate their major points.

Interactive simulations can also involve the student in contemporary environmental and political issues. For example, an educational game called SimEarth lets the player make decisions about ecological issues that affect the entire planet. Screen graphics show the effects of good and bad judgments immediately. A student can try out many different scenarios to find how to balance human consumption, ecological preservation, and political issues.

Students in the same classroom and in classrooms separated by thousands of miles can collaborate on projects with the help of communications networks such as the Internet. They can share video files with each other, or see each other in a video conference to review and expand their reports. The technology exists today for students to use an electronic camera to create virtual versions of their classrooms. Students and friends elsewhere can "move" around the electronic rooms, while watching the view on a computer screen.

At the Workplace

The multimedia-equipped personal computer is the centerpiece of interactive multimedia applications in the workplace. At first, it may seem odd that media such as animation, sound, and video would play a role in business, but there is an unstoppable trend occurring to enlist these media in many aspects of a company's primary activities.

For example, training is a never-ending task in large corporations, especially as companies expect their employees to master the latest computer technologies. As a replacement for, or supplement to classroom training, many companies have developed customized interactive training materials. These materials fall into a category of products called **computer-based training (CBT)**. Training courses on company policies, customized computer systems, and customer contact are of particular interest.

Sales and marketing are taking on new meaning in the age of multimedia. Information that used to be distributed only in printed catalogs may now be available in an interactive electronic catalog, mailed to customers in CD-ROM format, or presented on a company's World Wide Web site. A clothing company, for example, has the space on a CD-ROM to let the viewer select from all the available colors of a sweater, and see the model in the catalog change sweater colors instantly.

This computer-based training program is designed to teach Windows 95.

Companies are also beginning to allow customers to preview merchandise from an interactive catalog on the World Wide Web. Customers can place orders for merchandise by filling in an on screen order form. For many marketers, this is the ultimate in interactivity: presenting the merchandise electronically, and getting an electronic order in return. No stores, parking lots, or even toll-free operators come between the company and the customer.

However, the primary focus of multimedia in business is on communication—both within the corporation and in getting the company's message out to the rest of the world. Multimedia is also helping employees to work together, even when their locations or schedules prevent face-to-face contact.

Video conferencing is no longer only the province of specially equipped meeting rooms and studios. Compact, inexpensive cameras and microphones can sit atop the desktop computer monitor, allowing two or more people to see and speak with each other by

This screen shows an interactive multimedia catalog from Lands' End. The user can click on different colors to change the color of the woman's sweater.

means of their screens. Other kinds of software allow two people to view the same document simultaneously on two computers in different parts of the world. While talking to each other over the phone or computer network, one user can circle a part of the document with the mouse, and the circle will appear in the same place on the other user's monitor.

At Home

Reference materials, self-help instruction, and entertainment packages offer many opportunities for enhancement via multimedia productions. Regardless of the

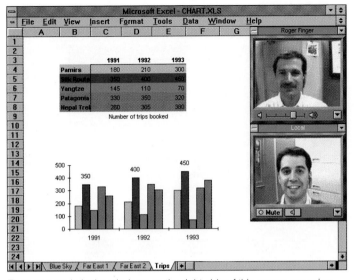

The two people in the windows on the right side of this screen are using video conferencing to discuss the information shown in the spreadsheet.

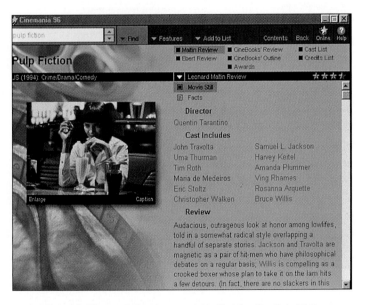

Here, Microsoft Cinemania has been used to find the film *Pulp Fiction*.

content, the goal is to engage the audience—to get the viewers to participate in the activity.

Perhaps you want some help in selecting a movie rental for the evening. Of course, you can read about a film you know by name in any of dozens of printed movie guides. However, an interactive guide such as Microsoft's Cinemania lets you search for movies by genre, performers, and other criteria that might interest you. For most of the films listed, you can often view clips or trailers, read reviews from multiple sources, and find out which other films might be related.

By far, the largest application for commercial multimedia is in the entertainment field. Video games sold on cartridges and CD-ROMs for dedicated game machines or for desktop computers are very popular. The large storage capacity of CD-ROMs often allows higher-quality animation, embedded video, lots of digital-quality sound, and a broader variety of game play.

Multimedia packages for managing money are becoming popular. For example, financial planning for retirement is not an easy task for most families. Today, you can use the Internet to connect to investment firms such as Fidelity Investments to get some guidance about planning a retirement portfolio. At Fidelity's World Wide Web site, you enter information about your current financial status, how much risk you are willing to take, and your retirement financial goals. While you are still connected, the Fidelity computer displays a report that recommends the right mix of investments to meet your requirements.

Other "how-to" multimedia offerings range from gardening to household repairs. The combinations of textual material, colorful graphics, animation, and videos of real people doing a job you are about to tackle gives you as much help as you need, and allows you to progress at your own pace.

Another interactive service is a technology called **interactive television**. In conjunction with a specially made computer connected to your television set, the remote control is used for more than just switching channels. On screen menus will allow you to select from vast libraries of movies stored in computers at your cable company office. Instead of going to the movie rental store or waiting for a cable TV movie to start at a certain time, you will be able to begin watching the movie of your choice when you want it. You even may be able to pause the transmission to cook up some more popcorn.

Careers in multimedia are as varied and as numerous as the medium itself. The sheer variety and range of what can be done in multimedia is astonishing. This can be both enlivening and overwhelming to the multimedia professional.

How is the enormity of work involved in a multimedia product accomplished? Multimedia work is usually done by teams. A project usually starts in the producer's office. The producer is the person who is responsible for initiating the project, obtaining the necessary funding, and assembling the project team. A producer may be an independent entrepreneur, or he or she may be a part of a larger company that produces multimedia projects either as its sole venture or as part of its business.

At the helm of a multimedia project is the creative director, who is responsible for developing and refining the overall design process from start to finish. The creative director is also responsible for integrating that design process into the developmental process of the company.

The team members of a multimedia project usually include some or all of the following:

- **Art Director**—directs the creation of all art for the project. This involves a variety of original media, such as drawings, computer-generated art, paintings, photographs, animation, video, even sculpture. All of this divergent art must wind up in digital form for manipulation on the modern artist's "canvas," the computer.
- **Technical Lead**—assures that the technological process of a project works, and that it accommodates all project components and media.
- **Interface Designer**—directs the development of the user interface for a product, which includes not only what users see, but also what they hear and touch.

Interface designers are concerned with information design (how the information is organized and presented), interaction design (how the user encounters and interacts with the information), and sensory design (how all the various media work together).

- **Instructional Designer**—designs the pedagogy, or instructional system for how material is taught, if the product is educational.
- **Visual Designer**—creates the various art forms, usually within a specialized area such as graphic design, calligraphy, illustration, photography, image manipulation, or typesetting.
- **Game Designer**—designs interactive games. A game may be an independent project, or part of a larger whole.
- **Interactive Scriptwriter**—a writer who weaves the project content among various media and forms of interactivity. A multimedia scriptwriter is part writer and part interactive designer.
- **Animator**—like the multimedia stars who made the dinosaurs come to life in *Jurassic Park*. Animators used to work from models, but today, the more economical 3-D computer-generated art is becoming increasingly popular. 2-D animators turn static images into a display of motion, minus the added dimension of depth found in 3-D animation.
- **Sound Producer**—part manager, part creative artist, and part programmer. A sound producer designs and produces all sounds within a product, including musical scores, vocals, voice-overs, and sound effects, and makes sure each sound interacts correctly with all the other media.
- **Videographer**—creates the video footage that interfaces with the interactive technology of the product. Video is often the most complex, time consuming, and resource-demanding media to create.
- **Programmer/Software Designer**—designs and creates the underlying software that runs a multimedia program and carries out the user's commands.

Multimedia products are usually produced by teams working in close coordination.

▶ THE NEW MEDIA

Traditional media companies—print publishing, music publishing, and broadcasting—have been in the business of delivering information and entertainment for a long time. With the recent popularity of consumer-priced multimedia computers, however, these companies have begun to search for ways to repackage their existing content to take advantage of the new technologies. Many companies are also developing content in a form that better matches the capabilities of the new computers. It is, therefore, not uncommon to hear multimedia frequently referred to as **new media**.

New media is a young industry, still groping to find the kind of material that will capture the imagination of millions of consumers. Another challenge in establishing new media as a mainstream entity is the frequent conflict of cultures between the traditional media companies (publishers, movie studios, and so forth) that own a lot of content and the computer software world. However, large new media products, such as an educational CD-ROM, often involve both kinds of companies: a publisher develops the content and a software company combines it into a cohesive multimedia product.

At the core of new media is a concept known as **digital convergence**. As computers are used to create all kinds of content, from plain text to video, more and more of the content is in digital form. All digital information, regardless of its content, can travel to the consumer along the same path—perhaps via a CD-ROM disk or a cable TV wire. Rather than delivering movies on film or videotape, music on tapes or compact disks, and books on the printed page, different kinds of content now can reach the computer or cable TV box in the same way. Thus, a variety of content comes together, converging into one digital stream.

Multimedia: Beyond Words

Print publishers were among the first to explore the possibilities of delivering their content in digital form for display on a personal computer. Consumers, however, quickly rejected the simple conversion of the printed page to the computer screen, perhaps because reading extensive amounts of text on a screen is not as convenient or as comfortable as reading the printed page. The task, then, was to make the electronic version of the content more engaging, utilizing the special powers that computers have to offer.

Adding Sound, Graphics, Animation, and Video

One way to make plain text and pictures inviting to an audience is to add time-based content, such as audio, cartoon animation, and video. It is, however, very important that the added media do more than merely mimic the static text and graphics content. It would be very boring indeed to watch a video of someone reading a passage of text that appears on the screen. But if the text is a scene from *Hamlet* and the video displays that same scene with Sir Laurence Olivier's film portrayal, then the video enlivens the printed text.

The First Person series of CD-ROMs, published by Voyager, are excellent examples of valuable multimedia additions to printed text. One volume consists of the book *The Society of Mind* by artificial-intelligence pioneer and MIT professor Marvin Minsky. When some passages of the book's text appear on screen, the user can click the mouse on an icon to receive a related mini-lecture by the author. Instead of the typically uninteresting "talking head" appearing in a small overlapping video window, the designers of this program make the author appear to walk around, lean against, and sit on graphic objects displayed on the screen. In other places, concepts are illustrated by animation—something that could never be accomplished in the printed version.

The multimedia encyclopedia, such as the one included in the Microsoft Bookshelf software, adds a number of sound, animation, and video clips to enliven several subjects. For example, in the article about rocketry, a click of the mouse on the cross-section diagram of a rocket's components starts a narrated animation that demonstrates the process of mixing the fuel components to cause propulsion. Many interactive multimedia products, such as this, also allow the viewer to examine different slices of the content. Instead of searching for a particular word or phrase, users can scan through all the sound clips or animations, stopping to listen to or view any item that stimulates the imagination.

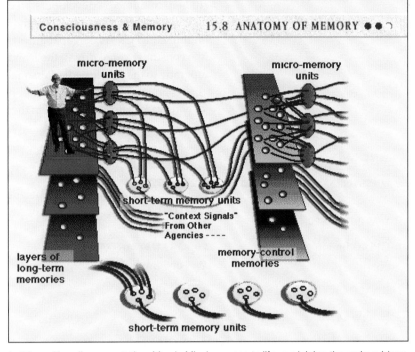

In this multimedia presentation, Marvin Minsky comes to life, explaining the various ideas that are being illustrated. Here, he appears to stand on top of a micro-memory unit.

A focus on the *content* of a multimedia program or presentation is essential. It is the content that the consumer pays for, or the audience comes to see. For example, the first feature-length computer-animated film, *Toy Story*, would have had limited appeal for just its technical wizardry. Because it also had an appealing story and strong character development, the film attracted children and adults alike.

Platform Considerations for Multimedia

The way in which content reaches its audience is a separate issue from the content itself. Because of the intensive amount of digital information that goes into building every second of a program, multimedia publishers must always consider the user's equipment—the platform on which the content will be displayed.

Today, PCs often come with all the necessary multimedia components already installed. These computers ease the start-up time for computer novices and home computer users because the users are not faced with complicated hardware issues, such as configuring a new CD-ROM player or installing a sound board. For older computers, however, it may be necessary to add one or more of the following components to turn the PC into a multimedia PC:

■ Sound card
■ Speakers
■ CD-ROM player

Additionally, a multimedia computer requires enough processing horsepower (a fast CPU chip) and memory (RAM) to accommodate multimedia programs.

Along with a fast CPU and plenty of RAM, a multimedia PC needs a CD-ROM drive, speakers, and a sound card.

To help multimedia developers predict how much multimedia power should be in users' computers, an industry standards group has defined minimum standards for multimedia PCs. As the capabilities of computers increase over the years and costs to the consumer come down, the standards become more rigorous. In 1995, the latest upgrade to the **Multimedia Personal Computer (MPC) standard**, called MPC Level 3, was announced to software and hardware makers. Table 12.1 shows a summary of hardware features specified in the two most recent standards for MPC computers.

TABLE 12.1

Multimedia PC Specifications (Level 2 and 3)

YEAR INTRODUCED	LEVEL 2 1993	LEVEL 3 1995
CPU (Min.)	25 MHz 486SX or compatible	75 MHz Pentium or equivalent
RAM (Min.)	4 MB	8 MB
Floppy Drive	Yes	Yes
Hard Drive (Min.)	160 MB	540 MB
Video Playback	None	MPEG
Two-Button Mouse	Yes	Yes
101-Key Keyboard	Yes	Yes
CD-ROM Drive	Double-speed; 300 KB per sec transfer rate; 400 ms average access time	Quad speed; 600 KB per sec ransfer rate; 250 ms average access time
Audio	16-bit digital; 44.1, 22.05, and 11.025 kHz sampling rates; microphone input	Compact audio disk playback 16-bit digital; 44.1, 22.05, and 11.025 kHz sampling rates; microphone input; wavetable support; internal mixing of four sources
Serial Port	Yes	Yes
Parallel Port	Yes	Yes
MIDI I/O Port	Yes	Yes
Joystick Port	Yes	Yes
Speakers	Yes	Two-piece stereo; 3 watts per channel
Operating System	Windows 3.0 plus Multimedia Extension; Windows 3.1	Windows 3.11

Source: Software Publishers Assn. Multimedia PC Working Group

Even though a modern multimedia PC is capable of displaying multimedia content, there are still other factors that must be considered by the multimedia developer. Perhaps the most important is the issue of data compression.

The problem here is that high-quality digital video requires that millions of bits be transmitted to the monitor every second. Remember, the monitor is attached to a video controller, which assigns 24 bits to each pixel on a full-color monitor. Monitors display a grid of pixels that measures at least 640×480, and video requires at least 15 image frames per second. If you multiply all these numbers together, you get the number of bits it takes to display digital video:

	24	bits per pixel
×	480	pixels vertically
×	640	pixels horizontally
×	15	frames per second
=	110,592,000	bits per second

It does not matter whether the information comes from a CD-ROM and is being displayed on a monitor, or comes through a cable box and is being displayed by the television—the wires connecting the components of the system usually are not capable of transmitting the digital information fast enough. The capacity for data transmission is known as **bandwidth**. Somewhere in a computer system, there is almost always a bottleneck in the bandwidth. When it comes to video, one potential solution is data compression.

Data compression typically uses mathematical analyses of digital source material to strip away unnecessary bits of data prior to sending it across the wire. At the receiving end (for example, inside a modern cable TV converter or direct-broadcast satellite receiver), the missing bits are quickly reinserted to produce a copy that is extremely close to the original in quality and detail.

An example of a simple compression algorithm is *run-length encoding*. Suppose we have a scanned image 20 pixels wide by 20 pixels high (see Figure 12.3).

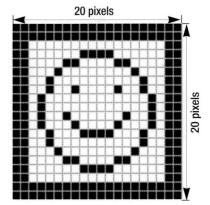

FIGURE 12.3
Scanned image.

It would require 400 numbers (20x20) to represent this image without compression. With run-length encoding, we will use pairs of numbers (referred to mathematically as "run-length pairs") to describe each continuous horizontal block of same-color pixels (otherwise known as a run). The first number in each pair represents color (in this case, black or white) and the other number represents the number pixels of that color in that particular run. If we use the number 255 to represent the color white and the number 0 to represent the color black, then the following pairs of numbers would represent the top eight lines in the scanned image.

line 1 (0,20)
line 2 (0,20)
line 3 (0,2)(255,16)(0,2)
line 4 (0,2)(255,6)(0,4)(255,6)(0,2)
line 5 (0,2)(255,4)(0,2)(255,4)(0,2)(255,4)(0,2)
line 6 (0,2)(255,3)(0,1)(255,8)(0,1)(255,3)(0,2)
line 7 (0,2)(255,2)(0,1)(255,10)(0,1)(255,2)(0,2)
line 8 (0,2)(255,2)(0,1)(255,2)(0,1)(255,4)(0,1)(255,2)(0,1)(255,2)(0,2)

For the first few lines, the algorithm performs well, since there are some long run-lengths (runs of the same color), and relatively few runs in each line. Using this compression algorithm, lines one through seven each require less than the 20 numbers it would take to represent the 20 pixels without compression. However, at line eight, the algorithm uses 22 numbers to represent 20 values, illustrating that this mode of compression does not work well for complex images with short horizontal run-lengths. Overall, this image can be represented by 120 pairs of numbers, for a total of 240 numbers instead of the 400 required to represent the image without compression. This results in a compression rate of 40%, since the encoded file is 60% of the original.

Among the most common multimedia compression schemes currently being used are **JPEG** (pronounced "jay-peg," for Joint Photographic Experts Group), **MPEG** (pronounced "em-peg," for Motion Picture Experts Group), and **MPEG-2**. Each scheme is sponsored by an industry consortium whose goal is to achieve high rates of compression and industry-wide agreement on standards. The push for standards is important, because it means that multimedia-equipped personal computers, cable TV boxes, and other hardware will have the requisite decompression facilities built in (usually requiring special integrated circuit chips and software—all of which work behind the scenes). The standards also allow multimedia developers to choose the right compression scheme for the target audience.

Hypermedia: User-Directed Navigation

A major challenge accompanies the large volume of multimedia content that arrives via a CD-ROM or through an online service—finding your way through the text, pictures, and other media available in the presentation. This is where the interactivity component comes into play. The user is responsible for deciding where and when to go to a particular place within the collection of data.

Wending your way through electronic information is commonly called **navigation**. The person who wrote the information is responsible for providing the user with on screen aids to navigate. In software that mimics the old format of books, the navigation aid might be a simple palette of left- and right-facing arrow icons to navigate backward or forward one page. Because authors of digital content are not bound by the physical constraints of pages, they also can provide buttons that allow you to jump to locations outside of the normal, linear sequence.

Figure 12.4 illustrates several common navigation methods at work on a single multimedia screen. Note that the figure shows only a few of the many commonly used navigation methods.

Each button along the top row of icons leads to a different electronic book (a label pops into view when the pointer is on each icon). In the text, there are linked words (in small capital letters and colored differently). When you click on a word, the program zips you to the page referring to that word. At the bottom right is a palette of navigation buttons that take you forward or backward by one page, or jump back to the previous page you viewed. In other programs, a click on a picture may turn that picture into a video or an audio track that explains the picture.

A new term has evolved to describe the environment that allows users to click on one type of media to navigate to the same or other type of media: that term is **hypermedia**. The word is a more modern version of a concept called **hypertext**.

TECHVIEW

How to Choose a Multimedia PC

Multimedia is an incredibly rich and wild art form. A wealth of instructional and educational products featuring digital sound, animation, full-motion video, and interactivity are taking over store shelves everywhere.

There's no question that multimedia expands the horizons of any product. A dance video becomes a personalized lesson. A dry encyclopedia becomes an audio-visual documentary. A game becomes Saturday afternoon at the movies.

But only if you have the right equipment. To view the eye-catching graphics, full-motion videos, and lively animations that come alive to the accompaniment of symphonic-quality scores, special sound effects, and crystal clear dialog, you need state-of-the-art equipment.

What features do you need on your PC to make sure that you can run the hottest new multimedia products? The quick answer is: as high-end as possible. Multimedia products are advancing in capabilities every day, as are the requirements they make on a PC. What will play today's multimedia products may prove to be underpowered very soon.

At a minimum, here is what to look for in a multimedia PC:

■ **System: Pentium PC, 75 megahertz or higher, 16 MB RAM or higher.** Multimedia applications demand lots of CPU power and storage space. The more you have, the quicker and smoother your CD-ROMs will perform.

■ **Hard disk: 1 GB minimum; 2 GB is preferable.**

■ **Sound Board: 16-bit with 44.1-KHz stereo sampling frequency.** This allows you to achieve genuine CD-quality sound on all kinds of multimedia audio.

■ **Video Card: Super Video Graphics Array (SVGA).** This will put those gorgeous graphics in a full spectrum of 65,000 colors with clear, sharp detail.

■ **Display: 17- or 20-inch monitor, SVGA compatible, with local bus graphics adapter.** A large monitor will lessen eyestrain and allow you to work with more windows open on your screen.

■ **CD-ROM Drive: Quad speed minimum, 8X preferable.**

■ **Speakers: Good quality right- and left-channel speakers.** Separate speakers allow flexible placement for optimal sound quality.

■ **Headphones:** Yes, especially if you have roommates or family whom you might disturb.

There are several ways to acquire a multimedia system. The easiest is to buy a new complete multimedia PC system, in which all of the above components come bundled together. Installation and setup time is minimal, and you will not have to mix and match components. All you do is plug it in and get started. Plus, many multimedia systems come with a wide sampling of software worth hundreds of dollars.

The second approach is an upgrade. Upgrade kits come with varying arrays of components. You must be careful that every component in the upgrade is compatible with your system. And, unless you are an electronics whiz, you will probably need to have the upgrade installed by a computer retailer.

The last approach is to buy components individually and piece together a custom system with the setup you already have. This approach is generally advisable for technical wizards only, or for those with considerable amounts of time for tinkering and technical support phone calls.

Whether you buy a brand-new system, an upgrade, or add components one step at a time, multimedia will take you into a whole new dimension of communication, learning, and entertainment.

TM & ©1995 Lucas Arts Entertainment Company. All rights reserved.

Rebel Assault II from Lucas Arts.

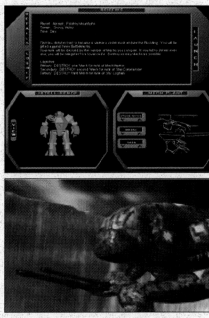

MechWarrior II from Activision/FASA Corp.

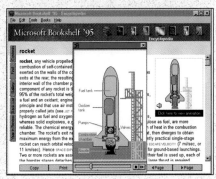

Microsoft Bookshelf.

363

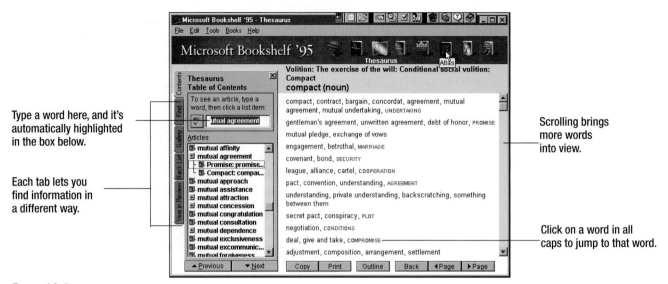

Type a word here, and it's automatically highlighted in the box below.

Each tab lets you find information in a different way.

Scrolling brings more words into view.

Click on a word in all caps to jump to that word.

FIGURE 12.4
Common navigation methods in multimedia programs.

In a 1945 *Atlantic Monthly* article, computing science pioneer Vannevar Bush wrote about the concept of associative links between ideas. At the time, crude computing power hindered the development of working models using this concept. It was not until the 1960s that computer scientists were able to experiment with working prototypes of associative links. In 1965, futurist Ted Nelson, writing in his book *Literary Machines,* coined the term "hypertext," defining it as "a body of written or pictorial material interconnected in a complex way that could not be conveniently represented on paper." Nelson's scheme predicted a world of interlinked computers and vast storage available to everyone. A click on a reference to a magazine article, for example, might bring up a display of the article from another computer halfway around the planet.

In some respects, the highlighted links you see in the World Wide Web pages on the Internet hint at hypertext and hypermedia as envisioned by Bush and Nelson. A click on such a link may automatically connect you to a related item on a computer in another country—and it appears on your screen as if it were coming from across the street.

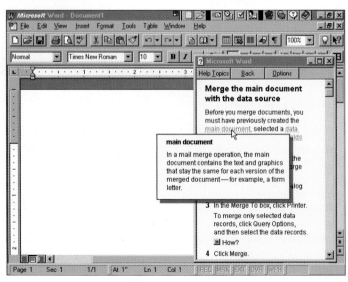

Hypermedia can also exist on a smaller scale. You may have already used hypermedia in the Windows Help system or some of the programs designed for Windows. Figure 12.5 shows a screen from Microsoft Word's Help system.

FIGURE 12.5
The Help system in Microsoft Word contains many hypertext links. Clicking on a green, underlined word displays the definition for that word.

The words "main document" are underlined (and are also displayed in a different color). Clicking anywhere on that link displays the popup window, which shows a definition of the term. At the end of step 3 is a small button next to the word "How?". Clicking on that button displays an entirely different screen from the Help system that explains how to select data records for merging. At the top of the Help window is a button labeled "Back," which steps you backward along your trail through the help process; the Help Topics button takes you all the way out to the Help system's table of contents.

Authors of interactive multimedia must be conscious that while hypermedia links often can be helpful, there are times when it is undesirable to let the user wander off to other locations, perhaps never to return. Some content must continue to exist in a linear fashion, at least for part of the time. Steps in a tutorial or a carefully crafted story, for example, must be told in an unalterable sequence for accuracy or the most dramatic impact. The author must decide when it is acceptable for the viewer to take control of the navigation process.

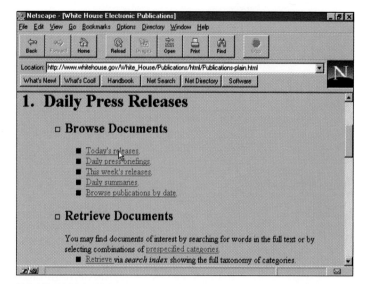

This World Wide Web page comes from the White House in Washington D.C. Clicking on "Today's releases" will display the press releases that have been put out by the Office of the President in the last 24 hours.

Presentation Software: Reaching Your Audience

For decades, the overhead projector and slide projector were the only display devices anyone had to illustrate concepts at public presentations. Presenters displayed on the screen, on the ceiling, or in the front of the room static text and the occasional graphic. Multimedia computers have changed all that.

Presentation software such as Microsoft PowerPoint and Adobe Persuasion make it a simple task to assemble not only distinctive static material, but also to add splashes of razzle-dazzle with visual effects during the transitions between screens; bulleted text lines that drift in from off-screen as the presenter makes each point; and even animation, video, and sound.

Although these types of programs generate primarily linear presentations that tell a story (or make a sales pitch), a multimedia presentation can include interactivity where appropriate. For instance, the author may predict that the audience will have questions about earlier parts of the presentation. By building in an icon or button on the screen that jumps back to the earlier part, the author or presenter can navigate as needed for each audience.

As evidenced by their popularity, presentation programs are easy to use and offer a quick, convenient way to create simple multimedia shows. For example, a history teacher might create a 20-minute interactive classroom presentation on the Vietnam War, including text bullets, scanned photo images, audio clips, and video clips of television news coverage from the period. A salesperson might develop a 30-minute pre-

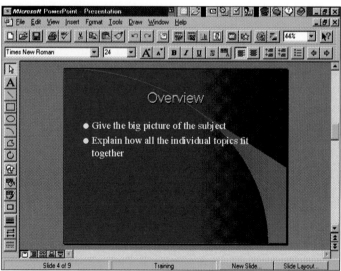

This screen from Microsoft PowerPoint shows how the program can guide you through the process of creating a presentation. The basic look of the screen was chosen from a list of templates.

sentation of a company's new product line. To help customers better understand the message, the presentation might include text, scanned photos of the new packaging, and video clips of the upcoming television advertising.

Creating multimedia presentations that will be displayed in a one-on-one environment is simple enough to do from the screen of a personal or laptop computer. Showing such a presentation to a group, however, requires more display equipment.

A number of transportable projector panels are available to fit on top of an overhead projector. The panels have translucent liquid crystal displays (LCDs), and use the projector's light source and lens to beam the output to the screen. The LCD panel connects to most desktop and laptop computers as if it were an external video monitor. In a few laptop computer models, the built-in LCD display can be converted into an overhead projector display panel. More sophisticated projection systems are currently being built into modern auditoriums, meeting rooms, school computer labs, and lecture halls. They, too, connect to computers like a video monitor, but they can provide a very large, high-quality display of the material on the computer.

This IBM ThinkPad has a convertible display panel that can be used with a projector.

Virtual Reality: Adding the Third Dimension

It could be said that the most effective computer navigation is when you have the feeling of traveling through a 3-dimensional world. Imagine, for example, that every chapter of a reference book were a room off a corridor. Then, if you use the computer to move the view down the corridor and turn into a particular room, you would have a unique spatial sense of that chapter of information. The recreation on a computer display of what appears to be physical space is called **virtual reality**. The images and sounds exist only in the RAM of the computer, but a user can enter this world using special devices such as head-mounted displays, stereoscopic glasses, data gloves, and sensor seats. These devices with motion sensors are connected to the computer. When a user walks or moves a hand, the sensors detect the motion and send data to the virtual reality program. The program processes the user's movements and projects the action into the virtual space.

Until recently, it was possible to experience virtual reality only with the help of mini- and mainframe computers. Increased personal computing power and clever software techniques now make it possible to see the effects at home. Presenting virtual reality is still quite difficult because it is the ultimate in user-directed navigation. With some of the wearable devices, a slight tilt of the head requires the computer to interpret the angle of movement, and recalculate and redraw a complex graphical scene based on the new point of view. To accomplish this in realistic animation at an acceptable speed is a significant engineering challenge.

At the moment, virtual reality is used predominantly for entertainment software. However, the time could come when you will travel by virtual reality links through space to jump from one piece of information to another.

Many of the virtual reality environments in use today create artificial, cartoon-like virtual worlds. Another technique, called QuickTime VR (developed by Apple Computer) takes the concept of virtual reality and applies it to the real world. To prepare a QuickTime VR scene, a digital camera on a special tripod takes a number of photographs in all directions from the same point. The QuickTime VR software

Courtesy of Autodesk

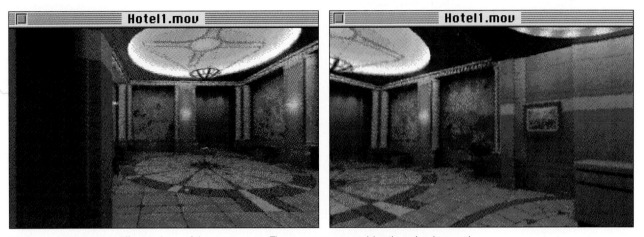

These pictures are two different views of the same room. The computer assembles them (and several more) so you can move through the virtual room and see how it would look from different perspectives.

then blends the individual photos into a continuous, 360-degree scene. As the viewer maneuvers the mouse around the window, the point of view changes as if the person were standing in that spot and turning around or looking upward or downward—not in jerky shifts, but in smooth movements. With another mouse action, the view magnifies, as if the person were walking toward the center point of the screen. In this case, the scene is virtual, but the photos are of real space.

Virtual reality is also invading the online world. Virtual Reality Modeling (VRML) is an authoring language used to create 3-dimensional environments on the World Wide Web. This tool allows the user to navigate through 3-D worlds, create or edit 3-D objects, and link them to other Web objects. Pioneer, made by Caligari Corporation, is one of the most widely used VRML authoring programs.

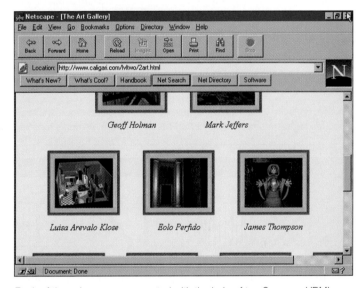

Each of these images was created with the help of trueSpace, a VRML authoring and 3-D graphics program from Caligari Corporation, which also makes Pioneer.

CREATING MULTIMEDIA

Because of the different types of media and the flexibility in navigation, creating effective multimedia is difficult. The development team usually involves people with a variety of skills, and the development process is complex. Figure 12.6 shows an overview of the multimedia development process.

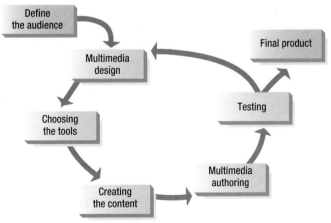

FIGURE 12.6

The multimedia development process involves a number of distinct steps before achieving a final product.

Defining Your Audience

Because a multimedia presentation or program can offer so much in the way of content, it is a valuable exercise to understand precisely who the audience is. Imagine you are about to compose a multimedia program. Then imagine yourself as someone using or viewing that program. Then ask yourself the following questions:

- ▨ How much should users know about the subject before the presentation or program begins?
- ▨ What do users expect to gain from their experience with the program? Is the goal to learn something? To be entertained?
- ▨ How much time will users want to spend going through this content?
- ▨ Will users get more out of this content if it is predominantly text, graphics, sound, animation, or video?
- ▨ What kind of interaction will users want with the program? Is their feedback via a touch screen, a keyboard and mouse, or a game controller?
- ▨ Will the content or presentation be engaging enough to make users want to linger and to come back again?

Having answers to these questions firmly in hand will help the multimedia author focus on the result.

Some programs, such as Scene Slate Storyboard, can guide the user through the process of creating a storyboard for a multimedia product.

Multimedia Design

Planning the overall design is often the longest part of the development process. Much of this work goes on without any computers.

A common way to start is by composing an outline of the sequences and blocks of information that will appear on the screen. This is the time to determine how much information—text, graphics, clickable objects—will be presented on each screen. It is also the time to establish a navigation methodology for the user. Will there be a navigation bar with arrows leading from scene to scene, or will there be text or graphic objects that the user will click on to jump around the entire program?

When a program includes a great deal of animation or many different scenes, the best design aid is the storyboard. Used by film directors for productions ranging from 30-second television commercials to feature-length motion pictures, the **storyboard** consists of sketches of the scenes and action. Mapping out a storyboard helps the author to recognize gaps in logic. Some multimedia authoring programs provide facilities for drawing and organizing the frames of a storyboard.

Choosing the Tools

Because multimedia includes different kinds of content, creating it involves many types of software. Creating text often requires a word processor; working with digital images requires graphics software; using video requires a video-capture program and editing software; sound often requires its own editing software. All of this software is used to generate the content. When the content is ready, it needs to be assembled in a process called **multimedia authoring**. This process requires still another type of software, which can understand all the different types of media, combine them, control the sequences in which they appear, and create navigational tools and an interface for the user.

It would be a mistake to select the tools before designing a multimedia extravaganza. It is better to imagine the ideal presentation in the design stage, and then locate the tools that let you come as close to that ideal as possible.

The variety of tools used for multimedia depends largely on the variety of media to be included. For a simple text-and-graphics slide show type of presentation, a presentation software program should suffice. You could enliven the offering by adding preexisting graphics from the hundreds of commercially available CD-ROM collections of clip art, clip sound, and clip video. These clip collections store small files in the proper file formats for use in a wide range of multimedia programs.

Adding animation, sound, or video that you need to create from scratch expands the number of tools you need. Although most multimedia PCs come equipped with basic hardware and software for sound recording, you may wish to use a more sophisticated sound editing program, which allows you to splice together segments or add sound effects electronically, for example, echoes, to the sounds you record. You can do the same kind of electronic editing for video (transferred from the camcorder to the computer via a video digitizer).

Other, even more specialized tools allow you to perform such multimedia tricks as morphing (developing a video sequence that appears to transform one scene into another via smooth stretching and contorting) and creating fractal art for screen backgrounds. Note that the editing of time-based media generally requires significant amounts of hard disk storage and computer RAM.

The Sound Recorder is a utility built into Windows that lets you capture and digitize sound from a microphone.

Macromedia Director is one of the most popular programs for combining all the elements of a multimedia presentation. In Director, the multimedia author assembles each element—text, graphics, sound, and video into separate "tracks." The program helps the author to synchronize all the elements, so that, for example, a crash sound effect is heard precisely when the two animated objects collide. The file that Director generates is the one that contains the entire multimedia presentation, ready for distribution on disk or CD-ROM, or to be played over an interactive television linkup or through the Internet (if your Internet browser software has the Director plug-in program, called ShockWave, installed).

Multimedia Authoring

Once all the content has been created (and converted to a digital form, if necessary), it is time to put it all together. For a complex product created with the use of a sophisticated tool such as Director, the multimedia authoring generally is performed by a skilled computer user, often referred to as the programmer.

Authoring proceeds more quickly and is more successful if the programmers have access to all of the content at the outset, and there is a clear and detailed storyboard telling the programmers how the content fits together.

Testing

If the multimedia program is to be used by other people—perhaps in a free-standing information kiosk in the lobby of a building or at various stations around a shopping mall—it is vital that the program be tested by the kinds of people who will be using it. By going through this testing, the programmer can locate any flaws ahead of time and repair them before unleashing the finished product on the world.

Just as with the testing of any software product, it is helpful for the program's author(s) to watch users navigate through the product. The kinds of problems to watch for are any locations in the product where the user does not know what to do next. Is the user struggling to read a font size too small for descriptive text? Are there sufficient controls to stop a video or audio clip if the user wants to move on without going through the entire clip? Is the user following navigational paths that lead quickly to the desired information, or do there appear to be times when the user seems lost in the multimedia maze?

Before a program is ready for release, it may need to go through several testing-and-revision cycles so that everyone is comfortable with the finished product. As part of the planning process, sufficient time must be built into the schedule for the testing cycles.

A program's author and the final user very often have different points of view. What the author believes to be very simple to use—having designed the interface and used it for weeks or months during development—might be totally bewildering to someone seeing the interface for the first time. The author must learn to regard any problems the user detects with the program as constructive criticism. The reason testing is so valuable is that it is all too easy to lose sight of the audience once the heavy-duty authoring starts.

▶ NORTON WORKSHOP: CREATING A MULTIMEDIA PRESENTATION

This workshop shows you a realistic example of how a multimedia presentation is created. In the following example, you will observe a team working on a presentation used to promote a fictional Pacific island country as a location for business conferences. To keep the example simple, the final product is created using presentation software rather than a more sophisticated multimedia authoring program such as Director.

The director of the Boston office of the Maru-Maru Chamber of Commerce, Carol Keihani, is invited to make presentations to groups of meeting planners at a local conference. The meeting planners, therefore, are the target audience. To help illustrate her talk, she wants to use a multimedia slide show, which will be projected on a screen at the front of the room.

Designing the Presentation

Carol knows she needs some help in pulling together the components of the presentation. She asks Rosa, a graphic designer who has experience with computer graphics tools, to help her with the visual images and overall appearance. One other person, Bryan, is added to the team because of his proven writing and organizational skills.

The three of them have a planning meeting in which they discuss the audience, the points to be made in the presentation, and the size of the budget allocated for the project. A presentation such as this must lead the audience through a logical sequence of thought. The purpose is not only to inform the audience, but also to convince them to act on what they have heard. Because the final product is a sales presentation rather than interactive multimedia, they decide to use presentation software. This choice will also allow them to design the look of the presentation after they create the text.

Entering and Formatting the Text

Because this is not a long presentation, Bryan starts drafting the text for the slides in an outliner function of the presentation software to be used for this project. The outline view, shown in Figure 12.7, allows Bryan to visualize how much textual information will be on each screen, the order of the points to be emphasized, and how long the presentation will be (Carol must limit her talk to 20 minutes).

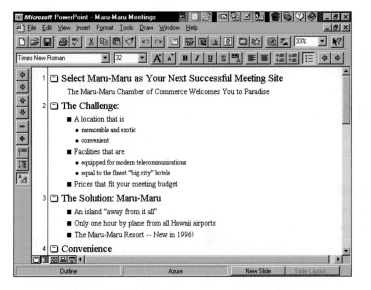

FIGURE 12.7
The presentation in outline view.

By clicking a button near the bottom left of the screen, Bryan can switch the view to the actual slide (although not in full-screen size) to see how the text he entered in the outline looks. The presentation program assigns a standard background design as a starting point. One change Bryan wants to make is to emphasize the island's name each time it appears in the text. The software allows editing of the text and styles either in the outline view or in the slide view. Clicking on a text block highlights that block and allows standard text editing. Bryan selects the island name and chooses a scriptlike font style. He also increases the size so that the name stands out even more, as shown in Figure 12.8. The change must be made to all instances of the name.

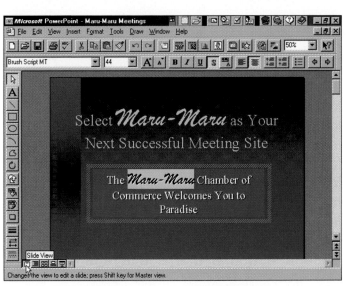

FIGURE 12.8
Formatting text.

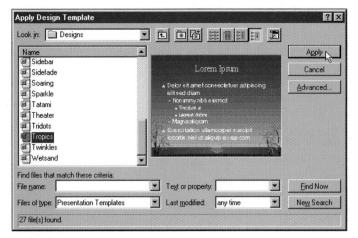

FIGURE 12.9
An appropriate template.

Adding Graphics

With the text content in place, the team begins the process of establishing the right appearance and choosing the images for the presentation. In consultation with Rosa, the designer, Bryan wants to change the background that will appear on all slides. There is not enough money in the budget for Rosa to design an entire background, so she looks through the design templates provided with the presentation software. One template, named Tropics (see Figure 12.9), has both fitting background art and a pleasing combination of text colors and interesting bullet characters for the main points.

After the template is selected from the dialog box, the new design becomes a part of the presentation, as shown in Figure 12.10.

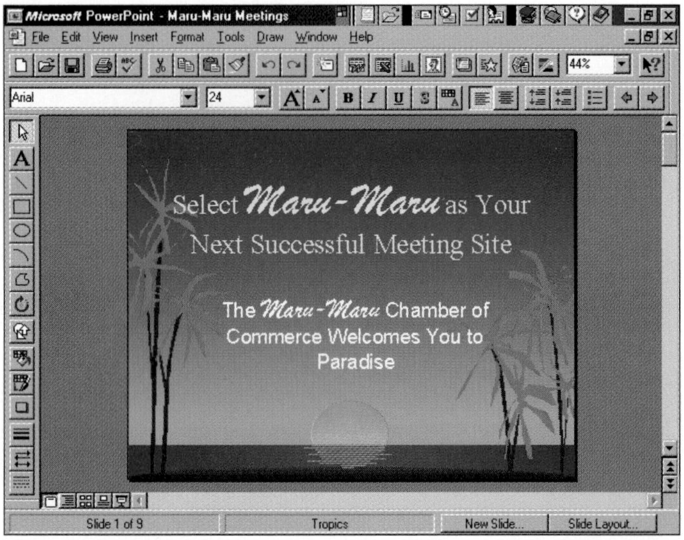

FIGURE 12.10
The template applied to the presentation.

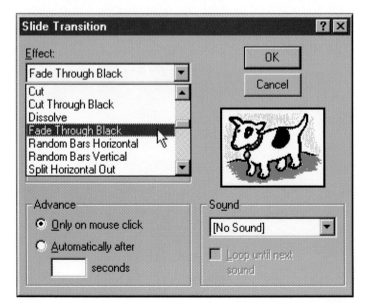

Before Rosa goes to work on some of the animation effects they have planned for other slides, she selects a transition visual effect between each slide. Unlike the standard slide projector, which whisks one slide out and another slide in, the electronic version can produce smooth, seamless transitions. As Rosa selects some of the transition effects, the program demonstrates a preview of the transition in the Slide Transition dialog box.

Rosa selects the effect that fades one slide out to a brief black screen, at which point the next slide begins to fade in. Control of the advance of the slides will be up to Carol, who must click the computer mouse to advance the slides. The completed dialog box is shown in Figure 12.11.

FIGURE 12.11
Controlling the transition between slides.

As part of Bryan's outline, he left space in one slide to include a map of a segment of the Pacific Ocean to help the audience understand where Maru-Maru is in relation to Hawaii. Another multimedia CD-ROM program in his library contains an atlas. Using that program's search capabilities, he finds a map of Oceania, which encompasses an area larger than he needs. That's fine, because he can crop the picture of the map later. As shown in Figure 12.12, this electronic atlas includes a button at the bottom of the screen that copies the map on screen to the Clipboard.

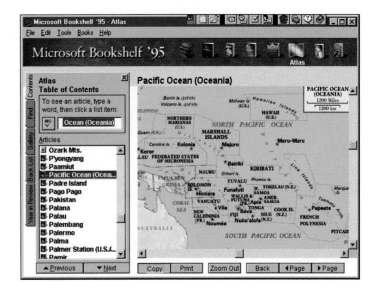

FIGURE 12.12

Copying a map from an electronic atlas.

Switching back to the presentation, and advancing to the edit window of one of the slides, Bryan pastes the map from the Clipboard into the slide. Using software tools in the Tools and Draw menu, he is able to crop the view to the upper-right corner of the map, and increase the scale to 200 percent, making the map very legible when the slide is shown full-screen (see Figure 12.13).

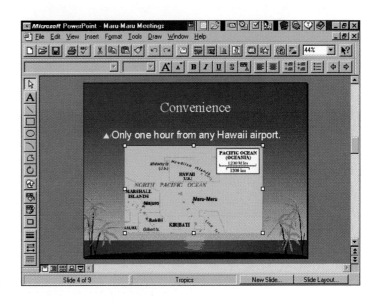

FIGURE 12.13

The map pasted into the presentation.

Next, it is Rosa's turn to work with the map. To both highlight Maru-Maru's location on the map and to emphasize the convenience of flying to the island from Hawaii, she uses the drawing tools in the presentation package to create an arrow leading from Hawaii to Maru-Maru. To do this with the most accuracy, she increases the magnification of the slide view on screen. Like most drawing programs, this one creates an object in a distinct layer on the screen. Each object can have any number of properties set to it, such as line thickness, color, and animation. First, Rosa sets the appearance of the arrow in the dialog box shown in Figure 12.14, and then she drags the mouse pointer to create the bent arrow shown in Figure 12.15.

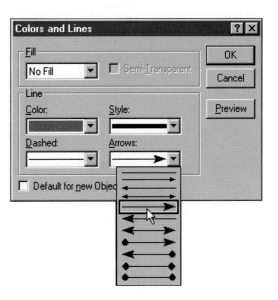

FIGURE 12.14

Controlling the appearance of the arrow.

To animate the arrow, Rosa makes selections in the Animation Settings dialog box for the arrow object. Because the arrow is to be hidden when the map slide

Figure 12.15
The arrow pasted on the slide.

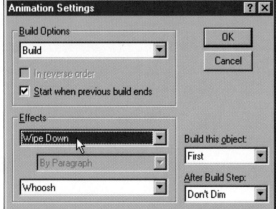

first appears, and then magically appears after a brief delay, the instructions are for the program to build the animation after the map slide is on the screen. The choice of visual effects for the animation must be carefully considered here. For some types of objects, such as a bulleted line of text or a horizontal arrow, it may be desirable to have the object fly to its position from off screen. For this arrow, however, Rosa wants the effect to look as if the arrow emanates from Hawaii and points down to Maru-Maru on the map. The closest choice that meets that requirement is called a Wipe Down effect. Unfortunately, the tip of the arrow will not really appear until the bottom part of the arrow is revealed in the wipe. However, by adding the "Whoosh" sound (one that comes with the presentation program or one that Rosa records on her multimedia PC), the audience may be visually tricked into believing that the arrow in fact grew out of Hawaii. These effects are created using another dialog box, shown in Figure 12.16.

Figure 12.16
Controlling animation effects.

On a slide that highlights the conference facilities, Carol suggests adding a bit of animation by having a picture of a satellite dish come flying in from one side of the slide. The slide should also list the current communications facilities available to conference participants. Because the list is changing rapidly, it is decided to link the list in a word processing document to the slide via Windows 95's object linking and embedding (OLE) technology. That way, to change the listing in the presentation, all Carol has to do is update the word processing document. This OLE link will act like an automatic hypermedia link, but will embed the linked data into the current slide, rather than navigating to another place.

The process of creating the OLE link involves inserting an object (available through the presentation program's windows) and selecting the word processing document file. The text from the document appears as an object, which can have animation assigned to it as well. Carol decides that she wants to wait until she reaches the point in the presentation that discusses the communications links. She will then click on the screen once to trigger the satellite dish flying in, automatically followed by the OLE object that contains the latest information. The result is shown in Figure 12.17. Rosa finds a promotional videotape with a number of idyllic scenes from Maru-Maru. Using a video digitizer board in her PC, Rosa captures a segment of the video showing one of the beaches at sunset, with a bright orange sun and illuminated clouds glistening off the gently rolling surf. She thinks it would be a nice illustration

FIGURE 12.17

Text linked to a word processing document.

to emphasize a point on one of Bryan's slides about the island's beaches. Once the video segment is saved as a video clip file, she uses the presentation program to import the video as an object. She has complete control over the location and size of the image. When Carol gives the presentation, all she will have to do is click on the still image to play the movie (which has its own soundtrack of the lapping waves) shown in Figure 12.18.

FIGURE 12.18

Clicking on the image plays the movie.

On the next-to-last slide, Bryan summarizes the main points of the presentation. This would be a good time in Carol's presentation to ask the audience if they would like to see any section again. Rosa designs two small pictures and selects one clip art picture that Bryan links to the start of each of these sections. Here Bryan sets a link of a cartoon showing people in a meeting to the sixth slide in the presentation. If Carol clicks once on that cartoon while giving the presentation, the navigation will jump back to slide number 6 about conference facilities. The link and the button that activates it are shown in Figures 12.19 and 12.20.

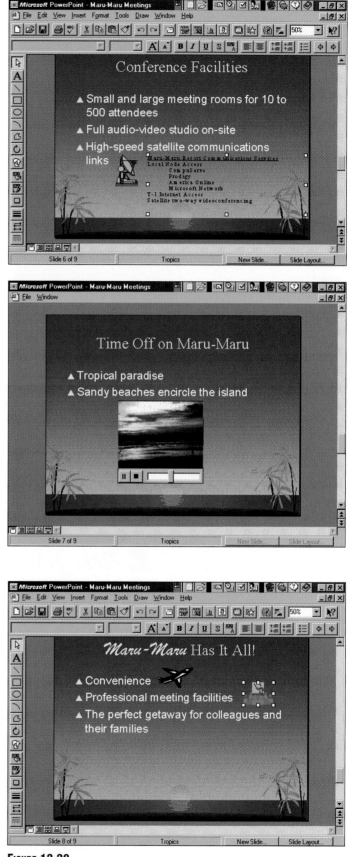

FIGURE 12.19

Creating a link between slides.

FIGURE 12.20

The button that initiates the link.

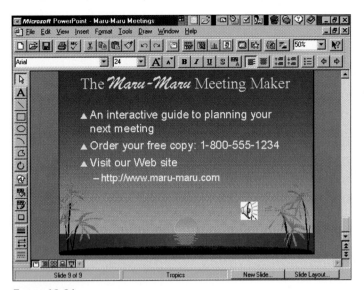

FIGURE 12.21

Clicking on the speaker icon plays a sound.

The final stage of authoring comes with the addition of a sound button in the last slide. Carol has many tape recordings of traditional island music from Maru-Maru. Connecting an audio cable between the line out jack of her tape recorder and the sound input jack on her multimedia PC, she is able to transfer and digitize a tune. With the sound saved as a Windows 95 sound file, Bryan can then insert it into the last slide. The presentation program assigns a speaker icon to the sound. If Carol feels the mood is right after her talk—as attendees file out—she can click the icon, shown in Figure 12.21, to play the island music. With the presentation completed, Rosa and Bryan turn it over to Carol for testing.

Presenting the Finished Product

Before giving this talk in front of the real audience, Carol must test the presentation program in rehearsals. Bryan, Rosa, and others should also attend. There may be places in the presentation that need additional work. Perhaps it is not clear where Carol should click for some animation effect to take place, or for some sound to play. Carol might prefer a slightly different organization of the entire program. Fortunately, the presentation software lets her view the slides as if they were in a rack. She can shuffle miniature versions of the slides into the order she prefers.

On the day of the presentation, she uses time during the lunch break to set up her computer and check the quality of the image being projected. No matter how good the presentation is, if there is a computer or projector malfunction, the audience will be distracted by these difficulties. Planning, testing, and preparation all pay off for Carol, who generates many leads from her presentation the first time she shows it.

▶ WHAT TO EXPECT IN THE FUTURE

New media will not be new forever. Interest in multimedia software will certainly increase in the near future, but it may no longer appear as a separate software category. Rather, the elements of multimedia—sound, video, interaction—will be integrated into all kinds of documents and programs. What is new media today will be the standard media in the not too distant future. Just as the printed page went from being a new medium in Gutenberg's day to the common medium shortly thereafter, so too will the electronic page become a commonplace way of communicating ideas.

Great strides in improving the realistic experience of virtual reality will occur in the next several years. Beyond heightening the visual and aural accuracy of computer-generated space, you may be asked to wear mechanical devices that not only respond to your movements, but will provide you with a sense of touch. For example, if you strike a pose of leaning against a wall with your hand in a virtual world, the glove you wear will exert slight pressure on your hand. You will feel as though you are leaning against a physical wall whose electronic image you see in the virtual reality helmet video screens.

Where the most rapid advances will occur, however, will be in the delivery of content containing multiple media and interaction. Sophisticated cable TV networks will beckon some households to join their interactive services. The importance of the CD-ROM could recede as more people are wired to the Internet or other online services offering Internet connectivity. Multimedia reference material will become readily available with up-to-the-minute changes; computers will be able to categorize video, audio, and graphics so you can search for time-based media as you now search for text; game opponents will be real humans elsewhere on the Internet; you will use the Internet to conduct international long-distance telephone calls via computerized video conferencing; and you will be able to hear the most recent hour's BBC World Service news program whenever you want.

▶ VISUAL SUMMARY

The Power of Interactivity

■ Interactivity allows viewers to participate in the action on the screen.

■ The popularity of video games demonstrates a widespread interest in interacting with content.

■ Broadcast and cable TV companies are still determining how best to produce and deliver interactive material.

■ The CD-ROM for personal computers and video games is the most popular interactive content delivery medium today.

■ Online delivery via commercial services and the Internet is growing rapidly.

■ Interactivity includes interaction between people as well as between people and computers.

■ Multimedia is the combination of text, still graphics, animation, video, sound, and interactivity.

■ In education, interactive multimedia can enrich the learning experience by engaging students in the content, connecting students in different locations, and simulating real-world actions and their consequences.

■ Businesses use interactive multimedia for training, video conferencing, and reaching customers with catalogs and customer support.

■ Home reference and how-to books come alive in interactive multimedia form.

■ Entertainment is the widest application of multimedia in the home today, but interactive television will allow the viewing of any content when you want it.

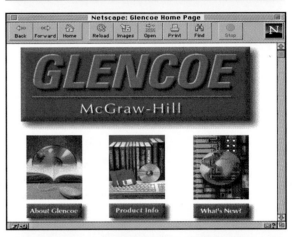

The New Media

■ Existing media companies are looking to new media for new markets.

■ Digital convergence implies that different kinds of data (voice, sound, video) can be delivered via a single medium, such as CD-ROM or the Internet.

■ Adding animation, video, and sound to what is normally print media makes it easier for many users to understand concepts.

■ Technical wizardry is not enough to sell a multimedia program: there must be content that the audience considers valuable.

■ Data compression allows more information—higher-quality content—to reach users via existing delivery vehicles such as CD-ROM, telephone wires, and TV cable.

■ There is an industry standard for what constitutes a multimedia-capable personal computer: the Multimedia PC (MPC) standard, which is currently in its third revision.

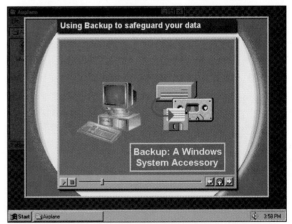

■ Designing a multimedia product requires designing a navigation system for users to find their way around the content.

■ A hypermedia link (derived from hypertext) connects one piece of media on the screen with perhaps a different kind of media, which may even be located on another computer along the network.

■ Highlighted links of World Wide Web pages exemplify hypermedia.

■ Software tools for creating presentations allow users to generate colorful and animated presentations by selecting ready-made art, video, and sounds from clip collections.

■ Personal computers are becoming powerful enough to create virtual reality—scenes and sounds that make you believe you are in a different place.

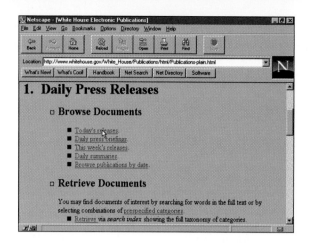

Creating Multimedia

■ Planning is the most time-consuming part of creating a multimedia program or presentation.

■ Understanding your audience is of paramount importance.

■ Before turning to the computer, sketch out an outline or storyboards of key scenes planned for the program.

■ Select authoring tools that best meet the needs of your planned program.

■ If possible, divide the content authoring among those with the most experience in writing, photography, video production, sound recording, and graphic design.

■ Test the program on small audiences before releasing it to the world.

▶ KEY TERMS

After completing this chapter, you should be able to define the following terms:

bandwidth, 361
computer-based training (CBT), 355
data compression, 361
digital convergence, 358
hypermedia, 362
hypertext, 362
interactive media, 350

interactive television, 356
JPEG, 362
MPEG, 362
MPEG-2, 362
media, 349
multimedia, 349
multimedia authoring, 369

Multimedia Personal Computer (MPC) standard, 360
navigation, 362
new media, 358
presentation software, 365
storyboard, 368
virtual reality, 366

▶ KEY TERM QUIZ

Fill in the blank with one of the terms listed in Key Terms.

1. Computers make it possible to create _____ in which people can respond to—and even control—what they see and hear.

2. _____ typically uses mathematical analyses of digital source material to strip away unnecessary bits of data prior to sending it across the wire.

3. Used by film producers for productions, a(n) _____ consists of sketches of the scenes and action.

4. The capacity for data transmission is known as _____.

5. Wending your way through electronic information is commonly called _____.

6. _____ is a new term that has evolved to describe the environment that allows users to click on one type of media to navigate to the same or other type of media.

7. The re-creation on a computer display of what appears to be physical space is called _____.

8. Text, graphics, animation, video, and sound can be combined to produce an engaging _____ presentation for any audience.

9. _____ describes the process by which a variety of content converges into one digital stream.

10. It is not uncommon to hear multimedia referred to as _____.

REVIEW QUESTIONS

1. What does the term "interactive media" mean?
2. What benefits can interactive multimedia bring to education?
3. List and describe at least three ways in which multimedia and communications have made significant contributions to businesses.
4. In what area is the biggest application of multimedia software?
5. Describe briefly what is meant by digital convergence.
6. List the basic steps involved in developing multimedia.
7. What are the key hardware components in a multimedia PC system?
8. Define data compression. Why is it such an important consideration for multimedia software developers?
9. Explain briefly how hypermedia allows a user to navigate through digital content without necessarily following a linear sequence.
10. Explain why a multimedia developer should not select software tools before beginning the design process.

DISCUSSION QUESTIONS

1. Why do you think animation, video, and audio are all described as "time-based media?" What problems might a multimedia developer face when integrating time-based media into a product?
2. Think about the issues that must be addressed by television and cable networks as interactivity becomes part of television broadcasting. What types of interactive programming can you envision? Will television programs and movies as we know them still exist in 30 years? To what extent should the government regulate the types of interactive programs that can be broadcast?
3. You have probably been exposed to some examples of multimedia educational software. Describe the examples you have seen. What were the strengths and weaknesses of this software? What suggestions can you make for improving educational multimedia? Can you suggest any specific products that would benefit students?

4. This chapter states that virtual reality is predominately used for entertainment applications. Do you think virtual reality has practical applications in other areas, such as engineering, science, business, and education? Provide at least two examples in which you envision virtual reality technology being applied to other, nonentertainment sectors of the economy.

NORTON INTERACTIVE

Complete the Norton Interactive module for this chapter.

APPENDIXES

CONTENTS

THE HISTORY OF MICROCOMPUTERS

IN THE BEGINNING

In 1971, Dr. Ted Hoff put together all the elements of a computer processor on a single silicon chip slightly larger than 1 square inch. The result of his efforts was the Intel 4004, the world's first commercially available microprocessor. It sold for $200 and contained 2,300 transistors. It was designed for use in a calculator, and Intel sold more than 100,000 calculators that ran on the 4004 chip. Almost overnight, the chip found thousands of uses. It paved the way for today's computer-oriented world, and for the mass production of computer chips now containing millions of transistors.

The first microprocessor, Intel's 4004, was a 4-bit computer containing 2,300 transistors that could perform 60,000 instructions per second. By contrast, the modern 32- and 64-bit PC microprocessors contain 5.5 million transistors and are capable of more than a million operations per second.

1975

The first commercially available microcomputer, the Altair 8800, was the first machine to be called a "personal computer". It had 64K of memory and an open 100-line bus structure. It was sold for about $400 in a kit to be assembled by the user.

Two young college students, Paul Allen and Bill Gates wrote the BASIC language interpreter for the Altair computer. It took them eight weeks, working night and day, to write the several thousand lines of code. During summer vacation they formed a company called Microsoft, now the largest software company in the world.

At Bell Labs, Brian Kernighan and Dennis Ritchie developed the C programming language, which became the most popular professional application development language.

1976

Steve Wozniak and Steve Jobs built the Apple I computer. It was less powerful than the Altair, but also less expensive and less complicated. Jobs and Wozniak formed the Apple Computer Company together on April Fool's Day, naming it after their favorite snack food.

Bill Millard, recognizing that people would rather buy pre-assembled computers in stores than put computers together themselves from kits, founded Computerland, the retail computer chain.

Intel introduced the 8088 microprocessor, featuring 16-bit internal architecture and an 8-bit external bus.

In the 1970s, computer chips were designed by etching circuits in clay models with X-Acto knives. Today's chip designers use the latest in CAD computer software and photo-lithography to develop their prototypes.

Motorola introduced the 68000 chip, used in early Macintosh computers.

The Apple II computer was unveiled. It came already assembled in a case with a built-in keyboard. Users had to plug in their own TVs for monitors. Fully assembled microcomputers hit the general market, with Radio Shack, Commodore, and Apple all selling models. Sales were slow since neither businesses nor the general public knew exactly what to do with them.

Software Arts, Inc. released VisiCalc, the first commercial spreadsheet program for personal computers, developed by Dan Bricklin and Bob Frankston. VisiCalc is generally credited as being the program that paved the way for the personal computer in the business world.

Datapoint Corporation announced ARCnet, the first commercial local area network (LAN) intended for use with microcomputer applications. It transmitted data over a coaxial cable at 3 million bits per second.

Bob Metcalf formed 3Com Corporation in Santa Clara, California, to develop Ethernet-based networking products. Metcalf developed Ethernet while at Xerox Corporation's Palo Alto Research Center (PARC), and it later evolved into the world's most widely used network protocol.

MicroPro International, founded by Rob Barnaby and Seymour Rubenstein, introduced WordStar, the first commercially successful word processing program for microcomputers.

IBM released the IBM 3800, the fastest printer to date, which could print 20,000 lines per minute.

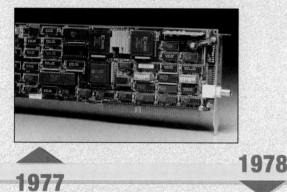

1977

1978

1979

Early commercial microcomputers were sold in kits and assembled by users, putting them in the domain of the electronic hobbyists. In the late 1970s, pre-assembled computers began to be sold in retail outlets, making them convenient for the average consumer.

Intel released the 8086 16-bit microprocessor, setting a new standard for power, capacity, and speed in microprocessors.

The first major microcomputer bulletin board, run by Ward Christensen and Randy Seuss, went online in Chicago, Illinois.

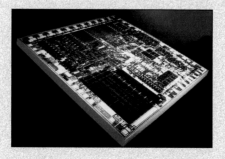

Epson announced the MX-80 dot-matrix printer, coupling high performance with a relatively low price.

IBM chose Microsoft (cofounded by Bill Gates, shown above, and Paul Allen) to provide the operating system for its upcoming PC, then under wraps as top secret "Project Acorn." Microsoft bought a program developed by Tim Patterson of Seattle Computer Products called Q-DOS (for Quick and Dirty Operating System), and modified it to run on IBM hardware. Q-DOS became PC-DOS, one of two operating systems eventually released with the IBM PC.

Bell Laboratories invented the Bellmac-32, the first single chip microprocessor with 32-bit internal architecture and a 32-bit data bus.

The Hercules Company introduced a graphics card allowing text and graphics to be combined on a display monitor at the same time.

Lotus Development Corporation unveiled the Lotus 1-2-3 integrated spreadsheet program combining spreadsheet, graphics, and database features in one package. The program was developed by Lotus president and founder, Mitch Kapor.

Intel released the 80286, a 16-bit microprocessor.

Peter Norton introduced Norton Utilities, a collection of software tools for the PC to help users recover corrupted files, clean up disk space, and increase the security of programs and data files.

When IBM introduced its Personal Computer, Apple Computer took out a full-page ad in *The Wall Street Journal* featuring the headline: "Welcome IBM. Seriously."

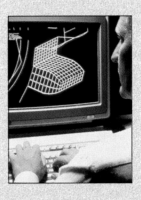

AutoCAD, a program for designing 2-D and 3-D objects, was released. AutoCAD revolutionized the architecture and engineering industries.

1980

1981

1982

IBM introduced the IBM PC, with a 4.77 MHz Intel 8088 CPU, 16 KB of memory, a keyboard, a monitor, one or two 5.25" floppy drives, and a price tag of $2,495.

Ashton-Tate developed dBase II, which set the standard for database programs.

Xerox unveiled the Xerox Star computer. Its high price doomed it to commercial failure, but its features inspired a whole new direction in computer design. Its little box on wheels (the first mouse) could execute commands on screen (the first graphical user interface).

Hayes Microcomputer Products, Inc. produced the SmartModem 300, which quickly became the industry standard.

Apple introduced the "user-friendly" Macintosh microcomputer.

Adobe Systems released its Postscript system, allowing printers to produce crisp print in a number of typefaces, as well as elaborate graphic images.

IBM shipped the PC AT, a 6 MHz computer using the Intel 80286 processor, which set the standard for personal computers running DOS

Early PC operating systems used text commands, requiring the user to know dozens of command sequences. The graphical user interface, which became popular after the introduction of the Macintosh in 1984, made computing simpler and more accessible to the nontechnical user.

Satellite Software International introduced the WordPerfect word processing program on several platforms.

1983
1984
1985

Time magazine featured the computer as the 1982 "Machine of the Year," acknowledging the computer's new role in society.

Apple introduced the Lisa, the first commercial computer with a purely graphical operating system and a mouse. The industry was excited, but its $10,000 price tag discouraged buyers.

IBM unveiled the IBM PC XT, essentially a PC with a hard disk drive and more memory. The XT was able to store programs and data on its built-in 10 MB hard disk drive.

The first version of the C++ programming language was developed, allowing programs to be written in reusable independent pieces called objects.

The Compaq Portable was released, the first successful 100 percent compatible PC clone. Despite its 28 pounds, it was the first computer to be lugged through airports.

Apple announced its "Kids Can't Wait" program, donating Apple II computers to 10,000 California schools.

Intel released the 80386 processor (also called the 386), a 32-bit processor with the ability to address over 4 billion bytes of memory—ten times faster than the 80286.

Aldus released PageMaker for the Macintosh, the first desktop publishing software for microcomputers. Coupled with Apple's LaserWriter printer and Adobe's PostScript system, the desktop publishing industry was born.

Hewlett-Packard introduced the Laser Jet laser printer featuring 300 dpi resolution.

Microsoft released the Windows 1.0 operating system, which featured the first graphical user interface for PCs.

IBM unveiled the new PS/2 line of computers featuring a 20-MHz 80386 processor at its top end.

IBM introduced its Video Graphics Array (VGA) monitor offering 256 colors at 320x200 resolution, and 16 colors at 640x480.

The Macintosh II computer, aimed at the desktop publishing market, was introduced by Apple Computer. It featured an SVGA monitor.

Apple Computer introduced HyperCard, a programming language for the Macintosh, which used the metaphor of a stack of index cards to represent a program—a kind of visual programming language.

Motorola unveiled its 68030 microprocessor.

Novell introduced its network operating system called NetWare.

1986

1987

1988

IBM delivered the PC Convertible, IBM's first laptop computer and the first Intel-based computer with a 3.5-inch floppy disk drive.

Microsoft sold its first public stock for $21 per share, raising $61 million in the initial public offering.

The First International Conference on CD-ROM technology was held in Seattle, hosted by Microsoft. Apple Computer introduced the Macintosh Plus, with increased memory and the capacity to connect an external hard drive.

IBM and Microsoft shipped OS/2 1.0, the first multitasking desktop operating system. High price, steep learning curve, and incompatibility with existing PCs contributed to its lack of market share.

Apple Computer filed the single biggest lawsuit in the computer industry against Microsoft and Hewlett-Packard claiming copyright infringement of its operating system and graphical user interface. Ashton-Tate sued Fox Software and Santa Cruz Operations alleging copyright infringement of dBase.

Hewlett-Packard introduced the first popular ink jet printer, the HP Deskjet.

 Steve Jobs' new company, NeXT, Inc., unveiled the NeXT computer featuring a 25-MHz Motorola 68030 processor. The NeXT was a pioneer computer introducing several "firsts" to the industry. It was the first computer to use object-oriented programming in its operating system and an optical drive instead of a floppy drive.

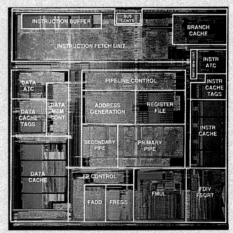

Apple introduced Apple CD SC, a CD-ROM storage device allowing access to up to 650 MB of data.

Intel released the 80486 chip (also called the 486), the world's first 1 million-transistor microprocessor. The 486 integrated a 386 CPU and math coprocessor onto the same chip.

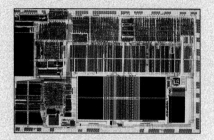

Tim Berners-Lee developed software around the hypertext concept, enabling users to click on a word or phrase in a document and jump either to another location within the document or to another file. This software laid the foundation for the development of the World Wide Web.

The World Wide Web was created at the European Particle Physics Laboratory for use by scientific researchers.

Apple Computer launched its new System 7.0 operating system and a product line featuring its new PowerBook series of battery-powered portable computers.

Apple, IBM, and Motorola signed a cooperative agreement to:

■ Design and produce RISC-based chips.
■ Integrate the Mac OS into IBM's enterprise systems.
■ Produce a new object-oriented operating system.
■ Develop common multimedia standards.

Symantec released Norton Desktop for Windows, a software package giving the user an improved desktop environment.

The ban on commercial business on the Internet was lifted.

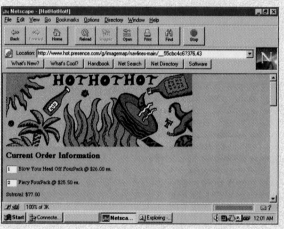

1989

1990

1991

Microsoft released Windows 3.0, shipping 1 million copies in four months.

A multmedia PC specification setting the minimum hardware requirements for sound and graphics components of a PC was announced at the Microsoft Multimedia Developers' Conference.

The National Science Foundation Network replaced ARPANET as the backbone of the Internet.

Motorola announced its 32-bit microprocessor, the 68040, incorporating 1.2 million transistors.

With an estimated 25 million users, the Internet became the world's largest electronic mail network.

Microsoft acquired Fox Software, including the popular Foxbase database management system.

In Apple Computer's five-year copyright infringement lawsuit, Judge Vaughn Walker ruled in favor of defendants Microsoft and Hewlett-Packard, finding that the graphical interface in dispute was not covered under Apple's copyrights.

Microsoft shipped its Windows 3.1 operating system, including improved memory management and TrueType fonts.

IBM introduced its ThinkPad laptop computer.

Apple announced its decision to license its System 7 operating system to other companies, opening the door for Macintosh clones.

Apple introduced the Power Macintosh line of microcomputers based on the PowerPC chip. This line introduced RISC to the desktop market. RISC was previously available only on high-end workstations.

Netscape Communications released the Netscape Navigator program, a World Wide Web browser based on the Mosaic standard, but with more advanced features.

Online service providers CompuServe, America Online, and Prodigy added Internet access to their services.

After 2 million Pentium-based PCs had shipped, a flaw in the Intel Pentium floating-point unit was found by Dr. Thomas Nicely. His report was made public on CompuServe.

1992

Mosaic, a point-and-click graphic Web browser, was developed at the National Center for Supercomputing Applications (NCSA), making the Internet accessible to those outside of the scientific community.

Intel, mixing elements of its 486 design with new processes, features, and technology, delivered the long-awaited Pentium processor. It had a 64-bit data path and more than 3.1 million transistors.

1993

Apple Computer expanded its entire product line, adding the Macintosh Color Classic, Macintosh LC III, Macintosh Centris 610 and 650, Macintosh Quadra 800, and the Powerbooks 165c and 180c.

Estimated total industry cost to produce the Pentium microprocessor: $1.5 billion. Average cost to manufacture one Pentium chip: $50

1994

Apple introduced the Newton MessagePad at the Macworld convention, selling 50,000 units in the first ten weeks.

Microsoft shipped its Windows NT operating system.

IBM shipped its first RISC-based RS/6000 workstation, featuring the PowerPC 601 chip developed jointly by Motorola, Apple, and IBM.

Intel announced the 200 MHz Pentium processor.

Microsoft added Internet connection capability to its Windows 95 operating system.

The number of Internet hosts has doubled every year since 1993. The number of hosts in 1993 was 1.1 million; 2.2 million in 1994; 4.8 million in 1995; and an estimated 9.5 million in 1996.

Digital Equipment Corp. launched Alta Vista, a Web search engine claimed to be the fastest online, with 36 million Web pages indexed.

Several vendors introduced VRML authoring tools that used simple interfaces and drag-and-drop editing features to create 3-dimensional worlds with colors, textures, motion video, and sound on the Web.

The U.S. Congress enacted the Communications Decency Act as part of the Telecommunications Act of 1996. The act regulated fines of up to $100,000 and prison terms for transmission of any "comment, request, suggestion, proposal, image or other communication which is obscene, lewd, lascivious, filthy, or indecent" over the Internet. The day the law was passed, millions of Web page backgrounds turned black in protest. The law was immediately challenged on Constitutional grounds.

1995

1996

Microsoft released its Windows 95 operating system with a massive marketing campaign, including prime time TV commercials. Seven million copies were sold the first month, with sales reaching 26 million by the end of the year.

Netscape Communications captured over 80 percent of the World Wide Web browser market, going from a start-up company to a $2.9 billion company in one year.

Power Computing shipped the first-ever Macintosh clones, the Power 100 series with a PowerPC 601 processor.

Intel released the Pentium Pro microprocessor.

Motorola released the PowerPC 604 chip, developed jointly with Apple and IBM.

TODAY

FROM THE VERY SMALL. . .

The microprocessor, which had its 25th anniversary in 1996, is the most complex consumer product in history. An estimated 10 billion microprocessors have been made worldwide over the product's quarter-century lifespan, and microcomputers are now an indisputable part of modern life. Technological advances in miniaturization have made it possible for computers to be inserted into almost any modern machine. Modern microprocessors contain millions of circuits, yet can fit through the eye of a needle...or a ring on your finger.

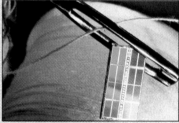

. . .TO THE VERY BIG

Intel has a contract with the U.S. Department of Energy to build the world's fastest supercomputer, which will contain 9,000 Pentium Pro microprocessors, each chip containing more than 5.5 million transistors. This new supercomputer will cost $45 million to build and will be capable of about 140 billion operations per second.

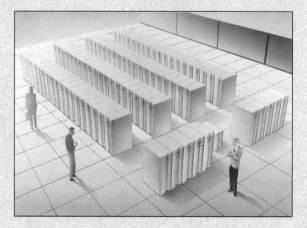

ERGONOMICS

Making the computer world hospitable means making computers easier, safer, and more comfortable to use. Ergonomics, the study of the physical relationship between people and their tools (such as their computers) addresses these issues.

Any office worker will tell you that sitting at a desk all day can become very uncomfortable. Sitting all day and using a computer can be even worse. Not only does your body ache from being in a chair too long, you can injure your wrists by keyboarding all day or strain your eyes by staring at a monitor for hours on end. Thanks to the publicity these problems have received over the years, most people now recognize the importance of ergonomically designed computer furniture.

▶ CHOOSING THE RIGHT CHAIR

A good, comfortable chair is an important piece of ergonomic computer furniture. You should look for three characteristics in any office chair: adjustable height, lower-back support, and arm rests.

▶ PREVENTING REPETITIVE STRESS INJURIES

Office workers have been demanding comfortable chairs for a long time. The field of ergonomics, however, did not receive much attention until repetitive stress injuries, a group of ailments caused by continually using the body in ways it was not designed to work, began appearing among clerical personnel who spend most of their time entering data on computer keyboards. One injury that is especially well documented is carpal tunnel syndrome, a wrist or hand injury caused by extended periods of keyboarding.

The carpal tunnel is a passageway in the wrist through which a bundle of nerves passes. In carpal tunnel syndrome, the tunnel becomes misshapen as a result of holding the wrist stiffly for long periods of time, as people tend to do at a keyboard. When the tunnel becomes distorted, it can pinch the nerves that run through it, causing numbness, pain, or an inability to use the hands. Carpal tunnel syndrome is the best known of the repetitive stress injuries. It can become so debilitating that employees suffering from it have to take weeks or even months off work.

Ergonomic chair.

The split layout of this keyboard allows the users' wrists to remain relaxed, because the hands remain in line with the forearms.

FIGURE B.1
A wrist support.

Several solutions have been proposed to make working at a keyboard more comfortable, which will help prevent carpal tunnel syndrome. The first is to set the keyboard at a proper height. When setting up their computer systems, most people just put their keyboards on their desks. The problem is that most desks are too high for good keyboard placement. Ideally, your hands should be at the same height as your elbows, or several inches lower, when they hover above the keyboard. To solve this ergonomic problem, many computer desks are slightly lower than traditional desks. Others are equipped with retractable shelves that position the keyboard at the correct height.

Another solution to wrist fatigue is to use a wrist support. The support can be built onto the keyboard or just placed in front of it, as shown in Figure B.1. A wrist support allows you to relax your arms and to use only your fingers to type.

One designer, Tony Hodges, realized that a flat keyboard is not well suited to the shape of our hands. After all, if you relax your arms, your thumbs tend to point up. Logically, then, keyboards should be designed with two sides, one for each hand. Hodges created just such a keyboard. Other manufacturers have followed his lead and designed ergonomic keyboards that allow the user's hands to rest in a more natural position.

A final solution is behavioral. You should take frequent breaks during an extended work period at a computer. Get up, walk around, stretch in your chair, and be sure to change positions frequently.

Protecting Your Eyes

Another area of concern for ergonomics is protecting people's vision. Staring at a computer screen for long periods can strain or even injure the eyes. Many users have found their vision deteriorating as a result of prolonged computer use. In fact, eyestrain is the most frequently reported health problem associated with computers.

Anti-glare screens cut down on light reflecting off the surface of the monitor, so they are useful in bright offices or where there is a window that faces the monitor.

If looking at the screen for fewer hours is not an option, here are some ways to reduce eyestrain:

- Avoid staring at the screen for long stretches. Maintaining your focus at the same distance for long periods tends to distort the shape of your eye's lens.

- Position your monitor between 2 and 2.5 feet away from your eyes. This is close enough for you to see everything on the screen but far enough away to let your eyes take in the whole screen at once.

- Try to position your monitor so that no bright lights, including sunlight, reflect off the screen. If you cannot avoid reflections, get an anti-glare screen.

- When shopping for a monitor, remember that most people prefer a relatively large screen (at least 14 inches, measured diagonally). A small screen encourages you to get too close to it.

- Look for a monitor that holds a steady image without appearing to pulsate or flicker. Make sure the dot pitch is no greater than .28 mm, and the refresh rate is at least 72 Hz.

Electromagnetic Fields

Electromagnetic fields (EMFs) are created during the generation, transmission, and use of low-frequency electrical power. These fields exist near power lines, in your home near electrical appliances, and in the office near any piece of equipment that has an electric motor. Currently, there is no convincing evidence to link EMFs with cancer. There is enough data, however, to raise suspicion. Given the pervasiveness of EMFs in our homes and workplaces, the issue cannot be ignored.

EMFs are composed of an electrical and a magnetic component. Of the two, the magnetic field is the one that raises the health concern. Electrical fields lose strength when they come in contact with barriers such as clothing and skin. A magnetic field, however, will penetrate most materials, even concrete or lead.

Populations that are deemed to be at the greatest risk include children, pregnant women, and anyone who spends many working hours near a piece of electrical equipment. This latter category, of course, includes many computer users.

Magnetic fields lose strength rapidly with distance. Options to reduce your risk from EMFs include:

- Taking frequent breaks away from the computer.

- Sitting an arm's length away from the terminal.

- Using a monitor with a liquid crystal display (LCD). These monitors do not radiate EMFs.

ETHICS

A new world is available to computer users—an electronic frontier called cyber-space, where data is stored, processed, and moved through vast data communications networks. Cyberspace is not just the name of a new chapter in the history books—it is a technological, cultural, and economic frontier that is growing all around us, and will continue to grow.

As with any new frontier, the taming of cyberspace presents many challenges and opportunities to computer users, corporate data professionals, information entrepreneurs, and others who make their living off this wild, new land. Laws must be written to define the particular qualities of ownership, property, and value in cyberspace. Ethics must be developed to govern how citizens treat each other, and standards must be first articulated and then accepted so we can live comfortably with one another and with this ever-changing technology.

► COMPUTER CRIME

Many things that take place in cyberspace are not addressed by the traditional body of law. For example, physical location has always been a fundamental concept in law: different laws govern depending on the jurisdiction of community, state, or country. In cyberspace, however, physical location is irrelevant, so which laws govern which transactions? Suppose, for example, that someone in Akron, Ohio, downloads an interesting short story from a computer in London. Has that person broken the law if the material is in the public domain in England but is still under copyright protection in the United States?

► SOFTWARE PIRACY

By far, the biggest legal problem affecting the computer industry today is software piracy, which is the illegal copying or use of programs. Piracy is a huge problem mainly because it is so easy to do. Some programs cost as little as $20 to $50, but most applications cost between $100 and $500. Highly specialized or very complex applications can cost several thousand dollars.

Copyright Laws Regarding Software

Part of the reason that piracy is so difficult to stop is that some kinds of copying are legal, a fact that tempts some people to gloss over the distinctions. For example, it is generally legal to copy software that you own so that you have a backup copy in case your original is damaged.

Anti-piracy safeguards such as copy protection and password protection are not completely effective. Consequently, many software developers simply rely on the law and people's respect for the law.

The principal law governing software piracy is still the Copyright Act of 1976. In 1983, a software Piracy and Counterfeiting Amendment was added. More recently, software piracy was upgraded from a misdemeanor to a felony.

Network Versions and Site Licenses

Businesses and organizations are the biggest purchasers of computer hardware and software. As a result, the greatest potential loss of revenue caused by piracy is from their abuse of the copyright laws.

Software companies have developed two solutions based on volume discount—site licenses and network licenses. A site license is an agreement through which a purchaser buys the right to use a program on a given number of machines for less than the price of buying a separate copy of the program for each computer.

The network license is based on the same principle as the site license but is intended for networked machines. The company buys a network license for commonly used applications, and then loads these applications onto the network server.

Software Forgeries

Sharing software illegally with friends or within a company is one issue. Blatant forgery with the intent to sell is another problem altogether. Forgery is big business in some parts of the world, including Europe and Asia. By one estimate, piracy cost U.S. software publishing and distribution companies $12.8 billion in 1994.

◪ COMPUTER VIRUSES

Although software piracy is by far the most prevalent computer crime, for many users the creation of computer viruses is a more disturbing crime. A virus is a parasitic program buried within another legitimate program or stored in a special area of a disk called the boot sector. Executing the legitimate program or accessing the disk activates the virus without the user's knowledge. The following list details a few of the activities that viruses have been programmed to do:

- Copy themselves to other programs.
- Display information on the screen.
- Destroy data files.
- Erase an entire hard disk.
- Lie dormant for a specified time or until a given condition is met.

Preventing Infection

Fortunately, safeguarding a system against viruses is not very difficult, given a little knowledge and some handy utility software. The first thing you need to know is when your system is in danger of infection.

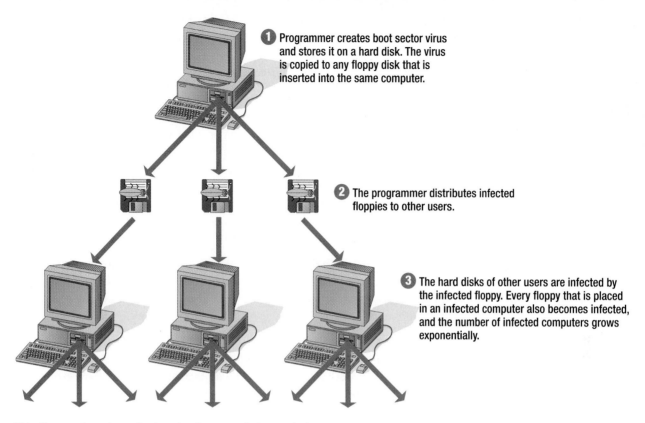

① Programmer creates boot sector virus and stores it on a hard disk. The virus is copied to any floppy disk that is inserted into the same computer.

② The programmer distributes infected floppies to other users.

③ The hard disks of other users are infected by the infected floppy. Every floppy that is placed in an infected computer also becomes infected, and the number of infected computers grows exponentially.

This diagram shows how a boot sector virus spreads from a single computer to many computers.

There are two common ways to pick up a virus:

- Receiving a disk from another user. In this case, the virus could be in the boot sector of the disk or in an executable file (a program) on the disk.

- Downloading an executable file from another user, an online service, or the Internet.

Checking for viruses requires antivirus software, which scans disks and programs for known viruses and eradicates them. Using such a program can be easy. Once it is installed on your system and activated, a good antivirus program checks for infected files automatically every time you insert any kind of disk or use your modem to retrieve a file. Several excellent antivirus programs are available. Some are even free.

Hackers

Hackers are experts in computer technology who take great pleasure in solving software problems, often by circumventing the established rules. Often, these experts are tempted by the power of their skills and become criminals. They can steal money or crash computer systems intentionally.

Colorful examples of computer crime abound. Credit card thieves using a personal computer broke into a database at TRW, a company that keeps credit histories, and gained access to the confidential credit records of 90 million people. Using a com-

Computer student Robert Morris planted a computer virus in the national defense computer. He was arrested and charged with a federal offense.

puter in his bedroom, a 17-year-old high school student broke into AT&T's computer network and stole $1 million worth of software before he was caught. Several employees of an East Coast railroad manipulated data to show that 200 railroad cars had been destroyed, and then they sold the cars.

One scheme is just a computerized twist on the crime of embezzlement, usually from an employer. Computer embezzlers manipulate a company's computerized accounts to divert funds for their own use. For example, a bank embezzler might instruct a computer system to round down all interest payments on customer accounts to two decimal places, then enter the difference into the embezzler's account. Although the amount of each fraudulent transaction always would be minuscule, making that transaction several million times a day would add up to quite a lot of money. FBI records show that, whereas a bank robber steals an average of $1600 per heist, a computer embezzler steals an average of $600,000.

Often, curious hackers are the ones who catch the criminals. In one celebrated case, a graduate student named Clifford Stoll followed up on a $0.75 account discrepancy at the Lawrence Berkeley Laboratory. He wound up tracking a computer intruder across international networks and uncovered a high-tech spy ring.

No one really knows the full extent of data theft that is occurring now, in part because companies do not want to admit that their computer systems have been breached. They fear the liability associated with that admission. By some estimates, though, the losses are huge, possibly as much as 5 percent of gross sales in some large companies. For the United States as a whole, a 1994 FBI estimate suggested the losses lie between $164 million and $5 billion. That range is as large as it is because only 1 percent, or less, of computer crime is even *detected*, much less solved.

There is no easy solution to the problem posed by computer crime. Data security is becoming more and more sophisticated, but so are criminals. To illustrate that point to the experts, a Dutch engineer first explained that computers emit TV-like signals that can be reconstructed with standard equipment and displayed. Then, to demonstrate his point, he set up his equipment in a basement and read the data from a PC located on the eighth floor of a neighboring office building.

Although stiff penalties can be imposed to guard against computer crimes, catching the culprits can be extremely difficult, and the methods used to do so sometimes carry their own set of ethical dilemmas. Crackdowns on suspected hackers have occasionally resulted in the arrest and prosecution of people engaged in perfectly legal activities.

For example, after an unexplained, nine-hour crash of AT&T's long-distance network in 1990, Secret Service agents arrested Craig Neidorf, a Georgia college student. Neidorf had once published an illicit copy of a telephone company document in his electronic newsletter as an amusing example of bureaucratic nonsense. Later, the government's case collapsed when it was discovered that the information Neidorf had published could be ordered for about $20. The story of the 1991 "hacker crackdown" was told in the book of the same name by Bruce Sterling.

10base-T an Ethernet network standard that uses twisted-pair wires to achieve data transfer speeds of up to 10 Mbps.

3-D modeling software graphics software used to create electronic models of 3-dimensional objects; includes surface, solid, polygonal, and spline-based modeling.

A

absolute cell reference a spreadsheet cell reference that does not change when copied to a new cell.

accelerator card a circuit board that fits into an expansion slot and enhances the processing speed of the CPU.

activate to initiate a command or to load a program into memory and begin using it; also, to choose.

active matrix LCD a liquid crystal display technology that assigns a transistor to each pixel; improves display quality and eliminates the submarining effect typical of a flat-panel monitor.

active window the program or area on the computer screen in which the next action taken by the user will occur; the title bar of the active window is highlighted.

address the location of a cell on a spreadsheet, named with the column letter and row number, such as A1.

address bus a set of wires connecting the CPU and RAM, across which memory addresses are transmitted; the number of wires determines the amount of memory that can be addressed at any one time.

Advanced Research Projects Agency Network (ARPANET) an early network developed by the Department of Defense to connect computers at universities and defense contractors.

alignment the orientation of the lines of a paragraph with respect to the margins; options include left, right, center, and justified or full justification.

alphanumeric field a database field that stores a string of alphanumeric characters; also called a text field or character field.

alphanumeric keys the part of the keyboard that includes the letters of the alphabet and other keys commonly found on a typewriter.

ALU *see* arithmetic logic unit.

American Standard Code for Information Interchange (ASCII) a 7-bit binary code developed by ANSI to represent symbols and numeric and alphanumeric characters; the most common character set for PCs.

anonymous FTP archives a compilation of programs and data files accessible to the public on the Internet; anyone can download a file from an FTP archive, using the account name "anonymous".

antivirus software *see* antivirus utility.

antivirus utility a program that scans disks and memory for viruses, detects them, and removes them.

application software any computer program that is used to create or process data, such as text documents, spreadsheets, graphics, and so on; examples include database management software, desktop publishing programs, presentation graphics applications, spreadsheets, and word processing programs.

Archie a catalog of file names maintained by McGill University in Montreal; the public can search and locate a file among thousands of directories listed on this service.

ARCnet *see* Attached Resource Computer Network.

argument (1) in a spreadsheet, the values (often cell references) within a formula on which the function performs its operation; (2) in programming, an item of information needed by a function or subroutine to carry out its instructions.

arithmetic logic unit (ALU) the component of the CPU that handles arithmetic and logic functions; instructions are passed from memory to the ALU.

ARPANET *see* Advanced Research Projects Agency Network.

ascending sort order arranged in alphabetical or numerical order.

ASCII *see* American Standard Code for Information Interchange.

Asynchronous Transfer Mode (ATM) a network protocol designed to send voice, video, and data transmissions over a single network; provides different kinds of connections and bandwidth on demand, depending on the type of data transmitted.

Attached Resource Computer Network (ARCnet) a LAN network standard that uses twisted-pair wire or coaxial cable to achieve data transfer speeds of up to 20 Mbps.

auditing the process of maintaining and confirming the contents of a spreadsheet for accuracy, using tools provided by the software.

automated fabrication a computer tool used in the manufacturing process that enables designers to make quick design changes to customize a product.

average access time the average amount of time it takes a storage device to position its read/write heads over any spot on the medium.

■ B

backbone the central structure that connects other elements of the network and handles the major traffic in the system.

backing up the process of creating a duplicate set of programs or data in case the originals become damaged.

backup software a program that enables the user to copy large groups of files from a hard disk to another storage medium.

bandwidth the amount of data that can be transmitted over a network, measured in bits per second.

bar code reader an input device that converts a pattern of printed bars into a number that a computer can read; a beam of light reflected off the bar code image into a light-sensitive detector identifies the bar code and converts the bar patterns into numeric digits; commonly used in retail stores.

BASIC *see* Beginners All-purpose Symbolic Instruction Code.

batch mode a processing method in which computer transactions are performed on a scheduled basis, daily, weekly, monthly, and so on.

BBS (bulletin board service) an online information service tailored to the needs of a specific discussion group.

Beginners All-purpose Symbolic Instruction Code (BASIC) a popular programming language used primarily as an educational tool.

Bezier tool a computer graphics tool that builds an image with a series of curves expressed as mathematical formulas; permits the reshaping and blending of an image with other graphics.

binary field a database field that stores binary objects, such as clip art, photographs, screen images, formatted text, sound objects, video clips, or OLE objects such as graphs or worksheets created with a spreadsheet or word processor.

Binary Large Object (BLOB) a graphic image file such as clip art, a photograph, a screen image, formatted text, a sound object, or a video clip; also an OLE object such as a graph or worksheet created with a spreadsheet or word processor; frequently used with object-oriented databases.

binary system a system for representing the two possible states of electrical switches, on and off ; also known as base 2.

bit the smallest unit of data; *bi*nary digi*t*.

bitmap a binary representation of an image in which each part of the image, such as a pixel, is represented by one or more bits in a coordinate system.

bits per second (bps) a measurement of modem transmission speed.

BLOB *see* Binary Large Object.

block a contiguous series of letters, words, sentences, or paragraphs in a word processing document, or a range of cells in a spreadsheet upon which an action, such as moving, formatting, or deleting, is performed.

BMP a graphics file format created by Microsoft and commonly used with Windows applications.

booting the process of starting a computer.

boot sector a part of the logical formatting process; contains a program that runs when the computer is first turned on and that determines whether the disk has the basic components necessary to run the operating system successfully.

border a paragraph format that displays a line on any side of a block; used to distinguish the block from regular text.

bps (bits per second) a measurement of modem transmission speed.

bridge a device that connects two LANs and controls data flow.

bulletin board *see* discussion group.

bus the path between components of a computer or nodes of a network; the width of the bus determines the speed at which data is transmitted; commonly refers to the data bus.

bus network a network topology in which all network nodes and peripheral devices are attached to a single conduit.

buttons symbols found in graphical environments that simulate a push button; the user clicks a button to initiate an action.

byte the amount of memory required to store a single character, a byte comprises 8 bits.

C

cache memory high-speed memory that resides between the CPU and RAM and stores data and instructions.

CAD *see* computer-aided drafting or computer-aided design.

CAE *see* computer-aided engineering.

CAM *see* computer-aided manufacturing.

card *see* circuit board.

carpal tunnel syndrome an injury of the wrist or hand commonly caused by repetitive motion, such as extended periods of keyboarding.

cathode ray tube (CRT) monitor a type of monitor or TV screen that uses a vacuum tube as a display screen; most commonly used with desktop computers.

CBT *see* computer-based training.

CD-recordable (CD-R) drive a peripheral device that allows the user to create customized CD-ROM disks that cannot be changed once created, but can be read by any CD-ROM drive; used to create beta versions and program masters and to archive data.

CD-ROM *see* compact disk, read-only memory.

cell the intersection of a spreadsheet row and column, forming a box into which the user enters numbers, formulas, or text.

cell pointer a square covering one cell of a spreadsheet that identifies the active cell; positioned by clicking the mouse on the cell or by using the cursor movement keys on the keyboard.

cell reference the address of a spreadsheet cell used in a formula.

central processing unit (CPU) the computer's processing hardware that interprets and executes program instructions and communicates with input, output, and storage devices; composed of the control unit and the ALU on a single chip of a PC's motherboard or on several circuit boards in larger computers.

Centronics interface the portion of a parallel printer cable that connects to the printer with a 36-pin plug; a standard developed by Centronics Corporation for the first dot-matrix printers.

character field *see* alphanumeric field.

chart *see* graph.

chat line an online service similar to a BBS in which users can conduct live group discussions; each keystroke is transmitted as it is entered.

choose *see* activate.

CIM *see* computer-integrated manufacturing.

circuit board a rigid rectangular card consisting of chips and electronic circuitry that ties the processor to other hardware; also called a card.

circuit-switched line a type of communications line in which access to the connection is constant until broken by either party; commonly used for telephone or modem transmission.

CISC processors *see* Complex Instruction Set Computing processors.

click to select an object or command on screen by pointing to the object and pressing and releasing the mouse button once.

client an application program on a user's computer that requests information from another computer through a network; also refers to the machine making the request.

client/server network a hierarchical network strategy in which the processing is shared by a server and numerous clients; clients provide the user interface, run applications, and request services from the server, which contributes storage, processing, and printing services.

Clipboard a holding area maintained by the operating system in memory; used for storing text, graphics, sound, or video that has been copied or cut from a document.

cluster a group of disk sectors treated as a storage unit.

CMYK separation *see* process color separation.

coaxial cable a cable composed of a single conductive wire wrapped in a conductive wire mesh shield with an insulator in between.

code the instructions or statements that are the basis of a computer program.

color monitor a computer screen that displays computer data in color; range and intensity are related to video bandwidth, dot pitch, refresh rate, and convergence.

color separation a computer process used to prepare full-color pages for printing; creates a separate page for each color found in the image.

column a vertically arranged series of cells in a spreadsheet, named with a letter or combination of letters.

command-line interface a user interface in which the user interacts with the software by typing strings of characters at a prompt.

common user access (CUA) a system that makes use of similar graphical tools in several software products; the level of consistency in the interface makes software easier to learn and to use.

communication device an input/output device used to connect one computer to another in order to share hardware and information; includes modems and network cards.

communications programs software used to transmit data between computers and terminals.

compact disk, read-only memory (CD-ROM) the most common type of optical storage medium; data is written in a series of lands and pits on the surface of a disk, which can be read by a laser in a CD-ROM drive; stores approximately 650 MB but cannot be altered.

comparison operator a component of a spreadsheet formula that compares the values or labels in two cells and returns an answer of either TRUE or FALSE; includes equals, does not equal, greater than, greater than or equal to, less than, and less than or equal to.

Complex Instruction Set Computing (CISC) processors processors designed to handle large and comprehensive instruction sets; commonly used in the Motorola and Intel microprocessor lines.

computer a machine composed of electronic devices used to process data.

computer-aided drafting or computer-aided design (CAD) the use of computers to create complex 2- or 3-dimensional models of products, including architectural, engineering, and mechanical designs.

computer-aided engineering (CAE) the use of software that allows designers to perform analyses on designs, such as structural analysis or electronic circuit analysis, and determine the optimum materials and design components.

computer-aided manufacturing (CAM) the use of software to create automated systems and to manufacture products, including the use of robotics.

computer-aided software engineering (CASE) tool software used to develop information systems; automates the analysis, design, programming, and documentation tasks.

computer-based training (CBT) the use of customized interactive computer tools to train employees in such areas as company policy, software, and personnel issues.

computer-integrated manufacturing (CIM) the use of software to design products and integrate the production process with the accounting system to control inventory, ordering, billing, and scheduling.

computer system an organization and analysis tool that consists of hardware, software, data, and a user.

configure to adapt a computer to specific needs by selecting from a wide range of hardware and software options.

control unit the component of the CPU that contains the instruction set; directs the flow of data throughout the computer system.

conversion the process of replacing an existing system with an improved version.

cooperative multitasking a multitasking environment in which programs periodically check with the operating system to see if other programs need the CPU and, if so, relinquish control of the CPU to the next program.

Copy an application command that makes a duplicate of data selected from an application and stores it in the Clipboard without removing the data from the original document.

copy protection an antipiracy technique that prevents the illegal duplication of software.

counter field a database field that stores a unique, incrementing numeric value (such as an invoice number) that the DBMS automatically assigns to each new record.

CPU *see* central processing unit.

crop marks marks that identify the precise corners of a page; used in desktop publishing.

CRT monitor *see* cathode ray tube monitor.

CUA *see* common user access.

cursor a graphic symbol on screen that indicates where the next keystroke or command will appear when entered; representations include a blinking vertical line or underline, a box, an arrow, or an I-beam pointer.

cursor movement keys the keys that direct the movement of the on screen cursor, including the up, down, left, and right arrows, and the Home, End, Page Up and Page Down keys.

Cut an application command that removes data selected from an application and stores it in the Clipboard; the data is no longer a part of the original document.

cyberspace a term used to describe a vast electronic network in which everyday tasks, such as banking, research, and communication, are conducted via computer.

cylinder all tracks bearing the same track number on both sides of a floppy disk or across all platters of a hard disk.

■ D

DAT *see* digital audiotape.

data raw facts, numbers, letters, or symbols that the computer processes into meaningful information.

data area the part of the disk that remains free to store information after the logical formatting process has created the boot sector, FAT, and root folder.

database a collection of related data organized with a specific structure.

database management software *see* database management system.

database management system (DBMS) computer program used to manage the storage, organization, processing, and retrieval of data in a database; also called database management software.

data bus an electrical path composed of parallel wires that connects the CPU, memory, and other hardware on the motherboard; the number of wires determines the amount of data that can be transferred at one time.

data communications the electronic transfer of data between computers.

data compression to reduce data volume and increase data-transfer rates using a mathematical algorithm that analyzes groups of bits and encodes repeating sequences of data.

data compression utility a program that reduces the volume of data by manipulating the way the data is stored.

data-encoding scheme the method that a disk drive uses to translate bits of data into a sequence of flux reversals, or changes in magnetic polarity, on the surface of a disk.

data recovery utility a program used to recover data files that have been mistakenly deleted or somehow rendered unusable; also called an unerase program.

data-transfer rate the rate at which a data storage device can read or write data; expressed as bytes, KB, MB, or GB per second.

date field a database field that stores a date.

DBMS *see* database management system.

decimal system the system that uses 10 digits to represent numbers; also called base 10.

defragmentation utility a program that reorganizes data on disk by rejoining parts of files split in the editing process and eliminating breaks between data units; speeds disk access.

density a measure of the quality of a magnetic disk's surface; the higher the density, the more closely the iron oxide particles are packed and the more data the disk can store.

DES *see* Data Encryption Standard.

descending sort order arranged in reverse alphabetic or numerical order, from Z to A or 9 to 0.

desktop (1) the graphical representation of a desktop in which all files, utilities, and programs are at the fingertips of the user. (2) the most common PC model, sized to fit on a desk, with a separate unit for the CPU and for the monitor.

desktop publishing (DTP) software a program used to enhance standard word processing documents; creates professional-quality documents and publications using design, typesetting, and pasteup features.

desktop publishing programs *see* desktop publishing software.

device any electronic component attached to or part of a computer; hardware.

digital the use of numbers, or digits, to express units of computer data.

digital audiotape (DAT) a magnetic storage medium that can store a very high density of data; read by a DAT drive that has two write heads that write data with opposite magnetic polarities on overlapping areas of the tape, and two read heads that each read only one polarity or the other.

digital camera a video camera that converts light intensities into digital data; used to record images that can be viewed and edited on the computer.

digital convergence   the process of combining digital text, graphics, video, and sound into a single product.

digital video disk (DVD)   a high-density optical medium that is capable of storing a full-length movie on a single disk the size of a CD.

direct conversion   the complete transfer of all data and users from an existing system to a new system at one time.

directory   a tool for organizing a disk; contains a list of files and other directories; also called a folder.

discussion group   an electronic storage space where users can post messages to other users, carry on extended conversations, and trade information; also called a bulletin board or a news group.

disk drive   a storage device that holds, spins, reads, and writes removable floppy disks or nonremovable hard disks.

diskette   a removable magnetic disk made of a thin piece of flexible plastic coated with iron oxide and encased in a plastic sleeve; used to load new programs or data on a hard disk, transfer data between computers, or make a backup copy of data from a hard disk; common sizes include 3.5" and 5.25"; also called a floppy disk or a floppy.

diskette drive   a device that holds a removable floppy disk when in use; read/write heads read and write data to the diskette.

distributed computing   a system configuration in which two or more computers in a network share applications, storage, and processing power; also called distributed processing.

DNS   *see* Domain Name System.

document   a computer file consisting of a compilation of data, including text documents, spreadsheets, graphics files, and so on.

domain   a name given for a computer and its peripherals connected to the Internet.

Domain Name System (DNS)   a naming system used for computers on the Internet, consisting of an individual name representing the institution or person and the domain name, which classifies the type of organization, such as .com for commercial enterprises; converts an e-mail address into the IP address for transmission.

dot pitch   the distance between phosphor dots on a monitor; the best monitors have the smallest dot pitch.

double-click   to select an object or activate a command on screen by pointing to the object and quickly pressing and releasing the mouse button twice.

downloading   retrieving a file from a remote computer.

downward (backward) compatibility   the ability of a hardware device or a software product to interact successfully with the same software or hardware used by its predecessor.

drag   to move an object on screen by pointing to the object, depressing the mouse button, and holding it down while dragging the object to a new location; also used to activate commands, as when moving files in the Windows 95 Explorer.

drag-and-drop editing   moving text from one part of the document to another by highlighting the block, holding down the mouse button, dragging the block to a new location, and releasing the mouse button.

DRAM   *see* dynamic RAM.

draw program   a graphics program that uses vectors to create an image; mathematical equations describe each line, shape, and pattern, allowing the user to manipulate all elements of the graphic.

drivers   programs that accept requests for action from the operating system and cause a device, such as a sound or video card, to execute the requests.

drop cap   an enlarged capital letter that occupies two or more lines of type at the beginning of a paragraph.

DTP   *see* desktop publishing software.

dual-scan LCD   an improved passive matrix technology for flat-panel monitors in which pixels are scanned twice as often, reducing the effects of submarining and blurry graphics.

DVD   *see* digital video disk.

dye-sub (dye-sublimation) printer   a printer that produces photographic-quality images by using a heat source to evaporate colored inks from a ribbon, which transfers the color to specially coated paper; variations in color are related to the intensity of the heat; also called thermal dye transfer and thermal dye diffusion.

dynamic RAM (DRAM)   the most common type of computer memory.

▪ E

EBCDIC   *see* Extended Binary Coded Decimal Interchange Code.

editing   making modifications to an existing document.

edutainment   a class of educational programs that are also entertaining, such as programs that teach children to do math, learn to read, or conduct science projects.

EFF *see* Electronic Frontier Foundation.

EISA bus *see* Extended Industry Standard Architecture.

electromagnet a magnet made by wrapping a wire coil around an iron bar and sending an electric current through the coil; reversing the direction of the current's flow reverses the polarity of the magnetic field; a part of the read/write heads.

electromagnetic field (EMF) a field of magnetic and electrical forces created during the generation, transmission, and use of low-frequency electrical power, as in that produced by a computer.

Electronic Frontier Foundation (EFF) an organization created to provide research, policy development, and legal services for issues related to the expansion of electronic communications.

electronic mail (e-mail) a system for exchanging written, voice, and video messages through a network.

electronic pen an input device that allows the user to write directly on or point at a special pad or the screen of a pen-based computer, such as a PDA.

Encapsulated Postscript (EPS) a file format based on the PostScript printing language.

enhanced small device interface (ESDI) a hard disk drive interface standard developed by Maxtor Corporation.

entertainment software computer programs such as flight simulators, children's tutorials, and games designed to amuse and interact with the user.

EPS *see* Encapsulated Postscript.

ergonomics the study of the physical relationship between people and their tools.

error-correction protocols standards for correcting errors that occur when static interferes with data transmitted over telephone lines; examples include MNP2, MNP3, MNP4, and V42.

ESDI *see* enhanced small device interface.

Ethernet the most common network protocol, commonly implemented using twisted-pair wires and star topology; requires each computer on the network take its turn to send data.

executable file the core program file responsible for launching software.

executing loading and carrying out a program or a specific set of instructions; also called running.

expansion slots the area of the motherboard into which circuit boards are inserted; connected to the bus in a PC.

Extended Binary Coded Decimal Interchange Code (EBCDIC) an 8-bit binary code developed by IBM to represent symbols and numeric and alphanumeric characters; commonly used today on IBM mainframe computers.

Extended Industry Standard Architecture (EISA) bus a PC bus standard created by a consortium of hardware developers that extends the 16-bit bus to 32 bits; capable of accessing 16-bit and 32-bit devices.

external modem a communications device used to modulate data signals; housed outside the computer and connected to the computer through a serial port and to the telephone system with a standard telephone jack.

F

FAQ *see* Frequently Asked Questions.

FAT *see* file allocation table.

fax modem a modem that can emulate a fax machine.

fiber-optic cable a thin strand of glass wrapped in a protective coating; transfers data by means of pulsating beams of light.

field the smallest unit of data in a database, used to group each piece or item of data into a specific category; arranged in a column and titled by the user.

field format a DBMS tool that converts or verifies the type of data entered in a field, accepting only valid characters and controlling the entry's display format; also called a mask or picture.

fiery printer a color laser printer typically used to produce high-quality graphics; used by print shops and publishing firms.

file a set of related computer data or program instructions that has been given a name.

file allocation table (FAT) a table log created in the logical formatting process that records the location of each file and the status of each sector.

file server the central computer of a network, used for shared storage; stores software applications and databases; also called network server or server.

file server network a hierarchical network strategy in which the server is used to store and forward files to the nodes; each node runs its own applications.

file transfer sending a file from one computer to another by modem.

File Transfer Protocol (FTP)   a set of rules or guidelines that dictate the format in which data is sent from one computer to another.

filter   a DBMS tool that allows the user to establish conditions for selecting and displaying a subset of records meeting those criteria.

find and replace   a text editing feature that searches a document for a particular string of data and replaces that string with a block of text specified by the user.

flatbed scanner   a scanner that can accommodate large pages and books; scanning heads move under a glass cover to copy data to the computer.

flat-file database   a database file consisting of a single data table; not linked to other databases.

flat-panel display   a thin, lightweight monitor used in laptop and notebook computers; most often uses LCD technology.

floating-point arithmetic   a method used to speed up the storage and calculation of numbers by reducing the number of decimal places through the use of scientific notation; function of a math coprocessor.

floppy   *see* diskette.

floppy disk   *see* diskette.

folder   *see* directory.

font   the style of the letters, symbols, and punctuation marks in a document.

form   a custom screen created in a database for displaying and entering data for one record at a time.

formatting   the process of magnetically mapping a disk with a series of tracks and sectors where data will be stored.

formula   a mathematical equation within a cell of a spreadsheet; begins with a special symbol, such as a plus sign, an equal sign, or a parenthesis.

formula bar   a special toolbar above the spreadsheet window that displays the active cell address and the formula or data entered in that cell.

FPU (Floating-Point Unit)   *see* math coprocessor.

fragmented   describes a file in which sections of the file have been stored on noncontiguous sectors of a disk.

frame   a small block of data to be transmitted over a network; includes an identifying header and the actual data to be sent; also called a packet.

Frequently Asked Questions (FAQ)   a document routinely developed by a news group that lists the most commonly

asked questions and answers; avoids repeatedly posting the same information to the group.

full duplex   the ability to send and transmit data simultaneously over a common data path or communications link.

function   (1) in a spreadsheet, a part of a cell formula used to perform complex operations, such as adding the contents of a cell range or finding the absolute value of cell contents; (2) in programming, a block of statements designed to perform a specific routine or task.

function keys   the part of the keyboard that can be used to quickly activate commands, designated F1, F2, and so on.

◼ G

gateway   a computer system that can translate one network protocol into another so that data can be transmitted between two dissimilar networks.

GB   *see* gigabyte.

GIF   *see* Graphics Interchange Format.

gigabyte (GB)   equivalent to approximately one billion bytes; typical measurement of storage.

goal seeking   a data analysis process that begins with a conclusion and calculates the values that will lead to the desired outcome, such as figuring a mortgage amount based on an affordable monthly payment.

Gopher   an Internet service that organizes resources into multilevel menus to make finding information easier; first created by the University of Minnesota to provide easy access to computers campus-wide.

grammar checker   a word processing tool that examines and evaluates a document for correct word usage, grammar, and writing style.

graph   a graphic representation of numbers created from spreadsheet data; also called a chart.

graphical user interface (GUI)   a user interface in which actions are initiated when the user selects an icon or an option from a pull-down menu with the mouse or other pointing device; also called a point-and-click interface.

Graphics Interchange Format (GIF)   a file format developed by CompuServe to display graphics; used to develop Web pages.

graphics program   software used to create and manipulate original images or those created in another application.

grayscale monitor   a monitor that displays colors ranging from white to black, including up to 256 shades of gray.

groupware   application software that allows multiple users on a network to cooperate on projects; includes scheduling and calendar software, e-mail, and document management software.

GUI   *see* graphical user interface.

H

hacker   an expert in computer technology who uses skill and innovative techniques to solve complex computing problems.

hand-held scanner   a scanner that can be held in the hand and used to scan narrow areas of data.

hard disk   a nonremovable magnetic storage device included in most PCs; a stack of aluminum or glass platters, each coated with iron oxide, enclosed in a hard disk drive.

hard disk drive   a device that consists of the hard disk platters, a spindle on which the platters spin, and a sealed chamber that encloses disk and spindle.

hardware   the physical components of a computer, including processors, memory, input/output devices, tapes, disks, modems, and cables.

head crash   the damage to a hard disk and the possible destruction of a read/write head that occurs when the head touches the disk.

Hertz (Hz)   the frequency of electrical vibrations, or cycles, per second.

hierarchical database   a database structure in which records are organized in parent-child relationships; each child type is related to only one parent type.

hierarchical file system   a structured file organization system in which the root folder may contain other folders, which in turn contain files.

highlighted   text that is displayed in a different color from the remaining text in a document, indicating that the text is selected.

home page   an organization's principal Web page that provides pointers to other Web pages with additional information.

hot-swappable hard disk   a magnetic storage device similar to a removable hard disk; a removable box encloses the disk, drive, and read/write heads in a sealed container; can be added or removed from a server without shutting the server down.

HTML   *see* Hypertext Markup Language.

HTTP   *see* Hypertext Transfer Protocol.

hypermedia   text, graphics, video, and sound linked and accessible in a hypertext format.

hypertext   a flexible software technology that provides fast and flexible access to information; the user can jump to a search topic by selecting it on screen; used to create Web pages and help screens.

Hypertext Markup Language (HTML)   a page description language used on the World Wide Web that defines the hypertext links between documents.

Hypertext Transfer Protocol (HTTP)   a set of file transfer rules used on the World Wide Web that control the way information is shared.

Hz   *see* hertz.

I

I-beam cursor   an on screen symbol shaped like a capital I that indicates the location of the next keyboard or mouse action.

icons   graphical screen elements that execute one or more commands when selected with a mouse or other pointing device.

IDE   *see* integrated drive electronics.

image scanner   an input device that converts printed images into electronic form; sensors determine the intensity of light reflected from the page, and the light intensities are converted to digital data that can be viewed and manipulated by the computer; also called a graphics scanner.

indent   the distance between the beginning or end of a line of text and the margin.

index   a table created by a database that stores an association between one field and the original record number assigned to that field; used by the DBMS to locate records when queried, regardless of the final record order.

Industry Standard Architecture (ISA) bus   a PC bus standard developed by IBM, extending the bus to 16 bits; capable of accessing 8-bit and 16-bit devices.

inference engine   software used with an expert system to examine data with respect to the knowledge base and to select an appropriate response.

infographic   an image developed using a variety of graphics tools and designed to impart the maximum amount of information to the viewer.

information superhighway the vast communications link that will allow access to government, industry, and educational data banks for all users; similar to the Internet, but will provide a single high-speed link in place of a network of systems.

initial cap an enlarged capital letter at the beginning of a paragraph that stands higher than the rest of the line.

initializing *see* formatting.

ink jet printer a printer that produces images by spraying ink onto the page; prints at moderate speeds and is cost effective.

input device computer hardware that accepts data and instructions from the user; includes the keyboard, mouse, joystick, pen, trackball, scanner, bar code reader, microphone, and touch screen.

insertion point *see* cursor.

install to transfer program components from a diskette or CD-ROM to a hard disk.

instruction set machine language instructions that define all the operations that the CPU can perform.

integrated drive electronics (IDE) a common hard disk interface standard developed by Compaq Computer; places most of the disk controller circuitry on the drive itself.

Integrated Services Digital Network (ISDN) a digital telecommunications standard that replaces analog transmissions and transmits voice, video, and data.

interactive the ability to react to and respond to external influences.

interactive media a software product that can react to and respond to input from the user.

interactive television a service that will allow viewers to select movies, shop, and participate in live broadcasts using phone lines, cable, and satellite communications.

interface *see* user interface.

internal modem a communications device used to modulate data signals; a circuit board plugged into one of the computer's expansion slots.

Internet Service Provider (ISP) an intermediary service between the Internet backbone and the user, providing easy and relatively inexpensive access to shell accounts, direct TCP/IP connections, and high-speed access through dedicated data circuits.

interrupt request a signal sent by the keyboard controller to the CPU to indicate that a complete keystroke has been received.

I/O (input/output) communication between the user and the computer or between hardware components that results in the transfer of data.

IP address a unique four-part numeric address assigned to each computer on the Internet, containing routing information to identify its location; each of the four parts is a number between 0 and 255.

IRIS printer a type of ink jet printer that sprays the ink on paper mounted on a spinning drum; can produce an image with a resolution of 1800 dots per inch.

ISA bus *see* Industry Standard Architecture bus.

ISDN *see* Integrated Services Digital Network.

ISP *see* Internet Service Provider.

J

joystick an input device used to control the movement of on screen components; typically used in video games.

JPEG (Joint Photographic Experts Group) format a bitmap file format commonly used to display photographic images; compresses the bitmap, resulting in a loss of clarity while increasing the image refresh rate.

K

KB *see* kilobyte.

kerning a text editing feature that adjusts the distance between individual letters in a word to make that word easier to read.

keyboard the most common input device; used to enter letters, numbers, symbols, punctuation, and commands into the computer; includes numeric, alphanumeric, cursor movement, modifier, and function keys.

keyboard buffer a part of memory that receives and stores the scan codes from the keyboard controller until the program can accept them.

keyboard controller a chip within the keyboard or the computer that receives the keystroke and generates the scan code.

keyboarding touch typing using a computer keyboard.

kilobyte (KB) equivalent to 1,024 bytes; common measurement of memory.

L

label descriptive text used in a spreadsheet cell to describe the data in a column or row.

LAN *see* local area network.

land a flat area on the metal surface of a CD-ROM that reflects the laser light into the sensor of an optical disk drive.

landscape orientation a document format in which the text is printed parallel to the widest page edge; the opposite of portrait orientation.

laptop a small, portable computer with an attached flat screen; typically battery or AC powered and weighing under 12 pounds.

laser printer a quiet, fast printer that produces high-quality output; a laser beam focused on an electrostatic drum creates an image to which toner adheres, and that image is transferred to paper.

LCD monitor *see* liquid crystal display monitor.

line spacing the distance between lines of text in a document; the most common examples include single-spaced and double-spaced.

liquid crystal display (LCD) monitor a flat-panel monitor on which an image is created when the liquid crystal becomes charged; used for notebook and laptop computers.

listserv an e-mail server that contains a list name and allows users to communicate with others on the list in an ongoing discussion.

local area network (LAN) a system of PCs that are located relatively near to one another and are connected by wire or a wireless link; permits simultaneous access to data and resources, enhances personal communication, and simplifies backup procedures.

logical field a database field that stores only one of two values, yes or no, true or false, on or off, and so on.

logical format (soft format) an operating system function in which tracks and sectors are mapped on the disk surface; mapping creates the boot record, FAT, root folder or directory, and the data area.

log on to access a computer system.

M

Macintosh operating system the operating system that runs on PCs built by Apple Computer; the first operating system to use a graphical user interface, utilize plug-and-play hardware compatibility, feature built-in networking, and support common user access.

macro a tool that allows the user to store and then automatically issue a sequence of commands or keystrokes.

magnetic disk a round, flat computer component that spins around its center and is the most common storage medium; data is written magnetically and can be recorded over and over.

magnetic storage a storage technology in which data is recorded when iron particles are polarized on a magnetic storage medium.

magneto-optical (MO) disk a storage medium that has the capacity of an optical disk but can be rewritten with the ease of a magnetic disk; data is written to disk when a laser melts the plastic coating encasing the magnetically sensitive metallic crystals, allowing a magnet to change the orientation of the crystals.

mail merge the process of combining a text document, such as a letter, with the contents of a database, such as an address list; commonly used to produce form letters.

mail server the server on which messages received from the post office server are stored until the recipients access their mailbox and retrieve the messages.

mainframe computer a large, multiuser computer system designed to handle massive amounts of input, output, and storage; usually composed of a powerful CPU connected to many terminals; typically used in businesses requiring the maintenance of huge databases or processing of multiple complex tasks.

margin the space between the edge of a page and the main body of the document; text cannot be entered within the margin.

mask *see* field format.

massively parallel processing a processing architecture that uses hundreds to thousands of microprocessors in one computer to perform complex processes more quickly.

master pages special pages created in desktop publishing software that contain elements common to all the pages in the document, such as page numbers, headers and footers, ruling lines, margin features, special graphics, and layout guides.

math coprocessor a computer chip separate from or part of the CPU especially designed to handle complex mathematical operations.

MB *see* megabyte.

MCA bus *see* Micro Channel Architecture bus.

MDTs *see* mobile data terminals.

megabyte (MB) equivalent to approximately one million bytes; measurement of memory and storage.

megahertz (MHz) a measurement of clock speed; equivalent to millions of cycles per second.

memo field a database field that stores text information of variable length.

memory a collection of chips on the motherboard or on a circuit board attached to the motherboard where all computer processing and program instructions are stored while in use; allows the CPU to store and retrieve data quickly.

memory address a number used by the CPU to locate each piece of data in memory.

menu a list of commands or functions displayed on screen for selection by the user.

menu bar a graphical screen element located above the application window on which a list of the types of commands available to the user are displayed; selecting an option from the menu bar will display a list of commands related to that menu option.

message a signal in an object-oriented program that is sent to an object, requesting it to perform a specific function.

Mhz *see* megahertz.

Micro Channel Architecture (MCA) bus a 32-bit PC bus standard developed by IBM; allows expansion boards to be configured by the software instead of manually.

microcode code that details the individual tasks the computer must perform to complete each instruction in the instruction set; a necessary level of translation between program instructions and elementary circuit operations.

microcomputer *see* PC (personal computer).

microphone an input device used with multimedia applications to digitally record audio data.

microprocessor an integrated circuit on a single chip that makes up the CPU, or brain, of the computer; composed of silicon or other material etched with many tiny electronic circuits.

millisecond equivalent to one thousandth of a second; used to measure access time.

minicomputer a midsize, multiuser computer capable of handling more input and output than a PC, but with less processing power and storage than a mainframe.

mobile data terminals (MDTs) display terminals used by law enforcement personnel in their cars to access information about a vehicle or an individual from a central computer.

modem an input/output device that allows computers to communicate through telephone lines; converts outgoing digital data into analog signals that can be transmitted over phone lines, and converts incoming audio signals into digital data that can be processed by the computer; short for modulator-demodulator.

modifier keys the part of a keyboard used in conjunction with other keys to execute a command; the PC keyboard includes Shift, Ctrl, and Alt.

MO disk *see* magneto-optical disk.

monitor a display screen used to provide computer output; examples include the cathode ray tube (CRT) monitor, color monitor, monochrome monitor, flat-panel monitor, and liquid crystal display (LCD).

monochrome monitor a monitor that displays only one color against a contrasting background.

monospace font a font in which each character uses exactly the same amount of horizontal space.

motherboard the main circuit board of the computer, composed of the CPU, memory, expansion slots, bus, and video controller; also called the system board.

mouse an input device operated by rolling it on a flat surface; used to control the on screen pointer by pointing and clicking, double-clicking, or dragging objects on screen.

MPC standard *see* Multimedia Personal Computer standard.

MPEG (Moving Pictures Experts Group) format a multimedia data compression standard used to compress full-motion video.

MPEG-2 format a multimedia data compression standard used to compress broadcast-quality video.

MS-DOS the command-line interface operating system developed by Microsoft for PCs; selected by IBM as the standard for early IBM and IBM-compatible machines.

multimedia elements of text, graphics, animation, video, and sound combined for presentation to the consumer.

multimedia authoring a process that combines text, graphics, animation, video, and sound documents developed with other software packages to create a composite product.

multimedia authoring software an application that allows the user to incorporate images, text, sound, computer animation, and video to produce a multimedia product.

multimedia PC a PC capable of producing high-quality text, graphics, animation, video, and sound; may include a CD-ROM drive, microphone, speakers, a high-quality video controller, and a sound card.

Multimedia Personal Computer (MPC) standard the minimum hardware and software requirements for a multimedia PC as defined by the Multimedia PC Marketing Council.

multitasking the ability of an operating system to load multiple programs into memory at one time and to perform two or more processes concurrently, such as printing a document while editing another.

N

navigation the process of moving through a software program.

network a system of interconnected computers that communicate with one another and share applications, data, and hardware components.

network database a database structure in which any record type can relate to any number of other record types.

networking the process of connecting computers that permits the transfer of data and programs between users.

network interface card (NIC) a circuit board that controls the exchange of data over a network.

network operating system (NOS) a group of programs that manage the resources on a network.

network protocol a set of standards used for network communications.

network server *see* file server.

network software a computer program that controls the hardware functions of a network.

network version an application program especially designed to work within a network environment; users access the software from a shared storage device.

new media *see* multimedia.

News a public bulletin board service on the Internet organized into groups representing specific topics of interest.

news group *see* discussion group.

NIC *see* network interface card.

nodes the individual computers that make up a network.

nonvolatile the tendency for memory to retain data even when the computer is turned off, such as for ROM; permanent and unchangeable.

NOS *see* network operating system.

notebook computer a smaller version of the laptop computer, weighing 5 to 7 pounds.

NSFnet a network developed by the National Science Foundation to accommodate the many users attempting to access the five academic research centers created by the NSF.

numeric field a database field that stores numeric characters.

numeric keypad the part of a keyboard that looks and works like an adding machine, with 10 digits and mathematical operators.

O

object embedding the process of integrating a copy of data from one application into another, as from a worksheet to a word processor; the data retains the formatting that was applied to it in the original application, but its relationship with the original file is destroyed.

object linking the process of integrating a copy of data from one application into another so that the data retains a link to the original document; a change in the original document also appears in the linked data.

Object Linking and Embedding (OLE) a Windows feature that combines object embedding and linking functions; allows the user to construct a document containing data from a single point in time or one in which the data is constantly updated.

object-oriented database a database structure in which data items, their characteristics, attributes, and procedures are grouped into units called objects.

OCR *see* optical character recognition.

OLE *see* Object Linking and Embedding.

online connected to, served by, or available through a networked computer system.

online service a telecommunications service that supplies e-mail and information search tools.

operating environment an intuitive graphical user interface that overlays the operating system but does not replace it, such as Microsoft Windows 3.0.

operating system (OS) the master control program that provides an interface for a user to communicate with the computer, manages hardware devices, manages and maintains disk file systems, and supports application programs.

operator the component of a formula that is used to specify the operation that you want to perform on the parts of a formula; includes arithmetic, comparison, and text operators.

optical character recognition (OCR) the technology that enables a computer to translate scanned data into character codes that can then be edited.

OS *see* operating system.

OS/2 a single-user, multitasking operating system with a point-and-click interface developed by IBM and Microsoft to take advantage of the multitasking capabilities of post-8086 computers.

outlining a spreadsheet tool that collapses spreadsheet data, so that only the cells with pertinent data, such as totals, are visible; used to analyze trends and view spreadsheet structure.

output device a hardware component, such as a monitor or printer, that returns processed data to the user.

P

packet *see* frame.

packet-switched line a type of communications line in which data is broken into distinct, addressed packets that can be transferred separately; access to the connection can be intermittent; commonly used for networks.

paint program a graphics program that creates images as a mosaic of pixels, or bitmaps, making precise changes to the graphic possible.

palmtop *see* personal digital assistant (PDA).

paragraph a series of letters, words, or sentences followed by a hard return.

parallel interface a channel through which 8 or more data bits can flow simultaneously, as for the computer bus; commonly used to connect printers to the computer; also called a parallel port.

passive matrix LCD liquid crystal display technology, used for flat-panel monitors, that relies on a grid of transistors arranged by rows and columns; the color displayed by each pixel is determined by the electricity coming from the transistors at the end of the row and the top of the column.

Paste an application command that copies data from the Clipboard and places it in the document at the cursor position.

payload the actual data that is being transmitted across a network or over telephone lines.

PC (personal computer) the most common type of computer found in an office, classroom, or home; designed to fit on a desk and be used by one person at a time; also called a microcomputer.

PC card a module the size of a credit card that fits into a laptop or notebook computer and is used to connect new components.

PCD *see* PhotoCD.

PCI bus *see* Peripheral Component Interconnect bus.

PDA *see* personal digital assistant.

peer-to-peer network a network environment in which all nodes on the network have equal access to at least some of the resources on all other nodes.

Pentium an Intel processor utilizing a 32-bit microprocessor and superscalar architecture.

Pentium Pro an Intel processor utilizing a 32-bit microprocessor; capable of processing three program instructions in a single clock cycle; utilizes dynamic execution, the ability to execute program instructions in the most efficient order.

Peripheral Component Interconnect (PCI) bus a PC bus standard developed by Intel that supplies a high-speed data path between the CPU and peripheral devices.

personal digital assistant (PDA) a very small portable computer designed to be held in one hand; used to perform specific tasks, such as creating limited spreadsheets or storing phone numbers; also called a palmtop.

PhotoCD (PCD) an imaging system developed by Kodak to digitally record and store photographic images on CD-ROM.

photo-manipulation program a multimedia software tool used to modify scanned photographic images, including adjusting contrast and sharpness.

PICT a Macintosh graphics file format that stores images in a vector format.

pit a depressed area on the metal surface of a CD-ROM that scatters laser light.

pixel one or more dots that express a portion of an image; *pic*ture *el*ement.

plotter an output device that uses a robotic arm to draw an image with colored pens on paper.

plug-and-play an operating system feature that enables the user to add hardware devices to the computer without performing technically difficult connection procedures.

pointer   an on screen object, usually an arrow, that is used to select text, access menus, move files, or interact with other programs, files, or data represented graphically on the screen.

Point to Point Protocol (PPP)   a communications protocol used for linking a computer directly to the Internet; features include the ability to establish or terminate a session, to hang up and redial, and to use password protection.

polarized   the condition of a magnetic bar with ends having opposite magnetic polarity.

polygonal modeler   a 3-D modeling program that builds images using an array of miniature polygons.

port   a socket on the back of the computer used to connect external devices to the computer.

portable   easily transferred from one platform to another.

portrait orientation   a document format in which the text is printed parallel to the narrowest page edge; the opposite of landscape orientation.

post office server   the server on which messages received from a sender's communications software are stored before being routed to the recipient's mail server.

Postscript   a printing language created by Adobe Systems that produces high-quality images ready for the printing press.

PPP   *see* Point to Point Protocol.

preemptive multitasking   a multitasking environment in which the OS prioritizes system and application processes and performs them in the most efficient order; can preempt a low-priority task with a more critical one.

presentation graphics application   software that allows the user to create professional-quality graphs and charts based on data imported from other programs, such as spreadsheets; images are presented on paper, on transparencies, or as automated slide shows with incorporated sound.

presentation software   *see* presentation graphics applications.

primary key   the element in a database table that determines the default or primary sort order; usually a single field.

printer   an output device that produces a hard copy on paper.

print preview   a feature that allows the user to display a document in reduced view so that a full page or facing pages can be seen on screen at one time; used to view page formatting before printing an entire document.

procedure   *see* function, definition 2.

process color separation   a color separation process used to prepare multicolor images for a printing press; the DTP software produces a separate film image for each of the three primary colors, cyan (blue), magenta (red), and yellow, as well as black.

processing   a complex procedure that transforms raw data into useful information.

processor   *see* central processing unit (CPU).

program   *see* software.

proportional font   a font in which the characters use varying amounts of horizontal space.

protocol   a set of rules and procedures that determine how a computer system receives and transmits data.

Q

QBE (query by example)   a database tool that accepts a query from a user and then creates the SQL code to locate data requested by the query.

query   a search question that instructs the program to locate records that meet specific criteria.

QWERTY   a standard keyboard arrangement; refers to the first six letters on the top row of the alphanumeric keyboard.

R

RAM (random access memory)   a computer's volatile or temporary memory built into the CPU; stores data and programs while they are being used and requires a power source to maintain its integrity.

range   a rectangular group of contiguous cells.

read-only memory (ROM)   a permanent, or nonvolatile, memory chip used to store instructions and data, including the computer's start-up instructions; its contents cannot be altered.

read/write heads   the magnetic devices within the disk drive that float above the disk surface and read, record, and erase data stored on disk; contains an electromagnet that alters the polarity of magnetic particles on the storage medium.

record   a database row composed of related fields; a collection of records makes up the database.

record number   a number displayed to the left of a record that refers to the position in which the record's data was originally entered.

Reduced Instruction Set Computing (RISC) processor a microprocessor design that simplifies the instruction set, using fewer instructions of constant size, each of which can be executed in one machine cycle.

refresh rate the number of times per second that each pixel on the screen is scanned; measured in hertz.

registers high-speed memory locations built directly into the ALU and used to hold instructions and data currently being processed.

registration marks marks inserted into a document by the DTP software and used to precisely align color separations and multiple-page layouts for the printing press.

relational database a database structure capable of linking tables; a collection of files that share at least one common field.

relative cell reference a spreadsheet cell reference that changes with respect to its relative position on the spreadsheet when copied to a new location.

removable hard disk a magnetic storage device that combines the speed and capacity of a hard disk with the portability of a diskette; a removable box encloses the disk, drive, and read/write heads in a sealed container that can be moved from computer to computer.

render to create an image of an object as it actually appears.

report a database product designed by the user that displays data satisfying a specific set of search criteria in a particular layout.

resolution the degree of sharpness of an image, determined by the number of pixels on a screen, expressed as a matrix.

right-click to use the right mouse button to select an object or command on screen.

ring topology a network topology in which network nodes are connected in a circular configuration; each node examines the data sent through the ring and passes on data not addressed to it.

RISC processor *see* Reduced Instruction Set Computing processor.

ROM *see* read-only memory.

rotating text a DTP feature that allows the user to set text at angles to normal text.

router a computer device that stores the addressing information of each computer on each LAN or WAN and uses this information to transfer data along the most efficient

path between nodes of a LAN or WAN.

row a horizontally arranged series of cells in a spreadsheet, named with a number.

RS-232 the standard serial port configuration used for communications between the computer and peripherals.

running *see* executing.

 S

sans serif a typeface without decorative finishing strokes on the tips of the characters; commonly used in headings.

scan code the code generated by the keyboard controller that tells the keyboard buffer which key has been pressed.

scanner an input device used to copy a printed page into the computer's memory and transform the image into digital data; can read text, images, or bar codes.

screen saver a utility program that displays moving images on the screen if no input is received for several minutes; originally developed to prevent an image from being etched into the screen.

scroll arrow an arrow at the top, bottom, right, or left of a scroll bar activated by a click of the mouse; allows the user to scroll the window up or down one line at a time or to the right or left a short distance.

scroll bar a vertical or horizontal bar displayed along the side and bottom of a window that allows the user to scroll horizontally or vertically through a document by clicking an arrow or dragging a box within the scroll bar.

scroll box a box located within a scroll bar; allows the user to move quickly through a document by dragging the box to a new position on the scroll bar.

scrolling the movement of an entire document in relation to the window view to see parts of the document not currently visible on screen.

SCSI *see* small computer system interface.

sector a segment or division of a track on a disk.

select to click once on an icon to initiate its action.

serial interface a channel through which a single data bit can flow at one time; used primarily to connect the mouse or communications devices; also called a serial port.

Serial Line Interface Protocol (SLIP) a method for linking a computer directly to the Internet by using a phone line connected to a serial communications port.

serif a typeface with decorative finishing strokes on the tips of the characters; commonly used in the main body of text.

server   *see* file server.

shading   a paragraph format that displays a pattern or color as a background to the text; used to emphasize a block of text.

shell account   a type of Internet access used by remote terminal connections; operates from a host computer running UNIX or a similar operating system.

SLIP   *see* Serial Line Interface Protocol.

small computer system interface (SCSI)   a device that extends the bus outside the computer, permitting the addition of more peripheral devices than normally could be connected using the available expansion slots.

software   a collection of electronic instructions that direct the CPU to carry out a specific task; created by programmers in a programming language; usually resides in storage.

software piracy   the illegal duplication of software for commercial or personal use.

solids modeler   a 3-D modeling program that depicts an object as an outer layer stretched over a wire frame and that incorporates the concepts of thickness and density.

sorting   arranging records in a particular order according to the contents of one or more fields.

sort order   the order in which records are sorted, either ascending or descending.

sound card   an expansion card that records and plays back sound by translating the analog signal from a microphone into a digitized form that the computer can store and process and then translating the modified data back into analog signals, or sound.

speech recognition   *see* voice recognition.

spelling checker   a text editing feature that checks document spelling.

spline-based modeler   a 3-D modeling program that builds objects using mathematically defined curves.

spot color separation   a color separation process used to print a specific color as a design element; the DTP software produces the graphic for the desired color as a separate piece of film.

spreadsheet   a grid of columns and rows used for recording and evaluating numbers; used primarily for financial analysis, record keeping and management, and to create reports and presentations.

spreadsheet program   application software that displays a grid of columns and rows into which a user enters text, num-

bers, or formulas for calculations; a computerized ledger or worksheet used for calculating and evaluating numbers; used primarily for financial analysis, record keeping, data entry, and management, and to create reports and presentations.

SQL   *see* Structured Query Language.

star network   a network topology in which network nodes connect to a central hub through which all data is routed.

Start button   a Windows 95 screen element, found on the desktop, which displays operating system options when selected; includes tools to locate documents, find help, change system settings, and run programs.

storage   the portion of the computer that holds data or programs while they are not being used; media include disks, tape, and cartridges.

storage media   the physical components, or materials, on which data is stored.

storyboard   a production tool that consists of sketches of scenes and actions that map a sequence of events; helps the author to edit and improve the presentation.

Structured Query Language (SQL)   the standard query language used for searching and selecting records and fields in a relational database.

style   a named collection of character and paragraph formats that determine the appearance of a text block.

style sheet   a collection of styles, or design elements, created for a specific document.

subdomain   a division of a domain address that specifies a particular level or area of an organization, such as a branch office.

supercomputer   the fastest, most powerful computer; often used for scientific and engineering applications and processing complex models using very large data sets.

superscalar architecture   a microprocessor architecture that allows more than one instruction to be processed in each clock cycle.

surface modeler   a 3-D modeling program that depicts an object as an outer layer stretched over a wire frame.

SVGA (Super VGA)   an IBM video display standard capable of displaying resolutions up to 1280x1024, with 16 million colors.

swap in   to load essential parts of a program into memory as required for use.

swap out   to unload, or remove, nonessential parts of a program from memory to make room for needed functions.

syntax the precise sequence of characters required in a spreadsheet formula or in a programming language.

system board *see* motherboard.

system call a feature built into an application program that requests service from the operating system, as when a word processing program requests the use of the printer to print a document.

system clock the computer's internal clock, used to time processing operations; time intervals are based on the constant, unchanging vibrations of molecules in a quartz crystal; measured in megahertz.

system software a computer program that controls the system hardware and interacts with application software; includes the operating system and the network operating system.

T

T1 a communications line that represents a higher level of the ISDN standard service and supplies a bandwidth of 1.544 Mbps; also called PRI.

T3 a communications line capable of transmitting a total of 44.736 Mbps.

tab stop a preset position in a document to which the cursor moves when the Tab key is pressed.

Tagged Image File Format (TIFF) a graphics file format developed by Microsoft and Aldus; expresses images as bitmaps.

tape drive a magnetic storage device that reads and writes data to the surface of a magnetic tape; generally used for backing up data or restoring the data of a hard disk.

target *see* registration marks.

Taskbar a Windows 95 screen element, displayed on the desktop, which includes the Start button and lists the programs that are currently running on the computer.

TCP/IP *see* Transmission Control Protocol/Internet Protocol.

telecommuting to work at home or on the road and have access to a work computer via telecommunications equipment, such as modems and fax machines.

teleconferencing live communications between two or more people using computers, telecommunications equipment, and e-mail software.

Telnet an Internet tool that provides a transparent window between the user's computer and a distant host system; data

is transmitted from the user's keyboard to the host, effectively taking control of the host computer to access data, transmit files, and so on.

template a preformatted document used to quickly create a standard document, such as a memo or report.

terminal an input/output device connected to a multiuser computer, such as a mainframe; consists of a monitor and keyboard but lacks its own CPU and storage.

text field *see* alphanumeric field.

text operator a component of a spreadsheet formula that combines two or more strings of text to create a single text string.

thermal-wax printer a printer that produces high-quality images using a heat source to evaporate colored wax from a ribbon, which then adheres to plain paper.

thesaurus a text editing tool that lists alternative words with similar meanings.

TIFF *see* Tagged Image File Format.

time field a database field that stores the time.

title bar an on screen element displayed at the top of every window that identifies the window contents; dragging the title bar changes the position of the window on screen.

Token Ring IBM's network protocol based on a ring topology, in which linked computers pass an electronic token containing addressing information to facilitate data transfer.

toner a substance composed of tiny particles of charged ink, used in laser printers; the ink particles stick to charged areas of a drum and are transferred to paper with pressure and heat.

topology the physical layout of wires that connect the computers in a network; includes bus, star, and ring.

touch screen an input/output device that accepts input directly from the monitor; the user touches buttons displayed on screen to activate commands.

trackball an input device that functions like an upside-down mouse, consisting of a stationary casing containing a movable ball that is operated by hand; used frequently with laptop computers and video games.

tracking adjusting letter spacing within blocks of text to make the text easier to read.

trackpad a stationary pointing device that the user operates by moving a finger across a small, touch-sensitive surface; used with laptop and notebook computers.

transistors   electronic switches within the CPU that exist in two states, conductive (on) or nonconductive (off); the resulting combinations are used to create the binary code that is the basis for machine language.

Transmission Control Protocol/Internet Protocol (TCP/IP)   the set of commands and timing specifications used by the Internet to connect dissimilar systems and control the flow of information.

trapping   a DTP process in which a tiny overlap of color is added to spot color separations to account for possible misalignment in the press.

twisted-pair wire   cable used in network connections that consists of four or eight copper strands, individually shrouded in plastic, twisted around each other in pairs and bound together in a layer of plastic insulation; also called unshielded twisted-pair (UTP) wire; twisted-pair wire encased in a metal sheath is called shielded twisted-pair (STP) wire.

typeface   *see* font.

U

UART   *see* Universal Asynchronous Receiver Transmitter.

unerase program   *see* data recovery utility.

Unicode Worldwide Character Standard   a character set that provides 16 bits to represent each symbol, resulting in 65,536 different characters or symbols, enough for all the languages of the world; a superset of ASCII.

Uniform Resource Locator (URL)   an Internet address used with HTTP in the format type://address/path; specifies the type of server on which the file is located, the address of the server, and the path or location within the file structure of the server.

Universal Asynchronous Receiver Transmitter (UART)   a chip that converts parallel data from the bus into serial data that can flow through a serial cable, and vice versa.

uploading   sending a file to a remote computer.

upward compatibility   the ability of a hardware device or a software product to interact successfully with all succeeding versions of software or hardware.

URL   *see* Uniform Resource Locator.

Usenet   a popular system of news groups accessible on the Internet and maintained by volunteers.

user interface   the on screen elements that allow the user to interact with the software.

users   the people who record and analyze data using the computer.

V

value   a numerical entry in a spreadsheet, representing currency, a percentage, a date, a time, a fraction, and so on, which can be used in formulas.

vector   a mathematical equation that describes the position of a line.

Veronica   Very Easy Rodent-Oriented Net-wide Index to Computer Archives; a keyword search tool that finds and displays items from Gopher menus.

VGA (Video Graphics Array)   an IBM video display standard capable of displaying resolutions of 640x480, with 16 colors.

video conferencing   live video communication between two or more people using computers and video conferencing software.

video controller   a circuit board attached to the motherboard that contains the memory and other circuitry necessary to send information to the monitor for display on screen; determines the refresh rate, the resolution, and the number of colors that can be displayed; also called the display adapter.

video RAM (VRAM)   memory on the video controller, called dual-ported memory, that can send a screen of data to the monitor while receiving the next data set.

virtual reality   a computer navigation tool that projects the user into 3-dimensional space using special devices designed to simulate movement and spatial dimension.

virus   a parasitic program developed as a prank that is buried within a legitimate program or stored in the boot sector of a disk; may be contracted when adding programs, copying data, or communicating online and will damage data, software, or the computer itself.

voice recognition   an input technology that can translate human speech into text.

volatile   the tendency for memory to lose data when the computer is turned off, such as for RAM; nonpermanent and alterable.

VRAM   *see* video RAM.

W

WAN   *see* wide area network.

Web page   a document developed using HTTP and found on the Internet; contains information about a particular subject with links to related Web pages and other resources.

what-if analysis   a data analysis process used to test how alternative scenarios affect numeric results.

wide area network (WAN)   a computer network in which two or more LANs are connected together across a wide geographical area.

window   an area on the computer screen in which an application or document is viewed and accessed.

Windows 3.0   an operating environment introduced by Microsoft in 1990 that could run 16-bit Windows and DOS applications, managed larger amounts of memory than its predecessors, and included the File Manager, Program Manager, and 3-dimensional screen elements.

Windows 3.1   an operating environment introduced by Microsoft in 1992 as an upgrade to Windows 3.0; capable of running 16-bit Windows and DOS applications as well as 32-bit Windows applications; supports multimedia, TrueType fonts, OLE, and drag-and-drop functions.

Windows 3.11   an upgrade to Windows 3.1; provides the basis for Windows for Workgroups, which includes built-in peer-to-peer networking and electronic mail capabilities.

Windows 95   a 32-bit operating system developed by Microsoft and released in 1995; features preemptive multitasking, plug-and-play capabilities, built-in networking, and the ability to access 16- and 32-bit applications.

Windows NT   a 32-bit operating system developed by Microsoft and released in 1993; designed for powerful workstations and restricted to running 32-bit applications; supports peer-to-peer networking, preemptive multitasking, and multiprocessing.

Winsock   Windows Sockets, a standard network interface that makes it possible to mix and match application programs from more than one developer to communicate across the Internet.

wireframe model   a CAD tool that represents 3-D shapes by displaying their outlines and edges.

wireless communication   communication via computers that relies on radio signals, including x-rays, ultraviolet light, the visible spectrum, infrared, microwaves, and radio waves, to transmit data.

word processing program   software used to create and edit text documents such as letters, memos, reports, and publications.

word size   the size of the registers in the CPU, which determines the amount of data the computer can work with at any given time; larger word sizes lead to faster processing; common word sizes include 16 bits, 32 bits, and 64 bits.

word wrap   a word processing feature that computes the length of each line of text as the text is entered.

worksheet   the data file created with spreadsheet software; also called a spreadsheet.

workstation   a fast, powerful microcomputer used for scientific applications, graphics, CAD, CAE, and other complex applications; usually based on RISC technology and operated by some version of UNIX.

World Wide Web (the Web or WWW)   an Internet service developed to incorporate footnotes, figures, and cross-references into online hypertext documents; created in 1989 at the European Particle Physics Laboratory in Geneva, Switzerland.

WORM (write once, read many) drive   a permanent optical storage device that uses a laser to read data from the surface of a disk; cannot be changed or rewritten.

WYSIWYG   a display mode that shows a document as it will appear when printed; stands for What You See Is What You Get.

INDEX

protocols
    for modem file transfers, 152
    for networks, 146–148
pull-down menus, 172
PV function in spreadsheets, 249

Q

QBE (query by example), 281–282
queries of databases, 280–282
QuickTime VR, 366–367
QWERTY keyboard layout, 66

R

RAID (Redundant Array of Independent
        Disks) devices, 122
RAM (random access memory), 19, 21, 48, 50
    DRAM (dynamic RAM), 83
    upgrade considerations, 57
    VRAM (video RAM), 57, 83
ranges of cells in worksheets, 248
read-only memory (ROM), 47–48
read-write heads, 21, 103
record numbers in databases, 277
records in tables, 268
recovery utilities, 185
refresh rate of monitors, 82
registers, 46–47, 49–50
registration marks in desktop publishing, 228
relational databases, 269–270
relative cell references in spreadsheet
        formulas, 250
removable storage devices
    hard disks/drives, 101, 111–113
    PC Cards, 118
rendering of images, 336
reports from databases, 282
resolution of monitors, 81–82
resume example, 205
right-clicking the mouse, 69
ring topology for networks, 143
RISC processors, 58, 60
RLL (run-length limited) data-encoding
        scheme, 120
ROM (read-only memory), 47–48
rotating text in desktop publishing, 225–226
ROUND function in spreadsheets, 249
routers for networks, 138, 139, 310
rows
    in spreadsheets, 240
    in tables, 268
RS-232 ports, 91
run-length limited (RLL) data-encoding
        scheme, 120

S

SAA (System Application Architecture), 191
sans serif fonts, 214
satellites, 146
saving documents (word processing
        software), 211
scan code, 68
scanners, 19, 20, 75–77, 231, 326
scientific uses of computers, 7
screens
    as menus, 171–172
    as monitors, 20, 78, 80–84
    as touch screens, 75
    See also user interface
screen savers, 186
scroll bars, arrows and boxes, 170, 171, 208
scrolling through documents (word
        processing software), 208
SCSI/Audio Multimedia Combo PC
        Cards, 118
SCSI (small computer system interface)
        devices, 93, 121, 123
Seagate Technology, 120
sectors
    on CD-ROMs, 115
    on magnetic disks, 106, 107–108
secure removable storage on PC Cards, 118
selecting
    blocks of text (word processing software),
        210
    icons, 168
serial interfaces, 90–91
Serial Line Interface Protocol (SLIP), 310
serif fonts, 214
servers, 132, 139, 140
    on Internet, 296–297
shared peripheral devices (networks), 132–133
shell accounts, 310
shielded twisted-pair (STP) wire, 144
Shift+key combinations, 73
shortcut keys for menu access, 172
Shugart Technology, 120
SIMMs (Single In-Line Memory Modules),
        50, 57
simultaneous access to networks, 130, 132
SLIP (Serial Line Interface Protocol), 310
small computer system interface (SCSI)
        devices, 93, 121, 123
Smartmodem, 149
SMDS (Switched Multimegabit Digital
        Service), 156
SMP (symmetric multiprocessing), 59
soft formatting of disks or diskettes, 108
software
    groupware, 132

network versions of, 130, 132
    for presentations, 365–366
    system, 183
    See also computer systems
software emulation, 192
software types
    application software, 23–27
    communications, 27
    database management, 24–25
    desktop publishing, 24
    education/entertainment (edutainment),
        26
    graphics, 25
    multimedia, 25
    network, 27
    operating systems, 22–23
    paint/draw, 25
    presentations, 25
    spreadsheets, 24
    utilities, 26
    word processor programs, 23–24
solids modelers, 337
sorting worksheet data, 255
sound cards, 88, 90
sound effects
    systems for, 88, 89, 90
    in word processing software, 222–223
    See also multimedia
sound studios, 90
speakers for multimedia, 360, 363
speech recognition, 20, 77, 79, 89, 94
speech synthesizers, 79
speed considerations
    factors affecting, 49–54
    pace of chips, 59
    parallel processing, 58–60
    storage drives, 117, 119–121, 123
spell checking (word processing software),
        211–212
Spielberg, Steven, 131
spline-based modelers, 338
spot color separations in desktop publish-
        ing, 227–228
spreadsheets
    analyzing data, 254–255
    auditing, 256
    described, 24, 240–241
    designing, 246
    editing, 249–251
    entering labels and numbers, 246
    examples, 243, 244
    formatting, 251–252
    formulas, 247–249
    future trends in, 260
    as graphs or charts, 241, 252–253
    macros, 255–256

Photo Credits

Table of Contents xv Courtesy of International Business Machines Corporation. Unauthorized use not permitted; xvi Intel Corporation; xvii Logitech; xviii Maxtor; xix Courtesy of International Business Machines Corporation. Unauthorized use not permitted; xxi Microsoft; xxv permission pending; xxvi Tom McCarthy/ SKA (*top*), courtesy of International Business Machines Corporation. Unauthorized use not permitted (*bottom*); xxvii BodyBilt Seating; xxxvii Courtesy of International Business Machines Corporation. Unauthorized use not permitted; xxix Tom McCarthy/ SKA; xxx CompUSA, Computer Superstores.

Part I 1 Lois & Bob Schlowsky/Tony Stone Images.

Chapter 1 2 Courtesy of International Business Machines Corporation. Unauthorized use not permitted (*inset*), Lois & Bob Schlowsky/Tony Stone Images (*background*); 4 D. Young-Wolff/ PhotoEdit (*top*), U. S. Department of Defense Camera Combat Center (*bottom*); 5 Courtesy of International Business Machines Corporation. Unauthorized use not permitted (*top left*), Chevron Corporation (*top right*), Tom Lippert Photography (*bottom left and right*); 6 Philippe Plailly/Photo Researchers, Inc. (*top*), Smithsonian Institution (*bottom*); 7 NASA; 9 Bettmann Newsphotos; 10 Chrysler Corporation (*top*), Levi Straus Co. (*bottom left and right*); 11 Lexis (*top*), Bob Daemmrich/The Image Works (*bottom*); 12 U. S. Department of Defense Camera Combat Center; 13 Phillippe Goutier/Image Works (*top*), Richard Pilbrow/ Theatre Projects Consultants (*bottom*); 14 Universal/The Kobel Collection (*left*), Walt Disney/The Kobel Collection (*right*); 15 Wide World; 16 Tom McCarthy/SKA; 19 Intel Corporation; 21 Tom McCarthy/SKA; 28 Cray Computer; 29 Courtesy of International Business Machines Corporation. Unauthorized use not permitted (*top and bottom*); 30 DEC (*top*), Courtesy of International Business Machines Corporation. Unauthorized use not permitted (*bottom*); 31 Courtesy of International Business Machines Corporation. Unauthorized use not permitted (*top left, top right, and center*), Fujitsu (*bottom*); 32 Philip Gould (*left*), Courtesy of International Business Machines Corporation. Unauthorized use not permitted (*right*); 33 Sun Microsystems; 34 Levi Straus Co.; 35 Courtesy of International Business Machines Corporation. Unauthorized use not permitted (*top and center*), Fujitsu (*bottom*).

Chapter 2 38 Intel Corporation (*inset*), Lois & Bob Schlowsky/Tony Stone Images (*background*); 44 Intel Corporation; 45 Timex Corporation (*top*), Dallas Semiconductor (*bottom*); 48 Intel Corporation (*left*), Kingston Technology Corporation (*right*); 50 Newer Technology (*left and right*); 52 Intel Corporation; 54 Intel Corporation (*top and bottom*); 55 Intel Corporation; 56 Intel Corporation; 57 Intel Corporation; 58 Photos courtesy of Motorola (*top two*), NEC Electronics, Inc. (*middle*); Sun Microsystems, Inc. (*bottom*); 59 Daystar Inc.; 62 Intel Corporation.

Chapter 3 64 Tom McCarthy/SKA (*inset*), Lois & Bob Schlowsky/Tony Stone Images (*background*); 67 NMB Technologies; 68 Courtesy of International Business Machines Corporation. Unauthorized use not permitted; 70 Photo courtesy of Hewlett Packard Co.; 72 Logitech (*top left*), Tom McCarthy/ SKA (*top middle*), Courtesy of International Business Machines Corporation. Unauthorized use not permitted (*top right and center*), NEC (*bottom*); 74 Courtesy of International Business Machines Corporation. Unauthorized use not permitted (*top*), courtesy of Apple Computer Inc. (*middle*), UPS (*bottom*); 75 Bob Daemmrich/ The Image Works (*top*), Courtesy of International Business Machines Corporation. Unauthorized use not permitted (*bottom left*), Federal Express (*bottom right*); 76 Ultima; 77 Photo courtesy of Hewlett Packard Co. (*right*), Visioneer (*left*); 79 Biolink; 81 Applied Optical Co.; 83 Photo courtesy of Hewlett Packard Co.; 85 Photo courtesy of Hewlett Packard (*top and bottom*); 87 Cal-Comp (*top*), IRIS Graphics (*bottom*); 88 Photo courtesy of Hewlett Packard Co.; 89 Digidesign; 92 Courtesy of National Instruments, Austin, Texas (*top left and center*), Courtesy of International Business Machines Corporation. Unauthorized use not permitted (*top right*), Courtesy of National Instruments, Austin, Texas (*bottom*); 93 Adaptec; 95 Courtesy of Apple Computer Inc.; 96 Photo courtesy of Hewlett Packard Co..

Chapter 4 98 Maxtor (*inset*), Lois & Bob Schlowsky/Tony Stone Images (*background*); 100 Courtesy of International Business Machines Corporation. Unauthorized use not permitted; 101 Seagate Technology (*left*), SyQuest (*middle*), Panasonic (*right*); 109 Maxtor (*left and right*); 112 Adaptec (*top*), SyQuest (*middle*), Iomega (*bottom*); 113 Seagate Technology (*top*), photo courtesy of Hewlett Packard Co. (*bottom*); 114 Courtesy of International Business Machines Corporation. Unauthorized use not permitted; 115 Tom McCarthy/SKA; 116 Photo courtesy of Hewlett Packard CO. (*top*), Courtesy of International Business Machines Corporation. Unauthorized use not permitted (*middle*), Maxoptix (*bottom*); 118 Kingston Technology Corp.; 121 Maxtor; 122 Kingston Technology Corp; 124 Seagate Technology; 125 Maxoptix (*top*), Maxtor (*bottom*).

Chapter 5 128 Courtesy of International Business Machines Corporation. Unauthorized use not permitted (*inset*), Lois & Bob Schlowsky/ Tony Stone Images (*background*); 130 Photo courtesy of Hewlett Packard Co.; 131 Allegheny General Hospital; 136 Photo courtesy of Motorola; 144 Tom McCarthy/ SKA (*top*), Property of AT&T Archives. Reprinted with permission of AT&T (*bottom*); 145 Property of AT&T Archives. Reprinted with permission of AT&T (*top*), Farallon (*bottom*); 146 Compaq; 149 Reproduced by permission of Hayes Microcomputer Products, Inc., © 1996; 150 U.S. Robotics; 151 Courtesy of International Business Machines Corporation. Unauthorized use not permitted (*top and middle*), Compaq (*bottom*); 153 Panasonic; 159 Tom McCarthy/SKA (*top*), Property of AT&T Archives. Reprinted with permission of AT&T (*middle right and left*); 160 U. S. Robotics.

Part II 162 FPG.

Chapter 6 164 Microsoft (*inset*), FPG (*background*); 166 Microsoft; 192 Artwork is provided courtesy of Miramar Systems Inc., manufacturers of Personal MacLan Connect, all rights reserved.

Chapter 7 203 FPG (*background*); 206 SKA; 213 Wright Strategies.

Chapter 8 239 FPG (*background*).

Chapter 9 265 FPG (*background*); 267 Unisys (*top*), NEC Electronics Inc.(*bottom*); 279 Courtesy of International Business Machines Corporation. Unauthorized use not permitted.

Chapter 10 293 FPG (*background*); 304 Courtesy of Apple Computer Inc.; 306 Paul Hurschmann.

Chapter 11 320 Tom McCarthy (*inset*), FPG (*background*); 322 Tom McCarthy/SKA; 323 Tom McCarthy (*top, right and middle*), Sun Microsystems (*bottom*); 324 Walt Disney/ Kobol; 326 Epson (*top*), Kodak (*bottom*); 327 Kodak; 328 Connectix (*left*), Kodak (*right*); 330 Fractal; 332 Fractal (*top right and left*), Corel (*middle*), Kino, DSP Productions (*bottom*); 337 Photo courtesy of Hewlett Packard Co. (*top*); 338 Autodesk (*top left, right and bottom*); 339 Graphsoft; 344 Sun Microsystems (*top left*), Walt Disney/Kobol (*top left*), Fractal (*bottom*).

Chapter 12 348 Courtesy of International Business Machines Corporation. Unauthorized use not permitted (*inset*), FPG (*background*); 350 FPG; 353 Photo courtesy of Hewlett Packard Co.; 354 NEC; 357 C/Net; 359 Courtesy of International Business Machines Corporation. Unauthorized use not permitted; 366 Courtesy of International Business Machines Corporation. Unauthorized use not permitted; 378 Courtesy of International Business Machines Corporation. Unauthorized use not permitted.

Appendixes 382 Superstock.

Appendix A: History of Microcomputers
384 Intel Corporation (*top two photos*), The Computer Museum, Boston (*left*), Property of AT&T Archives. Reprinted with permission of AT&T (*two photos*), Courtesy of Apple Computer Inc. (*right top*), Computerland (*bottom*); 385 Courtesy of Apple Computer Inc. (*top left*), Intel Corporation (*top right*), VisiCalc (*right*), Datapoint Corporation (*center left*), Intel Corporation (*bottom*); 386 Microsoft (*top left*), Intel Corporation (*top right*), Bell Laboratories (*center left*), Lotus (*center*), Kapor Enterprises, Inc. (*center bottom*), photo courtesy of Hewlett Packard Co. (*center left*), Courtesy of International Business Machines Corporation. Unauthorized use not permitted (*bottom left*), Xerox Corporation (*bottom right*); 387 Courtesy of Apple Computer Inc. (*top left*), Courtesy of International Business Machines Corporation. Unauthorized use not permitted (*top right*), Compaq (*center left*), Adobe (*center*), Intel Corporation (*center right*), Courtesy of Apple Computer Inc. (*bottom left*), Microsoft (*bottom center*), photo courtesy of Hewlett-Packard Co. (*bottom right*); 388 Courtesy of International Business Machines Corporation. Unauthorized

CREDITS

use not permitted (*top left*), Courtesy of Apple Computer Inc. (*top center*), Courtesy of International Business Machines Corporation. Unauthorized use not permitted (*left center*), Image provided courtesy of PhotoDisk, Inc. © 1996 PhotoDisk, Inc. All rights reserved (*bottom left*), logo courtesy of NeXT Computer, Inc. Reprinted with permission. (*bottom right*); **389** Intel Corporation (*top right*), Donna Coveney/MIT News Office (*top center*), Courtesy of Apple Computer Inc. (*top right*), Courtesy of International Business Machines Corporation. Unauthorized use not permitted (*bottom center*); **390** Microsoft (*top left*), Internet World (*top center*), courtesy of Apple Computer Inc. (*top right*), Courtesy of International Business Machines Corporation. Unauthorized use not permitted (*left center*), America Online (*center right*), Intel Corporation (*bottom left*), photo courtesy of Motorola (*bottom right*); **391** Microsoft (*top left*), Courtesy of International Business Machines Corporation. Unauthorized use not permitted (*top right*); Power Computing (*center left*), Intel Corporation (*center*), photo courtesy of Motorola (*bottom center*), Intel Corportion (*bottom right*).

Appendix B   **392**: Bodybilt; **393** Fellowes (*top and bottom*).

Appendix C   **396** Autodesk; **398**: Bettmann Newsphotos.

Screen Credits

Table of Contents
xxii, xxiii, xxiv Microsoft.

Chapter 1   **6** SimCity 2000™ and © 1994 Maxis, Inc. All rights reserved; **8** The Boeing Co. (*top*), USCO Distribution Services (*bottom*); **11** Reprinted with the permission of LEXIS-NEXIS, a division of Reed Elsevier Inc. LEXIS and NEXIS are registered trademarks of Reed Elsevier Properties Inc.; **12** Intuit, permission pending; **23** Microsoft (*bottom*); **24** Microsoft (*top, bottom*); **25** Macromedia, Inc., permission pending (*bottom*); **26** Microsoft (*top*), © 1966 SoftKey International Inc. and its licensors (*bottom*); **27** Microsoft (*top*).

Chapter 3   **67** Microsoft (*middle*); **69** Microsoft (*top*); **73** Microsoft (*left, right*); **90** Creative labs, permission pending; **90** Mindscape, permission pending.

Chapter 4   **102** Courtesy Danz Development Corp.; **109** Microsoft (*middle*).

Chapter 5   **132** Lotus Development Corporation, permission pending; **133** Qualcomm, permission pending; **134** Timbuktu is a registered trademark of Farallon Communications, Inc. Reprinted with permission.; **135** Cornell University, permission pending (*top*); Microsoft (*bottom*); **137** Microsoft (*top*); **148** Netware Login Dialog Box, Copyright 1987–1994, Novell, Inc. All rights reserved. Reproduced and used with permission; **157** Lotus Development Corporation, permission pending.

Chapter 6   **166** Microsoft (*bottom*); **167** Microsoft (*top*); **168** Microsoft (*top, middle, bottom*);

169 Microsoft (*top, bottom*); **170** Microsoft (*top, bottom*); **171** Microsoft (*top, middle,bottom*); **172** Microsoft (*top, bottom*); **173, 174, 175** Microsoft (*top, bottom*); **177** Microsoft (*top, middle, bottom*); **178** Microsoft (*top, bottom*); **179, 180** Microsoft (*bottom*); **181, 183** Microsoft (*top*); **184** Micro- soft (*middle, bottom*); **185** Microsoft (*top, middle*); **186** Star Trek The Screen Saver by Berkeley Systems, Inc.; **187** Microsoft (*top, bottom*); **188** Microsoft (*middle*); **189** Microsoft (*top, bottom*); **190** Apple Computer, permission pending; **191** IBM, permission pending (*top*), UNIX, permission pending (*bottom*); **193** Microsoft (*bottom*); **194, 195, 196, 197, 199** Microsoft (*top, middle, bottom*); **200** Microsoft (*middle*).

Chapter 7   **202** Microsoft (*inset*); **207** Microsoft (*top, bottom*); **208** Microsoft (*top*); **210** Microsoft (*middle*); **211, 212** Microsoft (*top, bottom*); **220** Microsoft (*bottom*); **221** Microsoft (*top left, top right, bottom*); **222** Microsoft (*top*); **223** Microsoft (*top, bottom*); **224** Microsoft (*left, right*); **227** Portions copyrighted 1986–1996 Quark, Inc. All rights reserved.; **229, 230, 231** Microsoft (*top, middle, bottom*); **232** Microsoft (*top*); **234, 235** Microsoft (*middle*).

Chapter 8   **238** Microsoft (*inset*); **240** Lotus Development Corporation, permision pending (*top*), Microsoft (*middle, bottom*); **241** Microsoft (*top, middle, bottom*); **244** Microsoft (*top*); **246, 250, 251** Microsoft (*top, bottom*); **252** Microsoft (*top, middle, bottom*); **252** Microsoft (*top, middle, bottom*); **253** DeltaGraph for MacIntosh, DeltaPoint, Inc.; **256** Microsoft (*top, middle left, middle right, bottom*); **257, 258, 259** Microsoft (*top, middle, bottom*); **261** Microsoft (*middle, bottom*); **262** Microsoft (*top, bottom*).

Chapter 9   **264** Microsoft (*inset*); **268** Microsoft (*top*); **273, 274** Microsoft (*top, bottom*); **275** Microsoft (*top*); **276** Microsoft (*top, bottom*); **276** (*middle*), **278** (*bottom*); **279 Borland ® Paradox ®** screen shots used by permission. Copyright © 1985, 1996 Borland International, Inc. All Rights Reserved. Paradox is a registered trademark of Borland International, Inc. Corporate Headquarters 100 Borland Way, ScottsValley, CA 95066-3249, (408) 431-1000. **Internet: http://www.borland.com** CompuServe: GO BORLAND. Offices in Australia, Canada, France, Germany, Hong Kong, Japan, Latin America, Mexico, The Netherlands, Taiwan, and United Kingdom; **278** Microsoft (*top*); **280** Microsoft (*top*); **281** Microsoft (*bottom*); **283, 284** Microsoft (*middle, bottom*); **285** Microsoft (*top, middle, bottom*); **286, 289** Microsoft (*top, middle*).

Chapter 10   **297** Microsoft (*bottom*); **303** Poultry Science Dept.–Texas A&M University (*top*), Microsoft (*bottom*); **304** AltaVista, permission pending; **305** The Paris Pages, permission pending (*top, bottom*); **306** The East Village (www.eastvilage.com) copyright 1996, Marinex Multimedia Corp.; **307** Text and artwork copyright © 1996 by Yahoo! Inc. Yahoo! and the Yahoo! logo are trademarks of Yahoo! Inc. (*top*), America Online, permission pending (*bottom*); **308** Permission granted by CompuServ, Inc. (*top*), reprinted with the permission of LEXIS-NEXIS, a division of Reed Elsevier Inc. LEXIS and NEXIS are registered trademarks

of Reed Elsevier Properties Inc.(*bottom*); **309** MapQuest™ (http://www.mapquest.com); **312** NETCOM On-Line Communication Services (*top*), The Daily Telegraph, permission pending (*bottom*); **313** The Daily Telegraph, permission pending (*top*), The Paris Pages, permission pending (*middle, bottom*); **314** The Paris Pages, permission pending (*top, middle, bottom*).

Chapter 11   **327, 329** Microsoft (*middle*); **330** Courtesy of Fractal (*top*), Fractal Design Painter, Auto Van Gogh tool (*bottom*); **336** Autodesk, permission pending (*top, middle, bottom*); **337** Cyan, permission pending.

Chapter 12   **351** Doom © 1993 Id Software, Inc.; **354** Microsoft (*top*); **355** Permission to reprint granted by Land's End, Inc. (*bottom*); **356** Microsoft (*top, bottom*); **359** Marvin Minsky, permission pending; **363** LucasArts, permission pending (*top*), MechWarrior is a registered trademark of FASA Corporation. Used with permission. (*middle*), Microsoft (*bottom*); **364, 365** Microsoft (*top, bottom*); **367** Autodesk, permission pending (*top right and left*); Reprinted with permission of Caligari Group (*bottom*); **368** Apple Computer, permission pending; **369** Microsoft (*middle*); **371** Microsoft (*top, bottom*); **372, 373** Microsoft (*top, middle, bottom*); **374** Microsoft (*top, bottom*); **375** Microsoft (*top, middle, bottom left, bottom right*); **376** Microsoft (*top*); **378** Microsoft (*bottom*).

Appendix A: History of Microcomputers
389 Presence, permission pending (*center*); Microsoft (*bottom left*); **390** America Online, permission pending (*center*).

References for History of the Microcomputer

The sources below provided general information for the timeline, in addition to the specific noted items.

1. Freed, Les, The History of Computers, Ziff-Davis Publishing Co. (Emeryville, CA), 1995.
2. Polsson, Ken, "Chronology of Events in the History of Microcomputers," May, 1996.
3. See Note 1.
4. Malone, Michael, "Chips Triumphant," Forbes ASAP magazine, February 26, 1996. (http://www.islandnet.com/~kpolsson/comphis8.html)
5. Internet Domain Survey, conducted by Network Wizards, January, 1996, (http://www.nw.com).
6. See Note 4.
7. See Note 4.
8. Poll by Times-Mirror Center for People and the Press, published in The Philadelphia Inquirer, November 19, 1995.
9. See Note 4.
10. See Note 5.